The Economics of Continuous-Time Finance

The Economics of Continuous-Time Finance

Bernard Dumas and Elisa Luciano

The MIT Press
Cambridge, Massachusetts
London, England

This book was set in Times Roman by diacriTech, Chennai. Printed and bound in the United States of America.

Library of Congress Cataloging-in-Publication Data

Names: Dumas, Bernard, author. | Luciano, Elisa, author.
Title: The economics of continuous-time finance / Bernard Dumas and Elisa Luciano.
Description: Cambridge, MA : MIT Press, [2017] | Includes bibliographical
    references and index.
Identifiers: LCCN 2016051903 | ISBN 9780262036542 (hardcover : alk. paper)
Subjects: LCSH: Finance–Mathematical models. | Finance–Econometric models.
Classification: LCC HG106 .D86 2017 | DDC 332.01/519233–dc23 LC record available at
https://lccn.loc.gov/2016051903

10   9   8   7   6   5   4   3   2

To those who gave me a second chance.
To my kids, who smile and fight.
—Elisa

To the memory of Professor Jack Hirshleifer whose textbook *Investment, Interest and Capital* illuminated my Ph.D. years.
—Bernard

Contents

1 Introduction

1.1 Motivation

The theory of continuous-time Finance is not new. It was developed in the 1970s and 1980s. It has inspired a lot of work by Finance academics and professionals, especially those specialized in the pricing of derivative securities, and it has been taken up for study by a large number of applied mathematicians. Our goal in this book is to highlight the applications of the approach to Economics, especially the more recent ones.

A number of highly qualified colleagues have already published crystal-clear textbooks in theoretical Finance. Doctoral students, Master of Science students, as well as advanced undergraduate students and Finance professionals—our main audience—have received valuable help in addressing the scope and complexity of the field and in enjoying the messages and insights of the asset pricing and equilibrium literature. Many of these textbooks either focus on the pricing of derivative securities, based on the principle of the absence of arbitrage, or emphasize the mathematical aspects of the topic.

We want to extract the economic message from the continuous-time approach so that it can then be used as a springboard to the construction of realistic economic models, especially when markets are incomplete.[1] Indeed, the more recent applications of the approach have endeavored to capture the imperfections and dysfunctions of financial markets, which have become more apparent than ever on the occasion of the "Great Recession" and the recent market turmoil.

Of course, before we take up that task, we need to lay the foundations. As most textbooks do, we use discrete time to illustrate the basic mechanisms but we limit that part to three chapters. Then we develop the continuous-time analog of these mechanisms so that we can use the powerful analytical tools of stochastic calculus. Eight chapters are dedicated to that.

We devote most of our energies to the study of markets in which some form of incompleteness, volatility puzzle, heterogeneity, friction, or behavioral subtlety arises. Here we go beyond other textbooks and we believe we do contribute by bringing order to a literature which is complex, growing, and sometimes unsettled.

---

1 See also the textbook by Back (2010).

Market incompleteness might have many sources. Agents can be restricted from participating in specific markets, and some risks can be hedgeable by no one. In that case, portfolio selection and equilibrium, the basic objects of asset pricing theory, are much more delicate, but perhaps more realistic, than in complete markets. A gamut of state prices are able to value securities and consumption streams. Even a simple model of restricted participation is able to cope to some extent with some of the empirical puzzles of financial markets, namely the fact that in a complete market individuals must be implausibly risk-averse, to explain the observed difference between risky and riskless securities' returns, or the observed level of interest rates.

Some other puzzling evidence in various asset classes is related to volatility, which is not constant, presumably stochastic, and excessively high in comparison with what calibrated theory would predict, this last being called the "excess volatility puzzle." We treat stochastic volatility in a manner that parallels our treatment of stochastic interest rates and the term-structure of interest rates.

Agents may be heterogeneous in many respects, in risk aversion and preferences, as well as in information and probability assignments. We study markets with agents who have incomplete information and "agree to disagree." No one has access to information that is deemed superior by other agents. They simply process public information differently and form different expectations. This feature, which seems so realistic to us, provides financial market models with the ability to capture the "excess" volatility, which has been growing in financial markets during the recent decades.

Market frictions may also be simpler than that. Some agents act as intermediaries in financial markets; some others use their services and pay a fee for that. The presence of fees, such as bid-ask spreads, explains that investors do not trade continuously in time but buy securities and hold them for a while. It offers a rationalization of volume and trade as observed in practice.

Last, we deal with two "behavioral" elaborations. We study habit formation, which is able to provide an alternative explanation for the observed difference between risky and riskless securities' returns, as well as for other pricing anomalies. We also study recursive preferences, which distinguish to some extent between the elasticity of intertemporal substitution in dynamic choice models and the risk aversion within each single point of time. This rich decision-theory approach is again better able to reproduce more sophisticated – even cyclical or time-dependent – patterns of prices in equilibrium, than traditional models do.

We venture far from the usual coverage of theoretical-Finance textbooks: into incomplete markets, volatility "puzzles" and modeling, heterogeneity in expectations, intermediated markets, habit formation, and recursive utilities. Equilibrium issues are our constant focus.

The emphasis on the economic interpretation of equations and results has had the regrettable consequence that, in some places, we may have sacrificed rigor somewhat, although to the smallest extent possible. We hope the reader will forgive us when we do. Another consequence is the length of the book. To cope with the last difficulty, we include a detailed outline and a short guide on using it.

1.2   Outline

This book develops the economic theory of dynamic security pricing and equilibrium under uncertainty, starting from intuition and progressively building a convenient modeling framework for it. In a financial market, there may exist securities that provide exactly the same opportunity to take on or, conversely, to hedge dimensions of risk as do other securities combined. These are called *redundant securities*. So, redundant securities are the ones the payoff of which may be obtained by combining other, *basic securities*, which can be, for instance, stocks and bonds. *Derivative securities* are securities written on other, *primitive or underlying securities*; they are sometimes redundant, sometimes not, so that one should not confuse derivative securities with redundant securities. We aim to obtain the prices of both redundant and basic securities either from the requirement that, in a well-functioning financial market, there should exist no arbitrage opportunities or from the assumption that investors act according to their preferences and the demand for securities equals their supply. We go beyond derivative pricing, and we discuss also the valuation of basic securities.

Part I: Discrete-Time Economies

In order to reach our goal, we work first in a static (two-points-in-time) and in a multi period but still discrete-time model, and we represent uncertainty by a finite number of states of the world in the future. The topic of "finite" uncertainty is covered in chapter 2. We introduce in that setting the notions of completeness, redundant-security pricing, and no arbitrage. We study the relations between them. Such a framework will provide the reader with economic intuition. We then switch to individual-investor optimality and, finally, to equilibrium, defined by equality between demand and supply of securities, and to the endogenous determination of prices and returns (chapters 3 and 4).

Parts II to IV: Continuous-Time Economies (Pricing of Redundant Securities, Investor Optimality, and Equilibrium)

We begin that topic by explaining how the limits to continuous time can be taken. As in the case of discrete-time, finite uncertainty, we study redundant-security pricing, optimality, and equilibrium. We develop most of the book material in continuous time and with "infinite" uncertainty, in our case a continuum, of states of the world. We do so because this framework, as compared to the discrete-time, finite-state uncertainty framework, is less cumbersome, more elegant, and easier to implement. Applications are the key motivation of our book.

In each of the previous market settings (discrete, continuous-time) we shall successively ask and, unfortunately, not always be able to answer, five questions:

- How do we define market "completeness"?
- How do we price redundant securities?
- What is the role of the no-arbitrage restriction?
- How do we obtain optimal portfolios?
- How do we determine the prices of primitive securities in equilibrium?

Part V: Applications and Extensions

Applications require first that we develop solution methods for control problems and related partial differential equations (PDEs). These methods are introduced in chapter 13. Equipped with them, we study portfolio optimization and equilibrium in incomplete markets (chapters 14 and 15). We then give an overview of interest-rate and fixed-income modeling (chapter 16). The methods introduced in the area of fixed income allow us to study stochastic volatility (chapter 17). We then proceed to models where investors form different beliefs or suffer frictions (represented mainly by bid-ask spreads that they must pay to intermediaries), form habits, or have recursive utilities. These are studied in chapters 18, 19, 20, and 21. We examine the effects not only on optimal portfolio choices, but also – and this is challenging – on equilibrium, namely on the price of primitive securities.

1.3   How to Use This Book

This book is written for advanced undergraduate and graduate students, with a background either in Economics and Finance or in Engineering, Physics, Statistics, Mathematics, and other natural sciences. The book is a compromise between the requirement of mathematical rigor and the need for economic interpretation, with a deliberate bias – in our very personal view – towards the second. Economists (other than mathematical economists) will accuse it of being too mathematical, and applied mathematicians will accuse it of lacking rigor. Hopefully, it will be appreciated by both constituencies as a bridge between them.

We suggest using parts I to IV for a one-semester course, or the entire book for a two-semester course.

Chapters 2 to 4 contain material that is covered in static and discrete-time courses in financial economics. The time to be devoted to them depends on the background of the students. However, since the continuous-time version that follows is based on these chapters, we suggest that they, at least, be read.

The content of chapters 5 and 7, as well as some sections of chapter 8, is usually covered in courses on stochastic calculus. The curriculum of the students should act as a guideline in deciding how to use this material.

Depending on their background, students may also be familiar with the notion of utility presented in Appendix A and/or with the dynamic programming approach of Appendix B. Please don't skip the afterword on page 569.

1.4 Apologies

Two apologies are in order. The first apology is about omissions. There are several aspects of continuous-time Finance that we have not covered or covered very little. We regret that very much, but the book is already quite long. Most of the models we present are models of a pure-exchange economy, without a production sector.[2] While chapter 18 considers markets in which investors have imperfect or incomplete information on the state of the economy, we do not present models in which investors receive private information.[3] Nor, most regrettably, do we cover international asset pricing (see Solnik (1974)). Finally, we never depart from the assumption that investors behave in a purely competitive fashion, which means we do not consider gaming and strategic behavior in continuous time.[4]

The second apology concerns errors. In a book this size, there are errors: typographical, computational, or even conceptual (although we hope not). We have done our best to weed them out, but some remain. Please, don't toss out the book because of them. Just forgive us and tell us what they are.

1.5 Acknowledgments

We are very grateful to Daniel Andrei, Suleyman Basak, Matthijs Breugem, Darrell Duffie, Christian Gollier, Michael Hasler, Julien Hugonnier, Andrew Lyasoff, Mavira Mancino, Emilio Osambela, Patrice Poncet, Dmitrii Pugachev, Lucie Tepla, Raman Uppal, Tan Wang, and the MIT Press anonymous referees, who have provided insightful comments and suggestions. A special thank you goes to Astrid Schornick for comments and for co-authoring chapter 18 and to Roberto Marfè for comments and for helping out with the exercises. Dumas is grateful to the University of Torino for awarding to him the AXA Chair in Socio-economic Risks and to Collegio Carlo Alberto and BI Norwegian Business School for their hospitality.

Bernard Dumas and Elisa Luciano, Fontainebleau and Torino, October 2016

---

2 In chapter 11, the equilibrium with production of Cox *et al.* (1985) is reviewed in detail and, in chapter 12, the two-person equilibrium of Dumas (1989) is also reviewed. Otherwise, the reader interested in production economies, can refer to: Cochrane (1991), Dumas (1992), Jermann (1998), Berk *et al.* (1999), Kogan (2001), Gomes *et al.* (2003), Kogan (2004), and Zhang (2005).

3 On that topic, the reader may want to refer to Kyle (1985), Wang (1993), Back (1992) and many others.

4 On that topic, the reader may want to refer to Kyle (1985), Grenadier (2002), and Back and Paulsen (2009).

I DISCRETE-TIME ECONOMIES

2 Pricing of Redundant Securities

In this chapter, we address an elementary problem, that of pricing redundant securities, in financial markets that are frictionless:

- trade occurs with full use of the proceeds: there are no transaction costs and no taxes
- short sales are admitted
- securities are infinitely divisible: even a small fraction of a security can be held
- and uncertainty is finite:[1] a finite number of different states of the world or states of nature may occur at each point in time.

We address the problem first in one-period economies, that is, when there are two dates only, 0 and 1; then in multiperiod, finite-horizon economies.

In the former setting, we start from a motivating example. Then we need a definition of redundant versus basic securities, together with that of a complete versus incomplete market. We provide necessary and sufficient conditions for the market to be complete. We study the consequences on redundant security pricing, both in incomplete and complete markets, introducing the fundamental notions of *state prices, stochastic discount factor, and risk-neutral probabilities*. Under complete markets, we show that state prices, as well as discount factors and risk-neutral probabilities, are uniquely obtainable from the prices of traded securities. We conclude the presentation of redundant security pricing in this setting by explaining two alternative methods: replication and hedging.

In multiperiod (but finite-horizon) economies we follow a similar procedure. However, at the outset, we need to explain how information is revealed over time and to distinguish two important notions of completeness: static versus dynamic.

Throughout this book, we maintain a *minimal assumption*: investors prefer more consumption to less. In other words, *there is no point of satiation in their preference ordering*.

---

1 In this book we use interchangeably the terms "risk" and "uncertainty."

Let the utility function $u(X)$ of an investor be a mapping from a high-dimensional space of strictly positive real vectors X representing a consumption stream to the space of real numbers.

Assumption 2.1 (of strong monotonicity): *(i) $u(X)$ is continuous*
(ii) for any pair X_1 and X_2 with semi-positive difference, $X_1 - X_2 \succ 0$, $u(X_1) > u(X_2)$.[2]

The goal of this chapter is to derive results about the pricing of securities that do not rely on any further specification of the utility function. This is in contrast to the next chapter, in which we restrict some more the utility function of an investor and proceed to derive his optimal consumption and portfolio-choice behavior.

The *Law of One Price* is a first example of a pricing principle that is based solely on the strong-monotonicity assumption. A single financial security cannot have two different prices. Otherwise, investors would sell it at the higher price and buy it at the lower one. The price pressure on supply and demand so created would lower the selling price and increase the buying price until they become one price. Distinct prices for the same security are ruled out.

2.1 Single-Period Economies

2.1.1 The Most Elementary Problem in Finance

A problem, which is encountered every time a new financial security is introduced in the market, is that of finding for it a price that is consistent with those of pre-existing securities. Let us consider a very simple market, in which two states of nature may occur at time 1 and in which there are at first two basic securities, a riskless bond and a stock. The price of the bond is normalized to one. It pays a face value of 1 plus the interest rate (here assumed to be 10%) in both states at time 1. The stock is worth 100 at date 0 and can either provide a payoff of 100 or a payoff of 150 at date 1. Collect the prices of basic securities in the vector

$$\begin{bmatrix} 1 \\ 100 \end{bmatrix}$$

and their payoffs in the following matrix

$$\begin{bmatrix} 1.1 & 1.1 \\ 100 & 150 \end{bmatrix}$$

Assume now that a derivative is introduced into this market.

---

2 A vector X is said to be "semi-positive," $X \succ 0$, if it has at least one strictly positive entry, with the others being non-negative. So, $X_1 - X_2 \succ 0$ means $X_1 \geq X_2$ *and* $X_1 \neq X_2$.

Definition 2.1   Derivative securities *have a payoff that is a (possibly nonlinear) function of the price or payoff of (one or more) securities called* primitive *or* underlying securities.

Options and futures are examples of derivative securities, which may sometimes be *redundant securities*. But the two terms are not synonymous.

Definition 2.2   *A security is* redundant *relative to a set of* basic securities *when its payoff can be obtained by combining the basic securities linearly into a portfolio of them.*

In the example considered now, any security whose payoff is a linear combination of the bond and the stock is redundant; that is, any "portfolio" (to be defined better below) of those basic securities is redundant.

Let the newly issued security be a call option on the stock. Because the new contract gives the holder the right to buy the underlying at a fixed price, called the "strike," the call will pay the difference between the stock and the strike at time 1, if positive. Let the strike be 100. As a consequence, the call will pay 0 when the stock is worth 100 and 50 when it is worth 150. So, the option on the stock has a payoff defined as a nonlinear function of the payoff of the stock. We shall have occasion (section 2.1.8) to show that, in the current situation, the option can be replicated by a portfolio of the underlying and the stock, and is, therefore, a redundant security. The enlarged vector of prices and matrix of payoffs are

$$
\begin{bmatrix} 1 \\ 100 \\ D \end{bmatrix} ; \begin{bmatrix} 1.1 & 1.1 \\ 100 & 150 \\ 0 & 50 \end{bmatrix}
$$

where we denoted with D the price (to be determined) of the call.

The price D must have "something to do" with the price of the other two securities. We now show that, for consistency, D must be equal to 9.09. Suppose it were, instead, equal to 9.00. One could exploit an "arbitrage opportunity" – to be defined formally below – as follows: buy the call for that price at time 0, so that 50 would be collected at time 1 in the second state. That would be the first leg of the arbitrage. On the second leg, one would sell, also at time 0, the stock short for 100, thereby committing to pay 100 and 150 in the respective states of time 1, use the proceeds in part to pay for the call, and invest the balance into the bond. On net, we would collect at time 1: $(100 - 9) \times 1.1 - 100 = 0.1$ and $(100 - 9) \times 1.1 + 50 - 150 = 0.1$ in the respective states. The arbitrageur would have been able to make money in both states with no initial outlay.

How did we come up with the number 9.09? Since it is a matter of pricing payoff units consistently across assets, we can imagine that there exist two positive "weights" for the payoffs of each basic security at time 1, which link their price today to their payoff tomorrow, that is, such that

$$
\begin{cases} 1 = 1.1 \times \phi(1) + 1.1 \times \phi(2) \\ 100 = 100 \times \phi(1) + 150 \times \phi(2) \end{cases} \tag{2.1}
$$

The price of the redundant security would have to be in the same relation with its own payoffs; that is, it would be true that

$$D = 0 \times \phi(1) + 50 \times \phi(2)$$

as otherwise there would exist an arbitrage opportunity.

Equivalently, define two new quantities, $\phi^*(1) = \phi(1) \times 1.1$, and $\phi^*(2) = \phi(2) \times 1.1$. Notice that $\phi^*(1) + \phi^*(2) = 1$, since $\phi(1) + \phi(2) = 1/1.1$, and $\phi^*(1) > 0$, $\phi^*(2) > 0$ since the ϕs are positive. So, these newly defined quantities can be interpreted as "fake" probabilities of the two states. With these new "weights," the price of each security today is the discounted expected value of its payoffs tomorrow. Indeed, using the newly defined quantities, the previous equations become

$$\begin{cases} 1 = \frac{1.1 \times \phi^*(1) + 1.1 \times \phi^*(2)}{1.1} \\ 100 = \frac{100 \times \phi^*(1) + 150 \times \phi^*(2)}{1.1} \end{cases} \tag{2.2}$$

which represent the prices of the two securities as expected values. The pseudo probabilities are named *martingale* probabilities because, except for discounting, the price today equates the expected value of the payoff tomorrow, that is, it is a martingale.[3]

This means that we can solve the system (2.1) in order to find the "weights," or, equivalently, the system (2.2) to solve for the "probabilities." In the first formulation we obtain[4]

$$\phi(1) = 0.7273; \quad \phi(2) = 0.1818$$

We can then find the price D as

$$D = 0 \times 0.7273 + 50 \times 0.1818 = 9.09$$

The next sections are going to provide necessary and sufficient conditions for the relations (2.1) and (2.2) to hold, so that the suggested technique for pricing the derivative security, using the same "weights," holds, or, equivalently, to justify the fact that there are positive weights such that

$$\begin{bmatrix} 1 \\ 100 \\ D \end{bmatrix} = \begin{bmatrix} 1.1 & 1.1 \\ 100 & 150 \\ 0 & 50 \end{bmatrix} \begin{bmatrix} \phi(1) \\ \phi(2) \end{bmatrix}$$

---

3 Martingales are defined in chapter 5. For the time being, the reader is asked to go along with the intuitive characterization just given.

4 If ϕ_1 or ϕ_2 had not been strictly positive, there would have existed an arbitrage opportunity between the two primitive assets already. The market would not have been "viable."

2.1.2 Uncertainty

In order to describe uncertainty, consider a complete *probability space* $(\Omega, \mathcal{F}, P)$.[5]

- Ω is the *sample space*, containing all possible *realizations*, describing at time 1 the conditions external to the decision maker. It is a complete description of the exogenous uncertainty. We might conceivably call *state of nature* an element of this space. However, given what he is able to observe at time 1, an investor may not be capable of distinguishing each and every element of the sample space. For instance, there are many phenomena occurring on planet Saturn that no investor would be able to observe and contingent on which, therefore, he could not write a contract with another investor or agree with him on a contingent security payoff. If so, it is pointless to develop a model that would recognize each and every element of Ω. Let us instead regroup into subsets all the elements of Ω that no investor can distinguish. A *partition* of a set Ω is a collection of disjoint (non-overlapping) subsets of it such that their union is Ω. Our assumption is that each investor will be able to tell which element of that partition has occurred at time 1. We call *state of nature* an element of the partition. For instance, in the extreme case in which investors could not observe anything at time 1, the partition would just be $\{\Omega\}$, which would mean that the only element of that partition is Ω itself, and there would be only one state of nature.

- $\mathcal{F}$ is a *σ-algebra* on Ω.[6] As compared to partitions, σ-algebras contain more elements than partitions, because they contain all the sets obtained by performing countable unions and complements. $(\Omega, \mathcal{F})$ is then a *measurable space*, and elements of $\mathcal{F}$ are the *events*. These are the subsets of the state space that belong to $\mathcal{F}$. A probability – or a probability measure – can then be assigned to all the elements of this σ-algebra.

- P is a *probability measure* on that space, that is, a bounded mapping, $P : \mathcal{F} \to [0, 1]$, such that $P(\Omega) = 1$ and the probability of a union of disjoint events is the sum of their probabilities.

- A real random variable $X(\omega)$ is a measurable mapping or set function, $X : \Omega \to \mathbb{R}$. For each state of the world that can take place, X takes a real value.[7]

---

5 Measurable subsets are those that have a probability measure assignment. *Complete* means that subsets of null sets (which have zero probability) are measurable, and have zero probability measure.

6 A σ-algebra over a set Ω is a non-empty collection of subsets of Ω that is closed under (that is, contains) the complements and the countable unions of its members. It includes at least Ω itself and its complement, the empty set $\varnothing$.

7 "Measurable" in the case of random variables means that the knowledge of a value of X would not convey any new information relative to what is already contained in the knowledge of the events that produce that value: $X^{-1}(\mathcal{B}) \in \mathcal{F}$, where $\mathcal{B}$ is any Borel set of $\mathbb{R}$. Borel sets are those obtained by union, complementation and intersection of intervals of $\mathbb{R}$.

In the case of *finite uncertainty*, the partition of the sample space is made of K states of nature at time 1, which we call ω_s or simply s; that is, $\Omega = \{\omega_s\}_{s=1}^{K}$. The σ-algebra is simply the set of all possible subsets of the partition of Ω. The probability measure is described by a K-dimensional vector of probabilities $\{\pi(s)\}$ assigned at time 0, the only vantage point from which uncertainty exists. In discrete time (chapters 2 to 4), we consider only states with positive probability of occurrence: $\pi(s) > 0, s = 1, .., K$.[8]

2.1.3   Securities Payoffs and Prices, and Investors' Budget Set

Consider a financial market composed of N securities, indexed by $i = 1, ..., N$. Their prices at time 0 are collected in the N-dimensional vector $S = \{S_i\}$.[9] Prices and payoffs are in units of the (unique) consumption good. The non-negative payoffs, or dividends, of the N securities in the K states at time 1 form an $N \times K$ matrix

$$\Sigma = \begin{bmatrix} q_1(1) \ q_1(2) & & q_1(K) \\ & q_i(s) & \\ q_N(1) & & \end{bmatrix}$$

In this matrix, each row gives the payoffs of a single security in all possible states of the world (security i in row $i, i = 1, .., N$), while each column gives the payoffs of all the securities in a single state of the world (state s in column $s, s = 1, .., K$). Later on, we denote by $\Sigma_i = \{q_i(s)\}_{s=1}^{K}$ the vector that collects the payoffs of security i (row i of matrix Σ) and by $q(s) = \{q_i(s)\}_{i=1}^{N}$ the vector that collects the payoffs of the N securities in state s (column s of matrix Σ).

Assume that the first security is a riskless one, the bond or bank account, which pays the same amount $q_1(s) = 1 + r$, for all s, where r is the rate of interest. The market is defined by the pair (S, Σ), which we call a *securities market*.[10]

We include in a "*basis*" and call "*basic*" a fixed set of securities that have linearly independent payoffs. This means that the payoffs of one basic security cannot be obtained by combining linearly the other basic securities. Redundant securities exist necessarily when there are more securities than states ($N > K$), since *at most* K of them can have linearly

---

8 The reason for which we consider only states with positive probability of occurrence: $\pi_s > 0, s = 1, .., K$ is that we consider as indistinguishable two random variables that differ only on zero-probability sets.

9 In the case of the static economy we henceforth omit the specification "time-0" price. Indeed, it is evident that in a one-period economy, ex-dividend prices of financial securities at time 1 are zero. Only prices at time 0, the ones at which trade occurs, are of interest.

10 Most of the book uses continuous time. For reasons that will become clear later, in continuous time it is preferable to consider separately the riskless and the risky securities. Therefore, in continuous time, we separate S into two different subvectors, $S = \{B, \mathcal{S}\}$. The first includes only the riskless security, the second the risky securities. In continuous time, for notational simplicity and mnemonic reasons, the number of *risky* securities – which here is $N - 1$, and is not relevant per se in formulating the results – will be denoted N. For the time being, we do not need to separate B from $\mathcal{S}$, and we can keep the total number of securities equal to N.

independent payoffs: $\text{rank}(\Sigma) \leq K$.[11] Suppose that $\text{rank}(\Sigma) = K$. Under this rank condition we are able to replicate any vector of payoffs in the possible states using a basis of the K-dimensional vector space. The securities that form a basis can be combined so as to mimic the redundant ones.

Since the payoffs of basic securities form a basis of the K-dimensional vector-space, and any space has several bases, we have many degrees of freedom in choosing basic securities. A typical example of basis is formed by the so-called *Arrow-Debreu securities* or state-contingent or simple claims, when they exist.

Definition 2.3 *The Arrow-Debreu security for state s pays 1 unit of consumption if state s occurs and zero otherwise.*

Arrow-Debreu securities have linearly independent payoffs, which are vectors in $\mathbb{R}^K$ that have the number 1 in only one place. All together, their vectors of payoffs form a payoff matrix equal to the identity matrix in $\mathbb{R}^K$:

$$I_K = \begin{bmatrix} 1 & 0 & & 0 \\ 0 & 1 & & \\ & & 0 & 1 \\ 0 & & & 1 \end{bmatrix}$$

An investor combines the securities into a portfolio $\Theta = \{\theta_i, i = 1, 2, ..N\}$ by taking a position θ_i in security $i = 1, ...N$. A position is a number of units of a security. It can be negative or positive. Negative positions represent short sales.[12]

The payoff X of a portfolio is equal to $\Sigma^{\mathsf{T}}\Theta$ at time 1.[13] Its price or initial cost is $S^{\mathsf{T}}\Theta$. The payoff matrix Σ^{T} establishes a linear mapping Σ^{T} that maps $\mathbb{R}^N$ into $\mathbb{R}^K$

$$\Sigma^{\mathsf{T}} : \Theta \in \mathbb{R}^N \to X \in \mathbb{R}^K \tag{2.3}$$

This linear mapping transforms portfolios $\Theta \in \mathbb{R}^N$ into payoff vectors $X \in \mathbb{R}^K$.

Because the initial cost of such a portfolio is $S^{\mathsf{T}}\Theta$, we define the investor's budget set, or set of all levels of consumption that are affordable, as

$$\mathbb{B}(S, \Sigma, e(0)) = \left\{ (X(0), X) \in \mathbb{R}_+^{K+1} : \exists \Theta \in \mathbb{R}^N : X \leq \Sigma^{\mathsf{T}}\Theta \text{ and } X(0) + S^{\mathsf{T}}\Theta \leq e(0) \right\}$$

---

11 Of course, even when $N \leq K$, the N securities may have linearly dependent payoffs, so that some of them may be viewed as redundant.

12 In continuous time, consistently with the split of the price vector S into $\{B, \mathcal{S}\}$, explained in footnote 10, we will use a special symbol for the position in the riskless security, α. The other positions will still be denoted with $\theta_i, i = 1, ..N$, since the risky securities will be N in number. We will collect the latter in a vector Θ. To help the reader distinguish the θ_i-discrete-time positions from the continuous-time ones, Θ will be replaced by $\{\alpha, \Theta\}$, and Θ will have N entries. $\Theta = \theta_1 = \theta$, meaning that Θ is replaced by θ only in the presence of a single risky asset.

13 The superscript "T" is the notation we use for a matrix transpose. See notational conventions at the end of the book.

where $e(0) \in \mathbb{R}_+$ is some number of consumption units with which the investor is endowed at time 0.

2.1.4 Absence of Arbitrage and Risk-Neutral Pricing

We are interested in arbitrage opportunities for reasons related to the minimal assumption of monotonicity of utility stated in the introduction. At the end of this section, we cite a theorem of Magill and Quinzii (1996) saying that, under that assumption on utility, *the absence of arbitrage opportunities is necessary and sufficient for the optimization problem of an investor to have a solution.* We now give necessary and sufficient conditions for the absence or arbitrage, or *no arbitrage*, and draw implications for the pricing of redundant securities.

We must start from a definition of an arbitrage opportunity. In common parlance, an arbitrage opportunity is the possibility of exploiting a deviation from the *Law of One Price*, by selling and buying the same security at a different price, thus reaping a profit from nothing. So, arbitrage opportunities under certainty are quite easy to describe, and the need for excluding arbitrage (or, at least, its prevalence in equilibrium) is as evident as its definition.

Under uncertainty, the definition of arbitrage is still based on the idea of reaping a certain gain at time 1 without any sacrifice at time 0. Here are two types of arbitrage opportunities:

Definition 2.4 *An arbitrage opportunity is a portfolio* $\Theta \neq 0$ *with either of the following properties*

$$S^\mathsf{T}\Theta \leq 0, \Sigma^\mathsf{T}\Theta \succ 0$$
$$S^\mathsf{T}\Theta < 0, \Sigma^\mathsf{T}\Theta \geq 0$$

An arbitrage opportunity of the first type is a portfolio whose initial value is non-positive, $S^\mathsf{T}\Theta \leq 0$ (which means that setting it up either generates a profit, equal to $-S^\mathsf{T}\Theta > 0$, or costs nothing: $S^\mathsf{T}\Theta = 0$), that yields a positive payoff in at least one state of the world, without yielding negative payoffs in the others. Since the vector that collects the portfolio payoffs in the future is $\Sigma^\mathsf{T}\Theta$, for the corresponding portfolio to be an arbitrage we need $\Sigma^\mathsf{T}\Theta$ to be semi-positive, a circumstance that we denote as $\Sigma^\mathsf{T}\Theta \succ 0$.[14] An arbitrage opportunity of the second type is a portfolio that has negative value at inception, $S^\mathsf{T}\Theta < 0$ (which means that setting it up generates a profit $-S^\mathsf{T}\Theta > 0$) and the final payoff $\Sigma^\mathsf{T}\Theta$ of which can be either positive or zero in each single state of the world. Since the payoffs can also be all equal to zero, we say that the vector $\Sigma^\mathsf{T}\Theta$ is non-negative and we write $\Sigma^\mathsf{T}\Theta \geq 0$.

Before addressing the relation between absence of arbitrage and other market features, let us ask ourselves whether the absence of arbitrage is the same thing as the *Law of One Price*. It turns out that absence of arbitrage is a more restrictive condition than the *Law of*

---

14 See also footnote 2 for the meaning of the semi-positive symbol.

One Price. An economy in which the *Law of One Price* holds may offer arbitrage opportunities. The next few lines explain why.

———————————————◆———————————————

Examples of economies in which the *Law of One Price* obtains but arbitrage opportunities exist can be provided. Consider the following.

Example 2.1   Assume a two-state economy, with two securities, the payoffs of which are $1 + r$ in both states and $(0, 1)$ respectively. The Σ matrix, with $r = 10\%$, is

$$\Sigma = \begin{bmatrix} 1.1 & 1.1 \\ 0 & 1 \end{bmatrix}$$

Assume that the security prices are respectively $S_1 = 1.09$ and $S_2 = 1$. Consider a portfolio made up by θ_1 units of the riskless security and θ_2 of the risky one. Assume that the *Law of One Price* holds. This portfolio must be priced $\theta_1 \times 1.09 + \theta_2$. In this market one can undertake an arbitrage by buying $\theta_1 > 0$ riskless securities and θ_2 risky securities, provided that $-\theta_1 \times 1.1 < \theta_2 < -\theta_1 \times 1.09$. The strategy has the following vector of payoffs

$$\Sigma^\mathsf{T}\Theta = \begin{bmatrix} \theta_1 \times 1.1, \theta_1 \times 1.1 + \theta_2 \end{bmatrix}$$

Both payoffs are positive, since $\theta_1 > 0$ and $\theta_2 > -\theta_1 \times 1.1$.

The price of the portfolio is $\theta_1 \times 1.09 + \theta_2 < 0$ since $\theta_2 < -\theta_1 \times 1.09$. This is indeed an arbitrage (type 1). For instance, if $\theta_1 = 1000$ and $\theta_2 = -1095$, then the payoffs are 1100 and 5, while the price is $\theta_1 \times 1.09 + \theta_2 = -5 < 0$.

———————————————◆———————————————

Assumption 2.1 implies that, if ever they existed, investors would exploit arbitrage opportunities. Hence they cannot exist. We are going to prove what is named the *fundamental theorem of security pricing:*[15] *the absence of arbitrage is a necessary and sufficient condition for the existence of a linear relation between prices of (basic as well as redundant) securities and their payoffs*

$$S = \Sigma\Phi$$

written with a strictly positive vector Φ, *called the vector of state prices.*

The fundamental pricing theorem is then recast into a "risk-neutral valuation formula," which serves to price all securities, redundant or not. The proof is at the end of the section.

Theorem 2.1 (Fundamental theorem of security pricing) *A securities market* (S, Σ) *with* $S \neq 0$ *does not offer arbitrage opportunities if and only if there exists a (at least one) strictly positive vector* $\Phi > 0$ *such that*

$$S = \Sigma\Phi \tag{2.4}$$

———————————————————————————

15 The original formulation of the fundamental theorem is in Ross (1978), even though the idea of risk-neutral pricing dates back to Arrow (1970) and made its first appearance in relation with positive pricing vectors in Ross (1973). In continuous time, Harrison and Kreps (1979), Harrison and Pliska (1981), who consider Ross (1976) as the single greatest stimulus for their work, are the seminal papers in the field.

Equation (2.4) says that the matrix Σ establishes a linear mapping from state prices $\Phi \in \mathbb{R}^K$ to securities prices $S \in \mathbb{R}^N$. The mapping is "adjoint" to mapping (2.3):

$$\Sigma : \quad \Phi \in \mathbb{R}^K \rightarrow S \in \mathbb{R}^N \tag{2.5}$$

Remark 2.1 *The vector Φ is a vector of prices of Arrow-Debreu securities, since the previous theorem applied to Arrow-Debreu securities gives $S = I_K \Phi = \Phi$ and I_K is the Arrow-Debreu payoff matrix.*

Since Φ has positive components, we can normalize them. Consider

$$\Phi^* \triangleq \frac{\Phi}{\sum_{s=1}^{K} \phi(s)}$$

These normalized prices Φ^* are strictly positive and smaller than one, since they sum up to one. As a consequence, they form a well-defined probability measure for the K states, equivalent to the initial one.[16]

If, among the N securities, there exists a riskless security, with payoff $1 + r$ and price 1, from the theorem statement (2.4) we get

$$1 = \sum_{s=1}^{K} \phi(s)(1 + r) \tag{2.6}$$

Then $\phi^*(s) = \phi(s) \times (1 + r)$ and we can rewrite (2.4) as

$$S_i = \frac{1}{1 + r} \sum_{s=1}^{K} \phi^*(s) q_i(s) \tag{2.7}$$

The RHS of this expression is the discounted expected value of the payoff of the securities, under the probabilities Φ^* representing a measure equivalent to the initial one. The formula says that the price today is computed as the expected value of the discounted payoff tomorrow, as would be done by a risk-neutral investor with Φ^* probability beliefs, or, equivalently, that securities prices are martingales, once payoffs are discounted. For that reason, we call the new measure a "risk-neutral" measure. We denote it P^* and denote $\mathbb{E}^*$ the expected value calculated under it. We then have the following *risk-neutral pricing* or *martingale-pricing* rule.

Proposition 2.1 (risk-neutral pricing rule) *In the presence of a riskless security with rate of return r, a securities market (Σ, S) does not offer arbitrage opportunities if and only if there exists an equivalent martingale measure $P^* = \{\phi^*(s)\}_{s=1}^{K}$ such that (2.7) holds.*

The probabilities $\{\pi(s)\}_{s=1}^{K}$ assigned to each state by the investors will be named *effective probabilities*. These may be the result either of a subjective assessment or of a

---

16 With a finite number of states, "equivalent" probabilities measures are those that assign positive probabilities to the same states (in the present case, all states since we assumed $\pi(s) > 0$).

frequency-related computation. We do not take a stand on a particular interpretation.[17] What matters is that they are the probabilities assigned to the states for some reason. We can take the ratios of the new to the old probabilities: $\eta(s) \triangleq \phi^*(s)/\pi(s); \eta(s) > 0$. The pricing rule of the fundamental theorem can be restated as

$$S_i = \frac{1}{1+r} \sum_{s=1}^{K} \pi(s)\eta(s)q_i(s)$$

The vector η effects a *change of measure,* from the old to the new probability measure.

Finally, we can also define $\xi(s) \triangleq \eta(s)/(1+r)$ and call the vector $\xi > 0$ the *stochastic discount factor.* We rewrite

$$S_i = \sum_{s=1}^{K} \pi(s)\xi(s)q_i(s)$$

The stochastic discount factor acts as an "exchange rate" that allows us to compute prices as expectations (under the effective measure), after having converted payoffs tomorrow into their value today. Because of this role, the term "discount factor" is used. The factor is *stochastic* since it is state-dependent (one value for each state).

So, *the fundamental pricing theorem and the pricing rule that follows from it justify the rule adopted for pricing the option in section 2.1.1.* A necessary and sufficient condition for the "weights" used there to exist, that is, for justifying that rule, is the absence of arbitrage in the financial market. The theorem and its pricing rule state that, *for any security i,* derivatives and riskless security included, the following equations hold

$$S_i = \sum_{s=1}^{K} \phi(s)q_i(s) = \frac{1}{1+r} \sum_{s=1}^{K} \phi^*(s)q_i(s) \tag{2.8}$$

$$= \frac{1}{1+r} \sum_{s=1}^{K} \pi(s)\eta(s)q_i(s) = \sum_{s=1}^{K} \pi(s)\xi(s)q_i(s)$$

The pricing rule is thus a restatement of (the necessary and sufficient condition for) no arbitrage. It applies to securities in both complete and incomplete markets. The difference between the two cases will be examined in the next section. Before doing that, we want to make two additional points.

First, when attempting to price a new security, one might want to extract state prices from the prices of already traded securities. That means inverting the relation

$$\underbrace{S}_{N \times 1} = \underbrace{\Sigma}_{N \times K} \underbrace{\Phi}_{K \times 1} \tag{2.9}$$

The theorem states that there exists a solution. There may actually be several. We now want to describe the set of possible solutions. To do so, suppose that $N \leq K$ and that the matrix

---

17 The following terms are synonyms: effective, physical, objective, or empirical probabilities.

Σ has full row rank N, which is not restrictive.[18] If there existed redundant securities, one could always eliminate securities (rows) so as to get a payoff matrix whose rows would be linearly independent.

We construct the matrix $\Sigma\Sigma^{\mathsf{T}}$ and observe that this matrix has rank N and admits an inverse, $(\Sigma\Sigma^{\mathsf{T}})^{-1}$. The general solution of equation (2.9), interpreted as an equation in unknown state prices, is

$$\underbrace{\Phi}_{K\times 1} = \underbrace{\Sigma^{\mathsf{T}}}_{K\times N} \underbrace{(\Sigma\Sigma^{\mathsf{T}})^{-1}}_{N\times N} \underbrace{S}_{N\times 1} + \underbrace{\Lambda}_{K\times 1} \qquad (2.10)$$

where Λ is any solution of the equation $\Sigma\Lambda = 0$, that is, any vector in the so-called "kernel" of the matrix Σ.[19] Hence, there are as many solutions for state prices as there are elements of the kernel.

Second, we justify our focus on the absence of arbitrage by observing, as did Kreps (1981), that, when a utility function is introduced, arbitrage may be loosely defined as the possibility of purchasing, at a zero or negative time-0 price, a supplement of time-1 good able to increase the agent's expected utility. With strictly increasing utility functions and a single good, the utility of an agent increases as soon as consumption of that good does in at least one state. Consumption may occur at time 0 ($X(0)$) or at time 1 (X, an vector in $\mathbb{R}^{K}$ with one entry for each state). Time-1 consumption is financed by the portfolio payoff $\Sigma^{\mathsf{T}}\Theta$, which has been purchased for the price of $S^{\mathsf{T}}\Theta$. To emphasize the tight connection between the focus on no arbitrage and the monotonicity assumption 1, we cite a theorem proven in Magill and Quinzii (1996, page 73), which expands the fundamental theorem:

Theorem 2.2 (Expanded fundamental theorem) *If investors' utility functions u satisfy Assumption 1, then the following conditions are equivalent:*

(i)   *The problem* $\max\{u(X(0),X)\}$ *subject to* $(X(0),X) \in \mathbb{B}(S,\Sigma,e_0)$ *has a solution*

(ii)   *The securities market* (S,Σ) *does not offer arbitrage opportunities*

(iii) *There exists a (at least one) positive vector* $\Phi > 0$ *such that:* $S = \Sigma\Phi$ *holds*

(iv)   *The budget set* $\mathbb{B}(S,\Sigma,e_0)$ *is compact.*

---

18 We cannot assume, however, that the matrix has full column rank K. In incomplete markets, the number of states is greater than the number of independent securities ($N < K$). We just know that the rank of Σ is not greater than the number of its columns, $\text{rank}(\Sigma) \leq K$. It is smaller in incomplete markets, equal to it in complete ones (see the next section).

19 By way of verification, observe that the first term of the general solution solves equation (2.9) since, substituting in the RHS of the equation, we get exactly the LHS

$$\Sigma\Sigma^{\mathsf{T}}(\Sigma\Sigma^{\mathsf{T}})^{-1}S = S$$

When the second term is included, (2.10) still solves the equation, since

$$\Sigma\Sigma^{\mathsf{T}}(\Sigma\Sigma^{\mathsf{T}})^{-1}S + \Sigma\Lambda = S + 0 = S$$

In small characters, we now give the proof of the fundamental theorem 2.1 above (which is part (ii) $\Longleftrightarrow$ (iii) in the expanded theorem).

———————————— ♠ ————————————

Proof:[20]

In $\mathbb{R}^N$, the columns $q(s)$ of Σ, for $s = 1, ..K$, define an open convex polyhedral cone H as follows[21]

$$H = \left\{ h; h = \Sigma \Phi; \Phi \in \mathbb{R}^K_{++} \right\}$$

where $\Phi \in \mathbb{R}^K_{++}$ means $\Phi > 0$ (as explained in the notations section of the book). This cone is not empty.

Consider now a point in $\mathbb{R}^N$ with coordinates given by the vector $S \neq 0$. There are only two mutually exclusive possibilities: $S \in H, S \notin H$.

In the first case, there exists a $\Phi > 0$ such that $\Sigma \Phi = S$.

In the second case, by virtue of the separating hyperplane theorem we can separate S from H by a linear functional on $\mathbb{R}^N$ (or a hyperplane in $\mathbb{R}^N$ passing through the origin) with coefficients $\Theta \in \mathbb{R}^N$ such that[22]

$$\text{either } S^\mathsf{T}\Theta \leq 0 \text{ and } h^\mathsf{T}\Theta > 0; \forall h \in H$$
$$\text{or } S^\mathsf{T}\Theta < 0 \text{ and } h^\mathsf{T}\Theta \geq 0; \forall h \in H$$
$$\text{or } S^\mathsf{T}\Theta \geq 0 \text{ and } h^\mathsf{T}\Theta < 0; \forall h \in H$$
$$\text{or } S^\mathsf{T}\Theta > 0 \text{ and } h^\mathsf{T}\Theta \leq 0; \forall h \in H$$

which, since $h = \Sigma\Phi$, is equivalent to

$$\text{either } S^\mathsf{T}\Theta \leq 0 \text{ and } \Phi^\mathsf{T}\Sigma^\mathsf{T}\Theta > 0; \forall \Phi > 0$$
$$\text{or } S^\mathsf{T}\Theta < 0 \text{ and } \Phi^\mathsf{T}\Sigma^\mathsf{T}\Theta \geq 0; \forall \Phi > 0$$
$$\text{or } S^\mathsf{T}\Theta \geq 0 \text{ and } \Phi^\mathsf{T}\Sigma^\mathsf{T}\Theta < 0; \forall \Phi > 0$$
$$\text{or } S^\mathsf{T}\Theta > 0 \text{ and } \Phi^\mathsf{T}\Sigma^\mathsf{T}\Theta \leq 0; \forall \Phi > 0$$

To see the equivalence, consider, for instance, the restriction $\Phi^\mathsf{T}\Sigma^\mathsf{T}\Theta > 0; \forall \Phi > 0$. Since the restriction must hold for all $\Phi > 0$, each element of $\Sigma^\mathsf{T}\Theta$ must be either equal to zero or strictly positive, with at least one positive; that is, $\Sigma^\mathsf{T}\Theta \succ 0$.

In all four cases, either Θ or $-\Theta$ is an arbitrage opportunity.   □

———————————————————————

20 A hyperplane in the space $\mathbb{R}^N$ is a subspace of dimension $N - 1$. The drop in dimension is imposed by one affine equation.

21 A cone in a vector space is such that, if x belongs to it, αx belongs to it as well, for any $\alpha > 0$. The cone H defined here is convex because it contains any convex linear combination of its elements. Because we have assumed that payoffs are non-negative and, obviously, that they are not all equal to zero, the origin $h = \mathbf{0}_{N \times 1}$ does not belong to the cone. We do not actually prove that the cone is open.

22 Functionals defined on $\mathbb{R}^n$ are mappings from that vector space to the real line, $f : \mathbb{R}^n \to \mathbb{R}$. If they are linear, they are also continuous, and there exists a vector Θ of the same space such that they can be represented as an inner product, as formalized in the text. We can identify functionals with vectors of the dual space. For this reason, we say that the functional belongs to the dual of $\mathbb{R}^n$, which is also $\mathbb{R}^n$.

2.1.5   Complete versus Incomplete Markets

The comparison between the number of securities N and the number of states K is key if we want to distinguish *complete* from *incomplete markets*, as we do now. In a complete market, every vector of payoffs in the K states can be attained by forming a portfolio of the basic securities with dividends Σ. To make the statement rigorous, consider a vector of payoffs $X \in \mathbb{R}^K$ at time 1.

Definition 2.5   *A payoff vector $X \in \mathbb{R}^K$ is said to be attainable or to be marketed or to belong to the marketed subspace $\mathbb{M} \subset \mathbb{R}^K$, if there exists a portfolio $\Theta \in \mathbb{R}^N$ such that $\Sigma^\mathsf{T}\Theta = X$.*

Using the notion of marketed payoff vector we can classify the financial market as complete or incomplete.

Definition 2.6   *A market is said to be complete if and only if every payoff vector $X \in \mathbb{R}^K$ is marketed.*

For the market to be complete, every vector in $\mathbb{R}^K$ should be obtainable as a linear combination of the columns of Σ^T, or, equivalently, should be obtainable from the linear mapping Σ^T described in (2.3). The completeness definition given above translates into the following requirement.

Proposition 2.2   *In a finite-state one-period economy, the market is complete if and only if the matrix Σ^T spans the whole space $\mathbb{R}^K$.*

Proof.   The proof is elementary. The market is complete if and only if

$$\forall X \in \mathbb{R}^K, \exists \, \Theta \in \mathbb{R}^N : \Sigma^\mathsf{T}\Theta = X$$

This is true if and only if the mapping characterized by Σ^T is surjective, that is, if and only if it spans the whole space, or its rank, which is also the rank of Σ, is K

$$\text{rank}(\Sigma^\mathsf{T}) = \text{rank}(\Sigma) = K \qquad \qquad \Box$$

A necessary condition for that is that Σ, which is $N \times K$, have at least as many rows as columns ($N \geq K$), that is, that there be at least as many securities as states. But the number of securities *per se* is not key; what matters is the number of securities that are linearly independent and can form a base, compared to the number of states.

As a consequence of the necessary and sufficient condition for market completeness, one can show easily that a market can be *completed* by introducing as many (nonredundant) derivatives as are needed to let the payoff matrix be of full column rank.[23]

---

23 For the result to hold, the derivative must be such that there exist two different states in which the payoffs on the underlying and its derivative are unequal.

2.1.6 Complete Markets and State-Price Uniqueness

In this section, we make the assumption that $N \leq K$ and that the matrix Σ has full row rank. When the market is incomplete, $N = \text{rank}(\Sigma) < K$ and the linear system $\Sigma \Lambda = 0$, which has to be understood as a system in Λ, has $\infty^{K-\text{rank}(\Sigma)}$ solutions described by equation (2.10).

When the market is complete, $N = \text{rank}(\Sigma) = K$ and the kernel contains only the vector zero: it alone solves $\Sigma \Lambda = 0$. Since the matrix Σ is square and has full (column and row) rank, it admits an inverse Σ^{-1} (which is also $\Sigma^{\mathsf{T}}(\Sigma\Sigma^{\mathsf{T}})^{-1}$). Equation (2.9) admits a unique solution

$$\underbrace{\Phi}_{K \times 1} = \underbrace{\Sigma^{-1}}_{K \times K} \underbrace{S}_{K \times 1} \tag{2.11}$$

Actually, completeness is a necessary and sufficient condition for uniqueness of state prices, as the following theorem shows.

Theorem 2.3 *A financial market is complete if and only if state prices are unique.*

Proof. If the market is complete, Σ has an inverse and the equality $S = \Sigma\Phi$, considered as a system of equations in the state prices, has a unique solution (2.11). The converse is proved as follows. If the solution of the equation $S = \Sigma\Phi$ is unique, it must be that rank $(\Sigma) = K$. Since rank $(\Sigma^{\mathsf{T}}) = \text{rank}(\Sigma)$, then Σ^{T} has rank K. If so, there exist one or several solutions Θ to the equation $\Sigma^{\mathsf{T}}\Theta = X$, for any X belonging to $\mathbb{R}^K$, whether the matrix Σ is square or not. □

It is immediate to show that, in a complete market, knowing the state prices or the financial-securities prices is equivalent, since[24]

Corollary 2.1 *In a complete market, state prices can be obtained from financial-securities prices and vice versa.*

Proof. Since Σ is a square, full rank matrix, it has an inverse, Σ^{-1}. In this case, we can solve $S = \Sigma\Phi$ for state prices: $\Phi = \Sigma^{-1}S$. This gives state prices from securities prices. Obviously, $S = \Sigma\Phi$, gives securities prices from state prices. □

In short, two cases exist. In one of them there are fewer independent vectors of payoffs than states, which makes up an incomplete market. In the second there are as many linearly independent payoffs as states, which makes up a complete market. In both cases, prices S must be equal to $\Sigma\Phi$ for some vector $\Phi > 0$ as, otherwise, there would exist *arbitrage opportunities*. In the incomplete-market case, for given securities prices there exists an infinity of state prices consistent with no-arbitrage, and one cannot infer state prices uniquely from security prices. In the complete market case, instead, the relation $S = \Sigma\Phi$ can be used in two different ways: either as providing security prices for given state prices,

---

24 The corollary says that the mapping (2.3) $\Sigma^{\mathsf{T}} : \Theta \in \mathbb{R}^N \to X \in \mathbb{R}^K$ is surjective when the mapping (2.5) $\Sigma : \Phi \in \mathbb{R}^K \to S \in \mathbb{R}^N$ of the fundamental theorem is injective and vice versa.

or as providing the state prices "implicit" in given security prices. In the second case we must use it in the version $\Phi = \Sigma^{-1}S$.

2.1.7 Benchmark Example

As an example of the derivation of state prices, assume that there are only two states and two securities. The payoff matrix is

$$\Sigma = \begin{bmatrix} q_1(1) & q_1(2) \\ q_2(1) & q_2(2) \end{bmatrix}$$

Suppose that you can observe the prices of the corresponding securities, S_1 and S_2. Then, it is possible to infer from those prices either the Arrow-Debreu prices ϕ, or the risk-neutral probabilities ϕ^*, or the stochastic discount factors ξ. Indeed, they are related by

$$S_i = \sum_{s=1}^{2} \phi(s)q_i(s) = \frac{1}{1+r}\sum_{s=1}^{2} \phi^*(s)q_i(s) = \sum_{s=1}^{2} \pi(s)\xi(s)q_i(s)$$

for $i = 1, 2$. Each one of the previous equalities is an equation in the state prices (risk-neutral probabilities and stochastic discount factors respectively), where the LHS, that is, the price of a security is given. Considering the two securities together we have a system of two equations in two unknowns (the two states prices, or the two risk-neutral probabilities or the two stochastic discount factors). We can state the problem of finding the state prices as that of solving for $\phi(1), \phi(2)$ the equations

$$\begin{cases} S_1 = \displaystyle\sum_{s=1}^{2} \phi(s)q_1(s) \\ S_2 = \displaystyle\sum_{s=1}^{2} \phi(s)q_2(s) \end{cases}$$

or, in a compact form, $S = \Sigma\Phi$, with Σ given above. We know that, trivially, $\Phi = \Sigma^{-1}S$. Considering that the discount factor is the sum of the state prices, that is, $1 + r = 1/(\phi(1) + \phi(2))$, the solution to the previous system gives also the risk neutral probabilities $\phi^*(s) = (1 + r)\phi(s) = \phi(s)/(\phi(1) + \phi(2))$. If the state probabilities are given, the system

$$\begin{cases} S_1 = \displaystyle\sum_{s=1}^{2} \pi(s)\xi(s)q_1(s) \\ S_2 = \displaystyle\sum_{s=1}^{2} \pi(s)\xi(s)q_2(s) \end{cases}$$

can be solved for the values of the stochastic discount factors. Equivalently, one can simply obtain them from the first system, using the fact that $\xi(s) = \phi(s)/\pi(s)$.

We suggest that the reader solve exercise 2.1.

2.1.8 Valuation of Redundant Securities

The fundamental theorem and its pricing rule allow us to price any security by means of *martingale pricing,* which consists in extracting the state prices from a collection of linearly independent or basic securities and applying the pricing rule.

While we are free to *extend* the pricing rule to *any* security, beyond those that served to calculate the state prices, the result may be not unique since there may be several solutions to equation (2.9), as equation (2.10) above demonstrates. But we show now that, for redundant securities, the price is unique even when the state prices are not.

In order to make computations simpler, consider the case in which there is a single redundant security, numbered $N + 1$. Form an enlarged matrix Σ^+ by stacking the matrix Σ, which collects the payoffs of the basic securities and has full row rank N, and the vector Σ_{N+1} of the payoffs of the redundant security

$$\Sigma^+ = \begin{bmatrix} \Sigma \\ \Sigma_{N+1} \end{bmatrix}$$

Form an enlarged vector of security prices similarly

$$S^+ = \begin{bmatrix} S \\ S_{N+1} \end{bmatrix}$$

We obtain the prices of redundant securities in the following way.

Martingale or Risk-Neutral Pricing
When the market is complete, we know that the kernel contains the 0 vector only; the state-price vector is unique and equal to $\Sigma^{-1}S$. In this case the redundant security price is unique too and equal to

$$S_{N+1} = \Sigma_{N+1}\Sigma^{-1}S$$

When the market is incomplete, the result we seek is less obvious. Applying to the redundant security the state prices (2.10) that came from basic securities prices gives

$$S_{N+1} = \Sigma_{N+1}\left[\Sigma^{\mathsf{T}}\left(\Sigma\Sigma^{\mathsf{T}}\right)^{-1}S + \Lambda\right] \tag{2.12}$$

Such is the price provided by risk-neutral pricing. It is not obvious that the very same number is obtained no matter which of the many possible values of Φ (or Λ) is being used in this formula. The next argument will prove that it is the case.

Replication
Since the $N + 1$st security is redundant, by definition there exists a replicating vector Θ such that

$$\Sigma_{N+1} = \Theta^{\mathsf{T}}\Sigma \tag{2.13}$$

From (2.13), the replicating portfolio is unique

$$\Sigma_{N+1}\Sigma^{\mathsf{T}} = \Theta^{\mathsf{T}}\Sigma\Sigma^{\mathsf{T}}$$
$$\Theta^{\mathsf{T}} = \Sigma_{N+1}\Sigma^{\mathsf{T}}(\Sigma\Sigma^{\mathsf{T}})^{-1}$$

so that, since $S_{N+1} = \Theta^{\mathsf{T}}S$,

$$S_{N+1} = \Sigma_{N+1}\Sigma^{\mathsf{T}}(\Sigma\Sigma^{\mathsf{T}})^{-1}S$$

which is obviously a unique price.

This shows that the pricing of redundant securities can be reduced to an exercise in linear algebra, consisting in *replicating* them by means of basic securities. The price obtained is, by construction, equal to the one obtained by martingale pricing.

Hedging

Another pricing approach is the following. Instead of replicating the redundant security, synthesize a riskless security using the redundant and the non-redundant securities, if possible. Fix the prices of redundant securities using the fact that a riskless security deserves a rate of return equal to r (the *Law of One Price* again). This approach consists in *hedging* the redundant securities, in that the whole portfolio is riskless or hedged.

More generally, we can synthesize one of the basic securities (say, the one numbered 1) using the other basic securities plus the redundant one. To illustrate, partition the matrices without the redundant security as

$$\Sigma = \begin{bmatrix} \Sigma_1 \\ \Sigma^- \end{bmatrix}; \quad S = \begin{bmatrix} S_1 \\ S^- \end{bmatrix}$$

and the ones with the redundant security as

$$\Sigma^+ = \begin{bmatrix} \Sigma_1 \\ \Sigma^- \\ \Sigma_{N+1} \end{bmatrix}; \quad S^+ = \begin{bmatrix} S_1 \\ S^- \\ S_{N+1} \end{bmatrix}$$

and recall that Σ_1, Σ_{N+1} are row vectors and S_1 and S_{N+1} are scalars. Assume that the matrix

$$\begin{bmatrix} \Sigma^- \\ \Sigma_{N+1} \end{bmatrix}$$

has full row rank N; otherwise undertake to synthesize a security other than security 1. Obtain a hedge portfolio

$$\begin{bmatrix} \underbrace{H^-}_{1\times(N-1)} & \underbrace{H_{N+1}}_{1\times 1} \end{bmatrix}$$

such that

$$\Sigma_1 = \begin{bmatrix} H^- & H_{N+1} \end{bmatrix} \begin{bmatrix} \Sigma^- \\ \Sigma_{N+1} \end{bmatrix} \tag{2.14}$$

That portfolio is unique. The *Law of One Price* implies that

$$S_1 = \begin{bmatrix} H^- & H_{N+1} \end{bmatrix} \begin{bmatrix} S^- \\ S_{N+1} \end{bmatrix}$$

Therefore

$$S_{N+1} = \frac{1}{H_{N+1}} (S_1 - H^- S^-)$$

$$S_{N+1} = \frac{1}{H_{N+1}} \begin{bmatrix} 1 & -H^- \end{bmatrix} S \tag{2.15}$$

The hedge portfolio H is related to the replicating portfolio Θ that solves (2.13)

$$\Theta^{\mathsf{T}} = \frac{1}{H_{N+1}} \begin{bmatrix} 1 & -H^- \end{bmatrix}$$

To verify this relation, postmultiply by Σ and observe that the LHS becomes equal to Σ_{N+1}, while the RHS can be obtained from (2.14)

$$\frac{1}{H_{N+1}} \begin{bmatrix} 1 & -H^- \end{bmatrix} \begin{bmatrix} \Sigma_1 \\ \Sigma^- \end{bmatrix} = \Sigma_{N+1}$$

Martingale pricing, replicating, and hedging then lead to the same price. They are the three approaches that we shall use for redundant-security pricing throughout the book, as straightforward consequences of making sure that arbitrage opportunities do not exist. To get the price of the redundant security, there has been no need, beyond strong monotonicity, to introduce assumptions on any particular market participant, such as his risk aversion. The same will happen throughout the book, and it is the reason why we shall start with redundant-securities pricing also in discrete, multiperiod, and continuous-time economies. When pricing basic securities, however, we shall need more structure. Above all, we shall need Economics in addition to algebra and the assumption of absence of arbitrage.

Before going on, we suggest that the reader solve exercise 2.2.

2.2   Multiperiod Economies

In order to attack the redundant-security pricing problem in discrete-time economies, we need to introduce some notions on the arrival of information over time and on stochastic processes. Here stochastic processes play the role that random variables such as security payoffs played above. But portfolio allocations will also be stochastic processes, since now there is not a single allocation at time 0 but an allocation at each point in time, the last one not included. The arrival of information will translate into conditional probabilities about the processes, that is, probabilities conditional on information revelation up to a given point in time.

2.2.1   Information Arrival over Time and Stochastic Processes

We now introduce some definitions that will be maintained both for discrete and continuous-time economies.

Consider a real parameter t representing time, $t \in \mathcal{T} = [0, T]$, which can be an interval of the real line or, for discrete-time economies, a time index running over the natural numbers, $\mathcal{T} \subset N$. The span of time $\mathcal{T}$ can be bounded or not, depending on whether one wants to describe finite or infinite-horizon economies. Our discrete-time economies will always have a finite horizon, $T < \infty$; assume the same for continuous-time economies. Both in discrete and continuous-time economies, Ω is the *sample space*, an element of which represents over time the external conditions faced by investors. It is a path over time.

In order to represent uncertainty in a multiperiod economy, we need information updating over time, which in turn requires the notion of filtration.

A *filtration* is a modeling tool for representing information arrival over time. Intuitively, the filtration at time t contains all the events *observable* at or before time t. At time t the decision maker can tell which element or event of a σ-algebra $\mathcal{F}(t)$ is true (that is, "has happened"). This is his information up to t.

Definition 2.7   *On the probability space $(\Omega, \mathcal{F}, P)$, a filtration*

$$\mathbf{F} = \{\mathcal{F}(t), t \in \mathcal{T}\}$$

is a family of σ-algebras with the properties listed below.[25]

- *every element of the filtration is contained in the σ-algebra $\mathcal{F}$, $\mathcal{F}(t) \subset \mathcal{F}$.*
  This means that one cannot acquire more information than the one contained in the overall σ-algebra,
- *the filtration is increasing, $\mathcal{F}(\tau) \subset \mathcal{F}(t)$ whenever $\tau \leq t$.*
  The increasing property means that one can accumulate information but one cannot forget anything. At time t, one knows everything he got to know up to that point, or $\cup_{\tau \leq t} \mathcal{F}(\tau) = \mathcal{F}(t)$,
- *the initial filtration is trivial, $\mathcal{F}(0) = \{\varnothing, \Omega\}$.*
  At time 0, one knows only that an element of the state space will become true. All elements of the sample space are deemed possible.

---

25 In this definition, the σ-algebras must also be "augmented." See footnote 26 below.

- *the entire information $\mathcal{F}$ is revealed when the final horizon T is reached: $\mathcal{F} = \mathcal{F}(T)$. At time T, one knows which element of the sample space became true. The filtration $\mathcal{F}(T)$ coincides with the σ-algebra $\mathcal{F}$, $\mathcal{F}(T) = \mathcal{F}$.*

The filtration is said to satisfy the *usual conditions* if it is right-continuous ($\mathcal{F}(t) = \wedge_{u>t}\mathcal{F}(u)$, $t < T$, where $\wedge_{u>t}\mathcal{F}(u)$ is defined as the largest σ-algebra contained in all elements of the filtration for $u > t$) and complete ($\mathcal{F}(0)$ contains all the elements of the σ-algebra $\mathcal{F}$ that have zero measure).[26]

Once a filtration has been introduced, the probability space $(\Omega, \mathcal{F}, P)$ becomes a *filtered probability space* $(\Omega, \mathcal{F}, P, \mathbf{F})$. An element of $\mathcal{F}(t)$ is called an event or a state of time t. For the case of *discrete-time economies*, we will denote the *state* – or the path that has been followed up to time t – as (s, t). We are also interested in the states that can be reached from state s, the successors of state s, which we denote as s^+. Conditioning at time t is done with respect to the filtration $\mathcal{F}(t)$. Using conditional probabilities, one can compute the conditional expectation of a process.

Definition 2.8   *The conditional expected value of a random variable X with respect to a σ-algebra $\mathcal{F}(t) \subset \mathcal{F}$, denoted as $\mathbb{E}[X \mid \mathcal{F}(t)]$ or $\mathbb{E}_t[X]$ for short, is the expected value formed using the probabilities updated on the basis of the filtration $\mathcal{F}(t)$. $\mathbb{E}[X \mid \mathcal{F}(t)]$ is (i) measurable with respect to $\mathcal{F}(t)$ and (ii) for every $b \in \mathcal{F}(t)$*

$$\mathbb{E}[\mathbf{1}_b \mathbb{E}[X \mid \mathcal{F}(t)] \mid \mathcal{F}(t)] = \mathbb{E}[\mathbf{1}_b X \mid \mathcal{F}(t)]$$

where $\mathbf{1}_b$ is the indicator of event b.

Property (i) says that the expectation can be formed (that is, it takes a specific value) only when the information available at time t comes. This is the sense in which it is conditional. Property (ii) formalizes the fact that, if an event b becomes true at time t, only realizations of the process consistent with that event matter in the computation of its expectation later on. *The initial filtration being trivial, the conditional expectation at time 0 is an unconditional expectation, and may be simply written as $\mathbb{E}[X]$, with no subscripts.*

The following "law of iterated expectations" holds: if $\tau > t$ (so that $\mathcal{F}(t) \subset \mathcal{F}(\tau) \subset \mathcal{F}$), then

$$\mathbb{E}[\mathbb{E}[X \mid \mathcal{F}(\tau)] \mid \mathcal{F}(t)] = \mathbb{E}[X \mid \mathcal{F}(t)]$$

---

26 "Augmented" σ-algebras contain the P-null sets, more loosely called "sets of zero measure." These are sets A such that:

$$\{A \subset \Omega : \exists G \in \mathcal{F}(t) \text{ with } A \subset G, P(G) = 0\}$$

In other words, these sets of zero measure are contained in sets that have zero probability while they themselves may or may not be measurable to start with. The σ-algebras of definition 2.7 are "augmented," when the P-null sets have been added to them. In some cases, the augmentation assumption serves to show that the filtration is right-continuous if the generating process (defined at the end of this section) is Markov. See Karatzas and Shreve (1991, page 89).

It says that, when conditioning on the information at time t, the expectation of the expectation of a random variable X at time τ, which will be based on knowledge up to that time, cannot be other that the expectation based on time-t information. The richer information that will come at τ is unknown at t. The best one can do is to use all the information available now.

While filtrations can be used in all cases to model information arrival, it is easiest to illustrate their meaning graphically *in the special case of discrete uncertainty*. In that case, an equivalent description is provided by an *event tree* containing nodes and branches. States coincides with nodes, and the successors and predecessors of a given node are indeed the ones that follow or precede it in the branch development. For instance, in figure 2.1, at time 0 there is only one node and the event-tree means that, at time 0, we just know that some outcome will occur by time 2. At later times, the nodes stand for elements of a partition of the sample space: at time 1, one gets to know that either $\{\omega_1, \omega_2, \omega_3\}$ (meaning "either ω_1 or ω_2 or ω_3") or $\{\omega_4, \omega_5\}$ takes place, while at time 2, one gets to know exactly which outcome occurred among the possible ones. Thus, the nodes of the event-tree of figure 2.1 reflect *partitions* of the set of all the possible outcomes. We start from a coarse partition $\mathcal{P}$, namely

$$\mathcal{P}(0) = \{\Omega\}$$

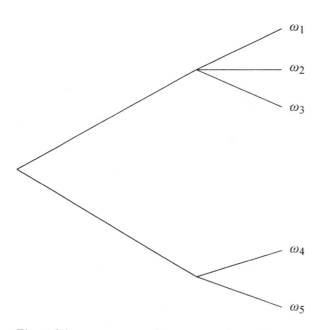

Figure 2.1
Event-tree with three points in time $(0, 1, 2)$, two nodes at time 1, five nodes at time 2.

go to a finer one at time 1

$$\mathcal{P}(1) = \{\{\omega_1, \omega_2, \omega_3\}, \{\omega_4, \omega_5\}\}$$

and to the finest possible at time 2

$$\mathcal{P}(2) = \{\{\omega_1\}, \{\omega_2\}, \{\omega_3\}, \{\omega_4\}, \{\omega_5\}\}$$

An equivalent representation of the information arrival process is the filtration:

$$\mathcal{F}(0) = \{\varnothing, \Omega\}$$

$$\mathcal{F}(1) = \{\{\omega_1, \omega_2, \omega_3\}, \{\omega_4, \omega_5\}, \varnothing, \Omega\}$$

$$\mathcal{F}(2) = \left\{ \begin{array}{c} \{\omega_1\}, \{\omega_2\}, \{\omega_3\}, \{\omega_4\}, \{\omega_5\}, \{\omega_1, \omega_2\}, \{\omega_2, \omega_3\}, .. \\ .., \{\omega_4, \omega_5\}, \{\omega_1, \omega_2, \omega_3\}, \varnothing, \Omega \end{array} \right\}$$

where $\mathcal{F}(2)$ includes all the possible unions and complements of subsets in $\mathcal{P}(2)$. In the filtration it is clear that one does not forget (for instance, $\{\omega_4, \omega_5\}$ is in $\mathcal{F}(1)$ and stays in $\mathcal{F}(2)$) and that if one is able to say whether, say, ω_1 is true, one can also tell whether $\{\omega_1, \omega_2\}$ is true.

In the tree formulation, at each point in time $t = 0, 1, ..T$ the economy finds itself at a node (s, t) of the tree, $s = 1, ...K_t$. K_t then is the number of nodes at t. We allow the number of nodes to change over time. Any node s at time t can evolve into nodes s^+ at time $t + 1$. We call $K_{s,t}$ the number of nodes that are *immediate* successors of node s of time t: $s^+ = 1, ...K_{s,t}$. $K_{s,t}$ is called the "splitting index" at s. When we want to keep track of paths in the tree, the predecessor at time $u < s$ of node (s, t) is called (s^-, u). In that context, therefore, (s^-, u) is a specific node s of time u.

Seen from time 0, the probability measure for time-t states is described by a K_t-dimensional vector of probabilities $\{\pi(s, t)\}$. These are the so-called unconditional probabilities. We can also introduce so-called conditional probabilities, which are assigned conditional on information that will arrive later in time. The conditional probability of being in state s^+ at time $t + 1$ given that state s prevailed at time t is equal to $\pi(s^+, t + 1)/\pi(s, t)$ (with the convention $\pi(0) = 1$).

In the context of continuous time we will assume that an infinite number of states can arise. We will refer to this circumstance as "continuous uncertainty." There, we shall be unable to describe the unveiling of uncertainty by means of event-trees.[27] But the definitions of partition, filtration, and their relation remain valid.

How does information revelation, be it described by event-trees, partitions, or filtrations, interact with financial decision making? In order to provide a formal answer, we need a more precise definition of stochastic processes and their properties.

In the single-period economy we had random variables, which represented the payoffs of the risky securities at time 1. In discrete-time economies, there are *stochastic processes* for

---

27 Even in discrete time, one cannot write a tree with a continuum of branches.

portfolio allocations and payoffs of the risky securities. There is also a stochastic process for prices. Formally,

Definition 2.9   *A real stochastic process is a family X of real random variables* $\{X(\omega, t)\}$ *indexed by* $t \in \mathcal{T}$.

Fixing $\omega \in \Omega$, the process can be viewed as a function of time $X(t)$; this function is called a sample path or a realization of the process. Fixing t, the process is a random variable $X(\omega, t)$. The process can also be understood as a mapping from the product space $\Omega \times \mathcal{T}$ into the real numbers. We write $X : \Omega \times \mathcal{T} \rightarrow \mathbb{R}$. The definition can obviously be extended to vector-valued or N-dimensional processes, which take values in $\mathbb{R}^n$, $n > 1$. The initial filtration being trivial, the value at time 0 of any process is a real number (a real vector if $n > 1$), not a random variable (or collection of random variables).

In order to deal with stochastic processes, we need some technical definitions.

- Two processes X and Y are *stochastically equivalent*, or one is a *version* of the other, if they are equal with probability one at every point in time. Up to now, in discrete time, we did not distinguish random variables that differed on a set of zero probability and, for that reason, in discrete time we did not take into consideration zero-probability states (π_s was assumed strictly positive). Similarly, we consider equivalent processes as being the same process. This convention allows us to omit some technical details.

- Two processes X and Y are *independent* if, for any m and any choice of intermediate dates $t_0 < t_1 < .. < t_m$, the random vectors $X(t_0), X(t_1),.., X(t_m)$ and $Y(t_0), Y(t_1),.., Y(t_m)$ are pairwise independent.

- A stochastic process is of *finite variation* if it is adapted (see below) and if its sample paths have finite variation, or, intuitively, if the length of any path is finite. This property holds for sure in discrete time, but may hold or not in continuous time.

- The filtration $\mathbf{F}^X = \{\mathcal{F}^X(t)\}$ *generated by a process* X is the family of σ-algebras with the following property. At each point in time t, $\mathcal{F}^X(t)$ is the smallest σ-algebra with respect to which all random variables $X(\tau), \tau \leq t$ are measurable.[28] $\mathcal{F}^X(t)$ is the filtration provided by the past history of the process, or the information an agent could have acquired by looking at that process only. The sample paths of the process determine all distinguishable events.

- A process $X(\omega, t)$ is said to be *adapted to the filtration* $\mathbf{F}$ if, for each t, the random variable $X(\omega, t)$ is measurable with respect to $\mathcal{F}(t)$. If adapted, therefore, we can write it

---

28 "Measurable" here means $X^{-1}(\mathcal{B}, t) \in \mathcal{F}(t)$, where $\mathcal{B}$ is any Borel-set of $\mathbb{R}^n$, $n > 1$. See footnote 7 for an interpretation. This measurability is slightly different from the measurability of the process X – viewed as a mapping $\Omega \times \mathcal{T} \rightarrow \mathbb{R}^n$ – with respect to $\mathcal{F} \times \mathcal{B}$. Indeed, in the second case measurability is jointly in ω and t. Every adapted, continuous process is measurable in ω and t.

as $X(s,t)$ in the case of discrete time. Intuitively, "adapted" means that the knowledge of the process at t does not reveal any more information than is available in $\mathcal{F}(t)$ up to time t. In particular, the process does not depend on information available strictly after t. This seems to be a very reasonable requirement for decision situations. If the process is a decision variable, such as a portfolio allocation, the decision is made knowing which event took place at t. It is not made on the basis of future realizations of a path, but only on the basis of probabilistic information regarding the future derived from the past, that is, the possible states and the probabilities conditional on the information available at t. For instance, in the discrete-time special case, agents will take their decisions at t knowing what happened up to t, but ignoring the future. Time-t portfolios $\Theta(s,t)$ are decided at time t and kept until $t+1$; their realization is known when time t arrives. They are adapted. In the sequel, including the case of continuous time, we always assume that stochastic processes are adapted to the filtration that is placed on the underlying space. This property holds by definition if the filtration is actually generated by the process itself.

2.2.2   Self-Financing Constraint and Redundant Securities

We now return to the specific case of discrete time. In the filtered probability space $(\Omega, \mathcal{F}, P, \mathbf{F})$, with a finite horizon T, we define a financial market, in which there are N long-lived securities with price processes $S(\omega, t)$, which are adapted and can, therefore, be written $S(s,t)$.[29] They remain available for trading at each point in time between time 0 and time $T-1$ and pay no dividends till the terminal date T. For parsimony of notation, we also call $S(s,T)$ the matrix of terminal payoffs of existing securities in all terminal states.

The first one of the securities has a one-step ahead deterministic behavior, namely

$$S_1(s,t) = S_1(0) \times \Pi_{u=0}^{t-1}(1 + r(s^-, u))$$

with $S_1(0) \in \mathbb{R}_{++}$. We normalize it at time 0, so that $S_1(0) = 1$. Recall that (s^-, u) is the notation for the node preceding (s,t) at time u.

We may form portfolios out of the N securities. Denote as $\Theta(\omega, t) = \{\theta_i(\omega, t),\ i = 1, 2, ..N\}$ the vector containing the number of units of riskless and risky securities that an investor decides at t to hold till date $t+1$. We impose that the process $\{\Theta(\omega, t), t \in [0, 1, ...T-1]\}$ be adapted to the filtration $\mathbf{F}$. For that reason, we write it as $\{\Theta(s,t), t \in [0, 1, ...T-1]\}$. The class of N-dimensional adapted processes is called $\bar{\Theta}$. The *value* of the pre-trade or entering portfolio at t is the investor's *financial wealth*, denoted in

---

29 What follows does *not* depend on the existence of long-lived securities. The same theory can be developed with securities that come to their maturity date and are replaced by newly issued securities. But the notation would be more cumbersome.

the sequel of the book indifferently with the symbols F or W. It is

$$F(s,t) \triangleq \Theta^{\mathsf{T}}(s^-, t-1)S(s,t) \qquad\qquad t = 1, ..T$$

where $(s^-, t-1)$ is the node just preceding (s,t), while the investor's after-trade or exiting portfolio is worth

$$\Theta^{\mathsf{T}}(s,t)S(s,t) \qquad\qquad t = 0, 1, ..T-1$$

Please, observe that the same prices $S(s,t)$ of time t are used in both quantities, all buy and sell trades being executed at the same prices of time t.

Among all admissible trading strategies, we are interested in those that entail neither new investment into the portfolio, nor withdrawals from it: $\Delta\Theta^{\mathsf{T}}(s,t)S(s,t) = 0$, with $\Delta\Theta(s,t) \triangleq \Theta(s,t) - \Theta(s^-, t-1)$. These strategies are said to be *self-financing*. At each time t, they are defined by the requirement that the post- and pre-trade portfolios have equal values

$$\Theta^{\mathsf{T}}(s,t)S(s,t) = F(s,t) \qquad\qquad t > 0 \qquad\qquad (2.16)$$

This means that any change in the position in a security is financed by a change in another one. With two securities only, for instance, the self-financing constraint becomes

$$\theta_1(s,t) \times S_1(t) + \theta_2(s,t) \times S_2(s,t)$$
$$= \theta_1\left(s^-, t-1\right) \times S_1(s,t) + \theta_2\left(s^-, t-1\right) \times S_2(s,t)$$

or

$$\Delta\theta_1(s,t) \times S_1(s,t) = -\Delta\theta_2(s,t) \times S_2(s,t)$$

The change in the allocation to security 1 must Finance the change in the allocation to security 2.[30]

Consider any point in time after the initial one. Since prices may have changed from $t-1$ to t, an investor arrives at time t with given portfolio positions $\Theta(s^-, t-1)$, but not with the same portfolio value as the one he or she had after trade at $t-1$. Since time $t-1$, he has made a gain (or loss) because prices have changed from $S(s^-, t-1)$ to $S(s,t)$. We accumulate these gains in the form of the so-called *gains* process G: $G(0) = 0$ and

$$G(s,t) - G(s^-, t-1) = \Theta^{\mathsf{T}}(s^-, t-1)\left[S(s,t) - S(s^-, t-1)\right]$$

---

30 One could define the "capital flow" into security i as
$$\left[\theta_i(s,t) - \theta_i\left(s^-, t-1\right)\right] \times S_i(s,t)$$

for $t > 0$. Setting $S(s,t) - S(s^-, t-1) = \Delta S(s,t)$, we get

$$G(s,t) = \sum_{u=1}^{t} \Theta^\mathsf{T}(s^-, u-1)\Delta S(s,u)$$

for $t > 0$, where $(s^-, u-1)$ is the predecessor of (s, u). The overall gain up to t is the sum of the accrued price-changes up to that point, considering that, between $u-1$ and u, price changes from $S(s^-, u-1)$ to $S(s, u)$ while the portfolio stays fixed at $\Theta(s^-, u-1)$.

When the portfolio is self-financing as per (2.16), the total value at time T, $\Theta^\mathsf{T}(s, T-1)S(s,T) = F(s,T)$, is simply the initial value plus accumulated gains:

$$\Theta^\mathsf{T}(s, T-1)S(s,T) = \underbrace{\Theta^\mathsf{T}(0)S(0)}_{F(0)} + \underbrace{\sum_{t=1}^{T} \Theta^\mathsf{T}\left(s^-, t-1\right)\Delta S(s,t)}_{G(s,T)} \tag{2.17}$$

or

$$F(s,T) = F(0) + G(s,T)$$

We are interested in self-financing trading strategies because, if we can take the prices of a set of basic securities as given (as we did in the one-period economy when we derived the state prices) and we can replicate a security that has a single payoff at time T with a self-financing portfolio, then its price at any point in time before T will be the price of the portfolio itself (to prevent violations of the *Law of One Price*).

Definition 2.10 *A single-payment security with time-T payoff $X(s) \in \mathbb{R}^{K_T}$ is said to be* redundant *relative to a set of* basic securities *when its payoff* can be replicated by a self-financing portfolio strategy of basic securities *(that is, if there exists a self-financing strategy $\Theta(s,t) \in \bar{\Theta}$ containing basic securities only, such that $\Theta^\mathsf{T}(s, T-1)S(s,T) = X(s)$).*

.

2.2.3   Arbitrage, No Arbitrage, and Risk-Neutral Pricing

The definition of arbitrage may be extended to the multiperiod context, with several nuances. First, we can define a multiperiod arbitrage in a "global" sense, as follows:

Definition 2.11 *An arbitrage opportunity starting at time 0 is a self financing portfolio strategy $\Theta(s,t) \neq 0; \Theta \in \bar{\Theta}, t = 0, .., T-1$ with either of the following properties:*

$$S(0)^\mathsf{T}\Theta(0) \leq 0, S(s,T)^\mathsf{T}\Theta\left(s^-, T-1\right) \succ 0$$
$$S(0)^\mathsf{T}\Theta(0) < 0, S(s,T)^\mathsf{T}\Theta\left(s^-, T-1\right) \geq 0, \forall s$$

Or using a similar, but "local" definition:

Definition 2.12 *An arbitrage opportunity starting at time* 0 *is a portfolio strategy* $\Theta(s,t) \neq 0; \Theta \in \bar{\Theta}, t = 0,..,T-1$ *with the following property*[31]

$$
\begin{bmatrix}
-S(0)^\mathsf{T}_{1 \times N}\Theta(0)_{N \times 1} \\
S(s,1)^\mathsf{T}_{1 \times N}\Theta(0)_{N \times 1} - S(s,1)^\mathsf{T}_{1 \times N}\Theta(s,1)_{N \times 1}; s = 1,..,K_1 \\
S(s,2)^\mathsf{T}_{1 \times N}\Theta(s^-,1)_{N \times 1} - S(s,2)^\mathsf{T}_{1 \times N}\Theta(s,2)_{N \times 1}; s = 1,..,K_2 \\
... \\
S(s,t)^\mathsf{T}_{1 \times N}\Theta(s^-,t-1)_{N \times 1} - S(s,t)^\mathsf{T}_{1 \times N}\Theta(s,t)_{N \times 1}; s = 1,...,K_t \\
... \\
S(s,T)^\mathsf{T}_{1 \times N}\Theta(s^-,T-1)_{N \times 1}; s = 1,...,K_T
\end{bmatrix} \succ 0
$$

Notice first that – according to (2.17) – arbitrage opportunities that satisfy definition (2.11) produce semi-positive final gains

$$G(s,T) = -S(0)^\mathsf{T}\Theta(0) + S(s,T)^\mathsf{T}\Theta(s^-,T-1) \succ 0$$

We prove that a "global" arbitrage in the sense of definition (2.11) entails a "local" arbitrage according to definition (2.12). A "global" arbitrage produces

$$G(s,T) = -S(0)^\mathsf{T}\Theta(0) + S(s,T)^\mathsf{T}\Theta(s^-,T-1) \succ 0$$

and requires self-financing strategies. Since strategies are self-financing, that is, $\Delta\Theta^\mathsf{T}S = 0$ for all t, all rows of the matrix of definition (2.12) are equal to zero, apart from the first and the last. Still, there is an arbitrage opportunity according to definition (2.12), since we have

$$
\begin{bmatrix}
-S(0)^\mathsf{T}_{1 \times N}\Theta(0)_{N \times 1} \\
0; s = 1,..,K_1 \\
0; s = 1,..,K_2 \\
... \\
0; s = 1,...,K_t \\
... \\
S(s,T)^\mathsf{T}_{1 \times N}\Theta(s^-,T-1)_{N \times 1}; s = 1,...,K_T
\end{bmatrix} \succ 0
$$

As for the converse, suppose that an arbitrage exists according to "local" definition (2.12) with $S(t)^\mathsf{T}\Theta(t) \leq 0$. Suppose also that the first line that is strictly positive in the corresponding matrix is the time-t line. That means there exist states over which

$$S(s,t)^\mathsf{T}\Theta(s^-,t-1) - S(s,t)^\mathsf{T}\Theta(s,t) > 0$$

---

31 Here the subscripts serve to remind the reader of the dimensions of the vectors and matrices.

This means that a strictly positive outflow occurs for the first time in some state s. That outflow can be reinvested into the riskless all the way till date T. If the amount reinvested was positive at date t, it will still be positive at date T with certainty in all the states that are descendents of s. The same thing can be done again later on whenever a positive outflow occurs. It follows that

$$S(s,T)^\mathsf{T} \Theta\left(s^-, T-1\right) \succ 0$$

that is, there exists an arbitrage opportunity in the "global" sense. A similar reasoning applies to the case $S^\mathsf{T}(t)\Theta(t) < 0$.

Overall, since there exists an arbitrage according to one definition if and only if there exists one according to the other, we can use either of them to study the relation between the absence of arbitrage and the existence of state prices. We use definition (2.12). Defining a matrix Σ^T with $1 + \sum_{t=1}^{T} K_t$ rows (column headings not counted as a row) and $N \times \left(1 + \sum_{t=1}^{T-1} K_t\right)$ columns:[32]

$$\Sigma^\mathsf{T} \triangleq$$

time 0	time 1					time $T-1$		
$-S(0)^\mathsf{T}$		...					...	
$S(1,1)^\mathsf{T}$	$-S(1,1)^\mathsf{T}$							
...	...							
$S(K_1,1)^\mathsf{T}$	0	$-S(K_1,1)^\mathsf{T}$						
	$S(1,2)^\mathsf{T}$							
	...							
	$S(K_{1,1},2)^\mathsf{T}$							
		...						
		$S(K_{K_1,1},2)^\mathsf{T}$						
			...					
				$-S(1,T-1)^\mathsf{T}$				
				...				
						$-S(K_{T-1},T-1)^\mathsf{T}$		
				$S(1,T)^\mathsf{T}$				
				...				
				$S(K_{1,T-1},T)^\mathsf{T}$				
						...		
						$S(K_{K_{T-1},T-1},T)^\mathsf{T}$		

---

32 Recall that we call $K_{s,t}$ the number of *immediate* successors of node s of time t: $s^+ = 1, ... K_{s,t}$. Recall also that K_t is the total number of nodes at time t: $K_{t+1} = \sum_{s=1}^{K_t} K_{s,t}$.

the condition in the definition can be rewritten in matrix form:

$$
\Sigma^{\mathsf{T}}
\begin{bmatrix}
\Theta(0)_{N\times 1} \\
\Theta(s,1)_{N\times 1}; s = 1,..,K_1 \\
\cdots \\
\Theta(s,t)_{N\times 1}; s = 1,...,K_t \\
\cdots \\
\Theta(s,T-1)_{N\times 1}; s = 1,...,K_{T-1}
\end{bmatrix}
\succ 0
$$

Corollary 2.2 (of Static fundamental theorem) *A securities market*

$$
(S(0) \neq 0, S(s,t) \neq 0; t = 1,...,T)
$$

does not offer arbitrage opportunities starting at time 0 if and only if there exists a (at least one) strictly positive vector process $\{\Phi(s,t) > 0; t = 1,...,T\}$ *such that*

$$
\Sigma
\begin{bmatrix}
1 \\
\Phi(1)_{K_1\times 1} \\
\cdots \\
\Phi(t)_{K_t\times 1} \\
\cdots \\
\Phi(T-1)_{K_{T-1}\times 1} \\
\Phi(T)_{K_T\times 1}
\end{bmatrix}
= 0
$$

holds.

There is no need for a proof. This is just an application of the one-period fundamental theorem.

Corollary 2.3 *The* Φ*'s compound over time and in each single period are ratios of state prices, so that:*

$$
S(s,t) = \sum_{s^+=1}^{K_{s,t}} \frac{\phi(s^+,t+1)}{\phi(s,t)} S(s^+,t+1)
$$

Proof. Corollary 2.2 above says:

$$
S(0)_{N\times 1} = S(\{s^+\},1)_{N\times K_1} \Phi(1)_{K_1\times 1}
$$

$$
S(s,1)_{N\times 1}\Phi(s,1)_{1\times 1} = S(\{s^+\},2)_{N\times K_{s,1}} \Phi(2)_{K_{s,1}\times 1}; s = 1,..,K_1
$$

$$
\cdots
$$

$$
S(s,t)_{N\times 1}\Phi(s,t)_{1\times 1} = S(\{s^+\},t+1)_{N\times K_{s,t}} \Phi(t+1)_{K_{s,t}\times 1}; s = 1,..,K_t
$$

where, say, $S(\{s^+\}, 1)_{N \times K_1}$ stands for $[S(1,1), S(2,1)..S(K_1,1)]$. Therefore, in each state of nature s of time t, calling $\phi(s,t)$ the element s of vector $\Phi(t)$,

$$S(s,t) = \sum_{s^+=1}^{K_{s,t}} \frac{\phi(s^+, t+1)}{\phi(s,t)} S(s^+, t+1) \qquad (2.18)$$

Call s^{++} the successors of state s^+. Substitute for

$$S(s^+, t+1) = \sum_{s^{++}=1}^{K_{s^+,t+1}} \frac{\phi(s^{++}, t+2)}{\phi(s^+, t+1)} S(s^{++}, t+2)$$

into the previous expression, to get

$$S(s,t) = \sum_{s^+=1}^{K_{s,t}} \frac{\phi(s^+, t+1)}{\phi(s,t)} \sum_{s^{++}=1}^{K_{s^+,t+1}} \frac{\phi(s^{++}, t+2)}{\phi(s^+, t+1)} S(s^{++}, t+2)$$

which shows the meaning of "compounding" in the current setting. $\qquad \square$

Thanks to this corollary, substituting from the terminal to the initial date, we can write the formula (2.18) using the ratio $\phi(s^+, T)/\phi(s,t)$. The two corollaries state that a price process $S(s,t), t = 0, ...T$ with $S \neq 0$ does not offer arbitrage opportunities if and only if there exists a (at least one) positive state-price process $\Phi(0) = 1; \phi(s,t) > 0; t = 0, ...T$ such that

$$S(s,t) = \sum_{s^+} \frac{\phi(s^+, T)}{\phi(s,t)} S(s^+, T)$$

Equivalently,

$$S(s,t) = \mathbb{E}^* \left[\Pi_{u=t}^{T-1}(1 + r(u))^{-1} S(T) \mid \mathcal{F}(t) \right] \qquad (2.19)$$

where the expectation is taken under the risk-neutral measure, defined by $\Phi^*(s,t) = \Phi(s,t)\Pi_{u=0}^{t-1}(1 + r(s,u))$, and, the expectation being a conditional one, all terminal states $s(T)$ that are not part of the current state s are excluded, exactly as in the previous formula.

Equivalently, there exists a process $\eta(s,t) \triangleq \phi^*(s,t)/\pi(s,t)$ such that

$$S(s,t) = \mathbb{E} \left[\frac{\eta(T)}{\eta(s,t)} \Pi_{u=t}^{T-1}(1 + r(u))^{-1} S(T) \mid \mathcal{F}(t) \right] \qquad (2.20)$$

Still equivalently, we can write the price using the stochastic discount factor $\xi(t)$:

$$S(s,t) = \mathbb{E} \left[\frac{\xi(T)}{\xi(s,t)} S(T) \mid \mathcal{F}(t) \right]$$

since $\xi(s,t) = \eta(s,t)\Pi_{u=0}^{t-1}(1 + r(s,u))$.

Equation (2.19) says that the price of any security at time 0 is equal to the expected value of the discounted dividend paid at time T, calculated under the new measure. That implies that discounted price processes are martingales under that measure:

$$S(s,t) = \mathbb{E}^* \left[\Pi_{u=t}^{\tau-1} (1 + r(u))^{-1} S(\tau) \mid \mathcal{F}(t) \right]; \forall \tau > t$$

a property otherwise written as

$$S(s,t) = \mathbb{E} \left[\frac{\eta(\tau)}{\eta(s,t)} \Pi_{u=t}^{\tau-1} (1 + r(u))^{-1} S(\tau) \mid \mathcal{F}(t) \right]; \forall \tau > t$$

2.2.4 Valuation of Redundant Securities

If we want to price redundant securities in a multiperiod economy, we can exploit the knowledge we acquired in a one-period economy, by reducing it to a sequence of one-period economies. In a market with no arbitrage opportunity, there exists a (generally more than one) martingale pricing measure Φ^* that applies to all securities and which can be extended beyond existing, basic securities to entirely new securities.

For an arbitrary new security, the price so obtained is generally not unique. For a redundant security, however, the price so obtained is unique, just as in the one-period case. An example is provided below in section 2.2.6.

If the market is already complete, then any additional security is necessarily redundant. We turn now to the definition of a complete market in a dynamic setting.

2.2.5 Statically versus Dynamically Complete Markets

The definition of completeness in multiperiod economies is twofold:

Definition 2.13 *A market is* statically complete *if every single-payment security X is attainable* without *rebalancing the portfolio over time. A market model is* dynamically complete *if every single-payment security is attainable,* possibly by rebalancing the portfolio over time.

In order to establish conditions for completeness, we must say when m assets are linearly independent at time t. We define linear independence as follows:

Definition 2.14 *m assets are linearly independent at time t in state s*

$$rank(S(\{s^+\}, t+1)) = m$$

where $S(\{s^+\}, t+1)$ is the matrix of the payoffs of the N securities at time $t+1$, in the successors of state s.

Recall also that uncertainty in the current context can be represented by a tree. We are going to prove the following:

Theorem 2.4   *The market is dynamically complete if and only if, at each node, the number of linearly independent securities is equal to the splitting index of that node.*

Proof. For the sake of simplicity, assume that – at a specific point in time – the splitting index is equal for all states : $K_{s,t} = K_t$. K_t is the splitting index common to all states at time t; m_t is the number of linearly independent securities at that time. Let $X(\{s^+\})$ be the subvector of payoffs of X which can be obtained starting from state s at t. It has K_t components. Consider completeness at the terminal date. Since the matrix $S(s, T)$ contains the payoffs of the N securities at T, in order for the market to be dynamically complete, for any starting state s at $T - 1$ and any payoff vector $X(\{s^+\})$ at time T there must exist a portfolio at time $T - 1$ such that

$$\Theta(s, T-1)^\mathsf{T} S\left(\{s^+\}, T\right) = X(s^+) \quad \forall s^+$$

This is a system of K_{T-1} equations in N unknowns, which has a solution (unique or not) if and only if

$$\mathrm{rank}(S\left(\{s^+\}, T\right)) = \mathrm{rank}(\left[S\left(\{s^+\}, T\right) \; X(\{s^+\})\right])$$

If the number of independent securities m_{T-1} is equal to the dimension of $X(\{s^+\})$, which is K_{T-1}, the two ranks are equal. So, the market is complete at the terminal date if and only if

$$m_{T-1} = \mathrm{rank}(S\left(\{s^+\}, T\right)) \geq K_{T-1}$$

for all s. A portfolio that solves the previous system – call it $\Theta^*(s, T-1)$ – costs

$$\Theta^*(s, T-1)S(s, T-1) = F^*(s, T-1)$$

Now consider a predecessor of s, let s^- be s at $T - 2$. In order to finance all the portfolios that will be needed starting from s, we need a portfolio $\Theta(s^-, T-2)$ such that, for all the K_{T-2} successors s of s^-

$$\Theta\left(s^-, T-2\right) S(s, T-1) = F^*(s, T-1) \quad \forall s^-$$

This is a system of K_{T-2} equations in N unknowns, which has a solution (unique or not) if and only if

$$\mathrm{rank}(S(s, T-1)) = \mathrm{rank}(\left[S(s, T-1) \; F^*(s, T-1)\right])$$

Recall that the dimension of $F^*(s, T-1)$ is K_{T-2}, so that the previous condition is satisfied if

$$m_{T-2} = \mathrm{rank}(S(s, T-1)) \geq K_{T-2}$$

Proceeding backwards one can show that, if ever the requirement in the theorem statement is violated for some node, we lack a solution and the market is not complete.   □

The number of states can be huge even with a small number of nodes at each time and over short horizons. The previous theorem is very powerful, since it dramatically lowers the number of basic securities one needs in order to complete the market.

The theorem is likely to become even more important as we move towards continuous time, where the number of states of the world is a continuum. We could hardly conceive an economy with a continuum of linearly independent securities. However, if that continuum entails a finite splitting index (as we will see, the notion of splitting index exists for continuous processes too), we can still hope for market completeness even in the presence of a finite number of traded, long-lived securities.

We demonstrate that:

Corollary 2.4 *If markets are dynamically complete, state prices are unique.*

Indeed, imagine again that the number of successors is equal across states at a specific time; that is, $K_{s,t} = K_t$. If the market is dynamically complete, eliminate assets in the relation

$$S(s,t)_{N \times 1} = S(t+1)_{N \times K_t} \frac{\Phi(t+1)_{K_t \times 1}}{\Phi(s,t)_{1 \times 1}}; s = 1,..,K_t$$

so as to get a matrix $S(t+1)_{m_t \times K_t}$ which contains only linearly independent payoffs and, if ever $K_t > m_t$, consider only its first K_t rows, so as to obtain $S(t+1)_{K_t \times K_t}$. Multiplying the RHS and LHS of the previous equation by its inverse, one obtains the unique state prices from asset prices:

$$\frac{\Phi(t+1)_{K_t \times 1}}{\Phi(s,t)_{1 \times 1}} = \left[S(t+1)_{K_t \times K_t} \right]^{-1} S(s,t)_{K_t \times 1}$$

2.2.6   Benchmark Example

The valuation of redundant securities will be made comparatively easy if we restrict ourselves to a simple case of multiperiod economy, namely the binomial tree of Cox, Ross, and Rubinstein (1979).

The finite horizon T is split into n equal steps of magnitude $\Delta t = T/n$, so that the dates at which we analyze the economy are $t = 0, \Delta t, 2\Delta t, ...(n-1)\Delta t, T$, or $k\Delta t, k = 0, 1, ..n$. Two securities are traded in the market: a *riskless* one, which earns a constant interest rate r each period, and a long-lived *risky* one. The riskless security is worth 1 at time 0 and $(1+r)^k$ at time $k\Delta t$. With a slight abuse of notation, call the price of the risky security $S(k)$, and let its initial value be $S(0) = S \in \mathbb{R}_{++}$. The risky security does not pay dividends on the way. It pays a dividend at T only. At each time step, independently of past behavior, the risky security can increase by a multiplicative factor $u > 0$ or decrease by a factor $d > 0$.[33] In order to avoid arbitrage, the constraint on u and d is

$$d < 1 + r < u$$

Overall, we can then represent the security dynamics as in figure 2.2.

This tree is *recombining* because successive moves determine an increase up or down of the same percentage amount. Although it is not essential for the reasoning, the recombining feature, while not changing the splitting index, reduces the total number of nodes as compared to the non-recombining case. Indeed, we have

- two states (characterized by u, d) at time Δt,
- three nodes ($d^2, ud = du, u^2$) at $2\Delta t$,
- $k + 1$ nodes ($u^j d^{k-j}, j = 0, 1, ..k$) at time $k\Delta t$,
- and finally $n + 1$ nodes ($u^j d^{n-j}, j = 0, 1, ..n$) at time $T = n\Delta t$.

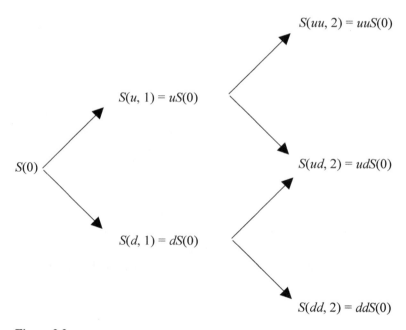

Figure 2.2
Stock price dynamics on a binomial tree.

---

33 We apologize for using the symbol u both for the up factor in the binomial model and for utility functions. By so doing, however, we keep the standard notation in both cases.

The node of the stock price tree is characterized by the number of up and down moves that occurred so far, not by the order with which they occurred or other properties of the whole "history" of the price process. Because of that property, the binomial price is Markovian. We defer until chapter 5 the exact definition of a Markovian process.

As for the probabilities attached to the up and down moves, they remain constant over the horizon $(0, T)$. Let us denote as $p > 0$ the probability of an up move, with $1 - p$ the probability of a down one. Because of independence of moves, the probability of any path characterized by j moves up and $k - j$ moves down at time $k\Delta t$ is $p^j(1 - p)^{k-j}$. The number of such paths is the number of ways in which one can select j places out of k, when the order does not matter:

$$\binom{k}{j} \triangleq \frac{k!}{j!(k - j)!}$$

Consequently, the probability attached to the node that is characterized by j moves up and $k - j$ moves down is

$$\pi(j, k) \triangleq \binom{k}{j} p^j (1 - p)^{k-j} \tag{2.21}$$

In this node the risky security is worth $Su^j d^{k-j}, j = 0, 1, ..k$.

Now, let us suppose that we want to price a derivative security in this setting. Let it be a European call option, with strike $\mathcal{K}$ and time to expiry T. Since the exercise will take place if and only if the resulting payoff is non-negative, the call has terminal value or payoff:

$$[S(T) - \mathcal{K}]^+ \triangleq \max[0, S(T) - \mathcal{K}] = \begin{cases} S(T) - \mathcal{K} \text{ if } S(T) > \mathcal{K} \\ 0 \text{ otherwise} \end{cases} \tag{2.22}$$

We can get its price in three ways: martingale pricing, replication, and hedging. In order to simplify the discussion, let us restrict the attention to the case in which $T = 2$, and let the time-step be equal to 1: $\Delta t = T/n = 1$. There are three possible final values for the option, namely

$$\left[Su^2 - \mathcal{K}\right]^+, [Sud - \mathcal{K}]^+, \left[Sd^2 - \mathcal{K}\right]^+$$

For the sake of simplicity, let $Su^2 - \mathcal{K} > 0$ and let the other two payoffs be null: the option is in the money only in state u^2. Call C_u, C_d the value that the option will take at time 1, node up and down respectively, and C its time-0 price. All of them have to be determined, and we will do this recursively. For the time being, we just pin them on the tree as in figure 2.3.

Martingale Pricing
Consider the following quantities:

$$p^* = \frac{(1 + r) - d}{u - d}$$

$$1 - p^* = \frac{u - (1 + r)}{u - d}$$

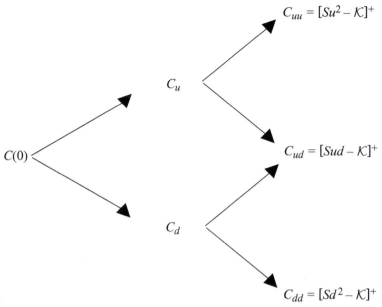

$C_{uu} = [Su^2 - \mathcal{K}]^+$

C_u

$C_{ud} = [Sud - \mathcal{K}]^+$

$C(0)$

C_d

$C_{dd} = [Sd^2 - \mathcal{K}]^+$

Figure 2.3
Option price dynamics on a binomial tree.

which are well defined, positive probabilities, under the condition $d < 1 + r < u$, since they are both positive and sum up to one. These are the probabilities that the fundamental theorem provides for the binomial tree. Indeed, with those probabilities, the price of the underlying at each node is the expectation of its payoff one period later. One can derive from them the Arrow-Debreu prices and the stochastic discount factor of the binomial model (see exercise 2.3 or later on in this section).

The same rule must hold, node by node, for the derivative. The expectation at u of the final payoff discounted is

$$
\begin{aligned}
C_u &= \frac{1}{1+r}\left[p^* \times \left(Su^2 - \mathcal{K}\right) + (1 - p^*) \times 0\right] \\
&= \frac{1}{(1+r)}\left(Su^2 - \mathcal{K}\right)\frac{1+r-d}{u-d}
\end{aligned}
$$

while the expectation at d, C_d, is zero. The time-0 expectation of C_u and 0 is

$$
C = \frac{1}{(1+r)^2}\left(Su^2 - \mathcal{K}\right)\frac{(1+r-d)^2}{(u-d)^2}
$$

In turn, this price can be written as the discounted expectation of the final payoff times the probability of the only path that leads to it, namely

$$C = \frac{1}{(1+r)^2} \left(Su^2 - K \right) \phi^*(2,2) = \frac{1}{(1+r)^2} \left(Su^2 - K \right) \binom{2}{2} (p^*)^2$$

where $\phi^*(2,2)$ is determined as in (2.21), which holds for the p^*-probabilities too:

$$\phi^*(j,k) \triangleq \binom{k}{j} p^{*j} (1 - p^*)^{k-j} \tag{2.23}$$

So, the derivative price at 0 is the expectation under the new probabilities of the final, discounted payoff.

Replication
To price the option by replication, start from considering C_u. Since the option is worth $\left[Su^2 - K \right]^+ = Su^2 - K$ if a further jump up occurs, while it is worth zero otherwise, one can think of replicating it with α bonds and θ stocks as follows. Choose α and θ so that the replicating portfolio pays $Su^2 - K$ in u^2, 0 in ud:

$$\begin{cases} \alpha(1+r)^2 + \theta Su^2 = Su^2 - K \\ \alpha(1+r)^2 + \theta Sud = 0 \end{cases}$$

This is a linear system in two equations, which can be easily solved, to get:

$$\begin{cases} \alpha^* = -\frac{d}{(1+r)^2} \frac{Su^2 - K}{u-d} \\ \theta^* = \frac{Su^2 - K}{Su(u-d)} \end{cases}$$

The price of such portfolio at time 1 gives C_u:

$$\begin{aligned} C_u &= \alpha^*(1+r) + \theta^* Su \\ &= \frac{1}{(1+r)} \left(Su^2 - K \right) \frac{1+r-d}{u-d} \end{aligned}$$

Consider C_d. Since the option will be worth nothing in both the nodes that can be reached from d, the replicating portfolio is the null portfolio, which contains no bonds and no stocks.

Now go one step backwards and consider a portfolio, to be set up at time 0, able to replicate C_u in state u and 0 in state d:

$$\begin{cases} \alpha(1+r) + \theta Su = C_u \\ \alpha(1+r) + \theta Sd = 0 \end{cases}$$

This portfolio is made of

$$\begin{cases} \alpha^* = -\frac{1}{(1+r)} \frac{dC_u}{u-d} \\ \theta^* = \frac{C_u}{S(u-d)} \end{cases}$$

and it can be bought at time 0 for the following price, which is the option price:

$$C = -\frac{1}{(1+r)}\frac{dC_u}{u-d} + \frac{C_u}{S(u-d)}S$$

$$= \frac{1}{(1+r)^2}\left[Su^2 - \mathcal{K}\right]\frac{(1+r-d)^2}{(u-d)^2}$$

As expected, this is the same price obtained under martingale pricing. Notice also that the number of stocks in the replicating portfolio is

$$\frac{C_u - C_d}{S(u-d)} = \frac{C_u}{S(u-d)} \tag{2.24}$$

at time 0, and similarly in the other nodes and times: $\Delta C/\Delta S$, where ΔC and ΔS are the differences in the call and stock value between the two successor nodes. It is the ratio of the change in the derivative price to that in the underlying, while the number of bonds is chosen so that all available resources are invested (self-financing).

Hedging

Hedging works similarly to replication, in a recursive way. The main difference is that now one wants to build a riskless portfolio at each node. Start from C_u. Since the option is worth $\left[Su^2 - \mathcal{K}\right]^+ = Su^2 - \mathcal{K}$ if a further jump up occurs at time 1, while it is worth zero otherwise, one can think of building a riskless portfolio for node u, which returns $1 + r$, with one option and h stocks, as follows. Let the portfolio initial value be P. In node u at time 1 choose h so that

$$\begin{cases} (Su^2 - \mathcal{K}) + hSu^2 = P(1+r) \\ hSud = P(1+r) \end{cases}$$

Now imagine being at node d. The portfolio built there, call its value Q, is riskless if one instant later it gives its initial value compounded in all states

$$\begin{cases} 0 + hSud = Q(1+r) \\ 0 + hSd^2 = Q(1+r) \end{cases}$$

At time 0, the portfolio, call its value R, is riskless if

$$\begin{cases} C_u + hSu = R(1+r) \\ C_d + hSd = R(1+r) \end{cases}$$

It is easy to verify that the portfolio built in such a way is hedged if $h = -\Delta C/\Delta S$. At node u we have $h = -(Su^2 - \mathcal{K})/S(u-d)$, at node d we have $h = 0$, at the initial node $h = -C_u/S(u-d)$. It is also easy to verify that the call values C_u, C_d, C obtained with the two previous methods do satisfy also the current equations. So, with the third method as well, we find the same price as above.[34]

---

34 One could wonder whether the portfolio is self-financing or not. We discuss the issue in continuous time, in chapter 6.

More Dates

Our benchmark example is still the binomial model, but with more dates. Since (2.23) holds, the risk-neutral probability for node $u^j d^{n-j}$ at time T, evaluated at time 0, is

$$\phi^*(j,n) = \binom{n}{j} p^{*j} (1-p^*)^{n-j}$$

The change of measure is

$$\eta(j,n) \triangleq \frac{p^{*j}(1-p^*)^{n-j}}{p^j(1-p)^{n-j}}$$

As a consequence, the time 0-state price for node $u^j d^{n-j}$ at time T is[35]

$$\phi(j,n) \triangleq (1+r)^{-T} \binom{n}{j} p^{*j}(1-p^*)^{n-j}$$

Last but not least, we can define the overall stochastic discount factor from time 0 to node $u^j d^{n-j}$ at T

$$\xi(j,n) \triangleq \frac{\phi(j,n)}{\binom{n}{j} p^j (1-p)^{n-j}}$$

$$= (1+r)^{-T} \eta(j,n)$$

$$= (1+r)^{-T} \frac{p^{*j}(1-p^*)^{n-j}}{p^j(1-p)^{n-j}}$$

The reason for combining single-period, conditional probabilities of going up or down the tree, $(1-p^*)$ and p^*, into unconditional probabilities over an n-period horizon of the $\phi^*(j,n)$ type has been sketched in section 2.2.4 above: there are $\binom{n}{j}$ mutually-exclusive ways to reach the node $u^j d^{n-j}$; each one has probability $p^{*j}(1-p^*)^{n-j}$. Probabilities combine exactly as discount factors do, that is, as products over a single path or branch of the tree, because we assume here that each jump up or down is independent of the past. For instance, the probability of going down and up over a single branch of the tree is $p^*(1-p^*)$, exactly as the discount factor over those two periods would be $(1+r)^{-2}$. However, there are two ways to get from any specific node S to a node $Sud = Sdu$ two periods later: either by going down and then up, or up first and then down. Each path has probability $p^*(1-p^*)$, the two of them are mutually exclusive, so that their probability is $2p^*(1-p^*)$, which is also

$$\binom{n}{1} p^*(1-p^*)^{n-1}$$

when $n = 2$. This means that when combining probability across path we cannot take the product. We must take the sum, because of mutual exclusion. So, the overall probability from time 0 to T is not the product of the probabilities, whereas the discount factor is: $(1+r)^{-T}$. This explains the functional form of state prices and stochastic discount factors too.

---

35 Note that this is not a state price from one state to another over successive instants in time, but an overall state price from a specific node at time T to time 0, where there is a unique state.

For any security whose payoff is a function of the underlying S, we have a pricing rule that generalizes the results we obtained in the first section of this chapter. Denote the payoff as $f(S(T))$, that is, $f(Su^j d^{n-j})$ in the state with j jumps up and $n-j$ jumps down. Then the corresponding price $f(S)$ can be written as its value "discounted" using the state prices:

$$f(S) = \sum_{j=0}^{n} \phi(j,n) f\left(Su^j d^{n-j}\right)$$

or as the discounted expectation under the risk-neutral probabilities ϕ^*. Let $\mathbb{E}^*$ be such time-0 expectation:

$$f(S) = (1+r)^{-T} \sum_{j=0}^{n} \phi^*(j,n) f(Su^j d^{n-j})$$
$$= (1+r)^{-T} \mathbb{E}^* \left[f(S(T)) \right]$$

It can also be written as the discounted expectation of the payoffs multiplied by the stochastic discount factor, with the expectation taken under the effective probabilities p. Let $\mathbb{E}$ be such a time-0 expectation:

$$f(S) = \sum_{j=0}^{n} \binom{n}{j} p^j (1-p)^{n-j} \xi(j,n) f(Su^j d^{n-j})$$
$$= \mathbb{E} \left[\xi f(S(T)) \right]$$

In all cases, substituting for the state prices, probabilities, and stochastic discount factors, we get, as expected, the same pricing rule:

$$f(S) = (1+r)^{-T} \sum_{j=0}^{n} \binom{n}{j} p^{*j} (1-p^*)^{n-j} f(Su^j d^{n-j})$$

which attaches to each realization of the payoff, that is, to each node, the risk-neutral probability of reaching that node. In the call option case, if the strike is $\mathcal{K}$, this gives the following call price at time 0:

$$C(0) = (1+r)^{-T} \sum_{j=0}^{n} \binom{n}{j} (p^*)^j (1-p^*)^{n-j} [S(0)u^j d^{n-j} - \mathcal{K}]^+ \tag{2.25}$$

Limit

With two dates, 0 and 1, the binomial model gives back the results of our one-period setting. If we think of increasing the number of periods and, at the same time, we imagine shrinking the length of each subinterval so as to approach continuous-time, we get two very interesting features: the model mimics a situation in which both the expectation of returns and its variance are linear in time. Since we divided the length of time T into n subperiods, of length $\Delta t = T/n$, by increasing n we make the length of each subinterval tend to zero, $\Delta t \to 0$. One can show that, when the single intervals become infinitesimal, the expected value of undiscounted, risk neutral returns in the binomial model is linear in time. Consider, indeed, undiscounted, gross returns over a short interval Δt, under the risk-neutral measure:

$$\frac{\Delta S}{S} = \frac{S(t + \Delta t)}{S(t)} = \begin{cases} u \text{ with probability } p^* \\ d \text{ with probability } 1 - p^* \end{cases}$$

and let $R \triangleq \ln(1 + r)$. The returns have expectation

$$\mathbb{E}^* \left[\frac{\Delta S}{S} \right] = up^* + d(1 - p^*) = u \frac{e^{R\Delta t} - d}{u - d} + d \frac{u - e^{R\Delta t}}{u - d} = e^{R\Delta t}$$

For $\Delta t \to 0$, the expectation becomes linear in Δt itself:[36]

$$\lim_{\Delta t \to 0} \mathbb{E}^* \left[\frac{\Delta S}{S} \right] = 1 + R\Delta t = 1 + r\Delta t$$

By an appropriate choice of the up and down factors u and d, also the variance of gross returns can be made linear in time. For instance, if $\sigma \in \mathbb{R}_{++}$ and we choose the up and down factors as follows:

$$u = e^{\sigma \sqrt{\Delta t}}, d = 1/u = e^{-\sigma \sqrt{\Delta t}}$$

then it can be demonstrated that both discounted and undiscounted returns over an interval Δt have variance $\sigma^2 \Delta t$. So, variance is linear in time. This will be important in order to understand the connection between this model and continuous-time models: a continuous-time model that, once discretized, gives back the binomial must have undiscounted returns and their variance which increase linearly in time.

2.3 Conclusion

The key notions introduced in this chapter are those of *state prices, stochastic discount factor, and risk-neutral probabilities*. They exist and take strictly positive values if and only if the market does not offer arbitrage opportunities. They are unique if and only if the market is complete.

Under strong monotonicity of the investors' utility functions, their existence will be shown in the next chapter to be equivalent to existence of a consumption plan that maximizes utility.

Prices of financial assets are weighted averages of final payoffs, where the weights are the state prices. They are also equal to expected values of those payoffs, discounted, under the risk-neutral probabilities. And they are also expected values of the same payoffs, multiplied by the appropriate discount factor, under the effective probability.

---

36 It follows that the same returns, once discounted, have no growth rate, as expected:

$$\lim_{\Delta t \to 0} \mathbb{E}^* \left[e^{-R\Delta t} \Delta S / S \right] = 1$$

Exercises

2.1 Consider a two-dates ($t = 0, 1$) economy where the interest rate is zero (the bond price $B(t) = 1$ for all t), the price of the risky stock at time 0 is $S(0) = 16$, and the payoff matrix is:

$$\Sigma = \begin{bmatrix} 1 & 1 \\ 20 & 12 \end{bmatrix}$$

We call the two states at time 1 an "up" and a "down" state, since the stock either moves up (to 20) or down (to 12). We could alternatively represent the situation with the following "tree:"

$$S(u, 1) = 20$$
$$S(0) = 16$$
$$S(d, 1) = 12$$

The probability of an up-move in the stock price is $\pi(1) = 0.6$ while that of a down move is $\pi(2) = 0.4$. Based on this information:

a. Find the prices at $t = 0$ of the set of state-contingent or Arrow-Debreu prices.

b. Determine the risk-neutral probabilities and the stochastic discount factor and verify by the corresponding pricing formulas that the correct prices for the bond and the stock are respectively 1 and 16.

 (Hint for a: use either the arguments in the text or the fact that Arrow-Debreu securities can be replicated via portfolios of bonds and stocks, which means that there exists (α_1, θ_1) such that α_1 units of the bond and θ_1 units of the stock allow us to replicate an Arrow-Debreu security with payoff 1 in state $s = 1$ at date $t = 1$. There also exists (α_2, θ_2) such that α_2 units of the bond and θ_2 units of the stock allow us to replicate an Arrow-Debreu security with payoff 1 in state $s = 2$ at date $t = 1$.)

2.2 Add to the economy of exercise 2.1 a European call option, $X(t)$, on the risky stock with strike price $\mathcal{K} = 8$ and maturity $t = 1$. Based on this information:

a. Determine the payoff matrix and the number of redundant securities.

b. Determine the call option price, $X(0)$, by using the three methods for pricing: replication, martingale pricing, and hedging.

2.3 Consider a three-dates ($t = 0, 1, 2$) economy where the interest rate is zero (the bond price $S_1(t) = B(t) = 1$ for all t) and the price of the risky stock, $S_2(s, t)$; $s = u$, d, uu, ud, dd, is as follows:

$$S_2(uu, 2) = 31.25$$
$$S_2(u, 1) = 25$$
$$S_2(0) = 20$$
$$S_2(ud, 2) = 20$$
$$S_2(d, 1) = 16$$
$$S_2(dd, 2) = 12.80$$

The probability of an up-move in the stock price is the same at all times (so that we are in the binomial model): $p = 0.6$. It follows that that of a down move is $1 - p = 0.4$. Based on this information:

a. Find the prices at $t = 0$ and $t = 1$, of the set of state-contingent or Arrow-Debreu claims.

b. Determine the risk neutral probabilities and the stochastic discount factor and verify by the corresponding pricing formulas that the correct prices for the bond and the stock are 1 and 20.

3 Investor Optimality and Pricing in the Case of Homogeneous Investors

In this chapter we progress from the pricing of redundant securities to the pricing of basic securities in a competitive market when the economy is an exchange economy. To do so we need to make explicit the preferences and the optimizing behavior of an investor who is a price taker. Conversely, if this investor is alone or all investors are identical, their behavior determines prices (which, however, are virtual since no trading actually takes place).

Again, we first consider a one-period economy. The investor is endowed with a utility function that represents his preferences over consumption at times 0 and 1. He consumes a unique good, used as numeraire. We make the following assumption, which will be maintained also in chapter 4.

Assumption 3.1 (of smooth preferences): *(i) the utility function $u(c(0), c(1))$: $\mathbb{R}_+ \times \mathbb{R}_+^K \to \mathbb{R}$ is increasing and strictly concave*[1]
(ii) u is differentiable twice, with continuous derivatives up to the second order (that is, class C^2)
(iii) the first derivatives are strictly positive, while the second ones are strictly negative
(iv) the Inada conditions (see Appendix A) are satisfied.

Because of *(i)*, we need not be concerned with sufficient conditions when studying maximization problems over non-empty domains. Because of *(iv)*, the first-order conditions in this chapter have a solution, which is a maximum. In order to preserve some level of generality, we do not assume that utility is separable in its two arguments, consumption today and consumption tomorrow.[2]

The investor receives endowments of consumption good (or securities) at times 0 and 1, and is allowed to transfer part of the time-0 endowment to time 1 by trading financial securities. In section 3.1.1 we start from the elementary case in which there is no

---

1 A function $f: \mathbb{R}^n \to \mathbb{R}$ is strictly concave if $f(tx + (1-t)y) > tf(x) + (1-t)f(y)$.

2 As Appendix A argues, this means that the level of consumption today may affect the investor's appreciation of tomorrow's consumption, as in the case of habit formation (explored below in chapter 20).

uncertainty, the case of the Fisher economy $(K = 1)$.[3] In section 3.1.2 we assume that the investor is faced with *finite uncertainty*, $1 < K < \infty$. We assume first that the investor has access to a riskless security, together with simple or Arrow-Debreu securities (section 3.1.3). Then we allow him to use more complex securities that pay dividends (section 3.1.4). We are able to capture some basic consequences of investor choice – mainly their implications for basic securities pricing – and to discuss their relation with the absence of arbitrage (section 3.1.5). Section 3.2 studies one-period optimality in the benchmark example.

We then examine a multiperiod economy, patterned after Lucas (1978). We set it up in section 3.3 and provide different optimization approaches in sections 3.3.2 and 3.3.3. In some cases, these approaches can be simplified by means of a so-called lifetime budget constraint, which is constructed in section 3.3.3. We draw some implications for security pricing in section 3.3.4 and revisit the benchmark case in section 3.4.

3.1 One-Period Economies

3.1.1 Investor Optimality and Security Pricing under Certainty

Consider the utility maximization problem of a single investor, or of a homogeneous group of investors. By "homogeneous" we mean that they are identical in terms of utility and endowments.

Let there be just one state of the world at time 1; endowment and consumption at time 1 can only take a single value: $(e(0), e(1))$ are the endowments at times 0 and 1, with $(c(0), c(1))$ the corresponding consumption levels.

- at time 0, the investor receives a non-random and non-negative endowment $e(0) \in \mathbb{R}_+$, consumes an amount $c(0) \in \mathbb{R}_+$ of the good and invests the difference between the two;[4]

- at time 1, he receives a new, non–random and non-negative endowment $e(1) \in \mathbb{R}_+$ and consumes it, together with accumulated savings, as $c(1) \in \mathbb{R}_+$.

In the absence of uncertainty, the transfer of resources from time 0 to time 1 can be done through the riskless security. We write down the investor's problem as an expected-utility maximization under the budget constraint. The budget constraint, which reflects the possibility of transferring funds over time by saving at the rate r, says that consumption at time 1 is the value of savings $e(0) - c(0)$ at time 0 plus interest on them, plus the

---

3 See Fisher (1930).

4 We mostly assume that investors receive endowments of goods only. But they could also be receiving endowments of securities.

time-1 endowment:[5]

$$c(1) = (e(0) - c(0))(1 + r) + e(1)$$

Dividing by $1 + r$, readjusting and denoting $\phi \triangleq 1/(1 + r)$, we can write it as an equality between total discounted consumptions and total discounted endowments

$$c(0) + \phi c(1) = e(0) + \phi e(1)$$

The latter make up the *total wealth* of the investor at time 0, which we denote with $\mathfrak{W}_0$:

$$\mathfrak{W}_0 \triangleq e(0) + \phi e(1)$$

The investor's optimality problem can be written as:[6]

$$\max_{c(0), c(1)} u(c(0), c(1))$$

subject to:

$$c(0) + \phi c(1) = \mathfrak{W}_0 \tag{3.1}$$

The Lagrangean is

$$L(c(0), c(1), \lambda_0) \triangleq u(c(0), c(1)) + \lambda_0(\mathfrak{W}_0 - c(0) - \phi c(1))$$

and the corresponding first-order conditions are:

$$\frac{\partial u(c(0), c(1))}{\partial c(0)} = \lambda_0$$

$$\frac{\partial u(c(0), c(1))}{\partial c(1)} = \lambda_0 \phi$$

$$c(0) + \phi c(1) = \mathfrak{W}_0$$

where λ_0 is the Lagrange multiplier for the budget constraint, or the shadow price of the resources at time 0. The first and second conditions say that the shadow price is both equal to the marginal utility at time 0 and the ratio of the marginal utility at time 1 to the discount factor. The conditions form a system of three (nonlinear) equations in three unknowns $c(0), c(1), \lambda_0$, which needs to be solved. For instance, we could solve the first two equations for $c(0)$ and $c(1)$ as functions of λ_0 and substitute into the third one (which is the budget constraint) to solve for λ_0.

---

5 Budget constraints are satisfied as equalities. Given that utility is strictly increasing, satiation never occurs. Also, we need not impose non-negativity of consumption. See proposition A.1. We do not take a stand, either here or in the rest of the book, unless specified otherwise, on the existence of the solution to maximization problems. As a general rule, this is guaranteed when the feasible set is non-empty, closed and bounded, that is, compact.

6 Here and in the rest of the book we use the notation "max" independently of whether the conditions for existence of a maximum are satisfied or not. A rigorous approach consists in writing "sup" and then verifying whether the supremum is reached (and finite). In the latter case we have a maximum. To concentrate on economic interpretation, we leave the conditions aside and use the max notation.

We can draw one implication without solving. By combining the first two conditions we get:

$$\phi = \frac{\frac{\partial u}{\partial c(1)}(c(0), c(1))}{\frac{\partial u}{\partial c(0)}(c(0), c(1))} > 0 \tag{3.2}$$

which says that the discount factor or bond price per unit of face value (on the LHS) is equal to the ratio of the investor's marginal utilities at times 1 and 0 (on the RHS). This ratio is the *marginal rate of substitution* (MRS) between time-0 and time-1 consumption. Since both marginal utilities are assumed to be positive, the discount factor is also. So, the price ϕ of the unique security that characterizes this economy is strictly linked to preferences: it is equal to the MRS. The more an investor appreciates an additional unit of consumption at time 1 relative to a unit today, the higher will be the security price, since it is by investing in the bond that he can increase his consumption tomorrow. By saying that consumption reveals the price that the investor puts on the security, we are anticipating on equilibrium (chapter 4). In the optimization problem, the price ϕ is given to the investor and he chooses his consumption accordingly.

In geometric terms, condition (3.2) states the equality between ϕ, the slope of the budget constraint, and the slope of indifference curves. The equation defining indifference curves is

$$u(c(0), c(1)) = \text{constant}$$

which implies

$$\frac{\partial u}{\partial c(1)}dc(1) + \frac{\partial u}{\partial c(0)}dc(0) = 0$$

while the equation defining the budget constraint 3.1 is in the form $c(0) = \mathfrak{W}_0 - \phi c(1)$. The optimum pair $(c(0), c(1))$ is the one where the highest indifference curve is tangent to the budget constraint. There the slope of the indifference curve, which is the MRS, is equal to the price of time-1 consumption ϕ, which is the slope of the budget constraint.

This extremely simple model is already capable of providing a method for pricing securities, quantifying returns, and defining wealth. Indeed, equation (3.2) provides the price of the unique security in terms of marginal rates of substitution. The price is strictly positive, since marginal utilities are. A stock entity such as wealth is well defined as soon as the MRS is. All in all, prices, returns, and stock entities such as wealth are defined in terms of investor preferences. Financial prices and their returns being determined by marginal rates of substitution, the same is true for wealth, so that pricing and optimizing are two faces of the same coin.

Remark 3.1 *A frequently used assumption is that utility is additive over time and that time factors out when "discounting" future utility to capture impatience in consumption, which, with an abuse of notation, we transcribe as*

$$u(c(0), c(1)) = u(c(0)) + \beta u(c(1))$$

Notation is abused since we use the same symbol u both for lifetime utility, defined on the consumption stream, and for the utility function defined on each period consumption (see also Appendix A). With this assumption on utility, marginal utilities are:

$$\frac{\partial u}{\partial c(1)}(c(0), c(1)) = \beta u'(c(1))$$

$$\frac{\partial u}{\partial c(0)}(c(0), c(1)) = u'(c(0))$$

which imply the following expression for the bond price and the budget constraint:

$$\phi = \frac{\beta u'(c(1))}{u'(c(0))} > 0$$

$$\mathfrak{W}_0 = c(0) + \sum_{s=1}^{K} \frac{\beta u'(c(s,1))}{u'(c(0))} c(s,1) = e(0) + \sum_{s=1}^{K} \frac{\beta u'(c(s,1))}{u'(c(0))} e(s,1)$$

As expected, the price ϕ is increasing in β, or decreasing in time impatience. The more impatient the investor is, the less he will be willing to pay for consumption in the future. The price ϕ is increasing in the marginal utility of time 1 and decreasing in that of time 0. Since marginal utility is decreasing, the lower consumption at time 1 relative to consumption at time 0, the higher is the price ϕ that the investor is willing to pay for one unit of consumption.

3.1.2 Investor Optimality and Security Pricing under Uncertainty

Consider now the utility maximization problem of an investor under finite uncertainty. The investor is either a single investor, or a homogeneous group of investors. Here, by "homogeneous" we mean that investors are identical in terms not only of utility and endowment, but also in terms of probability assessments over the states at time 1.[7] As before, the investor receives endowments at time 0 (a non-random one) and at time 1, and consumes at times 0 and 1. The time-1 endowment and accumulated savings take values that are random or state-contingent or state-dependent. From the vantage point of time 0, they are discrete random variables. Randomness is represented by K states of nature. The investor consumes $c(s) \in \mathbb{R}_+$ in state s. Consumption is random, since it is the time-1 endowment $e(s) \in \mathbb{R}_+$ plus accumulated savings. Utility is the expected, intertemporal utility in the Savage version of von Neumann-Morgenstern, as characterized in Appendix A:

$$\sum_{s=1}^{K} \pi(s) u(c(0), c(s))$$

with u increasing and strictly concave as in section 3.1.1. We also look at the special case of additivity over time.

The prices of securities are expressed in units of contemporaneous consumption.

---

7 In chapter 4, we shall learn that, if the market is complete, they need not be identical in their endowments for the formula of the current chapter to hold.

3.1.3 Arrow-Debreu Securities

Consider the investor's problem when both the riskless bond and K Arrow-Debreu securities are traded. Since contemporaneous consumption is the numeraire, the security for state s now provides a unit of consumption in state s. Recall that, in order to consume one unit in each state at time 1, the investor can buy either one Arrow-Debreu security for each state of the world, for a total of $\sum_{s=1}^{K} \phi(s)$, or the riskless bond, which has price $\phi = 1/(1+r)$, and this implies:

$$\sum_{s=1}^{K} \phi(s) = \frac{1}{1+r}$$

As in the economy of section 3.1.1, let us write down the budget constraint. We then examine how to maximize expected utility by choosing both time-0 consumption and consumption in each of the s states of the world at time 1.

Since a unit of consumption in state s at time 1 can be financed by purchasing a unit of the corresponding Arrow-Debreu security, the budget constraint becomes

$$c(0) + \sum_{s=1}^{K} \phi(s)c(s) = e(0) + \sum_{s=1}^{K} \phi(s)e(s) \tag{3.3}$$

and, since the only assets are the Arrow-Debreu ones, the LHS is also the investor's wealth, $\mathfrak{W}_0 = e(0) + \sum_{s=1}^{K} \phi(s)e(s)$.

The investor selects $c(0)$ and the vector of consumption in each state in the future $\{c(s)\}_{s=1}^{K}$ so as to maximize expected utility

$$\max_{c(0),\{c(s)\}} \sum_{s=1}^{K} \pi(s)u(c(0), c(s)) \tag{3.4}$$

subject to (3.3). He has $K + 1$ choice variables. The corresponding Lagrangean is

$$L(c(0), \{c(s)\}, \lambda_0) \triangleq \sum_{s=1}^{K} \pi(s)u(c(0), c(s))$$

$$+ \lambda_0 \left(\mathfrak{W}_0 - c(0) - \sum_{s=1}^{K} \phi(s)c(s) \right)$$

and the first-order conditions are similar to those of section 3.1.1:

$$\sum_{s=1}^{K} \pi(s)\frac{\partial u}{\partial c(0)}(c(0), c(s)) = \lambda_0 \tag{3.5}$$

$$\pi(s)\frac{\partial u}{\partial c(s)}(c(0), c(s)) = \lambda_0\phi(s) \tag{3.6}$$

$$c(0) + \sum_{s=1}^{K} \phi(s)c(s) = e(0) + \sum_{s=1}^{K} \phi(s)e(s) \tag{3.7}$$

These make up a non-linear system of $K+2$ equations in $K+2$ unknowns: $c(0)$, $\{c(s)\}_{s=1}^{K}$, λ_0.

By combining the first two conditions we get:

$$\phi(s) = \pi(s)\frac{\frac{\partial u}{\partial c(s)}(c(0), c(s))}{\sum_{s=1}^{K} \pi(s)\frac{\partial u}{\partial c(0)}(c(0), c(s))} > 0$$

Prices of state-specific single-payment securities, the so-called *state prices,* are equal to marginal rates of substitution, the MRS for state s being now defined as its probability times the ratio between marginal utility in that state and expected marginal utility from consumption at time 0. This is a natural extension of the Fisher's MRS (3.2), with a probability added in front.[8] The price of each security is increasing not only in the marginal utility of the state, as compared to today's utility, but also in the likelihood of the state itself. The vector of state prices $\Phi = \{\phi(s)\}$ is the *state-price vector* or *pricing functional.* Since we decided to disregard states of the world that have zero-probability, and marginal utilities are strictly positive, the pricing functional is strictly positive.

As in the case of the Fisher economy, if we substitute for $\phi(s)$ in the definition of wealth, the latter is still related to the marginal rates of substitution:

$$\mathfrak{W}_0 = c(0) + \pi(s)\frac{\frac{\partial u}{\partial c(s)}}{\sum_{s=1}^{K} \pi(s)\frac{\partial u}{\partial c(0)}}c(1) = e(0) + \pi(s)\frac{\frac{\partial u}{\partial c(s)}}{\sum_{s=1}^{K} \pi(s)\frac{\partial u}{\partial c(0)}}e(1)$$

The lesson that we draw from the Arrow-Debreu as well as the Fisher economy is that pricing and optimizing are again two faces of the same coin.

Remark 3.2 *If utility is additive and time factors out, according to Appendix A, we have*

$$\phi(s) = \pi(s)\beta\frac{u'(c(s))}{u'(c(0))} > 0$$

State prices behave as in the Fisher economy with respect to impatience and consumption. Furthermore, they are increasing in the probability assigned to state s.

3.1.3.1   Risk-Neutral Probabilities

Since all the state prices, interpreted now as MRS, are positive and sum up to the price of a riskless bond, we can normalize them by their sum and interpret them as "pseudo" probabilities:

$$\phi^*(s) \triangleq \frac{\phi(s)}{\sum_{s=1}^{K} \phi(s)} = \phi(s) \times (1+r)$$

$\Phi^* = \{\phi^*(s)\}_{s=1}^{K}$ forms a new set of probabilities, or a *new probability measure.* All $\phi^*(s)$ are strictly positive and not one is zero. The new measure is said to be *equivalent* to the

---

8 Actually, in Fisher's case the unique state of the world at time 1 had probability one. In the rest of the book, we adopt the convention that the MRS incorporates probability.

initial one. Still, we labeled the new probabilities "pseudo," since they are not the proba-bilities that each single risk-averse investor would assign to the states (these were called $\pi(s)$). One can also define the ratio of the new to the old measure, as we did in the previous chapter, formula (2.15):

$$\eta(s) \triangleq \frac{\phi^*(s)}{\pi(s)}$$

The change of measure is now based on utility maximization, instead of being justified by the absence of arbitrage opportunities. In order to understand the economic interpretation of the new probabilities, let us see how they enter the value today of consumption, endow-ments, and Arrow-Debreu securities. The value of future consumption, which enters the budget constraint, is its expected value under the new probabilities, discounted at the risk-less rate. Substituting $\phi^*(s)/(1+r)$ for $\phi(s)$, the LHS of the budget constraint can indeed be rewritten:

$$c(0) + \sum_{s=1}^{K} \phi(s)c(s) \equiv c(0) + \frac{1}{1+r} \sum_{s=1}^{K} \phi^*(s)c(s) \qquad (3.8)$$

where $\sum_{s=1}^{K} \phi^*(s)c(s)$ is the expectation of future consumption under the probabilities $\{\phi^*(s)\}$. Discounting is done by dividing by $1+r$, in a manner similar to what would do a risk-neutral investor, who does not care about the dispersion of the consumption values around their mean. An analogous restatement holds for current and future endowments, which enter the budget constraint as:

$$e(0) + \sum_{s=1}^{K} \phi(s)e(s) = e(0) + \frac{1}{1+r} \sum_{s=1}^{K} \phi^*(s)e(s) \qquad (3.9)$$

Since by definition an Arrow-Debreu security pays one unit of consumption in state s, its price today can be read as the discounted expected value of its payoff:

$$\phi(s) = \frac{1}{1+r} \times \left(\phi^*(s) \times 1\right) \qquad (3.10)$$

Like for consumption and endowment, discounting is done as a risk-neutral investor would do.

This is again the so called *martingale-pricing* result: the value of consumption, endow-ments, and the price of any security is equal to the expectation of its payoff, under the changed probability, discounted at the riskless rate. Or, under the probabilities $\{\phi^*(s)\}$, all assets have the same one-period expected rate of return equal to the short rate of interest r. As we know, because of the martingale-pricing result, the pseudo-probabilities $\{\phi^*(s)\}$'s are named *risk-neutral probabilities*. The remarkable power of martingale pricing is that it holds *independently* of the risk attitudes of the investor. We never assumed a risk-neutral investor. In fact, we took him to be risk-averse (u strictly concave, assumption 2, parts *(i)* and *(iii)*). We just reformulated the prices he puts on the assets, by creating pseudo-probabilities, so as to write them as an expected value. However, if ever there existed in the market a risk-neutral investor with those probability beliefs, he would price the security that way but using the effective probabilities. All other investors change their probability assessments into the pseudo ones before pricing.

Time-1 payoffs can be looked at as time-1 prices. Therefore, as in chapter 2, we can say that discounted future prices have expectation equal to their current value. From the economic point of view, under these probabilities there is no expected gain from trade. The investor pays today exactly what he expects to receive tomorrow, discounted, provided that the expectation is formed under the martingale measure. In that sense, markets are "efficient," because no expected gain from trade occurs.

3.1.3.2 Stochastic Discount Factor

As in the previous chapter, call *stochastic discount factor* or *state-price deflator* the Arrow-Debreu price per unit of probability, that is, the MRS between state-s and time-0 consumption per unit of probability. Denote it as $\xi(s)$:

$$\xi(s) \triangleq \frac{\phi(s)}{\pi(s)} = \frac{\frac{\partial u}{\partial c(s)}}{\sum_{s=1}^{K} \pi(s) \frac{\partial u}{\partial c(0)}}$$

The values at time 0 of consumption, endowments, and Arrow-Debreu securities can be written as expectations under the effective probabilities, provided that the corresponding time-1 cash flows are multiplied by the state-price deflator. We, indeed, have

$$c(0) + \sum_{s=1}^{K} \phi(s)c(s) \equiv c(0) + \sum_{s=1}^{K} \pi(s)\xi(s)c(s) \tag{3.11}$$

$$e(0) + \sum_{s=1}^{K} \phi(s)e(s) \equiv e(0) + \sum_{s=1}^{K} \pi(s)\xi(s)e(s) \tag{3.12}$$

The stochastic discount factor "discounts" in the sense that it transforms payoffs into today's units of marginal utility. If consumption is high in state s, by the properties of utility functions, utility is high and its marginal value is low. As a consequence, for those states in which future consumption is high, the stochastic discount factor is low, and the corresponding payoff does not receive a high appreciation by the investor. It is strongly discounted in forming the price. The opposite holds for low-consumption states. The expectation of the stochastic discount factor, under the effective probabilities, is the price of a riskless bond ϕ:

$$\sum_{s=1}^{K} \pi(s)\xi(s) = \sum_{s=1}^{K} \phi(s) = \phi$$

From this follows the following, important remark:

Remark 3.3   *If utility is additive and separable in time and consumption, the risk-neutral probabilities and stochastic discount factors become:*

$$\phi^*(s) = \pi(s)\frac{\beta u'(c(s))}{u'(c(0))}(1+r)$$

$$\xi(s) = \frac{\beta u'(c(s))}{u'(c(0))}$$

The ratio of the risk neutral to the effective probabilities depends on β and marginal utility in each state:

$$\eta(s) = \frac{\phi^*(s)}{\pi(s)} = \frac{\beta u'(c(1))}{u'(c(0))}(1+r) > 0$$

The price of a riskless bond is:

$$\phi = \sum_{s=1}^{K} \pi(s)\xi(s) = \sum_{s=1}^{K} \pi(s)\frac{\beta u'(c(s))}{u'(c(0))}$$

so that we end up with the following ratio of risk-neutral to effective probabilities:

$$\frac{\phi^*(s)}{\pi(s)} = \frac{u'(c(s))}{\sum_{s=1}^{K} \pi(s)u'(c(s))}$$

This makes clear that the twisting of probabilities is not a mere mathematical transformation, it depends on preferences. The above ratio is higher, the higher is the marginal utility in state s at time 1, that is, the lower is consumption in that state. Risk-neutral probabilities in this sense are pessimistic, in that they "put more weight" on low-consumption states.

To sum up, in this Arrow-Debreu economy every future payoff can be priced equivalently using state prices, risk-neutral probabilities, or state-price deflators. It is the expectation of its future realizations ($c(s), e(s), 1$ or 0 for Arrow-Debreu securities) computed

- either using the Arrow-Debreu prices *tout court*, as in (3.3)

- or using risk-neutral probabilities and discounting at the riskless rate, as in (3.8, 3.9),

- or using the effective probabilities, after having multiplied the future realization by the stochastic discount factor, as in (3.11, 3.12).

All together, using consumption as an example of a future payoff, we have:

$$\mathfrak{W}_0 \triangleq c(0) + \sum_{s=1}^{K} \phi(s)c(s) \equiv c(0) + \frac{1}{1+r}\sum_{s=1}^{K} \phi^*(s)c(s)$$

$$\equiv c(0) + \sum_{s=1}^{K} \pi(s)\xi(s)c(s)$$

An analogous expression holds for endowments and Arrow-Debreu prices themselves. These expressions are similar to the ones we obtained from the fundamental theorem of security pricing in chapter 2. Now, however, we have a link between utility and Arrow-Debreu prices (and consequently, risk-neutral probabilities and stochastic discount factors): each state price is a MRS.

We suggest that the reader solve exercise 3.1.

3.1.4 Complex or Real-World Securities

Consider now the case of N complex or real-world securities, as described by a payoff matrix Σ, which contains basic securities and may also contain redundant ones (for the time being, we do not take a stand on the magnitude of N relative to K). The investor chooses a portfolio, namely a number of units of securities of each type, that he wants to hold when exiting time $0, \Theta = \{\theta_i, i = 1, \ldots, N\}$. No constraint is imposed on purchases and sales; in particular short sales (that is, cases in which $\theta_i < 0$) are allowed. Inflows and outflows from security trades form the net amount of securities $\sum_{i=1}^{N} \theta_i S_i$ held, which can have any sign.[9]

Unlike in the Arrow-Debreu case, there are $K + 1$ budget constraints. The first says that, at time 0, consumption and net trade are equal to the endowment $e(0)$:[10]

$$c(0) + \sum_{i=1}^{N} \theta_i S_i = e(0) \tag{3.13}$$

The other K constraints say that, in each state s of time 1, the difference between consumption and endowment equates the portfolio payoff for that state

$$c(s) - e(s) = \sum_{i=1}^{N} \theta_i q_i(s) = \Theta^{\mathsf{T}} q(s) \quad s = 1, \ldots, K \tag{3.14}$$

or that consumption in each state must be financed by a portfolio mix: $c(s) = e(s) + \sum_{i=1}^{N} \theta_i q_i(s)$. The optimization problem still has expected utility maximization as an objective:

$$\max_{c(0), \{c(s)\}, \{\theta_i\}} \sum_{s=1}^{K} \pi(s) u(c(0), c(s)) \tag{3.15}$$

It is subject to the $K + 1$ budget constraints (3.13) and (3.14). Call $\lambda_0 \phi(s)$ the multipliers for the time-1 constraints.

---

9 The investor might also have been endowed with a number of units, $\bar{\theta}_i$, of security i at time 0, in which case the net trade would have been $\sum_{i=1}^{N} (\theta_i - \bar{\theta}_i) S_i$.

10 Again, if there was an initial endowment *of securities*, the value of that endowment should be added in at time 0.

The Lagrangean is:

$$L(c(0), \{c(s)\}, \{\theta_i\}, \lambda_0, \{\lambda_0\phi(s)\}) \triangleq \sum_{s=1}^{K} \pi(s)u(c(0), c(s)) \tag{3.16}$$

$$+\lambda_0 \left(e(0) - c(0) - \sum_{i=1}^{N} \theta_i S_i \right) + \lambda_0 \sum_{s=1}^{K} \phi(s) \times \left(e(s) - c(s) + \sum_{i=1}^{N} \theta_i q_i(s) \right)$$

This Lagrangean is to be maximized with respect to $c(0)$, $\{c(s)\}$, $\{\theta_i\}$, which we call "the primal variables," and *minimized* with respect to the Lagrange multipliers also called "the dual variables."[11]

For analogy with the Arrow-Debreu case, let us start by solving for consumption choices. The first-order conditions that are obtained by equating to zero the derivatives of the Lagrangean with respect to consumption at time 0 and consumption in the different states at time 1 are:

$$\sum_{s=1}^{K} \pi(s)\frac{\partial u}{\partial c(0)}(c(0), c(s)) = \lambda_0 \tag{3.17}$$

$$\pi(s)\frac{\partial u}{\partial c(s)}(c(0), c(s)) = \lambda_0\phi(s) \tag{3.18}$$

$$s = 1, 2, ..K$$

The first condition recognizes that, as in the Arrow-Debreu maximization problem, the time-0 Lagrange multiplier is the marginal utility at time 0, while the second ones say that the same holds for the marginal utility at time 1 in each single state, so that the ratio $\phi(s)$ is the marginal utility in state s:

$$\phi(s) = \frac{\pi(s)\frac{\partial u}{\partial c(s)}(c(0), c(s))}{\sum_{s=1}^{K} \pi(s)\frac{\partial u}{\partial c(0)}(c(0), c(s))} \tag{3.19}$$

The derivatives of the Lagrangean with respect to the portfolio choice $\{\theta_i\}$ are:

$$-\lambda_0 S_i + \lambda_0 \sum_{s=1}^{K} \phi(s) \times q_i(s) = 0 \tag{3.20}$$

Introduce the stochastic discount factor $\xi(s)$, as in section 3.1.3.2:

$$\xi(s) = \frac{\phi(s)}{\pi(s)} = \frac{\frac{\partial u}{\partial c(s)}(c(0), c(s))}{\sum_{s=1}^{K} \pi(s)\frac{\partial u}{\partial c(0)}(c(0), c(s))}$$

---

11 See Appendix B on the saddle-point property of the Lagrangean, which justifies here the appearance of a minimization.

With that notation, (3.20) can be restated as a "pricing" equation:

$$S_i = \sum_{s=1}^{K} \pi(s)\xi(s)q_i(s) \tag{3.21}$$

Finally the minimization with respect to Lagrange multipliers produces first-order conditions that are, as usual, just restatements of the constraints (3.13) and (3.14).

Consider now the case in which a complex security i coincides with an Arrow-Debreu security. For the Arrow-Debreu security for state s, which pays $q_i(s) = 1$ in state s and zero otherwise, the price becomes

$$S_i = \phi(s) = \pi(s)\frac{\frac{\partial u}{\partial c(s)}}{\sum_{s=1}^{K} \pi(s)\frac{\partial u}{\partial c(0)}} = \pi(s)\xi(s) > 0$$

The intermediate expression says that the Arrow-Debreu prices are still equal to the marginal rates of substitution. The last expression says that they are still the product of the effective probability and the stochastic discount factor. We can easily verify that the Arrow-Debreu prices are strictly positive. Indeed, positivity of the probabilities $\pi(s)$ and of the marginal utilities again implies that every $\phi(s)$ is positive.

Using the Arrow-Debreu prices we can write the prices of general complex securities simply as:

$$S_i = \sum_{s=1}^{K} \phi(s)q_i(s) \tag{3.22}$$

According to this expression, the price of security i is the sum of its payoffs, each one evaluated at the MRS for the corresponding state. The expression is the *Law of One Price* again: two securities with the same payoffs in each state, namely the complex asset and the basket of Arrow securities, have the same price. From the economic point of view, it says that, all else equal, securities that pay more in low-consumption (and high-marginal utility) states sell at a higher price than securities that pay out in high-consumption states, in which an additional unit of consumption is poorly appreciated.

Even when we start from complex securities, we can define risk-neutral probabilities

$$\phi^*(s) = \phi(s)(1+r) = \frac{\phi(s)}{\sum_{s=1}^{K} \phi(s)}$$

We can still call η the change of measure that leads to them, and which is the same we obtained for the corresponding economy under the assumption of no arbitrage possibilities, in the previous chapter:

$$\eta(s) \triangleq \frac{\phi^*(s)}{\pi(s)}$$

Last, note that, once we introduce complex securities, the maximization problem is more complicated, even though the pricing rule we obtain is the same as that obtained when dealing with Arrow-Debreu securities only.

If $N = K$ and the matrix Σ is non-singular, it is possible to write the portfolio selection problem in terms of a problem of the Arrow-Debreu type, since independent complex assets can be written in terms of any basis of $\mathbb{R}^K$, and the identity matrix of dimension K, which is the Σ matrix for the Arrow-Debreu securities, is just one of those bases (see also the next chapter). Below the reader can find a hint of the usefulness of the transformation from complex to Arrow-Debreu assets. Also, we suggest that he solve exercises 3.2 and 3.3.

———————————————◆———————————————

Notice that, in the maximization problem of the Arrow-Debreu economy:

1. the object of choice is future consumption $\{c(s)\}$, with no reference to portfolio allocation $\{\theta_i\}$;

2. the budget constraint connects the lifetime endowment and consumption streams, instead of relating endowment and consumption at each point in time, via portfolio choices;

3. as a consequence of 2, there is a single constraint instead of $K + 1$ constraints, namely one for each state and time.

Even though the difference between the one period and dynamic formulations is not very evident at this point, the reader can figure it out in the following way. Anticipating on the next section, allow for more than two dates. In the Arrow-Debreu case we will still have a constraint of the type

$$\mathfrak{W}_0 = c(0) + \sum_{t=1}^{T} \sum_{s=1}^{K} \phi(s,t)c(s,t)$$

where $c(s,t)$ is obviously consumption in state s at date t. But, in the complex-security statement the constraints are (3.13) and (3.14) at each state s *and* time t. That is why it will be important to find conditions under which one can transform a problem of investor optimization with complex securities into the corresponding problem with Arrow-Debreu securities. This will become even more important with heterogeneous investors. That is why also, in the next chapter, we make the condition explicit and explain how to make that transformation.

3.1.5   Relation with the No-Arbitrage Approach

In the presence of a utility function, arbitrage may be seen, as in Kreps (1981), as the possibility of purchasing at zero or negative price an incremental amount of good able to increase the investor's expected utility. Under assumption 1, the utility of an investor increases as soon as consumption increases in, at least, one state.

In compact matrix-vector notation, consumption is C and it is financed by the endowment E and by the portfolio payoff $\Sigma^{\mathsf{T}}\Theta$, which has been purchased at price $S^{\mathsf{T}}\Theta$. In order to understand how this compares to the risk-neutral pricing arguments of the fundamental theorem 2.1, take the complex-security case, which includes the previous ones as subcases. Let $C - E$ be the *net-trade* vector of time 1. The pricing rule (3.22), which has been obtained from the first-order conditions of consumption and portfolio choice (3.17) and (3.18), can be written as

$$S = \Sigma \Phi$$

while the budget constraints at time 1 (3.14) are:

$$C - E = \Sigma^{\mathsf{T}} \Theta$$

The former states that there exists a pricing functional Φ such that the matrix Σ maps into the vector of prices, S. The second characterizes the vector of net trades which are budget-feasible at time 0. As we know from linear algebra, the pricing functional Φ, which maps a matrix into a vector, is linear. As we know from our economic reading of the conditions above, Φ is positive, since it is given by the MRS computed at the optimal consumption. We have thus established the following result:

Theorem 3.1 *In a market populated by homogenous investors, who solve problem (3.15, 3.13, 3.14), there exists a pricing functional Φ, linear and positive.*

There is obviously a strong similarity between this result and the result of chapter 2 obtained from the assumption of absence of arbitrage. The reason for the similarity is theorem 2.2 which said that, under assumption 1, the optimization problem of each investor has a solution if and only if there do not exist arbitrage opportunities.

We collect in figure 3.1 below the results obtained so far.

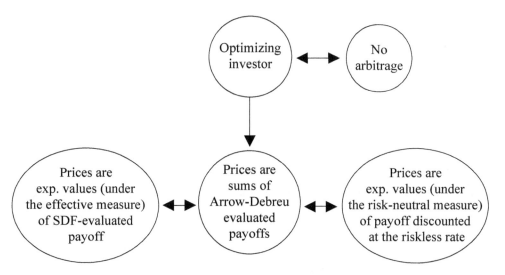

Figure 3.1
Individual optimality and asset pricing in the single-period model

3.1.6   The Dual Problem

The problem of maximizing (3.15) subject to the budget constraints (3.13) and (3.14) involves only primal variables $c(0)$, $\{c(s)\}$, $\{\theta_i\}$. Let us refer to it as the *primal problem*, to be distinguished from the corresponding *dual problem*, which we now define.

The Lagrangean (3.16) was linear in the portfolios $\{\theta_i\}$. The first-order condition (3.22) set equal to zero the derivative of the Lagrangean with respect to portfolio choice. Suppose that we instead impose (3.22) as a constraint written separately. The effect will be to cancel out of the Lagrangean (3.16) the terms involving $\{\theta_i\}$, thus causing portfolio choice to disappear:

$$\min_{\lambda_0,\{\phi(s)\}} \max_{c(0),\{c(s)\}} \sum_{s=1}^{K} \pi(s)u(c(0),c(s)) + \lambda_0 \left[e(0) - c(0) - \sum_{s=1}^{K} \phi(s)(c(s) - e(s)) \right]$$

subject to (3.22).

The above can be viewed as a partial Lagrangean formulation for the following problem called the *dual* problem, the constraints of which are just one budget condition and the pricing condition (3.22):[12,13]

$$\min_{\{\phi(s)\}} \max_{c(0),\{c(s)\}} \sum_{s=1}^{K} \pi(s)u(c(0),c(s)) \tag{3.23}$$

$$c(0) + \sum_{s=1}^{K} \phi(s) \times (c(s) - e(s)) = e(0) \tag{3.24}$$

$$S_i = \sum_{s=1}^{K} \phi(s)q_i(s) \tag{3.25}$$

In section 3.3.3.2 below and in later chapters, such as chapter 14, we shall have occasion to make use of this dual approach.

---

12 We mean that necessary conditions for the two programs are the same. We do not discuss sufficiency here.

13 This formulation is commonly called the "dual approach" because the choice of the primal variables (portfolios or quantities) Θ has been replaced in the problem below by the choice of the dual variables (prices) Φ. The problem below, however, is not the complete dual program; only portfolio choices, and not consumption, have been "dualized."

In order to get the full dual, one would need to use the convex conjugate utility function. The transformation of the objective function works as follows. Define the convex conjugate of the utility function

$$\tilde{u}(\lambda_0,\{\phi(s)\}) \triangleq \max_{c(0),\{c(s)\}} u(c(0),c(s)) - \lambda_0 [c(0) + \phi(s)c(s)]$$

and substitute into the quasi-dual (3.23). You obtain

$$\min_{\{\lambda_0,\phi(s)\}} \sum_{s=1}^{K} \pi(s)\tilde{u}(\lambda_0,\phi(s)) + \lambda_0 \left[e(0) + \sum_{s=1}^{K} \phi(s)e(s) \right]$$

subject to (3.25), where maximization with respect to consumption does not show up any more.

3.2 A Benchmark Example

3.2.1 Isoelastic Utility

Throughout this textbook, we revisit the benchmark example of an investor whose single-period utility is isoelastic or power:

$$u(c) = \frac{c^\gamma}{\gamma}; \qquad \gamma < 1$$

This utility function is a member of the so-called HARA (hyperbolic absolute risk aversion) class, discussed in Appendix A. The isoelastic utility is characterized by the following risk aversion coefficients:

$$A(c) = \frac{1 - \gamma}{c}$$
$$A_r(c) = 1 - \gamma$$

Its absolute risk aversion, therefore, is decreasing in consumption, while relative risk aversion is constant. That is why this utility function is also named CRRA (constant relative risk aversion). Both assumptions are commonly considered to be desirable and representative of a vast majority of investors' attitudes. The evidence on that question dates back to Friend and Blume (1975).

Noting that:

$$\lim_{\gamma \to 0} \left(\frac{c^\gamma - 1}{\gamma} \right) = \ln(c)$$

the so-called myopic or log investor case is obtained, up to a constant, as a limit as $\gamma \to 0$. The meaning of the term "myopic" will be apparent when, in later chapters, we discuss portfolio selection in intertemporal models.

In this textbook, the benchmark example of utility function for intertemporal choices is additive over time, with time factoring out and a power dependence on consumption. This means that the utility at time t is

$$u(t, c(t)) = \beta^t u(c(t)) = \beta^t \frac{(c(t))^\gamma}{\gamma}; \qquad \gamma < 1$$

In the Fisher economy this entails

$$u(c(0), c(1)) = \frac{(c(0))^\gamma}{\gamma} + \beta \frac{(c(1))^\gamma}{\gamma}$$

while in the single-period model under uncertainty this means that the expected utility function is

$$\sum_{s=1}^{K} \pi(s) u(c(0), c(s)) = \frac{(c(0))^\gamma}{\gamma} + \beta \sum_{s=1}^{K} \pi(s) \frac{(c(s))^\gamma}{\gamma}$$

The consequences for pricing of such a utility choice are described in the next section.

3.2.2 Securities Pricing

With isoelastic utility, the MRS in the Fisher economy is:

$$\phi = \beta \times \left(\frac{c(1)}{c(0)}\right)^{\gamma-1} > 0$$

As expected, the MRS is increasing in the time discount factor β or decreasing in time impatience, and increasing in the ratio between today and tomorrow's consumption, $c(0)/c(1)$. The more one consumes tomorrow compared to today, the lower is ϕ.

In an Arrow-Debreu economy, the marginal rates of substitution are similar:

$$\phi(s) = \pi(s)\beta \left(\frac{c(s)}{c(0)}\right)^{\gamma-1} > 0 \tag{3.26}$$

The corresponding equivalent martingale probabilities are

$$\phi^*(s) = \pi(s)(1+r)\beta \left(\frac{c(s)}{c(0)}\right)^{\gamma-1} > 0$$

Finally, the stochastic discount factor for an isoelastic investor becomes

$$\xi(s) = \frac{\phi(s)}{\pi(s)} = \beta \left(\frac{c(s)}{c(0)}\right)^{\gamma-1}$$

Both the marginal rates of substitution and martingale probabilities are increasing in the corresponding "true" probabilities. Both behave as the MRS of the Fisher economy in respect to the time-discount factor and consumption.

In the complex-security case, the marginal rates of substitution and stochastic discount factor become:

$$\phi(s) = \pi(s)\frac{\beta(e(s) + \Theta^\mathsf{T} q(s))^{\gamma-1}}{(c(0))^{\gamma-1}}$$

$$\xi(s) = \frac{\phi(s)}{\pi(s)} = \frac{\beta(e(s) + \Theta^\mathsf{T} q(s))^{\gamma-1}}{(c(0))^{\gamma-1}}$$

The same intuition as above applies to them, with the additional remark that tomorrow's consumption is expressed here in terms of endowments and portfolio outcomes. Since $\gamma < 1$, the better the portfolio is expected to perform in a given state (say, the higher are the dividends $q_i(s)$), the lower is the corresponding MRS and discount factor.

Also, complex security prices (3.22) turn out to be:

$$S_i = \sum_{s=1}^{K} \pi(s)\xi(s)q_i(s) = \sum_{s=1}^{K} \pi(s)\frac{\beta(e(s) + \Theta^\mathsf{T} q(s))^{\gamma-1}}{(c(0))^{\gamma-1}}q_i(s)$$

In this case there is a form of offset between the positive, direct effect via the payoff $q_i(s)$ and the negative effect on the corresponding state-price. Because the dividend contributes to future consumption, it is quite conceivable that the price of a security is reduced when its future dividend is increased. That happens when there is no future endowment, $\gamma < 0$ (risk aversion is greater than 1) and the security being priced is the whole stock market

$c(s) = q(s)$. An increase in the future growth of consumption reduces today's value of the stock market!

3.2.3 From Security Prices to State Prices, Risk-Neutral Probabilities, and Stochastic Discount Factors

In the derivations above we started from a utility function and we derived the corresponding Arrow-Debreu and complex security prices. Assume now that the market is complete and, for the sake of simplicity, that there are only two states and two securities. The payoff matrix is then

$$\Sigma = \begin{bmatrix} q_1(1) \ q_1(2) \\ q_2(1) \ q_2(2) \end{bmatrix}$$

Suppose that you can observe the prices of the corresponding securities, S_1 and S_2. Then, in the absence of a utility function, as we saw in the previous chapter, it is possible to infer from those prices either the Arrow-Debreu prices $\phi(s)$, or the risk-neutral probabilities $\phi^*(s)$, or the stochastic discount factors $\xi(s)$.

Here, starting from observed security prices, one can do more; that is, one can construct the optimal consumption path and the way to finance it through optimal portfolio allocation.

To build optimal consumption, one can proceed as follows. Exploiting (3.26), derive the optimal ratio $c(s)/c(0)$ between consumption $c(0)$ at time 0 and consumption $c(s)$ at time 1 in each state. Supposing that, from securities prices, we solved for the stochastic discount factors. From $\xi(s) = \beta(c(s)/c(0))^{\gamma-1}$ we get the consumption ratio as

$$\frac{c(s)}{c(0)} = \left(\frac{\xi(s)}{\beta} \right)^{1/(\gamma-1)} \tag{3.27}$$

This, together with the budget constraint

$$c(0) + \sum_{s=1}^{2} \pi(s)\xi(s)c(s) = \mathfrak{W}_0 \triangleq e(0) + \sum_{s=1}^{2} \pi(s)\xi(s)e(s)$$

gives the optimal consumption levels for the isoelastic investor at time 0 and in the two states a time 1. Indeed, the RHS of this budget constraint is known, since the endowment realizations are known and the state prices have been solved for. Substituting for (3.27) in the LHS, we get:

$$c(0) \times \left[1 + \sum_{s=1}^{2} \pi(s)\xi(s) \left(\frac{\xi(s)}{\beta} \right)^{1/(\gamma-1)} \right] = e(0) + \sum_{s=1}^{2} \pi(s)\xi(s)e(s)$$

which is a single equation in the optimal consumption at time 0,

$$c(0) = \frac{e(0) + \sum_{s=1}^{2} \pi(s)\xi(s)e(s)}{1 + \sum_{s=1}^{2} \pi(s)\xi(s) \left(\frac{\xi(s)}{\beta} \right)^{1/(\gamma-1)}}$$

For consumption at time 1, we use (3.27) again:

$$c(s) = \frac{e(0) + \sum_{s=1}^{2} \pi(s)\xi(s)e(s)}{1 + \sum_{s=1}^{2} \pi(s)\xi(s)\left(\frac{\xi(s)}{\beta}\right)^{1/(\gamma-1)}} \left(\frac{\xi(s)}{\beta}\right)^{1/(\gamma-1)}$$

To find the optimal portfolio allocation, recall that the relation $C - E = \Sigma^{\mathsf{T}}\Theta$ can be written as a two-equation, two-unknown system for the portfolio mix:

$$\left(\Sigma^{\mathsf{T}}\right)^{-1}(C - E) = \Theta$$

At the optimum

$$\begin{cases} \theta_1 = a_1(1) \times (c(1) - e(1)) + a_1(2) \times (c(2) - e(2)) \\ \theta_2 = a_2(1) \times (c(1) - e(1)) + a_2(2) \times (c(2) - e(2)) \end{cases}$$

where $a_i(j)$ are the elements of the inverse $(\Sigma^{\mathsf{T}})^{-1}$ of the payoff matrix. In this system, endowments and the elements of Σ, and therefore its inverse, are given. If one substitutes in optimal consumptions on the RHS too, the system provides the optimal portfolio on the LHS.

3.3   Multiperiod Model

This section describes a utility-based discrete-time model, due to Lucas (1978). The model is one of a pure-exchange economy in which a single investor decides his consumption and portfolio allocation over the horizon T. It is a pure-exchange economy because there is no production and each investor receives exogenous endowments. As in the binomial simplification of section 2.2.6, the market includes so-called *long-lived securities* for trade, which are securities that exist from 0 to T.

Since time is discrete and both consumption and portfolio decisions are taken at those discrete points in time, we let information evolve according to an *event-tree* as in section 2.2.1.

At state s of time t, securities pay non-negative dividends or payoffs that are collected in a matrix $\Sigma(s,t)$ and security prices are collected in the vector $S(s,t) \in \mathbb{R}^N$. Prices are ex-dividend, so that $S(s,T) = 0$ for all the states s. No payoffs are paid at 0. As usual, the first security is the riskless one.

At each node, the investor makes decisions having seen the dividends and prices of the securities in that state and knowing the dividend matrices at the successor states and being able to assign a probability to each successor state. Recall that $\pi(s,t)$ is the unconditional (or time-0) probability that the investor assigns to the event of being in state s at t. In the whole treatment of multiperiod economies, we denote as $c(t)$ the random variable that takes values $c(s,t)$. Analogous notation is used for the other random variables.

The investor's utility is:[14,15]

$$u(c(0),0) + \sum_{t=1}^{T} \sum_{s=1}^{K_t} \pi(s,t) u(c(s,t),t)$$

Let $\Theta(s^-, t-1) \in \mathbb{R}^N$ be the vector of post-trade security holdings in state s^- at time $t-1$. For the sake of simplicity, the investor is given an endowment $e(0)$ of goods at time 0 but no endowment of securities. As a consequence, considering that there is only one state at time 0, the budget constraint he faces at that point is

$$c(0) + \Theta(0)^{\mathsf{T}} S(0) = e(0) \tag{3.28}$$

It says that he can use the initial endowment in order to consume or save, using financial securities (as in the one-period model, there is no restriction on the sign of his positions; he could borrow or sell securities short in order to consume more than his endowment).

If we assume that the investor has *zero endowment* of goods or securities at any other point in time, his total wealth coincides with financial wealth, which is the total value of the securities of the investor that he bought or sold one period before, when he was in state s^-, plus the dividends he gets in state s at t:

$$W(s,t) \triangleq \Theta(s^-, t-1)^{\mathsf{T}} \times (q(s,t) + S(s,t)) \tag{3.29}$$

That is what he can use to finance consumption and the new portfolio holdings $\Theta(s,t)^{\mathsf{T}} S(s,t)$. Pre-trade wealth being called $W(s,t)$, his budget constraint at that time is

$$c(s,t) + \Theta(s,t)^{\mathsf{T}} S(s,t) = W(s,t) \tag{3.30}$$

We call these "*recursive*," "*dynamic*," or "*flow*" budget constraints. These work exactly in the way an accountant keeps track of debits and credits or records flows of funds during each period of time. They are, therefore, the primitive form of the budget constraints.

The amounts of consumption and the portfolio strategies in each state of each time t, namely

$$c(s,t), s = 1,.., K_t, t = 0,.., T$$

$$\Theta(s,t), s = 1,.., K_t, t = 0,.., T-1$$

are the investor's choice variables. Overall, his problem is that of maximizing lifetime utility

$$\max_{\{c(s,t)\}, \Theta(s,t)} u(c(0),0) + \sum_{t=1}^{T} \sum_{s=1}^{K_t} \pi(s,t) u(c(s,t),t) \tag{3.31}$$

subject to the $1 + \sum_{t=1}^{T} K_t$ constraints (3.28) and (3.30).

---

14 The original Lucas model has infinite uncertainty and an infinite horizon. These two features, however, can be changed without affecting the main implications (pricing and equilibrium) of the model. Notice that consumption is in a single good, whose price is, as usual, the numeraire.

15 On the one hand, additivity facilitates the use of a powerful solution method for optimization, dynamic programming. On the other hand, as we know from chapter 2, it restricts the generality of the results.

3.3.1   Optimization Methods

There are two methods to solve the intertemporal optimization problem: one consists in using dynamic programming and in solving the problem recursively by backward induction. Dynamic programming works by recursion and is described in Appendix B. The other solution method is global instead of recursive: it consists in considering all the constraints at the same time, and applying a Lagrangean technique to the problem of maximizing overall, or global, or lifetime utility.

We examine both techniques, since each has advantages and drawbacks. The dynamic programming technique has the advantage of being applicable, with no distinction, in complete as well as incomplete markets. In incomplete markets, the global approach requires special care (see chapter 14). For recursive techniques to be applicable, the structure of the problem must be recursive.[16] Nothing more is required for what follows. However, at the implementation stage dynamic programming will require some kind of Markov setting: one can solve period by period if and only if the state variables at each point in time are a sufficient statistic for the whole information content of state variable processes.[17] The global technique can be implemented in more general situations.[18]

3.3.2   Recursive Approach

We demonstrate the use of a recursive approach called dynamic programming. The method is recursive since one solves recursively or sequentially for *one* period at a time, moving backwards. Because it is sequential, the method only makes use of flow budget constraints and is applicable whether the market is complete or incomplete.

Consider the successors s^+ of state $s, s^+ = 1, \ldots K_{s,t}$. Define the value function J as the maximized value of the utility that the investor can get from a given point in time onwards, or *derived* utility. Bellman's principle of optimality, which we present in Appendix B, states that the value function today is the sum of current consumption and the expectation of the value function tomorrow, that is, it satisfies the recurrence relation

$$
J(W(s,t),s,t) \triangleq \max_{\{c(s,t)\},\Theta(s,t)} \left\{ u(c(s,t),t) \right.
$$
$$
\left. + \sum_{s^+=1}^{K_{s,t}} \frac{\pi\left(s^+,t+1\right)}{\pi(s,t)} J\left(W\left(s^+,t+1\right),s^+,t+1\right) \right\}
$$

---

16 The reader may refer to chapter 21 for the definition of recursive lifetime utility functions.

17 Please, refer to chapter 5 for the definition of Markov or Markovian processes.

18 In addition, in a Markov, continuous-time, complete-market setting, the global technique leads to linear differential equations instead of nonlinear ones (see chapter 10).

A priori, the maximization is subject to the dynamic budget constraints (3.28, 3.30), that is, to as many constraints as periods of time and states in the decision horizon, and to the condition that the value function coincides with the final utility at the terminal date:

$$J(W(s,T),s,T) = u(c(s,T),T)$$

To maximize the value function subject to the period constraints, we can work backwards, starting from period T. This is equivalent, as Appendix B explains, to embedding the original problem in a larger class of problems, parametrized by the arguments $\{W,s,t\}$ of the value function, and to choosing the solution path that corresponds to the particular problem with initial wealth: $\{e(0),0\}$. The procedure is followed in detail for the benchmark example at the end of this chapter.

Furthermore, since the optimization of the value function is under constraints, we can write a separate Lagrangean *for each point in time and each state*:

$$L(c(s,t), \Theta(s,t), \lambda(s,t); W(s,t), s, t) \triangleq u(c(s,t),t)$$

$$+ \sum_{s^+=1}^{K_{s,t}} \frac{\pi(s^+,t+1)}{\pi(s,t)} J\left(W(s^+,t+1), s^+, t+1\right)$$

$$+ \lambda(s,t) \times \left(W(s,t) - c(s,t) - \Theta(s,t)^\mathsf{T} S(s,t)\right)$$

where $\lambda(s,t)$ is the Lagrange multiplier of the time-t constraint, when state s is true. We can obtain the first-order conditions from all these Lagrangeans. In order to do that, we differentiate with respect to consumption $c(s,t)$ in each state and time, obtaining

$$\frac{\partial}{\partial c} u(c(s,t),t) = \lambda(s,t)$$

We also differentiate with respect to the portfolio weights of each security $\theta_i(s,t)$, $i = 1,..,N$, in each state and time $t \neq T$. Since asset i enters in wealth at time $t+1$ and state s^+, $W_{s^+,t+1}$, and contributes to it through dividends and prices, $q_i(s^+,t+1) + S_i(s^+,t+1)$, according to (3.29):[19]

$$W(s^+,t+1) = \Theta(s,t)^\mathsf{T} \times \left[q(s^+,t+1) + S(s^+,t+1)\right]$$

when we differentiate with respect to the portfolio weights we get:

$$\sum_{s^+=1}^{K_{t+1}} \frac{\pi(s^+,t+1)}{\pi(s,t)} \frac{\partial}{\partial W} J\left(W(s^+,t+1), s^+, t+1\right)$$

$$\times \left(q_i(s^+,t+1) + S_i(s^+,t+1)\right) = \lambda(s,t) S_i(s,t)$$

---

19 We write $\Theta(s,t)$ for the portfolio allocation vector and $\theta_i(s,t)$ for its entries. Similarly for prices and dividends.

Last, we differentiate with respect to the multipliers $\lambda(s,t)$ and, as usual, we get back the budget constraints.

As a whole, the first-order conditions for the recursive formulation are:

$$\frac{\partial}{\partial c}u(c(s,t),t) = \lambda(s,t); \ s = 1,..,K_t \tag{3.32}$$

$$\sum_{s^+=1}^{K_{t+1}} \frac{\pi(s^+,t+1)}{\pi(s,t)} \frac{\partial}{\partial W}J\big(W(s^+,t+1),s^+,t+1\big) \tag{3.33}$$

$$\times \big(q_i(s^+,t+1) + S_i(s^+,t+1)\big) = \lambda(s,t)S_i(s,t)$$

$$i = 1,..,N; \ s = 1,..,K_t$$

$$c(0) + \Theta(0)^\mathsf{T} S(0) = e(0) \tag{3.34}$$

$$c(s,t) + \Theta(s,t)^\mathsf{T} S(s,t) = W(s,t) \tag{3.35}$$

$$s = 1,..,K_t$$

$J(W(s,t),s,t)$ being the saddle point of the Lagrangean (see Appendix B), namely:

$$J(W(s,t),s,t) \triangleq \max_{\{c(s,t)\},\Theta(s,t)} \min_{\lambda(s,t)} L(c(s,t),\Theta(s,t),\lambda(s,t); W(s,t),s,t)$$

It follows from differentiation and the envelope theorem that the derivative of J in wealth is equal to the multiplier:

$$\frac{\partial}{\partial W}J(W(s,t),t) = \lambda(s,t) \tag{3.36}$$

The first-order condition (3.32), which states the equality between marginal utility of consumption and the multiplier, together with (3.36), which states the equality between marginal derived utility and the multiplier, say that the derivative of the value function with respect to accumulated wealth and the marginal utility of consumption are equal to each other, state by state. We call this the *marginality principle*:

$$\frac{\partial}{\partial W}J(W(s,t),t) = \frac{\partial}{\partial c}u(c(s,t),t) \tag{3.37}$$

Equality between the J and u derivatives plays a key role in the dynamic pricing literature, in discrete as well as in continuous time. It states a principle that is familiar in Microeconomics and Decision theory. In intertemporal problems, the marginal utility of current wealth, in terms of total discounted future utility, must equate the marginal utility of spending now, instead of saving. One unit of consumption saved now and spent in the future must have the same value to the investor as one unit of consumption spent today. What matters, in appreciating this consumption unit is its contribution to utility. As a consequence, it is the marginal utility of the unit of consumption tomorrow that is equated to its marginal utility today. As one would expect, intertemporal optimization involves the smoothing of marginal utility over time. Savings smooth utility, not literally consumption, over time. The investor can use both consumption and portfolio allocation to achieve his smoothing goal, taking security prices and initial endowment as given. The value that is common to current and future marginal utility assumes the usual meaning of shadow price of the resources and is, therefore, represented by a Lagrange multiplier (see Appendix B). Here the resource is wealth. There is a different value of the shadow price, $\lambda(s,t)$, across states and time depending on the level of marginal utility. This means that, at each point in time, the intrinsic value of wealth is higher (lower) in those states in which utility is low (high). These are, indeed, the states in which its marginal value is high (low).

3.3.3 Global Approach

3.3.3.1 Euler Conditions

The Lagrangean technique or global approach can also be adopted, keeping the period-by-period constraint, without using the value function. Indeed, if we form the Lagrangean directly from the problem (3.31), we get :

$$L(c(s,t), \Theta(s,t), \lambda(s,t)) \triangleq \qquad (3.38)$$

$$u(c(0),0) + \sum_{t=1}^{T} \sum_{s=1}^{K_t} \pi(s,t) u(c(s,t),t) + \lambda_0 \times (e(0) - c(0) - \Theta(0)^\mathsf{T} S(0))$$

$$+ \sum_{t=1}^{T} \sum_{s=1}^{K_t} \pi(s,t) \times \lambda(s,t) \times \left(W(s,t) - c(s,t) - \Theta(s,t)^\mathsf{T} \times S(s,t) \right)$$

where we gave the name $\pi(s,t) \times \lambda(s,t)$ to the Lagrange multipliers of the many constraints, just for conformity of notation with the previous section. The Lagrangean is to be maximized with respect to $c(0), \{c(s,t)\}, \Theta(0), \{\Theta(s,t)\}$ and minimized with respect to $\lambda_0, \{\lambda(s,t)\}$. Let us write the corresponding system of first-order conditions. As above, the first $1 + \sum_{t=1}^{T} K_t$ conditions are obtained by differentiating with respect to $c(0)$ and $c(s,t)$:

$$\frac{\partial u}{\partial c(0)}(c(0),0) = \lambda_0$$

$$\frac{\partial u}{\partial c(s,t)}(c(s,t),t) = \lambda(s,t)$$

The next conditions are obtained by differentiating with respect to each component $\theta_i(0)$ of $\Theta(0)$. Since, according to (3.30), at time 1, in each state s^+, $s^+ = 1, \ldots K_1$, wealth is given by

$$W(s^+,1) = \Theta(0)^\mathsf{T} \left(q_i(s^+,1) + S_i(s^+,1) \right)$$

the time-1 constraint in that state becomes

$$\Theta^\mathsf{T}(s^+,1) S(s^+,1) + c(s^+,1) = \Theta(0)^\mathsf{T} \left(q_i(s^+,1) + S_i(s^+,1) \right)$$

and the first-order condition with respect to $\theta_i(0)$ is

$$-\lambda_0 S_i(0) + \sum_{s^+=1}^{K_1} \pi(s^+, 1) \times \lambda(s^+, 1) \times (q_i(s^+, 1) + S_i(s^+, 1)) = 0$$

As in section 3.3.2, when we differentiate with respect to each component $\theta_i(s, t)$ of $\Theta(s, t)$, for all s and $t < T$, we must recall (3.29) and substitute it into the corresponding constraint, which becomes

$$\Theta^{\mathsf{T}}(s^+, t+1) S(s^+, t+1) + c(s^+, t+1) = \Theta(s, t)^{\mathsf{T}} (q(s^+, t+1) + S(s^+, t+1))$$

The RHS is the entering wealth at time $t + 1$, $W(s^+, t + 1)$, while the LHS is the post-trade wealth, in the same state and at the same point in time, plus consumption. As a consequence, each θ_i for each security, state s and time t, $\theta_i(s, t)$, appears twice, once on the RHS of the previous constraint, in the entering wealth $W(s^+, t + 1)$, multiplied by the corresponding dividends and price, $q(s^+, t + 1) + S(s^+, t + 1)$, and once in the exiting wealth for state s at time t, $\Theta(s, t)^{\mathsf{T}} S(s, t)$, in the constraint of one period before. The corresponding first-order condition is

$$-\pi(s, t) \times \lambda(s, t) S_i(s, t) + \sum_{s^+=1}^{K_{s,t}} \pi(s^+, t+1) \times \lambda(s^+, t+1) \times (q_i(s^+, t+1)$$
$$+ S_i(s^+, t+1)) = 0$$

Last, there are the budget constraints, which are the derivatives with respect to the Lagrange multipliers. As a whole, writing the first-order condition for all $t = 0, 1, 2, .., T$; $s = 1, .., K_t$; $i = 1, 2, .., N$, we have

$$\frac{\partial u}{\partial c(0)}(c(0), 0) = \lambda_0 \tag{3.39}$$

$$\frac{\partial u}{\partial c(s, t)}(c(s, t), t) = \lambda(s, t) \tag{3.40}$$

$$-\lambda_0 S_i(0) + \sum_{s^+=1}^{K_0} \pi(s^+, 1) \times \lambda(s^+, 1) \times (q_i(s^+, 1) + S_i(s^+, 1)) = 0 \tag{3.41}$$

$$-\pi(s, t) \times \lambda(s, t) S_i(s, t) + \sum_{s^+=1}^{K_{s,t}} \pi(s^+, t+1) \times \lambda(s^+, t+1) \tag{3.42}$$
$$\times (q_i(s^+, t+1) + S_i(s^+, t+1)) = 0$$

$$c(0) + \Theta(0)^{\mathsf{T}} S(0) = e(0) \tag{3.43}$$

$$c(s, t) + \Theta(s, t)^{\mathsf{T}} S(s, t) = W(s, t) \tag{3.44}$$

Substituting the first-order conditions of consumption choice (3.39) and (3.40) into the first-order conditions of portfolio choice (3.41) and (3.42), we get a set of equations called the "Euler conditions"

$$-\frac{\partial u}{\partial c(0)}(c(0),0)S_i(0)$$

$$+\sum_{s^+=1}^{K_1}\pi_{s^+,1}\frac{\partial u}{\partial c_{s,1}}(c_{s^+,1},1)\left(q_i(s^+,1)+S_i(s^+,1)\right)=0 \tag{3.45}$$

$$-\pi(s,t)\frac{\partial u}{\partial c(s,t)}(c(s,t),t)S_i(s,t)$$

$$+\sum_{s^+=1}^{K_{s,t}}\pi\left(s^+,t+1\right)\frac{\partial u}{\partial c(s,t)}(c(s^+,t+1),t+1)\times\left(q_i(s^+,t+1)+S_i\left(s^+,t+1\right)\right)=0 \tag{3.46}$$

Note that the Euler conditions (3.45, 3.46) can also be obtained from the dynamic programming approach by substituting the marginality equation (3.37) into the first-order condition for portfolio choice (3.33).

3.3.3.2 The Dual

Looking for ways to simplify the intertemporal optimization problem, one wonders whether there are conditions under which the recursive form of the budget constraint, which entails one constraint at each point in time, can be turned into the following *lifetime* constraint:[20]

$$c(0)+\sum_{t=1}^{T}\sum_{s=1}^{K_t}x(s,t)c(s,t)=e(0) \tag{3.47}$$

for some process $\{x(s,t)\}$ to be determined.

In the lifetime form, the budget constraint says that the present value of all future consumption must be equal to the present value of all future endowments (or vice versa). Discounting is not performed using the riskless rate, but via appropriate deflators $x(s,t)$, and the values of the deflators remain to be determined. This is a single constraint which replaces the $1+\sum_{t=1}^{T}K_t$ constraints of the recursive approach. In addition, portfolios financing consumption no longer show up in the constraint. Maximizing utility subject to

---

20 Or

$$c(0)+\sum_{t=1}^{T}\sum_{s=1}^{K_t}x(s,t)c(s,t)=e(0)+\sum_{t=1}^{T}\sum_{s=1}^{K_t}x(s,t)e(s,t)$$

in case investors receive future endowments of goods.

that constraint will lead to direct choice of consumption. So, the problem will be much simpler than before, if and when we know how to choose the deflators.

When the market is complete, statically or dynamically, we saw in theorem 2.3 that the state prices are unique (and vice versa). They can be used for evaluating consumption, endowments, payoffs of securities. So, we can use as deflators the Arrow-Debreu prices

$$x(s,t) = \phi(s,t)$$

Those are defined, consistently with the one-period case, as

$$\phi(s,t) = \frac{\pi(s,t)\frac{\partial u}{\partial c(s,t)}(c(0),c(s,t))}{\sum_{s=1}^{K_t}\pi(s,t)\frac{\partial u}{\partial c(0)}(c(0),c(s,t))} \tag{3.48}$$

By the definition of completeness, every consumption plan is marketed. Its market price, which is given by the state prices, can be used for the transformation. Whenever the unique budget constraint (3.47) is well defined, it can be used to obtain the global form of the investor's optimization problem. In a complete market, assuming no endowments after time 0, for simplicity, the optimization problem

$$\max_{c(0),\{c(s,t)\}} u(c(0),0) + \sum_{t=1}^{T}\sum_{s=1}^{K_t}\pi(s,t)u(c(s,t),t)$$

can be written subject to the lifetime budget constraint:

$$c(0) + \sum_{t=1}^{T}\sum_{s=1}^{K_t}\phi(s,t)c(s,t) = e(0)$$

This problem has many fewer unknowns than the dynamic problem, since it involves only consumption choices. The straightforward way to attack it is by writing the Lagrangean:

$$L(c(0),c(s,t),\lambda_0) \triangleq u(c(0),0) + \sum_{t=1}^{T}\sum_{s=1}^{K_t}\pi(s,t)u(c(s,t),t)$$

$$+\lambda_0\left(e(0) - c(0) - \sum_{t=1}^{T}\sum_{s=1}^{K_t}\phi(s,t)c(s,t)\right)$$

This Lagrangean is very simple, in that it has a unique constraint and a unique multiplier. Once we solve it for consumption and for the single Lagrange multiplier, we can reconstruct the portfolio weights that are able to deliver the optimal consumption, using at each point in time a replicating-portfolio reasoning, similar to the one we used in chapter 2 for replicating payoffs. We expound a similar approach for continuous time in chapter 10.

When the market is incomplete, state prices are not unique and the lifetime form of the budget constraint becomes less straightforward, because the present value of future consumption (minus future endowments, if any) is not known a priori. We show now that the dual problem remedies that difficulty.

Consider the Lagrangean (3.38) and imagine that the conditions (3.41) and (3.42) are imposed separately as constraints. Since the objective function is linear in the portfolios, once these conditions are satisfied, the problem becomes:

$$\min_{\lambda_0, \{\lambda(s,t)\}} \max_{c(0), \{c(s,t)\}} u(c(0), 0) + \sum_{t=1}^{T} \sum_{s=1}^{K_t} \pi(s,t) u(c(s,t), t)$$

$$+ \lambda_0 \times (e(0) - c(0)) - \sum_{t=1}^{T} \sum_{s=1}^{K_t} \lambda(s,t) \times c(s,t)$$

subject to (3.41) and (3.42). Writing $\lambda(s,t) = \lambda_0 \times \phi(s,t)$, thus introducing implied state prices $\phi(s,t)$, that problem admits the same Lagrangean as the following:

$$\min_{\{\xi(s,t)\}} \max_{c(0), \{c(s,t)\}} u(c(0), 0) + \sum_{t=1}^{T} \sum_{s=1}^{K_t} \pi(s,t) u(c(s,t), t)$$

subject to (3.41), (3.42) and subject to a single lifetime budget constraint:

$$e(0) - c(0) - \sum_{t=1}^{T} \sum_{s=1}^{K_t} \phi(s,t) \times c(s,t) = 0$$

We come back to that problem in chapter 14. In the meanwhile, the reader can solve exercises 3.4 and 3.5.

3.3.4   Securities Pricing

Whether we start from the recursive or the global approach, if the financial market is complete, or populated with one investor or a homogeneous group of investors, we can solve for securities pricing in the same way, using the marginality principle. Suppose that we are in an exchange economy with a stream of endowments so that consumption is given exogenously as $c(s,t) = e(s,t)$. If we start from the global approach, we can use the Euler equation (3.46) to get the following equilibrium price for marketed securities in state s at time t, as a function of what will happen in the successors s^+ of that state:

$$S_i(s,t) = \sum_{s^+=1}^{K_{t+1}} \frac{\pi(s^+, t+1) \frac{\partial}{\partial c} u(c(s^+, t+1), t+1)}{\pi(s,t) \frac{\partial}{\partial c} u(c(s,t), t)} \times \left(q_i(s^+, t+1) + S_i(s^+, t+1) \right) \quad (3.49)$$

Each security price is the sum of the dividends and prices in the successor nodes, weighted using the appropriate MRS for each state.

The same result obtains starting from the recursive approach, since the Euler condition can also be obtained from the dynamic-programming approach. Since (3.37) and (3.36) state that

$$\frac{\partial}{\partial W} J(W(s,t),t) = \frac{\partial}{\partial c} u(c(s,t),t) = \lambda(s,t)$$

we get

$$\sum_{s^-=1}^{K_{t+1}} \frac{\pi(s^+,t+1)}{\pi(s,t)} \frac{\partial}{\partial c} u\big(c\big(s^+,t+1\big),t+1\big)$$

$$\times \big(q_i\big(s^+,t+1\big) + S_i\big(s^+,t+1\big)\big) = \frac{\partial}{\partial c} u(c(s,t),t)S_i(s,t)$$

and consequently

$$S_i(s,t) = \sum_{s^+=1}^{K_{t+1}} \frac{\pi(s^+,t+1)\frac{\partial}{\partial c}u(c(s^+,t+1),t+1)}{\pi(s,t)\frac{\partial}{\partial c}u(c(s,t),t)} \times \big(q_i\big(s^+,t+1\big) + S_i\big(s^+,t+1\big)\big)$$

As usual, call "state prices" the MRSs. The (conditional) state price in state s for state s^+ is:

$$\frac{\phi(s^+,t+1)}{\phi(s,t)} \triangleq \frac{\pi(s^+,t+1)\frac{\partial}{\partial c}u(c(s^+,t+1),t+1)}{\pi(s,t)\frac{\partial}{\partial c}u(c(s,t),t)} \tag{3.50}$$

$$= \frac{\lambda(s^+,t+1)}{\lambda(s,t)} \frac{\pi(s^+,t+1)}{\pi(s,t)}$$

as for the discount factors:

$$\frac{\xi(s^+,t+1)}{\xi(s,t)} \triangleq \frac{\frac{\partial}{\partial c}u(c(s^+,t+1),t+1)}{\frac{\partial}{\partial c}u(c(s,t),t)} = \frac{\lambda(s^+,t+1)}{\lambda(s,t)}$$

Observe that all the discount factors differ from all the Lagrange multipliers by a constant of proportionality (which would be λ_0).

Using definition (3.50), the Lucas model also provides a positive pricing functional, which works unconditionally as $\Phi(s,t)$ and works conditionally (through the ratios $\phi(s^+,t+1)/\phi(s,t)$) as follows:

$$S_i(s,t) = \sum_{s^+=1}^{K_{t+1}} \frac{\phi(s^+,t+1)}{\phi(s,t)} \times \big(q_i\big(s^+,t+1\big) + S_i\big(s^+,t+1\big)\big) \tag{3.51}$$

The price of security i is the sum of next period's cum dividend prices, evaluated using the conditional state prices. The pricing formula of an investor resembles very much the one of the one-period economies, namely (3.22). Here, for all future dates but the last, the security price contains the price prevailing at $t+1$ in addition to the upcoming payoff. The price at

$t+1$ is the continuation value of the security, which did not show up in the single-period economy, for the obvious reason that there was no continuation. This extended version $q_i(s^+, t+1) + S_i(s^+, t+1)$ of next period's payoff is now endogenous.

Consider now the riskless security, that pays the interest rate $r(s,t)$ in state s at time t:

$$\frac{1}{1+r(s,t)} = \sum_{s^+=1}^{K_{t+1}} \frac{\phi(s^+, t+1)}{\phi(s,t)}$$

Define the normalized, conditional state prices:

$$\frac{\phi^*(s^+, t+1)}{\phi^*(s,t)} = \frac{\phi(s^+, t+1)}{\phi(s,t)} \times (1 + r(s,t)) \tag{3.52}$$

As in the single-period case, the corresponding unconditional probabilities are denoted $\{\phi^*(s,t)\}$ or, in a vector, $\Phi^*(s,t)$. They represent a measure that is equivalent to the initial one, since, given $\partial u / \partial c > 0$, each element $\phi^*(s^+, t+1)$ is positive if and only if the corresponding probability $\pi(s^+, t+1)$ is.

The above pricing formula has the following, nice interpretation in terms of expectation:

$$S_i(s,t) = \frac{1}{1+r(s,t)} \mathbb{E}^*_{s,t} \left[q_i(t+1) + S_i(t+1) \right] \tag{3.53}$$

where $\mathbb{E}^*_{s,t}$ denotes expectation under the probabilities in $\Phi(s,t)^*$ conditional on being in state s at time t. The price of security i is the discounted, expected value of its dividend and price one period ahead, under the adjusted probability. Discounting is performed using the riskless rate. This is *martingale pricing* again. In other words, (3.53) says that under the probability $\Phi^*(s,t)$ all assets have the same one-period expected rate of return equal at time t in state s to the short rate of interest $r(s,t)$. The formulation (3.53) resembles the martingale rule of the one-period economy, in which each security was the expectation of the final, discounted payoffs, under the martingale probability $S_i = \left(\sum_{s=1}^K \phi^*(s) q_i(s) \right) / (1+r)$.

Finally, define a stochastic discount factor by taking the ratio of unconditional state prices to unconditional probabilities, or the state prices per unit of (unconditional) probability. Call it $\xi(s,t)$:

$$\xi(s,t) \triangleq \frac{\phi(s,t)}{\pi(s,t)} \tag{3.54}$$

Substituting for it in (3.51) or (3.53), we get

$$S_i(s,t) = \mathbb{E}_{s,t} \left[\frac{\xi(t+1)}{\xi(s,t)} \times (q_i(t+1) + S_i(t+1)) \right] \tag{3.55}$$

where the expectation is computed under the probabilities $\pi(s,t)$ and $\xi(t+1)$ is the random variable that takes realizations $\xi(s^+, t+1)$. This corresponds to the third pricing possibility we presented for the one-period economy, namely (3.21). There, we interpreted it as the expectation of the payoffs under the effective measure, after the payoffs themselves have been translated into utils by means of the stochastic discount factor, or MRS over probability.

At time T there is no continuation value. Prices take the value zero: $S_i(s, T) = 0$. Using this terminal condition one can also write the security price at time t in (3.51) as

$$S_i(s,t) = \sum_{u=t+1}^{T} \sum_{s^+=1}^{K_{u,s,t}} \frac{\phi(s^+,u)}{\phi(s,t)} \times q_i(s^+,u) \tag{3.56}$$

where $K_{u,s,t}$ is the total number of nodes at time u in the *subtree* that stems from state s at time t. Prices at time t are the sum of future payoffs or dividends, evaluated using the Arrow-Debreu prices. Correspondingly, expressions (3.53) and (3.55) become:

$$S_i(s,t) = \sum_{u=t+1}^{T} \mathbb{E}_{s,t}^* \left[\frac{1}{\prod_{\tau=t}^{u-1}(1+r(\tau))} q_i(u) \right] \tag{3.57}$$

or

$$S_i(s,t) = \sum_{u=t+1}^{T} \mathbb{E}_{s,t} \left[\frac{\xi(u)}{\xi(s,t)} \times q_i(u) \right] \tag{3.58}$$

Prices are expectations, under the martingale measure, of future dividends, discounted at the riskless rate. They are also expectations, under the effective measure, of dividends translated into utils using the stochastic discount factor.

We suggest that the reader solve exercises 3.6 and 3.7.

The same pricing principles apply to wealth. If any endowments $e(s,t)$ are received after time 0, *total wealth* at time t and state s is given by the value of the portfolio with which one enters time t, $\Theta^\mathsf{T}\left(s^-, t-1\right)\left[q(s,t) + S(s,t)\right]$, that is, financial wealth, as described up to now, *plus* the discounted value of total endowments over time:

$$\mathcal{W}(s,t) \triangleq \Theta^\mathsf{T}\left(s^-, t-1\right)\left[q(s,t) + S(s,t)\right] + e(s,t)$$
$$+ \sum_{u=t+1}^{T} \sum_{s^+=1}^{K_{u,s,t}} \frac{\phi(s^+,u)}{\phi(s,t)} e(s^+,u)$$

The lifetime budget constraint (3.47) imposes that this new wealth be equal to the present value of current and future consumption:

$$c(s,t) + \sum_{u=t+1}^{T} \sum_{s^+=1}^{K_{u,s,t}} \frac{\phi(s^+,u)}{\phi(s,t)} c(s^+,u) = \mathcal{W}(s,t)$$

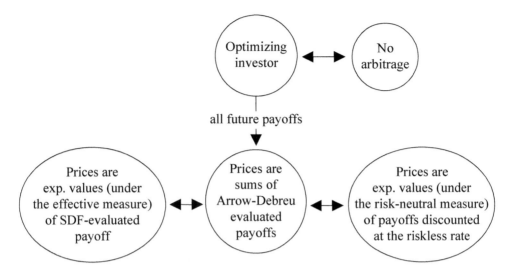

Figure 3.2
Individual optimality and asset pricing in the multiperiod model.

The stock form of the budget constraint can be rearranged so that it says that *financial wealth W* is equal to the present value of consumption minus endowments:

$$W(s,t) \triangleq \Theta^{\mathsf{T}}\left(s^{-},t-1\right)\left[q(s,t) + S(s,t)\right]$$

$$c(s,t) - e(s,t) + \sum_{u=t+1}^{T} \sum_{s=1}^{K_{u,s,t}} \frac{\phi\left(s^{+},u\right)}{\phi(s,t)} \times \left(c\left(s^{+},u\right) - e\left(s^{+},u\right)\right) = W(s,t)$$

The results obtained so far can be synthesized in figure 3.2, which updates figure 3.1.

3.4 Benchmark Example (continued)

As an example of utility maximization in a Lucas-tree economy, we use the binomial model of section 2.2.6. We explore briefly its optimization and security-pricing features in a binomial setting where the percentage increases and decreases of total output are called u and d ($u > d$). The Lucas problem covering the time span $(0, n)$ becomes[21]

$$\max_{\{c(j,k)\},\{\Theta(j,k)\}} u(c(0),0) + \sum_{k=1}^{n} \sum_{j=0}^{k} \pi(j,k)u\left(c(j,k),k\right)$$

---

[21] The authors apologize a second time for the notational conflict encountered here. The increases and decreases of total output are called u and d as in the binomial model, while the utility function is also called u.

subject to the constraints

$$c(0) + \Theta(0)^\mathsf{T} S(0) = e(0)$$
$$c(j,k) + \Theta(j,k)^\mathsf{T} S(j,k) = W(j,k); \quad j = 0,1,..k, k = 0,1,..n$$

For the numbering of nodes (in the tree, which is recombining), we adopt the following convention: node j of time k is followed by node $j+1$ of time $k+1$ in case of a u move and by node j of time $k+1$ in case of a d move. The first-order condition for this problem can be written down either using the Lagrangean approach, or using a dynamic programming technique. Either way, one obtains the Euler equations (3.46):

$$-\frac{\partial u}{\partial c}(c(j,k),k) \times S_i(j,k) + p\frac{\partial u}{\partial c}(c(j+1,k+1),k+1)$$
$$\times (q_i(j+1,k+1) + S_i(j+1,k+1))$$
$$+(1-p)\frac{\partial u}{\partial c}(c(j,k+1),k+1) \times (q_i(j,k+1) + S_i(j,k+1)) = 0$$

If the investor is alone in the financial market, therefore, the price at which he *would* be willing to trade is:

$$S_i(j,k) = p\frac{\frac{\partial u}{\partial c}(u \times e(j,k),k+1)}{\frac{\partial u}{\partial c}(e(j,k),k)} \times (q_i(j+1,k+1) + S_i(j+1,k+1))$$
$$+(1-p)\frac{\frac{\partial u}{\partial c}(d \times e(j,k),k+1)}{\frac{\partial u}{\partial c}(e(j,k),k)} \times (q_i(j,k+1) + S_i(j,k+1))$$

where $e(j,k)$ is the endowment in state j at time k that formula can be iterated forward all the way to the terminal date n, thus obtaining a closed-form formula for the price of security i.

For instance, if utility is isoelastic $(\beta^t c^\gamma / \gamma)$, we get

$$S_i(j,k) = p \times \beta \times u^{\gamma-1} \times (q_i(j+1,k+1) + S_i(j+1,k+1))$$
$$+(1-p) \times \beta \times d^{\gamma-1} \times (q_i(j,k+1) + S_i(j,k+1))$$

and, if the security being priced pays the total endowment $(q_i(j,k) = e(j,k))$, we get

$$S_i(j,k) = p \times \beta \times u^{\gamma-1} \times (u \times e(j+1,k+1) + S_i(j+1,k+1))$$
$$+(1-p) \times \beta \times d^{\gamma-1} \times (d \times e(j,k+1) + S_i(j,k+1))$$

State prices from one period to the next are $p \times \beta \times u^\gamma$ and $(1-p) \times \beta \times d^\gamma$ for the u and d moves respectively. Iterating forward, the ex-dividend price at time 0 is

$$S(0) = e(0) \sum_{k=1}^{n} \beta^k \sum_{j=0}^{k} \binom{k}{j} p^j (1-p)^{k-j} \left(u^j d^{k-j}\right)^\gamma$$

3.5   Conclusion

The chapter solved the investor's problem of consumption and portfolio choice, in a single period and in a multiperiod economy. The former problem was attacked using Lagrangeans, and the main message was that state prices, risk-neutral probabilities, and stochastic discount factors are marginal rates of substitution or depend on them.

To solve the investor's problem of consumption and portfolio choice in a multiperiod economy, two techniques are available. They are dynamic programming, which is recursive in time, and the global Lagrange technique, which writes a system involving all points in time and all states simultaneously. The latter is valid in all cases while the former requires additional assumptions. With both techniques, the first-order condition of portfolio choice is an Euler equation.

When all investors are alike, their Euler equation provides a simple way to price basic securities. Valuation equations are simply restatements of first-order conditions of portfolio choice.

Exercises

3.1. Consider a two-dates economy with a single individual, whose utility is log. There are three states at $t = 1$, equally likely. The investor has access to Arrow-Debreu securities only, his initial wealth is 100, and there is no endowment at time 1.

 a. Determine the prices of the Arrow-Debreu securities and the riskless rate.

 b. Determine the risk neutral probabilities, $\phi^*(s)$, and the stochastic discount factor components, $\xi(s)$.

3.2. In the economy of exercise 3.1, imagine that no Arrow-Debreu securities are traded. The traded securities are a riskless bond, $B(t) = S_1(t)$, and a risky one, $S_2(t)$, which pays $10, 12, 11$ in the three states.

 a. Which price should be assigned to the complex securities at time 0, if the numeraire is B?

 b. Is the market described complete?

 c. If we now add a call option with maturity 1 and strike 11, and call its value $S_3(t)$, is the market complete? What are the prices of the risky securities, $S_2(0), S_3(0)$?

3.3. Suppose that in the presence of the securities described in exercise 3.2 their prices are respectively

$$B(0) = S_1(0) = 1$$
$$S_2(0) = 11$$
$$S_3(0) = 0.1$$

and $r = 0\%$. Determine optimal consumption and securities holdings.

3.4. Consider an investor who wishes to maximize the sum of the utility from consumption at $t = 0$ and expected utility from consumption at $t = 1$. Also, to simplify matters, assume that the utility function is log, time-additive with zero time impatience. Finally, the initial wealth of the investor is $W_0 = 10$ and there is no endowment at $t = 1$.

Formally, the objective of the investor is to

$$\max_{c(0),c(1)} \{u(c(0)) + \mathbb{E}\, u(c(1))\} \quad \text{where} \quad u(c(t)) = \ln c(t), W_0 = 10$$

The investor can use Arrow-Debreu securities, which are priced as in exercise 2.3 in chapter 2. Based on this information:

a. Rewrite the portfolio problem of the investor in a global form (that is, all decisions are made at $t = 0$, and the budget equation is also in a lifetime form. This is a little bit artificial here, since there is a single time period, but is a useful exercise for the extension to more periods in the next exercises).

b. Using the global formulation, solve for the optimal $c(0)$ and the optimal number of state-contingent claims to hold at $t = 0$.

c. Find the optimal trading strategy involving the bond and the stock that finances, replicates, or generates the optimal $c(1)$.

3.5. In the economy of exercise 2.3 in chapter 2, consider an investor who wishes to maximize the sum of the utility from consumption at $t = 0$ and expected utility from consumption at $t = 1, 2$. Also, to simplify matters, assume that the utility function is time-additive with zero time impatience and log utility. Finally, the initial wealth of the investor is $W_0 = 100$ and there are no endowments at $t = 1, 2$. Formally, the objective of the investor is

$$\max \{u(c(0)) + \mathbb{E}\, u(c(1)) + \mathbb{E}\, u(c(2))\} \quad \text{where} \quad u(c(t)) = \log c(t), W_0 = 100$$

Based on this information:

a. Rewrite the portfolio problem of the investor in a global form (that is, all decisions are made at $t = 0$, and the budget equation is also in a lifetime form).

b. Using the global formulation, solve for the optimal $c(0)$ and the optimal number of state-contingent claims to hold at $t = 0$.

c. Find the optimal trading strategy involving the bond and the stock that finances, replicates, or generates the optimal c.

3.6. Consider the economy of exercise 2.3 in chapter 2. Interpret the stock price process as a binomial tree: starting from $S(0)$, assume in each time period the stock price either goes up by a factor $u > 1$ with probability p, or goes down by a factor $0 < d < 1$ with probability $1 - p$. The moves over time are IID. This is the binomial model, with $n = T$ and $\Delta t = 1$. For each t, $S(t) = S(0)u^{j(t)}d^{t-j(t)}$, where $j(t)$ represents the (stochastic) number of up moves up to t:

$$u = \frac{5}{4}$$
$$d = u^{-1}$$

Based on this information:

a. Show that the (unique) risk neutral probability of an up-move is given by

$$p^* = \frac{1+r-d}{u-d} = \frac{4}{9}$$

and use it to determine the distribution of $S(t)$.

b. Verify that the initial price obtained using Arrow-Debreu securities and risk-neutral probabilities coincide for any utility function.

3.7. Consider the binomial framework of exercise 3.6. Based on this information:

a. Determine the price process of a European call option on the stock with strike price $K = 18$ and maturity $T = 2$.

b. Determine the replicating portfolio for the call option at each node.

c. Use a hedging argument to derive the hedging portfolio and the same replicating portfolio at each node.

4 Equilibrium and Pricing of Basic Securities

This chapter adopts the discrete-time optimization models that were provided in the previous chapters but extends the corresponding equilibria to heterogeneous investors, specifically investors with different utility functions (thus deviating from the assumption made in chapter 3 when discussing prices).

Again we start from the one-period case, then go to the multiperiod case. In the one-period setting, we revisit the uniqueness of state prices that obtained in complete markets, when no investor choice was explicitly modeled (section 4.1). We study the consequences for Pareto optimality, the existence of a representative investor, as well as security prices and returns, leading to the so-called CAPM. Two further features of the equilibria are analyzed: the way equalization of state prices across different investors is achieved and the way they share risk (section 4.2). As an example, we then study the equilibrium of our benchmark complete-market economy (section 4.2.4).

In the multiperiod case, we extend to heterogeneous investors what we did in chapter 3. We then have to distinguish between Radner and Arrow-Debreu equilibria. We again analyze the equalization of state prices and risk sharing. That is done in section 4.4.

We conclude with a comment on the role of time-additivity in utility functions (section 4.4.5).

4.1 One-Period Economies

As soon as we want to describe a "realistic" market, we need to abandon the assumption of homogeneous investors. Investors may well differ in utility, endowment, and probability assessments.

It is natural to ask whether a notion of (unique) state price, risk-neutral probability, or stochastic discount factor is still workable, and whether a "representative investor" may be defined. What does the utility function of that investor look like? Is the outcome of a competitive equilibrium, in which every single investor maximizes his own utility, Pareto optimal? Is it equal to the outcome reached by the representative investor, if he maximizes his own utility or acts as a central planner?

These questions, which fall in the domain of Welfare Economics, are important also when financial choices are involved. In order to give an answer, go back to a one-period market and assume that M heterogeneous investors exist. Let

- u^m be the utility function of investor m, $m = 1,..,M$,
- $\pi^m(s)$ be his probability assignment for state $s, s = 1,..K$,[1]
- $e^m(0)$ and $E^m = \{e^m(s), s = 1,\ldots,K\}$ be his time-0 and time-1 endowments,
- $c^m(0)$, $C^m = \{c^m(s), s = 1,\ldots,K\}$ be his consumption at times 0 and 1,
- $\Theta^m = \{\theta_i^m, i = 1,\ldots,K\}$ be his portfolio allocation, in the presence of complex securities.

The optimal values of the decision variables solve the following problem:

$$\max_{c^m(0),\Theta^m} \sum_{s=1}^{K} \pi^m(s) u^m\left(c^m(0), c^m(s)\right) \tag{4.1}$$

subject to

$$c^m(0) + \left(\Theta^m\right)^{\mathsf{T}} S = e^m(0) \tag{4.2}$$

$$C^m - E^m = \Sigma^{\mathsf{T}} \Theta^m \tag{4.3}$$

where the matrix Σ is of full row rank (redundant securities having been removed from it). We know that the solution to this problem is centered upon the state prices for investor m:

$$\phi^m(s) = \pi^m(s) \frac{\frac{\partial u^m}{\partial c^m(s)}}{\sum_{s=1}^{K} \pi^m(s) \frac{\partial u^m}{\partial c^m(0)}}$$

The following theorem provides a necessary and sufficient condition for the equalization of state prices across investors.

Theorem 4.1 *With heterogeneous investors, state prices may differ from investor to investor if and only if the market is incomplete.*

Proof. The proof is merely a reinterpretation of what was done in chapter 2. Consider two investors 1 and 2. From the first-order conditions for their problems (4.1) subject to (4.2), (4.3) we have: $S = \Sigma \Phi^1 = \Sigma \Phi^2$. The vector S of market prices and the payoff matrix Σ are identical in the two equations. Read the latter as systems of N equations in the K unknowns Φ^1, Φ^2. We prove first that prices may differ in incomplete markets, then that they may not under market completeness.

If the market is incomplete, $\text{rank}(\Sigma) < K$. The previous systems have an infinity of solutions with multiplicity

$$K - \text{rank}(\Sigma) > 0$$

---

1 In order to make the treatment consistent with its extension to continuous-time, continuous-state economies, we assume that the agents' probability assessments are, to a limited degree, homogeneous. Agents face the same filtration and are not allowed to disagree on the states which have zero measure. Since we decided to consider only the states that have positive probability, this simply means that the number of states K is the same for every individual. So, the only homogeneity required here is a weak one. On states with positive probability, their probability assessments may be different.

As a consequence, an infinite number of state prices are admissible. In particular, two investors may have two different prices.

If the market is complete, however, rank$(\Sigma) = K$ and Σ admits an inverse. The equations have a unique solution $\Phi^1 = \Phi^2 = \Sigma^{-1}S$. Equal state prices are imposed on all investors. □

When the market is complete, whether or not investors are homogeneous, the results of chapter 2 obviously hold: (1) there exists a one-to-one relation between the prices of a collection of basic securities and state prices; (2) prices of redundant securities can be obtained by replication, martingale pricing, or hedging.

The situation can be summarized as in figure 4.1.

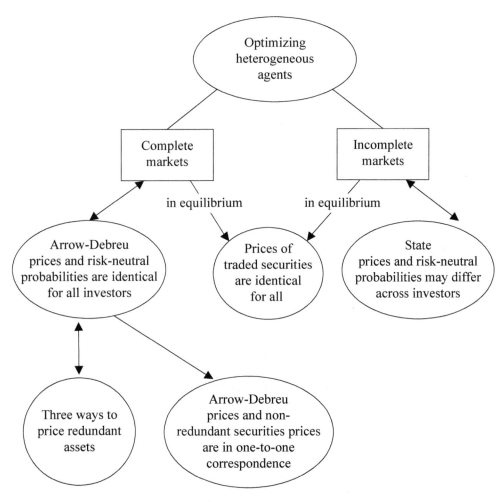

Figure 4.1
Complete and incomplete markets with heterogeneous agents in the single-period model.

4.2   Competitive Equilibrium

Now, we are interested in the equilibrium of a market in which a collection of heterogeneous investors trade. It will be an exchange equilibrium as in the Lucas economy,
since there will be no production, and each investor will receive exogenous endowments
at times 0 and 1, the latter time harboring several events. Let us consider the case in
which securities are in zero net supply.[2] Following the classic literature that originated
with Walras (1874), Arrow (1951, 1953, 1965), Arrow and Debreu (1954), and Debreu
(1959), we introduce the definition, applicable to the case in which securities are in zero net
supply:

Definition 4.1   *A competitive equilibrium is a vector of prices S, an allocation of consumption $\{c^m(0), c^m(s)\}$, a set of Lagrange multipliers $\{\lambda_0^m\}$, and a choice of portfolios
$\{\Theta^m\}$ for the various investors, $m = 1 \ldots M$, for which each investor's first-order conditions (3.17, 3.18, 3.20, 3.13, 3.14) are satisfied and all markets clear:*

$$\sum_{m=1}^{M} \Theta^m = 0 \tag{4.4}$$

$$\sum_{m=1}^{M} c^m(0) = \sum_{m=1}^{M} e^m(0) \tag{4.5}$$

$$\sum_{m=1}^{M} c^m(s) = \sum_{m=1}^{M} e^m(s) \qquad\qquad s = 1, \ldots, K$$

In equilibrium each investor is at its own optimum: the first five conditions are the first-
order conditions of the single-investor problem, which we have already seen in several
guises. The third (3.20), in particular, is the first-order condition with respect to portfolio
choice while the fourth and fifth are the usual budget constraints. The other conditions
impose market clearing. The sixth subset (4.4) of conditions, for instance, requires that
positions of different investors in the same security, θ_i^m for security i, sum up to zero, since
the net supply is zero.[3] Obviously, we have as many conditions of this type as securities.
The other market-clearing conditions, otherwise called Aggregate Resource Conditions
(ARC), equate consumption and endowments, both at time 0 and at time 1, in all states.
Walras' law says that one of the market-clearing conditions is redundant. For instance, (4.4)
implies (4.5).

---

2 In section 4.4.2 below we consider an exchange equilibrium in which there is exogenous output, which plays
the role of endowments. As long as output is exogenous, the two economies (pure endowment and production)
are equivalent. That is the reason why we keep an example of both.

3 If this is not the case, the RHS of the condition should be set equal to total supply. But, in that case, equation
(4.5) and following should also reflect dividends paid (otherwise called output) and not just endowments.

It will come as no surprise that, for each investor:

$$S_i = \frac{\sum_{s=1}^{K} \pi^m(s) \frac{\partial u^m}{\partial c^m(s)} (c^m(0), e^m(s) + (\Theta^m)^\mathsf{T} q(s)) q_{i,s}}{\sum_{s=1}^{K} \pi^m(s) \frac{\partial u^m}{\partial c_0} (c^m(0), e^m(s) + (\Theta^m)^\mathsf{T} q(s))} \qquad (4.6)$$

which, if we denote

$$\phi^m(s) = \frac{\pi^m(s) \frac{\partial u^m}{\partial c^m(s)} (c^m(0), e^m(s) + (\Theta^m)^\mathsf{T} q(s))}{\sum_{s=1}^{K} \pi^m(s) \frac{\partial u^m}{\partial c^m(0)} (c^m(0), e^m(s) + (\Theta^m)^\mathsf{T} q(s))},$$

is the familiar equation $S = \Sigma \Phi$.

We now make the assumption that:

Assumption 4.1   *Financial markets are complete.*

In this case, Σ is non-singular. As we saw in sections 3.1.4 and 3.3.3, if the market is complete, the portfolio choices and the flow budget constraints can be eliminated from the first-order conditions of equilibrium, which become (3.5), (3.6), and (3.7) with superscript m added.

They can also be eliminated from the market-clearing conditions to yield:

$$\sum_{m=1}^{M} c^m(0) = \sum_{m=1}^{M} e^m(0) \qquad (4.7)$$

$$\sum_{m=1}^{M} c^m(s) = \sum_{m=1}^{M} e^m(s) \qquad s = 1, \ldots, K \qquad (4.8)$$

Equations (3.5), (3.6), and (3.7) are the single investor's optimization conditions when he chooses directly current and future state-contingent consumption. The last two conditions, (4.7) and (4.8), are the ARCs that equate consumption and endowments. These last can also be seen as market-clearing conditions in the market for Arrow-Debreu state-contingent claims.

Definition 4.2   *An Arrow-Debreu competitive equilibrium is an allocation of consumption $\{c^m(0), c^m(s)\}$ to the various investors, $m = 1 \ldots M$, a set of state prices $\{\phi(s)\}$ and a set of Lagrange multipliers $\{\lambda_0^m\}$ for which first-order conditions (3.5), (3.6), (3.7), and goods-market clearing conditions (4.7) and (4.8) are satisfied.*

Since investor optimality is a necessary condition for equilibrium, it is clear that existence of equilibrium rules out arbitrage opportunities. But the definition of equilibrium requires more than the absence of arbitrage, since it entails market clearing.

We now ask whether a social planner can achieve the consumption allocation of the competitive equilibrium. Working on the first-order conditions of the equilibrium definition one proves that completeness is sufficient to guarantee that a representative investor exists. The result is very similar (and would follow from) the First Welfare Theorem (see for example, Mas-Colell, Whinston and Green (1995), chapter 16), which establishes the Pareto optimality of competitive markets and which is applicable to complete markets.

Theorem 4.2 *If the financial market is complete and a competitive equilibrium exists, there exists (that is, one can construct) a central planner who allocates consumption to investors, taking into account ARCs only and reaches the same allocation as in the equilibrium.*

Proof. Let the social planner allocate consumption c^m to investor m in a way that maximizes his utility, where his utility is the weighted sum of investors' utilities, with a set of weights $\{1/\lambda^m\}$. His problem is[4]

$$\max_{\{c^m(0)\},\{c^m(s)\}} \sum_{m=1}^{M} \frac{1}{\lambda^m} \sum_{s=1}^{K} \pi^m(s) u^m\big(c^m(0), c^m(s)\big) \,;\, \lambda^m > 0 \qquad (4.9)$$

$$\sum_{m=1}^{M} c^m(0) = \sum_{m=1}^{M} e^m(0) \qquad \sum_{m=1}^{M} c^m(s) = \sum_{m=1}^{M} e^m(s) \qquad (4.10)$$
$$s = 1, \ldots, K$$

The Lagrangean of the problem is

$$L(\{c^m(0)\}, \{c^m(s)\}, \mu, \mu\phi(s)) \triangleq \sum_{m=1}^{M} \frac{1}{\lambda^m} \sum_{s=1}^{K} \pi^m(s) u^m\big(c^m(0), c^m(s)\big)$$
$$+ \mu \times \left(\sum_{m=1}^{M} e^m(0) - \sum_{m=1}^{M} c^m(0)\right) + \mu \times \sum_{s=1}^{K} \phi(s) \left(\sum_{m=1}^{M} e^m(s) - \sum_{m=1}^{M} c^m(s)\right)$$

where μ is the Lagrange multiplier for the time-0 resource constraint and $\mu \times \phi(s)$ denotes the Lagrange multiplier for the state-s resource constraint. The first order conditions are

$$\frac{1}{\lambda^m} \sum_{s=1}^{K} \pi^m(s) \frac{\partial u^m}{\partial c^m(0)}\big(c^m(0), c^m(s)\big) = \mu \qquad (4.11)$$

$$\frac{1}{\lambda^m} \pi^m(s) \frac{\partial u^m}{\partial c(s)}\big(c^m(0), c^m(s)\big) = \mu\phi(s) \qquad (4.12)$$

$$\sum_{m=1}^{M} c^m(0) = \sum_{m=1}^{M} e^m(0), \quad \sum_{m=1}^{M} c^m(s) = \sum_{m=1}^{M} e^m(s) \qquad (4.13)$$

We want to show that, with a proper set of the weights that define the central planner, a solution of the system of equations defining equilibrium is also a solution of the above system. Since the market is complete, the maximization problem for each single investor

---

4 The problem is unchanged if all the weights $\{1/\lambda^m\}$ are multiplied by an arbitrary strictly positive number (homogeneity property).

can be written either using complex securities, as in definition 4.1, or using Arrow-Debreu securities, as in (3.5), (3.6), and (3.7). For the purpose of this proof, it is easier to use the latter.

Choose the central-planner weights $\{1/\lambda^m\}$ *to be equal to* the reciprocal of the Lagrange multipliers $\{\lambda_0^m\}$ *of the equilibrium problem.* Then comparing equations (3.5, 3.6, 3.7, 4.7 and 4.8) and (4.11 to 4.13), we see that these two sets of equations have a solution in common with $\mu = 1$. The theorem is proven. ☐

The weights $\{1/\lambda^m\} = \{1/\lambda_0^m\}$ appearing in the previous theorem are called *Negishi* weights,[5] while the utility function of the central planner is a *social welfare function* built as a simple weighted sum of the investor expected utilities. In this sum, every investor's utility or welfare enters with a weight which is higher, the lower is his multiplier, that is, his marginal utility at time 0. Since marginal utility is decreasing in consumption, investors with high consumption at time 0 have a low multiplier and are highly weighted. The competitive equilibrium makes no pretence of being guided by "justice."

The proof of theorem 4.2 establishes the correspondence from a competitive equilibrium, with given endowments, to a centralized economy. The reverse correspondence, from a central-planner optimum to a competitive equilibrium with given endowments, would be obtained by making sure, by adjusting the weights, that the optimal allocation of the former satisfies each investor's budget constraint (3.7). The mapping may be multivalued, which is an issue we do not address here. We synthesize the equilibrium results collected so far in figure 4.2.

We define the utility function $\bar{u}\left(\sum_{m=1}^{M} e^m(0), \sum_{m=1}^{M} e^m(s)\right)$ *of the "representative investor," which is the maximized utility of the central planner,* and his beliefs $\{\bar{\pi}(s)\}$ as being such that $\sum_s \bar{\pi}(s)\bar{u}\left(\sum_{m=1}^{M} e^m(0), \sum_{m=1}^{M} e^m(s)\right)$ is identical to the maximized value of the Pareto optimality problem (4.9) for all values of $\sum_{m=1}^{M} e^m(0)$ and $\sum_{m=1}^{M} e^m(s)$, namely:[6]

$$\sum_{s=1}^{K} \bar{\pi}(s)\bar{u}\left(\sum_{m=1}^{M} e^m(0), \sum_{m=1}^{M} e^m(s)\right)$$

$$= \max_{\{c^m(0)\},\{c^m(s)\}} \sum_{m=1}^{M} \frac{1}{\lambda_0^m} \sum_{s=1}^{K} \pi^m(s)u^m\left(c^m(0), c^m(s)\right)$$

---

5 See Negishi (1960).

6 While the overall objective function of the representative agent

$$\sum_s \bar{\pi}(s)\bar{u}\left(\sum_{m=1}^{M} e^m(0), \sum_{m=1}^{M} e^m(s)\right)$$

and its derivatives are thus well defined, we cannot claim that the utility function $\bar{u}$ and the probabilities $\bar{\pi}(s)$ are each uniquely defined. But that is immaterial for what follows.

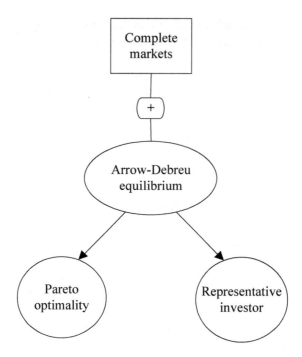

Figure 4.2
Arrow-Debreu equilibrium with complete markets.

subject to:
$$\sum_{m=1}^{M} c^m(0) = \sum_{m=1}^{M} e^m(0); \sum_{m=1}^{M} c^m(s) = \sum_{m=1}^{M} e^m(s)$$

In short, when a market is complete, one can define, *with weights* that are constant across states of nature, a representative investor who consumes the total endowment, and who will play a role in securities' pricing. The first-order conditions (4.11, 4.12) imply the values of marginal utilities and marginal rate of substitution of the representative investor:

$$\sum_{s=1}^{K} \bar{\pi}(s)\frac{\partial \bar{u}}{\partial c_0}\left(\sum_{m=1}^{M} e^m(0), \sum_{m=1}^{M} e^m(s)\right) = \mu$$

$$\bar{\pi}(s)\frac{\partial \bar{u}}{\partial c(s)}\left(\sum_{m=1}^{M} e^m(0), \sum_{m=1}^{M} e^m(s)\right) = \mu\phi(s)$$

so that:

$$\phi(s) = \bar{\pi}(s)\frac{\frac{\partial \bar{u}}{\partial c(s)}\left(\sum_{m=1}^{M} e^m(0), \sum_{m=1}^{M} e^m(s)\right)}{\sum_{s=1}^{K} \bar{\pi}(s)\frac{\partial \bar{u}}{\partial c_0}\left(\sum_{m=1}^{M} e^m(0), \sum_{m=1}^{M} e^m(s)\right)}$$

Notice that the marginal utilities of the representative investor are proportional to those of each and every investor.

With that in mind, we suggest that the readers solve exercise 4.1.

4.2.1 Equalization of State Prices

Let us point out the consequences of the previous theory for *equalization of state prices across investors*. We established in theorem 4.1 that, in a complete-market Pareto-optimal equilibrium with heterogeneous investors, state prices are equated across them. Let us see how.

From the first-order conditions of investor m in a market with heterogeneous investors, or from the price expression (4.6) specialized to Arrow-Debreu securities, we get the following expression for his state price:

$$\phi^m(s) = \frac{\pi^m(s) \frac{\partial u^m}{\partial c^m(s)}(c^m(0), c^m(s))}{\sum_{s=1}^K \pi^m(s) \frac{\partial u^m}{\partial c^m(0)}(c^m(0), c^m(s))}$$

We already know this expression from the homogeneous-investor case in chapter 3; it says that the state price of each investor is set equal to his MRS between time-1 consumption, in that state, and consumption at time 0. Investors may now differ in utility, endowments, and probability assignments. In principle, their state prices may well differ. However, theorem 4.1 implies that they must be equal across investors, as soon as the equilibrium is reached. This is achieved through consumption: each investor adjusts consumption $c^m(s)$ in all states, which enters his state price and determines it, so that, at the optimum, this is true.

Graphically, we can represent equalization of state prices using the traditional Edgeworth box. Consider an economy with two investors and two states of nature $s = u,d$ at time 1. Place on three axis the consumptions $\{c^m(0)\}_{m=1,2}$ at time 0 of the two investors $m = 1$ and $m = 2$, and their consumptions $\{c_u^m\}_{m=1,2}$ and $\{c_d^m\}_{m=1,2}$ in the two states. As is usual in an Edgeworth box, one investor's consumption is measured from the origin, the other's consumption in the opposite direction, so that the lengths of the edges of the box stand for total consumption, equal to total endowments. The four panels of figure 4.3 show various aspects of that box. In panel a, the indifference surfaces and the budget plane of both investors are represented. As usual, along an indifference surface:[7]

$$\frac{\partial u^m}{\partial c^m(0)} dc_0^m + \frac{\partial u^m}{\partial c^m(s)} dc_s^m = 0; s = u,d$$

for each investor m. Since both investors use the same state prices, $\phi(s)$, their budget sets in terms of Arrow-Debreu securities are similar:

$$c^m(0) + \phi_u c_u^m + \phi_d c_d^m = W_0^m$$

---

7 Here, dc is any small change in c. It does not mean $d \times c$.

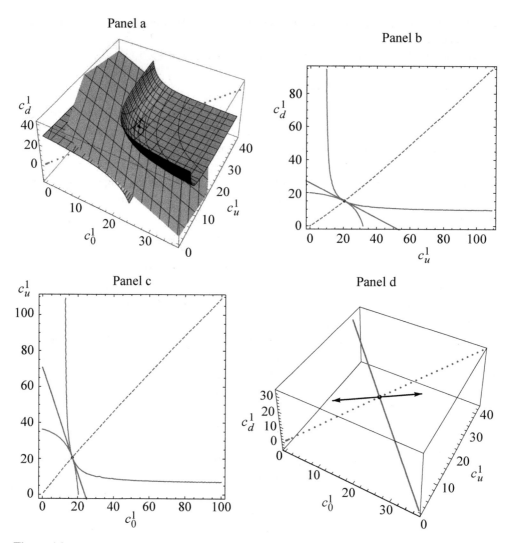

Figure 4.3

Complete-market Edgeworth box: a fragment of the entire 3D Edgeworth box is shown as a 3D picture (panel a). The indifference surfaces of the two investors are plotted. The plane is the (common) budget set of the two investors. Also shown are a 2D cut of the entire box at the equilibrium level of c_0 (panel b) and a 2D cut at the equilibrium level of c_d (panel c). In all four panels, the dotted or the dashed line is the complete-market contract curve. Panel d: the fragment of the 3D Edgeworth box again showing that the two marginal-utility vectors are aligned.

Each investor's indifference surfaces are tangent to his budget constraint at the optimum (this is condition (3.6)):

$$\phi_s = \frac{\frac{\partial u^m}{\partial c^m(s)}}{\frac{\partial u^m}{\partial c^m(0)}}; \, m = 1, 2; \, s = u, d$$

Taking the two investors together, it follows that their indifference curves are tangent with each other at the optimum. Recall that the set of all possible tangency points, obtained by changing investor endowments without changing their total, represents all the possible equilibrium trades. In the four panels of figure 4.3, the curves shown as dotted or dashed lines are the traditional complete-market *contract curve*. Panel d highlights the fact that the marginal-utility vectors of the two investors are aligned and that their state prices are equal.

♠

If utility is time-additive and time factors out, we have
$$u^m\big(c^m(0), c^m(s)\big) = u^m\big(c^m(0)\big) + \beta^m u^m\big(c^m(s)\big)$$
Equalization of Arrow-Debreu prices across investors becomes
$$\frac{\pi^1(s)\beta^1 \frac{\partial u^1(s)}{\partial c^1(s)}\big(c^1(s)\big)}{\frac{\partial u^1(s)}{\partial c^1(0)}\big(c^1(0)\big)} = \frac{\pi^2(s)\beta^2 \frac{\partial u^2}{\partial c^2(s)}\big(c^2(s)\big)}{\frac{\partial u^2}{\partial c_0^2}\big(c^2(0)\big)} \tag{4.14}$$
Write the previous expression in the following way:
$$\pi^1(s)\xi^1(s) = \pi^2(s)\xi^2(s)$$
where ξ^1 is the stochastic discount factor of investor 1, namely
$$\beta^1 \frac{\frac{\partial u^1}{\partial c^1(s)}\big(c^1(s)\big)}{\frac{\partial u^1}{\partial c^1(0)}\big(c^1(0)\big)}$$
and similarly for investor 2. In this second formulation, the equality says that, in a complete market, the product of the stochastic discount factors with the probabilities must be equated across investors. If ever two investors share the same probabilities, not only their state prices but also their stochastic discount factors are equal.

4.2.2   Risk Sharing

Equalization of state prices is a powerful result, but it is not the only consequence of a competitive equilibrium. If investors have homogeneous beliefs, that is, assign equal probabilities to states, an impressive result also obtains: the risk of individual-investor endowments (called idiosyncratic risk) is removed from investor consumption. Investors are exposed only to common risk. Only booms and bust in total resources, such as those arising from the business cycle, affect investors. This powerful result is known as *risk sharing*. A more precise statement of the risk-sharing result is the following.

Proposition 4.1   *When the allocation is Pareto optimal and everyone shares the same probability assessments ($\pi^m(s)$ constant over m), all risks are mutualized, in the sense that the consumptions of all people are monotonically related to each other across states of nature.*

Proof.   The first-order conditions (4.12) for two investors 1 and 2 imply, indeed, that their weighted marginal utilities are equal:
$$\frac{1}{\lambda_0^1}\pi^1(s)\frac{\partial}{\partial c^1(s)}u^1 = \frac{1}{\lambda_0^2}\pi^2(s)\frac{\partial}{\partial c^2(s)}u^2$$

With the same probability assignment,

$$\frac{1}{\lambda_0^1}\frac{\partial}{\partial c^1(s)}u^1 = \frac{1}{\lambda_0^2}\frac{\partial}{\partial c^2(s)}u^2 \tag{4.15}$$

This means that, when considering two states of nature s_1 and s_2, investors 1 and 2 have the same ratio of marginal utilities across states:

$$\frac{\dfrac{\partial u^1}{\partial c^1(s_1)}}{\dfrac{\partial u^1}{\partial c^1(s_2)}} = \frac{\dfrac{\partial u^2}{\partial c^2(s_1)}}{\dfrac{\partial u^2}{\partial c^2(s_2)}}$$

If s_2 is more favorable than s_1 for investor 1, in the sense that its marginal utility is, say, halved, the same holds for investor 2. Both ratios are equal to 2. The marginal utilities of the investors are said to be "comonotonic." Since marginal utilities are decreasing, consumptions are comonotonic too.   □

Risk mutualization means that the two investors are either better off or worse off *together* in the same state. The less risk-averse investor provides insurance to the more risk-averse one and, in the limit, if one investor is risk-neutral, he bears all the risk.

The risk-sharing effect is even clearer if utility is time-additive and time factors out. From (4.15) we, indeed, get

$$\frac{\beta^1}{\lambda_0^1}\frac{\partial u^1}{\partial c^1(s)}\left(c^1(s)\right) = \frac{\beta^2}{\lambda_0^2}\frac{\partial u^2}{\partial c^2(s)}\left(c^2(s)\right)$$

Invert the marginal utility of one of the investors, say 1, and denote the inverse as $\mathfrak{h}$: $\mathfrak{h} = \left(\partial u^1/\partial c^1(s)\right)^{-1}$. We get $c^1(s)$ as a function of $c^2(s)$ in each state s:

$$c^1(s) = \mathfrak{h}\left(\frac{\lambda_0^1}{\beta^1}\frac{\beta^2}{\lambda_0^2}\frac{\partial u^2}{\partial c^2(s)}\left(c^2(s)\right)\right)$$

Since both $\mathfrak{h}$ and $\partial u^2/\partial c^2(s)$ are decreasing (see Appendix A), the optimal consumption of investor 1 is an increasing function of the one of investor 2.

Figure 4.4 plots the equilibrium demand for future consumption as a function of the state price:[8]

$$c^m(s) = \mathfrak{h}\left(\lambda_0^m \times \xi(s)\right)$$

For given $\{\lambda_0^m\}$, the slope of the consumption demand *across states of nature* is:

$$\frac{dc^m(s)}{d\xi(s)} = \frac{1}{u''(c^m(s))}\lambda_0^m = -\frac{T^m(c^m(s))}{u'(c^m(s))}\lambda_0^m = -\frac{T^m(c^m(s))}{\xi(s)}$$

where T^m is the risk tolerance of investor m. More risk-tolerant people take more risks by adopting a consumption demand schedule that is more sensitive to differences in the

---

8 In case marginal utility u' is convex, the consumption function is also convex.

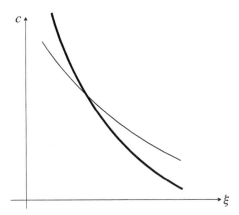

Figure 4.4
Plots the equilibrium demand for future consumption as a function of the state price ξ, which both investors face.

stochastic discount factor across states. More precisely, if we compare two people with different utility functions but the same initial wealth, the demand-schedule of one cannot be everywhere above that of the other since both must satisfy the same budget constraint. Marginal utility being a decreasing function, the two-demand schedule must cross in only one place. At that point, the slope of the schedule of the less risk-averse person is higher in absolute value than that of the other person.

We suggest that the reader solve exercise 4.2.

4.2.3 Security Pricing by the Representative Investor and the CAPM

Since each investor is at its optimum, the consequences on security prices are evident. Recall that the vector Σ_i collects the payoffs of security i (row i of matrix Σ). For each security i and each investor m, the relation $S_i = \mathbb{E}^m[\Sigma_i \xi^m]$ holds. It also holds for the representative investor: $S_i = \overline{\mathbb{E}}[\Sigma_i \bar{\xi}]$. This implies that payoffs are more appreciated as they covary less with consumption. To see this, denote as $\text{cov}(\cdot)$ the covariance under the effective measure. Using a generic notation for the beliefs and utility of any investor, including the representative one, the expected values of ξ and Σ_i are:

$$\mathbb{E}[\xi] = \sum_{s=1}^{K} \pi(s)\xi(s)$$

$$\mathbb{E}[\Sigma_i] = \sum_{s=1}^{K} \pi(s)q_i(s)$$

and the expectation of their product is

$$\mathbb{E}[\Sigma_i \xi] = \sum_{s=1}^{K} \pi(s)\xi(s)q_i(s)$$

Using the definition of covariance we can write each single price, which is the expected value of the product of payoffs and stochastic discount factors, as

$$S_i = \mathbb{E}[\Sigma_i \xi] = \mathbb{E}[\xi]\,\mathbb{E}[\Sigma_i] + \text{cov}\,(\xi, \Sigma_i) \tag{4.16}$$

For the riskless security, $i = 1$, expression (4.16) gives:

$$1 = S_1 = (1 + r) \times \mathbb{E}[\xi]$$

which says that the discount factor is the expectation of the stochastic discount factor:

$$1/(1 + r) = \mathbb{E}[\xi]$$

Substituting into (4.16) we get an expression for each security price that emphasizes the role of the expectation of future dividends versus their covariance with the stochastic discount factor:

$$S_i = \mathbb{E}[\Sigma_i \xi] = \frac{\mathbb{E}[\Sigma_i]}{1 + r} + \text{cov}\,(\Sigma_i, \xi) \tag{4.17}$$

Each price is the expectation of its payoffs, discounted at r, plus a "premium" due to its covariance with the stochastic discount factor. The latter is negatively correlated with consumption. This means that it is not pure *risk* – which we inevitably identify with variance – that matters, but the *co-risk*, which we measure through covariance, that does. A security that has high payoffs when consumption is high, or that covaries positively with consumption, receives a low market value compared to one that covaries negatively. The part of risk that matters is the component that covaries with consumption, that is, the "common" instead of the "idiosyncratic" or security-specific component.

Equation (4.17) holds for each investor. In this sense, the result could have been provided, with reference to investor consumption, already in chapter 3. However, we present it here because it holds as well for the representative investor, who by definition consumes the whole endowment of the economy – an exogenous quantity. In the complete market of this chapter, it holds in equilibrium. The next few lines trace the relation between this result and the one-period mean-variance CAPM explained in Appendix A, which holds under restrictive conditions on the utility function or on the probability distribution of the security returns.

Let us restate (4.17) in terms of the expected return that a security deserves, based on its "risk." Denote as $R_i \in \mathbb{R}^K$ the vector of the ratios between security net payoffs at time 1 and their price at time 0, so that the vector of returns is:

$$R_i \triangleq \frac{\Sigma_i - S_i}{S_i}$$

It follows from (4.17) that

$$1 = \mathbb{E}[(1 + R_i)\,\xi] = \mathbb{E}[1 + R_i]\,\mathbb{E}[\xi] + \text{cov}\,(\xi, 1 + R_i)$$

or, recognizing that the covariance between two variables is not affected by a constant $(\mathrm{cov}(\xi, 1 + R_i) = \mathrm{cov}(\xi, R_i))$

$$\mathbb{E}[R_i] - r = -\frac{\mathrm{cov}(\xi, R_i)}{\mathbb{E}[\xi]}$$
$$= -\frac{\mathrm{var}(\xi)}{\mathbb{E}[\xi]}\frac{\mathrm{cov}(\xi, R_i)}{\mathrm{var}(\xi)}$$

The first equality says that the difference between the expected return on security i and the riskless return, which is called the risk premium of security i (on the LHS) is proportional, according to $1/\mathbb{E}[\xi]$, to the covariance between the stochastic discount factor and the return of i itself (on the RHS). In the second equality we just multiply and divide by the variance of the stochastic discount factor $\mathrm{var}(\xi)$.

However, if we recognize that the ratio of the covariance $\mathrm{cov}(\xi, R_i)$ to that variance is the coefficient of a linear regression of R_i on the stochastic discount factor itself and if we write it as $-\mathfrak{b}_i$, we get the following relation between the return on a single risky security and the riskless return under optimality:

$$\mathbb{E}[R_i] = r + \mathfrak{b}_i \frac{\mathrm{var}(\xi)}{\mathbb{E}[\xi]}$$

which generalizes the Capital Asset Pricing Model (CAPM) of Sharpe (1964) and Lintner (1965), discussed in Appendix A, to the case in which the assumptions for mean-variance are not satisfied.

The next few lines study the specification with additive utility functions and the ensuing consumption-based CAPM.

───────────────── ♠ ─────────────────

Consider the case in which the utility function is additive and time factors out. The state price is

$$\xi(s) = \beta \frac{u'(c(s))}{u'(c(0))}$$

and the interest factor is

$$1 + r = \frac{1}{\beta \sum_{s=1}^{K} \pi(s) u'(c(s))/u'(c(0))} = \frac{u'(c(0))}{\beta \mathbb{E}[u'(c(1))]}$$

Define the vector of marginal utilities $u'(c(0)) \triangleq \{u'(c(s)), s = 1, .., K\} \in \mathbb{R}^K$. The risk premium $\mathbb{E}[R_i] - r$ becomes

$$\mathbb{E}[R_i] - r = -\frac{\mathrm{cov}(u'(c(1)), R_i)}{\mathbb{E}[u'(c(1))]}$$

and is the ratio of the covariance between the investor's marginal utility and the security returns, over the expected marginal utility at time 1. The equation holds for each single investor and for the representative investor. This is the so-called Consumption-based Capital Asset Pricing Model (CCAPM), which relates expected returns (or risk premia) to consumption in the future. It says that securities which pay more in low-consumption states have higher expected returns than securities which pay less in those states. The same is true symmetrically for securities that pay more in high-consumption states. If ever there is a security the covariance of which is zero, it deserves a zero risk premium.

4.2.4 The Benchmark Example (continued)

This section explores the equilibrium features of the benchmark example (isoelastic utility) introduced in chapter 3, with two investors.

In the presence of heterogeneous investors with different probability assessments, different time preferences, and different risk aversions, if the market is complete, we know that the optimal allocation of consumption is such that state-prices are equated across them. What form does this result take with power utilities? The equalization condition for state prices is:[9]

$$\pi^1(s)\beta^1\left(\frac{c^1(s)}{c^1(0)}\right)^{\gamma_1-1} = \pi^2(s)\beta^2\left(\frac{c^2(s)}{c^2(0)}\right)^{\gamma_2-1} \qquad s=1,\ldots,K$$

where γ_m is the utility parameter of investor m, $m=1,2$. In terms of probabilities this becomes

$$\frac{\pi^1(s)}{\pi^2(s)} = \frac{\beta^2\left(\frac{c^2(s)}{c^2(0)}\right)^{\gamma_2-1}}{\beta^1\left(\frac{c^1(s)}{c_0^1}\right)^{\gamma_1-1}}$$

On the RHS we have the stochastic discount factors. If ever risk and time preferences of the two investors coincide ($\gamma_1 = \gamma_2 = \gamma, \beta_1 = \beta_2$), the previous condition becomes:

$$\frac{\pi^1(s)}{\pi^2(s)} = \left(\frac{c^2(s)}{c^2(0)}\frac{c^1(0)}{c^1(s)}\right)^{\gamma-1}$$

which says that the ratio of probabilities is a transform of the ratios of future to current consumption. If ever the two investors have the same probability assessment, equality of the stochastic discount factors becomes

$$1 = \left(\frac{c^2(s)}{c^1(s)}\frac{c^1(0)}{c^2(0)}\right)^{\gamma-1}$$

that is, $c^2(s)/c^2(0) = c^1(s)/c^1(0)$, and the two investors reach the same state prices by equating future over current consumption state by state! This is an example of the way equalization of state prices obtains via consumption.

The risk mutualization condition (4.15) becomes:

$$\beta^1\frac{1}{\lambda_0^1}\left(c^1(s)\right)^{\gamma_1-1} = \beta^2\frac{1}{\lambda_0^2}\left(c^2(s)\right)^{\gamma_2-1}$$

---

9 This is (4.14) in small characters above.

In case risk and time preferences of two investors coincide ($\gamma_1 = \gamma_2 = \gamma, \beta^1 = \beta^2$), as above, it is true that:

$$\frac{1}{\lambda_0^1}\left(c^1(s)\right)^{\gamma-1} = \frac{1}{\lambda_0^2}(c^2(s))^{\gamma-1}$$

which can be simplified to:

$$c^2(s) = \left(\frac{\lambda_0^2}{\lambda_0^1}\right)^{\frac{1}{\gamma-1}} c^1(s)$$

Here as ever, it is clear from the last equation that consumption of investor 2 is a monotone increasing function of the consumption of investor 1, in each and every state. Not only does this hold, but the relation is linear. The ratio of the two consumptions is constant across states:

$$\frac{c^2(s)}{c^1(s)} = \left(\frac{\lambda_0^2}{\lambda_0^1}\right)^{\frac{1}{\gamma-1}}$$

Risk sharing for isoelastic investors takes an extreme form: the ratio of their consumptions in different states is constant, and one consumption is a linear function of the other.

4.3 Incomplete Market

In vector-matrix notation, we recall that (3.14) and (3.20) can be written as $C - E = \Sigma^\mathsf{T}\Theta$ and $S = \Sigma\Phi$. The first set of equations says that Σ^T establishes a linear mapping from portfolios Θ to the subspace of *marketed consumption bundles* $C - E$. This subspace is the *span* of the linear mapping Σ^T. What distinguishes incomplete markets from complete markets is the fact that the subspace of marketed consumption bundles $\Sigma^\mathsf{T}\Theta$, $\Theta \in \mathbb{R}^N$, is not the full space $\mathbb{R}^K$, because the payoff matrix has rank smaller than K.

The second system contains N equations in the K unknowns Φ. Since the matrix of dividends Σ has rank $N < K$, the system has ∞^{K-N} solutions. Each investor can pick one of these solutions. The condition says that, no matter how single investors determine state prices Φ, the linear combination of the columns of Σ via Φ must produce the same vector of prices S for the securities that are actually in the market. If there are two investors, they may very well be using different multipliers, or investor state-contingent-claim prices – Φ^1 may differ from Φ^2 – but their multipliers satisfy condition $S = \Sigma\Phi$ only if $\Phi^1 - \Phi^2$ is in the *kernel* of the linear mapping Σ. Call ν the difference between two possible solutions of the system $S = \Sigma\Phi$. We have $\nu \in \ker(\Sigma)$, which means

$$\Sigma\nu = 0 \qquad (4.18)$$

For this reason, $S = \Sigma\Phi$ – besides being a collection of first-order conditions of portfolio choice – is also named the *kernel condition*.

What does the kernel condition mean in the context of the Edgeworth box of figure 4.5 by which one represents possible contracts among different traders? Consider a two-state $(K = 2; s = u, d)$, one-security $(N = 1)$ case, with[10]

$$\Sigma = \begin{bmatrix} q_u & q_d \end{bmatrix}$$

Focus on the box for states u and d in the future (panel b of the figure). The budget constraints of the two investors are

$$c^m(0) + \phi_u^m c_u^m + \phi_d^m c_d^m = 0 \qquad m = 1, 2$$

or

$$c_d^m = -\left(c^m(0) + \phi_u^m c_u^m \right) / \phi_d^m$$

Slopes may differ, since they are $-\phi_u^1/\phi_d^1, -\phi_u^2/\phi_d^2$ respectively. The kernel condition now says that the difference between two state price vectors of different investors is in the kernel:

$$v = \Phi^1 - \Phi^2 \in \ker(\Sigma)$$

This means that

$$\Sigma v = q_u v_u + q_d v_d = 0 \tag{4.19}$$

or $v_d = -q_u v_u / q_d$. Then we can write the state prices of investor 2 in terms of the state prices of investor 1 and dividends, that is,

$$\Phi^2 = \Phi^1 + v = \begin{bmatrix} \phi_u^1 + v_u \\ \phi_d^1 - \frac{q_u}{q_d} v_u \end{bmatrix}$$

The marginal rate of substitution of investor 2 has the following slope, in terms of the slope for the other investor:

$$\frac{\phi_u^2}{\phi_d^2} = \frac{\phi_u^1 + v_u}{\phi_d^1 - \frac{q_u}{q_d} v_u}$$

Only for the specific choice $v_u = 0$ do the slopes for the two investors coincide, as in the complete-market case. This would be the case of effective Pareto optimality in which no utility improvement could be achieved for one investor without affecting the other investor's utility. Therefore, depending on the sign of v_u, the slope of investor 1's indifference curve at the optimum is smaller or larger than the one of investor 2 (in absolute value):

$$\frac{\phi_u^1}{\phi_d^1} < (>) \frac{\phi_u^2}{\phi_d^2}$$

if $v_u > (<)0$. All three panels of the figure illustrate that the indifference surfaces of the two investors are not tangent at the equilibrium point. Panel d highlights the fact that the

---

10 In the figure $q_u = q_d = 1$. That is, the security that is traded is a riskless one.

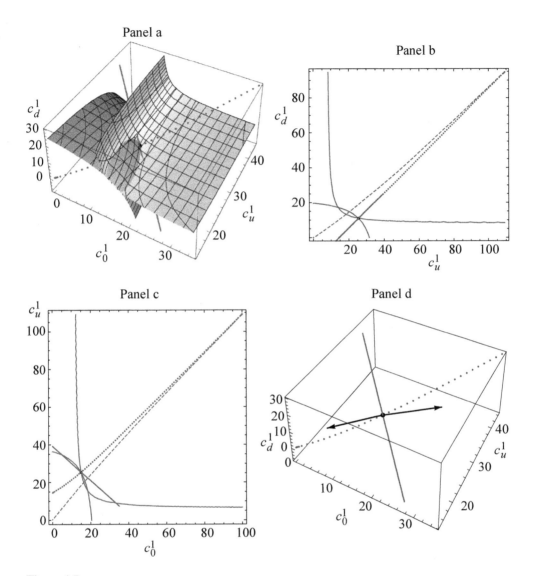

Figure 4.5

Incomplete-market Edgeworth box: represents an incomplete market in which only the riskless rate is traded (as in the Basak-Cuoco example of chapter 15). A fragment of the 3D Edgeworth box is shown as a 3D picture (panel a). The indifference surfaces of the two investors are plotted. The straight line is the (common) budget set of the two investors. Also shown are a 2D version of the entire box drawn for a fixed value of c_0 equal to its the equilibrium level (panel b) and a 2D version at the equilibrium level of c_d (panel c). The dashed line is the Pareto optimal contract curve shown (in the 2D panels only) for purposes of comparison only. The dotted line is the effective incomplete-market contract curve. Panel d: the fragment of the 3D Edgeworth box again showing the directions of the two marginal-utility vectors.

marginal-utility vectors of the two investors do not line up and that their state prices are unequal.

We revisit equilibria of incomplete markets and their properties in chapter 15.

4.4   Multiple-Period Economies

The Lucas model of chapter 3, under the assumption of market completeness, lends itself to a nice discussion of the implications of equilibrium, in a fashion similar to the single-period equilibrium of sections 4.1 to 4.2.4. However, as in the distinction between static and dynamic completeness, we are led to distinguish between Arrow-Debreu and *intertemporal or Radner equilibrium*, which is an "equilibrium of plans, prices and price expectations" (see Radner (1972)). In the Radner interpretation only the spot market for consumption of today's goods and the market for financial assets are open today. However, the equilibrium involves not only "prices" of consumption today and financial securities today but also "price expectations," that is, prices of consumption and financial securities in all the possible states in the future.[11]

This is in contrast to an *Arrow-Debreu* equilibrium, in which spot markets are open today for every possible state-contingent and time-stamped consumption in the future. In an Arrow-Debreu equilibrium one can go shopping today, at the currently known prices, and lock in every consumption and savings plan for the future. *That means we now define in an obvious way an extension of the Arrow-Debreu equilibrium definition 4.2 to any finite number of dates in the future.* For any given Radner equilibrium, namely any given number of consumption dates, and any given number of securities, the Arrow-Debreu equilibrium that can "mimic" it, by giving the same consumption plans and savings profile, must be open for many more contracts today, so as to fix the optimum consumption stream as of today.

In what follows, we define the first type of equilibrium, argue that under market completeness there is a unique Arrow-Debreu equilibrium for each Radner one, and study the relations between the two, as well as their properties in terms of (identical) state prices and risk sharing.

4.4.1   Radner Equilibrium

Dividends are another name for the output or payoff streams $\{q_i(s,t)\}_{i=1}^{N}$ paid by N firms. Aggregate output is a stochastic process with value in state s at time t

$$y(s,t) = \sum_{i=1}^{N} q_i(s,t)$$

---

11 These prices cannot be observed today, since the corresponding markets will open in the future. Investors assign a value to future prices, conditional on the state. One of the features of a Radner equilibrium is that all agents form the same belief on tomorrow's prices. There is more than that: these beliefs are correct. The price of consumption or a financial asset in a specific state is the one investors believed in, or predicted. Investors have perfect contingent foresight, state by state.

Let this be an exchange economy. Output is exogenous. We do not endogenize decisions that affect production.

We can extend Lucas' model to M *heterogeneous investors*, each one with a different utility function u^m, different probability assessments $\pi^m(s^+, t+1|s)$ for the successors s^+ of state s and different choices for consumption, $c^m(s,t)$, and portfolios, $\theta_i^m(s,t)$.[12] Recall that utility is time-additive in the Lucas' model.

We define an intertemporal, or stochastic, or Radner equilibrium as follows:

Definition 4.3   *A Radner equilibrium is an allocation of consumption and a portfolio selection for the various investors, states and points in time $\{c^m(s,t), \theta^m(s,t)\}$, for $m = 1 \dots M$, together with a vector price process for all points in time t, $\{S(s,t)\}$, such that each investor's first-order conditions, from (3.32), namely*

$$\frac{\partial}{\partial c} u^m = \lambda^m(s,t); \, m = 1, ..M$$

to (3.35) or from (3.39) to (3.43) are satisfied and all markets (for securities and consumption) clear:

$$\sum_{m=1}^{M} \theta_i^m(s,t) = 1 \tag{4.20}$$

$$\sum_{m=1}^{M} c^m(s,t) = y(s,t) \tag{4.21}$$

for all t, $i = 1, ..N, s = 1, ..K_t$.

The clearing condition (4.20) now requires that, at each time and in each state, portfolio positions summed over all investors be equal to one, since ownership of the production activity i by investors must be guaranteed at all times and states and the number of shares is normalized to one. Correspondingly, total consumption must sum up to total production in (4.21), since investors spend dividends they collect from productive units, apart from endowments of goods that they might receive along the way and which, for simplicity, we do not consider here.

In case all investors are identical, the first-order conditions in the Radner definition reduce to the ones of the single-investor economy, namely (3.32-3.35). The latter conditions, which boil down to the pricing formula (3.49), that is, to martingale pricing, are necessary and sufficient, together with the market-clearing requirements, to guarantee existence of an equilibrium, for strictly concave utility functions and bounded, positive production processes $\{y(s,t)\}$.

---

12 We assume only that they agree on the states which have zero probability, as explained in footnote 1.

4.4.2 State Prices and Representative Investor: From Radner to Arrow-Debreu Equilibria

This section outlines the way to write the Radner equilibrium in terms of the social welfare function of a representative investor. Using the second, we state the relation between Radner and Arrow-Debreu equilibria.

When the market is complete, it is possible to show that for each Radner equilibrium there exists a representative investor, or a central planner, whose single problem admits as solution the overall consumption process and portfolio allocations of the competitive Radner equilibrium. In other words, the representative investor holds an amount $\theta_i(s,t) = 1$ of security i at each point in time and state, while he consumes the whole production $c(s,t) = y(s,t)$. The utility function of the representative investor at time t is obtained in a way similar to the one-period case:

$$\sum_t \sum_s \bar{\pi}(s)\bar{u}(y(s,t),t)$$

It incorporates the constraint that the whole production must be consumed, or $y(s,t) = \sum_{m=1}^{M} c^m(s,t)$. The first-order condition for the representative investor gives us security prices, as usual:

$$S_i(s,t) = \frac{1}{\frac{\partial}{\partial c}\bar{u}(y(s,t),t)} \sum_{s^+=1}^{K_{t+1}} \bar{\pi}\left(s^+, t+1|s\right) \frac{\partial}{\partial c}\bar{u}\left(y\left(s^+,t+1\right),t+1\right)$$
$$\times \left(q_i\left(s^+,t+1\right) + S_i\left(s^+,t+1\right)\right) \tag{4.22}$$

If a Radner equilibrium exists and markets are complete then the state prices are well defined. They capture the marginal rates of substitution of the representative investor, and can be written as:

$$\phi\left(s^+,t+1|s\right) = \frac{\bar{\pi}\left(s^+,t+1|s\right)\frac{\partial}{\partial c}\bar{u}\left(y\left(s^+,t+1\right),t+1\right)}{\frac{\partial}{\partial c}\bar{u}(y(s,t),t)} \tag{4.23}$$

Once a state price holds for the representative investor, it must be shared by the single-investors. The equilibrium expression for state prices mimics the single-investor expression. State prices, however, depend on aggregate production fluctuations, instead of investor consumption fluctuations. For given probabilities, when total production in state s^+ at $t+1$ is high with respect to production at time t, then its marginal utility is lower than at time t and the corresponding state price is low, too.

The importance of the existence of the representative investor stems from its consequences for state prices, which we just outlined, and, above all, for transforming Radner into Arrow-Debreu equilibria, which we now examine.

Since a central planner exists, there is an Arrow-Debreu equilibrium implicit in the Radner one. The reasoning works as follows. Imagine that at time 0 all the M investors are allowed to trade all possible consumption streams. Consumption in state s^+ at time $t+1$

is marketed at price $\phi(s^+, t+1|s)$. Using state prices, investors can trade in one shot the consumption plan they reached via portfolios in the Radner equilibrium.

Vice versa, suppose that investors are allowed to trade at time 0 all possible consumption streams over the whole horizon, and that an equilibrium exists. The market is statically complete, by assumption. As such, it admits a representative investor. If we now allow for portfolio rebalancing and take the Arrow-Debreu state prices as state prices for the representative investor in the corresponding dynamic economy, we find a Radner equilibrium with the same consumption allocations.

We can sum up our reasoning as follows:

Proposition 4.2 *For any Arrow-Debreu equilibrium in a statically complete market, there exists a Radner equilibrium with the same consumption allocations. Vice versa, for any Radner equilibrium in a dynamically complete market, there exists an Arrow-Debreu equilibrium with the same consumption allocations. The state prices of the Arrow-Debreu equilibrium, which are the state prices of the Radner one, are equalized across investors.*

We can summarize the situation as in figure 4.6.

Even though the two types of equilibria typically produce allocations that coincide, they are conceptually quite different, especially in the assumptions made about the attitude of investors. In an Arrow-Debreu equilibrium, investors need not forecast future prices since all investment decisions are made at time 0. In a Radner equilibrium, they may have to revise their portfolio holdings all the time. Although technically that is not required by the definition, the most credible implementation scenario is one in which they anticipate the prices at which the revisions will occur. For that, they need to have in mind a model of the future behavior of other people.

4.4.3 Securities Pricing

The fact that, in a complete-market (Arrow-Debreu or Radner) equilibrium, state prices (4.23) are equated across investors, as in the single-period case, is of paramount importance for two reasons. First of all, prices can be written as in the single-investor case, using the representative investor utility and the $\phi(s^+, \tau)$ defined in (4.23):

$$S_i(s,t) = \sum_{\tau=t+1}^{T} \sum_{s^+=1}^{K_u} \phi(s^+, \tau)\, q_i(s^+, \tau) \tag{4.24}$$

As an alternative, we can use the formulations (3.57) or (3.58) in the previous chapter.

The last formulas generalize the single-period formulas of sections 4.1 to 4.2.4. We can price securities via

- state prices ϕ
- an expectation under the martingale probabilities $\mathbb{E}^*$, of payoffs discounted at the riskless rate,

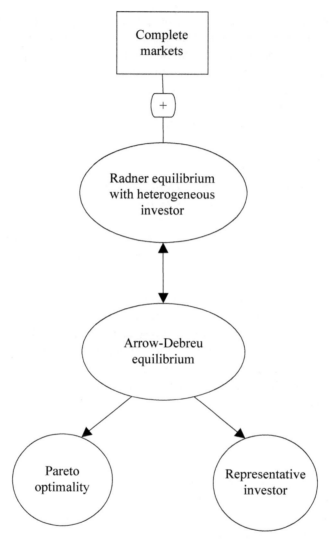

Figure 4.6
Arrow-Debreu and Radner equilibrium with multiperiod complete markets.

- an expectation under the effective probability $\mathbb{E}$, of payoffs translated into utils via the stochastic discount factor.

Second, starting from state prices, we can reconstruct market prices of basic traded securities, and vice versa. Going from prices of traded securities to state prices (or martingale probabilities or the stochastic discount factor) involves the inversion of formulas (4.24). The LHS is given, and the formulas are equations in the unknowns ϕ, which appear on the RHS. The actual feasibility of the procedure depends on the algebraic properties of the system. At any point in time, the condition on dynamic completeness guarantees that (4.24) can be inverted.

4.4.4 Risk Sharing

All investors, even if they start from different probability assessments, $\pi^m(s^+, t+1|s)$, $m = 1, \ldots M$, different utility functions and different consumption streams, agree on the equilibrium Arrow-Debreu implicit prices. Since it must be true, consistently with (3.48) in chapter 3, that

$$\phi(s^+, t+1|s) = \frac{\pi^m(s^+, t+1|s) \frac{\partial}{\partial c} u^m(c^m(s^+, t+1), t+1)}{\frac{\partial}{\partial c} u^m(c^m(s, t), t)} \tag{4.25}$$

for all m, for every couple of investors 1 and 2 we have:

$$\phi(s^+, t+1|s) = \frac{\pi^1(s^+, t+1|s) \frac{\partial}{\partial c} u^1(c^1(s^+, t+1), t+1)}{\frac{\partial}{\partial c} u^1(c^1(s, t), t)}$$

$$= \frac{\pi^2(s^+, t+1|s) \frac{\partial}{\partial c} u^2(c^2(s^+, t+1), t+1)}{\frac{\partial}{\partial c} u^2(c^2(s, t), t)}$$

It follows that the stochastic discount factors must be equated to the ratio of probabilities, across investors:

$$\frac{\frac{\partial}{\partial c} u^1(c^1(s^+, t+1), t+1)}{\frac{\partial}{\partial c} u^1(c^1(s, t), t)} \frac{\frac{\partial}{\partial c} u^2(c^2(s, t), t)}{\frac{\partial}{\partial c} u^2(c^2(s^+, t+1), t+1)} = \frac{\pi^2(s^+, t+1|s)}{\pi^1(s^+, t+1|s)}$$

If investors have the same probability assignments, then we obtain complete *risk sharing*, as in single-period economies.

As was true in the one-period economy, without the completeness assumption equalization of the budget constraints' slope is not guaranteed.

We are now interested in the way equalization of MRSs and risk sharing are implemented. That is done by adjusting optimal consumption appropriately. Consider, for instance, the case in which

$$u^m(c^m(s, t), t) = (\beta^m)^t u^m(c^m(s, t))$$

Equalization of state prices requires that

$$\phi(s^+, t+1) = \frac{\pi^m(s^+, t+1|s) \beta^m \frac{\partial}{\partial c} u^m(c^m(s^+, t+1))}{\frac{\partial}{\partial c} u^m(c^m(s, t))}$$

Equalization is achieved at time t by choosing consumption at time $t + 1$, state s^+, as:

$$c^m(s^+, t+1) = \mathfrak{h}\left(\frac{\phi(s^+, t+1|s)\frac{\partial}{\partial c}u^m(c^m(s, t))}{\pi^m(s^+, t+1|s)\beta^m}\right)$$

where $\mathfrak{h}^m \triangleq (\partial u^m/\partial c)^{-1}$ is the inverse of the marginal utility function of investor m. This is the same mechanism we encountered in the case of two points in time.

Here is a summary of our discussion of the implications of a multiperiod, discrete-time model à la Lucas. As in single-period models, in a market populated by identical investors, investor optimality implies that a positive pricing functional exists. Optimality and completeness imply that a representative investor with constant weights exists, even when the market is populated by heterogenous investors. In the last case, state prices are uniquely defined, and permit the pricing of traded securities. In the reverse, state prices can be inferred from traded securities' quotes. Risk sharing is achieved.

4.4.5   A Side Comment on Time-Additive Utility Functions

Having studied a multiperiod economy with a time-additive utility function, let us try to understand its advantages and drawbacks. This will also help us understand continuous-time economies, in which the additivity assumption is maintained.

The main drawback of additivity is the fact that the same mathematical properties of the utility function apply to different economic concepts or types of behavior.

Consider that the marginal rate of substitution between consumption at time 0 and consumption in state s of time 1, (3.19), when utility is additive, is equal to:

$$\phi(s) = \frac{\pi(s, 1)\frac{\partial}{\partial c}u(c(s, 1), 1)}{\frac{\partial}{\partial c}u(c(0), 0)} \tag{4.26}$$

Compute now the marginal rate of substitution between consumption in state s_2 of time 1 and consumption in state s_1 of time 1. It is equal to:

$$\phi(s_1, s_2) = \frac{\pi(s_1, 1)\frac{\partial}{\partial c}u(c(s_1, 1), 1)}{\pi(s_2, 1)\frac{\partial}{\partial c}u(c(s_2, 1), 1)} \tag{4.27}$$

This means that the shape of the function $u(\cdot, 1)$ plays a role in intertemporal as well as intratemporal or interstate choices, which in principle an economist would like to distinguish. This happens for each single-investor, as is apparent from the previous formulas, or for an economy populated with identical investors.

The drawback of additivity is especially apparent when $u(c(s, t), t)$ is simply equal to $\beta^t u(c(s, t))$. In this case, the previous expressions become

$$\phi(s) = \frac{\pi(s, 1)\beta u'(c(s, 1))}{u'(c(0))} \tag{4.28}$$

for intertemporal and

$$\phi(s_1, s_2) = \frac{\pi(s_1, 1)\, u'(c(s_1, 1))}{\pi(s_2, 1)\, u'(c(s_2, 1))} \tag{4.29}$$

for intratemporal substitution. The same derivative u' enters into both intertemporal and intratemporal substitution.

We also know that, when intertemporal discounting is done through the factor β, the derivatives of the utility function determine the Arrow-Pratt's coefficient $(-u''/u')$, which measures risk aversion. Risk aversion then affects both the allocation of consumption over time, for the same state, and over states. This shortcoming will be present in all the models in the first part of the book. In chapter 21 we come back to preferences and we relax the assumption of time additivity.

If the utility function is isoelastic, the drawbacks of additivity on which we commented above imply that the parameter γ plays a role both in intertemporal and in intratemporal substitution. The MRS between consumption at time 0 and consumption in state s at time 1, (4.28), is equal to:

$$\phi(s) = \beta \pi(s, 1) \left(\frac{c(s, 1)}{c(0)} \right)^{\gamma - 1}$$

The marginal rate of substitution between consumption in state s_2 at 1 and consumption in state s_1 of time 1, (4.29), is equal to:

$$\phi(s_1, s_2) = \frac{\pi(s_1, 1)}{\pi(s_2, 1)} \left(\frac{c(s_1, 1)}{c(s_2, 1)} \right)^{\gamma - 1}$$

As a consequence, an increase in risk aversion $1 - \gamma$, which means a decrease in γ, decreases both the first and the second MRS, when $c(s_1, 1) > c_0$, and $c(s_1, 1) > c(s_2, 1)$. Time additivity, therefore, gives to the parameter γ a role in allocation over time on top of its natural importance in allocation across states.

4.5 Conclusion

In a one-period economy, perfect risk sharing or perfect mutualization of risks is achieved if and only if the financial market is complete. In that case, the state prices are equated across investors. In a multiperiod economy, thanks to the possibility of trading and retrading, it is sufficient for the market to be dynamically complete for the same to be true.

Exercises

4.1. Write the central planner utility function for the case of two individuals with the same initial endowment, probability assessments, and power utility with exponents γ_1 and $\gamma_2 > \gamma_1$. Write down the first-order condition for the central planner and comment on their relation with the first-order conditions of each individual investor.

4.2. Go back to the economy described in exercise 2.1 of chapter 2 and imagine that two
investors exist, with rate of time preference 1 and utility function of the power type:

$$u(c(1)) = \begin{cases} (c(1))^{\gamma_1}/\gamma_1 & \text{for the first investor} \\ (c(1))^{\gamma_2}/\gamma_2 & \text{for the second investor} \end{cases}$$

Their Arrow-Debreu prices are equal, since the market is complete. They share the
same probability assessment $\pi(1) = 0.6, \pi(2) = 0.4$. Based on that, determine the
optimal consumption policies that ensure this equality. Write down the risk mutualization condition.

II PRICING IN CONTINUOUS TIME

5 Brownian Motion and Itô Processes

As we begin Part II of this book pertaining to the pricing of redundant securities in continuous time, and before we actually establish and comment some principles of Economics related to that topic, we need to make more precise a few mathematical concepts. In chapter 2 we defined filtrations and stochastic processes, but we provided only an intuitive definition of martingales. In chapter 3, we gave an intuitive definition of Markov processes. In section 5.1, we make these concepts more precise. We discuss the meaning of continuity for stochastic processes and introduce diffusions (section 5.2). We introduce Brownian motion, which conveys the economic intuition of a process with independent and Gaussian increments (section 5.3).

We next introduce Itô processes and stochastic differential equations (section 5.4). We provide the benchmark model for asset prices as an example (section 5.5). Lastly, we state Itô's lemma, the analog for stochastic processes of the rule of differential calculus, and the notion of Dynkin operator. We accompany them with some examples (section 5.6).

To start with, consider a complete, filtered probability space $(\Omega, \mathcal{F}, P, \mathbf{F})$. Let the parameter t cover the whole real interval $\mathcal{T} = [0, T]$, with T finite or not; that is, let time be continuous. Consider a (real or vector-valued) measurable stochastic process $X : \Omega \times \mathcal{T} \to \mathbb{R}^n, n \geq 1$. Let it be adapted.

Notation: from now on, unless doing otherwise is necessary for comprehension, we simplify the notation for processes. All processes are stochastic but we suppress the reference to the state ω. Therefore, $X(t)$ will actually mean $X(\omega, t)$. In special cases, we also use the notation $f(t)$ to refer to a deterministic function of time. When this happens, we say so explicitly.

5.1 Martingales and Markov Processes

We formalize the notion of martingale, which we used extensively in the previous chapters.

Martingales: Definition
The stochastic process $X : \Omega \times \mathcal{T} \to \mathbb{R}^n$ is integrable if its *conditional expectation* $\mathbb{E}_s[X(t)] = \mathbb{E}[X(t)|\mathcal{F}_s]$ is well defined; that is, the expectation of its value at time t,

conditional on the knowledge acquired up to time s, where $s \le t$, is finite (for any t and s). Following for instance Karatzas and Shreve (1988) we define it as follows:[1]

Definition 5.1   *A process X is said to be a martingale with respect to the filtration* **F** *if it is integrable, adapted, and its conditional expectation coincides with its current value with probability one:*

$$\mathbb{E}[X(t)|\mathcal{F}(s)] = X(s) \qquad \text{with probability one, } t \ge s$$

The current value $X(s)$ of the martingale is the best predictor of its future value, $X(t)$, no matter how far t is in the future. Martingales are intuitively presented in probability theory as fair games. In Finance, they can be interpreted as processes with no expected loss or gain: if $X(t)$ is a security price process and a martingale, on average, conditional on current information, we expect it neither to increase nor to decrease. We saw that in discrete time, once discounted at the riskless rate, security prices were martingales. That did not happen under the effective measure, assigned by the risk-averse investors that populate the financial market, but under another measure, which encapsulated the stochastic discount factor, that is, after translation into utils. Under these probabilities, securities returned the riskless rate.

In a number of circumstances, we need a definition of square-integrable martingale. A martingale is *square integrable* if

$$\mathbb{E}_s\left[X^2(t)\right] < \infty \qquad\qquad \forall t \in \mathcal{T}$$

which means that its second moment always exists. It follows that square-integrable martingales have finite (conditional) variance as well.

Local Martingales
We need the following:

Definition 5.2   *A stopping time τ relative to a filtration is a random variable, representing time, such that the event $\{\tau \le t\}$ belongs to the σ-field $\mathcal{F}(t)$ for every $t \ge 0$.*

In other words, whether the stopping time occurs or not (for example, whether a barrier is reached) is decided on the basis of existing information, and not information that will be revealed subsequently. As for every random variable, its realization is known ex post only. Ex ante, only probabilistic assessments on it can be done. The notion of stopping time is needed in order to formalize the distinction between martingales and local martingales (see Karatzas and Shreve (1988), page 36):

Definition 5.3   *A process X is said to be a* local martingale *relative to the filtration* **F** *if it is integrable and there is a sequence of non-decreasing stopping times $\tau_1, \tau_2, ..\tau_n, ..$ with*

---

1 As usual, all the equalities between random variables must be understood to hold almost surely.

$P(\lim_{n \to \infty} \tau_n = T) = 1$, *such that:*

$$\mathbb{E}[X(t \wedge \tau_n) | \mathcal{F}(s)] = X(s) \qquad\qquad s \leq (t \wedge \tau_n), \forall n$$

The expected value of the process stopped at a stopping time is equal to its value today.

The distinction between local martingales and martingales is subtle. It depends on whether any future expectation or only the expectation of the process randomly stopped coincides with the current value of the process. It will serve to specify security prices (see chapter 7).

Markov Processes: Definition

Another notion that is important in financial applications is the continuous-time version of the Markov property:

Definition 5.4   *A process X is said to be Markov or Markovian if for any Borel set $\mathcal{B}$ in $\mathbb{R}^n$ and any $t \geq s$,*

$$P[X(t) \in \mathcal{B} | \mathcal{F}(s)] = P[X(t) \in \mathcal{B} | X(s)]$$

This means that knowledge of the past behavior of the process X or any other element of $\mathcal{F}(s)$ adds no information beyond that contained in the current state of X. In order to form probability assessments for the future of X it is sufficient to look at its value today. We say that today's value is a "sufficient statistic" for the entire past and present values taken by the process. One can demonstrate that, for a Markov process, past and future are independent, when the present is given. The Markov property will turn out to be crucial in financial decision making, because it allows decisions to be made today (with repercussions in the future) with no information on the history of the process, its level today being sufficient.

For Markov processes, at any point in time s, we can define the probability of moving from the current value x to any value in a Borel set $\mathcal{B}$ at a future time t, $P[X(t) \in \mathcal{B} | X(s) = x]$, $x \in \mathbb{R}^n$. This conditional probability depends exclusively on $s, x, t, \mathcal{B}$: it is a function $P(s, x, t, \mathcal{B})$. It is called the *transition probability* of the Markov process. If this probability does not depend on the initial and final date, s and t, separately, but only on their difference $t - s$, then the process is said to be *time-homogenous*.

The transition probability enters the definition of a diffusion, one of the most important families of stochastic processes.

5.2   Continuity for Stochastic Processes and Diffusions

This section deals with continuity of stochastic processes, distinguishes continuous processes from just any continuous-time process, and introduces diffusions.

There are two ways in which a stochastic process can be continuous. First, the parameter, time t, is continuous, as we assumed at the beginning of the chapter. Second, its paths or trajectories are continuous. The latter will be called a continuous process *tout court*. Let us make this distinction precise.

As soon as we introduce a stochastic process in a continuous-time filtered probability space $(\Omega, \mathcal{F}, P, \mathbf{F})$ with $\mathcal{T} = [0, T]$, this process is a *continuous-time* process. This is the natural description of a phenomenon evolving in continuous time.

When considered as a function of time, a continuous-time process can be continuous or discontinuous. That is, it may have jumps. It is said to be a *continuous process* if its sample paths are continuous with probability one: you can draw them as functions of time without lifting the pen from the sheet.

Among continuous Markov processes, we distinguish *diffusions*. In addition to being continuous, they are characterized by two quantities, the drift vector f and the diffusion matrix F, to be defined below. K-dimensional diffusions are defined as follows:

Definition 5.5 *A continuous K-dimensional Markov process X is a diffusion when its transition probabilities $P(s, x, t, dy)$ satisfy the following conditions for every $s \in \mathcal{T}$, $x \in \mathbb{R}^K, \varepsilon \in \mathbb{R}_{++}, t \geq s$:*

$$\lim_{t \to s} \frac{1}{t - s} \int_{|y - x| > \varepsilon} P(s, x, t, dy) = 0$$

$$\lim_{t \to s} \frac{1}{t - s} \int_{|y - x| \leq \varepsilon} (y - x) P(s, x, t, dy) = f(s, x)$$

$$\lim_{t \to s} \frac{1}{t - s} \int_{|y - x| \leq \varepsilon} (y - x)(y - x)^\mathsf{T} P(s, x, t, dy) = H(s, x)$$

with $f : \mathcal{T} \times \mathbb{R}^K \to \mathbb{R}^K; H : \mathcal{T} \times \mathbb{R}^K \to \mathbb{R}^{K \times K}$.

The first condition says that jumps occur with vanishing probability: over short time periods, that is, when $t \to s$, the overall probability of non-small changes in the process, from x to y, with $|y - x| > \varepsilon$, is almost zero. The second and the third conditions concern small changes – those for which $|y - x| \leq \varepsilon$ – that occur over short time periods; that is, when $t \to s$. The conditions concern the expectation and variance of the small changes, or the "instantaneous" expectation and variance. H tells us "how dispersed" this movement is. The definition imposes that f and H exist and be functions only of the current time and state, s and x.

The expectation vector is denoted by f. The matrix H is a variance-covariance matrix; it is symmetric and positive semi-definite. f gives a measure of "where on average X goes," and makes this depend only on the current state and time. We call the vector f the *drift* of X. The variance-covariance matrix H can always be written in the form $H = FF^\mathsf{T}; F \in \mathbb{R}^{K \times \mathrm{rank}(H)}$. The matrix F is called the *diffusion* of the process. Both the drift $f(s, x)$ and the variance-covariance matrix $H(s, x)$ are conditional upon $\mathcal{F}(s)$. When dealing with diffusions, if we do not say otherwise, the variance and covariance are always the conditional, instantaneous ones.

As we will see below (see for instance section 7.1.2), *diffusions with zero drift are local martingales,* not necessarily martingales.

Most of the time, we deal with *Itô processes*, which may or may not be diffusions. Their definition requires the concept of Brownian motion. We introduce Brownian motion in the next section.

♠

Before doing that, notice that both the expectation and variance-covariance of the change in a diffusion, over small intervals of time, are locally linear in time. In order to see this, write the second and third condition in the definition of a diffusion X as:

$$\int_{|y-x|\le\varepsilon} (y-x)P(s,x,t,dy) = f\times(t-s)+o(t-s)$$

$$\int_{|y-x|\le\varepsilon} (y-x)(y-x)^{\mathsf{T}} P(s,x,t,dy) = H \times (t-s) + o(t-s)$$

where $o(t-s)$ is the standard notation for "infinitesimal of order strictly higher than one with respect to $t-s$." The first condition has the expected change of X on the LHS, the second has its variance-covariance matrix. The RHSs say that expectation and variance-covariance are approximately linear in time, with the coefficient of linearity being the drift and the variance-covariance matrix.

5.3 Brownian Motion

This section provides first an intuitive construction and a motivation for using Brownian motion in Finance and then its definition. The first part is less rigorous than the second, and works on the one-dimensional case, in which Brownian motion is a real process, while the second part encompasses the multidimensional case or a vector of Brownian processes.

5.3.1 Intuitive Construction

In order to understand the fine properties of Brownian motion and its definition, it is useful to think of it as the limit of a discrete-time process, the random walk. This construction helps us understand both the global behavior of the Brownian process, and its path-by-path properties.

We could start from a process which jumps by 1 or -1 in one unit of time, with independent jumps, and then shrink the time interval and the magnitude of the jump so that the latter is the square root of the former. Application of the Central Limit Theorem would provide us with the Brownian motion.

Below we let the process increase or decrease not by one unit, but by a Gaussian realization. But we maintain the idea of decreasing the length of time of each Gaussian increment in such a way that the mean and variance of each increment over a finite length of time are constant.

Begin with a "random walk" $B(t)$, that is, a discrete-time real process that starts from the value 0 at time 0, $B_0 = 0$, and is then constructed inductively by adding at each point in time a zero-mean random variable, independent of the previous ones. In other words, let its value at time $t + 1, t \in \mathbb{N}$, be the value it had one period before, at t, plus e_{t+1}

$$B(t + 1) = B(t) + e(t + 1)$$

where $e(t + 1)$ is a real-valued random variable with zero expected value conditional on $e(t), e(t - 1), ..e(1)$. The increments $e(t + 1)$ are identically distributed and independent (IID). We use indifferently the notation $e(t + 1)$ or the notation e without any time index. The increments are standard Gaussian: e is $\mathcal{N}(0, 1)$, with $\mathbb{E}(e) = 0$ and $\text{var}(e) = 1$. Let the filtration be generated by $B(t)$.

It follows from this construction, and the fact that the IID increments have zero mean, that the expectation of B at any point in time t, as computed at time 0, is equal to B_0, in the same way as the (conditional) expectation of its value at time $t > s$, given its value at time s, is equal to its value at s:

$$\mathbb{E}_s[B(t)] = \mathbb{E}_s \left[B(s) + \sum_{i=1}^{t-s} e(s + i) \right] = B(s) + \mathbb{E}_s \left[\sum_{i=1}^{t-s} e(s + i) \right] = B(s)$$

Equivalently, we can state that the expected *increments* of the process between s and t are equal to zero:

$$\mathbb{E}_s[B(t) - B(s)] = 0$$

Either way, a random walk is seen to be a martingale with respect to the filtration generated by itself.

Let us consider the behavior of the (conditional) variance of the random walk. Since the expectation is zero, and the increments are independent, the variance of $B(t) - B(s)$ is the expectation of the per-period squared increments:

$$\text{var}_s[B(t) - B(s)] = \mathbb{E}_s \left[\sum_{i=1}^{t-s} (B(s + i) - B(s + i - 1))^2 \right]$$

In turn, since each increment has unit variance, and they are independent over non-overlapping intervals, we have a total variance equal to the length of time, $t - s$:

$$\mathbb{E}_s \left[\sum_{i=1}^{t-s} (B(s + i) - B(s + i - 1))^2 \right] = \sum_{i=1}^{t-s} \mathbb{E}_s \left[(B(s + i) - B(s + i - 1))^2 \right] = \sum_{i=1}^{t-s} 1 = t - s$$

Now, let us reduce the interval of time that separates two successive values of B from 1 to $1/n$. Overall, we will have $n \times (t - s)$ small intervals in the period $t - s$. Let us do this in such a way that both the mean and the variance of the increment per unit of time remain constant. So, let the increments over the interval $1/n$ still have zero mean, but have variance $1/n$. A reasoning analogous to the previous one leads us to the conclusion that both the mean and the variance of the overall process are unaffected:

$$\mathbb{E}_s[B(t)] = B(s) + \mathbb{E}_s\left[\sum_{i=1}^{n(t-s)} e\left(s + \frac{i}{n}\right)\right] = B_s$$

$$\mathrm{var}_s[B(t) - B(s)] = \mathbb{E}_s\left[\sum_{i=1}^{n(t-s)} \left(B\left(s + \frac{i}{n}\right) - B\left(s + \frac{i-1}{n}\right)\right)^2\right] = n(t-s) \times \frac{1}{n} = t - s$$

(5.1)

By pursuing *ad infinitum* this process of subdivision, or letting n go to infinity, it can be shown (Donsker's theorem) that the resulting process B is adapted and has the following properties, which define Brownian motion (see also section 5.3.3):

1. $B(0) = 0$ with probability one

2. $B(t)$ is continuous

3. the increments over non-overlapping intervals are independent of each other

4. the increment $B(t) - B(s)$ is *normally distributed* with zero expected value and variance $(t - s)$.

As a consequence, B is a martingale. There are two more important properties that will enter the characterization of Brownian motion and which the construction can help rationalize: the process B has *infinite first (or total) variation* and *finite quadratic variation*.

To measure the first variation, take the sum of the (absolute value of the) increments of the process, over each single path, with finite n;

$$\sum_{i=1}^{n(t-s)} \left\| B\left(s + \frac{i}{n}\right) - B\left(s + \frac{i-1}{n}\right) \right\|$$

where $\|\;\|$ is the absolute value (it would be the Euclidean norm in the multidimensional case). Because the support of a Gaussian random variable is unbounded, each single increment $B(s + i/n) - B(s + (i-1)/n)$ can take any value. As n goes to infinity, the sum also contains an infinite number of terms, so that its maximum over all possible paths, that is, the *first variation* of the process, will not be finite:

$$\lim_{n\to\infty} \sup \sum_{i=1}^{n(t-s)} \left\| B\left(s + \frac{i}{n}\right) - B\left(s + \frac{i-1}{n}\right) \right\| = \infty$$

Quite intuitively, the same property holds over all the possible partitions of the interval $t - s$, even not equally spaced.[2] Brownian motion is extremely erratic, in the sense that it

---

2 Here, and below, with reference to the quadratic variation, we should prove that the statements do not depend on the fact that the partition of the interval $t - s$ is into subintervals of uniform length. An accurate proof would require consideration of all the partitions when the maximum amplitude of each subinterval tends to zero. We leave this aside.

is made of an infinity of small moves. Each one of them is allowed to be positive, negative, and potentially big. So, the length of any path (the variation over each single path) is infinite. The plots in figure 5.1 give an idea of this sort of unboundedness, generated by the infinite sequence of erratic moves. While continuous, the path is a non-differentiable function of time in the sense of ordinary calculus.[3]

Consider now the reason for which Brownian motion has finite quadratic variation. Define the quadratic variation in a way similar to the variation, with the sum of the squared changes instead of their absolute value:

$$\lim_{n \to \infty} \sup \sum_{i=1}^{n(t-s)} \left\| B\left(s + \frac{i}{n}\right) - B\left(s + \frac{i-1}{n}\right) \right\|^2$$

The expression is equal to $t - s$, in the sense that

$$P\left(\omega : \lim_{n \to \infty} \sup \sum_{i=1}^{n(t-s)} \left\| B\left(s + \frac{i}{n}\right) - B\left(s + \frac{i-1}{n}\right) \right\|^2 = t - s\right) = 1 \qquad (5.2)$$

so that the quadratic variation is finite. An intuitive proof is as follows. Take the difference

$$\sum_{i=1}^{n(t-s)} \left\| B\left(s + \frac{i}{n}\right) - B\left(s + \frac{i-1}{n}\right) \right\|^2 - t - s$$

and write ΔB_i for $B(s + i/n) - B(s + (i-1)/n)$. Observe that the previous difference can be written as

$$\sum_{i=1}^{n(t-s)} \left[\|\Delta B_i\|^2 - \left(s + \frac{i}{n} - s - \frac{i-1}{n}\right) \right] = \sum_{i=1}^{n(t-s)} \left[\|\Delta B_i\|^2 - \frac{1}{n} \right]$$

---

3 On the converse, it can be easily demonstrated that differentiable functions have finite first variation. Indeed, consider a function $f : \mathbb{R} \to \mathbb{R}$, with derivative f', construct the quantity

$$\sum_{i=1}^{n(t-s)} \left\| f\left(s + \frac{i}{n}\right) - f\left(s + \frac{i-1}{n}\right) \right\|$$

and use the Mean Value Theorem, which says that there exists a point $s^*(i) \in \left[s + \frac{i}{n}, s + (i-1)n\right]$ such that

$$f\left(s + \frac{i}{n}\right) - f\left(s + \frac{i-1}{n}\right) = f'(s^*(i))\frac{1}{n}$$

to transform it into

$$\sum_{i=1}^{n(t-s)} \|f'(s^*(i))\| \frac{1}{n}$$

so that

$$\lim_{n \to \infty} \sum_{i=1}^{n(t-s)} \|f'(s^*(i))\| \frac{1}{n} = \int_s^t \|f'(u)\| \, du < \infty$$

Boundedness follows from the boundedness of f'.

Each term has zero expectation, different terms are independent, so that the sum has zero expectation and variance equal to

$$\sum_{i=1}^{n(t-s)} \text{var}_s\left[\|\Delta B_i\|^2 - \frac{1}{n}\right]$$

$$= \sum_{i=1}^{n(t-s)} \mathbb{E}_s\left[\|\Delta B_i\|^4 - 2\left(\frac{1}{n}\right)\|\Delta B_i\| + \frac{1}{n^2}\right]$$

$$= \sum_{i=1}^{n(t-s)} \left[\frac{3}{n^2} - 2\frac{1}{n^2} + \frac{1}{n^2}\right]$$

$$= \sum_{i=1}^{n(t-s)} \frac{2}{n^2} = 2\frac{(t-s)}{n}$$

since the expectation of $\|\Delta B_i\|^4$, which is Gaussian with 0 mean and variance $1/n$, is $3/n^2$.[4] When $n \to \infty$, the variance tends to zero, and the difference between the quadratic variation and $t - s$ converges to 0, in the sense given by (5.2).

Overall, the resulting process has unbounded-variation paths, whose quadratic variation remains finite. It is important to distinguish the variations (first and quadratic) from the conditional mean and variance of the process. The variations are indeed path-by-path properties, while the mean and variances at any point in time are computed averaging over paths.

As anticipated, the random-walk construction helps us understand both the global behavior of the Brownian process (a martingale with independent, Gaussian increments, which have zero mean and finite variance), but also its path-by-path properties (infinite first variation, finite quadratic variation). Last, it helps us give a meaning to a quantity, the differential of B, which *per se* is difficult to conceive (and which is accurately defined only using the notion of stochastic integral, in chapter 7). First, B is a process; second, it has infinite first variation, while differentiable functions have finite variation.[5] How can we consider an infinitesimal change in it? By showing that it converges in some sense to a deterministic quantity.

When $n \to \infty$, the time intervals become a differential element which we may denote ds. With an abuse of notation, denote as $dB(s)$ or dB the random increase in B over the interval $(s, s+ds)$. This increment is not small in the sense of real numbers, since each infinitesimal increment is a Gaussian random variable. But it has two properties. First, its mean is zero and its square equals ds in expectation:

$$\mathbb{E}_s[dB] = 0$$
$$\mathbb{E}_s\left[dB^2\right] = ds \tag{5.3}$$

---

4 The fourth moment of a zero-mean Gaussian random variable is equal to three times its variance squared.

5 Each sample path of it is non-differentiable: there are mini-kinks everywhere.

where the second property follows from taking the limit in:

$$\mathbb{E}_s \left(B \left(s + \frac{i}{n} \right) - B \left(s + \frac{i-1}{n} \right) \right)^2 = \mathrm{var} \left(B \left(s + \frac{i}{n} \right) - B \left(s + \frac{i-1}{n} \right) \right) = \frac{1}{n} \quad (5.4)$$

Knowing that both the mean and the variance of dB have a finite limit, though, is not enough. We just stressed the importance of distinguishing moments from path-by-path behaviors, and we would like to characterize the convergence of dB beyond its moments. To this end, recall from (5.2) that the quadratic variation of Brownian motion over an interval $(t - s)$ converges to $t - s$, in the sense that the probability attached to paths on which the quadratic variation is not $t - s$ is equal to zero. In the limit, this says that the dB random variable, squared, tends *almost surely* towards the deterministic quantity ds:[6]

$$dB^2 = ds \quad (5.5)$$

Equation (5.5) is the result we do want to achieve: dB^2 tends almost surely to ds, not only in expectation. Note once more that the equality $dB^2 = ds$ is not an equality of real numbers.

5.3.2   A Financial Motivation

Suppose one wants to model returns on a security. Motivated in part by the martingale properties of securities' prices, in part by the Central Limit Theorem, one may want to make returns, defined as increments in a price process, independent and Gaussian, with zero mean and variance proportional to the length of time elapsed. If a large number of trades impacts on prices, indeed, the Central Limit Theorem is likely to make their change Gaussian. Zero mean can be justified, under some measures, by martingale properties. Call the return process B. If ε is $\mathcal{N}(0, 1)$, $\sqrt{t_2 - t_1} \times \varepsilon$ is a Gaussian random variable with zero mean and variance equal to $t_2 - t_1$. The requisite behavior is

$$B(t_2) - B(t_1) = \sqrt{t_2 - t_1} \times \varepsilon$$

In short, if Δt is the length of time we have in mind, $\Delta t = t_2 - t_1$, and ΔB is the return or change in the price process:

$$\Delta B = \sqrt{\Delta t} \times \varepsilon$$

Suppose, instead, one wants the mean return to be μ per unit of time, then one can write another process, $\bar{B}$:

$$\Delta \bar{B} = \mu \times \Delta t + \sqrt{\Delta t} \times \varepsilon$$

---

6 We say that a sequence of random variables X_n converges with probability one (or almost surely) to a random variable X if and only if the set of ω where

$$\lim_{n \to \infty} X_n = X$$

has probability 1:

$$P \left[\omega : \lim_{n \to \infty} X_n = X \right] = 1$$

which seems to be a reasonable extension of the discrete-time binomial model, since in that case returns had mean and variance proportional to the length of time elapsed.[7] We would like to take that process to the limit and give a meaning to the expression dB, by saying, for instance, that dB is Gaussian with mean 0 and variance dt

$$dB = \sqrt{dt} \times \varepsilon$$

The paths of Brownian motion, as our intuitive construction suggested, have infinite variation, so, the LHS is not a differential in the sense of ordinary calculus. However, we can go from the discrete-time change $\Delta B = \sqrt{\Delta t} \times \varepsilon$ to its "differential" dB if we understand the latter, as we did above, as the random variable that has zero expectation

$$\mathbb{E}_t[dB(t)] = 0$$

and variance equal to dt:

$$\mathbb{E}_t\left[dB(t)^2\right] = dt$$

So, the intuitive construction introduced above gives a way to model Gaussian returns in continuous time.

5.3.3   Definition

We can now provide a formal definition for the Brownian motion process that we have intuitively built and motivated.

Definition 5.6   *A K-dimensional standard* Brownian motion *in $(\Omega, \mathcal{F}, P)$, is a process*

$$B : \Omega \times \mathbb{R}^+ \to \mathbb{R}^K$$

such that:[8]

1. $B(0) = 0$ with probability one

2. $B(t)$ is continuous

3. increments over non-overlapping intervals are independent of each other: if $0 \leq s \leq t \leq \tau, B(t) - B(s)$ is independent of $B(\tau) - B(t)$

4. if $0 \leq s \leq t$, then the increment $B(t) - B(s)$ is *normally distributed* with zero expected value and covariance matrix $(t - s) \times I_K$.

If $K = 1$, we, indeed, get a process that starts at zero, is continuous, and has independent and identically distributed increments. These increments are Gaussian with variance equal to the length of time. With more than one dimension ($K > 1$), we just introduce

---

7 And, indeed, in the benchmark example below we show that this is the case, and that the distribution that characterizes the sum of the increments in a binomial tree tends to the Gaussian, when the intervals of time are small (with the limit to be qualified).

8 Note that we did not specify the filtration. The definition of Brownian motion must hold for every filtration. In particular, independency of increments must hold for any information about the past. See also the comparison with a Wiener process (in whose definition the filtration is specified, so that its properties hold only for that filtration) below, and Nielsen (1999), section 1.5.

a multivariate Gaussian. Each component has zero mean and variance dt, while the covariance is

$$dB_i(t) \times dB_j(t) = \begin{cases} dt & i = j \\ 0 & i \neq j \end{cases} \tag{5.6}$$

for $i, j = 1, ..K$. The Brownians are independent as per the definition. We could modify the starting point, by adding a constant to $B(0)$, or extend the definition so as to change the mean of the returns over $t - s$.

Definition 5.6 implies that:

(i) the Brownian motion is a *martingale*;

(ii) the Brownian motion is *square integrable;*

(iii) the Brownian motion is a *Markov* process. It is also called a *Gaussian Markov process*, since its transition probability at all time-intervals is normal;

(iv) the Brownian motion is a *diffusion.*

If the process represents accumulated gains, we know that being a martingale means that financial gains are fair bets. The square integrability provides a nice regularity on the martingale since it endows it with the variance at all points in time.

Last, a theorem by Paul Lévy (see below) guarantees that Brownian motion (a Gaussian process) is *the only type of continuous martingale* with variance proportional to time, if the filtration is the one generated by the Brownian itself, that is, in $(\Omega, \mathcal{F}, P, \mathbf{F}^B)$. The lines below give the definition of the Wiener process and the intuition of Lévy's theorem. This theorem is the reason why in this book we work most of the time on the filtration generated by the Brownian motion. For the rest of the chapter, for instance, we assume that $\mathcal{F}_t$ is the filtration generated by the Brownian motion, $\mathbf{F} = \mathbf{F}^B$. Under that filtration we can *use indifferently the terms Brownian motion and Wiener process, as well as the notations B or w*. Most of the time, we use the term Brownian motion and never use it for the notation B (which will refer to a riskless security), using w instead, so that $\mathbf{F}^B = \mathbf{F}^w$.

———————————————♠———————————————

Definition 5.7 Wiener process *A K-dimensional standard Wiener process with respect to the filtration* $\mathbf{F}$ *in* $(\Omega, \mathcal{F}, P, \mathbf{F})$ *is a K-dimensional process w such that:*

1. *$w(0) = 0$ with probability one*

2. *w is continuous*

3. *w is adapted to $\mathbf{F}$*

4. *w has normally distributed increments: $w(t) - w(s)$ is independent of $\mathcal{F}_s$ with zero mean and:*

$$var\left[(w(t) - w(s))(w(t) - w(s))^\mathsf{T}\right] = (t - s)I_K$$

The first two definitional properties of Brownian motion and Wiener processes are identical. Then a Wiener process – which is defined with a specific filtration in mind – is adapted and has standard Gaussian increments. This means that a process may be Wiener under a specific filtration and may not be such if you change the filtration, while a Brownian motion is such independently of the filtration. Lévy's theorem says that any Brownian motion is a Wiener process (at least) with respect to the filtration generated by itself. We also know that any process is a Wiener process with respect to a given filtration if and only if it is a standard Brownian motion, is adapted, and has independent increments.[9]

Note also that the fourth requirement in the definition of Wiener process could be substituted by the requirement that w be a square-integrable martingale and, for $t \geq s$:

$$\mathbb{E}_s\big[(w(t) - w(s))(w(t) - w(s))^\mathsf{T}\big] = (t - s)I_K$$

This requirement does not require Gaussian increments, but, together with the others, implies them.

5.4   Itô Processes

In the sequel of the book security prices – as well as returns, gains, and wealth – are always Itô processes. In order to properly define them we need the notion of *stochastic integral,* or integral in dw, and the notion of stochastic differential equation, which we present in chapter 7. For the time being, we just give an intuitive interpretation of integrals in dw as, for instance, the "gains" process G:

$$G(t) = \int_0^t b(s)dw(s)$$

where w is a real Wiener process. The "stochastic differential" version of the (well-defined) integral equation is

$$dG(t) = b(t)dw(t) \tag{5.7}$$

Per se, the last version is just a shortcut for the integral equation, which we shall define in chapter 7. If b is a vector and there are K Wiener processes, the gain is a scalar and the integral is a sum of integrals, one for each component of b:

$$G(t) = \sum_{i=1}^K \int_0^t b_i(s)dw_i(s)$$

If b is an $N \times K$ matrix, we consider several gains (say, on N different securities), and integration is performed term by term:

$$G_j(t) = \sum_{i=1}^K \int_0^t b_{ij}(s)dw_i(s)$$

---

9 See Nielsen (1999, pages 17 and following).

In all cases, conditional on b, or taking b as fixed at the beginning of a small interval $(t, t + dt)$, dG is Gaussian with zero mean. With one Wiener process, its variance will depend on the fact that the variance of dw is equal to dt, while with K Wiener processes we need to use the same property (5.6) as for Brownians. Overall, we can think of the integral, which represents cumulated gains from 0 to t, as a random variable with mean 0 and variance determined by the rich interplay of the Wiener processes.

Once this intuition is clear, it is not difficult, if the function a satisfies the usual properties for (path-by-path) Riemann integration, to interpret a gain process which has also a deterministic part. Its integral, correct representation is

$$G(t) = \int_0^t a(s)ds + \int_0^t b(s)dw(s)$$

while the differential one is

$$dG(t) = a(t)dt + b(t)dw(t)$$

This is what we call an *Itô process*. Again, G and a can be N-dimensional (*a vector of processes*), with b an $N \times K$ matrix (*of processes*), $N \geq 1, K \geq 1$.

A more delicate situation arises when, with all the dimensional caveats in place, both the terms a and b depend on the state of the world through the process G. In this case we must give a meaning to the equality

$$G(t) = \int_0^t a(G(s), s)ds + \int_0^t b(G(s), s)dw(s)$$

considered as an equation in G, or to

$$dG(t) = a(G(t), t)dt + b(G(t), t)dw(t)$$

This is a so-called *stochastic differential equation (SDE)*.

Chapter 7 will provide conditions under which this equation, together with an initial condition, of the type $G(0) = G_0 \in \mathbb{R}^N$, has a solution, for $N \geq 1, K \geq 1$. *Solutions of SDEs will be Itô processes.* They will be Markov if the functions a and b satisfy appropriate regularity (Lipschitz and growth) conditions. They will be Markov and diffusions under continuity of the functions a and b with respect to time. In that case, a will be the drift and b will be the diffusion matrix. This is why the coefficients of a SDE are named *drift* and *diffusion*. Most of the time a and b are named like that also when they are not continuous (and, therefore, the solution of the SDE is not necessarily a diffusion). In order to avoid the confusion arising from this potential misnomer, in the rest of the book, unless otherwise stated, we assume that the functions a and b are continuous with respect to time. The coefficient $a(G(t), t)$ represents the instantaneous expectation and $b(G(t), t)b^\mathsf{T}(G(t), t)$ represents the instantaneous variance-covariance matrix of G, because they are the expectation and the variance-covariance of its changes, dG, conditional on time-t information, and before you multiply times dt.

Suppose G include two processes, named X and Y, $\text{cov}(X(t), Y(t))$ – or simply $\text{cov}(X, Y)$, when the point in time is clear – are the instantaneous variances and covariances of *the increases* in the processes X and Y at time t. Total covariance over $(t, t + dt)$ is

$$\text{cov}(X, Y)dt = b(X, Y, t)b^\mathsf{T}(X, Y, t)dt$$

If the process X is real-valued, the variance-covariance matrix bb^T collapses into a real-valued product, the variance. So, in that case,

$$\text{var}(X)dt = b(X(t), t)b^\mathsf{T}(X(t), t)dt$$

In short, we could write

$$\text{cov}(X, Y) = \frac{dXdY}{dt}; \text{var}(X) = \frac{(dX)^2}{dt}$$

The meaning will be clear from Itô's lemma below and from the exact properties of the corresponding processes in chapter 7.

5.5   Benchmark Example (continued)

5.5.1   The Black-Scholes Model

Our benchmark example will be the *Black-Scholes (or strict-sense Black-Scholes)* model. We consider a riskless asset with constant rate of interest r, denoted by $B(t) = \exp(rt)$, and N non-dividend-paying stocks, with an equal number of underlying Wiener processes. Let us start from the case in which there is a single risky asset and a single Wiener process ($N = K = 1$) *and use the notation S for the Black-Scholes price (it will become $\mathcal{S}$ in the N-dimensional case).* The stock price process is

$$dS(t) = \mu \times S(t)dt + \sigma \times S(t) \times dw(t)$$

where μ and σ are two real constants, $\mu \geq 0, \sigma > 0$, $\mathbf{F}^w$ is the filtration generated by the Wiener process. As a consequence, prices are adapted to $\mathbf{F}^w$. Consider the random variable $S_t(\omega)$, for t fixed, which is a function of ω, as distinct from the process $S(t) = S(\omega, t)$, which is a function of both t and ω. At each point in time, we show in section 5.6.2 below that $S_t(\omega)$ has a lognormal distribution, which means that its log-returns are Gaussian. Indeed, in section 5.6.2 we will show that log-returns X_t, defined as the returns such that the value of prices in t is their value at 0 continuously compounded at the rate X_t

$$S_t = S(0)\exp(X_t)$$

are Gaussian with a specific mean and variance, both linear in time:

$$X_t \sim \mathcal{N}\left(\left(\mu - \frac{\sigma^2}{2}\right)t, \sigma^2 t\right) \tag{5.8}$$

From the economic viewpoint, Gaussian log returns can be very well interpreted as the sum of a myriad of trades or information releases, which by the Central Limit Theorem produce a Gaussian change in price. In chapter 7 we will label a process with lognormal distribution at each point in time a Geometric Brownian motion. The process of its logarithms, which are Gaussian at each point in time, will be an Arithmetic Brownian motion. So, the strict-sense Black-Scholes model has prices that follow a Geometric Brownian motion, and returns that follow an Arithmetic one. We give a visual representation of the Arithmetic Brownian motion, based on the intuitive construction of Brownian motion, and the fact that a random draw from any Arithmetic Brownian motion can be obtained from a standard Brownian draw by adding its drift and multiplying by its standard deviation. Similarly for the density of the random variable X_t. We proceed as follows.

First we simulate the paths of a number of Arithmetic Brownian motions, both with and without drift. These are obtained by discretizing the dynamics of w, using the device $\Delta w = \sqrt{\Delta t}\varepsilon$; $\varepsilon \sim \mathcal{N}(0, 1)$ and repeatedly sampling from a standard Gaussian. The left-hand panel of figure 5.1 below plots a sample path of a Brownian motion with and without drift, with the same volatility. Evidently, the Brownian motion with positive drift tends upwards over time, while the driftless one wanders around zero. By definition, their dispersion around the "trend" is the same. The right-hand panel of the same figure presents two Arithmetic Brownian motions with the same drift but different volatilities. The effect of increasing the volatility parameter is in the dispersion of the realizations around the trend. In both panels we observe the extremely kinky behavior of the trajectories, which makes them non-differentiable in the sense of ordinary calculus.

We then plot the density of the position at time 1 of some of the same processes, namely the driftless, low-volatility one as a dotted line, the low-volatility one with drift as a solid line, and the high-volatility one with drift as a dashed line. The representation is in the top panel of figure 5.2. Increasing the drift from zero to a positive number implies a

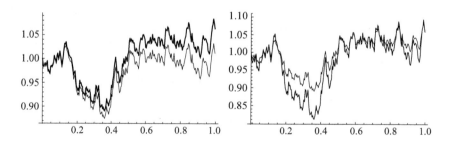

Figure 5.1

Left-hand panel: simulated behavior of a zero-drift and a non-zero-drift Brownian motion, with volatility $\sigma = 15\%$. The thin line is for $\mu = 0$; the thick one for $\mu = 5\%$. **Right-hand panel**: simulated behavior of the non-zero-drift Brownian motion for different volatility levels of volatility: $\sigma = 15\%$, $\sigma = 25\%$. The thin line is for $\sigma = 15\%$; the thick one for $\sigma = 25\%$.

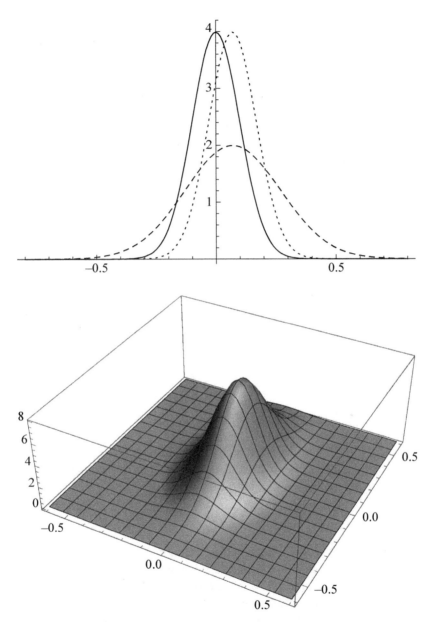

Figure 5.2

Top panel: time-1 density functions of the Brownian motions represented in figure 5.1. The solid line corresponds to the driftless, low volatility case with drift ($\mu = 0, \sigma = 10\%$), the dotted one is for the low volatility with drift ($\mu = 7\%, \sigma = 10\%$), the dashed one is for the high volatility case with drift ($\mu = 7\%, \sigma = 20\%$). **Bottom panel**: time-1 joint density function of the Brownian motions represented in the right-hand side of figure 5.1 ($\mu = 7\%, \sigma = 10\%$ and $\sigma = 20\%$, respectively from left to right and from back to front. Correlation is set to zero).

displacement of the distribution towards the right (from the solid line to the dotted line). Increasing the volatility enlarges the base of the bell (from the dotted to the dashed line). In the bottom panel, the figure presents the *joint* density function of the Brownian motions with drift (those with the dotted-line and the dashed-line densities), which is a multivariate Gaussian distribution. The resulting bell opens up more in the high-volatility case. Zero correlation is assumed. Overall, we have smooth, Gaussian densities, both univariate and multivariate, when we take a picture of the process at a single point in time looking to a finite distance into the future.

In the multidimensional case we still take the number of assets equal to the number of Wiener processes, $N = K$. The assumption on the riskless rate does not change. The strict-sense Black-Scholes model for stocks becomes

$$S(t) = S(0) + \int_0^t \text{diag}(S(s))\mu ds + \int_0^t \text{diag}(S(s))\sigma dw(s)$$

where $\text{diag}(S)$ is the $N \times N$ diagonal matrix which has the elements of S on the diagonal, μ is an expected-rate of return vector, and σ is an $N \times N$ constant matrix, which is positive definite. In differential form,

$$dS(t) = \text{diag}(S(t))\mu dt + \text{diag}(S(t))\sigma dw$$

which delivers

$$S(t) = \exp(X(t)) = S(0)\exp\left[\left(\mu - \frac{\check{\sigma}^2}{2}\right)t + \sigma w(t)\right]$$

where $\check{\sigma}^2$ is the vector that contains the norms of the rows of the matrix σ, namely $\check{\sigma}^2 = \{\|\sigma_i\|^2, \ i = 1, \ldots, N\}$. The same holds if we consider S as a random variable. Again, it entails prices growing at the rates μ in expectation. The joint distribution of log-returns is Gaussian, as in the bottom panel of figure 5.2.

5.5.2 Construction from Discrete Time

The strict-Black-Scholes model for a single security price may be obtained from a binomial tree, by letting the length of each interval approach zero. We prove the result for the case $\mu = 0$ and $r = 0$. The proof uses the Law of Large Numbers and the Central Limit Theorem, which we recall now. Consider the process that results from earning one unit of consumption during a unit of time if the stock goes up in a binomial tree, losing one if it goes down. Let M_n be its value after n jumps, n being an integer. By construction, M_n is the sum of n jumps each equal to $+1$ or -1, so that the values that M_n can take are

$$M_n = (1) \times j + (-1) \times (n - j); j \leq n$$

where j is the number of jumps up. The Law of Large Numbers says that the ratio of M_n to the number n of jumps tends to zero almost surely when n goes to infinity:

$$\frac{M_n}{n} \to 0 \qquad \text{with probability one}$$

while it follows from the Central Limit Theorem that the random variable $M_n/\sqrt{n}$ tends towards the standard Gaussian.

Now, let us consider the stock price at time T, after $n = T/\Delta t$ jumps, in a discrete binomial model, as in section 2.2.6. $S(T)$ is distributed as

$$S(0)u^j d^{n-j}$$

Set $S(0) = 1$ for simplicity and recall the expressions for the risk-neutral probabilities:

$$p^* = \frac{1-d}{u-d}; 1 - p^* = \frac{u-1}{u-d}$$

Choose either the parametrization

$$u = e^{\sigma\sqrt{\Delta t}}; d = \frac{1}{u} = e^{-\sigma\sqrt{\Delta t}}$$

or the parametrization

$$u = 1 + \sigma\sqrt{\Delta t}; d = 1 - \sigma\sqrt{\Delta t}$$

In the second case, $p^* = 1/2$ follows and the stock price at T is

$$S(T) = \left(1 + \sigma\sqrt{\Delta t}\right)^j \left(1 - \sigma\sqrt{\Delta t}\right)^{T-j}$$

Observe that the number of jumps up, j, can be written as $(n + M_n)/2$, while the number of jumps down $n - j$ is $(n - M_n)/2$, and n, the total number of steps or jumps, is equal to $T/\Delta t$. We, therefore, have

$$S(T) = \left(1 + \sigma\sqrt{\Delta t}\right)^{\frac{1}{2}(n+M_n)} \left(1 - \sigma\sqrt{\Delta t}\right)^{\frac{1}{2}(n-M_n)}$$

Taking the logarithm:

$$\ln S(T) = \frac{1}{2}(n + M_n)\ln\left(1 + \sigma\sqrt{\Delta t}\right) + \frac{1}{2}(n - M_n)\ln\left(1 - \sigma\sqrt{\Delta t}\right)$$

and using a Taylor series expansion truncated to terms of order $\sqrt{\Delta t}$, we obtain

$$\ln S(T) = -\frac{1}{2}\sigma^2 T + \sigma\sqrt{T}\left(\frac{M_n}{\sqrt{n}}\right) + \left(\frac{M_n}{n}\right)o\left(\sqrt{\Delta t}\right) + o\left(\sqrt{\Delta t}\right)$$

where $o\left(\sqrt{\Delta t}\right)$ is an infinitesimal of order $\sqrt{\Delta t}$. On the RHS,

$$\sqrt{T}\frac{M_n}{\sqrt{n}}$$

tends towards a Gaussian with standard deviation $\sqrt{T}$, or $w(T)$, while M_n/n tends towards zero. We end up with the following limit in distribution:

$$S(T) \to e^{\sigma w(T) - \frac{1}{2}\sigma^2 T}$$

which corresponds to the strict Black-Scholes distribution (5.8).

So, the binomial model produces the strict-sense Black-Scholes model as a continuous limit.

5.6 Itô's Lemma

Very often we need to describe the behavior over time of functions of Itô processes, such as functions of prices. Consider only smooth functions, with derivatives at least up to the second order. Do their values follow Itô processes? How do we compute their differentials and their integrals? Can we apply the chain rule of calculus? These are interrogations on *stochastic calculus*. The answer is provided by Itô's lemma, which states that the values of these smooth functions are also Itô processes and have a stochastic differential, in which both first (or gradient vectors) and second derivatives (or Hessian matrices) appear. We give a preview of the lemma starting from the case in which both the Itô process and its function are real-valued. We state the lemma for the general case in which the starting process is multi-dimensional and give the intuitive reason for which second-order derivatives show up. A few simple examples are then provided.

Consider a one-dimensional Itô process, namely a process of the type (5.7) with $N = 1$:

$$dX(s) = a(s)ds + b(s)dw(s)$$

and the process Y specified as a real function $g:\mathbb{R} \to \mathbb{R}$ of it:

$$Y = g(X)$$

Let g be twice differentiable with continuous derivatives, or C^2. Lemma 5.1, of Itô, says that the stochastic differential of Y is[10]

$$dY(s) = \left[g'(X(s))a(s) + \frac{1}{2}g''(X(s))b(s)^2 \right] ds + g'(X(s))b(s)dw(s)$$

Below, we provide an explanation for the peculiarity of this differential, as compared to ordinary calculus, which is the presence of the second-order derivative.[11]

---

10 Itô (1942, 1944). Bru and Yor (2002) point out that the German mathematician Wolfgang Döblin, who had taken French nationality under the name of Vincent Doblin, had already derived this formula in early 1940, shortly before the French debacle during which he committed suicide.

11 The lemma should really be stated in integral form:

$$Y(t) = g(X_0) + \int_0^t \left[g'(X(s))a(s) + \frac{1}{2}g''b(s)^2 \right] ds + \int_0^t g'(X(s))b(s)dw(s)$$

When Y is a real function of a multidimensional process, the lemma says:[12]

Lemma 5.1   *(Itô's lemma) Let X be an N-dimensional Itô process, $g : \mathbb{R}^N \to \mathbb{R}, g \in C^2$; let ∇g denote the gradient of g and $\nabla^2 g$, its Hessian matrix. Then the process $Y = g(X) \in \mathbb{R}$ is an Itô process with stochastic differential:*[13]

$$dY(s) = \left[\nabla g(X(s))a(s) + \frac{1}{2} trace\left(b(s)^\mathsf{T}\, \nabla^2 g(X(s))\, b(s) \right) \right] ds$$
$$+ \nabla g(X(s))b(s)dw(s)$$

The rule should really be written down and used in integral form:

$$Y(t) = g(X(t)) = g(X_0) + \int_0^t \left[\nabla g(X(s))a(s) + \frac{1}{2}\text{trace}\left(b(s)^\mathsf{T}\, \nabla^2 g(X(s))\, b(s) \right) \right] ds$$
$$+ \int_0^t \nabla g(X(s))b(s)dw(s) \tag{5.10}$$

As such, it shows that Y contains both a non-stochastic integral (a Riemann one, in ds, which is computed path by path) and a stochastic integral (the integral in dw). It is clear that, while the diffusion of Y is influenced only by the diffusion of X, *the drift of Y depends on both the drift and the diffusion of X*, unless the Hessian matrix is null. As in the unidimensional case, second-order terms are present. The next section will explain why this is the case.

---

12 Actually, one can also state the lemma for multidimensional functions of multivariate Itô processes. This is obtained simply by stacking the results in the next version of the lemma.

13 Recall that $\text{trace}\left(b(t)^\mathsf{T} \nabla^2 g(X(t))b(t) \right)$ is:

$$\sum_{k=1}^{K} \left[\sum_{i=1}^{N} b_{i,k}(s) \sum_{j=1}^{N} \frac{\partial^2}{\partial x_i \partial x_j} g(X(s))b_{j,k}(s) \right]$$

The triple summation can be written as:

$$\text{trace}\left(\nabla^2 g(X(t)) \times b(t)b(t)^\mathsf{T} \right)$$

which is:

$$\sum_{j=1}^{N} \sum_{i=1}^{N} \frac{\partial^2}{\partial x_i \partial x_j} g(X(s)) \left(\sum_{k=1}^{K} b_{i,k}(s)b_{j,k}(s) \right)$$

This means that the lemma can also be formulated as

$$dY(t) = dg(X(t)) = \left[\sum_{i=1}^{N} \frac{\partial}{\partial x_i} g(X(s))a_i(s) + \frac{1}{2}\sum_{i=1}^{N}\sum_{j=1}^{N} \frac{\partial^2}{\partial x_i \partial x_j} g(X(s)) \left(\sum_{k=1}^{K} b_{i,k}(s)b_{j,k}(s) \right) \right] ds \tag{5.9}$$
$$+ \sum_{i=1}^{N}\sum_{k=1}^{K} \frac{\partial}{\partial x_i} g(X(s))b_{i,k}(s)dw_k(s)$$

5.6.1   Interpretation

There are several ways to understand why, as an extension, as it were, of ordinary differential calculus, the second derivatives $\nabla^2 g$ appear in the drift of Y, which is the term in ds. We present three intuitive explanations.

First, recall that the chain rule of calculus can be viewed as a truncation of a Taylor expansion of the function g. In ordinary calculus, the second-order terms are dropped because they are negligible with respect to the first-order terms. But now, we know from section 5.3.1 that Wiener processes have infinite variation but finite quadratic variation, and we know that $dw(t)^2$ should be set equal to dt, where equality is understood to hold almost surely. As a consequence, the second-order term is no longer negligible. It is extremely important, and worth keeping in mind for the rest of the book, that the properties of Wiener process, the building block for Itô processes, make both the first and the second derivative matter when dt is small. Expectation and variance are likely to appear again and again in our results, much as they appear in static mean-variance frameworks, because our continuous-time theory is built on Wiener processes.

The second intuitive explanation rests on the properties of expectations of convex functions. The second derivative affects the expected value of Y because of *Jensen's inequality*. The inequality says that, if a real function g is strictly convex, then, for every non-degenerate random variable X, the expectation of the function is greater than the function computed at the expected value of X:

$$\mathbb{E}[g(X)] > g[\mathbb{E}(X)]$$

In differential terms, Jensen's inequality is

$$\mathbb{E}[dg(X)] > g[\mathbb{E}(X + dX)] - g[\mathbb{E}(X)]$$

It says that, in order to obtain the value on the LHS, or the expected change in $Y = g(X)$, we would need to increase the RHS by a positive amount, that is, by an amount that has the same sign as the second derivative of g (if it has a non-zero one, of course). That is why the second-order terms and the second derivative appear in Itô's lemma, for the calculation of the drift of Y. They adjust the latter, which is the expected value of the change in Y over the next period of time (the LHS above), in a way that depends on the sign of the second derivative.

The third way to understand why second derivatives show up consists in showing that the application of the standard rules of differentation of ordinary calculus would lead to results inconsistent with the properties of our building block, the Wiener process. The next lines give a more detailed rendering of that argument.

—————————————◆—————————————

To show inconsistency of ordinary calculus with the path properties of Wiener process, let us consider a very simple function of $w(t)$, namely its square, and let us show which inconsistencies ordinary calculus would give for it. The inconsistencies arise from the fact that, as we know, differentiation and integration should offset one another, in the following sense: by applying them sequentially, we should not destroy the properties of the functions involved.

So, for instance, if we differentiate the function w^2 and integrate it as we learned to do above, we should not change the expectation of the function itself. We know that its expected value is equal to t, by definition: $\mathbb{E}\left[w(t)^2\right] = t$. Suppose that we applied ordinary calculus to obtain the SDE for $w(t)^2$. We might calculate the differential of $w(t)^2$ as follows:

$$d\left[w(t)^2\right] = 2w(t) \times dw(t)$$

Computing the integral of $d\left[w(s)^2\right]$ we would get

$$\int_0^t d\left[w(s)^2\right] = 2\int_0^t w(t)dw(t)$$

By subdividing the interval $(0, t)$ into n subintervals of equal length, t/n, approximating the RHS with a discrete sum and taking the value of w at the beginning of each subinterval, we would obtain

$$\int_0^t d\left[w(s)^2\right] \approx 2\sum_{i=0}^{n-1} w\left(\frac{i \times t}{n}\right)\left[w\left(\frac{(i+1) \times t}{n}\right) - w\left(\frac{i \times t}{n}\right)\right]$$

This sum would have an expected value equal to zero, since

$$\mathbb{E}\left\{\sum_{i=0}^{n-1} w\left(\frac{i \times t}{n}\right)\left[w\left(\frac{(i+1) \times t}{n}\right) - w\left(\frac{i \times t}{n}\right)\right]\right\}$$

$$= \sum_{i=0}^{n-1} \mathbb{E}\left[w\left(\frac{i \times t}{n}\right)\right]\mathbb{E}\left[w\left(\frac{(i+1) \times t}{n}\right) - w\left(\frac{i \times t}{n}\right)\right] = 0$$

This is not right, since we know that the result must be t. So, if we apply ordinary calculus when taking the derivative and then integrate back, we do not obtain the desired result.

As an alternative, we could try to calculate the integral taking the value of w at the end of each subinterval, as follows:

$$\int_0^t d\left[w(s)^2\right] \approx 2\sum_{i=0}^{n-1} w\left(\frac{(i+1) \times t}{n}\right)\left[w\left(\frac{(i+1) \times t}{n}\right) - w\left(\frac{i \times t}{n}\right)\right]$$

$$= 2\sum_{i=0}^{n-1}\left\{w\left(\frac{i \times t}{n}\right) + \left[w\left(\frac{(i+1) \times t}{n}\right) - w\left(\frac{i \times t}{n}\right)\right]\right\}$$

$$\times \left[w\left(\frac{(i+1) \times t}{n}\right) - w\left(\frac{i \times t}{n}\right)\right]$$

But this would have an expected value equal to $2 \times t$! So, neither of the two approaches gives a result consistent with the properties of the Wiener process, namely $\mathbb{E}\left[w(t)^2\right] = t$. Only the application of Itô's lemma, that is, the computation of the differential by adjusting it with other terms that do not appear in ordinary differential calculus, would give a consistent result. Indeed, if we apply Itô's lemma to the function at hand, we get

$$d\left[w(t)^2\right] = 2w(t) \times dw(t) + \frac{1}{2}2dt$$

whose integral is

$$\int_0^t d\left[w(s)^2\right] = 2\int_0^t w(t)dw(t) + t$$

As we saw above and as we shall learn in chapter 7, the expectation of the first integral is equal to 0. Therefore, the whole expectation is t, as it should be.

5.6.2 Examples

Having provided some intuition, let us now give three small examples.

Example 5.1 Consider as argument of a function a single security price S, with

$$dS = [\mu(t) - \iota(t)] \, dt + \sigma(t)dw(t)$$

where $\mu(t)$ is the conditionally expected rate of return on that security and $\iota(t)$ the flow-dividend payment it makes. Assume that μ, ι, and σ do not depend on S. Consider as dependent variable Y the continuous returns on S, $Y = g(S) = \ln(S)$. Then $dg/dx = 1/S, d^2g/dx^2 = -1/S^2$ and the lemma says that the dynamics of Y is

$$d\ln(S(t)) = \left[\frac{\mu(t) - \iota(t)}{S(t)} - \frac{1}{2S(t)^2}\sigma^2(t)\right] dt + \frac{\sigma(t)}{S(t)}dw(t)$$

In this dynamics, the role of the second derivative is clear: it lowers expected return as compared to the value it would take by the laws of ordinary calculus, $(\mu(t) - \iota(t))/S(t)$, by an amount that is increasing in the variance of prices and decreasing in their level.

Example 5.2 The second-order effect disappears from dY only when the Y function is linear. Consider

$$dS = \mu(t)dt + \sigma(t)dw(t)$$

and define the function κ, which we shall recognize in chapter 8 as a market price of risk:

$$\kappa(S(t), t) \triangleq \frac{\mu(t) - r(t) \times S(t)}{\sigma(t)}$$

The κ function is linear in S, so that the first derivative is constant and the second is equal to zero: $d\kappa/dx = -r/\sigma, d^2\kappa/dx^2 = 0$. Applying Itô's lemma we have

$$d\kappa(t) = -r(t)\frac{\mu(t)}{\sigma(t)}dt - r(t)dw(t)$$

The second derivative disappears from the drift of κ.

Example 5.3   Consider the real-valued *strict-sense Black-Scholes model*:

$$dS(t) = \mu S(t)dt + \sigma S(t)dw(t)$$

with μ and σ constant and positive. Itô's lemma helps understand why the distribution of S at any point in time is lognormal. We can write $S(t)$ as

$$S(t) = S(0)e^{Y(t)} = e^{Y(t)}$$

with Y Gaussian with mean $\left(\mu - \sigma^2/2\right)t$ and variance $\sigma^2 t$. In order to motivate the last statement, we use Itô's lemma. Since Y is $\ln(S)$, we have

$$dY = \frac{1}{S}dS - \frac{1}{2}\frac{1}{S^2}(dS)^2$$

$$= \left(\mu - \frac{\sigma^2}{2}\right)dt + \sigma \, dw(t)$$

We know from the properties of the Wiener process that $\mathbb{E}[dw(t)] = 0$, so that

$$\mathbb{E}[dY] = \left(\mu - \frac{\sigma^2}{2}\right)dt$$

We know from the same properties that the Wiener process is such that

$$\mathbb{E}\left[dY^2\right] = \sigma^2 dt$$

Last, the Wiener process is made up of Gaussian increments, so that Y is Gaussian.

We suggest that the readers solve exercises 5.1, 5.2, 5.3, 5.4, 5.5, 5.6, and 5.7.

5.7   Dynkin Operator

An important notational tool for stochastic calculus – giving the expected value of changes – is the following:

Definition 5.8   *Consider a real function* $y(x,t) : R^K \times [0, T] \to R$, $y \in C^2$. *Let its partial gradient and Hessian matrix with respect to x be* ∇y *and* $\nabla^2 y$. *For any K-valued diffusion X with drift vector f and diffusion matrix F, the Dynkin operator is:*[14]

$$\mathcal{D}(y) = \nabla y f(x,t) + \frac{1}{2} F(x,t)^\mathsf{T} \nabla^2 y F(x,t)$$

---

14 It can be written in full as

$$\mathcal{D}(y(x,s)) = \sum_{i=1}^{K} f_i(x,s)\frac{\partial y}{\partial x_i} + \frac{1}{2}\sum_{i=1}^{K}\sum_{j=1}^{K}[H(x,s)]_{ij}\frac{\partial^2 y}{\partial x_i \partial x_j}$$

where $H = FF^\mathsf{T}$.

It can be proven that

$$\mathcal{D}(y) + \frac{\partial y}{\partial t} = \lim_{s \to 0+} \frac{1}{s} \int_{\mathbb{R}^K} (y(x, t+s) - y(x, t)) P(t, x, t+s, dy)$$

where P is the transition density of X. The RHS of this expression represents the expected change of the function y between t and $t+s$, when s tends to zero. As a consequence, the Dynkin approximates the instantaneous expected change of the function y due to changes in the variables other than time.

If the process X is real-valued and there is a single Wiener process, so that both the drift and diffusion are real-valued, the Dynkin becomes

$$\mathcal{D}(y) = \frac{\partial y}{\partial x} f(x, s) + \frac{1}{2} \frac{\partial^2 y}{\partial x^2} F^2$$

In the strict Black-Scholes example, $X = S$ and the Dynkin is

$$\mathcal{D}(y) = \frac{\partial y}{\partial x} \mu S(t) + \frac{1}{2} \frac{\partial^2 y}{\partial x^2} S^2(t) \sigma^2$$

5.8   Conclusion

In this chapter, we have defined, in continuous time, continuous processes, and, among them, the separate classes of Itô and diffusion processes, Markov processes, Brownian motions, and Wiener processes. These are very natural tools to model financial prices. We have seen that a form of differential calculus applies to them. Differentials now include second derivatives.

Exercises

5.1. Verify that:

$$X(t) = X_0 e^{\left(\mu - \frac{\sigma^2}{2}\right)t + \sigma w(t)}$$

where $w(t)$ is a unidimensional Wiener process and $\mu \in \mathbb{R}$, $\sigma \in \mathbb{R}_{++}$, is the solution to:

$$dX(t) = \mu X(t) dt + \sigma X(t) dw(t), \quad X(0) \text{ given.}$$

Calculate: $\mathbb{E}[X(t)|X(0) = x_0]$.

5.2. Let f be a strictly positive function. Find a solution to

$$dY(t) = \tfrac{1}{2} f(Y(t)) f'(Y(t)) dt + f(Y(t)) dw(t)$$

where $Y(0) = y \in \mathbb{R}$, w is a unidimensional Wiener process.

5.3. Let $dX(t) = \mu(t) dt + \sigma(t) dw(t)$ where w is a unidimensional Wiener process. Consider a function $Y = f(X)$. Compute $dY(t)$ for the following functions:

    a. $Y = X^\alpha$

    b. $Y = \ln(X)$

    c. $Y = \exp(X)$

5.4. Develop the analog for stochastic calculus of the multiplication rule of ordinary calculus.

5.5. Consider two diffusion, unidimensional processes X and Y. Prove the integration-by-parts formula:

$$\int_0^t X(s)dY(s) = X(t)Y(t) - X(0)Y(0)$$

$$- \int_0^t Y(s)dX(s) - \int_0^t dX(s)dY(s)$$

Demonstrate also that, if the diffusion coefficients of the two processes, σ_X, σ_Y, are constant, the last integral is equal to $\sigma_X \sigma_Y t$.

5.6. Compute $dY(t)$ for the following function

$$Y(t) = f(w_1(t), w_2(t)) = \exp(\alpha w_1(t) + \beta w_2(t))$$

where $\alpha, \beta \in \mathbb{R}$, w_1 and w_2 are two unidimensional Wiener processes. Consider both the cases of independence and of correlated Wiener processes.

5.7. Consider the following two-dimensional stochastic process

$$Y(t) = \begin{bmatrix} w_1(t) + w_2(t) - w_1(t)w_3^2(t) \\ w_1^2(t)w_2(t) + w_2(t) - w_2(t)w_3(t) \end{bmatrix}$$

where w_1, w_2, and w_3 are three independent, unidimensional Wiener processes. Use the multidimensional Itô's formula to write the differential of the process $Y(t)$ in the standard form

$$dY(t) = a(w_1, w_2, w_3, t)dt + b(w_1, w_2, w_3, t)dw(t)$$

for suitable choices of $a \in \mathbb{R}^N$, $b \in \mathbb{R}^{N \times K}$ and dimensions $N = 2$ and $K = 3$.

6 Black-Scholes and Redundant Securities

As we have seen, discrete-time, complete-market economies have three important features:

- prices of redundant securities, including derivatives, can be obtained by replication, martingale measures, or hedging;
- prices of basic securities are in a one-to-one correspondence with state prices, captured by the relations $S = \Sigma \Phi$ and $\Phi = \Sigma^{-1} S$;
- given securities prices, state prices are unique and take the same value across all investors.

This chapter shows that the same results obtain also in continuous-time economies. With a single Wiener process, the market is complete when there are two securities: a stock, the price of which follows strict Black-Scholes dynamics, and a short-term bond. Then a derivative security is redundant and can be priced by arbitrage.[1]

We first set up the notation and spell out the assumptions on the prices for the stock and the bond, as well as the requirements on the derivative price. Sections 6.1, 6.2, and 6.3 examine pricing of derivative securities – specifically, a call option on the stock – by means of replication, martingale measures, and hedging. In section 6.4 we examine the cases in which the underlying or the option pay a dividend. In section 6.5 we show that the pricing technique can be safely extended to the case of a generalized Black-Scholes setting. Section 6.6 addresses the correspondence between securities prices and state prices. Section 6.7 is devoted to market prices of risk, defined as excess expected returns per unit of risk, where risk is measured by the diffusion coefficient of asset prices.[2]

Consider a finite horizon T and a *one*-dimensional Wiener process w together with its complete, natural filtration $\mathbf{F}^w$. On the probability space $(\Omega, \mathbf{F}^w)$ two securities are defined: a short-term bond or bank account and a non-dividend paying stock. They are the *marketed*

---

1 We discuss completeness and incompleteness in more detail in chapter 8.

2 Reminder: unless doing otherwise is necessary for comprehension, we simplify the notation for processes. All processes are stochastic but we suppress the reference to the state ω. Therefore, $X(t)$ actually means $X(\omega, t)$. In special cases, we also use the notation $f(t)$ to refer to a deterministic function of time. When this happens, we say so explicitly.

securities. The bond or bank deposit B returns an instantaneous, constant rate of interest r:

$$\frac{dB(t)}{B(t)} = r\,dt$$

At time t, the value of the bank account $B(t)$ is then given by $B(t) = B(0)\exp(rt)$, a deterministic function of time, not a stochastic process. A bond, or a "unit" of this bank deposit, is defined by setting its value at time 0 equal to one: $B(0) = 1$.

The stock – which is, more generally, an *underlying or primitive security* of any sort on which a derivative is written – has a price S that follows a *strict Black-Scholes process* with constant drift μ and diffusion coefficient $\sigma > 0$:

$$\frac{dS(t)}{S(t)} = \mu\,dt + \sigma\,dw(t) \tag{6.1}$$

A "unit" or a *share* of this underlying is defined by setting $S(0) = 1$. We know that the solution of (6.1) is explicit:

$$S(t) = S_0 e^{mt + \sigma w(t)} \tag{6.2}$$

where $m = \left(\mu - \sigma^2/2\right)$.

Trade between the two securities S and B is frictionless. Only adapted strategies are allowed. Self-financing requirements will be added and discussed in due course.

Our goal is to determine the price at any point in time $0 \le t \le T$ of a derivative written on the time-T value of one share of stock. For the sake of simplicity, we focus on a European-type call maturing at T, with strike $\mathcal{K}$. The choice of the call payoff instead of any other function of the time-T value of S is immaterial, as it was in chapter 2, and is made only for expositional concreteness. What is material is the fact that the derivative payoff depends exclusively on the value of the underlying at a single point in time and not on the history of its values up to that point. The method we apply here does not work and would have to be generalized when the derivative is path-dependent.

The price of the call (the right to buy one unit of the underlying for a strike price $\mathcal{K}$) is denoted C.

Below we obtain C equivalently by means of replication, martingale probabilities, and hedging. The *replicating* argument leads to a partial differential equation (PDE), which, when solved, provides a value C. The *martingale approach* instead provides directly a value C as an expected value, its form being, therefore, explicit. The *hedging argument*, which is the argument originally given by Black and Scholes, leads to a PDE, too. We are going to show that the solution to the pricing problem is identical for all methods. Before doing that, we show in small characters that the use of a unique Wiener process is not restrictive.

The fact that the Wiener process w is one-dimensional is not a restriction, as long as the drift and diffusion are constant, for the following reason. Suppose that the stock price depended on a K-dimensional Wiener process $\hat{w}(t)$ and $\hat{\sigma} \in \mathbb{R}^K$:

$$\frac{dS(t)}{S(t)} = \mu dt + \hat{\sigma}^{\mathsf{T}} d\hat{w}(t)$$

Then we could get the Euclidean norm of the diffusion vector

$$\sigma \triangleq \|\hat{\sigma}\| = \sqrt{\hat{\sigma}^{\mathsf{T}}\hat{\sigma}} \in \mathbb{R}$$

and – provided it is not zero – use it to define a one-dimensional Wiener process

$$dw(t) \triangleq \frac{1}{\sigma}\hat{\sigma}^{\mathsf{T}} d\hat{w}(t)$$

Observe that $\hat{\sigma}^{\mathsf{T}} d\hat{w}(t) = \sigma dw(t)$. By so doing, we have reduced the price dynamics to a single Wiener process

$$\frac{dS(t)}{S(t)} = \mu dt + \sigma dw(t)$$

The single Wiener process has the same measurability requirements so that the reduced stochastic process for S is stochastically equivalent to the original one. In this chapter we, therefore, think of the underlying security as being driven by a single Wiener process, at least in the strict-sense Black-Scholes case. More generally, the number of Wiener processes we specify is always the *minimum number* needed to describe the process, in the meaning of the reduction just seen.

6.1 Replicating-Portfolio Argument

6.1.1 Building the Black-Scholes PDE

The typical argument for pricing derivatives in accordance with the *Law of One Price* consists in finding a replicating portfolio for the derivative itself. The derivative will receive the same price as this portfolio. For the specific case of call options on an underlying that follows an Itô process, this argument has been developed by Merton (1977). Merton constructs a portfolio of the two marketed securities – a share S and the bank deposit B – that has the same terminal payoff as the option, and which, like the option, has zero interim cash inflows and outflows, that is, is self-financing.[3]

One imposes the self-financing restriction on the portfolio on the basis of an argument similar to the one adopted in discrete time (section 2.2.2). At time t, let the post-trade portfolio contain θ shares of stocks and α units of the bank deposit. Let both holdings depend at most on the current stock value and time: $\theta = \theta(S,t), \alpha = \alpha(S,t)$. The value of the portfolio is

$$V(S,t) = \theta(S,t) \times S(t) + \alpha(S,t) \times B(t) \tag{6.3}$$

---

3 The replicating portfolio argument does not require that the call be marketed. The call is synthetized via the replicating portfolio. The latter must be traded.

Further, suppose that θ and α are C^2 functions. Consider the LHS, V. A simple application of Itô's lemma tells us that the change in V over the next instant, measured through its differential, dV, is equal to

$$dV = \frac{\partial}{\partial S}V(S,t)dS + \frac{1}{2}\frac{\partial^2}{\partial S^2}V(S,t)\sigma^2 S^2 dt + \frac{\partial}{\partial t}V(S,t)dt \qquad (6.4)$$

A similar application of Itô's lemma to the RHS, $\theta \times S + b \times B$, recognizes that it changes when prices or quantities do:

$$d(\theta S + \alpha B) = \theta \times dS + \alpha \times dB + d\theta \times (S + dS) + d\alpha \times (B + dB)$$

In view of the last expression, the change in V can be conceptually separated into two parts.[4] The first stems from pure portfolio gains, dG, and is given by the price changes on the time-t positions:

$$dG = \theta \times dS + \alpha \times dB \qquad (6.5)$$

The second part, $dV - dG$, is the cash flow from changes in quantities of assets, obtained from buying and selling securities:

$$dV - dG = d\theta \times (S + dS) + d\alpha \times (B + dB)$$

The post-trade number of shares in the portfolio being $\theta(S,t)$ at time t, the portfolio is adjusted next from θ to $\theta + d\theta$ at time $t + dt$, at which the price $S + dS$ prevails. Indeed, the formula reflects time $t + dt$ prices.

We are now ready to formalize the self-financing condition as the requirement that the change in V due to securities trading, $dV - dG$, is equal to zero:

$$dV - dG = 0 \qquad (6.6)$$

Substituting the expressions for dV obtained from Itô's lemma, (6.4) and the definition of dG (6.5), the self-financing condition becomes

$$dV - dG = \frac{\partial}{\partial S}V(S,t)(\mu(t)S(t)dt + \sigma(t)S(t)dw(t))$$

$$+\frac{1}{2}\frac{\partial^2}{\partial S^2}V(S,t)\sigma^2 S^2 dt + \frac{\partial}{\partial t}V(S,t)dt$$

$$-(\theta \times \mu(t)S(t)dt + \theta \times \sigma(t)S(t)dw(t) + \alpha \times rB(t)dt) = 0$$

Collecting terms and suppressing their dependence on time for notational simplicity, we have

$$\left[\left(\frac{\partial}{\partial S}V(S,t) - \theta\right)\mu S + \frac{1}{2}\frac{\partial^2}{\partial S^2}V(S,t)\sigma^2 S^2 + \frac{\partial}{\partial t}V(S,t) - r\alpha B\right]dt$$

$$+\left(\frac{\partial}{\partial S}V(S,t) - \theta\right)\sigma S dw = 0 \qquad (6.7)$$

---

4 See Merton (1982).

For equality to zero, both the diffusion and drift coefficients must be equal to zero. Consider first the random term:

$$\left(\frac{\partial}{\partial S}V(S,t) - \theta\right)\sigma S dw \tag{6.8}$$

It is zero if and only if the number of stocks in the replicating portfolio θ is set equal to the derivative of the value of the portfolio with respect to the underlying:

$$\theta = \frac{\partial}{\partial S}V(S,t) \tag{6.9}$$

The implied number of bonds α is

$$\alpha = \frac{V - \theta S}{B} = \frac{V - \frac{\partial}{\partial S}V(S,t)S}{B}$$

Consider then the drift term. Substituting for θ, α and canceling terms, the drift can be written as:

$$\frac{1}{2}\frac{\partial^2}{\partial S^2}V(S,t)\sigma^2 S^2 + \frac{\partial}{\partial t}V(S,t) - rV + \frac{\partial}{\partial S}V(S,t)Sr$$

The *self-financing condition* (8.5) then boils down to the following equation, called the *Black-Scholes PDE*:[5]

$$\frac{\partial}{\partial S}V(S,t)rS + \frac{1}{2}\frac{\partial^2}{\partial S^2}V(S,t)\sigma^2 S^2 + \frac{\partial}{\partial t}V(S,t) = rV(S,t) \tag{6.10}$$

We have thus proved the following

Proposition 6.1 *Any self-financing portfolio made up of the stock and the bank deposit, whose weights are twice differentiable functions of the stock price and time, has a value given by a function V(S,t) that satisfies the Black-Scholes PDE (6.10). If this equation has a solution, there exists a self-financing portfolio that replicates the option, and whose value is the option value:*

$$V(S,t) = \theta(S,t) \times S(t) + \alpha(S,t) \times B(t) = C(S,t) \tag{6.11}$$

It is characterized by

$$\begin{cases} \theta(S,t) = \frac{\partial V}{\partial S} = \frac{\partial C}{\partial S} \\ \alpha(S,t) = \frac{V - \frac{\partial V}{\partial S} \times S(t)}{B} \end{cases} \tag{6.12}$$

The numbers of stocks and bonds in the replicating portfolio have the same interpretation that they had in discrete-time (section 2.2.6): the number of shares of stock is the ratio of the change in the derivative price to the underlying price, while the number of bonds serves to make the portfolio self-financing.

If, in addition, we impose that $V(S,T) = [S(T) - \mathcal{K}]^+$, the self-financing portfolio replicates the option at the terminal date. Hence the two functions $C(S,t)$ and $V(S,t)$ must

---

5 The fact that the Black-Scholes PDE is a self-financing condition has been emphasized by He and Leland (1993) as well as Cox and Leland (2000).

coincide at any time and for any stock value. From the PDE point of view, we are asking that the function C satisfy the Black-Scholes PDE (6.10)

$$\frac{\partial}{\partial S} C(S(t), t) r S(t) + \frac{1}{2} \frac{\partial^2}{\partial S^2} C(S(t), t) \sigma^2 S^2(t) + \frac{\partial}{\partial t} C(S(t), t) = r C(S(t), t) \qquad (6.13)$$

together with its final condition $C(S, T) = [S(T) - \mathcal{K}]^+$. This is called a terminal-value problem.

Remark 6.1 *An important feature of equation (6.13) is that the expected rate of return μ of the underlying stock price appears neither in it, nor in its terminal condition. It has cancelled in the course of the derivation of (6.10). As a consequence, the option price, for a given value S of the underlying, is independent of the stock drift.*

Remark 6.2 *Note that the underlying and the call are perfectly correlated, because the latter is a (deterministic) function of the former and time.*

If we use the definition of the Dynkin or differential operator of the function $C(S, t)$, we can write the Black-Scholes PDE in a synthetic, suggestive way. It is, indeed, easy to recognize that the Black-Scholes PDE (6.13) can be written as

$$\mathcal{D}^*(C) + \frac{\partial C}{\partial t} = rC$$

where $\mathcal{D}^*$ is the Dynkin operator with the drift of S set at rS (see section 5.7). This tells us that, if the return on the underlying were equal to the riskless rate, the expected return on the call would also be equal to the riskless return.

For another application of the Dynkin operator, see exercise 6.1.

6.1.2 Solving the Black-Scholes PDE

There are at least two ways in which we can write explicitly the solution of the Black-Scholes PDE.

When the underlying price follows strict-sense Black-Scholes dynamics, the solution of the terminal-value problem exists, is unique and can be written in terms of the five variable and parameters $S(t), \sigma, T, \mathcal{K}, r$. Observe that the PDE (6.13) has constant coefficients. This PDE, together with its boundary condition, can be transformed into the heat equation of Physics. It admits a closed-form solution.

Proposition 6.2 *If the underlying price follows a Geometric Brownian motion, as in the strict-sense Black-Scholes model, the European call price, which solves (6.13) with the boundary condition $C(S, T) = [S(T) - \mathcal{K}]^+$, is*

$$C(S, t) = S \times N(d_1) - e^{-r(T-t)} \mathcal{K} \times N(d_2) \qquad (6.14)$$

where $N(\cdot)$ is the standard Gaussian cumulative distribution function, d_1 and d_2 are defined as

$$d_1 \triangleq \frac{\log\left(\frac{S}{\mathcal{K}}\right) + \left(r + \frac{\sigma^2}{2}\right)(T-t)}{\sigma\sqrt{T-t}}$$

$$d_2 \triangleq d_1 - \sigma\sqrt{T-t}$$

and $S = S(t)$.

There exists another way of writing the solution, which is more intuitive. Let $\mathbf{1}_{\{A\}}$ be the indicator function of the event A.

Proposition 6.3   *The solution (6.14) is also the discounted expectation of the final payoff of the option*

$$C(S,t) = \exp(-r(T-t))\mathbb{E}^*\left[[S(T) - \mathcal{K}]^+\right] \tag{6.15}$$
$$= \exp(-r(T-t))\left\{\mathbb{E}^*\left[S(T) \times \mathbf{1}_{\{S(T)>\mathcal{K}\}}\right] - \mathcal{K} \times \mathbb{E}^*\left[\mathbf{1}_{\{S(T)>\mathcal{K}\}}\right]\right\}$$

provided that the expected value $\mathbb{E}^*$ is calculated relative to a modified process for S:

$$\frac{dS(t)}{S(t)} = rdt + \sigma dw^*(t) \tag{6.16}$$

where w^* is a new Wiener process.[6]

Formula (6.15) is actually a special form of the Feynman-Kac formula, which we prove below in section 6.5. This expectation formulation corresponds to the one that we obtained as (2.25) in discrete-time. In the next sections we are going to call the modified process the "risk-neutral process" for S, because, as we argued at length in discrete time, a return equal to the riskless rate is the one that S would have in a world that would be populated by risk-neutral investors. The Black-Scholes formula for the solution of (6.13) will be equally valid under the martingale and hedging reasonings. Formula (6.15) can be proven using properties of Brownian motions and exponentials of Gaussian random variables.

Please note that – thanks to the properties of the Gaussian distribution – the solution we found is C^2, as assumed. In the last section of this chapter we will compute the derivatives of the call price with respect to the underlying up to the second order, calling them "delta" and "gamma." The reader will be able to verify their continuity in S.

6.2   Martingale-Pricing Argument

This section solves the call pricing problem using a process that makes the prices of traded securities martingales. This process, denoted ξ, will play a major role in the next chapters.

---

6 For the change of Wiener process, see the next chapter.

ξ is the product of usual discounting $1/B$ for the time value of money and of a change η to a martingale measure. Consistently with our approach in discrete time, we then call this a martingale-pricing approach. We recognize that the result coincides with the one obtained via replication.

Start by recalling that, for our stock, σ^{-1} exists since $\sigma > 0$. We can, therefore, define a "market price of risk" (which, in this one-dimensional case, is also a Sharpe ratio) as follows:

$$\kappa \triangleq \frac{\mu - r}{\sigma} \in \mathbb{R}$$

Define a process, called an exponential martingale, as follows:

$$\eta(t) \triangleq \exp\left[-\frac{1}{2}\int_0^t \kappa^2 ds - \int_0^t \kappa\, dw(s)\right]$$

We show that η plays the role that the change of measure $\eta(s,t)$ of chapter 2 (or $\eta(j, n-j)$ of section 2.2.6) played in discrete time. After introducing that factor on top of discounting for the interest rate by dividing by $B(t)$, the stock price becomes a martingale. To show that, call $\xi(t)$ the ratio $\eta(t)/B(t)$ and observe that, since

$$\frac{d\eta(t)}{\eta(t)} = -\kappa\, dw(t)$$

Itô's lemma gives as a differential of ξ

$$\frac{d\xi(t)}{\xi(t)} = -rdt - \kappa\, dw(t) \tag{6.17}$$

At the same time, observe that the initial value $\xi(0)$ of ξ is equal to 1, because both η and B take the value 1 at time 0. Now apply Itô's lemma to the product of ξ and the risky-security price. We get

$$d[\xi(t)S(t)] = \xi(t)S(t) \times (\sigma - \kappa) \times dw(t)$$

which says that the product $\xi \times S$ has a diffusion equal to $\xi S(\sigma - \kappa)$ and a drift equal to 0. It is a local martingale. Consider the bond price discounted the same way:

$$d[\xi(t)B(t)] = -\xi(t)B(t)\kappa\, dw(t)$$

So, ξ makes both the bond and the stock local martingales. In the Black-Scholes model, because a regularity condition to be introduced in chapter 8 below (called the Novikov condition) is satisfied, both securities are martingales and not just local martingales. If it were traded, the call price would be a martingale too, after multiplication by ξ. Otherwise, arbitrage opportunities would exist. We have

$$\xi(t)B(t) = \mathbb{E}_t[\xi(T)B(T)]$$
$$\xi(t)S(t) = \mathbb{E}_t[\xi(T)S(T)]$$
$$\xi(t)C(t) = \mathbb{E}_t\big[\xi(T)[S(T) - \mathcal{K}]^+\big]$$

Substituting for $\xi(t)$ and $\xi(T)$ in the last expression and simplifying, the martingale property of the call gives the option price straight away, as an expectation:

$$C(S,t) = \mathbb{E}\left\{ e^{-r(T-t)-\frac{1}{2}\int_t^T \kappa^2 ds - \int_t^T \kappa dw(s)} \times [S(T) - \mathcal{K}]^+ | S(t) = S \right\} \qquad (6.18)$$

Since the drift and volatility parameters and, therefore, the price of risk, are constant, the last expectation is easy to compute. It gives back the call price (6.14). The martingale approach then provides the value of the option directly, without writing a PDE and solving it.

We now have two values for the option, obtained via replication and martingale reasonings, namely (6.15) and (6.18). Both give back the Black-Scholes formula.

To summarize, using the exponential martingale we have developed a method that works in two steps:

1. Identify a discount factor from the riskless rate and the risk premium on the stock, as we did when defining ξ;

2. Get the value of the option as the expectation of the payoff translated via the exponential martingale, in the form (6.18), and recognize that that is equivalent to the more palatable form (6.15).

6.3   Hedging-Portfolio Argument

The original demonstration of the Black-Scholes PDE was given by Black and Scholes (1973) using a hedging, instead of a replicating, argument. We first price the option, then show how the hedging solution coincides with the replicating and martingale ones.

In the hedging approach, we assume that the call is traded and that its price depends at most on the underlying stock value and on time, $C = C(S,t)$, and we look for functions C that are C^2. We construct a portfolio of the share S and the option C that is instantaneously riskless, exactly as we did in section 2.2.6 for the discrete-time binomial model. Following Black and Scholes (1973), we impose that it *return the riskless rate of interest*. We get once again the Black-Scholes PDE.

Let the portfolio contain one option, written on one share, and $h(S,t)$ shares of stock. The value of the portfolio is

$$V_h(s,t) = C(S,t) + h(S,t) \times S(t)$$

In the absence of dividends, the *gains on the portfolio*, during a small period of time dt, are

$$dG_h = dC(S,t) + h(S,t) \times dS(t) \qquad (6.19)$$

Assuming that C is of class C^2, we know from Itô's lemma that the differential of the call is

$$dC(S,t) = \frac{\partial}{\partial S}C(S,t)dS + \frac{1}{2}\frac{\partial^2}{\partial S^2}C(S,t)\sigma(S,t)^2 S^2 dt + \frac{\partial}{\partial t}C(S,t)dt \qquad (6.20)$$

This, together with the SDE for S, implies that the gains differential on the hedging portfolio is

$$dG_h = \frac{\partial}{\partial S}C(S,t)[\mu(t)S(t)dt + \sigma(t)S(t)dw(t)]$$

$$+\frac{1}{2}\frac{\partial^2}{\partial S^2}C(S,t)\sigma(S,t)^2S^2dt + \frac{\partial}{\partial t}C(S,t)dt$$

$$+h(S,t)\times[\mu(t)S(t)dt + \sigma(t)S(t)dw(t)]$$

Collecting the random terms in the last expression we get

$$\left[\frac{\partial}{\partial S}C(S,t) + h(S,t)\right]\sigma(S,t)S(t)dw(t)$$

If we choose the number of shares to be

$$h(S,t) = -\frac{\partial}{\partial S}C(S,t) \tag{6.21}$$

the coefficients of the random part of dG_h vanish and we have:

$$dG_h = \left[\frac{1}{2}\frac{\partial^2}{\partial S^2}C(S,t)\sigma(S,t)^2S^2 + \frac{\partial}{\partial t}C(S,t)\right]dt$$

Gains are riskless! If we further suppose that the hedging portfolio is self-financing,[7] then $dV_h = dG_h$ and also V_h is instantaneously riskless. Because of the Law of One Price, it must then return the instantaneous rate of interest:

$$\frac{dV_h}{V_h} = \frac{\frac{1}{2}\frac{\partial^2}{\partial S^2}C(S,t)\sigma^2S^2 + \frac{\partial}{\partial t}C(S,t)}{C(S,t) + h(S,t)\times S(t)}dt = rdt \tag{6.22}$$

Canceling and collecting terms we get again the Black-Scholes PDE (6.13).

This equation must be solved under the terminal condition: $C(S,T) = [S(T) - \mathcal{K}]^+$. As an application of the Feynman-Kac formula, we can again state that the solution to this equation is the Black-Scholes formula (6.14) above.

We have obtained the same price as we did with the replication and martingale arguments. However, in contrast to the previous methods, the hedging argument has two weaknesses, on which we comment now.

———————————— ♠ ————————————

The hedging argument is weak on two counts. First, the call is assumed to be traded, whereas previously we only had to be able to replicate it.

Second, the portfolio $V_h = C + hS$ may not be self-financing. While writing the equation for its rate of return (6.22), we ignored any potential cash flows along the way, assuming, but not proving, that V_h is self-financing. Is this a problem? A priori yes, since the cash inflows (if positive) or outflows (if negative) of V_h are equal to:

$$S \times dh + dh \times dS$$

———————————————

7 See below the discussion of this issue, in small characters.

or

$$-S\left\{\frac{\partial^2}{\partial S^2}C(S,t)dS + \frac{1}{2}\frac{\partial^3}{\partial S^3}C(S,t)\sigma^2 S^2 dt + \frac{\partial^2}{\partial t \partial S}C(S,t)dt\right\}$$
$$-\frac{\partial^2}{\partial S^2}C(S,t)\sigma^2 S^2 dt \tag{6.23}$$

and this expression may not be equal to zero. How then did Black and Scholes, in their original 1973 article, not get an incorrect result? The reason is that, even though some cash flows come in and out of the hedging portfolio, their expected value under the risk-neutral process (6.16) is equal to zero. Indeed, consider the conditional expected value of (6.23)

$$-S\left\{\frac{\partial}{\partial S}\left[\frac{\partial}{\partial S}C(S,t)\right]rSdt + \frac{1}{2}\frac{\partial^2}{\partial S^2}\left[\frac{\partial}{\partial S}C(S,t)\right]\sigma^2 S^2 dt\right.$$
$$\left.+\frac{\partial}{\partial t}\left[\frac{\partial}{\partial S}C(S,t)\right]dt\right\} - \frac{\partial}{\partial S}\left[\frac{\partial}{\partial S}C(S,t)\right]\sigma^2 S^2 dt \tag{6.24}$$

and consider also that the Black-Scholes PDE (6.13) holds as an identity for all values of S, so that its derivative with respect to S is also a valid equality:[8]

$$\frac{\partial^2}{\partial S^2}C(S(t),t)rS(t) + \frac{1}{2}\frac{\partial^3}{\partial S^3}C(S(t),t)\sigma^2 S^2(t)$$
$$+\frac{\partial^2}{\partial S^2}C(S(t),t)\sigma^2 S(t) + \frac{\partial}{\partial t}\frac{\partial}{\partial S}C(S(t),t) = 0$$

This last equality says that (6.24) is equal to zero. So, the hedging portfolio for the strict-Black-Scholes case is self-financing, in an expected value sense.[9] This solves an issue we left pending in section 2.2.6.

6.3.1   Comparing the Arguments: Intuition

The three approaches listed so far bring us to the same price. That is not surprising, not only because they provided the same result for any security already in discrete time, but also in the light of the following, heuristic reasoning, due to Cox and Ross (1976).

An arbitrage opportunity is such for any investor, irrespective of his risk aversion. Similarly, if the rule of absence of arbitrage places a restriction on the prices of two assets, that restriction must be identical from the standpoint of any investor whatever be his risk aversion. If we want to obtain a relationship between the price of an option and the price of its underlying security, it is easiest to do that, as a thought experiment, for the case of a risk-neutral investor. Whether he actually exists or not, we know that such an investor *would require* from all securities the same expected rate of return, namely, the riskless rate. Accordingly, for him the underlying price *would abide* by the SDE (6.16) and he would

---

8 It is actually the PDE for the delta ($\delta_C \triangleq \partial C/\partial S$) of the option. See also sections 6.8 and 13.2.5.

9 It could be self-financing, if we allowed also the number of calls to vary at each point in time. We thank Patrice Poncet for having pointed this out.

price every security by its expected payoff discounted at the riskless rate. His price for the option would, therefore, be given by (6.15).

Any population of risk-averse investors trading in the market will price *both* the underlying and the option differently from the way a risk-neutral investor would price them (unless there actually is a risk neutral investor in the market, for he will impose his view) but, taking as given the stochastic process of the underlying, if we focus on the *relation* between the underlying price and the option price that will prevail in that market, we have to consider that it will be identical to the one a risk-neutral investor would impose.

6.4 Extensions: Dividends

This section shows how the Black-Scholes PDE can be generalized to the case in which the underlying or the option themselves pay dividends. This prepares the reader to the appropriate modification when valuing and optimizing in the presence of consumption and dividends, in more general continuous-time contexts such as those of chapter 9, where the self-financing condition will morph into a budget constraint.

6.4.1 Dividend Paid on the Underlying

Consider again the strict Black-Scholes case, but with the underlying paying a dividend continuously, at the constant rate ι. The stock price process is

$$dS(t) = [\mu S(t) - \iota]\, dt + \sigma S(t) dw$$

Using short hand for partial derivatives and suppressing arguments, the PDE for the corresponding non-dividend protected European call will be shown to be

$$\frac{\partial C}{\partial t}(S,t) + (rS - \iota)\frac{\partial C}{\partial S}(S,t) + \frac{1}{2}\sigma^2 S^2 \frac{\partial^2 C}{\partial S^2}(S,t) = rC(S,t) \qquad (6.25)$$

which differs from the one in the absence of dividends only in that the risk-neutralized drift on the underlying is reduced by the dividend rate (note that here we use the index for partial derivatives, too). Defining the Dynkin as

$$\mathcal{D}^*(C) = (rS - \iota)\frac{\partial C}{\partial S}(S,t) + \frac{1}{2}\sigma^2 S^2 \frac{\partial^2 C}{\partial S^2}(S,t)$$

the PDE remains

$$\mathcal{D}^*(C) + \frac{\partial C}{\partial t}(S,t) = rC(S,t)$$

This is true because the option is not dividend protected: dividends accrue to the owner of the underlying but not to the owner of the option.

To prove this, we use the replication argument. Let the replicating portfolio contain θ shares of stocks and α units of the riskless security. The value of the portfolio at time t is:

$$V(t) = \theta(t) \times S(t) + \alpha(t) \times B(t) \qquad (6.26)$$

and its differential is

$$dV = Sd\theta + \theta dS + d\theta \times dS + \alpha dB + Bd\alpha + d\alpha \times dB$$

The self-financing condition in replicating this portfolio at time $t + dt$ says, as usual, that the price of the portfolio purchased at $t + dt$ must equal the total worth at $t + dt$ of the portfolio purchased at t, or that the uses of wealth must equal the sources of wealth:

$$(\theta + d\theta)(S + dS) + (\alpha + d\alpha)(B + dB) = \theta(S + dS) + \theta\iota dt + \alpha(B + dB)$$

Expanding and subtracting V from both sides, we reach the following equality constraint (both sides of which stand for dV):

$$\theta dS + d\theta(S + dS) + \alpha dB + d\alpha(B + dB) = \theta dS + \theta\iota dt + \alpha dB$$

Equivalently,

$$dV - \theta dS - \alpha dB = \theta\iota dt$$

This equation guarantees that the dividend is fully reinvested:

$$\theta\iota dt = d\theta(S + dS) + d\alpha(B + dB)$$

and no cash flow goes in or out of the portfolio.

Consider only the portfolios that are functions of S and t: $\theta(S, t)$; $\alpha(S, t)$, so that the value of the portfolio is also a function of S and t only: $V(S, t)$. Applying Itô's lemma, we have

$$dV = \frac{\partial}{\partial S}V(S, t)dS + \frac{1}{2}\frac{\partial^2}{\partial S^2}V(S, t)\sigma^2 S^2 dt + \frac{\partial}{\partial t}V(S, t)dt$$

Hence

$$dV - (\theta dS + \alpha dB) = \frac{\partial}{\partial S}V(S, t)dS + \frac{1}{2}\frac{\partial^2}{\partial S^2}V(S, t)\sigma^2 S^2 dt$$

$$+ \frac{\partial}{\partial t}V(S, t)dt - (\theta dS + \alpha dB)$$

For this to be equal to $\theta\iota dt$, the random term must be equal to zero and the expected value must be equal to $\theta\iota dt$. First, the random term:

$$\frac{\partial}{\partial S}V(S, t) - \theta = 0 \tag{6.27}$$

Then, the expected value (we substitute (6.26) and (6.27)):

$$\frac{\partial}{\partial S}V(S, t)(\mu S - \iota) + \frac{1}{2}\frac{\partial^2}{\partial S^2}V(S, t)\sigma^2 S^2 + \frac{\partial}{\partial t}V(S, t)$$

$$- \frac{\partial}{\partial S}V(S, t)(\mu S - \iota) - \frac{V(S, t) - \frac{\partial}{\partial S}V(S, t)S}{B}rB = \frac{\partial}{\partial S}V(S, t)\iota$$

Cancelling and collecting terms, we get the appropriate PDE for the replicating portfolio V:

$$\frac{\partial}{\partial t}V(S, t) + \frac{\partial}{\partial S}V(S, t)(rS - \iota) + \frac{1}{2}\frac{\partial^2}{\partial S^2}V(S, t)\sigma^2 S^2 = rV(S, t) \tag{6.28}$$

or, with the appropriate definition of the Dynkin:

$$\mathcal{D}^*(V) = (rS - \iota)\frac{\partial V}{\partial S}(S, t) + \frac{1}{2}\sigma^2 S^2 \frac{\partial^2 V}{\partial S^2}(S, t)$$

the PDE remains

$$\mathcal{D}^*(V) + \frac{\partial V}{\partial t}(S, t) = rV(S, t)$$

Since the portfolio replicates the option, as we know, (6.28) is also the PDE – or *self-financing condition* – for the call.

6.4.2   Dividend Paid on the Option

Consider now the case in which the option, not the underlying, pays a dividend yield. We use the replication argument again. Let the replicating portfolio contain θ shares of stocks and α units of the bond. The value of the portfolio is $V = \theta \times S + \alpha \times B$ as above. Again, distinguish the change in value of the portfolio from the financial gains, $dG = \theta dS + \alpha dB$. The difference $dV - dG$ is the cash flow from buying and selling securities. Differently from above, we want to impose that this is equal to $-\iota dt$, since this is the dividend on the option, whose value must coincide with the replicating portfolio one, $V = C$. Stated otherwise, we want to impose that the gains from the replicating portfolio are its change in value plus dividends: $dG = dV + \iota dt$. Applying Itô's lemma, we obtain:

$$dV = \frac{\partial}{\partial S}V(S, t)dS + \frac{1}{2}\frac{\partial^2}{\partial S^2}V(S, t)\sigma^2 S^2 dt + \frac{\partial}{\partial t}V(S, t)dt$$

Hence:

$$dV - (\theta dS + \alpha dB) = \frac{\partial}{\partial S}V(S, t)dS$$

$$+ \frac{1}{2}\frac{\partial^2}{\partial S^2}V(S, t)\sigma^2 S^2 dt$$

$$+ \frac{\partial}{\partial t}V(S, t)dt - (\theta dS + \alpha dB)$$

For this to be equal to $-\iota dt$, the random term must be equal to zero and the expected value must be equal to $-\iota dt$. First, the random term:

$$\frac{\partial}{\partial S}V(S, t) - \theta = 0 \tag{6.29}$$

Then, the expected value (we substitute $V = \theta S + \alpha B$ and (6.29)) is

$$\frac{\partial}{\partial S}V(S, t)\mu S + \frac{1}{2}\frac{\partial^2}{\partial S^2}V(S, t)\sigma^2 S^2 + \frac{\partial}{\partial t}V(S, t)$$

$$- \frac{\partial}{\partial S}V(S, t)\mu S - \frac{V(S, t) - \frac{\partial}{\partial S}V(S, t)S}{B}rB = -\iota$$

Cancelling and collecting terms, we get the PDE for V:

$$\mathcal{D}^*(V) + \frac{\partial V}{\partial t}(S, t) = rV(S, t) - \iota$$

where now

$$\mathcal{D}^*(V) = rS\frac{\partial V}{\partial S}(S, t) + \frac{1}{2}\sigma^2 S^2 \frac{\partial^2 V}{\partial S^2}(S, t)$$

This is also the PDE for C. As expected, it is the risk-neutral return on the call that is now reduced by the amount of dividends.

6.5 Extensions: A Partially Generalized Black-Scholes Model

The generalized Black-Scholes price model, which we will analyze in depth in chapter 8, is characterized by N stocks, the prices of which still follow an Itô process. But the number of Wiener processes can be different from the number of stocks; the drift, diffusion, and the interest rate can be neither constant nor even deterministic. Here we take a partially generalized Black-Scholes model, in that we consider only one stock and, for reasons that will be clear in chapter 8, we assume that its price is driven by a single Brownian motion. The stock process follows the Itô process:

$$dS(t) = \mu(S, t)dt + \sigma(S, t)dw(t) \tag{6.30}$$

where μ is the expected consumption-unit, or absolute, return

$$\mu(S, t) : \mathbb{R} \times [0, T] \to \mathbb{R}$$

σ is the vector of instantaneous volatilities

$$\sigma(S, t) : \mathbb{R} \times [0, T] \to \mathbb{R}$$

w is a one-dimensional Wiener process and $\mathbf{F}^w$ its filtration, $S(0) = 1$. We assume that the volatility of the stock is not necessarily constant, but it depends on its current value and time at most, $\sigma(t) = \sigma(S(t), t)$, and that *the rate of interest is a deterministic function of time*. We claim that the pricing devices given above are still valid, and the call price is unique under some restrictions (to be elicited in chapter 8), which make the market complete.

6.5.1 Replicating-Portfolio Argument

The reasoning conducted in section 6.1 above, which led us to equation (6.10), is still valid, with the stochastic diffusion and $r = r(t)$. The solution of the PDE requires the use of the general Feynman-Kac formula, and generalizes the strict-Black-Scholes case, exactly as (2.19) in the discrete-time environment was the generalized version of the call option price in (2.25):

Proposition 6.4 (Feynman-Kac formula) *In the generalized case, a solution of (6.10) under the boundary condition $C(S,T) = [S(T) - \mathcal{K}]^+$ can be written explicitly as:*

$$C(S,t) = e^{-\int_t^T r(s)ds} \mathbb{E}_t^* \{ [S(T) - \mathcal{K}]^+ \} \tag{6.31}$$

$$= e^{-\int_t^T r(s)ds} \{ \mathbb{E}_t^* [S(T) \mathbf{1}_{\{S_T > \mathcal{K}\}}] - \mathcal{K} \mathbb{E}_t^* [\mathbf{1}_{\{S(T) > \mathcal{K}\}}] \}$$

provided only that the expected value $\mathbb{E}_t^*$ is calculated relative to a modified, risk-neutral process for S:

$$\frac{dS(t)}{S(t)} = r(t)dt + \sigma(S,t)dw(t)$$

A quite obvious remark is that the Black-Scholes formula does not provide the value of the call any more.

---♠---

The proof of the Feynman-Kac formula is as follows.

Proof. For a given $S(t) \in \mathbb{R}$, one can define the process $X(u)$ as the solution of

$$X(u) = S(t) + \int_t^u r(s)X(s)ds + \int_t^u \sigma(s)X(s)dw(s)$$

and observe that $X(t) = S(t)$. Let us apply Itô' lemma to $e^{-\int_t^s r(u)du} C(X(s),s)$:

$$e^{-\int_t^T r(s)ds} C(X(T),T) = C(X(t),t)$$

$$+ \int_t^T e^{-\int_t^s r(s)ds} \left[\frac{\partial}{\partial X} C(X(s),s)r(s)X(s)ds \right.$$

$$+ \frac{1}{2} \frac{\partial^2}{\partial X^2} C(X(s),s)\sigma(s)^2(X(s))^2 + \frac{\partial}{\partial s} C(X(s),s) - r(s)C(X(s),s) \right] ds$$

$$+ \int_t^T \frac{\partial}{\partial X} e^{-\int_t^s r(s)ds} C(X(s),s)\sigma(s)X(s)dw(s)$$

Let $C(S,t)$ be a solution of the Black-Scholes PDE, with the coefficients appropriate to this case, under the terminal condition $C(S,T) = [X(T) - \mathcal{K}]^+$. The content of the square brackets is null and the last expression turns into

$$e^{-\int_t^T r(s)ds} [X(T) - \mathcal{K}]^+ = C(S,t)$$

$$+ \int_t^T \frac{\partial}{\partial X} e^{-\int_t^s r(s)ds} C(X(s),s)\sigma(s)X(s)dw(s)$$

Taking the expectation on both sides we get exactly the representation for C we were searching for:

$$e^{-\int_t^T r(s)ds} \mathbb{E}^* \{ [X(T) - \mathcal{K}]^+ | S(t) = S \} = C(X(t),t) = C(S(t),t)$$

$\square$

6.5.2   Martingale-Pricing Argument

The reasoning we adopted in section 6.2 above holds also in the generalized case, and an appropriately modified version of formula (6.18) – which takes into account non-constant values for r and κ – still provides the option price. The price, thanks to proposition 8.1 in chapter 8, will be recognized to be the same as the one obtained with the replication argument, (6.31).

6.5.3   Hedging Argument

The hedging argument in section 6.3 above applies to the generalized case, leads to equation (6.10) modified in order to take into account that σ is stochastic and $r = r(t)$, and therefore the solution of the PDE is again (6.31). With the hedging argument, the call price can be recognized to be the same as with the replication argument straight away, since they solve the same PDE.

It is then true that, in the generalized Black-Scholes case as well, the option prices provided by the three methodologies are equal.

The reader can now solve exercise 6.2, which extends the above arguments to the case in which there is an additional state variable, and exercise 6.3, which discusses a case in which the interest rate is stochastic.

6.6   Implied Probabilities

In discrete-time, and in particular in one-period economies, we know that, provided markets are complete, risk-neutral probabilities and state prices can be obtained from any basket of basic security prices, and vice versa. What matters is to start from a basket of securities with linearly independent payoffs. Indeed, provided that the payoff matrix is non-singular, the relation $\Phi = \Sigma^{-1}S$ provides state prices, which can then be normalized into risk-neutral probabilities.

In all the methods for setting European option prices that we presented for the strict-Black-Scholes case and then extended to the general case, the process for the underlying is an input, while the value of the derivative, and consequently its dynamics, is an output. This section shows how to reverse the process, that is, how to go from the derivative price to the distribution of the underlying at a specific point in time, in the general Black-Scholes case. The expectation representation, following the Feynman-Kac approach in section 6.5, allows us to reconstruct the risk-neutral distribution of the underlying.

If one assumes, as we do in this chapter, that the underlying is driven by a single Wiener process, there is indeed a straightforward way to back out the density of the underlying price at T from the price of derivative securities. It is customary to refer to the probability density so obtained as being *implied* in the valuation of derivatives. We call it also the risk-neutral density, and denote it as p^*, its distribution being P^*.

Let us write the expectation in the call price in terms of the distribution function of the underlying at time T, $P^*(x)$, conditional on the time-t price. For simplicity, let the riskless rate be equal to zero and set $t = 0$:

$$
\begin{aligned}
C(S,t) &= \mathbb{E}^* \left\{ [S(T) - \mathcal{K}]^+ | S(t) = S \right\} \\
&= \int_0^{+\infty} (x - \mathcal{K})^+ dP^*(x) \\
&= \int_{\mathcal{K}}^{+\infty} x dP^*(x) - \mathcal{K} \int_0^{+\infty} dP^*(x) \\
&= \int_{\mathcal{K}}^{+\infty} x dP^*(x) - \mathcal{K}\left(1 - P^*(\mathcal{K})\right)
\end{aligned}
$$

If we now take the derivative twice with respect to $\mathcal{K}$, we get

$$
\frac{\partial C}{\partial \mathcal{K}} = -\mathcal{K}p^*(\mathcal{K}) - 1 + P^*(\mathcal{K}) + \mathcal{K}p^*(\mathcal{K})
$$

$$
\frac{\partial^2 C}{\partial \mathcal{K}^2} = p^*(\mathcal{K})
$$

By repeating the exercise when $\mathcal{K}$ runs over the support of S, we get the whole density of the underlying as

$$
p^*(x) = \left. \frac{\partial^2 C}{\partial \mathcal{K}^2} \right|_{\mathcal{K}=x}
$$

With a zero interest rate, this risk-neutral probability density is also the Arrow-Debreu price density of the event $S = \mathcal{K}$. Breeden and Litzenberger (1978) first recognized this result. Apart from its conceptual importance, their result has a practical application that is very well known to the Finance community. By collecting call option prices for different strikes, all others equal, one can approximate the derivatives $\partial^2 C / \partial \mathcal{K}^2$ with finite differences and obtain an approximation of the risk-neutral probability distribution of the underlying that is *implied* in option prices. This implied distribution can in turn be used to price other derivatives on the same underlying or to compute statistics for the underlying, such as its anticipated volatility, when the volatility does vary. (See chapter 17.)

6.7   The Price of Risk of a Derivative

There is a lesson on the pricing philosophy of Itô's models that we can draw from the derivations of this chapter, at the risk of belaboring the point. This lesson is of paramount importance for our understanding of security pricing in continuous time. It is the equality between the extra return per unit of risk of different securities.

Start from a (complete) market in which the basic securities are a stock, which follows a generalized Black-Scholes process, and a bond.

To demonstrate that the equality holds for a call and its underlying, we use Itô's lemma together with the Black-Scholes PDE. We have already demonstrated that, as a consequence of Itô's lemma, the function giving the price of the call satisfies the following SDE:

$$dC = \frac{\partial}{\partial S}C(S,t)[\mu S dt + \sigma S dw] + \frac{1}{2}\frac{\partial^2}{\partial S^2}C(S,t)\sigma^2 S^2 dt + \frac{\partial}{\partial t}C(S,t)dt$$

It follows that the (percentage) drift of the call, denoted as μ_c, is

$$\mu_c = \frac{1}{C}\left[\mathcal{D}(C) + \frac{\partial C}{\partial t}\right]$$

while its (percentage) diffusion, σ_c, is

$$\sigma_c = \frac{1}{C}\left[\frac{\partial}{\partial S}C(S,t)\sigma S\right]$$

The Black-Scholes PDE states that

$$\mathcal{D}^*(C) + \frac{\partial C}{\partial t} = rC$$

As a consequence, the drift can be written as

$$\mu_c = \frac{1}{C}\left[\mathcal{D}(C) - \mathcal{D}^*(C) + rC\right]$$
$$= \frac{1}{C}\left[\frac{\partial}{\partial S}C(S,t)(\mu - r)S + rC(S,t)\right]$$

while the market price of risk on the call $(\mu_c - r)/\sigma_c$ becomes

$$\frac{\mu_c - r}{\sigma_c} = \frac{\frac{\partial}{\partial S}C(S,t)(\mu - r)S}{\frac{\partial}{\partial S}C(S,t)\sigma S} = \frac{\mu - r}{\sigma}$$

which coincides with the same price on the stock, as announced.

Equalization of prices of risk follows directly from the Black-Scholes PDE. The equation itself can be interpreted as providing risk prices equated across securities.

The intuition for equalization stems from the central role of drift and diffusion in the Itô setting. In continuous time and with a single Wiener process – no matter how far from lognormal the diffusion process that represents security prices is (and then no matter how far its returns are from normality) – since it is an Itô process, the security is still priced, at least locally in terms of rates of return, on the basis of excess of drift per unit of standard deviation. Because the same Wiener drives them, the option and the underlying are perfectly correlated with each other. As a consequence of the Itô structure, and of its focus on drift and diffusion, or first and second moments, we are able to summarize the risk features of the different securities through excess return and standard deviation, combined into a market price of risk. As a consequence of the *Law of One Price*, these synthetic measures apply to all securities.

6.8   Benchmark Example (continued)

Pricing and hedging are two faces of the same coin. In this section we go back to the strict-sense Black-Scholes model and show how hedging can be performed, and how the hedging ratios or coefficients are linked to the Black-Scholes formula (6.14).

We have already seen that the weight of the underlying in the replicating portfolio is the derivative of the option value with respect to the underlying. It is known as the option "delta":

$$\delta_C \triangleq \frac{\partial}{\partial S} C(S(t), t) = N(d_1)$$

Consequently, the hedge ratio (6.21) for the hedging portfolio is the opposite of the option's delta:

$$h(S(t), t) = -\frac{\partial}{\partial S} C(S, t) = -N(d_1)$$

and the value of a portfolio that is either long $N(d_1)$ units of the underlying for each option held short, or is short the same quantity for each option held long, has a derivative with respect to S that is equal to 0.

In the Black-Scholes case it is customary to compute other derivatives of the call price. Together with the above delta, they are the so-called Greeks. Let $n(\cdot)$ be the standard Gaussian density function $(n(x) = e^{-x^2/2}/\sqrt{2\pi})$. Besides the delta, the Greeks are:

- the "gamma"

$$\gamma_C \triangleq \frac{\partial^2}{\partial S^2} C(S(t), t) = \frac{n(d_1)}{S(t)\sigma\sqrt{T - t}}$$

- "rho"

$$\rho_C \triangleq \frac{\partial}{\partial r} C(S(t), t) = \mathcal{K}(T - t)e^{-r(T-t)}N(d_2)$$

- and "theta"

$$\theta_C \triangleq \frac{\partial}{\partial t} C(S(t), t) = -\frac{\sigma S(t)n(d_1)}{2\sqrt{T - t}} - r\mathcal{K}e^{-r(T-t)}N(d_2)$$

Note that both delta and gamma are continuous in S, which shows that the Black-Scholes formula is C^2.

Remark 6.3   *Of the Greeks, δ_C and γ_C are sensitivities with respect to the underlying's price evolution; ρ_C tells us the impact of a different level of the interest rate; and θ_C measures the change in price over time, as time-to-maturity get closer. However, the interpretation varies from one Greek to the other: while the price S does vary over time in a stochastic way, the interest rate is assumed constant and the time-to maturity of the option evolves deterministically, as calendar time goes by.*

The signs of the previous Greeks are unambiguous: δ_C, γ_C, and ρ_C are positive; θ_C is negative. The Black-Scholes PDE itself can be written in terms of the Greeks as

$$\frac{1}{2}\gamma_C\sigma^2 S^2 + \theta_C - rC(S, t) + \delta_C rS = 0$$

The LHS of figure 6.1 and figures 6.2 and 6.3 show the behavior of the prices and that of some Greeks with respect to the underlying price. To be more precise, the behavior is plotted against the "moneyness" defined as $S/\mathcal{K}$. The call, if it were at maturity, would be

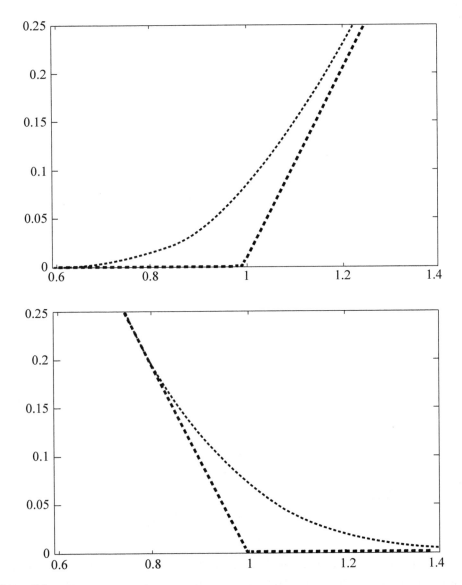

Figure 6.1

European call and put payoffs and prices in the Black-Scholes case, as a function of the moneyness $(S/\mathcal{K})$. The other parameters are set to $r = 1\%$, $\sigma = 20\%$, and $T = 1$. The top figure is for the call. The bottom figure is for the put.

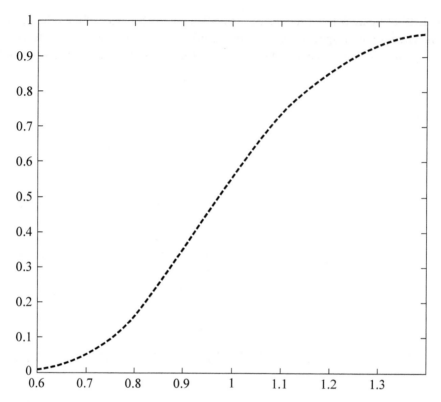

Figure 6.2
Delta of the European call in the Black-Scholes case, as a function of the so-called moneyness $(S/\mathcal{K})$.
The other parameters are set to $r = 1\%$, $\sigma = 20\%$, and $T = 1$.

worth exercising – we say that it is "in the money" – if $S/\mathcal{K} > 1$, while it is "out of the money" if the opposite inequality holds.

The European put with maturity T and strike $\mathcal{K}$ gives the right to sell the underlying at $\mathcal{K}$ when time T comes. It pays $[\mathcal{K} - S(T)]^+$. In the strict-sense Black-Scholes case, its price $P(S(t), t)$ is

$$
\begin{aligned}
P(S(t), t) &= e^{-r(T-t)}\mathbb{E}_t^*\{[\mathcal{K} - S(T)]^+\} \\
&= e^{-r(T-t)}\mathcal{K}\mathbb{E}_t^*\big[\mathbf{1}_{\{S(T)<\mathcal{K}\}}\big] - \mathbb{E}_t^*\big[S(T) \times \mathbf{1}_{\{S_T<\mathcal{K}\}}\big] \\
&= e^{-r(T-t)}\mathcal{K}N(-d_2) - S(t)N(-d_1)
\end{aligned}
$$

The European put price is linked to the price of the European call on the same underlying, with the same strike and maturity, by a no-arbitrage restriction, called *put-call parity*:

$$
P(S(t), t) + S(t) = C(S(t), t) + e^{-r(T-t)}\mathcal{K}
$$

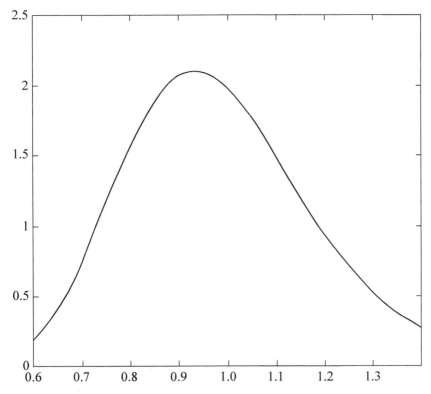

Figure 6.3
Gamma of the European call and put in the Black-Scholes case, as a function of the moneyness
$(S/\mathcal{K})$. The other parameters are set to $r = 1\%$, $\sigma = 20\%$, and $T = 1$.

In the case of the put, the weights of the replicating portfolio (6.12) would be:

$$\begin{cases} \theta(S,t) = \frac{\partial}{\partial S}P(S,t) = -N(-d_1) \\ \alpha(S,t) = \frac{V(S,t) - \frac{\partial}{\partial S}P(S,t) \times S(t)}{B(t)} = \mathcal{K}N(-d_2) \end{cases}$$

The hedge ratio for a long hedging position would be

$$h(S(t),t) = -\frac{\partial}{\partial S}P(S,t) = N(-d_1)$$

The put Greeks are

- its "delta"

$$\delta_P \triangleq \frac{\partial}{\partial S}P(S(t),t) = -N(-d_1) = N(d_1) - 1$$

- its "gamma"

$$\gamma_P \triangleq \frac{\partial^2}{\partial S^2} P(S(t), t) = \frac{n(d_1)}{S(t)\sigma\sqrt{T-t}}$$

- its "rho"

$$\rho_P \triangleq \frac{\partial}{\partial t} P(S(t), t) = -\mathcal{K}(T-t)e^{-r(T-t)}N(-d_2)$$

- and its "theta"

$$\theta_P \triangleq \frac{\partial}{\partial t} P(S(t), t) = -\frac{\sigma S(t)n(d_1)}{2\sqrt{T-t}} + r\mathcal{K}e^{-r(T-t)}N(-d_2)$$

The behavior of the put price and its gamma, as a function of the moneyness, is presented in the right bottom panel of figure 6.1 and in figure 6.3. The put is worth exercising – is "in-the-money" – if $S/\mathcal{K} < 1$ at maturity, while it is "out-of-the-money" if the opposite inequality occurs.

Some more cases of hedging are discussed in exercise 6.4.

6.9 Conclusion

In this chapter, the Black-Scholes miracle operated. That miracle now lies at the foundation of the whole of Continuous-time Finance.

A derivative security may or may not be redundant. But, in a market that is already complete, it is redundant by construction. The exemplar complete market we considered was one in which one risky security was driven by one Wiener process only and one riskless security was also available.

We described exhaustively the various reasonings that can serve to price the derivative. They were all based on one basic feature. When the same, single Wiener process drives the underlying security and the derivative written on it, the returns on these two are perfectly correlated. For that reason, their prices must be functionally related to each other.

Exercises

6.1. Recall the definition of the Dynkin operator (as in section 5.7):

$$\mathcal{D}f(x, t) = \frac{\partial}{\partial x}f(x, t)b(x, t) + \frac{1}{2}\sigma^2(x, t)\frac{\partial}{\partial x^2}f(x, t)$$

Suppose we are looking for the solution of the following PDE:

$$\mathcal{D}f(x, t) + \frac{\partial}{\partial t}f(x, t) = rf(x, t), \quad t \in [0, T]$$

with terminal condition:

$$f(x, T) = g(x)$$

Verify that if $f(x,t)$ is a solution, then

$$f(x,t) = \mathbb{E}\left[e^{-r(T-t)}g\left(X^{x,t}(T)\right)\right]$$

where:

$$X^{x,t}(u) = x + \int_t^u b\left(X^{x,t}(s),s\right)ds + \int_t^u \sigma\left(X^{x,t}(s),s\right)dw(s)$$

6.2. A considerable extension of the Black-Scholes securities market model can be achieved as follows. The processes for the price S of a security and a state variable Y jointly solve the SDE:

$$dS = \mu(S,Y,t)dt + \sigma(S,Y,t)dw$$
$$dY = \mu_Y(S,Y,t)dt + \sigma_Y(S,Y,t)dw$$

where w is a one-dimensional Wiener process and $\sigma(S,Y,t) > 0$ with probability one $\forall t$. The rate of interest r is given by a function $r(S,Y,t)$.

a. Is this a complete market? If yes, what is the stochastic discount factor ξ?

b. Write, in the form of a PDE, the restriction that would apply to the value $V(S,Y,t)$ of a self-financing portfolio made up of the risky security and the riskless security.

c. Give the value of the delta that would allow you to replicate a European call option written on the risky security and maturing at some date T.

6.3. (Option Pricing with Stochastic Interest Rate) Suppose that the stock price S follows a Geometric Brownian motion

$$dS(t) = \mu S(t)dt + \sigma S(t)dw(t)$$

Let $P(t,\tau)$ denote the price of pure discount bond maturing at date τ. Assume that

$$\frac{dP(t,\tau)}{P(t,\tau)} = \mu_P(\tau)dt + \sigma_P(\tau)dw_\tau(t)$$

where $w_\tau(t)$ is a Wiener process. Assume further the following correlations:

$$dw_\tau(t)dw_T(t) = \rho(\tau,T)dt; \quad dw_\tau(s)dw_T(t) = 0 \ (s \neq t);$$
$$dw(t)dw_\tau(t) = 0$$

a. Derive the PDE that the price a European call option on the stock must satisfy. Assume first that there is only one bond maturing at $\tau = T$, then extend to all $\tau \leq T$.

b. Attempt to solve the PDE.

c. Comment on whether the assumptions on the bond prices are realistic.

6.4. The hedging technique illustrated in the chapter is also known as delta-hedging. Actual hedging sometimes extends to higher-order variations or changes in variables different from the underlying, such as time or the interest rate. Focus on the strict-sense Black-Scholes dynamics and imagine being long a European call option. Considering that

$$dC = \delta dS$$

we learned that we can build a (delta) hedged portfolio V using the underlying. Such portfolio contains $h = -\delta = -N(d_1)$ shares per call, since in this case

$$dV = dC + hdS =$$
$$= dC - \delta dS = \delta dS - \delta dS = 0$$

a. Considering that

$$dC = \delta dS + \frac{1}{2}\gamma dS^2$$

we can build a delta-gamma hedged portfolio V using the underlying and another option. Suppose that you want to use another call option on the same underlying, with the same maturity and with a different strike ($\mathcal{K}_1$).

(i) Write down the conditions that give the appropriate number of underlying and calls with strike $\mathcal{K}_1$ in the portfolio. Determine whether there is a mix that allows the goal to be reached and whether it is unique.

(ii) Determine whether delta-hedging the underlying is different from hedging against variations up to the first order in dt and whether delta and gamma hedging the underlying is different from hedging against variations up to the second order in dt.

b. Consider now that the Black-Scholes PDE can be written in terms of the Greeks as[10]

$$dC = \delta dS + \frac{1}{2}\gamma dS^2 + \theta dt + \rho dr$$

we can build a delta-gamma-theta-rho hedged portfolio V using the underlying and other three options with the same maturity. Let the remaining ones have strike $\mathcal{K}_2$ and $\mathcal{K}_3$. Write down the conditions that give the appropriate number of underlying and calls in the portfolio. Determine whether there is a mix that allows the goal to be reached and whether it is unique.

c. There is another Greek, which we did not introduce in the text, the so-called vega, $dC/d\sigma$. Compute it, comment on its sign, and on its possible interpretation.

---

10 Recall the remark in the text on the different interpretation to be assigned to δ and γ as compared to the derivatives with respect to time and the interest rate, θ and ρ.

7 Portfolios, Stochastic Integrals, and Stochastic Differential Equations

We continue to pursue the goal of this part of the book, which is to re-do in continuous time what was done in chapter 2 for the case of discrete time. That means we aim to price redundant securities simply based on the assumption of no arbitrage in the financial market.

As before, an arbitrage opportunity is defined as an investment strategy that costs zero or a negative amount at some initial time 0 and delivers gains after some finite time T that have probability 1 of not being negative and a strictly positive probability of being strictly positive. But one difficulty arises that did not exist in discrete time. In continuous time, investors can trade an infinite number of times over a finite period of time. So, when we define gains, we need to have available a notion of integration over time of the increments of gain achieved upon each gain of each infinitesimal period. In order for the integral in question to be well defined, we may have to restrict the space of admissible strategies. To motivate that restriction, we provide in section 7.1 two examples of pathologies that can occur when an infinite number of rounds of trading is available, one of which is the "Doubling strategy."

To be able to discuss this issue, we posit again a filtered probability space as in chapter 5, and revisit the notions of stochastic integral and stochastic differential equation (SDE), which we took for granted there. These are used to describe strategies that replicate a given payoff and to represent security prices and financial gains. Stochastic integrals are defined in section 7.2, for a particular class of integrands. Section 7.3 defines admissible strategies. As usual, our modeling choices are motivated by economic meaning. Since we use Itô processes for prices and gains, we need to know whether, for a given SDE, there is an Itô process that solves it, whether Itô processes are Markov – thus facilitating the use of dynamic programming – and whether they are martingales. That is the content of section 7.4. In section 7.5, we show what dire consequences ensue when a PDE has more than one solution. In section 7.6, we state a theorem, called the "martingale-representation" theorem, which will allow us to spell out the replication strategies that are implicit in a martingale price. We conclude with examples.

The chapter is quite demanding, but provides a fairly rigorous foundation for the chapters to come. One immediate benefit of the added rigor is that we see clearly the need to rule out trading strategies – such as the Doubling strategy – that would enable gains for sure when trading is allowed to take place at any time on a continuous time scale. And we see the link between martingales and stochastic integrals over specific classes of functions.[1]

7.1   Pathologies

7.1.1   Doubling Strategies

To couch in more concrete terms the difficulty created by an infinite number of rounds of trading, we now provide an example of a pathological investment strategy.

Consider a portfolio choice in which the investor switches between cash and a bet on a coin toss. The player receives the bet in case he wins and pays it in case he loses. The investor can:

- start with no initial investment, or $b_0 = 0$.

- bet $b_1 = 1$ dollar on heads on the first toss. If he wins, he stops. If not, he bets $b_2 = 2$ dollars on heads on the second throw.

- on the nth toss, if the investor has lost on all preceding tosses, he bets $b_n = 2^{n-1}$ dollars on heads. If he wins, he stops; the gains will cover the preceding losses plus 1 dollar, since

$$2^{n-1} = 1 + 2 + 2^2 + \ldots + 2^{n-2} + 1$$

- If he loses, he bets $b_{n+1} = 2^n$ dollars in the next round, and so on, and so forth.

If the coin is fair, the probability of winning 1 dollar is equal to 1 minus the probability of losing on all tosses, which is $1/2^n$. This last probability tends towards zero when the number of tosses increases indefinitely. So the Doubling strategy just described leads to winning 1 with a probability that tends to one, with no initial investment. To achieve that, the investor is allowed to submit an infinite number of bets ($n \to \infty$), each single bet becomes infinite ($2^{n-1} \to \infty$), and the losses, which accumulate to negative wealth, may become infinite ($1 + 2 + 2^2 + \ldots + 2^{n-2} \to \infty$).

All the bets can be submitted on a finite time interval, provided one makes the time span between each bet and the next short enough. For instance, one can bet 2^n at time $T - 2^n$, so that all bets are submitted before time T comes.

It appears that, from a Doubling strategy, and by extension from any financial market in which Doubling strategies were allowed, a certain amount could be extracted with no

---

1 Reminder: unless doing otherwise is necessary for comprehension, we simplify the notation for processes. All processes are stochastic but we suppress the reference to the state ω. Therefore, $X(t)$ actually means $X(\omega, t)$. In special cases, we also use the notation $f(t)$ to refer to a deterministic function of time. When this happens, we say so explicitly.

capital outlay, on the condition of being allowed to play indefinitely, to place infinite bets, and to accumulate infinite negative wealth on the way, or equivalently, an infinite debt.

The strategy has been described in discrete time with an infinite number of rounds of trading. It has been a metaphor for the investor's ability, in continuous time, to trade an infinite number of times over a finite period of time. But the same example could also be fully presented in a continous-time setting.[2]

We must deem this kind of strategy to be inadmissible in the market-place. No financial investor would accept to be the counterparty to those bets and lose 1 with probability 1. In an equilibrium, such as the one of chapters 12 and 15, those bets would be excluded automatically, for lack of counterparty. But, when trying to obtain pure no-arbitrage results, or even when trying to optimize the out-of-equilibrium decisions of a small, purely competitive investor, we need to exclude them explicitly from the strategy set. We must decide which is the preferable formulation of this exclusion.

Given that, in continuous time, we want people to trade an infinite number of times over finite periods, it seems that we can avoid Doubling strategies either by putting constraints on bets b or by putting a lower bound on the sum of past bets, which is indebtedness, or (negative) wealth. The requirement on wealth is very sound: in the real world no one is ever granted infinite credit. The first requirement, on bets, is strictly linked to the second, as the example of Doubling strategies – even if is only meant to be suggestive – shows. Indebtedness becomes very large because each single bet does. The sum explodes because each term does. So, it seems that a constraint on cumulated bets would avoid both infinite bets and an infinite loss on the way. Placing technical requirements on strategies so that expected gains are null in expectation will imply bounding wealth from below. In order to spell out these requirements, we need to define gains properly.

7.1.2 Local Martingales

In the example of Doubling strategies, the coin was always the same, bet after bet. The pathology arose not from the behavior of the coin but from the bets taken by the investor and their size. But, it is also possible for the investment vehicle itself to be a source of pathology.

Consider the example of a share of stock, the price of which evolves as per the following zero-drift SDE:

$$dS(t) = \sigma S(t)^{\alpha} dw(t) \tag{7.1}$$

As will be indicated in chapter 13, one can obtain the probability density of transition by solving the associated Fokker-Planck forward PDE (13.4) with initial condition (13.5).

---

2 See footnote 14 below.

When $\alpha > 1$, one finds:[3]

$$\mathbb{E}[S(t)|S(0) = x] = x - x\frac{\Gamma[v, z(x, t)]}{\Gamma(v, 0)}$$

where $\Gamma(v, m) \triangleq \int_m^\infty e^{-l} l^{v-1} dl$ is called the "incomplete gamma function," $v = 1/2(\alpha - 1)$ and:

$$z(x, t) \triangleq \frac{1}{\sigma^2(1 - \alpha)}\frac{1}{(1 - \alpha)t}x^{2(1-\alpha)} \tag{7.2}$$

The important thing to notice is that:

$$\mathbb{E}[S(t)|S(0) = x] \neq x$$

so that the process S is not a martingale, even though its drift is equal to zero. One says that it is a local martingale, but not a martingale.[4]

The implication is that, even though at each time step (in the "short run") the expected gain from always holding one unit of this investment vehicle is equal to zero, the overall expected gain over a finite period of time (in the "long run") is not zero. That is also a type of gain or loss that we need to exclude in a well-functioning financial market.

7.2   Stochastic Integrals

Itô stochastic integrals are integrals in which the summation is over an integrand multiplied by time increments in the path of a Wiener process. In what follows, we provide a motivation for defining them, and we construct them, starting, as one does in ordinary calculus, from integrands that are step functions. Then we extend the notion to integrands that belong to wider spaces.

Most ubiquitously, in this book we use stochastic integrals – apart from the definition of a SDE – to represent the stochastic part of gains from trade. Recall the way in which we computed gains from trade in discrete time. Starting from an N-dimensional portfolio $\theta(t)$ worth $\theta^\top(t)S(t)$ at time t and holding it until $t + 1$ the gain was equal to

$$\theta^\top(t)(S(t + 1) - S(t)) = \theta(t)^\top \Delta S(t)$$

In the context of continuous time, we split the asset price vector S into $S = \{B, \mathcal{S}\}$, and split accordingly the vector of portfolio positions, $\theta = \{\alpha, \Theta\}$. For the single-security case, however, we use the notation S instead of the calligraphic $\mathcal{S}$.

---

3 Based on what comes below in this chapter, one can surmise that, when $\alpha > 1$, the Chapman-Kolmogorov backward equation (13.1) with terminal condition (13.2) has two solutions one of which only satisfies the initial condition.

4 One talks of a "strict local martingale." In section 15.5.1 below, we encounter another example of a strict local martingale.

If we reduce the length of each time interval to Δt, we can write the gains on the risky securities alone as $\Theta^{\mathsf{T}}(t)\Delta \mathcal{S}(t)$. It seems quite natural, therefore, to write gains over an infinitesimal interval dt as $\Theta^{\mathsf{T}}(t)d\mathcal{S}(t)$. In discrete time, the gains were

$$G(t) = \sum_{u=0}^{t-1} \Theta(u)^{\mathsf{T}} \Delta \mathcal{S}(u)$$

which in integral form is now expected to become

$$G(t) = \int_0^t \Theta(u)^{\mathsf{T}} d\mathcal{S}(u) \tag{7.3}$$

$$= \int_0^t \Theta(u)^{\mathsf{T}} (\mu(u)du + \sigma(u)dw(u))$$

The sum includes, besides a Riemann integral (in dt), a stochastic integral (in $dw(t)$). While in discrete time and with finite uncertainty, gains (the sum) were clearly defined, state by state, even if the portfolio and the prices were both stochastic processes, it is less evident to define the gains in continuous time, with infinite uncertainty. This is because of the second integral. It raises two concerns: the variable of integration w, which is not differentiable over time, and the integrand $\Theta(u)^{\mathsf{T}}\sigma(u)$, which is itself a stochastic process.

In order to give meaning to the stochastic integral, we first define it in the case in which $\Theta^{\mathsf{T}}\sigma$ – which for simplicity we now denote as b – is a "simple" function: one step or level for each small interval of time and a finite number of prespecified time intervals. Then we extend the definition to processes b that are not simple functions, letting the interval between two trades become infinitesimal, $(t, t+dt)$, so that the number of trades before T becomes infinite. We compute the gain of each interval with a diffusion matrix $\sigma(t)$ and portfolio decisions $\Theta(t)$ that are those of the beginning of the trading interval. Any surprise change of Θ over the interval is disallowed or is not credited into the gains. All positions in the financial market must be purchased (at the initial price $\mathcal{S}(t)$) prior to any price movement. *After a price movement has taken place, traders are not allowed to go back in time and reconsider their portfolios.* So, computing the $(t, t+dt)$ contribution to the integral using the time-t value of the process $\Theta(t)$ has a precise and realistic financial interpretation.

Define a simple process b:

Definition 7.1 *A one-dimensional process b on $\mathcal{T} = [0, T]$ is simple if there exist*

- *a fixed subdivision $0 = t_0 < t_1 < t_2 < ... < t_n = T$ of $[0, T]$ into n subintervals and*
- *$n + 1$ random variables β_i; $i = 0, ..., n$, with β_i measurable with respect to $\mathcal{F}(i)$ such that b has the form*

$$b(t) = \sum_{i=0}^{n-1} \beta_i \mathbf{1}_{\{[t_i, t_{i+1})\}} + \beta_n \mathbf{1}_{\{t_n\}}$$

The definition simply states that $b(t) = \beta_i$ when $t \in [t_i, t_{i+1})$, up to $t_{i+1} = t_n$, and $b(t) = \beta_n$ when $t = t_n$. In each interval the process has a constant value, which is known at the beginning of the interval, namely at time t_i. The process is said to be "non-anticipating".[5] To avoid technicalities, we assume that the first two moments of the random variables β_i are finite. With the integrand b a simple process and the variable of integration a Wiener process w, it is quite natural to give the following definition of the stochastic integral:

Definition 7.2   *When b is a simple process, the stochastic integral over $\mathcal{T}$ with respect to the one-dimensional Wiener process w is the random variable, denoted $\int_0^T b(t)dw(t)$, defined by*

$$\int_0^T b(t)dw(t) \triangleq \sum_{i=0}^{n-1} \beta_i(w(t_{i+1}) - w(t_i))$$

Since in each period the integral is defined using the level of the process $b(t)$ *at the beginning of the interval*, which is β_i, and the height of the simple process $b(t)$ is constant over $[t_i, t_{i+1})$, the integral is simply the sum of the products of the levels (β_i) times the change of the Wiener process over the time period $[t_i, t_{i+1}]$. Since the first two moments of the random variables β_i are finite, not only is the integral a well-defined random variable, its first two moments are also finite. Indeed, because the process b is simple and, therefore, non-anticipating, one can calculate the expected value of the integral by breaking it up into conditional expected values of its pieces, each of which is equal to zero. Hence, the expected value is:

$$\mathbb{E}\left[\int_0^T b(t)dw(t)\right] = 0 \tag{7.4}$$

The variance is finite and given by the time integral of the expectation of b^2:[6]

$$\mathbb{E}\left[\left(\int_0^T b(t)dw(t)\right)\left(\int_0^T b(t)dw(t)\right)\right] = \int_0^T \mathbb{E}\left[b^2(t)\right]dt \tag{7.5}$$

We can now extend the definition to non-simple processes, provided they can be "approximated" by simple processes, or, more exactly, that there is some sequence of simple processes that converges to the non-simple one. Figure 7.1 gives an intuitive understanding of the approximation of b by a simple process. As an example, it takes b itself to be a Wiener process and depicts one possible simple process that approximates b. Fixing the approximating process is like "cutting" the effective Wiener process and looking at it

---

5 Non-anticipating processes are close relatives of adapted processes (see section 2.2.1). The two notions differ only for processes with jumps. See Klebaner (2005), section 2.8 for the definition of an adapted process, and sections 8.2 and 8.13 for the non-anticipating or predictable ones.

6 For a proof, and also for the discussion of the enlargement to non-simple processes coming next, see for example Arnold (1974) or, with a slightly different notation, Nielsen (1999).

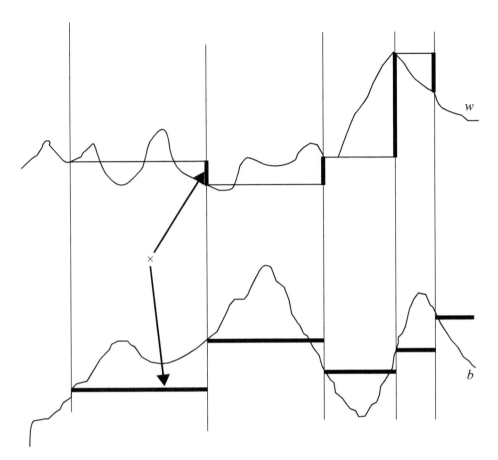

Figure 7.1
The picture examplifies the role of the simple process that approximates b in fixing, for each time subinterval, an initial value β_i, so as to permit integration over the Brownian Motion w.

as if it were a simple process (whose values are the values of the Wiener process at the leftmost points of the separate subintervals of time).

In this book, we focus on a class of processes that can be approximated in this way. Processes in the class called $\mathcal{H}^2$ are limits in mean-square of simple processes.[7]

---

7 Convergence in mean square to b of a sequence $\{b_n\}$, with b and b_n real processes, means that

$$\lim_{n \to \infty} \mathbb{E} \int_0^T |b(t) - b_n(t)|^2 \, dt = 0$$

Definition 7.3 *For a given probability space $(\Omega, \mathcal{F}, P)$, the $\mathcal{H}^2$ space[8] is the space of non-anticipating processes b that have a finite expected value of the integral up to T of the Euclidean norm $\|b\|$ squared:[9]*

$$\mathbb{E}\left[\int_0^T \|b(t)\|^2 dt\right] < \infty \quad \forall T \tag{7.6}$$

For each state of the world ω, the integral in this last definition is a standard (Riemann) integral of the function $\|b\|^2$, considered as a function of time. It is a pathwise integral and a function of ω. Considered over all states, it is a random variable. When defining $\mathcal{H}^2$, we are taking the expectation of that random variable and we are requiring that it be finite for all T.

We can define stochastic integrals for processes in $\mathcal{H}^2$. Convergence of the integrals of the simple functions to a random variable, which will be called the stochastic integral of the b process, is in mean square:[10]

Definition 7.4 *Let $b: \Omega \times \mathcal{T} \to \mathbb{R}, b \in \mathcal{H}^2$. Its stochastic integral with respect to the Wiener process w is the random variable*

$$\int_0^T b(t)dw(t) \triangleq \lim_{n\to\infty} \int_0^T b_n(t)dw(t)$$

where the convergence is understood in the mean-square sense, for every sequence $\{b_n\}$ of simple functions that converge in mean square to b.

Let us now consider the value of the stochastic integral for a variable upper bound of integration:

$$Y(t) \triangleq \int_0^t b(u)dw(u) \tag{7.7}$$

We are interested in it because the process for gains accumulated in the financial market is of that type (with $b = \Theta^\mathsf{T}\sigma$). The process $Y(t)$ is continuous, adapted, and differentiable. By definition, its differential dY is $b(t)dw(t)$. This means that differentiation and integration are still in the same relation as in non-stochastic calculus. Because of the non-anticipating nature of b, it follows that:

$$\mathbb{E}[dY(t)] = 0$$

---

8 We should write $\mathcal{H}^2(\Omega \times T)$, where $\Omega \times T$ is the product measure generated by states of the world ω and time t. The requirement comes from interpreting processes as mapping from pairs (ω, t) into real numbers or vectors. The notation $\mathcal{H}^2$ is a shortcut. Details can be found for instance in Duffie (1986).

9 If b is a matrix valued process, then $\|b\|^2$ means $\text{trace}(bb^\mathsf{T})$; in particular, for b an N-dimensional vector, $\|b\|^2$ is the classical Euclidean norm in $\mathbb{R}^N$.

10 See Itô (1944).

so that the process Y is a *local martingale*, at least. In fact, one can show that, if b belongs to $\mathcal{H}^2$, Y is a true *martingale*:[11]

$$\mathbb{E}[Y(t)] = 0$$

Furthermore, if b belongs to $\mathcal{H}^2$, the variance of the integral exists (in other words, Y is *square-integrable*) and can be computed as a time-integral:

$$\mathbb{E}\left[Y^2(t)\right] = \int_0^t \mathbb{E}\left[b^2(u)\right] du$$

Similar properties hold in higher dimensions.[12]

There exists another way to define stochastic integrals. Processes in a wider class called $\mathcal{L}^2$ are limits in probability of simple processes.[13]

Definition 7.5 *The $\mathcal{L}^2$ space is the set of adapted processes b that have, with probability 1, a finite value of the integral up to any T of the Euclidean norm $\|b\|$, squared:*

$$\int_0^T \|b(t)\|^2 dt < \infty \quad \text{with probability 1} \tag{7.8}$$

Like processes b in $\mathcal{H}^2$, processes in $\mathcal{L}^2$ do not vary "too much" over time. They are not too erratic, so that their pathwise integrals over a finite period of time are finite, almost surely. But they can reach more extreme values than in $\mathcal{H}^2$. One can find processes for which the integral of $\|b(t)\|^2$ is finite almost surely (while possibly infinite on a set of zero measure), and for which the expected value of the integral (7.6) is not finite. This means that the first class is smaller than the second; that is, $\mathcal{H}^2 \subset \mathcal{L}^2$. In this new class, the alternative definition of the stochastic integral is:

---

11 See Arnold (1974), pages 74 and 80.

12 They can be summarized in the following theorem.

Theorem 7.1 *Let $b \in \mathcal{H}^2$ be an $N \times K$-dimensional, matrix-valued process, ω a $K-$dimensional Wiener process. Then*

1. The N dimensional process $Y(t)$ in (7.7) is a martingale.

2. The $N \times N$ dimensional matrix valued process $Y(t)Y(t)^\mathsf{T}$ is integrable and:

$$\mathbb{E}\left[YY^\mathsf{T} \mid \mathcal{F}(s)\right] = \int_s^t \mathbb{E}\left[b(u)b(u)^\mathsf{T} \mid \mathcal{F}(s)\right] du$$

for $0 \leq s \leq t \leq T$.

13 Convergence in probability means that, for every $\varepsilon > 0$,

$$\lim_{n \to \infty} P(\{\omega \in \Omega : |b_n - b| \geq \varepsilon\}) = 0$$

Convergence with probability one implies convergence in probability, while the reverse is not true.

Definition 7.6 *Let $b: \Omega \times T \to R, b \in \mathcal{L}^2$. Its stochastic integral with respect to the Wiener process w is the random variable*

$$\int_0^T b(t)dw(t) \triangleq \lim_{n \to \infty} \int_0^T b_n(t)dw(t)$$

where the convergence is in probability, for every sequence $\{b_n\}$ of simple functions that converge in probability to b.

Unfortunately, the process Y defined on the basis of this last definition, while remaining a local martingale, would not generally be a martingale, which means that a process with zero expected change at each time step (a local martingale, therefore) could generate cumulated expected gains that are not equal to zero, a pathology reminiscent of the pathologies described in section 7.1.

The reader can solve exercises from 7.1 to 7.4 to get more familiar with the notion of stochastic integral.

7.3   Admissible Strategies

Given the above, what should be the rules of the game that we allow our investors to play? We need to fix a definition of "admissible strategies." In the next chapters we denote as $\mathfrak{M}$ the set of consumption and portfolio and terminal wealth processes that are admissible. Should their strategies be confined to the space $\mathcal{H}^2$ or be allowed to live in the space $\mathcal{L}^2$? The integral of $\|b(t)\|^2$ in $\mathcal{L}^2$ is finite almost surely, and is infinite on a set of measure zero: should we allow it to render the expected value of the integral (7.8) possibly infinite? It is certainly easiest to disallow those infinite values altogether and impose the following:[14,15]

Definition 7.7 *The strategies Θ are admissible if and only $b = \Theta^\top \sigma$ belongs to $\mathcal{H}^2$ and $\Theta^\top \mu$ belongs to $\mathcal{L}^1$.*

Remark 7.1 *Admissibility includes a condition on the process of the product $\Theta^\top \sigma$ where, however, Θ is the strategy to be chosen by the investor whereas σ is given to him. It could*

---

14 Without the restriction to $\mathcal{H}^2$, pathological opportunities could be pursued. Indeed, there exists a theorem due to Dudley (1977) – cited by Jeanblanc *et al.* (2009), page 60 – saying that every real random variable (including the real number 1, which is the profit from a strategy of the Doubling strategy type) measurable with respect to Wiener process paths can be written as a stochastic integral $\int_0^1 b(u)dw(u)$ where b is a non-anticipating functional, the stochastic integral being, however, defined in the sense of definition 7.6. See also Nielsen (1999), page 148.

15 The $\mathcal{L}^1$ space is the set of adapted, measurable processes a that have, with probability 1, a finite value of the integral up to any T of the Euclidean norm $\|a\|$:

$$\int_0^T \|a(t)\|dt < \infty \quad \text{with probability 1}$$

very well be that, for a given σ process, there does not exist a Θ such that $\Theta^\top\sigma$ belongs to $\mathcal{H}^2$. For instance, that is true if σ itself does not belong to $\mathcal{H}^2$. Then we say by extension that σ itself is not admissible. We have seen that situation already in section 7.1.2 and we go back to it below (see remark 7.4).

There might be one drawback to the $\mathcal{H}^2$ space. The definition contains an expected value, so that it is not invariant to the probability measure. In the theory of continuous-time Finance, there are many occasions on which a change of probability measure is called for and the stochastic integral needs to be defined on any probability measure that might be needed. In particular, one should be concerned that the process Y might be a martingale under one probability measure and that its random part may be only a local martingale under the other. This may not be a problem if we make sure that the change of measure is itself a martingale, a question to which we return in the next chapter (see definition 8.9 and what follows).

There is one great benefit to the strategies being in $\mathcal{H}^2$. We know from theorem 7.1 that the stochastic integral representing gains (7.7) is a martingale; that is, there is no expected gain from trade. Gains over each tiny interval have zero mean, their cumulated value has also zero mean, because the regularity of an $\mathcal{H}^2$-strategy is such that a local martingale (the tiny, zero-mean gain from t to $t + dt$, $b(t)dw(t)$) is a martingale in the large, when integrated from 0 to T. If, for instance, a strategy delivers a sure payoff (as in the example of the Doubling strategy of section 7.1.1), the gains being a martingale, its expected value at any time prior to the payoff date must be equal to the sure payoff and no smaller. The starting value cannot be equal to zero. Hence, when the only allowed strategies are those in $\mathcal{H}^2$, *there is no need to place a lower bound on wealth.*

The lower bound on wealth could, however, be imposed separately on strategies belonging to the wider class $\mathcal{L}^2$. On occasion, therefore, one can introduce an alternative definition of admissible strategies:

Definition 7.8 (Admissible strategies (alternative)) *The strategies Θ are admissible if and only if $b = \Theta^\top\sigma$ belongs to $\mathcal{L}^2$, $\Theta^\top\mu$ belongs to $\mathcal{L}^1$ and the financial wealth accumulated by the strategy admits a finite lower bound.*

Dybvig and Huang (1987) derive a theorem (their theorems 4 and 5) saying that the restriction to $\mathcal{H}^2$ is equivalent to placing a lower bound on wealth on strategies belonging to the wider class $\mathcal{L}^2$. However, to do that, they assume (their assumption 1) the existence of an equivalent martingale measure. Whether or not such a measure exists will be discussed in chapter 8.

Having carefully restricted admissible strategies, we can update for the continuous-time setting the definition of arbitrage that we provided in chapter 2.[16]

---

16 The self-financing requirement was explained in section 6.1, formula (6.6).

Definition 7.9 *An arbitrage is an admissible, self-financing strategy that costs zero or a negative amount at some initial time 0 and delivers gains after some finite time T that have probability 1 of not being negative and a strictly positive probability of being strictly positive.*[17]

7.4 Itô Processes and Stochastic Differential Equations

7.4.1 Itô Processes

In chapter 5, we introduced heuristically Itô processes as representations of gains from trade, both with zero-mean random price change $(b \times dw)$ and with non-zero mean ones $(a \times dt + b \times dw)$. We now give a more formal definition. We give it for the $\mathcal{L}$ spaces. Since we intend to restrict our integrands b to be in $\mathcal{H}^2$, the requirements of the definition are satisfied.[18]

Definition 7.10 *Consider the filtered probability space* $(\Omega, \mathcal{F}, P, \mathbf{F}^w)$, *with a K-dimensional Brownian motion, the filtration* $\mathbf{F}^w$ *being generated by the Brownian motion, and let a and b be two* $N \times 1$ *and* $N \times K$-*dimensional processes respectively,* $a \in \mathcal{L}^1$ *and* $b \in \mathcal{L}^2$. *An N-dimensional process X is an Itô process if it is of the form:*

$$X(t) = X(0) + \int_0^t a(s)ds + \int_0^t b(s)dw(s)$$

where X(0) is a random vector that is measurable with respect to $\mathcal{F}_0$.

For simplicity, in what follows we take $X(0) = X_0 \in \mathbb{R}^N$.

By construction, an Itô process is a continuous process, that is, a process with continuous sample paths, because it is the sum of a Riemann integral and a stochastic integral of the type as above.

7.4.2 Stochastic Differential Equations

In some cases, the processes a and b are functions of the current value of $X : a = f(X,t), b = F(X,t)$. We must give a precise meaning to a stochastic differential equation where the unknown is the process X, as anticipated in section 5.4.

Definition 7.11 *A stochastic differential equation (SDE) is an equation of the form*

$$dX(t) = f(X(t),t) \times dt + F(X(t),t) \times dw(t)$$

---

17 Conversely, a strategy that produces a loss for sure is sometimes called a "suicide strategy."

18 This entire section 7.4 follows closely chapters 6, 7, and 8 of Arnold (1974).

which stands for

$$X(t) = \int_0^t f(X(s), s)ds + \int_0^t F(X(s), s)dw(s) \tag{7.9}$$

where the functions f and F are assumed to be defined and measurable on $\mathbb{R}^N \times \mathcal{T}$ and to depend on ω only via the process X itself.[19]

$X(0) = X_0 \in \mathbb{R}^N$ is the initial condition.[20]

Definition 7.12 *A process $X(t)$ is said to be a strong solution – a solution, for short – to this equation if:*[21]

- *$X(t)$ is adapted to the filtration generated by w,*
- *The processes $\bar{f}(t) = f(X(t), t)$ and $\bar{F}(t) = F(X(t), t)$ are $\mathcal{L}^1$ and $\mathcal{L}^2$ respectively,*
- *Equation (7.9) holds for every t with probability one.*

The fact that the values of the integrands of the deterministic and stochastic part, $\bar{f}$ and $\bar{F}$, are well-behaved, makes the solution(s) an Itô process. The regularity conditions are, indeed, the ones that appeared in the definition of an Itô process. We can, therefore, state that:

Proposition 7.1 *Every strong solution of a SDE is an Itô process.*

Every time economic modeling leads us to a SDE, and the SDE has a solution, that solution is an Itô process.

Observe that it is not possible to verify that $\bar{f}(t) = f(X(t), t) \in \mathcal{L}^1$ and $\bar{F}(t) = F(X(t), t) \in \mathcal{L}^2$ until one knows the solution. We need conditions for existence of the solution that do not depend on the solution, but only on the functions f and F. In addition, we may be interested in uniqueness of the solution, for almost every choice of $X(0) = X_0$ and almost

---

19 The above SDE *simultaneously* means:

$$\mathbb{E}[dX(t)|\mathcal{F}(s)] = f(X(t), t)dt$$

and

$$dX(t)dX(t)^\mathsf{T} = F(X(t), t)F(X(t), t)^\mathsf{T}dt$$

For a detailed discussion, see, for instance, Karatzas and Shreve (1998).

20 Sometimes, we shall need more than the initial conditions and the SDE to characterize a process. In case of stopped or reflected processes we need also boundary conditions (see the discussion of optimal stopping and transactions costs later in chapter 19).

21 There exists also a concept of weak solution of SDEs in which the specific Wiener process w and its filtration are not given. Instead, the solution consists of a pair $\{X, w\}$ for which the SDE holds. The processes X of two weak solutions can at best be identical in law; that is, they have the same probability distribution but their sample paths will typically be different (because the Wiener process w will be different).

every Wiener path w, that is, uniqueness of the solution depending on X_0 and w. The function itself is determined by f and F. We would like to know when the solution is unique in that sense. The next theorem (see for instance Arnold (1974), page 105) provides an answer.

Theorem 7.1 *If there exists a constant C such that:*

1. *(Lipschitz condition) for all $t \in \mathcal{T}$, $x \in \mathbb{R}^N$, $y \in \mathbb{R}^N$,*

$$\|f(x,t) - f(y,t)\| + \|F(x,t) - F(y,t)\| \le C\|x - y\|$$

2. *(Growth condition) for all $t \in \mathcal{T}$, $x \in \mathbb{R}^N$,*

$$\|f(x,t)\|^2 + \|F(x,t)\|^2 \le C^2\left(1 + \|x\|^2\right)$$

then equation (7.9) has on $\mathcal{T}$ a unique solution, continuous with probability 1, that satisfies the initial condition $X(0) = c$.

The Lipschitz condition is a weak form of continuity and smoothness with respect to the values of the process, imposed on the functions f and F. It guarantees path-by-path uniqueness of the solution. The growth condition limits the growth of these functions. Along with the Lipschitz condition, it guarantees existence of the solution in the sense of the probability limit.

Remark 7.2 *The Lipschitz is a sufficient condition for uniqueness. It is by no means necessary. For instance, we have already given the probability distribution for the process (7.1). That distribution is unique. In fact, the SDE (7.1) admits a unique strong solution, while it violates the Lipschitz condition (exercise 7.5).*[22]

The reader is now ready to solve exercises 7.5 and 7.6.

7.4.3 When Are Itô Processes Markov Processes? When Are They Diffusions?

The first corollary below says that, if the solution of the SDE exists because the conditions in theorem 7.1 are true, then that solution is Markov. The second corollary says that, if the coefficients of the SDE are continuous functions, then the solution is a diffusion (see Arnold (1974), pages 146 and 152 respectively).

Conditions for the solution to a SDE to be Markov are just the Lipschitz and growth properties of its coefficients f and F with respect to X:

Corollary 7.1 *When the hypotheses of theorem 7.1 are satisfied, the solution to equation (7.9) is a Markov process.*

---

22 We are grateful to Julien Hugonnier for this remark.

Conditions for being a diffusion (defined previously in 5.5) pertain, instead, to the continuity of the functions f and F as functions of time. To get an intuition for the relationship between being a diffusion and continuity, recall from definition 5.5 that, in order to define a diffusion, we took limits over small intervals of time. The following corollary states that, if the coefficients of a SDE are continuous in time, the process is a diffusion:

Corollary 7.2 *When both the function $f(x, t)$ and $F(x, t)$ are continuous with respect to t, the solution to equation (7.9) is a diffusion process, with drift f and diffusion matrix F.*

The corollary gives us a representation for the drift and diffusion coefficients of the solution, whenever it is a diffusion. It tells us that the drift vector is equal to f, while the diffusion matrix is equal to F. That is why the coefficients of a SDE are also called *drift* and *diffusion*. Mostly they are named like that also when the hypotheses of corollary 7.2 are not satisfied (and, therefore, the solution of an SDE is not necessarily a diffusion). In order to avoid the confusion arising from this misnomer, in the rest of the book, unless otherwise stated, we will only distinguish the Itô case from the Markov case. We always assume that the functions f and F are continuous in time.

With the above definitions, we are ready to model in a quite general way gains and prices in continuous-time financial markets. In the rest of the book, sometimes we model security prices as solutions of a SDE. We do so in chapters 8, 10, and 12. When we want to use dynamic programming we require Markov security prices. This was the case in chapter 6 and will be the case in chapters 9 and 11.

Example 7.1 A typical example of SDE is the linear one. The coefficients $f(x, t), F(x, t)$ are linear affine in $x \in \mathbb{R}^N$, with the appropriate dimensions:[23]

$$f(x, t) = A(t)x + a(t),$$
$$F(x, t) = [B_1(t)x + b_1(t), B_2(t)x + b_2(t), .., B_K(t)x + b_K(t)]$$

where $A(t)$ is an $N \times N$-valued matrix function of time, $a(t) \in \mathbb{R}^N, B_l(t)$ is an $N \times N$-valued matrix function of time, $b_l(t) \in \mathbb{R}^N, l = 1, 2, ..K$ are also functions of time. In this case, the SDE, together with the initial condition $X(0) = X_0$, has a solution under mild measurability conditions. We will discuss some specifications in the last section of this chapter. The linear SDE has a unique global solution if the functions A, a, B_l, b_l are constant. If, in addition, $B_l = 0$ for every l, so that X does not show up in the diffusion, the solution is a Gaussian process. It turns out to be very similar to the solution of similar, non-stochastic equations. A basic example of Gaussian process is the log return of the strict-sense Black-Scholes

---

23 A function $f : \mathbb{R}^n \to \mathbb{R}$ is linear if it is of the type $f(x; t) = A(t) \times x$ where $A(t)$ is deterministic (that is, a function of time only). It is linear affine, or simply affine, if it includes a term constant in x, $f(x; t) = A(t) \times x + a(t)$.

price process. Another outstanding example of Gaussian process is the process (16.9) of chapter 16 postulated by Vasicek.

———————————————♠———————————————

In the rest of the book, not only do we adopt continuous time, but we also use continuous processes of the Itô type. In the benchmark example, they will be Gaussian. Empirical evidence on returns, however, is hardly consistent with the Gaussian hypothesis, and the presence of jumps, which violates continuity of paths, cannot be excluded, since in any case we observe real-world prices discretely. A whole strand of literature assumes instead that returns on financial assets are continuous in so-called business time, while they have discontinuities in calendar time. It models the change from one timescale to the other as stochastic. Returns are not Brownian motions, but time-changed Brownian motions.

The economic idea underlying the distinction between business and calendar time is the following: business time is driven by information arrival, mainly by order arrivals and trade taking place. It runs faster in comparison with calendar time when a lot of information arrives and trades are executed. The latter arrive in a stochastic fashion so that the time change is stochastic. So, even if prices and returns are continuous in business time, they might have discontinuities if the change of time from business to calendar time is stochastic.

The mathematical property underlying the representation of prices as time-changed Brownian motions is a theorem by Monroe (1978), which states that any semimartingale can be represented as a time-changed Brownian motion.[24] And the Mathematical Finance literature has established that the class of semimartingales is the widest class of processes for returns consistent with the absence of arbitrage. So, time-changed Brownian motions capture all possible representations of arbitrage-free returns.

While time change is interesting for a single price, it is more interesting in the large, when one has to model the time changes of all the securities in a market. A paper in this literature is Luciano and Schoutens (2006). There is a whole spectrum of possibilities: one may assume that trade in different assets is the same (a unique time change), or, at the opposite, that trades are independent (and the changes of time too). A third possibility, which seems economically and empirically better grounded, is that there exists a common, market-driven component to trade in all assets, together with one or more idiosyncratic components. This modeling approach leads to a wide range of price processes, which fit empirical observations on equity markets quite well. For a survey of their theoretical properties, as well as their fit on empirical data, see Luciano and Semeraro (2010a, 2010b), Luciano, Marena, and Semeraro (2015).

In spite of the promising nature of these models for prices, for the time being they do not obtain as a result of equilibria. This is the reason why we do not cover them in this textbook.

———————————————

24 A process is said to be a semimartingale with respect to a given filtration if it admits a decomposition into a local martingale and a finite-variation process. Every martingale, every local martingale, and every finite-variation process is a semimartingale. Semimartingales include not only continuous, but also jump processes, such as the Poisson process. Conversely, not all processes that can be constructed from the Wiener (or the Poisson) process are semimartingales.

7.5   Bubbles

In this section, we illustrate the effect of the multiplicity of solutions of the PDE associated with a stochastic process. The multiplicity of solutions can be given the picturesque name of "bubble." It is commonly believed that, from time to time, bubbles appear in financial markets. We introduce the notion of bubble, as difference between two hypothetical valuations of a security. We consider an underlying or fundamental security that follows an SDE that violates the Lipschitz condition, and a redundant derivative that solves a Black-Scholes type PDE. Both exhibit a bubble.

Remark **7.3**   *The conditions for existence of bubbles are quite distinct depending on whether we look at them out of or in equilibrium. In the present context (no equilibrium requirement), the process for some basic security is given, we assume absence of arbitrage opportunities and we obtain the prices of redundant securities. By contrast, in equilibrium we solve for utility maximizing strategies and the process for the basic securities is endogenized. Since we just addressed in chapter 6 the pricing of derivative securities without embedding it into the market equilibrium, we now study the former problem. The latter will be examined in chapter 15. In this section, we consider situations in which any portfolio strategy including the underlying or the option in any amount would violate the $\mathcal{H}^2$ property because the underlying market itself is not admissible, irrespective of any portfolio strategy.*

We say that a bubble exists when there are two prices for the same security. Formally, we write:

Definition 7.13   (Heston *et al.* (2007))   *A security has a bubble if there is a (at least one) self-financing portfolio, which not only has non-negative (pathwise) value, but that costs less than the security and replicates its payoff. The difference between the security price and the replicating portfolio with lowest value is the bubble.*

To see that a bubble may arise when the PDE for a fundamental security has multiple solutions, consider the example of the so-called Constant Elasticity of Variance (CEV) process (for which a pathology was already found in section 7.1.2). Its dynamics under a given risk-neutral measure P^* is

$$dS(t) = rS(t)dt + \sigma S(t)^{\alpha} dw^*(t) \qquad (7.10)$$

where α and $\sigma > 0$ are constants and w^* is a Wiener process under P^*.

With $\alpha > 1$, the associated PDE admits more than one solution. Consider derivative securities – including the underlying itself – that satisfy the Black-Scholes backward PDE, under appropriate terminal conditions. A well-known example of multiple solutions for the option PDE is the call option written on a CEV underlying.

Example 7.2   Consider the CEV process (7.10) in the case $\alpha > 1$. With this process for the underlying, the backward Black-Scholes PDE (imposing the self-financing condition) is:

$$\frac{1}{2}\sigma^2 S^{2\alpha}\frac{\partial^2}{\partial S^2}C(S,t) + rS\frac{\partial}{\partial S}C(S,t) + \frac{\partial}{\partial t}C(S,t) - rC(S,t) = 0 \qquad (7.11)$$

Emmanuel and MacBeth (1982) have found a solution of the PDE that satisfies the terminal condition for a call: $C(S,T) = [S - \mathcal{K}]^+$. They have proposed that solution as the value of a call option. Let us call it $C^{EM}(S,t;\mathcal{K})$. It is given by:

$$C^{EM}(S,t;\mathcal{K}) = Sp_1(S,t) - \mathcal{K}\exp(-r(T-t))p_2(S,t)$$

where $p_1(S,t)$ and $p_2(S,t)$ are complementary cumulative and cumulative non-central chi-square distributions, respectively, with $v = 1/(\alpha - 1)$ degrees of freedom.[25] The two non-centrality parameters of the two distributions depend on the time to maturity, the strike, and the parameters of the underlying, including the interest rate. Thus the value of the option depends on α, the initial underlying value S, its parameters, including the interest rate, and the time to maturity $T - t$.

Heston *et al.* (2007) pointed out that the solution C^{EM} of the PDE (7.11) is not the expected value of the final payoff of the option, discounted and taken under the risk-neutral measure. There exists another solution of the previous PDE that is equal to that discounted value. Call it C. It is equal to

$$C(S,t;\mathcal{K}) = C^{EM}(S,t;\mathcal{K}) - S\frac{\Gamma[v,z(S,t)]}{\Gamma(v,0)}$$

where z is as in (7.2) above:

$$z(S,t) \triangleq \frac{2r}{\sigma^2(1-\alpha)}\frac{e^{2r(1-\alpha)(T-t)}}{e^{2r(1-\alpha)(T-t)} - 1}S^{2(1-\alpha)}$$

Observe that $C < C^{EM}$ since, under the standard assumption on the interest rate, $r > 0$, the gamma function is positive.

So, in the example, two bubbles are present, which are exactly equal to each other. There is a bubble on the option, equal to

$$C^{EM}(S,t;\mathcal{K}) - C(S,t;\mathcal{K}) = S\frac{\Gamma[v,z(S,t)]}{\Gamma(v,0)}$$

---

25 For the properties of this special function, see, for instance, Johnson and Kotz (1970), chapter 28.

the value of which depends on maturity T (via z) but does not depend on the strike. But there is also a bubble on the underlying, the underlying being a special option with zero strike.[26]

In the CEV example the price C, which, once discounted at the rate r, is a martingale, is smaller than the price C^{EM}, at any point in time before T. One would be tempted to think that the lower of the two prices will prevail. Indeed, if an investor bought and held the underlying or the call option, thus buying the bubble, he would be sure to turn a positive value (the gap $C^{EM} - C > 0$) into zero value, since the terminal value is the same no matter what the purchase price might have been ($z(S, T) = \infty$):

$$C^{EM}(S, T, \mathcal{K}) - C(S, T, \mathcal{K}) = S \frac{\Gamma(v, z(S, T))}{\Gamma(v, 0)} = 0$$

However, that reasoning cannot be right for two reasons. For one, it could be turned on its head by considering the case of an investor who shorts the underlying or the call option or who buys and holds the put option. The lower value of the put and the lower value of the call would not together satisfy the no-arbitrage relation called "put-call parity."

The other reason is more general. Any investor holding the underlying would be holding a position that does not satisfy the $\mathcal{H}^2$ restriction. Because of the diffusion σS^α, which can become very large when $\alpha > 1$, an investor holding or shorting a bubble runs into potentially infinite losses before expiry. The price gap can be exploited, and the initial profit $C^{EM} - C$ locked in, with no final payoff, if and only if one is allowed to run into infinite losses on the way.

Remark 7.4 *In other words, as announced, the underlying price process (7.10) with $\alpha > 1$ is not admissible in the sense of definition 7.7.*

7.6 Itô Processes and the Martingale-Representation Theorem

In the finite-uncertainty setting of chapter 2 we gave sufficient conditions for prices to be martingales, under a measure that was equivalent to the initial one. To set the stage for a similar result in continuous time (which will be given in section 8.3), we are now interested in answering the following questions about Itô processes: when are they continuous-time martingales and when can martingales be represented as Itô processes?

The first question is easy to solve: we know from section 7.2 that, when b belongs to $\mathcal{H}^2$, stochastic integrals are martingales. They are also square integrable, in the sense that their variance exists, that is, is finite, for all t.

What about the second? Can we state that any martingale or any financial strategy with no expected gain can be represented as an Itô integral with a strategy $b \in \mathcal{H}^2$? The answer

---

26 Please, observe that, while the underlying security has no maturity, the bubble on it has one. The bubble termination date is T.

is positive, if it is square integrable; that is, if it has finite variance. The $\mathcal{H}^2$-technical condition is the basis for the following version of the *martingale-representation theorem*:

Theorem 7.2 *Let w be a K dimensional standard Wiener process and $\mathbf{F}^w$ its filtration. If X is a square-integrable martingale with respect to $\mathbf{F}^w$, then there exists a process $b \in \mathcal{H}^2$ such that:*

$$X(t) - X(0) = \int_0^t b(s)dw(s)$$

Putting the two results together, we can state that a process is a square integrable martingale in the filtration generated by a Wiener process if and only if it is a stochastic integral, and the integrand is in $\mathcal{H}^2$. In differential form it has zero drift $(a = 0): dX(t) = b(t)dw(t)$.

The martingale-representation theorem is of paramount importance when it comes to finding portfolios that replicate a given security. It will be key in proving the conditions for market completeness in continuous time (see section 8.4.1). To understand this, go back to the setting of section 6.5, when we were pricing a call option on an underlying that followed a generalized Black-Scholes process.[27] We showed that the three available methods – replication, martingale pricing, and hedging – provided the same option price (written as an expectation). The first and the third method produced a portfolio of their own, while the second one did not. If we are interested in replicating the option while using the martingale approach to price it, we can apply the *martingale-representation theorem*. Without loss of generality, take $r = 0$. Since the underlying price is a martingale, we have:

$$S(T) = \mathbb{E}_t[S(T)] + \int_t^T \sigma(s)S(s)dw(s) = S(t) + \int_t^T \sigma(s)S(s)dw(s) \qquad (7.12)$$

where $\sigma(s)$ is the percentage diffusion of the underlying. Since the call is also a martingale, there must exist a diffusion coefficient m such that:[28]

$$C(T) = \mathbb{E}_t[C(T)] + \int_t^T m(s)dw(s) = C(t) + \int_t^T m(s)dw(s) \qquad (7.13)$$

But by Itô's lemma

$$dC(S,t) = \frac{\partial}{\partial S}C(S,t)dS + \frac{1}{2}\frac{\partial^2}{\partial S^2}C(S,t)\sigma(S,t)^2 S^2 dt + \frac{\partial}{\partial t}C(S,t)dt \qquad (7.14)$$

where dS is given by $S \times (\mu(t)dt + \sigma(t)dw(t))$. It follows that the diffusion coefficient m of the call is the product of the partial derivative of the call with respect to the underlying with the diffusion of the underlying

$$m = \frac{\partial}{\partial S}C(S,t)\sigma(S,t)S(t)$$

---

27 A fortiori, the reasoning will be valid for the strict-Black-Scholes case.

28 Since C is a martingale, and not just a local martingale, m must be a process in $\mathcal{H}^2$.

and that $\partial C/\partial S$ is the amount of the underlying to be held in order to replicate the option. The representation theorem gives as a replicating portfolio exactly the (unique) one we had obtained under the replication approach to the Black-Scholes (strict and generalized) problem. That can be seen by comparing the above to equation (6.9). So, the martingale approach does provide a replication strategy also.

♠

As we saw, when the weaker condition $b \in \mathcal{L}^2$ is imposed, the stochastic integral may only be a local martingale. In that case a martingale-representation theorem still holds but in a weaker version:

Theorem 7.3 *Let w be a K dimensional Wiener process and let $\mathbf{F}^w$ be its filtration. If X is a local martingale with respect to $\mathbf{F}^w$, then there exists a process $b \in \mathcal{L}^2$ such that :*

$$X(t) - X(0) = \int_0^t b(s)dw(s)$$

7.7 Benchmark Example (continued)

This section comments again on the probabilistic properties of the strict-sense Black-Scholes model, based on its representation in terms of stochastic integrals, as announced in example 7.1. The assertions made when we introduced the model and the relation between returns and prices it entails as an example of Itô's lemma are, indeed, rigorously based on the stochastic integral. The properties of stochastic integrals are what provides the differential result.

As we know, the log returns for the strict-sense Black-Scholes model are defined by the following SDE:

$$X(t) = \int_0^t \left(\mu - \frac{\sigma^2}{2} \right) ds + \int_0^t \sigma \, dw(s)$$

where $\mu, \sigma > 0$ are real-valued and X is interpreted as the logarithm of the underlying price S. The equation is linear, with constant coefficients. It follows from theorem 7.1 that it admits a unique continuous solution, defined for all t. Since the first integral is a Riemann integral and the second reduces to

$$\sigma \int_0^t dw(s) = \sigma w(t)$$

the solution is the following:

$$X(t) = \left(\mu - \frac{\sigma^2}{2} \right) t + \sigma w(t)$$

Any SDE with constant drift and diffusion defines an Arithmetic Brownian motion. So, log returns in the Black-Scholes model follow an Arithmetic Brownian motion. At time t, they are Gaussian with mean $\left(\mu - \sigma^2/2 \right) t$ and variance $\sigma^2 t$.

If we use a scalar Arithmetic Brownian motion X as a model for returns, the security's price becomes $S(t) = S(0)\exp(X(t))$. The corresponding equation for $S(t)$

$$S(t) = S(0) + \int_0^t S(s)\mu ds + \int_0^t S(s)\sigma dw(s)$$

is still linear, but its coefficients are not constant. They are proportional to S according to a constant, or linear affine in S. Any SDE with linear affine drift and diffusion defines a Geometric Brownian motion, exactly as an SDE with constant coefficients defined an Arithmetic Brownian motion.

The SDE for S, as any SDE for Geometric Brownian motions, admits a unique solution. With the notation for S, the solution is:

$$S(t) = S(0)e^{\left(\mu - \frac{\sigma^2}{2}\right)t + \sigma w(t)}$$

It follows from the properties of the Gaussian random variable that the mean of $S(t)$ is

$$S(0)\mathbb{E}\left[e^{X(t)}\right] = S(0)e^{\mathbb{E}[X(t)] + \frac{var[X(t)]}{2}}$$

$$= S(0)e^{\left(\mu - \frac{\sigma^2}{2}\right)t + \frac{\sigma^2}{2}t} = S(0)e^{\mu t}$$

Prices grow in expectation at the rate μ.

The reader could do a similar calculation in the multidimensional case. We suggest that the reader solve exercise 7.7 as well.

7.8   Conclusion

Gains obtained in the financial market from a portfolio strategy are formulated as stochastic integrals. In a well-functioning market, gains or losses should *not be allowed to become infinite* in finite time. In this chapter, we have stated conditions guaranteeing that stochastic integrals satisfy that requirement.

In the reverse, when the *expected* gains from trade are equal to zero, which means that the gains are a martingale, the martingale-representation theorem tells us that there exists a portfolio strategy producing those gains.

Using the machinery of stochastic integrals, we also defined Itô processes and stated conditions under which they are Markov processes and conditions under which they are diffusions. In the rest of the book, unless otherwise stated, we will only distinguish the Itô case from the Markov case. All Itô processes will be diffusions: they will have a drift and a diffusion coefficient (which is a matrix in the case of more than one Wiener process).

Exercises

7.1. Let w be a unidimensional Wiener process. Calculate:

$$\mathbb{E}\left\{\left[\int_t^u w(\tau)d\tau\right]^2 \middle| w(t) = x; t \le u\right\}$$

and prove that it differs from

$$\mathbb{E}\left\{\left[\int_t^u w^2(\tau)d\tau\right] \middle| w(t) = x; t \le u\right\}$$

7.2. Consider the following pair of processes:

$$dX(t) = \mu(t)dt + \sigma_X dw_X(t)$$
$$d\mu(t) = \sigma_\mu dw_\mu(t)$$

where w_X and w_μ are two independent, unidimensional Wiener processes and σ_X, $\sigma_\mu \in \mathbb{R}_{++}$. Calculate:

$$\mathbb{E}[X(t)|X(0) = x_0, \mu(0) = \mu_0; 0 \le t]$$
$$\text{var}[X(t)|X(0) = x_0, \mu(0) = \mu_0; 0 \le t]$$

7.3. Solve the following SDE and find the mean, variance, and distribution at time t of the unidimensional process X:

$$dX(t) = (\beta - \alpha X(t))dt + \sigma\,dw(t)$$

when $X(0) = X_0$, $\alpha, \beta, \sigma \in \mathbb{R}$ and $\alpha \neq 0$.

7.4. Evaluate:

$$\int_t^{t+h} [w(s) - w(t)]dw(s)$$

where w is a unidimensional Wiener process.

7.5. (Arnold (1974), page 111 [example due to Girsanov]). Show that the integral equation:

$$X(t) = \int_0^t |X(s)|^\alpha ds; \alpha > 1$$

where X is unidimensional, violates the Lipschitz condition. Prove the same in the stochastic-differential case when the diffusion coefficient is a power function:

$$dX(t) = X(t)^\alpha dw(t); \alpha > 1$$

7.6. (Arnold (1974), page 112). Show that the differential equation:

$$dX = X^2 dt$$

where X is unidimensional, violates the growth condition.

7.7. Let the SDE for nominal prices on equity be:

$$S(t) = S_0 + \int_0^t S(s)\mu \, ds + \int_0^t S(s)\sigma \, dw(s)$$

and the SDE for the prices of goods be:

$$P(t) = P_0 + \int_0^t \mu_P P(s) ds + \int_0^t \sigma_P P(s) dz(s)$$

where w and z are two unidimensional Wiener processes, possibly correlated with each other and $\mu, \mu_P \in \mathbb{R}$, $\sigma, \mu_P, S_0, P_0 \in \mathbb{R}_{++}$. Find the SDE for the deflated price of equity S/P.

8 Pricing Redundant Securities

When we priced redundant securities in chapter 6, we used three equivalent arguments:

- discounting by a factor that makes securities' prices martingales
- replication
- hedging.

In this chapter, we show that the price today of any security (basic or redundant) and of any future payoff stream, may be obtained by taking its expected, discounted value, after an appropriate change of probability measure. The existence of that change of probability measure is essentially equivalent to the absence of arbitrage opportunities. That statement is valid in continuous time, as it was in discrete time. It applies both in complete and incomplete markets, as can be surmised from what was said in discrete time. In complete markets, the change of measure is unique.

We first set up, in section 8.1, the generalized Black-Scholes market-model. *We do not assume completeness.* We explain how to change the measure in that market in section 8.2. That is done by means of the so-called exponential martingale built from the market price of risk and by applying the Girsanov theorem. We then report on the equivalence between the existence of a change of measure that makes security prices martingales and the absence of arbitrage opportunities (section 8.3).

The second part of the chapter, beginning with section 8.4, focuses on complete markets. We provide the necessary and sufficient condition for completeness in section 8.4.1. In section 8.4.2 we show that the corresponding state prices, as well as stochastic discount factors and the equivalent martingale measure, are unique. In section 8.5 we introduce a notion of completeness that parallels and enriches the previous, traditional one, namely *"asset-specific completeness."* As usual, applications to our benchmark example conclude the chapter.[1]

---

1 Reminder: unless doing otherwise is necessary for comprehension, we simplify the notation for processes. All processes are stochastic but we suppress the reference to the state ω. Therefore, $X(t)$ actually means $X(\omega, t)$. In special cases, we also use the notation $f(t)$ to refer to a deterministic function of time. When this happens, we say so explicitly.

8.1 Market Setup

This section introduces our baseline, generalized Black-Scholes continuous-time market. It is rich of technical assumptions, which we recall and collect here, and will keep unchanged until Part V of the book.

Consider, as in the previous chapter, a time interval $\mathcal{T} = [0, T], T < \infty$, a complete probability space $(\Omega, \mathcal{F}, P)$, and a K-dimensional standard Wiener process $w(\omega, t)$, $t \in \mathcal{T}$, written $w(t)$ for short.[2] The space is endowed with the filtration generated by w, $\mathbf{F}^w = \{\mathcal{F}^w(t)\}$.

To characterize the market, we introduce in this space:

- the riskless security with price B and N long-lived risky securities with prices $\mathcal{S}$,[3]
- admissible, self-financing strategies (α, Θ),
- a definition of wealth,
- single-payment securities X and their replicating strategies.

The riskless security and N long-lived risky securities

There are $N + 1$ securities available in the market. A *bank account* B yields an instantaneously riskless rate r:[4]

$$B(t) = B(0)e^{\int_0^t r(s)ds} \tag{8.1}$$

or

$$dB(t) = r(t)B(t)dt$$

for which, without loss of generality, we assume $B(0) = 1$. And N *risky securities* pay dividends. Their SDE is:

$$\mathcal{S}(t) + \int_0^t \iota(s)ds = \mathcal{S}(0) + \int_0^t \mu(s)ds + \int_0^t \sigma(s)dw(s) \tag{8.2}$$

where $\mathcal{S}(0) = \mathcal{S}_0 \in \mathbb{R}^N$, ι and μ are the N-dimensional vectors of dividend yields and conditionally expected returns (in units of consumption, as opposed to percentages), σ is the $N \times K$ matrix of (consumption-unit) instantaneous volatilities. We take no stance on whether the number of securities is greater than or equal to the number of Wiener processes, and we simply assume existence of a solution to the SDE (8.2). In this way, $\mathcal{S}$ is well defined, not

---

2 As in the strict-Black-Scholes case of chapter 6, whenever, for a given number of securities, the number of Wiener processes can be reduced to a minimum, K has to be understood as the minimum number of Wieners necessary to describe the securities' dynamics.

3 As in discrete time, it is not really necessary to consider long-lived securities only. They only simplify the notations. If some securities come to their maturity date, they can be replaced by newly issued assets or we must consider that the number of outstanding assets N_t varies over time.

4 The process of r is assumed to be in $\mathcal{L}^1$, so that the value at time t of the riskless security is well defined.

necessarily Markovian, and its first two moments are finite.[5] We assume that securities' prices cannot go negative (that could be, for instance, because of limited liability).

Admissible, self-financing strategies

To characterize the portfolio strategies, assume, as we did in discrete time, that:

- trade can occur continuously in time *without any friction*: no transaction costs and no taxes,
- no portfolio constraints exist; in particular, no margin deposits or collateral is required and short sales are admissible, with full use of the proceeds,
- securities are infinitely divisible.

Denote as $\alpha(t)$ and $\Theta(t)$ the quantities of riskless and risky security held in a portfolio. $\alpha(t)$ is a scalar; $\Theta(t)$ is an N-dimensional vector. Its entries are, as usual, $\theta_i(t), i = 1, ..N$, with $\theta_i(t) < 0$ representing the holding of securities short (as a liability). A *trading strategy* is a pair (α, Θ). We now define its gain process and self-financing trading strategies, thus generalizing to the case of dividends being paid what we did in sections 6.1 and 6.4. The corresponding gains process is:

$$G(t) = \int_0^t \left[\alpha(s) \times dB(s) + \Theta^\mathsf{T}(s) \left(dS(s) + \iota(s)ds \right) \right] \tag{8.3}$$

$$= \int_0^t \left(\alpha(s) \times B(s) \times r(s) + \Theta(s)^\mathsf{T} \mu(s) \right) ds + \int_0^t \Theta(s)^\mathsf{T} \sigma(s) dw(s)$$

These gains are well defined provided the trading strategies are *admissible* in the sense of definition 7.7, that is, provided that the integrands $\alpha \times B \times r + \Theta^\mathsf{T} \mu$ and $\Theta^\mathsf{T} \sigma$ belong respectively to $\mathcal{L}^1$ and $\mathcal{H}^2$, which is what we assume throughout the book, unless otherwise indicated.

Financial wealth

Once strategies are defined, one can also introduce the concept of *financial wealth*, denoted as $W(t)$. By definition, this is the total value of financial securities held by the investor, both at time 0 and at later points in time:

$$W(t) \triangleq \alpha(t)B(t) + \Theta^\mathsf{T}(t)S(t) \tag{8.4}$$

We take initial financial wealth as given: $W(0) = W_0$. To simplify notations, we assume that the investor does not receive any endowment after time 0. We must then assume that W_0 is strictly positive, because the investor must have something to live on.

---

5 Since equation (8.2) is written in terms of absolute returns, we shall write the portfolio composition in terms of number of units held (and collect them in a vector Θ). In other places (such as chapter 9), when the parameters μ, σ in the price equation are percentage returns, the portfolio composition – represented then by a vector x – is viewed as a consumption amount held as a fraction of wealth, not as a vector of numbers of units of securities held. The relation between the two is spelled out in equation (9.10).

Definition 8.1   *An admissible strategy is* self-financing *if it consists in reinvesting the proceeds from dividends and net sales of risky securities and funding the cash needs for net purchases from the riskless security.*

In integral form, wealth at time t must equal wealth at time 0 plus the value of the gains process at that point, the gains process being as defined above:[6,7]

$$\underbrace{\alpha(t) \times B(t) + \Theta^{\mathsf{T}}(t)\mathcal{S}(t)}_{W(t)} = \underbrace{\alpha(0) \times B(0) + \Theta^{\mathsf{T}}(0)\mathcal{S}(0)}_{W(0)} + G(t) \qquad (8.5)$$

Single-payment securities and their replicating strategies
Within the context of the market just described, below we price single-payment securities (also called (state-)contingent claims):

Definition 8.2   *A single-payment security gives the right to a non-negative payoff $X(\omega)$ at time T if state $\omega \in \Omega$ realizes. $X(\omega)$ is a random variable measurable with respect to $\mathcal{F}(T)$, which we write $X(T)$ for short.*

We assume that the first two moments of X are finite, that is, that X is square-integrable.

Definition 8.3   *A self-financing trading strategy* replicates *the security X if its value at T (which is on the LHS of the upcoming equation) is equal to X for all states ω:*

$$\alpha(T)B(T) + \Theta^{\mathsf{T}}(T)\mathcal{S}(T) = X(T)$$

It can be easily proved that, if two self financing strategies $(\alpha_1, \Theta_1), (\alpha_2, \Theta_2)$ replicate the same security, they must have the same value in any state and at any point in time $t \leq T$:

$$\alpha_1(t) \times B(t) + \Theta_1^{\mathsf{T}}(t)\mathcal{S}(t) = \alpha_2(t) \times B(t) + \Theta_2^{\mathsf{T}}(t)\mathcal{S}(t)$$

We do not demonstrate the result, since the reader can rely on the *Law of One Price* to justify it.

8.2   Changes of Measure

In one-period economies, since the probability of all states at time 1 was positive, changing the measure simply meant finding a vector of positive numbers, normalized to sum up to one, which could be interpreted as a probability distribution, equivalent to the initial one.

---

6 The result can be demonstrated with the same reasoning used in sections 6.1 and 6.4.

7 It can easily be shown that, if a strategy is self financing, it remains such if we normalize the security prices by, say, the risky bond price, that is, the equality is equivalent to

$$\alpha(t) + \Theta^{\mathsf{T}}(t)\mathcal{S}(t)B(t)^{-1} = \alpha(0) + \Theta^{\mathsf{T}}(0)\mathcal{S}(0)B(0)^{-1}$$

$$+ \int_0^t (\alpha(s)r(s) + \Theta^{\mathsf{T}}(s)\mu(s)B(s)^{-1})ds + \int_0^t \Theta^{\mathsf{T}}(s)\sigma(s)B(s)^{-1}dw(s)$$

That vector made it possible to write prices as expectations of (discounted) payoffs. In discrete-time multiperiod economies, we could again produce a change of measure from final states to initial ones that permitted us to write securities prices as expectations of (discounted) payoffs.

Also in continuous time, when we consider a single-maturity, non-negative payoff $X(T)$, we may be interested in getting its price at time 0 in the form of an expectation. To do so, we proceed as follows. First, we introduce equivalent measures in continuous time. We characterize the object that makes the change of measure possible, the Radon-Nikodym derivative, and retrieve it in discrete-time, finite-uncertainty economies. Then, we define exponential martingales and show that they are the Radon-Nikodym derivative for the generalized Black-Scholes case. The risk-neutral measure is obtained. As usual, we accompany the shift to the risk-neutral measure with the elicitation of stochastic discount factors.

8.2.1   Equivalent Measures and the Radon-Nikodym Derivative

Let P and P^* be two probability measures on the real line and use the notation $\mathbb{E}$ for expectation under P and $\mathbb{E}^*$ for expectation under P^*. Note that, for the time being, P^* is any measure, not necessarily the risk-neutral one. We first define measures that are *equivalent* and then the *Radon-Nikodym derivative* of one measure relative to another.[8]

Definition 8.4   *Two probability measures P^* and P on the probability space $(\Omega, \mathcal{F})$ are equivalent if and only if they have the same null sets (that is, sets with zero probability of occurrence).*

As a special case, of course, they are equivalent if both are strictly positive: $P(A) > 0$ and $P^*(A) > 0$ for every set A of the σ-algebra.

A theorem in Measure Theory says that if two probability measures are equivalent, there exists an almost surely positive real random variable η on the real line such that:

$$P^*(A) = \mathbb{E}\big[\eta \times \mathbf{1}_{\{A\}}\big]$$

and vice versa:

$$P(A) = \mathbb{E}^*\left[\frac{1}{\eta} \times \mathbf{1}_{\{A\}}\right]$$

for every set A of the σ-algebra. That random variable η is called a Radon-Nikodym derivative:

Definition 8.5   *The Radon-Nikodym derivative, or density, of a probability measure P^* with respect to P is the random variable, denoted dP^*/dP, such that*

$$P^*(A) = \mathbb{E}\left[\left(\frac{dP^*}{dP}\right) \times \mathbf{1}_{\{A\}}\right] \tag{8.6}$$

for every set A of the σ-algebra.

---

8 Recall that the indicator function of the event $A, \mathbf{1}_{\{A\}}$, evaluates to 1 if A is true, 0 otherwise.

In our case the relevant σ-algebra is $\mathcal{F}^\omega(T)$. Together with the Radon-Nikodym deriva-tive, which is a *random variable,* we will also need its conditional expectation at any time $t \leq T$, which is an adapted *process:*

Definition 8.6   *The* likelihood ratio or density process *of the Radon-Nikodym derivative, which we call g(t), is its conditional expectation under P:*

$$g(t) = \mathbb{E}\left[\frac{dP^*}{dP} \mid \mathcal{F}(t)\right] \text{ so that } g(T) = \frac{dP^*}{dP}.$$

The Radon-Nikodym derivative and its expectation have a number of properties. If both measures are strictly positive, the derivative is positive. The most important property indi-cates how to connect expected values under P to expected values under P^*:

Proposition 8.1   *Expectations under P and P* are in the following relation:*

$$\mathbb{E}^*[X(T)] = \mathbb{E}\left[\frac{dP^*}{dP}X(T)\right] = \mathbb{E}\left[g(T)X(T)\right] \tag{8.7}$$

$$\mathbb{E}^*[X(T) \mid \mathcal{F}(t)] = \frac{1}{g(t)}\mathbb{E}\left[g(T)X(T) \mid \mathcal{F}(t)\right] \tag{8.8}$$

The first equality says that, at time 0, the expectation of any time-T random variable X under the new measure is the expectation, under the old measure, of the product of the Radon-Nikodym derivative with the random variable itself. The second property extends the idea to conditional expectations taken at points in time t posterior to 0 and prior to T, using the density process $g(t)$. It makes use of Bayes' rule for conditional expectations which states that, for any event A in the filtration $\mathcal{F}(t)$,

$$\mathbb{E}^*\left[X(T) \times \mathbf{1}_{\{A\}} \mid \mathcal{F}(t)\right] = \mathbb{E}^*\left[\frac{1}{g(t)}\mathbb{E}\left[g(T)X(T)\right] \times \mathbf{1}_{\{A\}} \mid \mathcal{F}(t)\right] \tag{8.9}$$

The proof of this version of Bayes' rule is given below, in small characters.

Remark 8.1   *Recall the Radon-Nikodym derivative for the change from the effective to the risk-neutral measure in the discrete-time, discrete-state settings covered in Part I of the book.*
In one-period models, the Radon-Nikodym derivative which converted events to the risk-neutral measure was simply the ratio of the new, risk-neutral probability $\phi^*(s)$ to the old, effective probability $\pi(s)$. Trivially, we had $\phi^*(s) = \pi(s) \times (\phi^*(s)/\pi(s))$, or

$$\frac{dP^*}{dP} = \frac{\phi^*(s)}{\pi(s)}$$

which satisfies definition 8.5:[9]

$$P^*(\omega_s) = \mathbb{E}\left[\left(\frac{\phi^*(s)}{\pi(s)}\right) \times \mathbf{1}_{\{\omega_s\}}\right] = \pi(s) \times \left(\frac{\phi^*(s)}{\pi(s)}\right) = \phi^*(s)$$

In discrete, multiperiod settings, the Radon-Nikodym derivative towards the risk-neutral measure was simply the ratio

$$\eta(t) \triangleq \frac{\phi^*(t)}{\pi(t)}$$

Indeed, when we discussed the fundamental theorem of security pricing, we introduced that process η, whose value at 0, $\eta(0)$, is equal to 1, and we proved that the expectation under the risk-neutral measure could be written as the expectation under the effective measure, provided that the integrand was multiplied by the change of measure, as in (2.19) and (2.20):

$$S(0) = \mathbb{E}^*\left[\prod_{u=0}^{T-1}(1 + r(u))^{-1}S(T)\right]$$

$$= \mathbb{E}\left[\frac{\eta(T)}{\eta(0)}\prod_{u=0}^{T-1}(1 + r(u))^{-1}S(T)\right]$$

$$= \mathbb{E}\left[\eta(T)\prod_{u=0}^{T-1}(1 + r(u))^{-1}S(T)\right]$$

This shows that η is the change to the risk-neutral measure. To confirm that, take $r = 0$ and a security paying one in state s and zero otherwise (an Arrow-Debreu security). We have the probability of the state on the LHS, $P^*(\omega_s)$ and $\mathbb{E}[\eta(T) \times \mathbf{1}_{\{\omega_s\}}]$ on the RHS, which tells us again that $\eta(T)$ is the Radon-Nikodym derivative, which satisfies definition 8.5:

$$P^*(\omega_s) = \mathbb{E}[\eta(T) \times \mathbf{1}_{\{\omega_s\}}] = \pi(T) \times \frac{\phi^*(T)}{\pi(T)} = \phi^*(T)$$

Finally, in discussing the binomial model, we defined a quantity, which had exactly the same purpose as the change of measure ϕ^*_s/π_s in the one-period setting. Indeed, the effective probability probability for node $u^j d^{n-j}$ at time T, evaluated at time 0, denoted as $\pi_{n,j}$, was $\binom{n}{j}p^j(1-p)^{n-j}$, while the risk-neutral one was

$$\binom{n}{j}p^{*j}(1-p^*)^{n-j}$$

The ratio of the risk neutral to the effective probability; that is, the Radon-Nikodym derivative, was

$$\eta_{n,j} \triangleq \frac{p^{*j}(1-p^*)^{n-j}}{p^j(1-p)^{n-j}}$$

---

9 The Radon derivative was, indeed, a random variable, since its value depended on the state.

This provided a change of measure, which worked from time 0 to a specific state $u^j d^{n-j}$ at time T. The probability of state $u^j d^{n-j}$ after the change of measure was:

$$P^*(u^j d^{n-j}) = \mathbb{E}\left[\eta \times \mathbf{1}_{\{u^j d^{n-j}\}}\right] = \binom{n}{j} p^j (1-p)^{n-j} \frac{p^{*j}(1-p^*)^{n-j}}{p^j(1-p)^{n-j}}$$

$$= \binom{n}{j} p^{*j}(1-p^*)^{n-j}$$

and satisfied definition 8.5.

━━━━━━━━━━━━━━━━ ♠ ━━━━━━━━━━━━━━━━

To demonstrate version (8.9) of Bayes' rule, start from (8.7) and substitute it into the right-hand side of (8.9). We get:

$$\mathbb{E}^*\left[\frac{1}{g(t)}\mathbb{E}_t\big[g(T)X(T)\big] \times \mathbf{1}_{\{A\}}\right] = \mathbb{E}\left[\frac{g(T)}{g(t)}\mathbb{E}_t\big[g(T)X(T)\big] \times \mathbf{1}_{\{A\}}\right]$$

By the Law of Iterated Expectations introduced in section 2.2.1 and by (8.7), this becomes:

$$\mathbb{E}\left\{\mathbb{E}_t\left[\frac{g(T)}{g(t)}\mathbb{E}_t\big[g(T)X(T)\big] \times \mathbf{1}_{\{A\}}\right]\right\} = \mathbb{E}\left\{\mathbb{E}_t\big[g(T)X(T)\big] \times \mathbf{1}_{\{A\}}\right\}$$

$$= \mathbb{E}\left\{\big[g(T)X(T)\big] \times \mathbf{1}_{\{A\}}\right\}$$

$$= \mathbb{E}^*\big[X(T) \times \mathbf{1}_{\{A\}}\big]$$

which is the left-hand side of (8.9). So, Bayes' rule holds.

8.2.2 Girsanov's Theorem: How to Shift to the Risk-Neutral Measure in Black-Scholes Economies

Extending what we did in the strict-sense Black-Scholes, univariate case of chapter 6, we introduce the definitions of the market price of risk and of the exponential martingale for N securities, K Wiener processes:

Definition 8.7 *A market-price of risk process κ is a $\mathbb{R}^K$-valued process such that:*[10]

$$\sigma(t)\kappa(t) \triangleq \mu(t) - r(t) \times \mathcal{S}(t) \tag{8.10}$$

If the number N of securities is equal to the number of Wiener processes K, a circumstance we will examine below, and rank$(\sigma(t)) = K$ at all times, the matrix σ is square and

---

10 Notice that we have the difference between μ and rS on the right-hand side and σ on the left-hand side, since both the drift μ and the diffusion σ are in units of consumption, not in percentage terms. For consistency, the riskless return also must be applied to an amount of units of consumption; hence $r \times S$. If we specified the price process in percentage returns, we would subtract the percentage riskless rate. Consider the one-Wiener case for simplicity. If we wrote

$$dS(t) = \mu(t)S(t)dt + \sigma(t)S(t)dw(t)$$

where the parameters μ and σ were percentage returns, the market price of risk would be computed from percentage returns: $(\mu(t) - r(t))/\sigma(t)$.

non-singular. The vector of market prices of risk is then unique, in the sense that equation (8.10) admits a unique, explicit solution:

$$\kappa(t) = \sigma(t)^{-1}[\mu(t) - r(t) \times \mathcal{S}(t)]$$

This is a multivariate generalization of the familiar Sharpe ratio (see Sharpe (1966, 1994)).

Even when κ is not unique, thanks to (8.10), it can be interpreted in the same way as in single-period models: it is the excess return investors earn per unit of risk, for each dimension of risk.

Now, introduce the following process based on the market prices of risk:

Definition 8.8 *The exponential local martingale of $\kappa(t)$ is the real-valued process $\eta(t)$*

$$\eta(t) \triangleq \exp\left\{ -\int_0^t \kappa(s)^\mathsf{T} dw(s) - \frac{1}{2}\int_0^t \|\kappa(s)\|^2 \times ds \right\} \tag{8.11}$$

The exponential local martingale is strictly positive and such that $\eta(0) = 1$. The name is justified by the fact that it is at least a local martingale. This can be seen applying Itô's lemma:

$$d\eta(t) = -\eta(t)\kappa(t)^\mathsf{T} dw(t) \tag{8.12}$$

It is apparent from the differential of η that it has zero drift. A sufficient condition for making it a martingale is the Novikov condition:

Definition 8.9 *The process κ satisfies the **Novikov** condition if and only if*

$$\mathbb{E}\left[\exp\left\{ \frac{1}{2}\int_0^T \|\kappa(s)\|^2 ds \right\} \right] < \infty \tag{8.13}$$

Proposition 8.2 *Under the Novikov condition, the exponential martingale η, which is a positive Itô process with initial value $\eta(0) = 1$ and zero drift, is a martingale.*

Proof. The proof that the Novikov condition makes η a martingale is in Liptser and Shiryayev (1977, theorem 6.1). Duffie (1988, Lemma E21) provides an easier proof, *based on the stronger assumption that the market price of risk itself is bounded.* So, the Novikov condition holds. Thanks to the boundedness of κ, also the following condition holds, for all t, including T:

$$\mathbb{E}\left[\left(\int_0^t \eta^2(s)\kappa^\mathsf{T}(s)\kappa(s)ds \right)^2 \right] < \infty$$

It says that $\eta(s)\kappa^\mathsf{T}(s) \in \mathcal{H}^2$. Consider now η. It follows from Itô's lemma, integrating (8.12), that

$$\eta(t) = 1 + \int_0^t \eta(s)\kappa^\mathsf{T}(s)dw(s)$$

Since the integrand is in $\mathcal{H}^2$, the integral is a martingale, as needed. $\qquad\square$

With the Novikov condition in force, the exponential martingale is not only a local martingale, but a martingale (which can be shown to be square integrable). As a consequence, $\mathbb{E}[\eta(T)] = \eta(0) = 1$. *From now on, we assume, as usual in this field, that the (sufficient) Novikov condition holds. As a consequence, the process η is a martingale.*

Thanks to the fact that the random variable $\eta(T)$ is positive and has unit expectation, it is a good candidate for being assigned as a probability measure on the space $(\Omega, \mathcal{F})$, according to

$$P^*(A) = \mathbb{E}\big[\eta(T) \times \mathbf{1}_{\{A\}}\big]$$

for all events $A \in \mathcal{F}$. If we compare this probability assignment with the definition of the Radon-Nikodym derivative 8.5, we can state that $\eta(T)$ *is the Radon-Nikodym derivative for the generalized Black-Scholes model*, which brings from P to a measure that we called P^*. In terms of expectations, we then have

$$\mathbb{E}^*[X(T)] = X_0$$

if and only if

$$\mathbb{E}[\eta(T)X(T)] = X_0$$

What has still to be demonstrated is that the new measure is a risk-neutral one, that is, that undiscounted securities' prices, under the new measure, return the riskless rate. This follows from the following theorem:

Theorem 8.1 (Girsanov theorem) *Let P^* be the probability that has density $g(t) = \eta(t)$ with respect to P. If the Novikov condition holds,*

$$w^*(t) = \int_0^t \kappa(s)ds + w(t) \tag{8.14}$$

is a Wiener process with respect to $\mathbf{F}^{w^*}$ and P^*.

To apply the theorem, all we have to do is to actually implement this substitution. Take any Itô price process:

$$d\mathcal{S}(t) = \mu(t)dt + \sigma(t)dw(t) \tag{8.15}$$

and perform the substitution (8.14):

$$d\mathcal{S}(t) = \mu(t)dt + \sigma(t)\big[dw^*(t) - \kappa(t)dt\big]$$
$$= r(t)\mathbf{1}dt + \sigma(t)dw^*(t)$$

where $\mathbf{1}$ is a vector of ones with the same number N of elements as μ. Equivalently, we could have proved that securities' prices discounted using B^{-1} are driftless:

$$d\left(\mathcal{S}(t)B^{-1}(t)\right) = B^{-1}(t)\sigma(t)dw^*(t)$$

So, Girsanov theorem serves to show that the change of measure based on the exponential martingale gives the risk-neutral measure.

A measure P^* with the above properties will be called an "equivalent martingale measure (EMM)."

The theorem thus gives us a convenient way to change the measure to a risk-neutral one *when writing down SDEs for prices*: the change of measure is obtained by turning the securities' drift into the riskless rate, and the theorem guarantees that the diffusion term contains the same coefficient σ as before, multiplied times a process w^* which is still a Wiener process, under the new measure. From this we obtain the rule: *"change the drift in order to change the measure,* and leave the diffusion unchanged," a rule which makes continuous-time very easy to work with.

On the technical front, notice that the Girsanov theorem says that, under the Novikov condition, the change of measure changes the drift but *does not change the diffusion.* Hence, under that condition, if a process has a diffusion that belongs to the $\mathcal{H}^2$ class under one measure,[11] as we have imposed on admissible strategies, it also belongs to the $\mathcal{H}^2$ class under the other measure as well.[12]

For other applications of the theorem, we refer the reader to section 8.6 below, where the constant-coefficient (or Black-Scholes strict sense) process is examined, to exercise 8.1, which examines the most ubiquitous application of Girsanov theorem and to exercise 8.2, which examines a case in which the theorem cannot be applied.

8.2.3   Change of Measure, Stochastic Discount Factors, and State Prices

The role of the exponential martingale in continuous-time economies with generalized Black-Scholes securities is pervasive. First of all, η is also a discount factor, exactly as it was in discrete-time economies. Generalizing the method we adopted in chapter 6 for the single-security case, we can easily prove that, once securities prices are discounted using the riskless rate and the exponential martingale, their discounted values $B^{-1}\eta S$ are (local) martingales under P. Indeed, the stochastic process for η being (8.12), the diffusion matrix of the discounted prices $B^{-1}\eta \mathcal{S}$ is

$$B(t)^{-1}\eta(t) \times \left(-\mathcal{S}(t)\kappa(t)^{\mathsf{T}} + \sigma(t)\right)$$

and

$$d(B(t)^{-1}\eta(t)S) = B(t)^{-1}\eta(t) \times \left(-\mathcal{S}(t)\kappa(t)^{\mathsf{T}} + \sigma(t)\right) dw(t)$$

The proof is in exercise 8.3.

We can also define the stochastic discount factor as the product of the discount factor for the time value of money and the exponential martingale

$$\xi \triangleq B^{-1}\eta$$

---

11 Recall from chapter 7 that the definition of the $\mathcal{H}^2$ class referred to a particular probability measure; that is, it should have properly been called $\mathcal{H}^2(P)$.

12 For admissibility, we have assumed that drifts are in $\mathcal{L}^1$. They are in that class irrespective of the probability measure, among measures that are equivalent.

It is easy to verify that

$$d\xi(t) = -\xi(t)r(t)dt - \xi(t)\kappa(t)^\mathsf{T}dw(t) \qquad (8.16)$$

– so that the instantaneous rate of interest is given by minus the percentage drift in ξ – and to see that prices discounted at ξ are (local) martingales under P:

$$d(\xi(t)S(t)) = \xi(t) \times \left(-S(t)\kappa(t)^\mathsf{T} + \sigma\right)dw(t) \qquad (8.17)$$

Under the Novikov condition, assuming σ bounded, both local martingales are martingales.

We can interpret the quantities

$$\xi(T)dP(\omega)$$

as *Arrow-Debreu or state prices*. Indeed, formula (8.18) in the next section shows that ξdP is the price at time 0 of a single-payment security that pays 1 at T in state ω, and 0 otherwise:

$$\mathbb{E}[\mathbf{1}_\omega \times \xi(T)] = \xi(T)dP(\omega)$$

The existence of these state prices is a simple consequence of ruling out arbitrage opportunities and is not based on any equilibrium assumption or optimality condition, as we see in the next section.

So, defining η and introducing some technicalities, such as the Novikov condition, one can show, as we did in the previous section, that securities' prices have drift r under the new measure P^*. This means that, once discounted by B^{-1}, they are martingales under that measure. One can also show that prices discounted using B^{-1} and η, or using ξ, are martingales under the effective measure, as we did just above. Using η and the Fundamental theorem one can reconstruct state prices.

But if we do take into consideration optimality conditions, the stochastic discount factor is still the transfer price – or the transformation into utils – that allows us to price any unit of numeraire received at time t. It can still be split into discounting for the time value of money, via B^{-1}, and discounting for risk aversion, via η. This is the sense in which η is a discount factor in addition to being a change of measure.

For other applications of η, the reader can see exercises 8.4 and 8.5.

8.3   Fundamental Theorem of Security Pricing

We just "reconstructed" in a (generalized) Black-Scholes economy the results we had obtained in discrete time for risk-neutral probabilities and discount factors. Reconstructing the relation between existence of a martingale measure and absence of arbitrage is more subtle.

Theorem 8.2   *Let investors have access to admissible strategies only and let the Novikov condition be satisfied. There is an equivalent martingale measure P^* for the generalized Black-Scholes model only if no arbitrage strategy is available in the market, where arbitrage strategies are as in definition (7.9).*

Recall that the gain process and portfolio value are

$$G(t) = \int_0^t (\alpha(s)dB(s) + \Theta(s)d\mathcal{S}(s))$$

$$V(t) = \alpha(t)B(t) + \Theta^\mathsf{T}(t)S(t)$$

It is straightforward to show that the existence of an equivalent measure P^* implies absence of arbitrage. Any strategy, including any arbitrage strategy, would have a price at time 0 given by the expected value under P^*. That expected value for any admissible, self-financing strategy ($V(t) = V(0) + G(t)$ for every t) in $\mathcal{H}^2$ that produces at time T gains that have P-probability 1 of not being negative and a strictly positive P-probability of being strictly positive, would be a strictly positive number (under both measures P and P^*).

The converse theorem that we would like to have available is the following. Unfortunately, it is, as far as we know, only a conjecture:

Conjecture 8.1 Let investors have access to admissible strategies only and let the Novikov condition be satisfied. There is an equivalent martingale measure P^* for the generalized Black-Scholes model if no arbitrage strategy is available in the market, where arbitrage strategies are as in definition (7.9).

Historically, Harrison and Kreps (1978) proved a theorem of that kind but restricting portfolio policies Θ to being simple strategies. Then Harrison and Pliska (1981) proved the same theorem restricting all portfolio policies to being *quasi-simple* strategies. This means that transactions are finite in number, but can occur at random or stopping times $\tau_0 = 0 < \tau_1 < \tau_2 < .. < \tau_T = T$. As was true for simple strategies, the portfolio remains unchanged between two dates.[13] Delbaen and Schachermayer (1994) also proved a theorem for price processes that are more general than Itô processes but for a restricted class of quasi-simple strategies, with a different definition of no arbitrage called *"no free-lunch with vanishing risk."* That theorem is, at once, very restrictive on the policies and more general than we need on the price processes. We know of no proof of the conjectured statement 8.1 for strategies in $\mathcal{H}^2$ in general.[14]

---

13 Since strategies are quasi-simple, they may be written as

$$\Theta(t) = \sum_{i=0}^{T-1} \Theta(\tau_i)\mathbf{1}_{\{[\tau_i,\tau_{i+1})\}} + \Theta(\tau_T)\mathbf{1}_{\{\tau_T\}}$$

Similarly for α.

14 Nor is there a proof for strategies in $\mathcal{L}^2$ with a lower bound on wealth, which would be admissible under the alternative definition 7.8.

If the conjecture is correct, the absence of arbitrage implies that there is a martingale pricing measure P^* under which the price at time t of any attainable claim $X(T)$ is given by:

$$P_X(t) = S_0(t)\mathbb{E}^*\left[\frac{X(T)}{S_0(T)} \mid \mathcal{F}(t)\right] \tag{8.18}$$

where S_0 is the price of a traded reference security (often called a numeraire),[15] provided its price process is adapted and stays positive. Otherwise said, the price of $X(T)$ normalized by S_0 is a martingale. If, as assumed in the previous sections, S_0 is a bank account on which the instantaneously riskless interest rate $r(t)$ accrues:

$$S_0(t) = S_0 \exp\left(\int_0^t r(s)ds\right) \tag{8.19}$$

the formula in the previous theorem becomes:

$$P_X(t) = \mathbb{E}^*\left[X(T)\exp\left(-\int_t^T r(s)ds\right) \mid \mathcal{F}(t)\right]$$

which we also write as

$$P_X(t) = B(t)\mathbb{E}^*\left[\frac{X(T)}{B(T)} \mid \mathcal{F}(t)\right]$$

or, using the original measure and the notation $\eta/B = \xi$, as

$$\xi^{-1}(t)\mathbb{E}[\xi(T)X(T) \mid \mathcal{F}(t)]$$

which parallels the expressions we wrote in discrete time.

If we need to price a security that yields not only a final payoff, but provides also dividends on the way, at a continuous but stochastic rate ι, and this rate is instantaneously risky too, the pricing formula may be adjusted as follows:

$$P_X(t) = \mathbb{E}^*\left[\exp\left(-\int_t^T r(s)ds\right)X(T) + \int_t^T \exp\left(-\int_t^u r(s)ds\right)\iota(u)du \mid \mathcal{F}(t)\right]$$

8.4 Market Completeness

8.4.1 Necessary and Sufficient Condition

Our discussion of completeness started in the *one-period* setting: in that stylized economy, we showed that, in the absence of arbitrage opportunities, a necessary and sufficient

---

[15] In our setup, S_0 should also be given in terms of the effective numeraire, which is price of the unique consumption good.

condition for completeness was the equality between the number of states of the world and the number of linearly independent securities, including the riskless one. From completeness followed uniqueness of states prices, their equality across investors in equilibrium, and a one-to-one relation between the prices of basic securities and state prices. This allowed us to price redundant securities. With more than two dates, the technical condition for *multiperiod dynamic* completeness was the equality between the splitting index and the number of linearly independent securities, including the riskless one, at each point in time. The splitting index is the number of immediate successor nodes.

This section shows that, when security prices are Itô processes, a market is complete, in its *continuous-time*, dynamic meaning, if and only if the number of independent Wiener processes is equal to the number of linearly independent securities minus one, at each point in time. So, the analogy with the discrete-time case remains if we consider separately the riskless security and ask for equality between the number of "sources of uncertainty" and the number of linearly independent risky securities. Linear independence of the risky securities is based on the rank of their diffusion matrix σ, while, in discrete time, it was based on the rank of the payoff matrix Σ.

In later sections we also show that, in a complete market, state prices are unique. We do not yet assume equilibrium nor equalize state prices across investors, as the notion of equilibrium in continuous time is postponed to chapter 12.

Let us start from the definition of *market completeness*. The definition updates the discrete-time one. We go back to the notation B and S, where the vector S collects risky securities only, with the strategies collected in (α, Θ):

Definition 8.10 *The continuous-time market is dynamically complete if all single-payment securities X can, at some finite initial cost, be replicated using strategies (α, Θ) that are admissible and self-financing.*

In a complete market, any $\mathcal{F}(T)$-measurable contingent claim can be replicated or attained. One of the appropriately selected (and technically valid) strategies will do the job, exactly as a static replication did it in a one-period framework. The existence of replicating strategies makes the market complete. That is why, in the proof of the condition for market completeness, the crucial role is played by *dynamic replication* of the security. At the end of the section, in small characters, we prove the following:

Theorem 8.3 *Consider a generalized Black-Scholes market with as many risky securities as Wiener processes, $N = K$. Let the Novikov condition hold. The market is dynamically complete if and only if the risky-security diffusion matrix $\sigma(t)$ is of full rank for almost every (ω, t).*

One important property of the proof is that it makes use of the Novikov condition and of integrability of (the stochastic part) of trading gains, which is feasible thanks to the fact that, for all stochastic integrals, we take for granted that the integrand is in $\mathcal{H}^2$. In the proof, the integrand is a linear combination of rows of the diffusion matrix in (8.17), $\xi \times (-\mathcal{S}\kappa^\mathsf{T} + \sigma)$.

When we start from a number of risky securities greater than the number of Wiener processes ($N > K$), what matters is still the equality between the number of risky independent securities and the number of independent sources of uncertainty (the Wiener processes). It is easy to demonstrate, by modifying slightly the previous proof, that the following property holds:

Corollary 8.1   *In a generalized Black-Scholes market with more risky securities than Wiener processes, that is, $N > K$, which satisfy the Novikov condition, completeness holds if and only if the rank of the risky-security diffusion matrix $\sigma(t)$ is equal to the number of Wiener processes, $\text{rank}(\sigma) = K$ for almost every (ω, t).*

For instance, if incompleteness just arises from the inequality between the number of securities available to all investors and the number of Wiener processes (and not from restricted participation or transaction costs, as will happen in chapters 15 or 19), any market can be made complete by introducing an appropriate number of *non-redundant* options, although we shall see in chapter 17 that it is not straightforward to specify option diffusions in a way that ensures that no arbitrage opportunities are created.

The equality between the number of independent, risky securities and the number of Wiener processes rests on the same replication idea as in the one-period and multiperiod settings. A Wiener process, as our discussions in the benchmark example have shown, is in an implicit correspondence with the binomial model in discrete time. At each single point, each Wiener process, once discretized, behaves "similarly" to a binomial tree. So, what matters is the comparison between these sources of risk and the number of independent securities that can span them.

$$\spadesuit$$

The proof of theorem 8.3, the necessary and sufficient condition for market completeness, is as follows.

Proof.   We prove first that, if the rank condition is satisfied, completeness holds, that is, each payoff $X(T)$ can be replicated. Recall that in such a circumstance the market price of risk process κ and its exponential martingale η become unique. We assumed in the market setup above that contingent claims are square integrable. Under this technical assumption, $X(T)$ has finite conditional expectation $\mathbb{E}_t[X(T)]$. The same is true for the discounted process $X(T)\xi(T)$, where $\xi = \eta/B$ and η is the exponential-martingale process. Which is a true martingale because of the Novikov condition. Since the conditional expectation is a martingale, a version of the martingale representation theorem (see theorem 7.2) states that, for $T > t > s$, there exists a process $b \in \mathcal{H}^2$ such that

$$\mathbb{E}_t[X(T)\xi(T)] = \mathbb{E}_0[X(T)\xi(T)] + \int_0^t b(s)^\mathsf{T} dw(s) \tag{8.20}$$

Notice that, taking the previous expression for $t = T$, we also have

$$X(T)\xi(T) = \mathbb{E}_0[X(T)\xi(T)] + \int_0^T b(s)^\mathsf{T} dw(s) \qquad (8.21)$$

The process b takes values in $\mathbb{R}^K$. Since the rank condition is satisfied, at each point in time s the rows of the diffusion matrix of X are a basis of $\mathbb{R}^K$. But also the rows of any other non-singular matrix obtained from σ are a basis. Let us take as a basis the rows of the diffusion matrix of security prices, discounted using ξ. Under the Novikov condition, equation (8.17) states that these discounted prices are martingales, with diffusion $\xi(-\mathcal{S}\kappa^\mathsf{T} + \sigma)$. Call $\bar{\sigma}^j(s)$ the rows of the matrix $\xi(-\mathcal{S}\kappa^\mathsf{T} + \sigma)$, so that

$$d(\xi(u)S(u)) = \bar{\sigma}^j(u)dw(u) \qquad (8.22)$$

At any point in time s, we will always be able to find K (unique) coefficients $\vartheta_j(s)$ which give $b^\mathsf{T}(s)$ as a linear combination of those rows:

$$b(s)^\mathsf{T} = \sum_{j=1}^K \vartheta_j(s)\bar{\sigma}^j(s) \qquad (8.23)$$

Knowing that $X\xi$ admits the representation (8.20), let us build a portfolio in which the riskless security enters with the following weight at time 0 and s respectively:

$$\alpha(0) = \mathbb{E}_0\left[X(T)\xi(T)\right] - \sum_{j=1}^K \vartheta_j(0)S_j(0)\xi(0) \qquad (8.24)$$

$$\alpha(s) = \mathbb{E}_0\left[X(T)\xi(T)\right] \qquad (8.25)$$

$$+ \sum_{j=1}^K \left[\int_0^s \vartheta_j(u)d(S_j(u)\xi(u)) - \vartheta_j(s)S_j(s)\xi(s)\right]$$

Let the risky securities weights be $\{\vartheta_j(s), s \geq 0\}$, collected in the vector $\Theta(s)$. We can easily demonstrate that this portfolio is self-financing and replicates X. Indeed, thanks to the expressions (8.24) and (8.25) for α, we have

$$\alpha(s) + \sum_{j=1}^K \vartheta_j(s)S_j(s)\xi(s) =$$

$$\alpha(0) + \sum_{j=1}^K \vartheta_j(0)S_j(0)\xi(0) + \sum_{j=1}^K \int_0^s \vartheta_j(u)d(S_j(u)\xi(u))$$

which shows that the portfolio is self-financing, and

$$\alpha(T) + \sum_{j=1}^{K} \vartheta_j(T) S_j(T) \xi(T) = \mathbb{E}_0 \left[X(T) \xi(T) \right]$$

$$+ \left[\sum_{j=1}^{K} \int_0^T \vartheta_j(u) d(S_j(u)\xi(u)) - \vartheta_j(T) S_j(T) \xi(T) \right]$$

$$+ \sum_{j=1}^{K} \vartheta_j(T) S_j(T) \xi(T)$$

$$= \mathbb{E}_0 \left[X(T) \xi(T) \right] + \sum_{j=1}^{K} \int_0^T \vartheta_j(u) d(S_j(u)\xi(u))$$

Since (8.22) and (8.23) hold, we have

$$\alpha(T) + \sum_{j=1}^{K} \vartheta_j(T) S_j(T) \xi(T)$$

$$= \mathbb{E}_0 \left[X(T) \xi(T) \right] + \sum_{j=1}^{K} \int_0^T \vartheta_j(u) \bar{\sigma}^j(u) dw(u)$$

$$= \mathbb{E}_0 \left[X(T) \xi(T) \right] + \int_0^T \Theta^{\mathsf{T}}(u) dw(u)$$

On the RHS, according to (8.21), we have $X(T)\xi(T)$:

$$\alpha(T) + \sum_{j=1}^{K} \vartheta_j(T) S_j(T) \xi(T) = X(T) \xi(T)$$

The last expression, once we multiply the LHS and the RHS times $B(T) = \eta(T)/\xi(T)$, becomes

$$\alpha(T) B(T) + \sum_{j=1}^{K} \vartheta_j(T) S_j(T) \eta(T) = X(T) \eta(T)$$

or

$$\alpha(T) B(T) + \sum_{j=1}^{K} \vartheta_j(T) S_j(T) = X(T)$$

and proves that the portfolio we built is a replicating one, which is what we aimed to obtain.

The reverse implication (that in a complete market with as many risky securities as Wiener processes the diffusion matrix has full rank) is proved by showing that, if the matrix does not have full rank, the market is not complete. Indeed, assume that there is at least a point in time s when the diffusion matrix has not full rank. Then it is not possible to write all possible vectors with K entries, that is, all possible $b(s)$, as linear combinations of the columns of that matrix, and there are securities for which the replicating portfolio written above is not defined any more. They cannot be replicated, so that the market is not complete any more.   □

8.4.2   Martingale Measure, Stochastic Discount Factor, and State-Price Uniqueness

Recall the definition of state prices, $\xi(T)dP(\omega) = \eta(T)B^{-1}(T)dP(\omega)$. If the market is complete, there is a unique price of risk and a unique exponential martingale $\eta(T)$. It is immediate to verify that:

Theorem 8.4   *In a complete market, state prices are unique.*

These prices retain the properties they had in one-period and discrete-time complete markets, since

- they can still be factored into a probability and a *stochastic discount factor*,
- they can be transformed into *risk-neutral probabilities (or a risk-neutral probability measure)*, under which discounted security prices are martingales.

These results provide intuition and are extremely important for the analysis of complete markets. In spite of the more complicated formal setting, complete markets still have the nice uniqueness properties we exploited in one-period and discrete-time economies.

It follows from uniqueness of the martingale measure and the fact that the exponential martingale permits to change the measure that

Theorem 8.5   *In a complete market, the pricing measure η being unique, the price at time 0, $P_X(0)$, of any single-payment security X, is unique:*

$$
\begin{aligned}
P_X(0) &= \mathbb{E}_0^*\!\left[X(T)B^{-1}(T)\right] \\
&= \mathbb{E}_0\!\left[\eta(T)X(T)B^{-1}(T)\right] \\
&= \mathbb{E}_0[\xi(T)X(T)]
\end{aligned}
$$

We prove at the end of this section, in small characters, that this is also the price one would obtain with a replication argument. Exercise 8.6 shows to the reader how the previous rule, when applied to derivative securities, gives back the Black-Scholes PDE, for generalized Black-Scholes securities. See also exercise 8.7.

Finally, observe that, as a consequence of market completeness, there is a *linear, one-to-one relation* between Arrow-Debreu prices on the one hand and security prices, S and B on the other. The one-to-one property is simply a consequence of the fact that prices are well defined, once the market price of risk is fixed, and vice versa. Linearity of the mapping is evident form the expression: $P_X(0) = \mathbb{E}_0[\xi(T)X(T)]$ and the fact that expectations are linear operators. Already in one-period and discrete-time economies, the relation between state prices and security prices (S and B), was one-to-one and linear.

————————————————♠————————————————

In order to demonstrate that the pricing formula

$$P_X(0) = \mathbb{E}_0^* \left[X(T)B^{-1}(T) \right]$$

also follows from replication, start by recognizing that, since the payoff X can be replicated by the portfolio (α, Θ) described in the proof of theorem 8.3, its price at time 0 is the time-0 value of that portfolio:

$$P_X(0) = \alpha(0)B(0) + \sum_{j=1}^{K} \vartheta_j(0)S_j(0)$$

Since we established in the proof of theorem 8.3 that the weight of the riskless security is

$$\alpha(0) = \mathbb{E}_0[\xi(T)X(T)] - \sum_{j=1}^{K} \vartheta_j(0)S_j(0)\xi(0)$$

$$= \mathbb{E}_0^* \left[X(T)B^{-1}(T) \right] - \sum_{j=1}^{K} \vartheta_j(0)S_j(0)\xi(0)$$

and we know that $B(0) = 1$, $\xi(0) = 1$, the price of security X at time 0 is

$$P_X(0) = \mathbb{E}_0^* \left[X(T)B^{-1}(T) \right] - \sum_{j=1}^{K} \vartheta_j(0)S_j(0) + \sum_{j=1}^{K} \vartheta_j(0)S_j(0)$$

$$= \mathbb{E}_0^* \left[X(T)B^{-1}(T) \right]$$

8.5   Asset-Specific Completeness

This section introduces a situation of *asset-specific completeness,* in which the market is complete with respect to one or more payoffs – in the sense that *these* can be replicated and hedged – without being complete in the sense considered so far, which was that *any* payoff can be replicated.

Asset-specific completeness is important in that derivatives written on some underlying security, when their payoff can be replicated, can still be priced, as if the market were "truly" complete, or marketwide complete.

To start with, consider the following example.

Example 8.1   In an economy with two dates and three states, two securities, a stock and a call option on it, are traded. The stock pays $\{1, 2, 3\}$, the call has strike 1 and therefore pays $\{0, 1, 2\}$. The market defined by the two previous securities is incomplete, in that the payoff matrix

$$\Sigma = \begin{bmatrix} 1 & 2 & 3 \\ 0 & 1 & 2 \end{bmatrix}$$

has rank $N = 2$, in the presence of $K = 3$ states.

However, the market exhibits asset-specific completeness, since one can get a riskless pay-off, equal to one in each state of the world, $\{1, 1, 1\}$, by going long the stock and short the call.

To highlight the difference between asset-specific and marketwide completeness, observe that the above market can be completed by introducing a second call option on the stock, with strike 2, and therefore payoff $\{0, 0, 1\}$. The payoff matrix becomes

$$\Sigma = \begin{bmatrix} 1 & 2 & 3 \\ 0 & 1 & 2 \\ 0 & 0 & 1 \end{bmatrix}$$

and the market becomes complete, since $N = K = 3$.

In continuous time, the equivalent idea is that of adding securities. Along the way, the market can turn out to exhibit asset-specific completeness. Consider the following example.

Example 8.2   The market contains one riskless security, with a value of one all the time, and two risky securities, their percentage drift and diffusion coefficients are constant and different from each other:

$$\begin{cases} \dfrac{dS_1(t)}{S_1(t)} = \mu_1 dt + \sigma_{11} dw_1(t) + \sigma_{12} dw_2(t) \\[2mm] \dfrac{dS_2(t)}{S_2(t)} = \mu_2 dt + \sigma_{21} dw_1(t) + \sigma_{22} dw_2(t) \end{cases}$$

Let the Wiener processes w_1 and w_2 be independent. If both securities are traded, with $\sigma_{11}\sigma_{22} - \sigma_{12}^2 \neq 0$, the market is complete ($K = N = 2$). If only the first security is traded, the market is incomplete, since the rank of the diffusion matrix of traded securities ($\mathrm{rank}(\sigma) = N = 1$) is not equal to the number of independent Wiener processes ($K = 2$). Nonetheless, if $\sigma_{12} = 0$, every derivative on the first security can be priced, since the price of risk is well defined and equal to $(\mu_1 - r)/\sigma_{11}$. There is asset-specific completeness.

The resemblance between asset-specific completeness and completeness is useful in that *option pricing* problems can be solved under asset-specific completeness with the same tools one uses for completeness. What matters, when pricing a derivative contract, is completeness with respect to the risks of the underlying, or the Wiener processes affecting its underlying. If the market is incomplete when we take into account Wiener processes that do not affect a specific underlying, we can still use the tool kit of complete-market pricing and replication.

However, for market equilibrium, that is, for chapter 12, the notion of completeness one needs for equilibrium is instead the traditional, or marketwide one, since all securities, all markets and all sources of uncertainty (Wiener processes) are considered at the same time. In this sense, asset-specific completeness is useful for partial, not for general equilibrium.

Exercises 8.8 and 8.9 present examples of asset-specific completeness, related to the example above, which the reader can work out in order to fully digest the distinction between the traditional or marketwide, and asset-specific cases. They examine further the example, distinguishing the cases $\sigma_{12} = 0$ and $\sigma_{12} > 0$.

8.6   Benchmark Example (continued)

Consider the complete, strict-sense Black-Scholes model with N securities and as many Wiener processes as securities, a riskless security with constant interest rate $r > 0$ and σ non-singular. In this section we use percentage returns instead of absolute returns in units of consumption. We start with a single Wiener process, for which we have also a graphical representation, and then extend to multiple Wiener processes. We give the market price of risk, the exponential martingale, the stochastic discount factor, the Wiener process in the Girsanov theorem; we ask whether the Novikov condition holds and provide a graphical representation of the risk-neutralized process.

Univariate case
Since for $N = K = 1$

$$dB(t) = rB(t)dt$$
$$dS(t) = \mu S(t)dt + \sigma S(t)dw(t)$$

with $\sigma > 0$, the market price of risk is simply

$$\kappa = \frac{\mu - r}{\sigma}$$

the exponential martingale is

$$\eta(t) = \exp\left\{-\frac{\mu - r}{\sigma}w(t) - \frac{1}{2}\left(\frac{\mu - r}{\sigma}\right)^2 t\right\}$$

and the Novikov condition holds, since

$$\mathbb{E}\left[\exp\left\{\frac{1}{2}\int_0^t \|\kappa(s)\|^2 ds\right\}\right] = \exp\left\{\frac{1}{2}\left(\frac{\mu - r}{\sigma}\right)^2 t\right\} < \infty$$

As a consequence, the Girsanov theorem applies, and the Wiener process under a measure equivalent to the initial one, generated by dw, is

$$dw^*(t) = \frac{\mu - r}{\sigma}dt + dw(t)$$

Substituting into the equation for the stock price, we get

$$dS(t) = \mu S(t)dt + \sigma S(t)dw(t) \tag{8.26}$$

$$= \mu S(t)dt + \sigma S(t)\left(dw^*(t) - \frac{\mu - r}{\sigma}dt\right)$$

$$= rS(t)dt + \sigma S(t)dw^*(t)$$

which shows, indeed, that, under the new measure, the risky security has the same diffusion coefficient as before, and a new drift, equal to the riskless rate, as we anticipated in chapter 6 and below Girsanov's theorem, in section 8.2. In integral form, the risky-security price under the changed and effective measure would be

$$S(t) = S(0)e^{\left(r - \frac{\sigma^2}{2}\right)t + \sigma w^*(t)} \tag{8.27}$$

$$= S(0)e^{\left(\mu - \frac{\sigma^2}{2}\right)t + \sigma w(t)} \tag{8.28}$$

The change of measure is identified by the Radon-Nikodym derivative $\eta(T)$, its density process $\eta(t)$, while the stochastic discount factor at t, according to our previous expression, is

$$\xi(t) = \frac{\eta(t)}{B(t)} = \exp\left\{-rt - \frac{\mu - r}{\sigma}w(t) - \frac{1}{2}\left(\frac{\mu - r}{\sigma}\right)^2 t\right\}$$

To appreciate the effect of the (unique) change of measure in the Black-Scholes model, we present in figure 8.1 an example of Black-Scholes price dynamics, obtained by discretization, as discussed in chapter 5. We do this for undiscounted prices, both under the initial and the martingale measure, that is, we plot a discretization of two paths of the risky security price, under the effective and the martingale measure. We use the same parameter

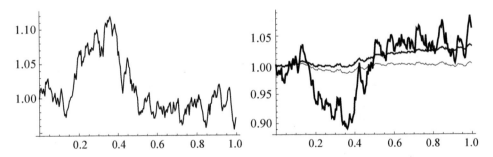

Figure 8.1
Right-hand panel: Simulated behavior of the asset price with Brownian Motion returns as in the thin line on the right-hand side of figure 5.1 ($\mu = 5\%$ and $\sigma = 15\%$), when $S_0 = 1$. The thick line presents a path under the initial measure (identical to the thin line of figure 5.1). The medium-thickness line represents the same path under the martingale measure ($r = 3\%$) (equal to the $\eta \times S$ under the effective measure). The thinnest line presents the path of the discounted asset price S/B also under the martingale measure. **Left-hand panel**: the path of the change-of-measure variable η.

values as in figure 5.1, right-hand panel, thin line, that is, $\mu = 5\%, r = 3\%, \sigma = 15\%$, so that the market price of risk is $\kappa = 2/15$. Observe that, as expected, security prices grow more under the initial measure than under the risk-neutral one (drifts are respectively 5% and 3%). In both cases, however, there is a trend, a tendency to increase over time, with a typical wander due to the Wiener component. We plot also the discounted price dynamics (8.26). By so doing, we consider the probability measure P^*, equivalent to P, which has Radon-Nikodym derivative $\eta(T)$ with respect to P, where

$$\eta(t) = \exp\left[-\frac{2}{15}w(t) - \frac{1}{2}\left(\frac{2}{15}\right)^2 t\right]$$

and the Novikov condition holds, as expected. As we know, η effects a "change of measure" from P to P^*, and the discounted price behaves as a martingale, that is, does not present a trend any more. This change is visible from the figure, where discounted security prices under the changed measure wander around the horizontal line, instead of showing a trend.

Multivariate case

Consider now the multivariate case, that is, $N = K > 1$, with

$$d\mathcal{S} = \mathrm{diag}\,(\mathcal{S})\,\mu dt + \mathrm{diag}\,(\mathcal{S})\,\sigma dw\,(t)$$

where μ is a vector in $\mathbb{R}^K$ and σ is a $(K \times K)$ non-singular matrix. The market price of risk is an $\mathbb{R}^K$ vector, equal to $\kappa = \sigma^{-1}(\mu - r\mathbf{1})$. Since the market price of risk is constant, the Novikov condition (8.13) is satisfied:[16]

$$\mathbb{E}\left[\exp\left\{\frac{1}{2}\int_0^t \left\|\sigma^{-1}(\mu - r\mathbf{1})\right\|^2 ds\right\}\right] = \exp\left\{\frac{1}{2}\left\|\sigma^{-1}(\mu - r\mathbf{1})\right\|^2 t\right\} < \infty$$

Girsanov's theorem again applies, with

$$dw^*(t) = \sigma^{-1}(\mu - r\mathbf{1})dt + dw(t)$$

The hypotheses of theorem 8.3 are still satisfied for every t, since the Novikov condition holds and the diffusion matrix is non-singular. In the multivariate case, we define the Radon-Nikodym density as:

$$\eta(t) \triangleq \exp\left\{-(\mu - r\mathbf{1})^\mathsf{T}\left(\sigma^{-1}\right)^\mathsf{T} w(t) - \frac{1}{2}\left\|\sigma^{-1}(\mu - r\mathbf{1})\right\|^2 t\right\}$$

The corresponding stochastic discount factor is

$$\xi(t) = \frac{\eta(t)}{B(t)} = \exp\left\{-rt - (\mu - r\mathbf{1})^\mathsf{T}\left(\sigma^{-1}\right)^\mathsf{T} w(t) - \frac{1}{2}\left\|\sigma^{-1}(\mu - r\mathbf{1})\right\|^2 t\right\}$$

and the dynamics of undiscounted securities under the martingale measure is, as expected:

$$d\mathcal{S} = \mathrm{diag}\,(\mathcal{S})\,rdt + \mathrm{diag}\,(\mathcal{S})\,\sigma dw^*\,(t) \tag{8.29}$$

---

16 Recall that $\left\|\sigma^{-1}(\mu - r\mathbf{1})\right\|^2 = (\mu - r\mathbf{1})^\mathsf{T}\left(\sigma^{-1}\right)^\mathsf{T}\sigma^{-1}(\mu - r\mathbf{1})$.

In order to represent graphically the effect of the change of measure, we should proceed by representing one security at a time, exactly as we did in the previous picture.

8.7 Conclusion

In continuous time, the change to the risk-neutral measure is again in one-to-one correspondence to the absence of (appropriately defined) arbitrage opportunities. That measure, together with its state prices and stochastic discount factors, requires a restriction on the price-of-risk processes that are admissible (the Novikov condition). Whether we consider securities' prices or portfolios, unless we place restrictions on the processes of the underlying securities and/or the processes of the portfolio strategies that are admissible, the concept of payoff replication can go awry. For instance, the replication strategy can undergo a period of infinite losses. Or a bubble may arise, as in the previous chapter.

Market completeness still means that any terminal payoff can be replicated by means of admissible portfolio strategies and entails uniqueness of the risk-neutral measure (and state prices and discount factors). We have seen under what conditions the market is complete. The strict-sense Black-Scholes market is complete.

Exercises

8.1. (Adapted from Karatzas and Shreve (1998) pages 196 and 197). The following is the most ubiquitous application of Girsanov theorem. Consider a Wiener process w. The first passage time τ_b to the level $b \neq 0$ has density at t:

$$f(t) = \frac{|b|}{\sqrt{2\pi t^3}} \exp\left[-\frac{b^2}{2t}\right]$$

Apply Girsanov theorem to obtain the first-passage density of a Brownian motion with drift μ.

8.2. Consider the Brownian bridge process on $[0, T]$ as a model of the behavior of the price of a bond:

$$Z(t) = \int_0^t \frac{T-t}{T-s} dw(s)$$

In an attempt to price options written on bonds, some researchers have suggested applying Girsanov theorem to find the equivalent martingale probability measure corresponding to two underlying securities: a riskless security with zero interest rate and a bond of fixed maturity T following a Bridge process. Show that the Novikov condition is violated in this case, so that the Girsanov theorem may not be applicable. (Answer due to Cheng (1991)).

8.3. Applying Itô's lemma to ξ, $\mathcal{S}$, and B as defined in the chapter, show that the securities prices (risky and riskless) normalized by ξ – where $\xi(t) = \eta(t)/B(t)$ – are local martingales, that is, have zero drift:

$$d\left(\xi(t)\mathcal{S}(t)\right) = \left[-\mathcal{S}(t)\xi(t)\kappa^{\mathsf{T}}(t) + \xi(t)\sigma(t)\right]dw(t)$$
$$d\left(\xi(t)B(t)\right) = -\xi(t)\kappa^{\mathsf{T}}(t)B(t)dw(t)$$

Recall that the matrix σ has an inverse at each point in time.

8.4. Consider the riskless security with constant interest rate and a risky security with the following dynamics:

$$d\mathcal{S}(t) = \varrho\left(\bar{S} - \mathcal{S}(t)\right)dt + \sigma\,dw(t)$$

where w is a unidimensional Wiener process, $\varrho \in \mathbb{R}_+, \bar{S} \in \mathbb{R}$, and $\sigma \in \mathbb{R}_{++}$. This is an Ornstein-Uhlenbeck process. Show that

a. the market characterized by those securities satisfies the assumptions of theorem 8.3; that is, it is complete;

b. the risk premium is

$$\kappa(t) = \sigma^{-1}(\varrho\bar{S} - (\varrho + r)\mathcal{S}(t))$$

c. the Novikov condition (8.13) is satisfied:

$$\mathbb{E}\left[\exp\left\{\frac{1}{2}\int_0^t \|\kappa(s)\|^2\,ds\right\}\right] < \infty.$$

d. Compute the (unique) stochastic discount factor, $\xi(t) = \eta(t)/B(t)$ as in the text, the corresponding change of measure $\eta(t)$ and the lifetime budget constraint.

8.5. Write the dynamics of undiscounted and discounted securities under the martingale measure in the previous exercise.

8.6. The fundamental theorem says that securities prices are turned into martingales by ξ. In differential form, this is

$$\mathbb{E}_t[d(\xi\mathcal{S})] = \mathbf{0}$$
$$\mathbb{E}_t[d(\xi B)] = 0.$$

Since a call option can be replicated using the stock and the bond, it must also be true that the call is a martingale, once discounted via the stochastic-discount factor process, ξ:

$$\mathbb{E}_t[d(\xi C)] = 0$$

Show that the last equality, indeed, gives the Black-Scholes PDE for $C(S, t)$.

8.7. Show how one would derive a PDE for the function $C(\xi, t)$, instead of the function $C(\mathcal{S}, t)$.

8.8. Develop the example in section 8.5. Consider a market with one riskless security, whose value is one all the time, and two risky securities, whose percentage drift and diffusion coefficients are constant:

$$
\begin{cases}
\dfrac{dS_1(t)}{S_1(t)} = \mu_1 dt + \sigma_{11} dw_1(t) + \sigma_{12} dw_2(t) \\[2ex]
\dfrac{dS_2(t)}{S_2(t)} = \mu_2 dt + \sigma_{21} dw_1(t) + \sigma_{22} dw_2(t)
\end{cases}
$$

There is zero correlation between w_1 and w_2. If both securities are traded, the market is complete ($K = N = 2$). Suppose now that $\sigma_{12} = 0$. Show that, if only the first security is traded, the market is incomplete, but there is asset-specific completeness.

8.9. Consider the securities of exercise 8.8 and assume that only the first security is traded. Discuss the case $\sigma_{12} > 0$.

III   INDIVIDUAL OPTIMALITY IN CONTINUOUS TIME

9   Dynamic Optimization and Portfolio Choice

As we enter Part III of this book, the problem to be addressed is no longer that of an investor who is choosing a portfolio strategy to replicate or reach a target payoff in continuous time. The investor now wants to solve a broader problem. He wishes to choose his consumption stream and portfolio strategy to maximize his lifetime utility.

This chapter extends to continuous time the portfolio-selection problem we already addressed in single-period and discrete-time models (chapter 3). The investor solves an intertemporal optimization problem. His choice variables are (i) how much to consume or save at each point in time, (ii) how much to invest in each security. The behavior of securities' prices is still given and exogenous. The approach used is dynamic programming.

In later chapters we shall attack the same problem with a Lagrangean approach, with the aim of writing the Lagrangean formulation as a *global* one. At that point we shall need to distinguish between complete (chapter 10) and incomplete (chapter 14) markets. In the present chapter, the assumption of completeness is not made except where explicitly mentioned.

A number of economic assumptions are crucial for the current chapter. First, we assume, as in the previous chapters, that markets are frictionless. Second, we assume that investors are price-takers.

Another crucial assumption, which justifies the optimization technique applied in the chapter, namely the dynamic programming principle, is the Markovian property of securities' prices. We take prices to be continuous Itô processes that follow the generalized Black-Scholes model *and* are Markov (whereas the global approach of chapter 10 will not require the Markov assumption).

The results we present are mainly borrowed from the seminal contributions of Merton (1969, 1971, 1973a, 1977) and Breeden (1979).

In the course of the exposition, we point out, and provide intuition for two main issues: correspondence between intertemporal choices and mean-variance, static choices on the one hand, and fund separation on the other.

First, we point out the situations in which there is equivalence between intertemporal and *static, mean-variance portfolio choices,* which arise in single-period settings. These choices were taken as a background in the book and are reviewed in Appendix A. Equivalence will obtain as long as returns are IID.

Second, we stress the so-called *mutual-fund theorems*, which state the equivalence between investing in the effective marketed securities and in an appropriate number of synthetic funds. We will prove that some mutual-fund results hold whether one considers the IID case or not. What distinguishes the different cases is the number of funds.

The chapter unfolds as follows: in section 9.1 we write down the continuous-time budget constraint for intertemporal optimization and study the single and IID risky-security problem; in section 9.2 we add a riskless security; in section 9.3 we extend to multiple securities with IID returns; in section 9.4 we study multiple, non-IID risky security. In section 9.5 we study the case of complete markets. The last section (section 9.6) is devoted, as usual, to the application of the chapter material to the benchmark example.

9.1   A Single Risky Security

As in Merton (1969), we consider an investor with horizon T. For the time being, suppose $T < \infty$. For simplicity, assume that he receives an endowment e_0 at time 0 but no further endowment later on. Denote wealth as $W(t)$.[1] The investor derives utility from consumption of a unique good, which is used as usual as numeraire.[2] Let $c(\omega, t)$, or $c(t)$ for short, be the adapted process representing the rate of consumption at time t, and let the utility function $u(c(t), t)$ have the properties listed in chapters 2 and 3, including the fact of being strictly increasing, strictly concave in consumption and belonging at least to the class C^2. In order to prevent zero consumption at the optimum, let the Inada conditions be satisfied for every t.[3] In order to incorporate the bequest motive, let us assume that the investor has also a bequest function $\wp$ defined over his terminal wealth $W(T)$.[4] Let the function $\wp$ be increasing and strictly concave in W. Let us work in a filtered probability space where the filtration is the Wiener one, $(\Omega, \mathcal{F}, P, \mathbf{F}^w)$. Overall, the investor optimality problem is:

$$\max_{\{c(t)\}} \mathbb{E}_0 \left\{ \int_0^T u(c(t), t) dt + \wp(W(T)) \right\} \tag{9.1}$$

subject to a budget constraint to be written down and for a given initial wealth, W_0.

---

1 Reminder: unless doing otherwise is necessary for comprehension, we simplify the notation for processes. All processes are stochastic but we suppress the reference to the state ω. Therefore, $X(t)$ actually means $X(\omega, t)$. In special cases, we also use the notation $f(t)$ to refer to a deterministic function of time. When this happens, we say so explicitly.

2 This implies, as in discrete time, that the numeraire evolves as a process. It is not constant over time.

3 The Inada conditions also guarantee existence of solution for consumption. See proposition A.1.

4 The bequest function, as the name says, represents the desire to leave a bequest to one's heirs. The utility coming out of the bequest may differ from the one deriving from one's own consumption. This is why we represent it with a different function. Extensions to bequest functions which depend on time in addition to wealth are possible.

Because of the Inada conditions, the non-negativity constraint, $c(t) \geq 0$ with probability one, is automatically satisfied as long as it is feasible. To make it feasible in the absence of endowments, we impose $W(t) \geq 0$. The relations between non-negativity of wealth, non-negativity of optimal consumption and its existence, for the case in which the securities are IID Geometric Brownian motions and the utility function is isoelastic, are discussed in exercise 9.1, point a).

9.1.1 Budget Constraint

We start with a simple formulation of the problem in which the only security available is a risky one:

$$\frac{dS(t)}{S(t)} = \mu(S,t)dt + \sigma(S,t)dw(t) \tag{9.2}$$

under the initial condition $S(0) > 0$. The coefficients μ and σ are real-valued, adapted processes. They are also assumed to satisfy the Lipschitz and growth conditions. These guarantee existence and uniqueness of a solution to (9.2). Under these conditions, theorem 5.3 guarantees that the *price process is Markov*. We are considering a subcase of the generalized Black-Scholes model.

The investor's financial wealth at time t, or the value of his portfolio holdings, before he chooses how many securities to hold for the period $(t, t + dt)$ and before he provides for consumption over the same period, is called $W(t)$. That wealth is used to consume and to buy a new portfolio:

$$\theta(t)S(t) + c(t)dt = W(t)$$

From time t to $t + dt$, his post-asset allocation and post-consumption wealth increases just because asset prices change. This means that he arrives at time $t + dt$ with the following resources:

$$W(t + dt) = \theta(t) \times [S(t) + dS(t)]$$

Taking the difference:

$$W(t + dt) - W(t) = \theta(t)dS(t) - c(t)dt$$

or

$$dW(t) = \theta(t)dS(t) - c(t)dt$$

We end up with the continuous-time budget constraint:

$$dW(t) = [\mu(t)W(t) - c(t)] \, dt + \sigma(t)W(t)dw(t) \tag{9.3}$$

which can be integrated as:[5]

$$W(t) = e_0 + \int_0^t \theta(s)dS(s) - \int_0^t c(s)ds$$

$$= e_0 + \int_0^t \theta(s)[\mu S(s)ds + \sigma S(s)dw(s)] - \int_0^t c(s)ds$$

where $W(0) = e_0 > 0$.

Distinguishing, as we did in section 6.1.1, the change in value of the portfolio from the gains, which we define as usual as the part of the value change due to movements in prices $dG(t) = \theta(t)dS(t)$, the difference $dW - dG$ is the cash flow from buying and selling securities. $dW - dG > 0$ means that the portfolio is taking in cash flows; $dW - dG < 0$ means that the portfolio is paying out a cash flow. In the sections on derivative replication, we imposed a *self-financing* constraint: $dW - dG = 0$. Here instead, we want the portfolio to finance consumption equal to $c(t)dt$. Stated otherwise, we want to impose that $dW - dG = -cdt$ or that the change in the value of wealth equals the gains minus the consumption expenditure: $dW = \theta dS - cdt$, or that consumption over the interval $(t, t + dt)$ is financed by the sale of securities at price $S + dS$: $cdt = -d\theta(dS + S)$. The budget constraint is exactly analogous to the self-financing restriction with the addition of a cash throw-off called "consumption."

In discrete time, the accounting was similar: securities acquired at time t to form the portfolio $\Theta(t)$ were resold at time $t + 1$ at price $S(t + 1)$. Please, refer back to section 3.3.

Exercise 9.2 serves to write down the budget constraint in the presence of dividends.

9.1.2 IID Returns and Dynamic Programming Solution

Let us assume that μ and σ are constant, with the latter positive, and we are in the *Geometric Wiener process or strict Black-Scholes* case. As we know from chapters 5 and 7, this causes rates of return to be IID over time and lognormal over any finite period of time. In agreement with the dynamic programming verification theorem in Appendix B, we regard the optimization problem starting at 0 as a special case of an optimization problem starting at t. For the latter we can define the function J, called the *value or Bellman function* of the program:

$$J(W, t) \triangleq \max_{\{c(t)\}} \mathbb{E}_t \left\{ \int_t^T u(c(s), s)ds + \wp(W(T)) \right\}; t < T$$

$$J(W, T) = \wp(W(T)) \tag{9.4}$$

Recall that in utility-maximization problems, the value function is the so called "indirect" or "derived" utility. In continuous time the value function is assumed to be of class C^2.

---

[5] This assumes that $\int_0^t \theta(s)dS(s)$ is well defined, that is, the portfolio strategy is admissible in the sense of definition 7.7, and that consumption is in $\mathcal{L}^1$.

Thanks to the C^2 smoothness property we can apply Itô's lemma.[6] Doing so, we can establish that a necessary condition of optimality is that the function $J(W, t)$ solves the following partial differential equation (PDE), called the *Hamilton-Jacobi-Bellman (HJB) equation*:

$$\max_{c(t)} \left\{ u(c,t) + \frac{\partial J}{\partial W}(W,t) \times (\mu W - c) + \frac{1}{2}\frac{\partial^2 J}{\partial W^2}(W,t)\sigma^2 W^2 + \frac{\partial J}{\partial t} \right\} = 0 \qquad (9.5)$$

which can be written as

$$\max_{c(t)} \left\{ u(c,t) + \mathcal{D}(J) + \frac{\partial J}{\partial t} \right\}$$

with the Dynkin (see section 5.7) defined under the effective measure:

$$\mathcal{D}(J) = \frac{\partial J}{\partial W}(W,t) \times (\mu W - c) + \frac{1}{2}\frac{\partial^2 J}{\partial W^2}(W,t)\sigma^2 W^2$$

In the HJB equation the drift of the process J, namely $\mathbb{E}_t(dJ)/dt$, shows up as the sum of three terms, as commanded by Itô's rule:

$$\frac{\mathbb{E}_t(dJ)}{dt} = \frac{\partial J}{\partial W} \times (\mu W - c) + \frac{1}{2}\frac{\partial^2 J}{\partial W^2}\sigma^2 W^2 + \frac{\partial J}{\partial t}$$

What the HJB equation requires is that, under the optimal consumption policy, the *total utility change* between t and $t + dt$, as measured, per unit of time, by its direct value, $u(c,t)$, and by the expected change in its indirect value, $\mathbb{E}_t(dJ)/dt$, be *equal to zero*. In the absence of intermediate consumption ($u = 0$), the HJB equation becomes

$$\frac{\mathbb{E}_t(dJ)}{dt} = D(J) + \frac{\partial J}{\partial t} = 0$$

It says that the value of the *value function is a local martingale*. In the pricing problems of the previous chapter, the martingale property held for discounted security prices. However, it held under a risk-neutral or pricing measure. The utility-maximization problem is different from the pricing one in that the martingale property now holds – for the value function of the dynamic program – with the effective drift for wealth, $\mu W - c$.

9.1.3   The Marginality Condition

The first-order condition for the choice of an interior (positive) consumption rate is obtained by differentiating the HJB equation with respect to consumption. It is the

---

6 A more heuristic, but perhaps more intuitive reasoning is provided by Merton (1969). He writes:

$$J(W,t) \equiv \sup_{\{c(t)\}} u(c(t),t)dt + \mathbb{E}_t\{J(W + dW, t + dt)\}$$

and expands $\mathbb{E}_t\{J(W + dW, t + dt)\}$ using Itô's lemma. He gets (9.5) immediately.

marginality condition, which is an *algebraic* equation where the unknown is current consumption c:

$$\frac{\partial u}{\partial c}(c,t) = \frac{\partial J}{\partial W}(W,t) \tag{9.6}$$

The marginality condition says that the marginal utility of *current* consumption must be equal, at each point in time, to the marginal utility of wealth, which represents *future* consumption. The same condition held in the discrete-time model of Lucas (chapter 3). In continuous time, this apparently innocuous condition will enable us to reinterpret the optimization results in a number of ways. In particular, it will permit us to obtain a single-beta CAPM.

Given the assumptions on $u(c,t)$, equation (9.6) has a positive solution c. Let us write it as:

$$c(W,t) = \mathfrak{h}\left(\frac{\partial J}{\partial W}(W,t),t\right) \tag{9.7}$$

where $\mathfrak{h}(x,t)$ is the inverse of the marginal utility function and can also be called the demand function.[7] For the sake of readability, we sometimes suppress its arguments, which are the marginal utility of wealth and time.

Substituting the first-order condition into the HJB equation (9.5) we get the following PDE:

$$u\left(\mathfrak{h}\left(\frac{\partial J}{\partial W}(W,t),t\right),t\right) + \mathcal{D}(J) + \frac{\partial J}{\partial t}(W,t) = 0 \tag{9.8}$$

where

$$\mathcal{D}(J) = \frac{\partial J}{\partial W}(W,t)\left[\mu W - \mathfrak{h}\left(\frac{\partial J}{\partial W}(W,t),t\right)\right] + \frac{1}{2}\frac{\partial^2 J}{\partial W^2}(W,t)\sigma^2 W^2$$

This nonlinear PDE must be solved for the unknown function $J(W,t)$ subject to the boundary condition (9.4) and the condition on wealth, $W(t) \geq 0$. Once that is done, the consumption decision c that does satisfy the first-order condition can be obtained from (9.7).

9.1.4   Subcases and Examples

Three issues are worth mentioning, in relation with this version of the continuous-time portfolio-selection problem.

First, when the utility function is additive and time factors out:

$$u(c,t) = \exp(-\rho t)u(c)$$

---

7 For its existence and properties, see proposition A.1 and the text that follows.

the finite-horizon assumption can be safely relaxed, in which case the limit condition:

$$\lim_{T \to \infty} J(W(T), T) \exp(-\rho T) = 0$$

is imposed. This condition guarantees that the lifetime optimization problem (9.1) is well defined (that is, that the objective function at any finite point in time remains finite) even when the horizon becomes infinite. It means that the derived utility can also go to infinity, as time becomes large, but that time impatience, as represented by the discount factor $\exp(-\rho T)$, must be such that utility increments far in time are perceived as negligible by the investor. The *discounted* value function, indeed, converges to zero. Derived utility can grow at any finite rate, provided that the rate is smaller than time impatience ρ.

Second, since we specified the security price process to be strict-sense Black-Scholes, and then with IID returns, if it is true that the utility function is additive and time factors out, the same is true for the function J, in the infinite-horizon case and, under appropriate conditions, in the finite-horizon case as well.[8]

Third, with additive utility and infinite horizon, the HJB equation becomes an ordinary differential equation (ODE). The ODE admits an explicit solution if $u(c)$ is in the so-called hyperbolic absolute risk aversion (HARA) class, namely if its Arrow-Pratt measure of risk aversion is hyperbolic (see Appendix A). For the isoelastic, or constant-relative risk aversion (CRRA), function of our benchmark example, coupled with the assumption that:

$$\wp(W(T)) = \epsilon^{1-\gamma} \exp(-\rho T) \frac{W(T)^\gamma}{\gamma} \qquad \epsilon \in [0, 1] \qquad (9.9)$$

there exists an explicit solution for the HJB equation, as well as an explicit consumption policy, which we discuss in section 9.2.2. Properties of the value function and existence of an optimal consumption policy are in exercise 9.1.

9.2 A Single Risky Security with IID Returns and One Riskless Security

Add to the optimality problem of the previous section the possibility of investing in a riskless security $B(t) = S_0(t) \neq 0$, which provides a constant rate of return r smaller than the expected rate of return of the risky security, $r < \mu$:

$$dS_0(t) = rS_0(t)dt$$

Let x be the adapted process that represents the *proportion* of wealth invested in the risky security, that is, its weight, defined as:[9]

$$x(t) \triangleq \frac{\theta(t)S(t)}{W(t)} \qquad (9.10)$$

---

8 Merton (1969) specifies the bequest function in such a way that the result holds also in the finite-horizon case. See section 9.2.2 below.

9 x can take any value, since both purchases and short sales of the risky asset are allowed, and correspondingly both borrowing and lending are admitted.

The budget constraint becomes:

$$dW(t) = [r + x(\mu - r)] W(t)dt - c(t)dt + \sigma x(t)W(t)dw(t)$$

Controls include x, so that the optimization problem is

$$\max_{\{c(t),x(t)\}} \mathbb{E}_0 \left\{ \int_0^T u(c(t),t)dt + \wp(W(T)) \right\}$$

and the HJB equation becomes (using short hand for partial derivatives and suppressing arguments)

$$\max_{c,x} \left\{ u(c,t) + \frac{\partial J}{\partial W} [rW + W(\mu - r)x - c] + \frac{1}{2}\frac{\partial^2 J}{\partial W^2} W^2 x^2 \sigma^2 + \frac{\partial J}{\partial t} \right\} = 0 \qquad (9.11)$$

Noting that the drift of the value function is now

$$\frac{\mathbb{E}_t(dJ)}{dt} = \mathcal{D}(J) + \frac{\partial J}{\partial t}(W,t)$$

where

$$\mathcal{D}(J) = \frac{\partial J}{\partial W} \{rW + W[\mu - r]x - c\} + \frac{1}{2}\frac{\partial^2 J}{\partial W^2} W^2 x^2 \sigma^2$$

we can still write the PDE as follows:

$$\max_{c,x} \left\{ u(c,t) + \mathcal{D}(J) + \frac{\partial J}{\partial t}(W,t) \right\} = 0$$

However, since the weight of the risky security can now also be chosen optimally, a new first-order condition is included. The first-order condition results from differentiating the HJB equation with respect to the weight:

$$(\mu - r)\frac{\partial J}{\partial W} + \frac{\partial^2 J}{\partial W^2}\sigma^2 xW = 0 \qquad (9.12)$$

This equation must be substituted in the HJB equation before solving it. It is linear in the portfolio weight. The weight is found to be Markowitz-style, that is, proportional to the risk premium and inversely proportional to the variance, in the spirit of the static mean-variance analysis:

$$x = -\frac{\frac{\partial J}{\partial W}}{\frac{\partial^2 J}{\partial W^2} W} \frac{\mu - r}{\sigma^2} \qquad (9.13)$$

Substituting in the HJB equation for the risky-security weight, the latter becomes

$$\max_c \left\{ u(c,t) + \frac{\partial J}{\partial W}(rW - c) - \frac{1}{2}\frac{\left(\frac{\partial J}{\partial W}\right)^2}{\frac{\partial^2 J}{\partial W^2}}\left(\frac{\mu - r}{\sigma}\right)^2 + \frac{\partial J}{\partial t} \right\} = 0$$

which is nonlinear in the derivatives of the unknown function J. Substituting for optimal consumption we get

$$
u\left[\mathfrak{h}\left(\frac{\partial J}{\partial W}(W,t),t\right),t\right] + \frac{\partial J}{\partial W}\left(rW - \mathfrak{h}\left(\frac{\partial J}{\partial W}(W,t),t\right)\right)
$$

$$
- \frac{1}{2}\frac{\left(\frac{\partial J}{\partial W}\right)^2}{\frac{\partial^2 J}{\partial W^2}}\left(\frac{\mu - r}{\sigma}\right)^2 + \frac{\partial J}{\partial t} = 0
$$

which is nonlinear in two places: where the consumption decision was and where the portfolio decision was. The boundary condition $J(W,T) = \wp(W)$ and the non-negativity condition on wealth remain in force. The subcases and examples mentioned in the previous section – namely, infinite horizon, additivity, and time-factoring out of the derived utility and presence of an explicit solution for HARA functions – still work out the same way.

9.2.1 Myopic Portfolio Weights

The optimal weight x of the risky security given in equation (9.13) is directly proportional to the ratio of excess return to the variance of the return. The coefficient of proportionality:

$$
-\frac{\partial J}{\partial W}\left(\frac{\partial^2 J}{\partial W^2}W\right)^{-1} > 0 \tag{9.14}
$$

is the reciprocal of relative risk aversion, the so-called risk tolerance, computed, however, from the derived utility function. Therefore, it measures tolerance towards riskiness of the whole wealth, instead of current consumption. It follows that all risk-averse investors, in that specific sense of risk aversion, go long the risky security. But portfolios are different across investors if their relative risk tolerances are also different. More risk-averse investors hold less of the risky security, in proportion to their wealth, than do more risk-averse ones.

For each investor, the portfolio composition $x(t)$ varies over time since the value function does. One can say that the optimal portfolio weights are "myopic" because the investor optimally behaves as if his horizon were very short and he took into consideration immediate, instantaneous rates of return only. His allocation is similar to the one that obtains in static, mean-variance portfolio problems (see Appendix A). This is because we have assumed the strict Black-Scholes model, which features *IID Gaussian log-returns*. It goes without saying that the myopic nature of the portfolio allocation opens the way to establishing a CAPM-like result in intertemporal economies. We postpone it to later sections.

9.2.2 Examples Revisited

This section specializes to CRRA utility functions the results just obtained. It does so first with a finite, then with an infinite horizon.

Finite horizon

Consider the *finite-horizon* CRRA example mentioned in section 9.1.4. The risk tolerance ratio that appears in the myopic portfolio weight becomes the constant $1/(1-\gamma)$. The risk tolerance of the derived utility, for any level of wealth, coincides with the one of the point-in-time utility, the latter being constant. This result holds with or without a bequest function, and is independent from wealth and from the length of the investor horizon. It follows that the *optimal portfolio* weight is constant too, independent of bequest, wealth, and the horizon:

$$x = \frac{\mu - r}{(1-\gamma)\sigma^2}$$

The optimal portfolio policy of an isoelastic investor is a benchmark rule in portfolio allocation: it is not only proportional to the ratio of excess return to variance. It is also a *constant multiple* of it. This means that investment policies do not change over time for the same investor and do not differ across investors with different horizons. They simply vary across investors depending on their risk tolerance.[10]

Consider for instance the case in which $\mu = 7\%$, $r = 1\%$, and $\sigma = 20\%$, so that the ratio of excess return to variance is extremely high: 150%. Two investors with risk aversion A_r equal to 2 and 11, which means $\gamma = -1\,(A_r = 2)$, $\gamma = -10\,(A_r = 11)$ would hold respectively 75% and 13.6% of their wealth in the risky security at each point in time, independent of their bequest, wealth, and investment horizon.

This constant allocation of CRRA investors does not exclude that consumption be a hump-shaped function of time over the lifetime of the investor. People can accumulate wealth until a given age and disaccumulate after, as intuition would suggest. In order to see that, define a constant a that incorporates the parameters of the problem, namely security returns, risk aversion, time impatience, and volatility:

$$a \triangleq \frac{1}{1-\gamma}\left[\rho - \gamma\left(\frac{(\mu-r)^2}{2\sigma^2(1-\gamma)} + r\right)\right] \tag{9.15}$$

We require that $a \geq 0$.[11] Recall from (9.9) that ϵ, the parameter that determines the importance of the bequest motive for the CRRA investor, belongs to the interval $[0,1]$. The higher is ϵ, the more important is the weight of his bequest function.

---

10 The optimal portfolio policy for the logarithmic investor can be computed taking the limit of the previous expression when $\gamma \to 0$.

11 The condition $\rho > \gamma\left(\frac{(\mu-r)^2}{2\sigma^2(1-\gamma)} + r\right)$ must be satisfied in the case of an infinite horizon for the present discounted value of consumption to be finite.

As can be verified by substitution into the HJB equation (9.11), the *optimal consumption policy* of any CRRA investor for $T < \infty$ is (Merton (1969)):

$$c\,(t) = \frac{aW(t)}{1 + (a\epsilon - 1)e^{a(t-T)}} \tag{9.16}$$

when $a \neq 0$ and

$$c\,(t) = \frac{W(t)}{T - t + \epsilon}$$

when $a = 0$.

When $a \neq 0$, consumption can exhibit different behaviors. Savings can be hump-shaped, with no bequest ($\epsilon = 0$). The savings behavior depends on the magnitude of t and the rate of growth of optimally invested wealth

$$\alpha^* \triangleq r + x(\mu - r)$$

If there exists a t^* in $[0, T]$ such that

$$t^* = T + \frac{1}{a}\log\left(1 - \frac{a}{\alpha^*}\right)$$

then the investor spends less than the increment $\alpha^* W(t)$ in his wealth before t^* and more later. When $a = 0$ the same result holds if

$$t^* = T - \frac{1}{\alpha^*}$$

Everything else equal, relative consumption, or marginal propensity to consume, c/W is higher for less risk-averse investors. To illustrate this fact, figure 9.1 presents the behavior of the optimal consumption rate c/W in (9.16) for the couple of risk-averse investors described above, as a function of their age (t). It is understood that, in order to apply the formulas just derived, there is no bequest ($\epsilon = 0$). We consider a numerical case, $T = 10$, where there is no hump-shape ($T < t^*$), since α^* is equal respectively to 5.5% and 1.81% and a to 3.13% and 1.55%. The reader can easily see that consumption is higher for less risk-averse investors. In addition, as age increases, consumption increases as well. Given that no bequest is left, the investor "eats up" his whole cake which, because of the independence of x from age, is constantly split in the same proportion between the risky and riskless securities.

Consider now a log (or myopic) investor, which was not considered in the above pictures. Since $a = \rho$, his optimal consumption depends on time impatience only, even in the presence of a bequest motive:

$$c\,(t) = \frac{\rho W(t)}{1 + (\rho\epsilon - 1)e^{\rho(t-T)}}$$

The market price of risk or its components, μ, r, and σ, have no impact. For the myopic investor consumption is decreasing with age t and decreasing with respect to the willingness to bequest, as measured by ϵ.

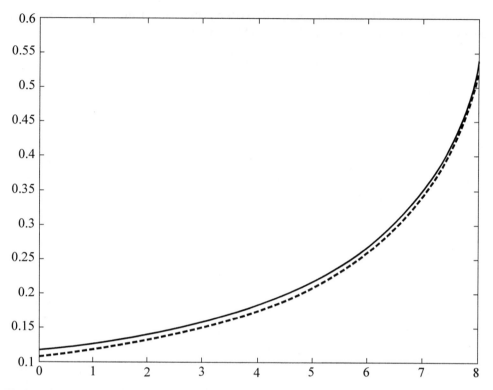

Figure 9.1

Optimal consumption behavior of CRRA investors as a function of age t, in the presence of a single, Geometric Brownian motion risky asset and a finite horizon $T = 10$, without bequest ($\varepsilon = 0$). The continuous line corresponds to $\gamma = -1$ ($A_r = 2$); the dotted one to $\gamma = -10$ ($A_r = 11$). The other parameters are set to $\mu = 7\%$, $r = 1\%$ (so that the risk premium is 6%), $\rho = 3\%, \sigma = 20\%$, which implies $a = \{3.13\%, 1.55\%\}$.

Infinite horizon

With an *infinite horizon*, the *optimal portfolio* decision rule is unchanged. Here the assumption $a \geq 0$ is crucial. Provided that there is no bequest, which means $\epsilon = 0$, and that the time preference parameter is positive for investors less risk-averse than the log investor, and smaller than the risk-aversion parameter for the remaining, risk-averse investors

$$\begin{cases} \rho > 0 & \gamma \leq 0 \\ \rho > \gamma & 0 < \gamma < 1 \end{cases}$$

then the *optimal consumption* policy is exactly the limit for $T \to \infty$ of the finite horizon policies:

$$c(t) = aW(t)$$

For the log investor $c(t) = \rho W(t)$. The marginal propensity to consume stays constant respectively at a level that depends on all the parameters, in accordance with a and the time impatience ρ. The hump-shaped behavior is excluded.

As an illustration, figure 9.2 compares the optimal c/W of two risk-averse investors, in the absence of hump-shaped behavior, with a finite and an infinite horizon. For the case in which the investors have finite horizon, the rate is plotted as a function of the horizon T, fixing $t = 0$. The horizon varies from 0 to 30 years. The behavior is symmetric to the one in the previous picture: the larger is the horizon, the less the investor consumes today. This effect is more pronounced the higher the risk aversion. The optimal infinite horizon policy is obviously shown as a horizontal line. Within each case (finite versus infinite horizon), less risk-averse investors consume more. Finite-horizon investors consume more

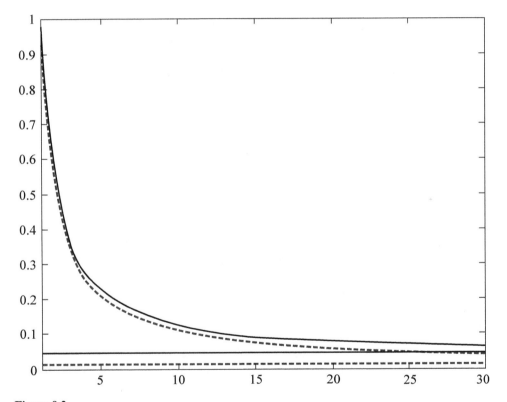

Figure 9.2

Finite-horizon optimal consumption behavior (consumption/wealth ratio) of CRRA investors as a function of the life-horizon $T(t = 0)$ in the presence of a single, geometric Brownian motion risky asset. The continuous line corresponds to $\gamma = -1$ ($A_r = 2$); the dotted one to $\gamma = -50$ ($A_r = 51$). The corresponding horizontal asymptotes are the infinite horizon policies. The other parameters are set at $\mu = 10\%$, $r = 1\%$ (so that the risk premium is 9%), $\rho = 3\%$, $\sigma = 20\%$, and $\varepsilon = 0$ (no final bequest).

than the infinite-horizon ones, even if they have the same risk aversion. Once again, myopic portfolio weights do not preclude a rich consumption behavior.

———————————————♠———————————————

We finish this section with a remark on the relation with discrete-time results, as obtained for CRRA investors by Samuelson (1969). As observed by Merton (1969), the continuous-time results confirm Samuelson's theory. For isoelastic preferences, the portfolio mix x is independent of the consumption decision c but not vice versa. The higher is the time preference ρ, the higher is the consumption rate. If, in addition, the decision maker is optimally myopic ($\gamma = 0$), the consumption decision is independent of the risky security drift and diffusion. It depends only on the current level of wealth. Under an infinite horizon, a log investor consumes a percentage of his wealth equal to his rate of time preference. So, the IID, strict Black-Scholes case is an extension of the discrete-time results.

9.3   Multiple, Correlated Risky Securities with IID Returns Plus One Riskless Security

Now we assume a multiplicity of risky securities or stocks, $\mathcal{S} = \{S_i, i = 1...N\}$. Each one has IID returns (Geometric Wiener process or strict Black-Scholes):

$$\frac{dS_i(t)}{S_i(t)} = \mu_i dt + \sigma_i dw(t) \qquad\qquad i = 1,..N \qquad (9.17)$$

where $\mu_i > r$ and σ_i is a K-dimensional and positive row-vector, row i of the matrix σ. Assume that rank$(\sigma\sigma^\mathsf{T}) = N$. Under this rank condition we know that *no redundant security* exists.

Define the security allocation weights $x_i(t)$ as above and collect them in a vector $x \in \mathbb{R}^N$. These are the adapted processes representing the *proportions* of wealth invested in each single risky security, so that

$$1 - \sum_{i=1}^{N} x_i$$

is the proportion invested in the riskless security. Allowing again for short sales, we impose no constraint on the sign of the fractions or portfolio weights x_i.

The budget constraint becomes:

$$dW(t) = W(t) \sum_{i=1}^{N} x_i \frac{dS_i}{S_i} + W(t) \left[1 - \sum_{i=1}^{N} x_i(t) \right] rdt - c(t)dt \qquad (9.18)$$

$$= rW(t)dt + W(t) \sum_{i=1}^{N} x_i \left(\mu_i - r \right) dt - c(t)dt$$

$$+ W(t) \sum_{i=1}^{N} x_i \sum_{k=1}^{K} \sigma_{i,k} dw_k(t)$$

or, in vector notation:

$$dW(t) = W(t)x^\mathsf{T} (\mu - r\mathbf{1}) \, dt - c(t)dt + W(t)x^\mathsf{T} \sigma \, dw(t)$$

The optimization problem is:

$$\max_{\{c(t),x(t)\}} \mathbb{E}_0 \left\{ \int_0^T u(c(t),t)dt + \wp(W(T)) \right\}$$

Its first-order conditions are the marginality one and N conditions similar to (9.13):

$$x = -\frac{\frac{\partial J}{\partial W}}{\frac{\partial^2 J}{\partial W^2} W} \left[\sigma \sigma^\mathsf{T} \right]^{-1} [\mu - r \times \mathbf{1}] \tag{9.19}$$

These conditions say that the investor can either, and indifferently, hold the individual securities, or invest in only two funds, built out of them. This result is the simplest *mutual-fund or fund-separation theorem*. The two funds are:

- the riskless security, whose weight can be positive or negative. In the first case the investor lends money, in the second he borrows;

- the diversified portfolio, in which securities enter with weight

$$\left[\sigma \sigma^\mathsf{T} \right]^{-1} [\mu - r \times \mathbf{1}] \in \mathbb{R}^N$$

and which is myopic. Each security enters in it with a weight that is constant over time.

The first fund determines the portfolio total risk, the second its level of diversification. The exposure of each investor to each fund is dependent on his risk tolerance, which is variable over time t. The entries of the optimal portfolio depend on the whole variance-covariance matrix. Covariance becomes important here, as in one-period and discrete-time markets; see section 4.2.3. With IID returns, we are again in the presence of a Markowitz-style portfolio choice: the introduction of multiple securities has simply substituted the unique security weight of the previous section with an exposure in a single fund. In the frictionless market that we are examining, this fund could be set up by an intermediary. Investors do not need to have access to the individual securities.

9.4   Non-IID, Multiple Risky Securities, and a Riskless Security

In this section, following Merton (1971, 1973), Breeden (1979), Cox, Ingersoll, and Ross (CIR, 1985a), we extend the portfolio problem so as to represent a *stochastic investment opportunity set*. First, we consider a riskless security with price S_0 whose rate of interest is only instantaneously riskless, instead of being constant or deterministic over time. Second, we consider a multiplicity of risky securities $\mathcal{S}$, whose returns are not IID. Their distributions vary over time.

Stochastic opportunity set

Intuitively, the instantaneously riskless rate and stock returns could vary as a function of past returns, the distribution of wealth, the state of activity or inactivity of some industries, the overall phase of the economic cycle, or other economic indicators. We take the typical *state-variables* approach. These variables are assumed to drive the returns' distribution. We collect them in a vector $Y(t)$ of dimension H. The other state variable needed to formulate the investment problem is wealth W. Current securities prices may be state variables and be included in the vector Y. In order to permit the use of dynamic programming, the joint process (W, Y) is assumed to be not only Itô, but also *Markov*. The dynamics of Y are in the form:

$$dY(t) = \mu_Y(Y(t), t)dt + \sigma_Y(Y(t), t) \times dw(t) \tag{9.20}$$

where μ_Y is an adapted process, $w(t)$ is a K-dimensional standard Wiener process, and the matrix-valued process σ_Y is of dimension $H \times K$. To make the problem non-degenerate, the matrix $\sigma_Y \sigma_Y^T$ is taken to be different from the null matrix. The instantaneous correlation between the state variables is not zero. We have thus described what, in the technical jargon, is known as a *stochastic opportunity set*. "Stochastic" here means that the conditions – drift and diffusion or volatility – at which investors can invest, as represented by the state variables, are liable to change over time, in a random way. Knowledge of these conditions is subject to the usual filtration mechanism and affects portfolio choices of rational investors, in the sense that they will try to hedge the additional channels of randomness.

Optimization

Letting the portfolio weights x be such that the integral in dS is well defined, the wealth dynamics can be written as in the IID case:

$$dW(t) = r(Y, t)W(t)dt + W(t)[\mu(Y, t) - r(Y, t)\mathbf{1}]^T x dt \tag{9.21}$$
$$- c(t)dt + W(t)x^T \sigma(Y, t)dw(t)$$

The optimization problem to be solved is again

$$\max_{c(t),\{x_i(t)\}} \mathbb{E}_0 \left\{ \int_0^T u(c(t), t)dt + \wp(W(T)) \right\} \tag{9.22}$$

subject to $W(0) = e_0$, to the non-negativity constraint on wealth, and to the terminal condition $J(W, Y, T) = \wp(W)$. Its dynamic programming solution involves again the definition of the value function. For notational convenience, we drop the dependence of the value function on (W, Y, t). The HJB equation is

$$\max_{c,x} \left\{ u(c, t) + D(J) + \frac{\partial J}{\partial t} \right\} = 0 \tag{9.23}$$

In order to expand it, observe that:

1. the Hessian matrix of the value function with respect to the $1 + H$ arguments (W, Y) is naturally partitioned as:[12]

$$
\underbrace{G_{WY}}_{(1+H)\times(1+H)} = \left[\begin{array}{cc} \underbrace{\dfrac{\partial^2 J}{\partial W^2}}_{1\times 1} & \underbrace{\dfrac{\partial^2 J}{\partial Y \partial W}}_{1\times H} \\[2em] \underbrace{\dfrac{\partial^2 J}{\partial W \partial Y}}_{H\times 1} & \underbrace{\dfrac{\partial^2 J}{\partial Y}}_{H\times H} \end{array} \right]
$$

2. the diffusion matrix b of (W, Y) can be partitioned as:

$$
\underbrace{b}_{(1+H)\times K} = \left[\begin{array}{c} \underbrace{W^2 x^{\mathsf{T}} \sigma}_{1\times K} \\[1em] \underbrace{\sigma_Y}_{H\times K} \end{array} \right]
$$

3. matrix multiplication can be performed by blocks, and the trace of a sum of matrices is the sum of their traces. This means that the trace of the matrix $(b^{\mathsf{T}} G_{WY} b)$, which is needed in Itô's lemma for J, is:

$$
\frac{\partial^2 J}{\partial W^2} W^2 x^{\mathsf{T}} \sigma \sigma^{\mathsf{T}} x + \text{trace}\left[\sigma_Y^{\mathsf{T}} \frac{\partial^2 J}{\partial Y^2} \sigma_Y \right] + 2\frac{\partial^2 J}{\partial Y \partial W} W \sigma_Y \sigma^{\mathsf{T}} x
$$

Using these results the HJB equation can be written as :

$$
\begin{aligned}
\max_{c,x} \Bigg\{ &u(c,t) + \frac{\partial J}{\partial W}\left\{ r(Y,t)W + W[\mu(Y,t) - r(Y,t)\times \mathbf{1}]^{\mathsf{T}} x - c\right\} \\
&+ \frac{\partial J}{\partial Y}\mu_Y(Y,t) + \frac{1}{2}\frac{\partial^2 J}{\partial W^2} W^2 x^{\mathsf{T}}\sigma\sigma^{\mathsf{T}} x + \frac{1}{2}\text{trace}\left[\sigma_Y^{\mathsf{T}} \frac{\partial^2 J}{\partial Y^2}\sigma_Y\right] \\
&+ \frac{\partial^2 J}{\partial Y \partial W} W\sigma_Y\sigma^{\mathsf{T}} x + \frac{\partial J}{\partial t} \Bigg\} = 0
\end{aligned} \tag{9.24}
$$

The first-order conditions with respect to consumption and portfolio selection are the usual marginality condition and the portfolio allocation first-order condition:

$$
\frac{\partial u}{\partial c} = \frac{\partial J}{\partial W} \tag{9.25}
$$

$$
\begin{aligned}
\frac{\partial J}{\partial W}[\mu(Y,t) - r(Y,t)\times \mathbf{1}] + \frac{\partial^2 J}{\partial W^2} W\sigma(Y,t)\sigma(Y,t)^{\mathsf{T}} x \\
+ \sigma(Y,t)\sigma_Y(Y,t)^{\mathsf{T}} \frac{\partial^2 J}{\partial W \partial Y} = 0
\end{aligned} \tag{9.26}
$$

---

12 We suppose that J belongs to C^2. Note that any Hessian matrix is symmetric.

An economic interpretation of these first-order conditions is offered now. The reader may wish to examine also section 11.3.

9.4.1 Myopic and Hedging Portfolios

Suppose here again that there are no redundant securities, namely that the variance-covariance matrix of securities' returns has full rank:

$$\text{rank}(\sigma(Y,t)\sigma(Y,t)^{\mathsf{T}}) = N.$$

Then it admits an inverse, and from the first-order condition (9.26) we get the following explicit solution for portfolio allocations, where, for notational convenience, we drop the dependence of the drift and diffusion coefficients on the state variables Y and time t:

$$x = -\frac{\frac{\partial J}{\partial W}}{\frac{\partial^2 J}{\partial W^2} W} \left[\sigma\sigma^{\mathsf{T}}\right]^{-1} \times [\mu - r \times \mathbf{1}] \tag{9.27}$$

$$-\frac{1}{\frac{\partial^2 J}{\partial W^2} W} \left[\sigma\sigma^{\mathsf{T}}\right]^{-1} \sigma\sigma_Y^{\mathsf{T}} \frac{\partial^2 J}{\partial W \partial Y}$$

The vector of weights has two components, namely

- A diversified component, which resembles the myopic, *static*, Markowitz-style portfolio choice with IID returns:

$$-\underbrace{\frac{\frac{\partial J}{\partial W}}{\frac{\partial^2 J}{\partial W^2} W}}_{1 \times 1} \underbrace{\left[\sigma\sigma^{\mathsf{T}}\right]^{-1}}_{N \times N} \underbrace{[\mu - r \times \mathbf{1}]}_{N \times 1} \tag{9.28}$$

- An *intertemporal-hedging component,* which depends on risk aversion and on risk, as measured by the diffusion matrices σ and σ_Y:

$$-\underbrace{\frac{1}{\frac{\partial^2 J}{\partial W^2} W}}_{1 \times 1} \underbrace{\left[\sigma\sigma^{\mathsf{T}}\right]^{-1}}_{N \times N} \underbrace{\sigma\sigma_Y^{\mathsf{T}}}_{(N \times K) \times (K \times H)} \underbrace{\frac{\partial^2 J}{\partial W \partial Y}}_{H \times 1} \tag{9.29}$$

The myopic portfolio represents *short-term or "tactical" investing* based on securities' predictability in the short run. The intertemporal hedging portfolio represents *long-term investing.* It smooths consumption over time by hedging good or bad states in the future via changes in wealth. It is a preparation for the *risks faced when reinvesting.*

To understand this, define as a "good" state or favorable shift in the investment opportunity set an increase in one of the state variables, say $dY_j > 0$, such that consumption increases:

$$\frac{\partial c}{\partial Y_j} > 0$$

We show that the hedging weights are such that this increase is counterbalanced by a decrease in wealth, which keeps the overall marginal utility constant. Indeed, recall that marginal-utility smoothing is a feature of intertemporal optimization. The increase in Y_j is, therefore, "good news," even if it is accompanied by an independent decrease $dW < 0$ in wealth. The hedging portfolio weights combine such occurrences. They stabilize utility by obtaining decreases in wealth in good states ($dY_j > 0$) and increases in wealth in bad states ($dY_j < 0$).

The impact of smoothing on portfolio weights depends also on the sign of the covariance between the state variable Y and the single securities' prices, as measured by the elements of the $N \times H$ matrix $\sigma \sigma_Y^\top$. Consider for simplicity a single security, single-state variable case ($\sigma_Y \in \mathbb{R}, \sigma > 0$). The hedging weight becomes

$$-\frac{\frac{\partial^2 J}{\partial W \partial Y}}{\frac{\partial^2 J}{\partial W^2} W} \left[\sigma \sigma^\top\right]^{-1} \sigma \sigma_Y$$

With a favorable shift in Y ($dY > 0$) the ratio

$$-\frac{\frac{\partial^2 J}{\partial W \partial Y}}{\frac{\partial^2 J}{\partial W^2} W}$$

is negative. If $\sigma_Y > 0$, the hedging weight is negative and its total weight in the optimal portfolio is negatively affected. The hedging motive, which arises when introducing a stochastic opportunity set instead of a constant one, is again based on co-risk instead of risk. A security receives a smaller or greater weight not based on its riskiness *per se*, but on the interaction with the overall wealth behavior and the resulting consumption stream (σ and σ_Y). Specifically, the hedging weight is negative for securities positively correlated to "good news."

In order to show this property, first recall that, because of the marginality condition, saying that consumption increases as a consequence of a change in Y_j, or $\partial c / \partial Y_j > 0$, is equivalent to stating that the ratio of the second mixed derivative of the value function to the second derivative of u is positive:

$$\frac{\partial c}{\partial Y_j} = \frac{\frac{\partial^2 J}{\partial W \partial Y_j}}{\frac{\partial^2 u}{\partial c^2}} > 0$$

Since we assumed that the utility function is strictly concave, with $\frac{\partial^2 u}{\partial c^2} < 0$, it follows that $\frac{\partial c}{\partial Y_j} > 0$ if and only if the marginal utility of wealth decreases when Y_j goes up, and vice versa:

$$\frac{\partial^2 J}{\partial W \partial Y_j} < 0 \tag{9.30}$$

Since J is strictly concave,

$$\frac{\partial^2 J}{\partial W^2} < 0 \tag{9.31}$$

Together with decreasing marginal utility of wealth when Y_j goes up, this means that *a favorable shift* in a state variable entails

$$-\frac{\frac{\partial^2 J}{\partial W \partial Y_j}}{\frac{\partial^2 J}{\partial W^2}} < 0 \tag{9.32}$$

Consider now the total change in marginal utility:

$$d\frac{\partial J}{\partial W} = \frac{\partial^2 J}{\partial W^2} dW + \frac{\partial^2 J}{\partial W \partial Y} dY$$

We are able to attain a zero change in marginal utility if we can find a change in wealth that solves the equation

$$d\left(\frac{\partial J}{\partial W}\right) = \frac{\partial^2 J}{\partial W^2} dW + \frac{\partial^2 J}{\partial W \partial Y} dY = 0$$

This is

$$dW = -\underbrace{\frac{\frac{\partial^2 J}{\partial W \partial Y_j}}{\frac{\partial^2 J}{\partial W^2}}}_{<0} \underbrace{dY_j}_{>0} < 0$$

which is negative because of (9.32) and of the sign of dY_j. Faced with a shift in the state variable Y, such decrease in overall wealth is able to maintain total derived utility unaffected, or marginal utility constant.

The conjunctions:

Good state	Bad state
$dY_j > 0$	$dY_j < 0$
$dW < 0$	$dW > 0$

are what an investor targets in order to smooth utility. The hedging portfolio combines such occurrences.

9.4.2   Fund Interpretation

The optimal portfolio result can equivalently be stated as follows. Individuals can either, and indifferently, hold, together with the riskless security S_0, the N securities S_i, or invest in $H+2$ funds, built out of them. This result is another *mutual-fund or fund-separation theorem.*

We discuss first the mix and number of funds, then the amount each investor should keep in them.

As for the *mix*, the funds are:

- the riskless security, which can still be positive (lending) or negative (borrowing),
- the myopic portfolio, which invests

$$\left[\sigma\sigma^{\mathsf{T}}\right]^{-1}\left[\mu - r\mathbf{1}\right]$$

in each primitive risky security and is held in an amount equal to the risk tolerance ratio,

- as many intertemporal hedging funds as state variables, H. Their weights in the effective securities are represented by the columns of the matrix:

$$\underbrace{\left[\sigma\sigma^{\mathsf{T}}\right]^{-1}\sigma\sigma_Y^{\mathsf{T}}}_{(N\times N)(N\times K)(K\times H)}$$

The risky funds invest in the N risky securities, but according to weights that are independent of preferences. We expect each single investor to place his wealth in the funds according to his risk tolerance, while the fund is the same for every investor and therefore preference-independent. The weights depend on the (instantaneous, conditional) variance-covariance matrix of S and Y, $\sigma\sigma^{\mathsf{T}}$ and $\sigma\sigma_Y^{\mathsf{T}}$. The hedging funds have maximal correlation with the state variables (see Breeden (1979)).

As for the *number* of funds, the two funds that characterized an IID, non-stochastic investment set have become $2 + H$ in number, when hedging needs arise, because of the existence of state variables which affect derived utility. In a random-changing opportunity set, on top of diversifying and adjusting total risk, investors hedge against state variables modifications. As for the *weight* that each investor should have in each fund, he can either invest x_i directly in each security, $i = 1, ..N$, or invest according to his risk tolerance:

$$-\frac{\frac{\partial J}{\partial W}}{\frac{\partial^2 J}{\partial W^2}}W \in \mathbb{R}$$

in the myopic portfolio and:

$$-\frac{\frac{\partial^2 J}{\partial W\partial Y}}{\frac{\partial^2 J}{\partial W^2}}W \in \mathbb{R}^H$$

in the H hedging funds. The exposure in the single funds is then determined by investor preferences, as in the IID case.

An enlightening example with a single state variable and isoelastic utility is discussed as exercise 9.3.

9.4.3   Optimization and Nonlinear PDE

Coming back to the optimization problem with a stochastic opportunity set, the first-order conditions (9.25) and (9.26) must be substituted into the HJB equation (9.24). In this case, as in the IID one, substitution of the first-order conditions produces a nonlinear PDE for the unknown function J. The equation has to be solved under the boundary condition $J(W, T) = \wp(W)$ and keeping non-negativity of wealth into account. The HJB equation is:

$$u\left(\mathfrak{h}\left(\frac{\partial J}{\partial W}, t\right), t\right) + \frac{\partial J}{\partial W}\left[r(Y, t)W - \mathfrak{h}\left(\frac{\partial J}{\partial W}, t\right)\right] \qquad (9.33)$$

$$+ \frac{\partial J}{\partial Y}\mu_Y - \frac{1}{2}\left[\frac{\partial J}{\partial W}(\mu - r \times \mathbf{1}) + \sigma\sigma_Y^{\mathsf{T}}\frac{\partial^2 J}{\partial W \partial Y}\right]^{\mathsf{T}}$$

$$\times \frac{1}{\frac{\partial^2 J}{\partial W^2}}\left[\sigma\sigma^{\mathsf{T}}\right]^{-1}\left[\frac{\partial J}{\partial W}(\mu - r \times \mathbf{1}) + \sigma\sigma_Y^{\mathsf{T}}\frac{\partial^2 J}{\partial W \partial Y}\right]$$

$$+ \frac{1}{2}\mathrm{trace}\left[\sigma_Y^{\mathsf{T}}\frac{\partial^2 J}{\partial Y^2}\sigma_Y\right] + \frac{\partial J}{\partial t} = 0$$

where $\mathfrak{h}$ is the consumption-smoothing solution of the first-order condition for consumption and the optimal portfolio weights have been substituted in.

Only when this PDE is solved do we have a solution of the optimization problem. Specific utility functions, namely the isoelastic choice, permit this solution explicitly. Apart from the isoelastic case, the non-linearity of the HJB equation in correspondence to the optimal controls, which we have found over all our specifications so far, makes the intertemporal optimization problem awkward. We now show how to simplify it.

In the aforementioned example, the solution Bellman function will be found by solving exercise 9.3.

9.5   Exploiting Market Completeness: Building a Bridge to Chapter 10

This section shows

- how to simplify the HJB equation (9.33) in the case of complete markets, when the total number of securities N is equal to the number of Wiener processes K,
- under which conditions the equation is linear,
- how to obtain optimal portfolios in the simplified case.

Simplified equation

Sometimes, nonlinear PDEs can be simplified by a change of dependent variable, that is, a change of unknown function. This can be done when the dependent variable, which here is the function J, is part of a nonlinear term whereas one of the independent variables, which here is wealth W, appears in a linear way. Engineering mathematicians call this the *hodograph transformation,* which is used to solve problems in Mechanics, specially Fluid Mechanics. Since it was introduced for the first time in Financial Economics by Cox and Huang (1989), it is known in this field as the *Cox-Huang transformation.* It consists in reading the HJB equation not as an equation in the unknown function J, but as an equation in wealth W as an unknown function, considering that the two are linked. The Cox-Huang change of unknown function is from:

$$\frac{\partial J}{\partial W}(W, Y, t) \triangleq \lambda$$

to

$$W = F(\lambda, Y, t)$$

with the F function unknown.

Assume that J is strictly concave, differentiate both sides of the HJB equation (9.33) with respect to W and operate the change of unknown. The appendix to the current chapter shows that, suppressing the arguments of F for notational simplicity, we get:

$$rF = \mathfrak{h} - \frac{\partial F}{\partial \lambda}\lambda r + \frac{\partial F}{\partial t} + \frac{1}{2}\frac{\partial^2 F}{\partial Y^2}\sigma_Y\sigma_Y^{\mathsf{T}} + \frac{\partial F}{\partial Y}\mu_Y \tag{9.34}$$

$$+ \left[\frac{1}{2}\frac{\partial^2 F}{\partial \lambda^2}\lambda + \frac{\partial F}{\partial \lambda}\right][\mu - r \times \mathbf{1}]^{\mathsf{T}}\left[\sigma\sigma^{\mathsf{T}}\right]^{-1}[\mu - r \times \mathbf{1}]\lambda$$

$$- \left[\frac{\partial F}{\partial Y} + \frac{\partial^2 F}{\partial \lambda \partial Y}\lambda\right][\mu - r \times \mathbf{1}]^{\mathsf{T}}\left[\sigma\sigma^{\mathsf{T}}\right]^{-1}\sigma\sigma_Y^{\mathsf{T}}$$

$$+ \left[\frac{1}{2}\frac{\frac{\partial^2 F}{\partial \lambda^2}\frac{\partial F}{\partial Y}}{\frac{\partial F}{\partial \lambda}} - \frac{\partial^2 F}{\partial \lambda \partial Y}\right]\sigma_Y\left\{I_K - \sigma^{\mathsf{T}}\left[\sigma\sigma^{\mathsf{T}}\right]^{-1}\sigma\right\}\sigma_Y^{\mathsf{T}}\frac{\frac{\partial F}{\partial Y}}{\frac{\partial F}{\partial \lambda}}$$

where I_K is, as usual, the identity matrix of size K.

Linear equation

When the combination of the diffusions of the prices in the last row, namely the matrix:[13]

$$\underbrace{\sigma^{\mathsf{T}}}_{K \times N}\underbrace{\left[\sigma\sigma^{\mathsf{T}}\right]^{-1}}_{N \times N}\underbrace{\sigma}_{N \times K} \tag{9.35}$$

is an identity matrix I_K for all t with probability 1, the last line of the above equation cancels out and one is left with a *linear* PDE in F (as the ones in chapters 6 and 8 were), which is very convenient for numerical as well as analytical solutions. It has to be solved under the boundary condition:

$$F(\lambda, Y, T) = \mathfrak{G}(\lambda)$$

where $\mathfrak{G}$ is the inverse function of $\partial\wp(W)/\partial W$.

---

[13] The condition is not an identity, in contrast to:

$$\sigma\sigma^{\mathsf{T}}\left[\sigma\sigma^{\mathsf{T}}\right]^{-1} = \left[\sigma\sigma^{\mathsf{T}}\right]^{-1}\sigma\sigma^{\mathsf{T}} = I_N$$

which would be, for any vector σ.

A very important case in which the equation becomes linear is the complete market case, $N = K$. In that case one can easily verify, premultiplying both sides of

$$\sigma^{\mathsf{T}}\left[\sigma\sigma^{\mathsf{T}}\right]^{-1}\sigma = I_K$$

by σ, that the equality is true.

Solving for the optimal portfolio

Let us now point out the consequences for the optimal portfolio weights x of turning the HJB equation into a linear equation for F. Once (9.34) is solved, one has two ways to obtain the optimal portfolio. One consists in substituting for F and its derivatives in (9.27), using the correspondence between F and J, as well as its derivatives and the ones of J. We get:

$$x\ (\lambda, Y, t) = -\left[\sigma\ (Y, t)\,\sigma(Y, t)^{\mathsf{T}}\right]^{-1}$$
$$\times \left\{ \frac{\partial F}{\partial \lambda}\lambda\left[\mu(Y, t) - r(Y, t) \times \mathbf{1}\right] - \frac{\partial F}{\partial Y}\sigma(Y, t)\sigma_Y(Y, t)^{\mathsf{T}} \right\}$$

The alternative consists in recovering the function J by inversion from the function F and applying (9.27).

9.6 Benchmark Example (continued)

The portfolio selection case analyzed in section 9.3 corresponds to the strict Black-Scholes set up with $N = K$. If we add an assumption of isoelastic utility function, the portfolio selection first-order conditions give

$$x = \frac{1}{1 - \gamma}\left[\sigma\sigma^{\mathsf{T}}\right]^{-1}\left[\mu - r \times \mathbf{1}\right]$$

since the risk tolerance of the derived utility function is constant and equal to $1/(1 - \gamma)$. It follows that, with an isoelastic utility function, the exposure to the myopic, risky portfolio $\left[\sigma\sigma^{\mathsf{T}}\right]^{-1}\left[\mu - r \times \mathbf{1}\right]$ is constant over time and independent of the bequest, wealth, and time discounting, exactly as in the single-risky security cases examined above.

If we maintain the isoelastic assumption for the utility function but extend our example to generalized Black-Scholes securities, as in section 9.4, we know that the portfolio weights will have both a myopic component and an intertemporal hedging one, namely (9.28) and (9.29). We discuss here an example provided by Ingersoll (1987).

Suppose there is a single risky security, whose expected rate of return is equal to the interest rate, which in turn is the state variable ($Y = r$). The instantaneous variance of both the risky return and the interest rate are constant. The drift of the interest rate is zero.

We have:

$$dS(t) = r(t)S(t)dt + \sigma S(t)dw_1(t)$$

$$dr(t) = sdw_2(t)$$

with $\sigma, s \in \mathbb{R}_{++}$. Let us assume also that the Wiener processes w_1, w_2 are perfectly negatively correlated. The model makes the risky security a perfect hedge for the state variable, while giving to it no role in providing expected extra returns. This is the consequence of the correlation being equal to -1, while the percentage drift of S is equal to the interest rate. The purpose of the example is to show that the hedging demand for S is different from zero, while the myopic demand for it is null. All else equal, that security would be held by no one in a single-period model.

To further simplify the model, assume that consumption takes place at time T only and assume that the rate of time preference is zero. The optimization problem (9.22) becomes

$$J(W, r, t) = \max_{x(s)} \mathbb{E}_t \left[\frac{W(T)^\gamma}{\gamma} \right]$$

under the security dynamics specified above. Ingersoll guesses a solution for J of the type

$$J(W, r, t) = Q(r, t)\frac{W(t)^\gamma}{\gamma}$$

Assuming such a solution, the HJB equation becomes the following PDE for $Q(r, t)$

$$\frac{\partial Q}{\partial t} + \gamma r Q + \frac{\gamma}{2(1 - \gamma)} s^2 \frac{1}{Q} \left(\frac{\partial Q}{\partial r} \right)^2 + \frac{1}{2} s^2 \frac{\partial^2 Q}{\partial r^2} = 0$$

with the terminal condition $Q(r, T) = 1$. The equation admits as a solution

$$Q(r, t) = \exp \left[\left(\gamma r (T - t) + \frac{s^2 \gamma^2}{6 \times (1 - \gamma)} \right) (T - t)^3 \right]$$

It follows that the optimal portfolio policy for this investor is

$$x = -\frac{\gamma(T - t)s}{(1 - \gamma)\sigma}$$

Figure 9.3 illustrates the behavior of the portfolio over time. The variation of the risky-security holding with respect to γ is opposite to the usual static demand. This means that investors who are less risk-averse than the myopic one, that is, that have γ positive, will be short the risky security. The opposite holds for the investors who are more risk-averse than the log investor. Everything else equal, the risky security demand, in absolute value, is decreasing in the remaining lifetime $T - t$ and in the volatility of the interest rate s, while it is increasing in the volatility of the risky security itself σ. Investors more risk-averse than the myopic one will, therefore, hedge more, the riskier is the state variable and the safer is the risky security. This incorporates the essence of hedging demand, in a particularly simple setting.

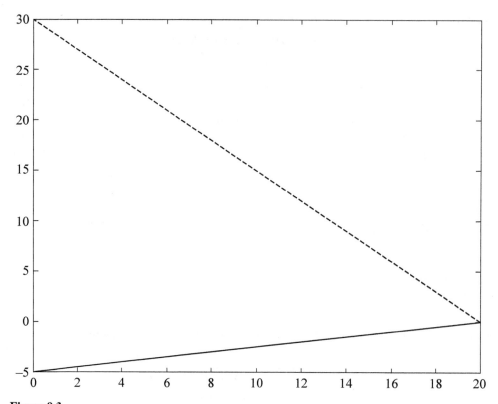

Figure 9.3
Optimal risky asset holding for CRRA investors as a function ot time t, under the asset specifications of Ingersoll's example and under the parameter choice of figure 9.1: $s = \{10\%, 30\%\}, \sigma = 20\%$. The continuous line corresponds to $\gamma = -1$ ($A_r = 2$); the dotted one to $\gamma = -10$ ($A_r = 11$).

9.7 Conclusion

Dynamic programming in continuous time has been used extensively to derive the behavior of an optimizing investor. In the general case of incomplete market considered here, the investor solves simultaneously for the amount he wishes to consume and for his choice of a portfolio. The portfolio contains two components. One is the myopic portfolio, the composition of which is identical to the portfolio chosen by a Markowitz investor in a one-period setting. That component of the portfolio is based on, and exploits, the securities' returns of the immediate period of time. It is purely "tactical." The other is the intertemporal-hedging portfolio, which aims to prepare the portfolio for *reinvestment* next period when the investment opportunity set has shifted. It reflects the longer-run, "strategic" behavior of the investor.

9.8 Appendix: The Link to Chapter 10

In this appendix we assume that the value function is at least of class C^3, which implies F being of class C^2. We want to prove equation (9.34). Given that the definition $\lambda \equiv \partial J / \partial W$ is an identity, take the derivatives of its LHS and RHS (and suppress the dependence of $F(\lambda, Y, t)$ and $J(W, Y, t)$ on their arguments, for notational simplicity) with respect to λ and Y:

with respect to λ:

$$1 \equiv \frac{\partial^2 J}{\partial W^2} \times \frac{\partial F}{\partial \lambda} \tag{9.36}$$

with repect to Y:

$$0 \equiv \frac{\partial^2 J}{\partial W \partial Y} + \frac{\partial^2 J}{\partial W^2} \times \frac{\partial F}{\partial Y} \tag{9.37}$$

Continue taking the derivative of (9.36) and (9.37) with respect to λ, of (9.37) with respect to Y:

$$0 \equiv \frac{\partial^3 J}{\partial W^3} \times \left(\frac{\partial F}{\partial \lambda}\right)^2 + \frac{\partial^2 J}{\partial W^2} \times \frac{\partial^2 F}{\partial \lambda^2}$$

$$0 \equiv \frac{\partial^3 J}{\partial W^3} \times \frac{\partial F}{\partial \lambda} \times \frac{\partial F}{\partial Y} + \frac{\partial^3 J}{\partial W^2 \partial Y} \times \frac{\partial F}{\partial \lambda} + \frac{\partial^2 J}{\partial W^2} \times \frac{\partial^2 F}{\partial \lambda \partial Y}$$

$$0 \equiv \frac{\partial^3 J}{\partial W \partial Y^2} + 2 \frac{\partial^3 J}{\partial W^2 \partial Y} \frac{\partial F}{\partial Y} + \frac{\partial^2 J}{\partial W^2} \frac{\partial^2 F}{\partial Y^2} + \frac{\partial^3 J}{\partial W^3} \frac{\partial F}{\partial Y} \tag{9.38}$$

From the previous identities we get the following expressions for the value function derivatives, in terms of the new function F and its own derivatives:

$$\frac{\partial^2 J}{\partial W^2} = \left(\frac{\partial F}{\partial \lambda}\right)^{-1}$$

$$\frac{\partial^2 J}{\partial W \partial Y} = -\frac{\partial F}{\partial Y} \left(\frac{\partial F}{\partial \lambda}\right)^{-1}$$

$$\frac{\partial^2 J}{\partial W \partial t} = -\frac{\partial F}{\partial t} \left(\frac{\partial F}{\partial \lambda}\right)^{-1}$$

$$\frac{\partial^3 J}{\partial W^3} = -\frac{\partial^2 F}{\partial \lambda^2} \left(\frac{\partial F}{\partial \lambda}\right)^{-3}$$

$$\frac{\partial^3 J}{\partial W^2 \partial Y} = \frac{\partial^2 F}{\partial \lambda^2} \left(\frac{\partial F}{\partial \lambda}\right)^{-3} \times \frac{\partial F}{\partial Y} - \left(\frac{\partial F}{\partial \lambda}\right)^{-1} \times \frac{\partial^2 F}{\partial \lambda \partial Y}$$

$$\frac{\partial^3 J}{\partial W \partial Y^2} = -2 \frac{\partial F}{\partial Y} \left(\frac{\partial F}{\partial \lambda}\right)^{-2}$$

$$\times \left[\frac{\partial^2 F}{\partial \lambda^2} \left(\frac{\partial F}{\partial \lambda}\right)^{-1} \times \frac{\partial F}{\partial Y} - \frac{\partial^2 F}{\partial \lambda \partial Y}\right]$$

$$- \left(\frac{\partial F}{\partial \lambda}\right)^{-1} \frac{\partial^2 F}{\partial Y^2} + \frac{\partial^2 F}{\partial \lambda^2} \left(\frac{\partial F}{\partial \lambda}\right)^{-3} \left(\frac{\partial F}{\partial Y}\right)^2$$

Differentiate (9.24) with respect to W:

$$0 = \frac{\partial^2 J}{\partial W^2}\left[r(Y,t)\,W - \mathfrak{h}\left(\frac{\partial J}{\partial W},t\right)\right] + \frac{\partial J}{\partial W}r(Y,t) + \frac{\partial^2 J}{\partial W \partial Y}\varkappa(Y,t)$$

$$+ \frac{1}{\frac{\partial^2 J}{\partial W^2}}\left\{\frac{1}{2}\frac{1}{\frac{\partial^2 J}{\partial W^2}}\frac{\partial^3 J}{\partial W^3}\left\{\frac{\partial J}{\partial W}[\mu(Y,t) - r(Y,t)\times\mathbf{1}]\right.\right.$$

$$\left.\left. + \frac{\partial^2 J}{\partial W \partial Y}\sigma(Y,t)\sigma_Y(Y,t)^{\mathsf{T}}\right\}^{\mathsf{T}}\right.$$

$$\left. - \left\{\frac{\partial^2 J}{\partial W^2}[\mu(Y,t) - r(Y,t)\times\mathbf{1}] + \frac{\partial^3 J}{\partial W^2 \partial Y}\sigma(Y,t)\sigma_Y(Y,t)^{\mathsf{T}}\right\}^{\mathsf{T}}\right\}$$

$$\times \left[\sigma(Y,t)\sigma(Y,t)^{\mathsf{T}}\right]^{-1}\left\{\frac{\partial J}{\partial W}[\mu(Y,t) - r(Y,t)\times\mathbf{1}]\right.$$

$$\left. + \frac{\partial^2 J}{\partial W \partial Y}\sigma(Y,t)\sigma_Y(Y,t)^{\mathsf{T}}\right\}$$

$$+ \frac{1}{2}\frac{\partial^3 J}{\partial W \partial Y^2}\sigma_Y(Y,t)\sigma_Y(Y,t)^{\mathsf{T}} + \frac{\partial^2 J}{\partial W \partial t}$$

that is,

$$0 = \frac{\partial^2 J}{\partial W^2}\left[rW - \mathfrak{h}\left(\frac{\partial J}{\partial W},t\right)\right] + \frac{\partial J}{\partial W}r \qquad (9.39)$$

$$+ \frac{\partial^2 J}{\partial W \partial Y}\zeta + \frac{\varpi}{\left(\frac{\partial^2 J}{\partial W^2}\right)^2} + \frac{1}{2}\frac{\partial^3 J}{\partial W \partial Y^2}\sigma_Y\sigma_Y^{\mathsf{T}} + \frac{\partial^2 J}{\partial W \partial t}$$

where, suppressing also the dependence of the drifts and diffusions on the state variables and time:

$$\varpi \triangleq \left[\frac{1}{2}\frac{\partial^3 J}{\partial W^3}\frac{\partial J}{\partial W} - \left(\frac{\partial^2 J}{\partial W^2}\right)^2 \quad \frac{1}{2}\frac{\partial^3 J}{\partial W^3}\frac{\partial^2 J}{\partial W \partial Y} - \frac{\partial^2 J}{\partial W^2}\frac{\partial^3 J}{\partial W^2 \partial Y}\right]$$

$$\times \begin{bmatrix} [\mu - r]^{\mathsf{T}}[\sigma\sigma^{\mathsf{T}}]^{-1}[\mu - r] & [\mu - r]^{\mathsf{T}}[\sigma\sigma^{\mathsf{T}}]^{-1}\sigma\sigma_Y^{\mathsf{T}} \\ \sigma_Y\sigma^{\mathsf{T}}[\sigma\sigma^{\mathsf{T}}]^{-1}[\mu - r] & \sigma_Y\sigma^{\mathsf{T}}[\sigma\sigma^{\mathsf{T}}]^{-1}\sigma\sigma_Y^{\mathsf{T}} \end{bmatrix} \times \begin{bmatrix} \frac{\partial J}{\partial W} \\ \frac{\partial^2 J}{\partial W \partial Y} \end{bmatrix}$$

Substituting the previously calculated derivatives, we get an expression that is equivalent to (9.39):

$$0 = \frac{1}{\frac{\partial F}{\partial \lambda}}(rF - c) + \lambda r + \left[-\frac{\frac{\partial F}{\partial Y}}{\frac{\partial F}{\partial \lambda}}\right]\mu_Y + \varpi\left(\frac{\partial F}{\partial \lambda}\right)^2 - \frac{\frac{\partial F}{\partial t}}{\frac{\partial F}{\partial \lambda}}$$

$$+ \frac{1}{2}\left\{-2\frac{\frac{\partial F}{\partial Y}}{\left(\frac{\partial F}{\partial \lambda}\right)^2}\left[\frac{\partial^2 F}{\partial \lambda^2}}{\frac{\partial F}{\partial \lambda}}\times\frac{\partial F}{\partial Y} - \frac{\partial^2 F}{\partial \lambda \partial Y}\right] - \frac{1}{\frac{\partial F}{\partial \lambda}}\frac{\partial^2 F}{\partial Y^2} + \frac{\frac{\partial^2 F}{\partial \lambda^2}}{\left(\frac{\partial F}{\partial \lambda}\right)^3}\frac{\partial F}{\partial Y}\right\}\sigma_Y\sigma_Y^{\mathsf{T}}$$

where

$$
\varpi \triangleq
$$

$$
\begin{bmatrix} -\dfrac{1}{2}\dfrac{\frac{\partial^2 F}{\partial \lambda^2}}{\left(\frac{\partial F}{\partial \lambda}\right)^3}\lambda - \left(\dfrac{1}{\frac{\partial F}{\partial \lambda}}\right)^2 \dfrac{1}{2}\dfrac{\frac{\partial^2 F}{\partial \lambda^2}\frac{\partial F}{\partial Y}}{\left(\frac{\partial F}{\partial \lambda}\right)^3} - \dfrac{1}{\frac{\partial F}{\partial \lambda}}\begin{bmatrix} \dfrac{1}{\frac{\partial F}{\partial \lambda}}\begin{bmatrix} \dfrac{\frac{\partial^2 F}{\partial \lambda^2}}{\left(\frac{\partial F}{\partial \lambda}\right)^3} \times \dfrac{\partial F}{\partial \lambda} \\ \\ \times \dfrac{\partial F}{\partial Y} - \dfrac{1}{\frac{\partial F}{\partial \lambda}} \times \dfrac{\partial^2 F}{\partial \lambda \partial Y} \end{bmatrix} \end{bmatrix} \end{bmatrix}
$$

$$
\times \begin{bmatrix} [\mu - r]^\mathsf{T}\,[\sigma\sigma^\mathsf{T}]^{-1}\,[\mu - r] & [\mu - r]^\mathsf{T}\,[\sigma\sigma^\mathsf{T}]^{-1}\,\sigma\sigma_Y^\mathsf{T} \\ \sigma_Y\sigma^\mathsf{T}\,[\sigma\sigma^\mathsf{T}]^{-1}\,[\mu - r] & \sigma_Y\sigma^\mathsf{T}\,[\sigma\sigma^\mathsf{T}]^{-1}\,\sigma\sigma_Y^\mathsf{T} \end{bmatrix} \times \begin{bmatrix} \lambda \\ -\dfrac{\frac{\partial F}{\partial Y}}{\frac{\partial F}{\partial \lambda}} \end{bmatrix}
$$

Simplify:

$$
0 = rF - c + \frac{\partial F}{\partial \lambda}\lambda r - \frac{\partial F}{\partial t} - \frac{\partial F}{\partial Y}\varkappa - \frac{1}{2}\frac{\partial^2 F}{\partial Y^2}\sigma_Y\sigma_Y^\mathsf{T} + \varpi \left(\frac{\partial F}{\partial \lambda}\right)^3
$$

$$
- \frac{\frac{\partial F}{\partial Y}}{\frac{\partial F}{\partial \lambda}}\left[\frac{1}{2}\frac{\frac{\partial^2 F}{\partial \lambda^2}}{\frac{\partial F}{\partial \lambda}} \times \frac{\partial F}{\partial Y} - \frac{\partial^2 F}{\partial \lambda \partial Y}\right]\sigma_Y\sigma_Y^\mathsf{T}
$$

Consider that:

$$
\varpi \left(\frac{\partial F}{\partial \lambda}\right)^3 = -\left[\frac{1}{2}\frac{\partial^2 F}{\partial \lambda^2}\lambda + \frac{\partial F}{\partial \lambda}\frac{1}{2}\frac{\frac{\partial^2 F}{\partial \lambda^2}\frac{\partial F}{\partial Y}}{\frac{\partial F}{\partial \lambda}} - \frac{\partial^2 F}{\partial \lambda \partial Y}\right]
$$

$$
\times \begin{bmatrix} [\mu - r]^\mathsf{T}\,[\sigma\sigma^\mathsf{T}]^{-1}\,[\mu - r] & [\mu - r]^\mathsf{T}\,[\sigma\sigma^\mathsf{T}]^{-1}\,\sigma\sigma_Y^\mathsf{T} \\ \sigma_Y\sigma^\mathsf{T}\,[\sigma\sigma^\mathsf{T}]^{-1}\,[\mu - r] & \sigma_Y\sigma^\mathsf{T}\,[\sigma\sigma^\mathsf{T}]^{-1}\,\sigma\sigma_Y^\mathsf{T} \end{bmatrix}
$$

$$
\times \begin{bmatrix} \lambda \\ -\dfrac{\frac{\partial F}{\partial Y}}{\frac{\partial F}{\partial \lambda}} \end{bmatrix}
$$

By so doing, one obtains:

$$
rF = \mathfrak{h} - \frac{\partial F}{\partial \lambda}\lambda r + \frac{\partial F}{\partial t} + \frac{1}{2}\frac{\partial^2 F}{\partial Y^2}\sigma_Y\sigma_Y^\mathsf{T} + \frac{\partial F}{\partial Y}\varkappa
$$

$$
+ \left[\frac{1}{2}\frac{\partial^2 F}{\partial \lambda^2}\lambda + \frac{\partial F}{\partial \lambda}\right][\mu - r]^\mathsf{T}\,[\sigma\sigma^\mathsf{T}]^{-1}\,[\mu - r]\lambda
$$

$$
- \left[\frac{\partial F}{\partial Y} + \frac{\partial^2 F}{\partial \lambda \partial Y}\lambda\right][\mu - r]^\mathsf{T}\,[\sigma\sigma^\mathsf{T}]^{-1}\,\sigma\sigma_Y^\mathsf{T}
$$

$$
+ \left[\frac{1}{2}\frac{\frac{\partial^2 F}{\partial \lambda^2}\frac{\partial F}{\partial Y}}{\frac{\partial F}{\partial \lambda}} - \frac{\partial^2 F}{\partial \lambda \partial Y}\right]\sigma_Y\sigma^\mathsf{T}\,[\sigma\sigma^\mathsf{T}]^{-1}\,\sigma\sigma_Y^\mathsf{T}\left[-\dfrac{\frac{\partial F}{\partial Y}}{\frac{\partial F}{\partial \lambda}}\right]
$$

$$
+ \frac{\frac{\partial F}{\partial Y}}{\frac{\partial F}{\partial \lambda}}\left[\frac{1}{2}\frac{\frac{\partial^2 F}{\partial \lambda^2}}{\frac{\partial F}{\partial \lambda}} \times \frac{\partial F}{\partial Y} - \frac{\partial^2 F}{\partial \lambda \partial Y}\right]\sigma_Y\sigma_Y^\mathsf{T}
$$

which is reproduced as (9.34) in the text.

Exercises

9.1. An individual investor has a single risky investment opportunity:

$$dP = \mu P dt + \sigma P dw$$

Suppose his utility function is isoelastic with $\gamma < 1$, $\gamma \neq 0$ and he lives forever.

a. Show that his wealth is non-negative as soon as consumption is.

b. Show that the value function for the problem at hand is homogeneous of degree γ.

c. Find a sufficient condition to ensure the existence of an optimal (non-negative) consumption strategy during his entire lifetime.

9.2. Suppose that there is only one stock and one risk-free security. Here, as opposed to the generalized Black-Scholes model, the stock pays dividends at the rate of $\{\iota(t)\}$; that is, over the small time interval $[t, t + dt]$, the dividend paid is $\iota(t)dt$. Let $\{S(t)\}$ be the price process of the stock given by the following equation

$$dS(t) = [\mu(t)S(t) - \iota(t)]\, dt + \sigma(t)S(t)dw(t)$$

Suppose further that all of the income that the investor has comes from holding the securities and an initial wealth W_0. Write down the SDE for the investor's budget constraint.

9.3. Consider an investor with an infinite horizon and an isoelastic utility function, which is time-additive with a rate of discount equal to zero. He has access to two investment opportunities. One investment opportunity is a stock security with the following rate of return specification (in the absence of dividends).

$$\frac{dP(t)}{P(t)} = \alpha Y(t)dt + \sigma\sqrt{Y(t)}dw(t), \quad P(0) > 0$$

where the state variable Y evolves as

$$dY(t) = \sigma_Y [Y(t)]^{\frac{3}{2}}\, dw_Y(t)$$

while w and w_Y are two (possibly correlated) Wiener processes. The other investment opportunity is a riskless instantaneous bank deposit with a rate of interest equal to $r \times Y$. The quantities α, σ, σ_Y, the correlation between the two Wiener processes, and the coefficient r are constants.

a. Write the optimal investment problem of this investor and the associated HJB equation and first-order conditions.

b. Solve for the value function (assuming that the objective function of the investor is a convergent integral).

10   Global Optimization and Portfolio Choice

This chapter studies the reformulation into global problems of dynamic-optimality, continuous-time problems, such as the ones in the previous chapters, which we solved so far by recursive, backward-induction methods. Along the way (section 10.3) we comment on the advantages and disadvantages of the reformulation in comparison with the recursive approach.

Recall from chapter 3, section 3.3.3 what we said regarding multi-period, discrete-time economies. In a *complete* market, we were able to write the investor's optimization problem, which originally involved portfolio choice, as a direct choice of consumption in each state of the world. It was simply a matter of changing variables. By eliminating security prices and portfolio choices we wrote it as:

$$\max_{c(0),\{c(s)\}} \sum_{s=1}^{K} \pi(s)u(c(0),c(s)) \tag{10.1}$$

subject to:

$$c(0) + \sum_{s=1}^{K} \phi(s)c(s) = e(0) + \sum_{s=1}^{K} \phi(s)e(s) \tag{10.2}$$

where $\phi(s)$ is the Arrow-Debreu or state price for state s. We extended the approach to the multiperiod problem, and got an Arrow-Debreu price $\phi(s,t)$ for each state at each point in time. As compared to the primitive formulation, the reformulated multiperiod problem was characterized by the fact that

1. the object of choice was overall, or lifetime, consumption $c(0), \{c(s,t)\}$, instead of being consumption *and* portfolio allocation $\{c(s,t)\}, \{\theta(s,t)\}$;

2. the budget constraint bound the lifetime endowment and consumption to each other, instead of relating endowment and consumption, at each point in time and in each state, to portfolio policy;

3. as a consequence of 2, there remained a single, lifetime constraint instead of $\sum_{t=1}^{T-1} K_t$ of them.

The single, lifetime constraint made the solution much easier, while solving directly for consumption did not prevent us from determining subsequently which portfolio strategies were able to generate or finance the chosen consumption path. As a result, the move from the recursive to the global portfolio choice was a win-win strategy (see end of section 3.3.3). In the equilibrium context of chapter 4, to which we return in chapter 12, we were also able to handle heterogeneous investors. Indeed we proved that in a complete market there existed a representative investor and that Arrow-Debreu prices were unique. They were those of the representative investor, but also those of each and every investor, since they were equated across investors.

The challenge now is to extend this same idea to the continuous-time, continuous-state setting. The task was performed by Cox and Huang (1989) and Karatzas, Lehoczky, Shreve (1987). Their great achievement was made possible by the technique of Pliska (1986) and was somewhat anticipated by the martingale approach in Harrison and Kreps (1979), Harrison and Pliska (1981), and Kreps (1981). After Cox and Huang, a whole stream of literature built on their method. While in their paper, as well as here, the key variables for the transformation are interpreted not only as changes of measure, but also as state prices and stochastic discount factors, in a large bulk of the literature that followed, the emphasis has been on the change of measure. We know that the Radon-Nikodym process and the state prices are related, so that the double interpretation comes as no surprise.

The chapter proceeds as follows: section 10.1 provides the setting and the reformulation of the problem from recursive to global. Section 10.2 illustrates the consumption and portfolio-optimization solution method. Section 10.3 illustrates the properties of the global approach. Section 10.4 addresses the non-negativity constraint on consumption and terminal wealth. Section 10.5 studies the portfolio called "growth-optimal" and derives a quasi-CAPM model. Section 10.6 contains the usual benchmark application.

10.1   Model Setup

Let time t be on an interval $\mathcal{T} = [0, T]$, with $T < \infty$, and a complete probability space (Ω, P). Let $w(\omega, t)$, or $w(t)$ for short, be a K-dimensional standard Wiener process in (Ω, P) and let the filtration $\mathbf{F}^w$ be that generated by w. One investor trades in the financial market, in which both a riskless security, numbered zero, and N long-lived risky securities are defined. The number of risky securities equates the number of Wiener processes, $N = K$. The market is then *complete*. As compared to chapter 9, where we examined the portfolio choice problem for one investor in a Markovian setting, we want our derivations, as far as possible, to be valid when securities are any Itô process, Markovian or not, driven by a finite or an infinite number of state variables. Only at a later stage, when we study the allocation to the risky securities instead of consumption versus savings, in section 10.2, do we specify a Markovian structure.

The setup is the complete-market one of chapter 8. The riskless security $B = S_0$ is riskless instantaneously only, the interest rate $r(t)$ (truly $r(\omega, t)$) being stochastic:

$$dB(t) = r(t)B(t)dt \tag{10.3}$$

The risky security prices $\mathcal{S}$ are generalized Black-Scholes, that is, Itô, adapted to $\mathbf{F}^w$, but not necessarily Markovian:

$$d\mathcal{S}(t) = [\mu(t) - \iota(t)]dt + \sigma(t)dw(t) \tag{10.4}$$

and wealth is as usual

$$W(t) = \alpha(t)B(t) + \Theta^{\mathsf{T}}(t)\mathcal{S}(t); \ t \in [0, T] \tag{10.5}$$

Investors do not receive *endowments* after time 0. As in chapter 8, admissible portfolio strategies must have the boundedness, or integrability, properties that guarantee that the wealth process is well-defined ($\mathcal{H}^2$). As usual, there is one *consumption* good, which is the numeraire. We want consumption and final wealth to be non-negative. We denote as $\mathfrak{M}$ the set of consumption and portfolio and terminal wealth processes that are admissible in the sense of definition 7.7. The optimization problem to be solved is then:

$$\max_{\{c(t)\}, \{\alpha(t), \Theta(t)\}, W(T) \in \mathfrak{M}} \mathbb{E}\left\{\int_0^T u(c(t), t)dt + \wp(W(T))\right\} \tag{10.6}$$

with initial wealth being given by $W_0 = e_0 > 0$ and final wealth-consumption plan being financed by (α, Θ), which means:[1]

$$\alpha(t)B(t) + \Theta(t)^{\mathsf{T}}\mathcal{S}(t) + \int_0^t c(s)ds \tag{10.7}$$

$$= W_0 + \int_0^t \left[\alpha(s)B(s)r(s) + \Theta^{\mathsf{T}}(s)\mu(s)\right]ds$$

$$+ \int_0^t \Theta^{\mathsf{T}}(s)\sigma(s)dw(s); \forall t \in [0, T]$$

$$W(T) = \alpha(T)B(T) + \Theta^{\mathsf{T}}(T)\mathcal{S}(T) \tag{10.8}$$

---

1 The flow budget constraint written below includes no endowment stream. In the current complete-market setting, there would be no difficulty at all in including one. Where c appears in the constraints, $c - e$ would appear instead and everything would proceed the same way. Non-negativity constraints on wealth would have to be readjusted. Of course, only c would still appear in the objective function.

If an endowment flow were present, one would need to be careful in the definition of wealth. Wealth can be defined either as financial wealth (value of securities on hand, denoted W or F) or as total wealth (value of securities on hand plus present value of future endowments, denoted $\mathfrak{W}$). The calculations could be carried out using one definition or using the other.

We assume that the initial wealth is positive (solvency constraint). If the first Inada condition is satisfied, that will be enough to guarantee solvency at all times. If an endowment stream were present, the solvency constraint would be that initial total wealth must be strictly positive.

where (10.7) represents an infinite number of budget constraints, and could be written also in the differential form used in the previous chapter (9.21). Note that the form is similar, even though the assumptions are different (Markov versus Itô and non-dividend paying assets versus dividend-paying ones). The lines below explain why this is the correct flow budget constraint on wealth, in spite of the presence of dividends, which were not in the previous chapter.

---- ♠ ----

In order to understand the budget constraint (10.7), which includes dividends, we must remember the definition of gains (8.3). Consider the differential form of the budget constraint, namely

$$
\begin{aligned}
dW + c \times dt &= dG + \Theta^\mathsf{T} \iota dt \tag{10.9} \\
&= \left[\alpha \times B \times r + \Theta^\mathsf{T}(\mu - \iota) \right] \times dt + \Theta^\mathsf{T} \iota \times dt + \Theta^\mathsf{T} \sigma dw(t) \\
&= \left[\alpha \times B \times r + \Theta^\mathsf{T} \mu \right] \times dt + \Theta^\mathsf{T} \sigma dw(t)
\end{aligned}
$$

Its first line says that the change in wealth plus the expenditure for consumption (on the LHS) must be equal to capital gains and dividends (on the RHS), at each point in time (we could, instead, have redefined gains G to include dividends). No leakage, that is, inflows or outflows other than consumption, is permitted. The second and third lines just show that capital gains plus dividends add up to the riskless rate on the riskless part of the portfolio, plus the return on the risky part. The corresponding integral form is the one reported in the main text.

10.1.1   Lifetime versus Dynamic Budget Constraint

To solve the optimization problem setup above, we implement a Lagrangean approach, with a unique budget constraint. We want to collapse the infinite number of "flow" or dynamic constraints (10.7) into a single, "lifetime" one. In discrete time, we made use for that purpose of completeness, together with the corresponding state prices. In continuous time a similar technique applies. The dynamic budget constraints (10.7) are transformed into a single, lifetime one, using the exponential martingale η and its stochastic discount factor ξ, which in complete markets is well defined and unique (see section 8.2):

$$
W_0 = \mathbb{E}\left[\int_0^T c(t)\xi(t)dt + W(T)\xi(T) \right] \tag{10.10}
$$

Although the "miraculous" properties of the exponential martingale have been highlighted above, this result is not at all trivial, and is the main contribution of Cox and Huang (1989). It is illustrated in the lines below in small characters. The converse transformation – from a global to a recursive or flow budget constraint – is feasible thanks to the martingale representation theorem. In order to see how this converse result obtains as well, read the next lines.

To go from an infinite number of budget constraints to a single one, consider the infinity of constraints in differential form:

$$dW + c \times dt = \left[\alpha \times B \times r + \Theta^{\mathsf{T}} \mu \right] \times dt + \Theta^{\mathsf{T}} \sigma \, dw \qquad (10.11)$$

Substitute the Wiener process w^* for w, where, as we know (from equation (8.14)),

$$dw = dw^* - \kappa \, dt$$

and $\kappa = \sigma^{-1}(\mu - rS)$. One gets

$$\begin{aligned} dW + c \times dt &= \left[\alpha \times B \times r + \Theta^{\mathsf{T}} \mu \right] \times dt + \Theta^{\mathsf{T}} \sigma \, dw^* - \Theta^{\mathsf{T}}(\mu - rS) dt \\ &= \left[\alpha \times B + \Theta^{\mathsf{T}} S \right] \times rdt + \Theta^{\mathsf{T}} \sigma \, dw^* \end{aligned}$$

Discount wealth using the riskless rate, and apply Itô's lemma to discounted wealth W/B:

$$d\left(\frac{W}{B} \right) = \frac{1}{B} dW + W \left(-\frac{1}{B^2} \right) dB$$

or

$$d\left(\frac{W}{B} \right) + \frac{c}{B} dt = \left[\alpha + \frac{1}{B} \Theta^{\mathsf{T}} S \right] \times rdt + \frac{1}{B} \Theta^{\mathsf{T}} \sigma \, dw^*(t) - \frac{\alpha \times B + \Theta^{\mathsf{T}} S}{B} rdt$$

$$d\left(\frac{W}{B} \right) + \frac{c}{B} dt = \frac{1}{B} \Theta^{\mathsf{T}} \sigma \, dw^*(t)$$

$$d\left(\alpha + \Theta^{\mathsf{T}} \frac{S}{B} \right) + \frac{c}{B} dt = \frac{1}{B} \Theta^{\mathsf{T}} \sigma \, dw^*(t)$$

Integrating over time,

$$\begin{aligned} &\frac{W(T)}{B(T)} + \int_0^T \frac{c(t)}{B(t)} dt \\ &= \alpha(T) + \Theta(T)^{\mathsf{T}} \frac{S(T)}{B(T)} + \int_0^T \frac{c(t)}{B(t)} dt \\ &= \alpha(0) + \Theta(0)^{\mathsf{T}} S(0) + \int_0^T \frac{\Theta^{\mathsf{T}}(t) \sigma(t)}{B(t)} dw^*(t) \end{aligned}$$

We know that, under the Novikov condition, the integral on the RHS, being a stochastic integral, is a martingale. This means

$$\mathbb{E}^* \left[\frac{W(T)}{B(T)} + \int_0^T \frac{c(t)}{B(t)} dt \right] = \alpha(0) + \Theta(0)^{\mathsf{T}} S(0) = W_0$$

The relation between expectations under the new and the old measure is

$$\mathbb{E}^* \left[\frac{W(T)}{B(T)} + \int_0^T \frac{c(t)}{B(t)} ds \right] = \mathbb{E} \left[\xi(T) W(T) + \int_0^T \xi(t) c(t) dt \right]$$

Combining the last two equalities gives (10.10), which is a single, lifetime budget constraint, as desired.

Now, let us start from the lifetime constraint and go back to a sequence of flow constraints. In differential form, (10.10) says that the expected change in wealth is consumption, if both are evaluated using the stochastic discount factor ξ:

$$\mathbb{E}_t d[\xi(t)W(t)] + \xi(t)c(t)dt = 0$$

Under the Novikov condition, this means that $\xi \times W$ is a martingale except for the drift $-\xi(t)c(t)$. By the martingale representation theorem, there exists a vector b in $\mathbb{R}^K$, with the appropriate technical properties, such that

$$d[\xi(t)W(t)] + \xi(t)c(t)dt = b(t)dw(t) \tag{10.12}$$

By Itô's lemma,

$$d[\xi(t)W(t)] + \xi(t)c(t)dt = W(t)d\xi(t) + \xi(t)dW(t) \tag{10.13}$$
$$+ d\xi(t)dW(t) + \xi(t)c(t)dt$$
$$= \left\{ \left[\alpha(t)B(t)r(t) + \Theta(t)^\mathsf{T}\mu(t) \right]dt \right.$$
$$+ \Theta(t)^\mathsf{T}\sigma(t)dw(t) - W(t)\kappa(t)^\mathsf{T}dw(t) - W(t)r(t)dt \Big\} \xi(t)$$
$$- \xi(t)\kappa(t)^\mathsf{T}\sigma(t)^\mathsf{T}\Theta(t)dt$$

Also, we know from the definition of κ that

$$0 = \alpha(t)B(t)r(t) + \Theta(t)^\mathsf{T}\mu(t) - W(t)r(t) - \kappa(t)^\mathsf{T}\sigma(t)^\mathsf{T}\Theta(t)$$

so that (10.13) becomes

$$d[\xi(t)W(t)] + \xi(t)c(t)dt = \xi(t)\left[\Theta(t)^\mathsf{T}\sigma(t) - W(t)\kappa(t)^\mathsf{T}\right]dw(t) \tag{10.14}$$

The last expression is consistent with (10.12) if and only if we take

$$b(t) = \xi(t)\left[\Theta(t)^\mathsf{T}\sigma(t) - W(t)\kappa(t)^\mathsf{T}\right]$$

On the LHS of

$$d[\xi(t)W(t)] + \xi(t)c(t)dt = \xi(t)\left[\Theta(t)^\mathsf{T}\sigma(t) - W(t)\kappa(t)^\mathsf{T}\right]dw(t)$$

substitute again for $W(t)d\xi(t), \xi(t)dW(t)$ and $d\xi(t)dW(t)$ as in (10.13), use again the fact that

$$\alpha(t)B(t)r(t) + \Theta(t)^\mathsf{T}\mu(t) = W(t)r(t) + \kappa(t)^\mathsf{T}\sigma(t)^\mathsf{T}\Theta(t)$$

and divide by ξ. You get (10.11), which is the flow budget constraint at time t.

10.2   Solution

With the single budget constraint at hand, the optimization problem becomes

$$\max_{[\{c(t)\}, W(T)] \in \mathfrak{M}} \mathbb{E}\left\{ \int_0^T u(c(t), t)dt + \wp(W(T)) \right\}$$

subject to (10.10), where $\mathfrak{M}$ is the set of consumption and wealth processes defined above. This is the global formulation, in contrast to the primitive, recursive one.[2]

Call λ_0 the Lagrange multiplier of the lifetime budget constraint and write down the Lagrangean

$$L(\{c(t)\}, W(T), \lambda_0) = \mathbb{E}\left\{\int_0^T u(c(t), t)dt + \wp(W(T))\right\}$$
$$+\lambda_0\left\{W_0 - \mathbb{E}\left[\int_0^T c(t)\xi(t)dt + W(T)\xi(T)\right]\right\}$$

Here, as in the discrete-time counterpart of the problem we examined in chapter 3, a solution to the original problem is a saddle point of the Lagrangean. Examine its first-order conditions. Ignoring for the moment any non-negativity constraints on consumption, the first-order conditions of optimality for consumption and terminal wealth are extremely simple:

$$\frac{\partial}{\partial c}u(c(t), t) = \lambda_0\xi(t) \tag{10.15}$$

$$\frac{\partial}{\partial W}\wp(W(T)) = \lambda_0\xi(T) \tag{10.16}$$

The previous conditions say that the process ξ is proportional to the marginal utility of consumption for $t < T$, and to the marginal utility of final wealth at T. The system (10.10, 10.15, 10.16) fully determines the time path of consumption and final wealth. We can solve for consumption and wealth as soon as we know the stochastic discount factor ξ and the Lagrange multiplier.

The calculation can be *separated into two steps*, as it could be in chapter 3. We can determine optimal consumption (step one) before addressing the portfolio composition issue (step two). The separation into two steps did not arise in dynamic programming problems, where first-order conditions for portfolio and consumption had to be substituted jointly into the PDE for the unknown derived utility. But here the assumption of market completeness produces the separation.

How do we solve for optimal consumption and final wealth? As in the previous chapter, denote as[3]

$$c(t) = \mathfrak{h}(\lambda_0\xi(t), t)$$

the solution for $c(t)$ of the first-order condition (10.15). Correspondingly, let $\mathfrak{G}$ be the inverse function of the derivative of the final utility, $\mathfrak{G} = (\partial\wp/\partial W)^{-1}$. The solution of the first-order condition (10.16) for $W(T)$ is:

$$W(T) = \mathfrak{G}(\lambda_0\xi(T))$$

---

2 Cox and Huang show that any solution of the static problem in $\mathfrak{M}$ is a solution of the original, dynamic one. Conversely, if all the solutions to the static problem stay in $\mathfrak{M}$, and if the dynamic problem has a solution, then it is also a solution of the static problem.

3 The inverse function exists. See proposition A.1.

The consumption and final wealth decisions $\mathfrak{h}$ and $\mathfrak{G}$ can be substituted into the lifetime budget constraint; the resulting equation can then be solved for λ_0. This means that, as intuition would suggest, the initial value of marginal utility depends on the initial endowment $W(0) = W_0$. To simplify the notation in future derivations, we define:[4]

$$\lambda(t) \triangleq \lambda_0 \xi(t)$$

and write:

$$c(t) = \mathfrak{h}(\lambda(t), t); \ W(T) = \mathfrak{G}(\lambda(T))$$

The biggest task may yet be to obtain the portfolio strategy (α, Θ) that finances the above consumption/wealth program. Let us now consider the Markov case. We already know that *solving for optimal portfolios is merely a payoff replication problem of the Black-Scholes variety*, of the kind studied in chapter 6. It leads to a *linear PDE*, exactly as in chapter 6 and in chapter 9. Exactly as in the last case, what needs to be done is to view wealth at time t as a derivative security written on the state variables that determine future opportunity sets (namely, the drift and diffusions of the securities), and the variable λ. In this way we obtain a linear PDE for maximized wealth and derive from it the optimal portfolio strategy.

10.2.1 Optimal Wealth

We impose now only a Markovian setting, but we also assume that Y collects the state variables relevant for information updating,[5] as we did in chapter 9.[6] Applying the Girsanov theorem, or substituting for dw^* (from equation (8.14)), the state variables of chapter 9 (equation (9.20)) satisfy the following SDE under the risk-neutral EMM:

$$Y(t) = Y(0) \tag{10.17}$$

$$+ \int_0^t [\mu_Y(Y(s), s) - \sigma_Y(Y(s), s)\kappa(Y(s), s)] \, ds$$

$$+ \int_0^t \sigma_Y(Y(s), s) dw^*(s)$$

Consider total, optimized wealth $W(t)$ at time t as the present value of future consumption. Under the risk-neutral measure it means that financial wealth $W(t)$ is equal to

$$F(\lambda(t), Y(t), t) \triangleq B(t)\mathbb{E}_t^*\left[\int_t^T B(s)^{-1}\mathfrak{h}(\lambda(s), s)ds + B(T)^{-1}\mathfrak{G}(\lambda(T))\right] \tag{10.18}$$

Using the same proof that permitted us in chapter 6 to show that the solution of the Black-Scholes PDE was given by the Feynman-Kac formula, one can obtain a PDE for

---

4 The SDE for λ is identical to the SDE for ξ (in section 8.2). Only the initial condition is different.

5 These include current securities prices, if needed.

6 We impose Lipschitz and growth conditions insuring existence and uniqueness of the solution of the SDEs for state variables.

optimized wealth F. This is the point at which the Markovian setting is used. Suppressing the dependence of F on its arguments, this PDE turns out to be as in chapter 8:

$$\mathfrak{h}(\lambda(t),t) - r(Y(t),t)F + \mathcal{D}^*(F) + F_t = 0 \tag{10.19}$$

but $\mathcal{D}^*$, the Dynkin of F under P^*, now includes terms in the state variables:

$$\mathcal{D}^*(F) = \frac{1}{2}F_{\lambda\lambda}(\lambda)^2\kappa^{\mathsf{T}}\kappa + \frac{1}{2}\text{trace}\left(F_{YY}\sigma_Y^{\mathsf{T}}\sigma_Y\right)$$
$$-F_{Y\lambda}^{\mathsf{T}}\sigma_Y\lambda\kappa + F_Y^{\mathsf{T}}[\mu_Y - \sigma_Y\lambda] - F_\lambda\lambda(r - \kappa^{\mathsf{T}}\kappa)$$

The PDE is subject to the usual terminal condition:

$$F(\lambda(T), Y(T), T) = \mathfrak{B}(\lambda(T))$$

This PDE has one main feature: it is *linear*, unlike the HJB PDE of dynamic programming. Equation (10.19) is also identical to equation (9.34) of chapter 9, which was obtained from dynamic programming by a Cox-Huang change of variables.

It is evident from that fact that the global approach – when restricted to the Markov setting and applied to cases in which non-negativity of consumption or wealth is not an issue – provides the same solutions as the recursive or dynamic-programming one, and that it does so in a much simpler way. Not only are consumption and final wealth straightforward to obtain, but also portfolio policies are easier to get. Under the global approach one has to solve a linear, instead of a nonlinear, PDE.

Some purely practical difficulties remain. On the first step, consumption and final wealth have to be obtained by inversion of marginal utility functions. And an expected value – or the solution of a linear PDE – has to be computed on the second one. The computational difficulties inherent in these inversions and solutions will be addressed in chapter 13.

10.2.2   Portfolio Mix

Once we have computed the function F that solves the linear PDE above, obtaining portfolios is quite straightforward, as we anticipated in chapter 9. Apply Itô's formula to F, while using the dynamics, especially the random part, of Y and λ, as given by equations (10.17) and (8.16):

$$F(\lambda(t), Y(t), t) - F(\lambda(0), Y(0), 0)$$
$$= \int_0^t \left[\mathcal{D}^*(F) + F_t(s)\right]ds + \int_0^t \left[F_Y^{\mathsf{T}}(s)\sigma_Y(Y(s),s) - F_\lambda(s)\lambda(s)\kappa(Y(s),s)^{\mathsf{T}}\right]dw^*(s)$$

Now compare the random part of the previous expression with (10.7) re-written under the risk-neutral EMM. The martingale representation theorem indicates that the coefficients of the Wiener process w^* must, at all points in time, be identical between the two expressions:

$$\Theta(t)^{\mathsf{T}}\sigma(Y(t),t) = F_Y(t)^{\mathsf{T}}\sigma_Y(Y(t),t) - F_\lambda(t)\lambda(t)\kappa(Y(t),t)^{\mathsf{T}}$$

For each t, this is a system of K algebraic equations in K unknowns $\Theta(t)$. Suppressing the dependence on the state variables Y and on λ, and substituting for the market price of risk κ in terms of the security parameters, their solution, in row and column form respectively, is

$$\Theta(t)^\mathsf{T} = F_Y(t)^\mathsf{T}\sigma_Y(t)\sigma^{-1}(t) - F_\lambda(t)\lambda(t)\kappa(t)^\mathsf{T}\sigma^{-1}(t) \tag{10.20}$$
$$= F_Y(t)^\mathsf{T}\sigma_Y(t)\sigma^{-1}(t)$$
$$- F_\lambda(t)\lambda(t)[\mu(t) - r(t) \times \mathcal{S}(t)]^\mathsf{T}\sigma^{-1}(t)^\mathsf{T}\sigma^{-1}(t)$$
$$\Theta(t) = \sigma^{-1}(t)^\mathsf{T}\sigma_Y(t)^\mathsf{T}F_Y(t)$$
$$- F_\lambda(t)\lambda(t) \times \sigma^{-1}(t)^\mathsf{T}\sigma^{-1}(t)[\mu(t) - r(t) \times \mathcal{S}(t)] \tag{10.21}$$

The solution can be interpreted in the following way. Portfolio allocations in the risky securities depend on the sensitivities $F_Y(t)$ and $F_\lambda(t)$ of maximized wealth with respect to the state variables Y and λ. The term in $F_\lambda(t)$ is the myopic, Markowitz-style part of the portfolio. The intertemporal-hedging part is the term in $F_Y(t)$. For each additional unit of wealth that would result from a change in the state variables Y, there is today an additional allocation in the risky securities proportional to their risk premium per unit of risk, $\sigma^{-1}(t)^\mathsf{T}\sigma_Y(t)^\mathsf{T}$. Of course, the allocation in the riskless security is such that the whole wealth is invested in securities: $\alpha(t)B(t) = F(t) - \Theta(t)^\mathsf{T}\mathcal{S}(t)$. We have, therefore, obtained explicitly α and Θ in terms of the solution F to the linear PDE.

The reader can now solve exercises 10.1 and 10.3.

10.3   Properties of the Global Approach

We want to emphasize a number of properties of the global problem. Let us start from the advantages, concentrate also on practical implementation, and list the disadvantages.

In general, the advantages of the global approach are:

a. The procedure is a *two-step* one, allowing us to solve first for optimal consumption and financial wealth, and then for portfolio policies as a pure replication problem.

b. In the Markov, or even diffusive, case, sufficient or necessary conditions for the existence of a solution are *easier* to find than in dynamic programming. In some applications, it is impossible to do that with dynamic programming, while it is possible with the global approach.

c. In the Markov case, explicit solutions are also *easier* to obtain.

d. It makes it possible to study optimization even outside the Markov case.

Property a) is clear from the above discussion. Regarding *Property b)*, under the assumption that $\sigma(t)$ is of full rank (with probability one) for every t (theorem 8.3 in chapter 8), *sufficient conditions for the existence of a solution can be found.* Cox and Huang (1989) mention a number of conditions of this type. These conditions are about security prices on the one hand and the utility function on the other. Security prices that satisfy a regularity, a uniform growth and local Lipschitz conditions, together with a utility function strictly concave and with risk aversion bounded from below in the limit are sufficient for a solution to exist. These conditions replace the compactness of controls, which is the main condition for guaranteeing existence of a solution to a dynamic programming problem, when direct verification does not apply. They are much *easier* to verify (see Krylov (1980)). We show below that the global approach can accommodate non-negativity constraints, and, therefore, makes it possible to show existence of solutions to Markov portfolio optimization even when dynamic programming does not.

Regarding *Property c)*: it is certainly much *easier* to solve a single-constraint problem than a problem with an infinite number of constraints. As long as we are interested in solving for *consumption*, there is no doubt that the global approach is easier to use. As seen in chapter 9, and now again, the Markov case makes it easier to solve for *portfolio strategies*, since it leads to a linear instead of a nonlinear PDE.

Regarding *Property d)*: the lifetime constraint can be built and the global problem can be studied with no Markovian requirement, while the problem can be dealt with by means of dynamic programming only under the assumption that security prices are Markovian. Without Markovianity, there is no other way to tackle the optimization problem than using the global approach.

Summarizing, the linearity of the PDE to be solved in the Markov case and the possibility of handling non-Markovian settings are the main practical advantages of the global approach. They explain that, in the remainder of this part of this book, when we examine equilibrium, we are able to characterize it much better with the global approach. With dynamic programming, we are able to give only restrictions that must hold in equilibrium, not to fully characterize the equilibrium itself.

The apparent drawback of the global approach is the assumption of a *complete* market. We examine incomplete markets and reconsider these issues in Part V (chapters 14 and 15) of the book.

10.4 Non-negativity Constraints on Consumption and Wealth

Suppose that, absent the Inada assumptions, the above solution leads to some negative consumption or negative final wealth at some time and/or in some states of nature. We may force the investor to buy insurance so that negative consumption or final wealth will not occur. Consider the following put-option payoffs:

$$[-c(t)]^+$$
$$[-W(T)]^+$$

and imagine that these options are written on the optimal consumption/wealth program so far calculated, $(c(t), W(T))$.

Their total price at time 0 is:

$$P(0) = \mathbb{E}\left[\int_0^T [-c(t)]^+ \xi(t)dt + [-W(T)]^+ \xi(T)\right]$$

$$= \mathbb{E}^*\left[\int_0^T \frac{[-c(t)]^+}{B(t)}dt + \frac{[-W(T)]^+}{B(T)}\right]$$

Imagine that, at time 0, the investor had a wealth level equal to $W_0 + P(0)$ instead of W_0. Then the unconstrained solution we have obtained would have been the constrained optimal program of this richer investor under the non-negativity constraints. By iteration, we can adjust the imagined initial level of wealth of the investor so that his imagined initial level (assumed strictly positive) plus $P(0)$ will equal his actual initial wealth.

This is a portfolio-insurance program (at zero strike) in which some amount of investment in the underlying securities must be sold off in order to pay for the cost of the implied puts. This is also the way in which the global program of section 10.2 with positive initial wealth can be adjusted, absent the Inada condition, so as to give positive consumption and wealth all the time.

10.5   The Growth-Optimal Portfolio

The stochastic discount factor ξ has served to perform in one fell swoop the discounting of future cash flows and the probability adjustment that accounts for the risk aversion of the marketplace. Here we would like to interpret it as the value of a portfolio and show the consequences for the choice of portfolio funds. A quasi-CAPM will result.

Recall that, as a consequence of equation (10.18):

$$W(t) = \mathbb{E}_t\left[\int_t^T c(s)\frac{\xi(s)}{\xi(t)}ds + W(T)\xi(T)\right] \qquad (10.22)$$

it is also true that:

$$\frac{W(t)}{\lambda^{-1}(t)} = \mathbb{E}_t\left[\int_t^T \frac{c(s)}{\lambda^{-1}(s)}ds + \frac{W(T)}{\lambda^{-1}(T)}\right]$$

Dividing by $\lambda^{-1}(t)$ can, therefore, be viewed as a change of reference security, provided we can interpret λ^{-1} as the value of a security or a portfolio. Indeed, we can. Merton (1990, chapter 6) shows that $\lambda^{-1}(t)$ is proportional to the value of the portfolio chosen by an investor endowed with a logarithmic utility function of terminal wealth, $\wp(W) = \ln W$, and $u(c) = 0.$[7] This investor's objective is:

$$\max_{c(s)} \mathbb{E}_t[\ln W(T)]$$

---

7 One can also say that this person maximizes the *expected average rate of growth* of his wealth:
$$\frac{\mathbb{E}_t[\ln W(T) - \ln W(t)]}{T - t}$$

The first-order condition provides a non-negative solution for optimal wealth.[8] It is simply:

$$W(T) = \frac{1}{\lambda(T)}$$

Now, compute this investor's wealth at time $t < T$. Substituting zero consumption on the way and terminal wealth equal to $\lambda^{-1}(T)$ in (10.22) we get *his* interim wealth as:

$$W(t) = F(t) = \lambda^{-1}(t)\mathbb{E}_t\left[\frac{\lambda(T)}{\lambda(T)}\right] = \lambda^{-1}(t)$$

which shows that λ^{-1} is the value of a portfolio of securities, namely the portfolio that would be optimally chosen by a log investor.

Examine also the portfolio allocation of the log investor, Θ^L. Since, *for this investor*, $F_Y = 0$, $F_\lambda = -1/\lambda^2$, equation (10.21) specializes to

$$\Theta^L(t) = \lambda^{-1}(t)\left[\sigma(t)\sigma(t)^\mathsf{T}\right]^{-1}\left[\mu(t) - r(t) \times \mathcal{S}(t)\right]$$

This is the one-period, mean-variance optimal portfolio.[9]

Substitute into equation (10.21) in order to express the optimal allocation of *any other investor* in terms of $\Theta^L(t)$. One gets:

$$\Theta(t) = \left[\sigma(t)^\mathsf{T}\right]^{-1}\sigma_Y(t)^\mathsf{T}F_Y(t) - F_\lambda(t)\lambda^2(t)\Theta^L(t) \tag{10.23}$$

which says that, in a complete market, any investor's optimal portfolio is a linear combination of the Y-hedging portfolio (the first term in (10.23)) and the logarithmic portfolio.

A quasi-CAPM restriction follows. In Merton's CAPM of the next chapter each investor hedges against Y and invests in the market.

10.6 Benchmark Example (continued)

We now enrich our understanding of the benchmark example, with CRRA utility function and strict Black-Scholes risky securities, by showing

a. the expression for the lifetime budget constraint with strict Black-Scholes securities;

b. that the corresponding intertemporal optimization problem has solutions for both HARA and CRRA functions. In the latter case, non-negativity of wealth holds;

c. that the former solutions are explicit.

---

8 For such a person we do not need to worry about non-negativity of consumption, since he consumes at T only and $W_0 > 0$: the Inada condition is satisfied.

9 Observe that the porfolio choice, once again, is myopic, with unit relative risk aversion.

The Black-Scholes example is, therefore, of paramount importance in showing the ability of the global method to generalize – in this case to HARA utilities or CRRA and non-negativity constraints – the results of the dynamic-programming approach presented in chapter 9.

We know from previous chapters that, with strict Black-Scholes securities, the ratio of the exponential martingale η to the value of the bank account B becomes

$$\xi(t) = \exp\left\{-rt - (\mu - r\mathbf{1})^\mathsf{T}\left(\sigma^{-1}\right)^\mathsf{T} w(t) - \frac{1}{2}\left\|\sigma^{-1}(\mu - r\mathbf{1})\right\|^2 t\right\}$$

The lifetime budget constraint simplifies into:

$$W_0 = \int_0^T \exp\{-rt - \frac{1}{2}\left\|\sigma^{-1}(\mu - r\mathbf{1})\right\|^2 t\} \times \mathbb{E}_0\left[c(t)\exp\left\{-(\mu - r\mathbf{1})^\mathsf{T}\left(\sigma^{-1}\right)^\mathsf{T} w(t)\right\}\right] dt$$

$$+ \exp\{-rT - \frac{1}{2}\left\|\sigma^{-1}(\mu - r\mathbf{1})\right\|^2 T\} \times \mathbb{E}_0\left[W(T)\exp\left\{-(\mu - r\mathbf{1})^\mathsf{T}\left(\sigma^{-1}\right)^\mathsf{T} w(T)\right\}\right]$$

with obvious simplifications in the univariate case.

Under mild conditions, a solution exists to the global optimization problem in the presence of an HARA utility function and securities that are diffusions. If the utility function is strictly increasing, strictly concave and bounded from below, then it suffices that ξ belongs to $\mathcal{H}^2$.

Consider explicit solutions. Cox and Huang reminded us that negative wealth and negative consumption may be encountered when solving optimization problems à la Merton, in the presence of HARA utility functions and Black-Scholes prices. They show that, as soon as non-negativity constraints are taken into consideration, as in their approach, the solution for both wealth and the derived utility function takes a completely different form. Without the constraints, Merton showed that – at least for a CRRA investor – consumption is linear in wealth (Merton (1969), as recalled in section 9.2.2). With the constraints, that is true only as wealth approaches infinity. A crucial role in making consumption and wealth explicit is obviously played by ξ and the exponential martingale η. Consider the combined case of constant riskless interest rate and a single Black-Scholes risky security. Since $d\eta/\eta = -\kappa dw$, the higher the volatility of the security, the lower the percentage diffusion of the exponential martingale.

The reader can solve exercise 10.4 for the single-risky security case. A richer example with a "reference" consumption level is discussed as exercise 10.5.

10.7   Conclusion

The global, Lagrangean approach to optimization finds its most pleasing application when the financial market is complete. In that case, it allows us to solve for the investor's optimal consumption path, abstracting completely from his choice of investment portfolio. Once the optimal consumption path is chosen, the optimal portfolio is a pure replication exercise, identical to the one we performed in Part II to replicate target payoffs and to value redundant securities.

Exercises

10.1. Solve explicitly by the method of this chapter – namely under the lifetime budget constraint (10.10) – the following portfolio optimization problem:

$$\max_{\{c(t)\},\{\alpha(t),\Theta(t)\}} \mathbb{E}\left\{\int_0^T e^{-\beta s} \ln c(s)ds + \wp(W(T))\right\}$$

Wealth evolves as in (10.7), namely there are multiple securities. Assume that their percentage expected returns, as well as the riskless rate, are constant.

10.2. Solve explicitly the following portfolio optimization problem using the martingale representation method:

$$\max_{\alpha(t),\Theta(t)} \mathbb{E}\left[\frac{(W(T))^\gamma}{\gamma}\right]$$

given W_0, with $\gamma < 1$ and $\gamma \neq 0$. The stock price follows an Itô process:

$$\frac{dS(t)}{S(t)} = \mu(t)dt + \sigma dw(t)$$

where σ is a positive constant while the risk-free rate of interest $r(t)$ is time varying. Let the Sharpe ratio be $X(t) = [\mu(t) - r(t)]/\sigma$ and assume that $X(t)$ satisfies

$$dX(t) = -\varrho\left(\overline{X} - X\right)dt - \sigma_X dw(t)$$

where $\overline{X}, \sigma_X$ and ϱ are constants. The Wiener process in this last equation is the same as in the stock price equation so that the Sharpe ratio and the return are perfectly negatively correlated with each other. Hint: there exists a fully explicit formula for the wealth function and the portfolio weights. You may not succeed in reaching it but you should at least write down all the equations that would have to be solved to obtain them.

10.3. Show that, in the special case of Markov process and complete markets, the optimal portfolio obtained in equation (10.21) is identical to the portfolio we obtained by dynamic programming in chapter 9.

10.4. Suppose that there is only one stock and one risk-free security. The stock price follows a Geometric Brownian motion and the risk-free rate of interest is constant. Solve the following utility maximization problems using the martingale representation approach:

a.

$$\max_{\{\alpha(t),\Theta(t)\}} \mathbb{E}\left[\frac{W^\gamma(T)}{\gamma}\right]$$

where $W(T)$ is financed by $\{\Theta(t)\}$, given W_0, with $\gamma < 1$, and $\gamma \neq 0$.

b.

$$\max_{\{c(t)\},\{\alpha(t),\Theta(t)\}} \mathbb{E}\left(\int_0^T e^{-\rho t}\frac{(c(t))^\gamma}{\gamma}dt\right)$$

where $\{c(t)\}$ is financed by $\{\Theta(t)\}$, given W_0, with $\gamma < 1$, and $\gamma \neq 0$.

c.

$$\max_{\{c(t)\},\{\alpha(t),\Theta(t)\}} \mathbb{E}\left(\int_0^T e^{-\rho t}\frac{(c(t))^\gamma}{\gamma}dt + \frac{(W(T))^\gamma}{\gamma}\right)$$

where $\{c(t)\}$ and $W(T)$ are financed by $\{\Theta(t)\}$, given W_0, with $\gamma < 1$, and $\gamma \neq 0$.

Compare with the solutions obtained via dynamic programming (chapter 9).

10.5. The Endowment Management Committee (EMC) is in charge of managing the endowment of the school. They have access to a riskless security whose price of a share is denoted B and a number of risky securities whose price per share is represented by the vector S. These follow stochastic processes described by the following set of SDEs:

$$B(t) = B(0)e^{\int_0^t r ds}, \quad B(0) = 1,$$

$$S(t) + \int_0^t \iota(s)ds = S(0) + \int_0^t \mu S(s)ds$$

$$+ \int_0^t \sigma S(s)dw(s),$$

$$S(0) = 1$$

where μ (an vector in $\mathbb{R}^N$), σ (a $N \times N$ matrix) and r (a scalar) are constant over time and w is a standard Wiener process in $\mathbb{R}^N$. The initial value of EMC's endowment, in the form of financial securities in the portfolio, is denoted W_0. The task of the committee is simultaneously to determine how much money c should be spent out of the endowment (the *spending rule*) and to determine the optimal mix of securities (α, Θ) to be held in the portfolio (the *investment rule*; α being the number of shares of the riskless security and Θ the vector of the number of shares of the risky securities). EMC has spending needs $\underline{c}$ and also outside income (for example, tuition fees) and donations e. By "spending needs" is meant the minimum amount of spending $\underline{c}$ that can possibly be tolerated, or the "survival" amount of spending. This requirement is embedded in the objective function of the school, which is:

$$\max_{\{c(t)\},\{\alpha(t),\Theta(t)\}} \mathbb{E}\left\{\int_0^T \frac{(c(t) - \underline{c})^\gamma}{\gamma}dt\right\}$$

Assume that $\underline{c}$ is constant and that EMC receives no outside income ($e = 0$).

a. Use the global method to determine explicitly the optimal spending and investment rules. Formulate your final answer in the form of a function indicating how much should be spent at any given time as a function of the current value of the endowment and how much should be invested in each security also as a function of the current value of the endowment.

b. How would your answer be affected if the minimum spending needs $\underline{c}$ were growing at a constant rate $g < r$ over time? Or if the minimum spending needs followed a Geometric Brownian motion with constant drift and diffusion matrix, driven by the same Wiener process w?

c. How would your answer be changed (compared to the previous answers) if EMC received an outside income e following a Geometric Brownian motion with constant drift and diffusion matrix, driven by the same Wiener process w?

IV EQUILIBRIUM IN CONTINUOUS TIME

11 Equilibrium Restrictions and the CAPM

As we enter Part IV of the book, we leave an analytical framework, in which the prices of basic securities and their processes were given, to build one in which those prices are endogenized.

But the present chapter is really a transition chapter. It establishes equilibrium price restrictions instead of a full description of the equilibrium dynamics of securities' prices. Full descriptions will be achieved in chapters 12 and 15, but also in section 11.4 below for a specific setting.

In the first part of the chapter, devoted to the Capital Asset Pricing Model (CAPM), the demand for securities equals the supply and we solve for the expected returns on securities, given the risk of their rates of return. This is a form of *partial equilibrium*. In a full description, the price is a function of state variables and, through it, both the risk and the expected value of return would be obtained. In the second part, devoted to the Cox-Ingersoll-Ross (1985) economy, demand equals supply, prices are endogenous, as in general equilibrium, but investors are assumed to be identical to each other.[1] The result is not really a general equilibrium with heterogeneous investors in a dynamic setting, that is, a Radner equilibrium. However, the progressive introduction of restrictions helps us understand the economic and formal properties of equilibrium, which will be treated in chapter 12.

The chapter unfolds as follows. In section 11.1 we show that, once we aggregate investor demands, we obtain an *Intertemporal Capital Asset Pricing Model (ICAPM)*. In section 11.2 we comment on the role of covariance or co-risk. In section 11.3 we switch to the consumption-version of the equilibria restrictions, the *Consumption-Based Capital Asset Pricing Model (CCAPM)*, which we already know in its one-period version. In section 11.4 we examine the Cox-Ingersoll-Ross (CIR) equilibrium. In section 11.5 we conclude with a special formulation of the CIR equilibrium that fits the benchmark example.

---

1 In the next chapter, we give the conditions for a set of heterogeneous investors to price assets the way a representative investor does.

11.1 Intertemporal CAPM and Betas

Let there be H state variables Y, driven by K Wiener processes w. Let us work on the filtration generated by those Wiener processes. Let S_0 be the riskless security, with drift $r(Y,t)$, and let $\mathcal{S}(t)$ be an N-dimensional adapted process that collects the prices of risky securities:

$$dS(t) = \operatorname{diag}(\mathcal{S}(t)) \times \mu(Y(t),t)dt + \operatorname{diag}(\mathcal{S}(t)) \times \sigma(Y(t),t) \times dw(t)$$

In equilibrium, the expected securities' returns $\mu \in \mathbb{R}^N$, in relation with the level of the interest rate $r \in \mathbb{R}$, will be determined by the equality of the demand for securities with the supply. Apart from that, the dynamics of risky security prices are still taken to be *exogenous* in that only an *algebraic* equation for the numerical value μ of the drift – not the price $\mathcal{S}$ – is solved for.

There are M investors, indexed by $m = 1, 2, .., M$. Each one acts as a price taker and solves the continuous-time optimization problem with stochastic opportunity set discussed in chapter 9. The appendix to the current chapter shows how to aggregate across investors the first-order conditions in equation (9.26), to yield a restriction on security returns that must hold in equilibrium, when demand and supply of each security are equal. The restriction links the excess return on the risky securities, $\mu - r\mathbf{1}$, to the other model parameters. It is the intertemporal form of the CAPM, or ICAPM, introduced by Merton (1973). To spell it out, call x^{M} the market-portfolio composition. The ICAPM provides the following expression for excess returns on marketed securities, $\mu - r\mathbf{1}$:

$$\underbrace{\mu(Y,t) - r(Y,t) \times \mathbf{1}}_{N \times 1} = \underbrace{\sigma(Y,t)\sigma(Y,t)^{\mathsf{T}}x^{\mathrm{M}}}_{N \times 1}\Lambda_{\mathbb{M}}(t) + \underbrace{\sigma(Y,t)\sigma_Y(Y,t)^{\mathsf{T}}}_{N \times H}\underbrace{\Lambda_Y(t)}_{H \times 1} \qquad (11.1)$$

where $\Lambda_{\mathbb{M}}(t)$ (a scalar) and $\Lambda_Y(t)$ (a vector) are given in this chapter's appendix and are commented upon below. According to expression (11.1), excess returns are the sum of two premia or sets of premia. The first is proportional to the covariance $\sigma\sigma^{\mathsf{T}}x^{\mathrm{M}}$ of each security with the market portfolio. The coefficient of proportionality $\Lambda_{\mathbb{M}}(t) \in \mathbb{R}$ is the reciprocal of the aggregate risk tolerance, namely the weighted-average of relative risk tolerances, the weights being investor wealths:[2]

$$\frac{1}{\Lambda_{\mathbb{M}}}(t) \triangleq \bar{T} = \frac{-\sum_{m=1}^{M} W^m \frac{\frac{\partial J^m}{\partial W}}{\frac{\partial^2 J^m}{\partial W^2}W^m}}{\sum_{m=1}^{M} W^m}$$

2 Recall that risk tolerances are the reciprocal of risk aversion coefficients, be they absolute or relative. Here, risk aversion is calculated on wealth and the indirect utility function $J(W)$.

So, the first component of excess-returns explains them across the several securities the way the traditional CAPM does. Assets command an excess return proportional to market risk according to Λ_M.

The second set of premia is proportional to the covariance matrix $\sigma\sigma_Y^\mathsf{T}$ of the securities with the state variables. The coefficients $\Lambda_Y(t) \in \mathbb{R}^H$ can be interpreted as weighted-averages of the changes in marginal utility, due to changes in the state variables. The weights are absolute risk tolerances. The second premia, similar to the hedging factor that entered portfolios in chapter 9, are positive for state variables, high realizations of which represent bad news.

In order to facilitate our understanding of the ICAPM, we write (11.1) for the case in which there is one risky security, a single state variable against which to hedge, and a single Wiener process:

$$\mu(Y,t) - r(Y,t) = \Lambda_M \sigma^2(Y,t)x^M + \Lambda_Y \sigma(Y,t)\sigma_Y(Y,t)$$

It is even more evident from this formulation that, motivated as they are by their desire to *hedge reinvestment risk*, investors prefer stocks that will do well when subsequent returns, as well as wealth and consumption, driven by the state variable, will be low. They demand more of these securities, increase prices, and depress returns. So, if Λ_Y is positive and the covariance is negative, then the security is a natural intertemporal hedge, which investors demand while accepting a lower return for it. If Λ_Y and the covariance $\sigma\sigma_Y$ are positive, then the security requires a boost of extra return in order to be attractive to investors.

11.2   Co-risk and Linearity

The CAPM is centered upon the notion of *covariance* and the *linearity* of excess returns with respect to the covariance or co-risk terms. We understood since chapter 3, in which we examined single-period economies, that what matters for security pricing was not the risk of a security *per se*, but its co-risk against the portfolio, or wealth. This principle holds for one and all investors and, therefore, in equilibrium. The result was confirmed in chapter 4, in the discrete-time, multiperiod model à la Lucas. Again it is covariances that matter now, many of them being computed against the state variables Y. As Cochrane (2001, chapter 9) notes, "*modern security pricing starts when we realize that investors care about portfolio returns, not about the behavior of specific securities.*" The variance of the portfolio shows up because of risk aversion. The ICAPM model formalizes, in a very general setting, the fact that investors do care about portfolios. Given that we are in an Itô setting, investors care about the instantaneous mean and variance of the portfolio. The prices Λ_M, Λ_Y derive from risk aversion. As such, they transform into utils the change in portfolio variance contributed by each security and encapsulate non-linearities due to risk aversion.

11.3   Consumption-Based CAPM

The multiple-premia of the intertemporal CAPM can be coalesced into a single premium, by means of the marginality condition. The expected excess return on any security turns out to be proportional to its beta or covariance against aggregate consumption. This idea, which goes back to Breeden (1979), is known as the consumption-based CAPM or CCAPM.

Consider, as we did in chapter 9, only one investor and call ξ the ratio between his marginal utilities at times t and 0, which, using the marginality condition, is also the normalized ratio of the marginal indirect utilities of wealth:

$$\xi(t) \triangleq \frac{\frac{\partial u}{\partial c}(c(t),t)}{\frac{\partial u}{\partial c}(c(0),0)} = \frac{\frac{\partial J}{\partial W}(W(t),Y(t),t)}{\frac{\partial J}{\partial W}(W_0,Y(0),0)} \tag{11.2}$$

Using the second expression for ξ, we study its drift and the drift of security prices once they are discounted using this marginal rate of substitution, which converts prices into today's utils. We show that the CCAPM holds and that the drifts of discounted prices are equal to zero; that is, they are a (local) martingale, under the effective measure. The last two properties are equivalent.

In order to compute those drifts, differentiate the HJB equation (9.24) with respect to W. To simplify notation, suppress the dependence of J on W, Y, t:

$$0 = \frac{\mathbb{E}\left(d\frac{\partial J}{\partial W}\right)}{dt} + \frac{\partial J}{\partial W}\left\{r(Y,t) + [\mu(Y,t) - r(Y,t) \times \mathbf{1}]^{\mathsf{T}} x\right\} \tag{11.3}$$

$$+ \frac{\partial^2 J}{\partial W^2} W x^{\mathsf{T}} \sigma(Y,t)\sigma(Y,t)^{\mathsf{T}} x + \frac{\partial^2 J}{\partial Y \partial W}\sigma_Y(Y,t)\sigma(Y,t)^{\mathsf{T}} x$$

and apply the first-order condition (9.26), for optimal portfolios. The terms containing the choice variables x cancel out and we are left with:

$$0 = \frac{\mathbb{E}(d\xi)}{dt} + \xi r(Y,t)$$

which gives the following expression for the expected, percentage change in discounted marginal utility ξ per unit of time:

$$-\frac{1}{\xi}\frac{\mathbb{E}(d\xi)}{dt} = r \tag{11.4}$$

The percentage drift of marginal utility equals the opposite of the riskless rate.[3] When wealth is optimally invested, marginal utility grows at a rate equal to minus the riskless rate.[4]

Consider now the drift $\mathbb{E}[d(\xi S_i)]$ of securities' prices discounted using the ratio of marginal utilities. Itô's lemma, as applied to ξ, gives:

$$\frac{d\xi}{\xi} = -rdt + \frac{\frac{\partial^2 J}{\partial W^2}[dW - \mathbb{E}dW] + \frac{\partial^2 J}{\partial Y \partial W}[dY - \mathbb{E}dY]}{\frac{\partial J}{\partial W}}$$

while, as applied to discounted prices ξS_i, it gives us:

$$\frac{d(\xi S_i)}{\xi} = S_i \frac{d\xi}{\xi} + dS_i + \frac{d\xi}{\xi} dS_i$$

Substituting the first in the second expression and taking expectations, which means dropping the random part, we get the following expression for the expected change in discounted prices ξS_i:

$$\frac{\mathbb{E}[d(\xi S_i)]}{\xi} = (\mu_i - r) S_i dt + \frac{d\xi}{\xi} dS_i \tag{11.5}$$

where we write $d\xi dS_i / dt$ for the covariance between the security and the marginal derived utility of wealth. The first-order condition (9.26) in effect says that the RHS of (11.5) is equal to zero. We get the alternative to the multiple-premia CAPM, in terms of marginal utility:

$$\mu_i - r = -\frac{1}{\xi S_i} \frac{d\xi dS_i}{dt} \tag{11.6}$$

Naturally, the LHS of (11.5) is zero as well:

$$\mathbb{E}[d(\xi S_i)] = 0$$

that is, *security prices, once multiplied by the marginal utility of wealth, are (local) martingales* under the effective measure. So, the (local) martingale property of security prices and the CAPM are identical properties.

---

3 We could also introduce the process η as the undiscounted value of ξ:

$$\eta \triangleq \xi \exp\left(\int_0^t r(s)ds\right) = \xi B$$

Using it, equation (11.4) becomes

$$0 = -\frac{1}{\eta} \frac{\mathbb{E}(d\eta)}{dt}$$

It says that undiscounted marginal utility is a (local) martingale.

4 It is analogous to the result in Fisher's (single good, no uncertainty) economy of chapter 3, namely:

$$\frac{1}{1+r} = \mathbb{E} \frac{\frac{\partial u}{\partial c_1}(c_1, 1)}{\frac{\partial u}{\partial c_0}(c_0, 1)}$$

It is clear that ξ, which here is the ratio of marginal utilities, plays the same role as the stochastic discount factor ξ of previous chapters.

The main advantage of the CAPM (11.6), which is Breeden's (1979) formulation, is that it contains a single driver for the excess return $\mu_i - r$, namely $d\xi dS_i/dt$, the covariance between the security and the derived utility of wealth, which is, of course, a scalar. The investor and the market need not consider on the one hand the covariance with the market portfolio and, on the other hand, the covariance with the state variables capturing the long-run changes in the opportunity set as we did in section 11.1. *Marginal derived utility ξ is all that is needed for determining risk premia.*

A major drawback of this representation for the CAPM is that the marginal derived utility is not observable, while we would like a version of the CAPM that is amenable to empirical testing. To obtain it, view again ξ as $\frac{\partial u}{\partial c}(c(t),t)/\frac{\partial u}{\partial c}(c(0),0)$. The following representation of the random component of its dynamics holds:

$$\frac{d\xi}{\xi} = \frac{\frac{\partial^2 u}{\partial c^2}}{\frac{\partial u}{\partial c}} \times [dc - \mathbb{E}dc]$$

Substituting into equation (11.6) we obtain the following form of Breeden's CCAPM:

$$\mu_i - r = -\frac{dS_i}{S_i}\frac{\frac{\partial^2 u}{\partial c^2}}{\frac{\partial u}{\partial c}}\frac{dc - \mathbb{E}dc}{dt}$$

The reader is reminded that a utility function of the von Neumann-Morgenstern type has been assumed all along. When, in additon, the utility function is additive and time factors out, the ratio of the utility function's derivatives is, in absolute value, the Arrow-Pratt coefficient of risk aversion, $A(c)$. It follows that:[5]

$$\mu_i - r = \frac{dS_i}{S_i}A(c)\frac{dc - \mathbb{E}dc}{dt}$$

With several investors, let $\bar{c}$ be the aggregate consumption, which is observable in principle, and $\bar{T}$ be the aggregate risk tolerance, Breeden's CAPM can be aggregated to yield:[6]

$$\mu_i - r = \frac{1}{\bar{T}}\frac{dS_i}{S_i}\frac{d\bar{c} - \mathbb{E}d\bar{c}}{dt} \tag{11.7}$$

In this form, the extra-return on security i is directly proportional to the covariance between the risky security price and aggregate consumption. A security that positively covaries with aggregate consumption is required to have a higher rate of return. We call that security *procyclical*. A security that is countercyclical can be sold at low excess return. This is because the former pays more when marginal utility is low and the latter pays less.

---

5 Exploiting the relationship between absolute and relative risk aversion, we can write also:

$$\mu_i - r = \frac{dS_i}{S_i}A_r(c)\frac{dc - \mathbb{E}dc}{cdt}$$

6 Please, observe that, in discrete-time economies, no such aggregation is feasible.

---------------------------♠---------------------------

Last, observe that the consumption-based model can be expressed in terms of betas and written as:

$$\mu(Y,t) - r(Y,t) \times \mathbf{1} = \frac{\beta_{S,\bar{c}}}{\beta_{M,\bar{c}}} \left[\mu_{\bar{c}}(Y,t) - r(Y,t) \right]$$

where $\beta_{S,\bar{c}}$ and $\beta_{M,\bar{c}}$ are the regression betas of all securities returns and of the market return on aggregate consumption growth, while $\mu_{\bar{c}}(Y,t)$ is the expected value of the ratio of growth of consumption conditional on Y. In this form Breeden's CAPM is expressed in terms of observable quantities.

11.4   The Cox-Ingersoll-Ross Equilibrium

In both Merton's multiple-premia CAPM (11.1) and Breeden's single premium consumption CAPM (11.7), prices remain exogenous. Only their drifts are determined by equating demand and supply. Now our goal is to endogenize prices as *functions of state variables*. We determine conditions satisfied by security prices that support equilibrium, when decision makers behave as price takers in a continuous-time portfolio model. Formally, this means that the first-order conditions of those models now become *functional equations* for the price processes. This change of perspective means that we are moving towards a *general-equilibrium approach*, instead of a partial-equilibrium one.[7] However, we assume that a representative investor exists, instead of demonstrating, as we did in discrete-time, that aggregation is possible. The equilibrium we study is due to Cox-Ingersoll-Ross (CIR, 1985a).

The discussion of the equilibrium unfolds as follows. We set up the model and we discuss the equilibrium riskless return and then the risky returns and prices.

11.4.1   Model Setup

In the CIR model, a representative investor is assumed to exist.[8] He faces a portfolio choice problem à la Merton, with a stochastic opportunity set. Let the horizon be finite. The only restriction imposed *a priori* on security prices is that they are diffusion processes, since they are supposed to be (twice differentiable) functions of the H state variables Y, which are diffusions themselves, and are driven by the same equation as in chapter 9, with K Wiener processes:

$$dY(t) = \mu_Y(Y(t),t)dt + \sigma_Y(Y(t),t) \times dw(t)$$

---

7 The same change of perspective was adopted in section 4.4, when shifting from the first-order conditions for portfolio-selection in multiperiod, discrete-time to the equilibrium conditions of the Lucas (1978) model.

8 Other than all investors being identical, the most justifiable assumption that will cause that condition to hold is the completeness of the financial market ($N \geq K$, with the rank of the volatility matrix of the securities—in equilibrium—being equal to K at all points in time). See chapter 12.

Let $S_0(t)$ be the price of the riskless security (in zero-net supply) and let $S(t)$ be an N-dimensional adapted process that collects the prices of risky securities, with the same SDE as in section 9.4. Subject to technical conditions, the functional dependence of the riskless rate and security prices on Y will be an equilibrium result.

The N-dimensional risky-security vector S is broken down into two parts, of dimensions n and k respectively.

The first n components are in positive net supply. They are *physical-output processes or productive or "outside" securities*. The vector process for their price is called S_Q; their expected return is the $\mathbb{R}^n$-vector μ_Q; their $n \times K$ diffusion matrix is σ_Q. The dynamic behavior of outside securities is given as:

$$dS_Q(t) = \text{diag}(S_Q(t)) \times \mu_Q(Y(t),t)dt + \text{diag}(S_Q(t)) \times \sigma_Q(Y(t),t) \times dw(t)$$

Not only are these securities in positive supply, they are also in *infinitely elastic supply*, which means that there is no cost of installing capital and the technology exhibits constant returns to scale. The technology imposes the returns. The market capitalizations of these securities are equal to the physical capital stocks accumulated in the firms.[9]

The last k risky securities are in zero net supply. They are *purely financial or "inside" or derivative – but not necessarily redundant – securities*. Their payoff processes are collected in the vector $\delta(Y(t),t)$; their market price forms the $\mathbb{R}^k$-vector S_F. Their dynamic behavior must be derived. As a pure matter of notation, it is written as:

$$dS_F(t) = \left[\text{diag}(S_F(t)) \times \mu_F(Y(t),t) - \delta(Y(t),t)\right]dt$$
$$+\text{diag}(S_F(t)) \times \sigma_F(Y(t),t) \times dw(t)$$

with evident meaning of the $\mathbb{R}^k$-vector μ_F and of the $k \times K$ diffusion matrix σ_F.

The individual investor treats the same way inside and outside securities. However, the equilibrium characterizations of inside versus outside prices is very different. The behavior of outside prices is given while that of inside prices is to be obtained.

Let us denote as $a_i(t) \times W$ the investment of the representative investor into production process $i, i = 1, ..n$, where W is the current stock of physical capital. Denote as $a(t)$ the vector of those outside security investments. Also, let $b(t)$ be the vector of investments in the derivative securities. Let $x \in \mathbb{R}^N$ be the block vector of investment weights in risky inside and outside securities, formed by a and b:

$$x \triangleq \begin{bmatrix} a \\ b \end{bmatrix}$$

---

9 We do not assume that the representative agent himself faces a "complete-market opportunity set": n is allowed to be smaller than K.

The weight of the riskless security is:

$$1 - \sum_{i=1}^{n} a_i - \sum_{i=1}^{k} b_i$$

With this setup, the following definition of equilibrium is introduced:

Definition 11.1 *At time t, an equilibrium is an allocation a(t) of capital to productive securities, a consumption level c(t), a rate of interest r(t), and a k-tuple of financial-security prices $S_F(t)$, such that the representative investor is at the optimum and all markets (for inside and outside securities, as well as for the riskless security) clear.*

Market-clearing conditions are as follows:

1. the zero-net supply condition for inside securities:

$$x = \begin{bmatrix} a^* \\ 0 \end{bmatrix}$$

where a^* is the optimal choice of a made freely by the representative investor

2. the supply-equals-demand condition for outside securities:

$$\sum_{i=1}^{n} a_i^* = 1$$

The two conditions together imply the absence of net investment in the riskless security:

$$1 - \sum_{i=1}^{N} x_i = 1 - \sum_{i=1}^{n} a_i^* = 0$$

The representative investor faces the following maximization problem, which he can solve by choosing his consumption path and securities allocation:

$$J(W, Y, 0) = \max_{\{c(t)\}, \{x_i(t)\}} \mathbb{E}_0 \left\{ \int_0^T u(c(t), t) dt \right\} \tag{11.8}$$

The program includes the dynamic budget constraints:

$$dW(t) = r(Y, t)W(t)dt + W(t)[\mu(Y, t) - r(Y, t)\mathbf{1}]^{\mathsf{T}} x dt - c(t)dt$$
$$+ W(t)x^{\mathsf{T}}\sigma(Y, t)dw(t)$$

where $\sigma(Y,t)$ is the $(n+k) \times K$ diffusion matrix obtained stacking up $\sigma_Q(Y,t)$ and $\sigma_F(Y,t)$. Suppressing the dependence of J on W, Y, t, the HJB equation is:

$$
\begin{aligned}
0 = \max_{c,x} \Bigg\{ & u(c,t) + \frac{\partial J}{\partial W} \{ r(Y,t)W + W[\mu(Y,t) - r(Y,t)\mathbf{1}]^\mathsf{T}x - c \} \\
& + \frac{\partial J}{\partial Y}\mu_Y(Y,t) + \frac{1}{2}\frac{\partial^2 J}{\partial W^2}W^2 x^\mathsf{T}\sigma(Y,t)\sigma(Y,t)^\mathsf{T}x \\
& + \frac{1}{2}\frac{\partial^2 J}{\partial Y^2}\sigma_Y(Y,t)\sigma_Y(Y,t)^\mathsf{T} \\
& + \frac{\partial^2 J}{\partial W \partial Y}W\sigma_Y(Y,t)\sigma(Y,t)^\mathsf{T}x + \frac{\partial J}{\partial t} \Bigg\}
\end{aligned}
\tag{11.9}
$$

The first-order conditions include the usual marginality condition:

$$
\frac{\partial u}{\partial c} = \frac{\partial J}{\partial W}
\tag{11.10}
$$

and the investment-choice condition (which is identical to (9.26)):

$$
\frac{\partial J}{\partial W}W[\mu(Y,t) - r(Y,t)\mathbf{1}] + \frac{\partial^2 J}{\partial W^2}W^2\sigma(Y,t)\sigma(Y,t)^\mathsf{T}x
$$

$$
+ W\sigma(Y,t)\sigma_Y(Y,t)^\mathsf{T}\frac{\partial^2 J}{\partial W \partial Y} = 0
\tag{11.11}
$$

Let (c,x) be the solutions of (11.10, 11.11) when markets clear. In equilibrium, the expected rate of return on invested wealth is:

$$
\mu(Y,t)^\mathsf{T}x = \mu_Q(Y,t)^\mathsf{T}a^*
\tag{11.12}
$$

and the variance of invested wealth is equal to:

$$
x^\mathsf{T}\sigma(Y,t)\sigma(Y,t)^\mathsf{T}x = a^{*\mathsf{T}}\sigma_Q(Y,t)\sigma_Q(Y,t)^\mathsf{T}a^*
\tag{11.13}
$$

What needs to be done in order to characterize the equilibrium is to solve (11.9) for the function J after having substituted both first-order conditions (11.10) and (11.11) and the behavior of aggregate invested wealth. From now on, we assume that this is done and that the function J, more specifically its derivative $\partial J/\partial W$, is available as a basis for pricing securities. That is, the key to the valuation of the riskless and risky securities is the process for optimal marginal utility of wealth, which is also the marginal utility of consumption. That means that both can be viewed as being proportional to the stochastic dicount factor ξ. The characterization of equilibrium proceeds in three steps: the rate of interest, the risky security returns, and their prices.

11.4.2   The Riskless Security

We obtain the representation of the rate of interest in terms of the drift of ξ. We then transform it in the spirit of the covariance representations for the CAPM. Applying Itô's lemma to $\partial J/\partial W$ we get:

$$d\frac{\partial J}{\partial W} = \frac{\partial^2 J}{\partial W^2}\mathbb{E}(dW) + \mathbb{E}(dY)\frac{\partial^2 J}{\partial W \partial Y}$$

$$+\frac{1}{2}\frac{\partial^3 J}{\partial W^3}dW^2 + \frac{1}{2}dY^2\frac{\partial^3 J}{\partial W \partial Y^2} + dWdY\frac{\partial^3 J}{\partial W^2 \partial Y}$$

Let us focus on the drift of $\partial J/\partial W$. Differentiating the HJB equation (11.9) with respect to W we get the following expression for the drift, which coincides with (11.3):

$$\frac{\mathbb{E}\left(d\frac{\partial J}{\partial W}\right)}{dt} = -\frac{\partial J}{\partial W}\left\{r(Y,t) + [\mu(Y,t) - r(Y,t)\mathbf{1}]^\mathsf{T}x\right\} \qquad (11.14)$$

$$-\frac{\partial^2 J}{\partial W^2}Wx^\mathsf{T}\sigma(Y,t)\sigma(Y,t)^\mathsf{T}x - \frac{\partial^2 J}{\partial Y \partial W}\sigma_Y(Y,t)\sigma(Y,t)^\mathsf{T}x$$

Pre-multiply the first-order condition (11.11) by x^T:

$$x^\mathsf{T}\left\{\frac{\partial J}{\partial W}W[\mu(Y,t) - r(Y,t)\mathbf{1}] + \frac{\partial^2 J}{\partial W^2}W^2\sigma(Y,t)\sigma(Y,t)^\mathsf{T}x\right.$$

$$\left. +W\sigma(Y,t)\sigma_Y(Y,t)^\mathsf{T}\frac{\partial^2 J}{\partial W \partial Y}\right\} = 0$$

and rearrange:

$$\frac{\partial J}{\partial W}[\mu(Y,t) - r(Y,t)\mathbf{1}]^\mathsf{T}x$$

$$+\frac{\partial^2 J}{\partial W^2}Wx^\mathsf{T}\sigma(Y,t)\sigma(Y,t)^\mathsf{T}x + \frac{\partial^2 J}{\partial Y \partial W}\sigma_Y(Y,t)\sigma(Y,t)^\mathsf{T}x = 0$$

The LHS is part of (11.14). Since it is zero, (11.14) simplifies as follows:

$$0 = \frac{\mathbb{E}(d\xi)}{dt} + \xi r(Y,t)$$

Rearranging we have the desired relation between the riskless rate and the marginal derived utility:

$$r = -\frac{1}{\xi}\frac{\mathbb{E}(d\xi)}{dt} \qquad (11.15)$$

As in partial equilibrium, *the rate of interest is equal to (the opposite of) the expected rate of growth of the marginal derived utility of wealth.*

Partial equilibrium gave us an ICAPM or Breeden's CCAPM. Obviously, we can reconstruct a CAPM result also in the CIR model. Applying it to the expected value of the return on wealth, it is also true that *the rate of interest is equal to the expected rate of return on wealth plus the covariance of the rate of return on wealth with the rate of change in the marginal derived utility of wealth:*

$$r = \mathbb{E}\left(\frac{dW}{W}\right) + \frac{\text{cov}(W, \frac{\partial J}{\partial W})}{W \frac{\partial J}{\partial W}} \qquad (11.16)$$

11.4.3 The Risky Securities

Let us consider now the equilibrium return processes and then the price processes for risky securities. Once more, the key variable is the process ξ.

11.4.3.1 Returns

A simple application of Itô's lemma shows that the SDE for the price processes "deflated" by means of the marginal derived utility of wealth, ξS_i, contains three terms:

$$d(\xi S_i) = S_i d\xi + \xi dS_i + d\xi dS_i$$

for $i = 1..N$. We know that its drift, namely

$$\xi(\mu_i - r) S_i dt + dS_i d\xi$$

is equal to zero by the first-order condition (11.11). Rearranging, we have:

$$\xi(\mu_i - r) S_i + \frac{d\xi dS_i}{dt} = 0 \qquad (11.17)$$

$$\mu_i - r = -\frac{\text{cov}\left(S_i, \frac{\partial J}{\partial W}\right)}{\frac{\partial J}{\partial W} S_i} \frac{1}{dt}$$

The last expression is a CAPM similar to equation (11.7). In the single-investor equilibrium of CIR, each security pays a premium over the riskless rate, that is proportional to the instantaneous covariance of its percentage returns (dS_i/S_i) with respect to the rate of change in his marginal derived utility of wealth, $d\frac{\partial J}{\partial W} / \frac{\partial J}{\partial W}$.

11.4.3.2 Prices

Focus on inside securities. Single out the last k components of the vector $\mathcal{S}$. For these securities, if we write F for $\mathcal{S}_F(W, Y, t)$ in vector terms, F_i for S_{F_i} in single-component terms, equation (11.17) can be written as:

$$\left(\mu_{F_i} - r\right) F_i = -\underbrace{\left[\underbrace{\frac{\partial^2 J}{\partial W^2}}_{1\times 1} \quad \underbrace{\frac{\partial^2 J}{\partial W \partial Y}}_{1\times H}\right]}_{1\times(H+1)} \underbrace{\Omega}_{(H+1)\times(H+1)} \underbrace{\left[\begin{array}{c} \underbrace{\frac{\partial F_i}{\partial W}}_{1\times 1} \\ \underbrace{\left[\frac{\partial F_i}{\partial Y}\right]^{\mathsf{T}}}_{H\times 1} \end{array}\right]}_{(H+1)\times 1} \qquad (11.18)$$

where:

$$\Omega \triangleq \begin{bmatrix} \underbrace{\text{var}(W)}_{1\times 1} & \underbrace{\text{cov}(W,Y)^{\mathsf{T}}}_{1\times H} \\ \underbrace{\text{cov}(W,Y)}_{H\times 1} & \underbrace{\text{var}(Y)}_{H\times H} \end{bmatrix}$$

The quantities $\text{var}(W)$ and $\text{cov}(W,Y)$ have been defined above, while $\text{var}(Y)$ is $\sigma_Y(Y,t)\sigma_Y(Y,t)^{\mathsf{T}}$. In words, the returns on financial securities are again dictated by the variance-covariance properties of wealth and the state variables.[10]

Now, let us rephrase these results in terms of prices, instead of returns. An application of Itô's lemma to obtain the expected return μ_{Fi} on financial securities gives:

$$\mu_{Fi}F_i = \underbrace{\nabla F_i}_{1\times(H+1)} \underbrace{\begin{bmatrix} \underbrace{W\mu_F(Y,t)^{\mathsf{T}}a^* - c^*}_{1\times 1} \\ \underbrace{\mu_Y(Y,t)}_{H\times 1} \end{bmatrix}}_{(H+1)\times 1} \qquad (11.19)$$

$$+\frac{\partial F_i}{\partial t} + \frac{1}{2}\text{trace}\left(\Omega \times \nabla^2 F_i\right) + \delta_i(Y,t)$$

where ∇F_i is the gradient of the price,

$$\nabla F_i = \begin{bmatrix} \underbrace{\frac{\partial F_i}{\partial W}}_{1\times 1} & \underbrace{\frac{\partial F_i}{\partial Y}}_{1\times H} \end{bmatrix}$$

$\nabla^2 F_i$ is its Hessian matrix, namely

$$\nabla^2 F_i = \begin{bmatrix} \underbrace{\frac{\partial^2 F_i}{\partial W^2}}_{1\times 1} & \underbrace{\frac{\partial^2 F_i}{\partial W\partial Y}}_{1\times(H} \\ \underbrace{\frac{\partial^2 F_i}{\partial W\partial Y}}_{H\times 1} & \underbrace{\frac{\partial^2 F_i}{\partial Y^2}}_{H\times H} \end{bmatrix}$$

---

10 In the presence of a single-state variable and a single contingent claim, for instance, the previous expression reduces to:

$$\frac{\frac{\partial^2 J}{\partial W^2}}{\frac{\partial J}{\partial W}}\frac{\partial F}{\partial W}\text{var}(W) + \frac{\frac{\partial^2 J}{\partial W\partial Y}}{\frac{\partial J}{\partial W}}\frac{\partial F}{\partial W}\text{cov}(W,Y) + \frac{\frac{\partial^2 J}{\partial W^2}}{\frac{\partial J}{\partial W}}\frac{\partial F}{\partial Y}\text{cov}(W,Y) + \frac{\frac{\partial^2 J}{\partial W\partial Y}}{\frac{\partial J}{\partial W}}\frac{\partial F}{\partial Y}\text{var}(Y)$$

in which the variance-covariance is split into its different components in an explicit way.

Substituting (11.19) into (11.18) we finally get the equation for the inside prices. It is the following PDE:

$$0 = \frac{1}{2}\text{trace}\left(\Omega \times \nabla^2 F_i\right) + \frac{\partial F_i}{\partial W}\left[r(Y,t)W - c\right] \tag{11.20}$$

$$+\frac{\partial F_i}{\partial Y}\left\{\mu_Y - \left[-\frac{\frac{\partial^2 J}{\partial W^2}}{\frac{\partial J}{\partial W}} \quad -\frac{\frac{\partial^2 J}{\partial W \partial Y}}{\frac{\partial J}{\partial W}}\right]\left[\begin{matrix}\text{cov}(W,Y)\\ \text{var}Y\end{matrix}\right]\right\}$$

$$+\frac{\partial F_i}{\partial t} - rF_i + \delta_i$$

Equation (11.20) is a linear PDE in the price function $F(W, Y, t)$. It gives the equilibrium price of any security as a function of the exogenous variables in the economy. In effect it treats the financial securities as derivatives written on W and Y. The replication machinery we introduced in chapter 6 is at work. The equation can, indeed, be recognized as a Black-Scholes equation for a derivative that pays a flow δ_i on the state variables and an underlying security W that pays a flow c. It will be accompanied by appropriate boundary conditions. The boundary conditions and the specificity of the equation itself will determine existence and uniqueness of a solution.

The principal contribution of CIR has been to regard the intertemporal CAPM of Merton as a functional equation where the unknown is a price function, as opposed to an expected-return number.

We suggest that the reader develop the model solution for the single state-variable case, following exercise 11.1.

Remark 11.1 *One interesting aspect of the last equation is the drift of Y, which is adjusted by the derivatives of the value function J of the optimization program:*

$$-\left[-\frac{\frac{\partial^2 J}{\partial W^2}}{\frac{\partial J}{\partial W}} \quad -\frac{\frac{\partial^2 J}{\partial W \partial Y}}{\frac{\partial J}{\partial W}}\right]\left[\begin{matrix}cov(W,Y)\\ var(Y)\end{matrix}\right]$$

It may be interpreted as the covariance between marginal utility and the state variables,

$$\frac{1}{\frac{\partial J}{\partial W}}cov\left(\frac{\partial J}{\partial W}, Y\right)$$

It is an equilibrium, as opposed to an arbitrage, result, and concerns Y. If we think of the equilibrium prices of all claims as the expectation of their payoffs, discounted, we realize that the expectation must be taken after reducing the drift of state variables in a way proportional to the "risk appreciation," given by the covariance between marginal utility and the state variables.

11.5   Benchmark Example (continued)

Assume that the utility function of the single investor is isoelastic. His optimization problem (11.8), starting at t, becomes:

$$J(W, Y, t) = \max_{\{c(s)\},\{x_i(s)\}} \mathbb{E}_t \left\{ \int_t^T e^{-\rho s} \frac{c(s)^\gamma}{\gamma} ds \right\}$$

One can verify that a value function of the form

$$J(W, Y, t) = B(Y, t) e^{-\rho t} \frac{W(t)^\gamma}{\gamma} + C(Y, t)$$

solves the PDE (11.9) after having substituted both first-order conditions (11.10) and (11.11) and the behavior of aggregate invested wealth, provided the functions $B(Y, t)$ and $C(Y, t)$ solve appropriate PDEs.

Consequently, risk aversion, measured in terms of the indirect utility function, is constant, as in the basic IID equilibrium of Merton (using short hand for partial derivatives and suppressing arguments):

$$-\frac{W J_{WW}}{J_W} = 1 - \gamma \tag{11.21}$$

At the same time, since

$$-\frac{J_{WY}}{J_W} = -\frac{B_Y}{B} \tag{11.22}$$

the rate of change of marginal utility with respect to the state variables does not depend on wealth, which is not an argument of the function B. The entire equilibrium, including the allocation a^* to outside securities, is independent of wealth, as a result of the isoelastic form of the utility function and the constant returns to scale of the production system. The same is true for the interest rate. Indeed, using (11.16):

$$r = \mu_Q^\mathsf{T} a^* + \frac{1}{\frac{\partial J}{\partial W}} \left[\frac{\partial^2 J}{\partial W^2} W a^{*\mathsf{T}} \sigma_Q \sigma_Q^\mathsf{T} a^* + \frac{\partial^2 J}{\partial Y \partial W} \sigma_Y \sigma_Q^\mathsf{T} a^* \right]$$

and substituting in it (11.21) and (11.22), we get

$$r = \mu_Q^\mathsf{T} a^* + \left[(\gamma - 1) a^{*\mathsf{T}} \sigma_Q \sigma_Q^\mathsf{T} a^* - \frac{B_Y}{B} \sigma_Y \sigma_Q^\mathsf{T} a^* \right]$$

If, furthermore, the utility of the representative investor is logarithmic:

$$J(W, Y, t) = \max_{\{c(s)\},\{x_i(s)\}} \mathbb{E}_t \left\{ \int_t^T e^{-\rho s} \ln c(s) ds \right\}$$

the function J is of the form:

$$J(W, Y, t) = B(t) e^{-\rho t} \ln W(t) + C(t) Y + D(t)$$

where:

$$B(t) = \frac{-e^{-\rho T} + e^{-\rho t}}{\rho}$$

$C(t)$ and $D(t)$ are deterministic functions of time. The representative investor holds only the myopic portfolio, which is independent of the state variables Y. The optimal portfolio allocation to the outside securities is easily calculated and is, in fact, identical to the Markowitz portfolio of a log investor (see Appendix A, equation (A.5)):

$$a^* = \left(\sigma_Q \sigma_Q^{\mathsf{T}}\right)^{-1} \mu_Q + \frac{1 - \mathbf{1}^{\mathsf{T}}\left(\sigma_Q \sigma_Q^{\mathsf{T}}\right)^{-1} \mu_Q}{\mathbf{1}^{\mathsf{T}}\left(\sigma_Q \sigma_Q^{\mathsf{T}}\right)^{-1} \mathbf{1}} \left(\sigma_Q \sigma_Q^{\mathsf{T}}\right)^{-1} \mathbf{1}$$

This allocation does not depend on total wealth. The evolution of aggregate wealth follows from (11.12), (11.13), and (11.10), where the latter implies a consumption equal to:

$$c^* = \frac{\rho W}{1 - e^{-\rho(T-t)}}$$

For the log investor, because $B_Y = 0$, the rate of interest simplifies to:

$$r = \mu_Q^{\mathsf{T}} a^* - a^{*\mathsf{T}} \sigma_Q \sigma_Q^{\mathsf{T}} a^*$$

$$= \frac{\mathbf{1}^{\mathsf{T}}\left(\sigma_Q \sigma_Q^{\mathsf{T}}\right)^{-1} \mu_Q - 1}{\mathbf{1}^{\mathsf{T}}\left(\sigma_Q \sigma_Q^{\mathsf{T}}\right)^{-1} \mathbf{1}} \tag{11.23}$$

A major consequence of the previous independence results is that in equilibrium any financial security whose payoff does not depend on wealth has a valuation equation, (11.20), that is very much simplified. For each of them, the Hessian matrix $\nabla^2 F$ is equal to zero. CIR use this as a starting point for their model of the term structure of interest rates, which we discuss below (chapter 16).

Exercise 11.2 gives the reader an opportunity to calculate the equilibrium for the case in which the investor has a logarithmic utility.

11.6   Conclusion

In this chapter, which has been a transition towards general equilibrium, some properties of rates of return were given and other properties derived. In the first part, the risk properties of securities' returns were taken as given and their expected values were obtained in the form of an *Intertemporal CAPM*. In this sense, the ICAPM is an algebraic restriction *providing us with numbers*, namely the expected returns. The terms in the ICAPM equation reflect one for one the components in the investor's portfolio, which we saw in the last chapter.

The myopic component generates a CAPM risk premium that is identical to the one-period CAPM of mean-variance portfolio theory. The other risk premia reflect the desire to hedge reinvestment risk intertemporally.

In the second part of the chapter (starting with section 11.4), a production system fixed the returns on some physical facilities. Investors decided how much to invest in each physical facility, as was done before under optimal portfolio choice. And the prices and returns of other securities were found to be restricted by a PDE that was identical to the ICAPM, the main conclusion being that the CAPM can be seen as a functional equation, in which *the unknowns are the prices* as functions of state variables.

11.7   Appendix: Aggregation Leading to the CAPM

Start from the first-order condition for portfolio weights, equation (9.26), which is satisfied by x:

$$
\frac{\partial J}{\partial W}[\mu(Y,t) - r(Y,t) \times \mathbf{1}] + \frac{\partial^2 J}{\partial W^2} W\sigma(Y,t)\sigma(Y,t)^\mathsf{T} x
$$

$$
+\sigma(Y,t)\sigma_Y(Y,t)^\mathsf{T} \frac{\partial^2 J}{\partial W \partial Y} = 0
$$

Assume that J is strictly concave, with $\frac{\partial^2 J}{\partial W^2}$ different from zero for all t with probability one. Divide by this quantity:

$$
\frac{\frac{\partial J}{\partial W}}{\frac{\partial^2 J}{\partial W^2}}[\mu(Y,t) - r(Y,t) \times \mathbf{1}] + W\sigma(Y,t)\sigma(Y,t)^\mathsf{T} x
$$

$$
+\frac{1}{\frac{\partial^2 J}{\partial W^2}}\sigma(Y,t)\sigma_Y(Y,t)^\mathsf{T} \frac{\partial^2 J}{\partial W \partial Y} = 0
$$

Sum over all investors:

$$
\left(\sum_{m=1}^{M} \frac{\frac{\partial J^m}{\partial W}(W^m, Y, t)}{\frac{\partial^2 J^m}{\partial W^2}(W^m, Y, t)}\right)[\mu(Y,t) - r(Y,t) \times \mathbf{1}]
$$

$$
+\sigma(Y,t)\sigma(Y,t)^\mathsf{T} \sum_{m=1}^{M} W^m x^m
$$

$$
+\left(\sum_{m=1}^{M} \frac{1}{\frac{\partial^2 J^m}{\partial W^2}(W^m, Y, t)}\right)\sigma(Y,t)\sigma_Y(Y,t)^\mathsf{T} \frac{\partial^2 J^m}{\partial W \partial Y}(W^m, Y, t) = 0
$$

Divide by the first factor and rearrange:

$$\mu(Y,t) - r(Y,t) \times \mathbf{1} \tag{11.24}$$

$$= -\frac{\sum_{m=1}^{M} W^m}{\sum_{m=1}^{M} \frac{\frac{\partial J^m}{\partial W}(W^m,Y,t)}{\frac{\partial^2 J^m}{\partial W^2}(W^m,Y,t)}} \sigma(Y,t)\sigma(Y,t)^\mathsf{T} \frac{\sum_{m=1}^{M} W^m x^m}{\sum_{m=1}^{M} W^m}$$

$$- \frac{\sum_{m=1}^{M} \frac{1}{\frac{\partial^2 J^m}{\partial W^2}(W^m,Y,t)}}{\sum_{m=1}^{M} \frac{\frac{\partial J^m}{\partial W}(W^m,Y,t)}{\frac{\partial^2 J^m}{\partial W^2}(W^m,Y,t)}} \sigma(Y,t)\sigma_Y(Y,t)^\mathsf{T} \frac{\partial^2 J^m}{\partial W \partial Y}(W^m,Y,t)$$

In order to simplify (11.24), we define two variables, $\Lambda_\mathbb{M}$ and Λ_Y, and recognize the presence in the previous expression of the market portfolio $x^\mathbb{M}$.

Define the real-valued process $\Lambda_\mathbb{M}$ as follows:

$$\Lambda_\mathbb{M} \triangleq \frac{\sum_{m=1}^{M} W^m}{-\sum_{m=1}^{M} W^m \frac{\frac{\partial J^m}{\partial W}}{\frac{\partial^2 J^m}{\partial W^2}} W^m}$$

It is the wealth-weighted harmonic-mean of investor risk aversions, with risk aversion measured in terms of derived utility. Equivalently, $1/\Lambda_\mathbb{M}$ is the weighted average of risk tolerances, or the aggregate risk tolerance $\bar{T}$

$$\frac{1}{\Lambda_\mathbb{M}} = \bar{T} = \frac{-\sum_{m=1}^{M} W^m \frac{\frac{\partial J^m}{\partial W}}{\frac{\partial^2 J^m}{\partial W^2}} W^m}{\sum_{m=1}^{M} W^m}$$

Define also the $\mathbb{R}^H$-valued process Λ_Y:

$$\Lambda_Y \triangleq -\frac{\sum_{m=1}^{M} \frac{\frac{\partial^2 J^m}{\partial W \partial Y}}{\frac{\partial^2 J^m}{\partial W^2}}}{\sum_{m=1}^{M} \frac{\frac{\partial J^m}{\partial W}}{\frac{\partial^2 J^m}{\partial W^2}}}$$

which can be interpreted as a weighted average as follows. Then:

$$\Lambda_Y = -\frac{\sum_{m=1}^{M} \frac{\frac{\partial^2 J^m}{\partial W \partial Y}}{\frac{\partial J^m}{\partial W}} \frac{\frac{\partial J^m}{\partial W}}{\frac{\partial^2 J^m}{\partial W^2}}}{\sum_{m=1}^{M} \frac{\frac{\partial J^m}{\partial W}}{\frac{\partial^2 J^m}{\partial W^2}}}$$

which says that Λ_Y is a weighted-average of the percentage changes in the marginal utility of wealth, when the state variables change:

$$\frac{\frac{\partial^2 J^m}{\partial W \partial Y}}{\frac{\partial J^m}{\partial W}} \tag{11.25}$$

Also in this case the weights are the risk tolerances in terms of derived utility, $\frac{\partial J^m}{\partial W} / \frac{\partial^2 J^m}{\partial W^2}$. The last step in order to simplify (11.24) consists in recognizing that the market portfolio $x^\mathbb{M}$ shows up in it.

It is indeed true that

$$\frac{\sum_{m=1}^{M} W^m x^m}{\sum_{m=1}^{M} W^m}$$

is the weighted-average of each investor's optimal portfolio (in percentage terms). The weight for investor m is his wealth. $\sum_{m=1}^{M} W^m x^{\,m}$ is the total demand for each financial security (in dollar terms). In equilibrium total demand must equal total supply, or the market portfolio. In dollar terms, this is $x^{\mathbb{M}} \sum_{m=1}^{M} W^m$. It follows that:

$$\frac{\sum_{m=1}^{M} W^m x^{\,m}}{\sum_{m=1}^{M} W^m} = x^{\mathbb{M}}$$

Substituting for $\Lambda_{\mathbb{M}}, \Lambda_Y, x^{\mathbb{M}}$ in (11.24) we get expression (11.1) in the main text.

Exercises

11.1. Consider the CIR model with a single state variable, Y, and a single derivative or inside security, $\mathcal{S}_F$. Write down in full:

a. the expected return on the financial security, $\mu_F \mathcal{S}_F$, in equation (11.19),

b. the PDE for asset pricing, (11.20).

Comment on the interpretation of the PDE in spirit of the Black-Scholes model.

11.2. Consider the CIR model in the presence of a single log investor and a single state variable Y.

a. Verify that
$$J(W, Y, t) = B(t) \log W(t) + C(t) Y(t) + D(t)$$
is the value function solving the HJB equation (11.9).

b. Show that the optimal consumption and portfolio allocation are
$$c^* = \frac{\rho W}{1 - e^{-\rho(T-t)}}$$
$$a^* = [\sigma_Q \sigma_Q^\top]^{-1} (\mu_Q - r)$$

c. Show that $\mathrm{cov}(J_W, Y)/J_W$ and r do not depend on W.

12 Equilibrium in Complete Markets

In chapter 4, while studying a simple single-period model, we established that, in a complete market, a direct calculation of an equilibrium was straightforward. We also showed that a representative investor, defined with constant weights, existed. His first-order conditions were all that was needed to characterize securities' prices. Indeed, his marginal utility, which was the marginal utility of aggregate consumption, could be used to obtain equilibrium prices starting from security payoffs. While studying discrete-time multiperiod economies, we again characterized complete-market equilibria via a representative investor, following Lucas' approach. In total similarity with the single-period model, his marginal derived utility was the fundamental pricing device, since it made it possible to obtain prices from security payoffs.

In this chapter, we are interested in the general equilibrium of continuous-time complete markets. We want to show how that equilibrium can be obtained by direct calculation. We also want to demonstrate that, when we start with a population of heterogeneous investors, a representative investor exists and that his marginal derived utility is again all that is needed for security pricing. As usual, security prices will be obtained by discounting payoffs using marginal indirect utility. The task is not trivial because we are interested in equilibria of markets where prices are Itô, but not necessarily Markov. This means that we need to use the global approach of chapter 10.

The chapter proceeds as follows: in section 12.1 we recall and partially restate the setting of chapter 10. The restatement is needed because security prices are now endogenous, instead of being exogenous. In section 12.2, we recall conditions under which the equilibrium exists. In section 12.3.2, we determine under what conditions a representative investor can be defined. In section 12.4, we study the security-pricing consequences of his existence. In section 12.4.2, we establish that the CAPM holds even when prices are not Markov. Up to that point, the development of the chapter is quite similar to that of chapter 11, with two differences: first, existence of the representative investor is now established instead of being an assumption; second, prices are Itô, not necessarily Markovian. Section 12.5 specifies the conditions under which prices are Markov processes. Section 12.6 addresses the interpretation of the state variables that drive prices and consumption paths. Section 12.7 revisits the benchmark example and applies to it the equilibrium results.

12.1   Model Setup: Exogenous and Admissible Variables

As usual, consider a time interval $\mathcal{T} = [0, T]$, with $T < \infty$, and a complete probability space (Ω, P). Let $w(\omega, t)$ be a K-dimensional standard Wiener process in (Ω, P) (written $w(t)$ for short) and let the filtration $\mathbf{F}^w$ be generated by w.[1] We study a pure-exchange economy populated by M investors, denoted by $m = 1, ..M$, who have homogeneous expectations over prices; they share the same information and process it in the same way.[2]

There is a riskless security and $N = K$ risky securities.[3] The *riskless security*, which is numbered zero, is only instantaneously riskless and its return $r(t)$ is endogenous, an Itô process, but not necessarily a Markovian one. The i-th *risky security* pays an *exogenous* dividend rate $\iota_i(t), i = 1, ..N$. Dividend processes are assumed to be well-defined Itô processes. While dividends are exogenous, prices, relative to the price of the unique consumption good, are *endogenous* and will be determined in equilibrium. The conditions we now state on security prices characterize the set of *admissible* prices. The only prices that are *admissible* are those that follow the usual Itô dynamics (Markov or not), adapted to $\mathbf{F}^w$, that is,

$$\mathcal{S}(t) = \mathcal{S}(0) + \int_0^t [\mu(s) - \iota(s)]\, ds + \int_0^t \sigma(s)\, dw(s) \qquad\qquad t < T$$

and for which $\sigma(s)$ is in $\mathcal{H}^2$ and $\mu(s)$ is in $\mathcal{L}^1$ (see definition 7.7 above). Returns, dividends, and variance-covariances collected in the vectors $\mu, \iota \in \mathbb{R}^N$ and in the matrix $\sigma\sigma^\mathsf{T} \in \mathbb{R}^{N \times N}$ are *in consumption units,* not percentages. Clearly, the expected-return vector inclusive of dividends is μ.[4]

Each investor receives an endowment process $e^m(t)$. So, in contrast to the previous chapters, we consider the possibility of positive endowments after time 0. The investor takes as given the securities' prices $(S_0(t), \mathcal{S}(t))$. The investor's choice variables are

---

1 Reminder: unless doing otherwise is necessary for comprehension, we simplify the notation for processes. All processes are stochastic but we suppress the reference to the state ω. Therefore, $X(t)$ actually means $X(\omega, t)$. In special cases, we also use the notation $f(t)$ to refer to a deterministic function of time. When this happens, we say so explicitly.

2 We can actually do without homogeneity of expectations and assume equivalence of the probability measures of the agents: see Duffie (1986) and chapter 18 below.

3 Assuming that the number of risky assets N equals the number of Wiener processes and that a riskless asset exists amounts to assuming straight away market completeness, if we also assume that the volatility matrix of the risky asset prices is non-singular. Notice, however, that the diffusion matrix is endogenous.

4 This market is dynamically complete, as desired, if the volatility matrix of securities, which is endogenous, is non-singular at every point in time. Therefore, the equilibria of Huang (1987), Duffie (1986), and those of the whole strand of literature stemming from them, need a "verification" of non-singularity of the security volatility matrix – a result referred to as "endogenous completeness." The verification is difficult, especially in heterogeneous agents' economies. A very recent strand of literature concentrates on conditions that guarantee endogenous completeness of financial markets with $N = K$ risky securities. The seminal papers in this field are Anderson and Raimondo (2008) and Hugonnier, Malamud, Trubowitz (2012).

his consumption rate and the portfolio allocations to the riskless and risky securities, $c^m(t) \in \mathbb{R}, \alpha^m(t) \in \mathbb{R}, \Theta^m(t) \in \mathbb{R}^N$. Consumption paths $c^m(\omega, t)$ are *admissible* if they are adapted to the filtration $\mathbf{F}^w$ and greater than zero with probability one. The portfolio allocations of investor m to the riskless and risky securities are restricted to be *admissible* in the sense of definition 7.7. Short sales are allowed. In order to define a plan that is not only admissible, but also *feasible*, in the sense of respecting a budget constraint, we define capital gains, in the same way as we did in chapter 8. As usual, let financial wealth W be the value of financial securities held. A *budget feasible plan* is such that at any point in time the change in investor m's wealth W^m results from net gains (including dividends) from financial securities, minus consumption plus endowments:

$$dW^m(t) = \left[\alpha^m(t)B(t)r(t) + \Theta^{m\mathsf{T}}(t)\mu(t) - c^m(t) + e^m(t)\right] dt$$
$$+ \Theta^{m\mathsf{T}}(t)\sigma(t)dw(t); \ W(0) = W_0$$

where W_0 is given.

Investor m chooses a budget-feasible consumption process $c^m(t)$ and a portfolio allocation process $\Theta^m(t)$, so as to maximize his total utility over the horizon $[0, T]$. The *utility functions* u^m are increasing, strictly concave, and satisfy the Inada conditions. Individual investor m solves a problem with time-additive utility:

$$\max_{\{c^m(t), \alpha^m(t), \Theta^m(t)\}} \mathbb{E}\left[\int_0^T u^m\left(c^m(t), t\right) dt\right] \tag{12.1}$$

with $c^m(t)$ positive, $\alpha^m(t), \Theta^m(t)$ admissible, subject to the dynamic budget constraints.

12.2 Definition and Existence of Equilibrium

The natural definition of equilibrium in the previous setting is the *dynamic or Radner* one. This section specializes the definition of Radner equilibrium to the above setup, states conditions for its existence, and shows how to define a corresponding *Arrow-Debreu* equilibrium.

Definition 12.1 *A Radner equilibrium is a collection of securities prices $\mathcal{S}$ and B and a set of consumption and portfolio allocations $(c^m, \alpha^m, \Theta^m)$, $m = 1..M$, such that*

- *for every investor m and for all t,*

$$W^m(t) \triangleq \alpha^m(t)B(t) + \Theta^{m\mathsf{T}}(t)\mathcal{S}(t)$$
$$= W_0 + \int_0^t \left[\alpha^m(s)B(s)r(s) + \Theta^{m\mathsf{T}}(s)\mu(s)\right] ds$$
$$- \int_0^t \left[c^m(s) - e^m(s)\right] ds + \int_0^t \Theta^{m\mathsf{T}}(s)\sigma(s)dw(s); \tag{12.2}$$

and each investor's consumption c^m is optimal. That is, for all $\check{c}^m$ such that

$$\mathbb{E}\left\{\int_0^T u^m(\check{c}^m(t),t)dt\right\} > \mathbb{E}\left\{\int_0^T u^m(c^m(t),t)dt\right\}$$

there exists a time t such that (12.2) is violated, and

- *goods markets and financial markets clear at all time:*[5]

$$\sum_{m=1}^M c^m(t) = \sum_{m=1}^M e^m(t); \ \sum_{m=1}^M \alpha^m(t) = 0; \ \sum_{m=1}^M \Theta^m(t) = 0$$

Obviously, a Radner equilibrium guarantees that the consumption plan of every investor is optimal, in the sense that it maximizes expected utility among all admissible plans. Market clearing for consumption and financial securities is also required. Here initial financial wealth W_0 is taken to be equal to zero.

A sufficient condition for the existence of a Radner equilibrium is that, at each point in time, the volatility matrix of dividends integrated over time have rank N. Given these assumptions, Duffie and Zame (1989) prove the existence of a Radner equilibrium in two steps.

First, they show that an Arrow-Debreu equilibrium exists; the equilibrium is defined as follows

Definition 12.2 *An Arrow-Debreu equilibrium is a linear pricing functional $\psi : c^m \to \mathbb{R}$ and a set of consumption processes c^m such that, for every investor m,*

$$\psi(c^m) \leq \psi(e^m) \tag{12.3}$$

$$\forall \check{c}^m : \mathbb{E}\int_0^T u^m\left(\check{c}^m\right) dt > \mathbb{E}\int_0^T u^m\left(c^m\right) dt \Rightarrow \psi(\check{c}^m) > \psi(c^m) \tag{12.4}$$

and goods markets clear:

$$\sum_{m=1}^M c^m(t) = \sum_{m=1}^M e^m(t) \tag{12.5}$$

---

5 Here we write market clearing in the form that applies when all securities are in zero net supply and dividends are payments from a person shorting the stock to one holding it long. Positive supply is also possible, in which case dividends would have to be added to aggregate resources:

$$\sum_{m=1}^M c^m(t) = \sum_{m=1}^M e^m(t) + \sum_{i=1}^N \iota_i(t); \ \sum_{m=1}^M \alpha^m(t) = 0; \ \sum_{m=1}^M \Theta^m(t) = 1$$

In the Arrow-Debreu equilibrium, as expected, securities are assumed to exist but do not appear explicitly in the definition. For every investor, the value of the equilibrium consumption path $\psi(c^m)$ is not greater than the value of the endowment $\psi(e^m)$, and any consumption plan that has greater utility than the equilibrium one costs more than it. The consumption goods market, which in the Arrow-Debreu formulation is the unique market, clears at all times.

When the market is complete, the stochastic discount factor ξ is equated across investors. The price functional, being linear, admits a representation as an expectation of payoffs transformed via the stochastic discount factor:

$$\psi(x) = \mathbb{E}\left[\int_0^T \xi(t)x(t)dt\right] \tag{12.6}$$

Considering that utility functions are strictly increasing, the first condition (12.3) is satisfied as an equality

$$\mathbb{E}\left[\int_0^T c^m(t)\xi(t)dt\right] = \mathfrak{W}_0 \tag{12.7}$$

where $\mathfrak{W}_0$ is the investor's overall wealth:

$$\mathfrak{W}_0 \triangleq \mathbb{E}\left[\int_0^T e^m(t)\xi(t)dt\right]$$

Alternatively, their starting financial wealth is equal to zero:

$$\mathbb{E}\int_0^T \left[c^m(t) - e^m(t)\right]\xi(t)dt = 0$$

These conditions, when compared with the lifetime budget constraint of chapter 10, also show that the Arrow-Debreu equilibrium can be implemented as a Radner one. The technology for implementing it is the martingale representation theorem together with market completeness. This is the *second* step in Duffie and Zame's derivation. The mechanism is similar to the one we described for each single investor in chapter 10.

12.3   Obtaining Equilibrium

12.3.1   Direct Calculation

As was done by means of (12.7) and as we did in chapter 10, we reformulate the investor problem as a lifetime problem using a single budget constraint. Call λ_0^m the Lagrange multiplier for the lifetime budget constraint of investor m.[6] According to section 10.2, the first-order conditions for investor optimality are:

$$\frac{\partial}{\partial c}u^m\big(c^m(t),t\big) = \lambda_0^m \frac{\eta(t)}{B(t)} \triangleq \lambda_0^m \xi(t) \tag{12.8}$$

which we invert to get demand functions as:

$$c^m(t) = \mathfrak{h}^m\big(\lambda_0^m \xi(t),t\big) \tag{12.9}$$

We then impose market clearing in the goods market at each point in time and each state of nature as in (12.5):

$$\sum_{m=1}^{M} e^m(t) = \sum_{m=1}^{M} \mathfrak{h}^m\big(\lambda_0^m \xi(t),t\big)$$

If an equilibrium exists, that equation can be solved for the equilibrium stochastic discount factors:

$$\xi(t) = \xi\Big(\bar{c}(t),t; \{\lambda_0^m\}_{m=1}^{M}\Big) \tag{12.10}$$

where $\bar{c}(t) \triangleq \sum_{m=1}^{M} e^m(t)$. One will be left with the task of finding the collection of Lagrange multipliers that is such that each investor's budget constraint is satisfied.

12.3.2   The Representative Investor

As soon as sufficient conditions for existence of an equilibrium are assumed to hold, a question arises. Can a representative investor be identified? Can his preferences be represented by means of expected utility, with a utility function increasing and strictly concave? The answer was provided by Huang (1987).

Starting from an Arrow-Debreu equilibrium in which the Lagrange multipliers take values $\{\lambda_0^m\}$, we can construct a representative investor whose utility is time-additive and state independent. This is a consequence of the fact that the equilibrium is Pareto optimal.

Define the representative investor or central planner as being an investor with an objective that is a weighted average of the objective functions of the population of investors ($m=1\ldots M$), with weights $\{1/\lambda_0^m\}$. His derived time-t utility $\bar{u}(\bar{c},t)$ is the maximized value of his objective function

$$\bar{u}(\bar{c}(t),t) \triangleq \max_{\{c^m(t)\}} \sum_{m=1}^{M} \frac{1}{\lambda_0^m} u^m\big(c^m(t),t\big) \tag{12.11}$$

---

6 The Lagrange multipliers λ_0 differ, indeed, across investors, since their endowments and utility functions do.

subject to the aggregate resource conditions (ARCs) holding at each point in time t:

$$\sum_{m=1}^{M} c^m(t) = \bar{c}(t) \tag{12.12}$$

The ARCs state that, at each point in time, the whole endowment is consumed. The derived utility is a well-defined, strictly increasing, strictly concave (and continuous) utility function.

The first-order conditions for the maximum are:

$$\frac{1}{\lambda_0^m} \frac{\partial u^m(c^m(t), t)}{\partial c^m(t)} = \xi(t) \tag{12.13}$$

where, in this context, we call $\xi(t)$ the Lagrange multiplier of the constraint at t. A comparison of (12.8) and (12.13) indicates that the two systems have a solution in common obtained for the value $\xi(0) = 1 \ (= \bar{u}_c(\bar{c}(0), 0))$ in the second one. For that solution, the allocation of consumption computed by the representative investor is identical at all times in all states of nature to the one that prevails in the competitive equilibrium.

In the reverse, there exists usually an infinity of decentralized equilibria that correspond to a Pareto optimum. These equilibria fit different distributions of endowments in the population.

Since we already know the consumption $\bar{c}(t)$ of the representative investor, the envelope theorem gives us the value of the marginal utility of the representative investor:

$$\frac{\partial}{\partial \bar{c}} \bar{u}(\bar{c}(t), t) = \xi(t) \tag{12.14}$$

The Arrow-Debreu prices per unit of probability or *stochastic discount factors* turn out to be equal to the *marginal derived utility* of the representative investor, as in discrete time and as we assumed in the CIR continuous-time pseudo-equilibrium. Notice once again that, in the present setting, thanks to the one-shot global optimization, we have obtained the results *without the Markov* assumption.

It is clear by simple comparison of (12.8) and (12.14) that, from an arbitrary, decentralized multiple-investor equilibrium we have constructed a centralized, representative investor that prices securities the same way as each and every individual investor. As in chapter 4, we can represent the situation as in figure 4.6.

To calculate an equilibrium allocation, therefore, all we have to do is solve the system formed by (12.12) and (12.13) to get $\{c^m(t)\}_{m=1}^{M}$ and $\xi(t)$ as functions of $\sum_{m=1}^{M} e^m(t)$ and $\{1/\lambda_0^m\}_{m=1}^{M}$, thus getting (12.10). *There is one such system to be solved for each point in time and each current state of nature.* The scalars $\{1/\lambda_0^m\}$ can then be obtained to satisfy the investor budget constraints (12.7).

In this, the crucial simplification does not so much emerge from the representative-investor concept but from the global Lagrange formulation, which bypasses entirely the prices of traded securities and portfolio decisions.

12.4 Asset Pricing in Equilibrium

The stochastic discount factors $\xi(t)$ are all we need to price all securities, that is, to derive the riskless rate r dynamics as well as the price level S for securities paying a continuous dividend process $\iota(t)$.

Since the ξ process is strictly positive, we know that it can always be written as an exponential martingale. Actually, it can always be written as the product of an artificial discount factor, which is positive, and an exponential martingale. This simple reasoning suggests to us separating the process ξ into two processes: $\xi = \eta/B$ where η is the exponential martingale for some adapted market-price-of-risk process κ. To separate ξ into η and B, apply Itô's lemma to ξ in the form (12.10) on the one hand, to $\xi = \eta/B$ on the other, and compare the SDE coefficients. That separation provides, as we know, the SDE (6.17) for $\xi(t)$ and gives us some information on the interest rate, and risk premium, in equilibrium.

We assume an exchange, not a production, economy, so that the SDE coefficients of aggregate consumption $\bar{c}$, which is defined as the sum of aggregate endowment and dividends, are exogenously given:

$$\bar{c}(t) = \bar{c}(0) + \int_0^t \mu_{\bar{c}}(s)ds + \int_0^t \sigma_{\bar{c}}(s)dw(s) \tag{12.15}$$

Applying Itô's lemma to both sides of (12.14), and recalling from equation (6.17) or (8.16) the SDE for $\xi(t)$ we get:

$$\bar{u}_{\bar{c},t}(\bar{c}(t),t)dt + \bar{u}_{\bar{c},\bar{c}}(\bar{c}(t),t)\mu_{\bar{c}}(t)dt$$

$$+\frac{1}{2}\bar{u}_{\bar{c},\bar{c},\bar{c}}(\bar{c}(t),t)\sigma_{\bar{c}}(s)\sigma_{\bar{c}}(s)^{\mathsf{T}}dt + \bar{u}_{\bar{c},\bar{c}}(\bar{c}(t),t)\sigma_{\bar{c}}(t)dw(t)$$

$$= -r(t)\xi(t)dt - \xi(t)\kappa(t)^{\mathsf{T}}dw(t)$$

Identifying terms, the price of risk κ and the rate of interest r are given by:

$$\kappa(t)^{\mathsf{T}} = -\frac{\bar{u}_{\bar{c},\bar{c}}(\bar{c}(t),t)}{\bar{u}_{\bar{c}}(\bar{c}(t),t)}\sigma_{\bar{c}}(t) \equiv \bar{A}(\bar{c}(t),t)\sigma_{\bar{c}}(t) \tag{12.16}$$

$$r(t) = -\frac{\bar{u}_{\bar{c},t}(\bar{c}(t),t)}{\bar{u}_{\bar{c}}(\bar{c}(t),t)} - \frac{\bar{u}_{\bar{c},\bar{c}}(\bar{c}(t),t)}{\bar{u}_{\bar{c}}(\bar{c}(t),t)}\mu_{\bar{c}}(s) - \frac{1}{2}\frac{\bar{u}_{\bar{c},\bar{c},\bar{c}}(\bar{c}(t),t)}{\bar{u}_{\bar{c}}(\bar{c}(t),t)}\sigma_{\bar{c}}(s)\sigma_{\bar{c}}(s)^{\mathsf{T}}$$

$$= -\frac{\bar{u}_{\bar{c},t}(\bar{c}(t),t)}{\bar{u}_{\bar{c}}(\bar{c}(t),t)} + \bar{A}(\bar{c}(t),t)\mu_{\bar{c}}(s) \tag{12.17}$$

$$-\frac{1}{2}\bar{P}(\bar{c}(t),t)\bar{A}(\bar{c}(t),t)\sigma_{\bar{c}}(s)\sigma_{\bar{c}}(s)^{\mathsf{T}}$$

where $\bar{A}$ is the absolute risk aversion of the representative investor and $\bar{P}$ is his absolute prudence.[7]

12.4.1 The Riskless Security

Equation (12.17) says that the equilibrium interest rate is the sum of the following:

- the rate of impatience,[8]

- a term proportional to the drift of aggregate consumption $\mu_{\bar{c}}$ with a coefficient equal to the representative investor's (or aggregate) risk aversion. With positive risk aversion this adjustment is positive, and the equilibrium interest rate is greater than the rate of impatience. To hold the riskless security, risk-averse investors require a greater return. Here, risk aversion really stands for the (inverse of) the elasticity of intertemporal substitution, which is defined in section 20.3.

- a term proportional to the instantaneous variance of consumption $\sigma_c \sigma_c^{\mathsf{T}}$, with a coefficient equal to the central planner's risk aversion times his prudence. With positive risk aversion and prudence the second adjustment is negative, and the equilibrium interest rate is reduced as compared to the case in which there is no volatility in aggregate consumption ($\sigma_c^{\mathsf{T}} \sigma_c = 0$). Prudence, if positive, lowers the riskless rate with respect to the zero-prudence level. Prudence depends on concavity of marginal utility. With positive prudence the representative investor has an additional positive demand for savings that is analogous to the *precautionary demand for savings* (see Kimball (1990) and section A.1.2 in appendix A), and the riskless rate is smaller than with zero prudence. Similar comments hold for the other combinations of signs of prudence and risk aversion.

The higher the expected growth rate of output $\mu_{\bar{c}}$, the higher the interest rate must be to prevent excess aggregate demand for borrowing that would be undertaken to invest into the risky asset. Conversely, the higher $\sigma_c \sigma_c^{\mathsf{T}}$, which means the more risky the output process is, the lower interest rates have to be as investors will have a desire to save more, thus lowering interest rates.

---

7 Had we done this derivation starting from individual investors' first-order conditions, instead of the representative agent, we would have been led to define aggregate absolute risk aversion and absolute prudence as follows:

$$\bar{A} \triangleq \frac{1}{\sum_{m=1}^{M} \frac{1}{A^m}}; \quad \bar{P} \triangleq \sum_{m=1}^{M} \left(\frac{\bar{A}}{A^m}\right)^2 P^m$$

8 Indeed, when time factors out as an exponential, the first term would be equal to ρ.

12.4.2   The Market Prices of Risk: CAPM without Markovianity

Equation (12.16) says that the market-price of risk vector κ is equal to the diffusion vector of aggregate consumption, $\sigma_{\bar{c}}$, times aggregate risk aversion. For given dynamics of aggregate resources, the higher is risk aversion in the economy, the higher are both the riskless rate and the risk premium. We turn to them below.

The reader recalls that, in chapter 11, we made the assumption of a Markov setting and derived from it, by dynamic programming, Merton's static and hedging demands, and from them the intertemporal CAPM. If we can draw a CAPM consequence from the current equilibrium, we can conclude that the Markov assumption, initially used by Merton in deriving his CAPM, is actually not needed. We follow Duffie and Zame (1989) in obtaining such a result.

Recalling that $\kappa = \sigma^{-1}(\mu - r\mathcal{S})$, where μ is the vector of returns on risky securities, σ their diffusion matrix and $\mathcal{S}$ their prices, and σ^{-1} exists because of market completeness, we get from (12.16) the following risk-premium vector:

$$\sigma^{-1}(\mu - r\mathcal{S}) = \bar{A}(\bar{c}, t)\sigma_{\bar{c}}^{\mathsf{T}}$$

Recall that SDE coefficients of prices are so far in consumption units. If instead μ and r were percentages, or rates of return, with the volatility matrix redefined the same way we would get:

$$\sigma^{-1}(\mu - r) = \bar{A}(\bar{c}, t)\sigma_{\bar{c}}^{\mathsf{T}} \tag{12.18}$$

which could be written, still in vector notation, as

$$\mu - r = \bar{A}(\bar{c}, t)\sigma \sigma_{\bar{c}}^{\mathsf{T}}$$

where the vector $\sigma\sigma_{\bar{c}}$ contains the covariances between security returns and aggregate consumption, individually denoted as $\sigma_i\sigma_{\bar{c}}$. The last expression says that the excess return on the risky assets is proportional to their covariance with aggregate consumption. The coefficient of proportionality is the absolute risk aversion of the representative investor, who consumes the aggregate consumption $\bar{c}(t)$. Taking one component at a time ($i = 1, .., N$), we can write the excess return of each security i as

$$\mu_i - r = \bar{A}(\bar{c}, t)\sigma_i\sigma_{\bar{c}} \tag{12.19}$$

This is the consumption CAPM (11.17) again.

We suggest that the reader solve exercise 12.1 on this topic.

12.4.3   The Risky Securities

Since stochastic discount factors ξ are now available to us, every consumption stream can be priced taking the expectation of its payoffs discounted for time and preferences, via ξ. This holds for risky assets and wealth. The price process for all securities is given by the equation:

$$S(t) = \frac{1}{\xi(t)} \mathbb{E}_t \left[\int_t^T \xi(s) \iota(s) ds \right] \tag{12.20}$$

$$= \frac{1}{\xi(\bar{c}(t); \{\lambda_0^m\})} \mathbb{E}_t \left[\int_t^T \xi(\bar{c}(s); \{\lambda_0^m\}) \iota(s) ds \right]$$

At each point in time, for given dividends, the previous expression establishes a linear mapping between the N processes that represent dividends and the N processes that represent security prices.

In particular, the total wealth and the financial wealth of investor m can be calculated as:

$$\mathfrak{W}^m(t) = \frac{1}{\xi(\bar{c}(t); \{\lambda_0^m\})} \mathbb{E}_t \left[\int_t^T \xi(\bar{c}(s); \{\lambda_0^m\}) c^m(s) ds \right] \tag{12.21}$$

$$W^m(t) = \frac{1}{\xi(\bar{c}(t); \{\lambda_0^m\})} \mathbb{E}_t \left[\int_t^T \xi(\bar{c}(s); \{\lambda_0^m\}) \left(c^m(s) - e^m(s) \right) ds \right]$$

At this point, we should verify that both the interest rate and the risky securities prices – and, as a consequence, wealth – are Itô processes. This can be done using the fact that the stochastic discount factor ξ is an Itô process, as equation (12.10) says.

We suggest that the reader solve exercises 12.2 and 12.3, in which examples of equilibrium in a complete market with two heterogeneous investors are given.

12.5 Diffusive and Markovian Equilibria

In this section, differently from the rest of the book, we make a distinction between diffusions and Itô processes. Since the relevant quantities of the equilibrium are endogenous, we cannot assume that the continuity in time of the SDE coefficients which guarantees coincidence of the two notions is indeed satisfied.

Let us define a Markovian equilibrium as an equilibrium in which the decisions of all investors and the prices of all securities, jointly with a finite set of state variables, form a Markov process. Define a diffusive equilibrium in an analogous way. We saw above that equilibrium prices are Itô processes. Under which conditions is the equilibrium Markovian? When is it diffusive, and, in particular, when are prices diffusion processes?

The lines below provide an intuitive answer, while the full exposition can be found in Huang (1987).

———————————◆———————————

We know from corollary 7.2 that continuity of the coefficients of a SDE is a sufficient condition for its solution to be a diffusion. The marginal utility of a representative investor is computed as a function of aggregate consumption and the latter equals aggregate endowment. The stochastic discount factor has continuous SDE coefficients if and only if aggregate endowment is a continuous process. If dividends are also diffusion processes, securities' prices are diffusions.

Indeed, Huang proves, in the presence of state variables (that is, $\bar{c}$ is a function of Y and Y behaves as in (9.20)), that, once some technical conditions are met, security prices are diffusions if the following conditions are satisfied:

1. aggregate endowment is a twice differentiable function of the current values of the state variables;

2. the equilibrium consumption of all investors is a strictly positive process;

3. the dividend price process of each and every security is continuous.

Once equilibrium prices are diffusions, we wonder which additional conditions are imposed for the equilibrium to be Markovian. The condition is:

4. the investor endowment process and the risk premium are deterministic functions of the current realization Y_t of the state variables (path independency).

The four conditions above produce a Markovian equilibrium.

Under Markovian assumptions, the process $\mathcal{S}$ in (12.20), can be obtained as a conditional expected value or as the solution $\mathcal{S}(Y, \bar{c}; \{\lambda_0^m\})$ of a linear PDE.

12.6   The Empirical Relevance of State Variables

In this book, we do not devote space to empirical studies of asset pricing. Nevertheless, it might be useful to indicate what role would play, in actual implementations of CAPMs, the state variables Y, which were explicit in chapter 11 and remained implicit (in the form of the abstract and hidden ω) in the current chapter. We might like to know what concrete interpretation they have.[9]

As the name indicates, state variables are variables that describe so exhaustively the state of the economy that we can consider that the economy jointly with the state variables form a Markov stochastic process. In that case, we say that the state variables are "sufficient statistics."

State variables can be of various types. As far as the theoretical model of the economy is concerned, the state variables can be exogenous or endogenous. The borderline between these two categories depends on the model's degree of inclusiveness. If the model is only a model of the financial market taking the rest of the structure of the economy as a given, macroeconomic variables, monetary and fiscal policy variables, and stages of the business cycles would be good examples of exogenous state variables while, in a more ambitious model, some of these might be endogenized. Sometimes, endogenous state variables can proxy for exogenous state variables. For instance, the rate of interest and the slope of the

---

9 We do not synthetize here the results of empirical tests of the CAPM. For an extensive discussion, we suggest Cochrane (2000).

CAPM cross-sectional relation (the so-called "security market line") are sometimes used as state variables.[10]

As far as the empirical implementation is concerned, state variables can be observed or latent. They are observed when the empiricist actually goes out and measures them before he implements the CAPM he wants to test. That would be the case when, for instance, stages of the business cycle are used as state variables. They are latent when the empiricist backs out their behavior – without necessarily giving them a name or interpretation – from the behavior of securities' returns. Then they are "dark matter" that must be there to make sense of the securities' returns, but which we do not observe directly. They could even be unobserved by market participants themselves; see chapter 18.

In the empirical implementation, state variables play *two roles*. First, they help investors forecast future returns that are not IID. In the CAPM all the statistics such as expected returns and covariances are conditional statistics, calculated conditional on the current value of state variables. Second, when state variables are stochastic, investors behave as described in chapter 9. They anticipate future shifts in the state variables, positioning their portfolios for reinvestment risk and trying to hedge against those shifts of the investment opportunity set. We called the portfolio components thus created "intertemporal hedging" portfolios, there being one for each state variable. We have seen in chapter 11 that these generated risk premia or "priced risk factor" (as in Merton's Intertemporal CAPM or ICAPM (11.1)) over and beyond the risk factor created by the market portfolio. We have also seen that, with time-additive utility, all the risk premia could be collapsed into one, which was the consumption risk premia (11.7), so that the state variables did not create additional risk premia over and beyond consumption risk. When implementing the consumption CAPM, the second role of state variables disappears but the first role remains.

In general equilibrium, even the return on the market portfolio can be endogenized (see above section 12.4.3) and expressed as a function of changes in state variables, so that all risk premia can be regarded as premia for the risks contained in state variables only. In this sense, state variables can be regarded as risk factors as in the *factor model* (or Arbitrage Pricing Theory) of Ross (1978). In implementations of this approach, state variables remain latent. Factor models link expected returns to state-variables, the so-called factors, in a linear way.[11] They have been extensively tested on data. Expected returns of investor securities or portfolios are the dependent variable, while covariances with (or betas against) factors are the independent or explanatory variables.

So, there are now two implementation possibilities: either use a factor model with more than one factor, in the spirit of the Arbitrage Pricing Theory of Ross, or use an intertemporal CAPM (ICAPM) with well-specified state variables. What is the difference? The most

---

10 See Nielsen and Vassalou (2006).

11 For an extensive treatment, see for instance Singleton (2006).

important single issue is probably the one pointed out by Brennan, Wang, and Xia (2004). The state variables in ICAPM models should be able to predict future returns. They should not be simply correlated with them contemporaneously, as in empirical factor models. Surprisingly, ICAPM models are still in their infancy. The main contributions are Campbell (1993), Vassalou (2003), and Brennan, Wang, and Xia (2004).

Campbell (1993) produces a linearization of the pricing model in the presence of state variables, and suggests to test the restrictions placed by the approximate intertemporal model on cross-sectional prices of risk factors.

Vassalou starts from one of the most well-known factor models, Fama and French (1993). Fama and French obtain explanatory power with a factor model in which the factors are the spread between returns for firms with an high-market-to-book ratio and firms with a low ratio (the HML factor) and the spread between returns of small versus big firms (the SMB factor). They argue that HML and SMB act as state variables in the context of Merton's (1973) ICAPM.

Vassalou (2003) shows that news related to future GDP growth, with evident macroeconomic interpretation, constitute important factors in equity returns, and much of the ability of the Fama-French factors to explain the cross section of equity returns is due to news they contain related to future GDP growth. One can tentatively conclude that what matters, after all, is the growth of GDP, and not the Fama and French factors *per se*.

Brennan *et al.* (2004) evaluate an ICAPM with just two factors, which are the short-term rate of interest and the maximum Sharpe ratio that can be achieved instantaneously by forming a portfolio of existing securities. Assuming that both these state variables can be described by an Ornstein-Uhlenbeck process, and taking as dataset the returns on several bond-and-stock US portfolios, including the Fama-and-French ones, over the time span 1952-2000, Brennan *et al.* find that their two-factor ICAPM does a good job in explaining returns. Its performance is at least as good as that of the Fama and French factor model.

Overall, as we see from Vassalou's and Brennan *et al.*'s paper, there is a trend towards reconciling purely empirical factor models and ICAPMs as far as stock returns are concerned. This trend parallels the search for an empirically tested, satisfactory relation between excess returns in the bond market and their theoretical determinants, which we will summarize in chapter 16.

12.7 Benchmark Example (continued)

The study of equilibrium in complete markets when investors have a power utility function has at least two subcases: one in which investors are homogeneous, in the sense that they have the same risk aversion and time preference parameters γ and ρ, and one in which they are heterogenous in those parameters. The homogeneous case can be written as the single-investor production model of CIR, which we treated in chapter 11 or it can be treated as in section 12.7.1 below. The case in which investors are heterogeneous will be treated in section 12.7.2 below.

12.7.1 Equilibria with Black-Scholes Securities

He and Leland (1993) provide the conditions under which strict-sense Black-Scholes prices can prevail in general equilibrium. They examine a complete, finite-horizon market, with a single risky security and a representative investor whose utility function is additive over time, with time factoring out. Taking the percentage volatility σ of the unique stock price S as given and constant, they first show that, for any given utility function, there exists a percentage drift $\mu(S, t)$ that makes the corresponding price an equilibrium one. A necessary and sufficient condition is that μ solve the PDE

$$\frac{1}{2}\sigma^2 S^2 \mu_{SS} + S\mu\mu_S + \mu_t = 0 \tag{12.22}$$

with terminal condition

$$\mu(S, T) = r + \sigma^2 A_r(S)$$

where A_r is the relative risk aversion of the representative investor.

We can verify that a power utility function ($A_r = 1 - \gamma$) admits Geometric Wiener process as a solution. Indeed, substitute $\mu = r - \sigma^2(\gamma - 1)$ into the PDE (12.22), and observe that for this drift $\mu_t = \mu_S = \mu_{SS} = 0$, since the drift is constant with respect to both the price level and time. The LHS of the PDE equals zero all the time, so that it is trivially satisfied.

A similar result can be obtained by letting the horizon go to infinity and allowing for a slightly more general utility function.

We suggest that the reader solve exercise 12.4.

12.7.2 Equilibria with Heterogeneous Power-Utility Investors

Consider an economy in which power-utility investors differ in their relative risk aversions, as in Dumas (1989). The setting is slightly different from the above, since the horizon is infinite and the economy is a production and not an exchange economy.

Investors belong to two groups: they are either logarithmic investors ($\gamma \to 0$) or CRRA investors with $\gamma < 1$. Denote with $c^m, m = 1, 2$, the consumption of the CRRA investor and log investor. Their optimization problems, as described by (12.1) are

$$\max_{\{c^1(t)\}} \mathbb{E}\left\{\int_0^\infty e^{-\rho t}\frac{(c^1(t))^\gamma - 1}{\gamma}dt\right\} ; \max_{\{c^2(t)\}} \mathbb{E}\left\{\int_0^\infty e^{-\rho t}\log c^2(t)dt\right\}$$

Consumers have access to an instantaneous riskless bond in zero net supply, for which we use the notation $S_0(t)$, and to a risky investment the price of which is $S(t)$. The market value of the risky investment is equal to the physical capital stock invested in a constant-returns-to-scale technology. This means that the dynamics of S is

$$dS = \left(\mu S - c^1 - c^2\right) dt + \sigma S dw$$

with $\mu, \sigma \in \mathbb{R}_{++}$. The market is complete so that there exists a representative investor whose utility function is described by (12.11). With two investors, his utility is

$$\bar{u}(\bar{c}, t) \triangleq \max_{\{c^1(t), c^2(t)\}} (1 - \varpi)e^{-\rho t}\frac{c^1(t)^\gamma - 1}{\gamma} + \varpi e^{-\rho t} \log c^2(t)$$

where ϖ is the welfare weight of the log investor, subject to:

$$c^1(t) + c^2(t) = \bar{c}(t)$$

Unlike in an exchange economy, the representative investor solves a dynamic program because he must decide how much to invest into the physical system. Dumas (1989) writes down the following ODE for the undiscounted value function $L(S)$ or lifetime utility of the representative investor:

$$0 \equiv \varpi e^{-\rho t} \log c^2(t) + (1 - \varpi)e^{-\rho t}\left(c^1(t)^\gamma - 1\right)/\gamma - \rho L(S)$$

$$+L'(S)\left(\alpha S - c^1 - c^2\right) + \frac{1}{2}L''(S)\sigma^2 S^2$$

The ODE is solved (numerically) with the following first-order conditions:

$$L'(S) = \varpi c^2(t)^{-1} = (1 - \varpi)c^1(t)^{\gamma - 1}$$

The portfolio selection and consumption decisions of log investors are straightforward. That makes it easy to determine the way the wealth is shared between the two groups of investors (the *wealth-sharing rule*) as well as the evolution (contraction or expansion) of the economy over time. For most parameter configurations, the equilibrium is not stationary in that the less risk-averse investor ultimately captures all the wealth and the consumption. But some configurations are found for which the equilibrium is stationary.

The rate of interest follows from the lifetime utility of the representative investor in a way similar to equation (12.18) above:

$$\mu - r(t) = -\frac{L''(S(t))}{L'(S(t))}S(t)\sigma^2$$

The rate r is always an increasing function of S so that the correlation between output shocks and the rate of interest is equal to $+1$. Since μ is fixed, the opposite holds for the risk premium. An example of its drift and diffusion of the interest rate is presented in figure 12.1.

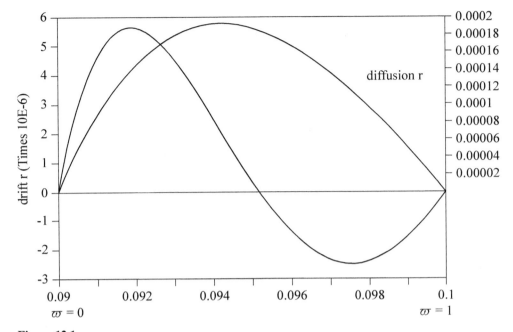

Figure 12.1

"Phase diagram" of the rate of interest in the Dumas (1989) two-person dynamic equilibrium. The diagram shows the drift and diffusion of the equilibrium rate of interest as a function of the rate of interest itself, the value of which is on the x-axis. The range of possible values of the rate of interest is set by the extremes $\varpi = 0$ and $\varpi = 1$ of the welfare weight of the log investor.

12.8   Conclusion

From the point of view of Economics, the problem of equilibrium in a complete financial market is basically solved. As we know, in such a market, investors are able, in a first stage of their optimization, to calculate their optimal consumption path, separate from portfolio choice, securities prices, and even the menu of existing securities. Therefore, it is a simple matter to first solve for the equilibrium in the market for goods. Consumption demand is equated to the aggregate endowment and the solution of that equation provides the consumption sharing rule and state prices. There exists a representative investor but the solution can be obtained with or without making use of it.

Once state prices are known, the prices of existing securities and the financial wealth of all investors, by martingale pricing, are just expected values to be computed. Once these are known, the paths of securities prices and the paths of financial wealths can be compared with each other to back out the portfolios that implement or finance or replicate, for each investor, his equilibrium consumption plan, exactly as was done in previous chapters to replicate contingent claims.

There only remain practical or computational difficulties. The consumption sharing rule is often only obtainable in an implicit form only, so that a numerical solution will be needed. And some of the expected values may not be at all straightforward to compute, technically speaking.

Exercises

12.1. Postulate an Itô process for the aggregate endowment such as:

$$d\bar{c}(t) = \mu_{\bar{c}}(t)dt + \sigma_{\bar{c}}(t)^\mathsf{T}dw(t)$$

From the ARCs:

$$\sum_{m=1}^{M} c^m(t) = \bar{c}(t) \tag{12.23}$$

and the first-order conditions for individual optimality

$$\frac{\partial}{\partial c}u^m\left(c^m(t), t\right) = \lambda_0^m \xi(t)$$

obtain an expression for the equilibrium rate of interest r and for the equilibrium price of risk κ. Hint: in the text, the equilibrium interest rate and price of risk were obtained from the representative investor solution. Here obtain them directly from the individual-investor problem. Consider the clearing condition (12.23) and substitute the first-order condition for consumption in it, equate the coefficients of their SDEs, differentiate with respect to time, equate the stochastic discount factors of all individuals, and substitute back in the time differentials.

12.2. Consider an economy with two investors featuring power utility but heterogeneous preference parameters, that is,

$$u^m(c^m, t) = e^{-\rho^m t}\frac{c^{\gamma^m} - 1}{\gamma^m}, \quad m = 1, 2$$

Let the sum of their risk aversions be equal to 1. There are N risky securities – with price vector S – paying a continuous dividend $\iota_i, i = 1, \ldots, N$ and an aggregate endowment process $\bar{c}$, depending on a K-dimensional Wiener process:

$$d\bar{c}(t) = d(\iota^\mathsf{T}(t)\mathbf{1}_N) = \mu_{\bar{c}}(t)dt + \sigma_{\bar{c}}(t)^\mathsf{T}dw(t)$$

Assuming $N = K$, determine the equilibrium stochastic discount factor and state the conditions for its existence and uniqueness.

12.3. Consider the same setup as in the previous exercise and investigate the equilibrium solution when the relative risk aversion of the first investor is twice that of the second one; in particular consider the case in which $\gamma^1 - 1 = 2 \times (\gamma^2 - 1) = 4$.

12.4. Recall the HARA utility introduced in section A.1.3:

$$u(x) = \frac{1-\gamma}{\gamma}\left(\eta + \frac{\delta x}{1-\gamma}\right)^{\gamma}$$

where $\gamma \neq 1, \delta > 0, \eta + \frac{\delta x}{1-\gamma} > 0, \eta = 1$ if $\gamma \to -\infty$.
Consider the following choice of parameters:

$$\delta = 1, \gamma = 0, \eta \geq 0$$

We know from section 12.7.1 that a necessary and sufficient condition for a constant-volatility equilibrium price is that the expected instantaneous return, $\mu(S,t)$, satisfy PDE (12.22) and its associated boundary condition.
For the sake of simplicity, assume a riskless rate equal to zero.

a. Show that absolute tolerance is not only affine in consumption x, as for any HARA function, but increasing in it.

b. Show that the equilibrium expected instantaneous return is

$$\mu(S,t) = \sigma^2 \frac{S}{S+\eta}$$

V APPLICATIONS AND EXTENSIONS

13 Solution Techniques and Applications

As we enter Part V of this book, which will be devoted to various applications of increasing complexity, we need to enrich our toolbox.

With the notable exception of the celebrated Black-Scholes formula (see chapter 6), problems in Financial Economics rarely lend themselves to explicit and analytical solutions, one among many reasons being the lack of linearity resulting from the optimization of a concave utility function. It is, therefore, often necessary to resort to approximations, or to numerical or simulated solutions.

Although there exist several excellent and detailed textbooks, written by authors more competent on this matter than we are,[1] the economist might still find use for a rapid overview of that field, so that, after having written down the system of equations to be solved, he or she will not find himself or herself in a *cul-de-sac*. This chapter will not expose a well-structured body of methodology. It will be more like a somewhat disparate toolbox.

We refer to four types of solution techniques, with a section for each:

- probabilistic methods (section 13.1) aim to compute quantities of interest, such as security prices, which are conditional expected values, directly from the joint probability distribution of the processes under consideration when it is known,

- simulation methods (section 13.2) may be viewed as numerical analogs of the probabilistic methods: they aim to compute conditional expected values by taking an average over many paths obtained from random draws,

- analytical methods (section 13.3) provide the needed quantities as solutions of ODEs or PDEs,

- numerical methods (section 13.5) are the last resort to obtain numerical estimates of quantities of interest, be they solutions of differential equations or the direct result of discrete formulations of economic problems.

---

1 See Quarteroni, Sacco, and Saleri (2000) and Fusai and Roncoroni (2008). A hands-on exposition of many of these methods is available in Shaw (1998).

13.1 Probabilistic Methods

Conceptually, it is very helpful to keep track of the movement of underlying processes, in the form of transition probabilities. If the solution for a quantity of interest is the conditional expected value of a random variable, that is already a big step towards the final solution. It only remains to then compute that expected value. The reader is reminded of the Feynman-Kac formula (6.31), which creates a link between the solution of PDEs written on a process and conditional expected values of future values of that process. As an application of the formula (or as an application of the "martingale" reasoning), one way to obtain the value of an option is to obtain the probabilities of transition of the stochastic process. When they are known (for example, lognormal distribution for Geometric Brownian motion, densities of the Ornstein-Uhlenbeck process (see the Vasicek term-structure model in section 16.2.1), densities of the square root process (see the Cox-Ingersoll-Ross term-structure model in section 16.2.3 etc.), the problem is solved. But where are they known from? The transition densities being a type of conditional expected value, they can be known as solutions of differential equations, in which case probabilistic methods are a by-product of analytical methods. Or they can be known via the device of integral transforms. We discuss each in the next subsections.

13.1.1 Probabilities of Transitions as Solutions of PDEs

13.1.1.1 PDEs for transition densities

As an illustration, consider the simple one-dimensional Markovian case with drift $r(S, t)S$ and diffusion $\sigma(S, t)S$. Denote by $p(x, t; y, T)$ the probability density of a transition of the process S from level x at time t to level y at time T; $T \geq t$. This density function can be viewed in two ways (the two corresponding PDEs are called "adjoint equations"):

1. Holding the terminal point (y, T) fixed, the density function $p(x, t; y, T)$ can be viewed as a function of x and t. This is the "backward approach." The function $p(x, t; y, T)$ satisfies the so-called Chapman-Kolmogorov equation:

$$r(x, t)x\frac{\partial p}{\partial x}(x, t; y, T) + \frac{1}{2}\sigma^2(x, t)x^2\frac{\partial^2 p}{\partial x^2}(x, t; y, T) + \frac{\partial p}{\partial t}(x, t; y, T) = 0 \qquad (13.1)$$

subject to the boundary (or *terminal*) condition:

$$p(x, T; y, T) = \delta_0(y - x) \qquad (13.2)$$

where $\delta_0(\cdot)$ is the Dirac function located at zero. This boundary condition arises from the requirement that:

$$\int_{-\infty}^{y} p(x, T; u, T)du = \begin{cases} 0 \text{ if } x \geq y \\ 1 \text{ if } x \leq y \end{cases}$$

The Chapman-Kolmogorov equation is a direct result of the Law of Iterated Expectations (section 2.2.1). The conditional expected value of a random variable viewed as a function of the current time, must be a martingale. Here $\int^y p(x, t; u, T)du$ is the conditional expected value of the random variable that takes the value 1 when the process started at x at time t reaches a value lower than or equal to y at time T and takes the value 0 otherwise. Applying Itô's lemma to write that the drift of the density is equal to zero, it can be seen easily that (13.1) follows.

2. Holding the initial point (x, t) fixed, the same density function $p(x, t; y, T)$ can be viewed as a function of y and T.[2] This is the "forward approach." The function $p(x, t; y, T)$ satisfies the so-called Fokker-Planck equation:

$$-\frac{\partial}{\partial y}\left[r(y, T)yp(x, t; y, T)\right] \tag{13.4}$$

$$+\frac{\partial^2}{\partial y^2}\left[\frac{1}{2}\sigma^2(y, T)y^2 p(x, t; y, T)\right] = \frac{\partial p}{\partial T}(x, t; y, T)$$

subject to the boundary (or *initial*) condition:

$$p(x, t; y, t) = \delta_0(y - x) \tag{13.5}$$

The Fokker-Planck equation is obtained from the Chapman-Kolmogorov equation by integration by parts. The reader will derive it by solving exercise 13.1.

In cases in which the process admits a long-run stationary density $\pi(y)$ (for example, when $r(S, t) = r$ and $\sigma(S, t) = \sigma$), the stationary density function (defined by $\partial p/\partial T = 0$)[3] can be obtained by solving the following Fokker-Planck equation:

$$-\frac{\partial}{\partial y}\left[r(y)y\pi(y)\right] + \frac{\partial^2}{\partial y^2}\left[\frac{1}{2}\sigma^2(y)y^2\pi(y)\right] = 0 \tag{13.6}$$

subject to:

$$\pi(y) \geq 0; \int \pi(y)dy = 1$$

The reader can solve exercise 13.2.

The Black-Scholes PDE is a backward-type equation for the calculation of the conditionally expected payoff of the option. For European options, it is possible to derive a "forward" option pricing PDE analogous to the Fokker-Planck equation that applies to the

---

2 Here is another way of saying the same thing. The Chapman-Kolmogorov integral equation relates the transitions at three points in time t_1, t_2, t_3 in that order on the time line, exploiting the Markov property:

$$p(x, t_1; y, t_3) = \int p(x, t_1; z, t_2) \times p(z, t_2; y, t_3)\, dz \tag{13.3}$$

Letting t_2 approach t_3, this integral equation gives the forward or Fokker-Planck differential equation (13.4). Letting t_2 approach t_1, this integral equation gives the backward or Chapman-Kolmogorov differential equation (13.1).

3 A weaker definition is: $\partial p/\partial x = 0$ (independence of initial conditions).

density $p(x, t; y, T)$. It would apply instead to the function giving the price of an option as a function of the strike and the maturity date (see exercise 3). For a given value of the price of the underlying at a fixed point in time t, the solution function of the forward equation gives in one go the prices at time t of options of all maturities and strikes.

13.1.1.2 Boundary conditions

Sometimes, the process S is not free to roam over the entire real line in accordance with the SDE that describes it. Note first that, if $x > 0$, $r \geq 0$, and $\sigma > 0$, the process can never reach the point $S(t) = 0$ at any time t. That point is called a "natural" or "unattainable" boundary. This type of boundary is imbedded in the SDE and requires no further treatment.

Sometimes, however, some boundary behavior will be superimposed on the SDE. The process may at some point be either "absorbed" or "reflected" (for instance, arrangements must set the fate of a investor who is bankrupt). Then the PDE holds on a restricted domain only. On the boundaries of that domain, boundary conditions (that is, *side* conditions) are then appended to the PDEs (13.4) and (13.1). For instance, for the backward equation, they are:

- "upper" reflection at point a: the domain of the function p being restricted to: $x \leq a$; $y < a$, the boundary condition is

$$\frac{\partial p}{\partial x}(a, t; y, T) = 0$$

By way of justification of the boundary condition, recall that $\int_{-\infty}^{y} p(x, t; u, T) du$ is the expected value of a random variable that takes the value 1 when the process that started at x at time t reaches a value lower than or equal to y at time T, and the value 0 otherwise. That expected value, seen as a process over t, is a martingale. When the variable x takes a value in a neighborhood of a, the expected value is based on the knowledge of the fact that the current position of the process is close to the reflection point. It is known that the process is going to be reflected there and temporarily halted. Hence, at that point the expected value must be unchanging (stationary).

- "upper" absorption at point b ($x \leq b$; $y < b$): the domain of the function p being restricted to: $x \leq b$; $y < b$, the boundary condition is

$$p(b, t; y, T) = 0 \text{ for any } T \geq t$$

By way of justification, recall also that $\int_{-\infty}^{y} p(b, t; u, T) du$ is the probability of the process that started at b at time t reaching a value lower than or equal to y at time T. Since $y < b$, if the process is absorbed at b, it is true that: $\int_{-\infty}^{y} p(b, t; u, T) du = 0$.

Corresponding boundary conditions could be appended to the forward equation.

The reader can solve exercise 13.4, which involves two such boundary conditions, holding, however, not at a preset point but at a floating point, which means "a point to be determined."

13.1.2 Integral Representation of the Solution (Characteristic Functions)

Sometimes, the transition densities of the process cannot be obtained but their characteristic functions can. Then, a conditional expected value, such as the price of a European option, can be obtained from a Fourier inversion.

Definition 13.1 *For parameters x, t, u, the "characteristic function" of a process X is a function of χ equal to:*

$$\mathbb{E}\left[e^{\chi X(u)}|X(t) = x\right] \tag{13.7}$$

The characteristic function is a "Fourier transform" of the transition density when χ is a pure imaginary number (such as $i \times \chi$, where i is the unit complex number).[4] The previous definition is easily extended to multidimensional processes X (in that case, χ is a vector).

The characteristic function of the probability distribution of the terminal value of the *logarithm* of the stock price is:

$$\varphi(x, t; \chi, T) \triangleq \mathbb{E}\left\{e^{i\chi \ln S(T)}|S(t) = x\right\} \tag{13.8}$$

or:

$$\varphi(x, t; \chi, T) \triangleq \mathbb{E}\left\{S^{i\chi}(T)|S(t) = x\right\}$$

Note that the integral (the expected value) is taken over the terminal stock price.

It is obvious from its definition that the function $\varphi(x, t; \chi, T)$, viewed as a function of x and t only, being a conditional expected value, must satisfy the *backward* equation:[5]

$$r(x, t)x\frac{\partial \varphi}{\partial x}(x, t; \chi, T) + \frac{1}{2}\sigma^2(x, t)x^2\frac{\partial^2 \varphi}{\partial x^2}(x, t; \chi, T) + \frac{\partial \varphi}{\partial t}(x, t; \chi, T) = 0 \tag{13.9}$$

with the boundary condition:

$$\varphi(x, T; \chi, T) = e^{i\chi \ln x} \tag{13.10}$$

---

4 When χ is a real number, this is a Laplace transform.

5 This method of characteristic functions is distinct from the textbook Fourier-transform technique for solving PDEs. In that technique, one applies the Fourier transformation to the unknown function, integrating over the exogenous variable (here, x). In equation (13.9), that is not what we are doing. Had we started from a forward equation, however, and transformed it the textbook way, we would have obtained the same (13.9).

After solving the PDE, the transition probability density is obtained by a Fourier inversion (canned Fast Fourier Transform codes for integration are available):[6]

$$p(x,t;y,T) = \frac{1}{2\pi} \int_{-\infty}^{\infty} \text{Re}\left[e^{-i\chi \ln y} \varphi(x,t;\chi,T)\right] d\chi$$

The power of the method arises from the terminal condition (13.10) defining the characteristic function. It is smooth, unlike the boundary conditions (13.5, 13.2) of the direct transition-probability problem.

As an example, consider the special case in which the "coefficients" r and σ are constant, one can guess a solution of the form:

$$\varphi(x,t;\chi,T) = e^{H(T-t)+i\chi \ln x} \tag{13.11}$$

where $H(\cdot)$ is a function for which the boundary condition (13.10) is $H(0) = 0$. Substituting (13.11) into (13.9) gives:

$$ri\chi - \frac{1}{2}\sigma^2\left(i\chi + \chi^2\right) + H'(T-t) = 0$$

which is an easily solvable ODE for the unknown function H of time.

That example is not convincing testimony to the power of the method since the solution for the transition probability, in the case of the example, is known anyway. We shall encounter a more convincing example when we study Heston's stochastic volatility model (section 17.2.2) and affine processes below in section 13.3.2.

The reader should consider solving exercise 13.5.

13.1.3   Other Uses of Integral Representations

A number of expansion methods allow the empiricist to obtain approximations to the distribution function without performing a Fourier inversion. The ancestor of expansion methods is the Gram-Charlier expansion, introduced into the field of Finance by Jarrow and Rudd (1978).[7] Consider the first coefficients of an expansion of the logarithm of the characteristic function against $i\chi$:[8]

$$\ln \mathbb{E}\left[e^{i\chi X}\right] = \kappa_1 i\chi - \frac{1}{2}\kappa_2 \chi^2 + \frac{1}{3!}\kappa_3 (i\chi)^3 + \frac{1}{4!}\kappa_4 \chi^4 + \cdots$$

---

6 Equivalently, the cumulative probability of transition $P(x,t;y,T) \triangleq \int_y^{\infty} p(x,t;u,T)du$ is given by the Lévy formula:

$$P(x,t;y,T) = \frac{1}{2} + \frac{1}{\pi} \int_0^{\infty} \text{Re}\left[\frac{e^{-i\phi \ln y} \varphi(x,t,\phi,T)}{i\phi}\right] d\phi$$

This is, in fact, the formula used by Heston (see chapter 17). See, for instance, Fusai and Roncoroni (2008).

7 See also Backus *et al.* (1997) and Jondeau and Rockinger (2001).

8 The logarithm of the characteristic function is often called the "cumulant generating function."

It is shown in Statistics that the coefficients are the "cumulants" of the unknown distribution of X, which are defined as:

$$\kappa_1 \triangleq \mathbb{E}[X]$$
$$\kappa_2 \triangleq \mathbb{E}\left[(X - \kappa_1)^2\right] = \sigma^2$$
$$\kappa_3 \triangleq \mathbb{E}\left[(X - \kappa_1)^3\right]$$
$$\kappa_4 \triangleq \mathbb{E}\left[(X - \kappa_1)^4\right] - 3(\kappa_2)^2$$

The cumulants are related to skewness γ_1 and kurtosis γ_2 of X by the definitions of the latter:

$$\gamma_1 \triangleq \frac{\kappa_3}{(\kappa_2)^{\frac{3}{2}}}; \gamma_2 \triangleq \frac{\kappa_4}{(\kappa_2)^2}$$

A Gram-Charlier expansion generates an approximate density for a random variable that differs from the standard normal in having potentially non-zero skewness and excess kurtosis. It defines an approximate density for a variable u with zero expected value and unit standard deviation as being equal to:

$$n(u) - \gamma_1 \frac{1}{3!} n'''(u) + \gamma_2 \frac{1}{4!} n''''(u)$$

where $n(u) \triangleq (2\pi)^{-1/2} \exp(-u^2/2)$ is the standard normal density. If u were normal, only the first term of this sum would be present. The price of an option, for instance, can then be obtained as a deviation from the Black-Scholes formula, to the degree that the state-price density differs from the normal distribution:

$$C(x, t) \simeq SN(d(x)) - KN(d(x) - \sigma)$$
$$+ Sn(d(x)) \times \sigma \times \left[\frac{\gamma_1}{3!} (2\sigma - d(x)) - \frac{\gamma_2}{4!} \left(1 - d(x)^2 + 3d(x)\sigma - 3\sigma^2\right)\right]$$

where $N(\cdot)$ is the standard Gaussian cumulative distribution function.

Chiarella *et al.* (2004) have extended the method to American options. Ian Martin (2013) has applied a related technique to obtain equilibrium security prices in an exchange economy where the growth of the payouts on the securities is IID over time. More general expansion forms are called "saddlepoint approximations." See Aït-Sahalia and Yu (2006) and Rogers and Zane (1999).

The reader can now solve exercise 13.6.

13.2 Simulation Methods

The calculation of an expected value can be conveniently done by simulation. The expected value is approximated by the *average across paths* of the values reached by a random variable at a fixed point in the future. When valuing European options, all that is needed is the distribution of the terminal payoff. If the distribution is known, the simulation of a random variable presents no special difficulty. In some cases, however, the distribution is not known or it is necessary to *simulate paths* of stochastic processes. This requires a great deal of care.[9]

13.2.1 Euler-Matsuyama Scheme

Consider a SDE:

$$dX(t) = a(X(t), t)dt + \sigma(X(t), t)dw(t)$$

A simple simulation method, which is called the Euler-Matsuyama scheme, consists in discretizing the variation of X over the interval of time $[t, t+h]$. It amounts to assuming falsely that a and σ are constant over the interval of time:

$$X(t+h) = X(t) + a(X(t), t) \times h + \sigma(X(t), t) \times \varepsilon(h)$$

where $\varepsilon(h)$ is a normally distributed random variable with variance h, which has the same distribution as $w(t+h) - w(t)$. This "explicit" scheme – that is, involving the unknown $X(t+h)$ on the LHS of the equation only – would not be accurate because any error made on the second term (arising from the variation of σ) would have an *expected value of its square* of order of magnitude h, compared to the drift term, which would contain a squared error of order h^2.

13.2.2 Mil'shtein's Scheme

It is possible to refine the simulation scheme to achieve higher orders of convergence so that fewer time steps are needed without a sacrifice on accuracy and convergence.[10] Focusing on the variation of σ, by repeated application of Itô's lemma, Mil'shtein has shown that the

---

9 For extensive treatments and surveys of this delicate matter, see: Kloeden and Platen (1999), Talay (1994), and Higham (2001).

10 In order to quantify the size of the error in relation to the size of the time step, two concepts of "convergence" have been introduced. Kloeden and Platen (1992) define them as follows:

We shall say that an approximating process Y converges in the strong sense with order $\gamma \in (0, \infty]$ to the true process X if there exists a finite constant K and a positive constant δ_0 such that

$$\mathbb{E}(|X(t) - Y(t)|) \le K\delta^\gamma$$

for any t and any time discretization with maximum step size $\delta \in (0, \delta_0)$.

We shall say that a time discrete approximation Y converges in the weak sense with order $\beta \in (0, \infty]$ to the true process X if, for any function g of no more than polynomial growth, there exists a finite constant K and a positive constant δ_0 such that

$$|\mathbb{E}(g(X(t))) - \mathbb{E}(g(Y(t)))| \le K\delta^\beta$$

for any time t and any time discretization with maximum step size $\delta \in (0, \delta_0)$.

It has been shown that the Euler scheme delivers strong order of convergence equal to $\gamma = 1/2$ and weak order of convergence $\beta = 1$. When weak convergence only is sought, it is not necessary for the random variable ε to be normally distributed. A binary variable $\varepsilon = \{-1, +1\}$ with equal probability on each value will deliver the same order of weak convergence. Implementing the simulation with binary variables is called a weak scheme.

In practice, only a few polynomial function g are ever used in the implementation of weak convergence, so that weak convergence basically only involves a restriction on the moments of the distribution of X. Strong convergence is, in fact, a restriction on the entire distribution of X.

following scheme has an expected value of the square of its error which is of order $h^{1.5}$.

$$X(t+h) = X(t) + \left[a(X(t),t) - \frac{1}{2}\sigma(X(t),t)\frac{\partial}{\partial x}\sigma(X(t),t) \right] \times h$$

$$+ \sigma(X(t),t) \times \varepsilon(h) + \frac{1}{2}\sigma(X(t),t)\frac{\partial}{\partial x}\sigma(X(t),t) \times \varepsilon^2(h)$$

$$\text{(13.12)}$$

A yet more accurate scheme could be derived.

———————————————♠———————————————

Proof. The justification for approximation (13.12) runs as follows (we drop the time variable t which is not central here):

$$X(t+h) - X(t) = \int_t^{t+h} aX(s))ds + \int_t^{t+h} \sigma(X(s))dw(s)$$

but then also:

$$X(s) = X(t) + \int_t^s a(X(\tau))d\tau + \int_t^s \sigma(X(\tau))dw(\tau)$$

Substituting and expanding:

$$X(t+h) - X(t) = \int_t^{t+h} a\left[X(t) + \int_t^s [a(X(\tau))d\tau + \sigma(X(\tau))dw(\tau)] \right] ds$$

$$+ \int_t^{t+h} \sigma\left[X(t) + \int_t^s [a(X(\tau))d\tau + \sigma(X(\tau))dw(\tau)] \right] dw(s)$$

$$\simeq \int_t^{t+h} a[X(t)]ds + \int_t^{t+h} \left\{ \sigma[X(t)] \right.$$

$$+ \sigma'[X(t)] \times \sigma(X(t)) \times \left[\int_t^s dw(\tau) \right] \right\} dw(s)$$

$$= a[X(t)]h + \sigma[X(t)] \times [w(t+h) - w(t)]$$

$$+ \sigma'[X(t)]\sigma(X(t)) \int_t^{t+h} \left[\int_t^s dw(\tau) \right] dw(s)$$

$$= a[X(t)]h + \sigma[X(t)] \times \varepsilon(h)$$

$$+ \sigma'[X(t)]\sigma(X(t)) \left\{ \int_t^{t+h} [w(s) - w(t)]dw(s) \right\}$$

Recall that:

$$d\left(w^2\right) = 2wdw + dt$$

or, in the integral form:

$$\int_t^{t+h} d\left(w^2(s)\right) = 2\int_t^{t+h} w(s)dw(s) + h$$

so that:

$$\int_t^{t+h} d\left(w^2(s)\right) - 2w(t) \int_t^{t+h} dw(s) = 2 \int_t^{t+h} [w(s) - w(t)]dw(s) + h$$

$$w^2(t+h) - w^2(t) - 2w(t)[w(t+h) - w(t)]$$

$$= 2 \int_t^{t+h} [w(s) - w(t)]dw(s) + h$$

$$[w(t+h) - w(t)]^2 = 2 \int_t^{t+h} [w(s) - w(t)]dw(s) + h$$

Hence:

$$\int_t^{t+h} [w(s) - w(t)]dw(s) = \frac{1}{2}\left\{ [w(t+h) - w(t)]^2 - h \right\}$$

$\square$

13.2.3 Stability

Besides their degree of convergence as time steps go to zero, various simulation schemes are also different in their *stability*, which is the degree to which they remain close to the solution when the number of time steps is increased, while each time step remains of the same size, thereby covering a longer time span. To improve convergence, *"implicit"* schemes are used. For instance, the *implicit* Euler-Matsuyama scheme is:

$$X(t+h) = X(t) + a(X(t), t) \times h + \sigma(X(t+h), t) \times \varepsilon(h)$$

It requires a solution by iteration because the unknown $X(t+h)$ appears on both sides of the equation. While unconditionally stable, the scheme would still contain a *squared error* of order h.

A reasonable compromise between explicit and implicit schemes would be of the so-called "Crank-Nicholson" type:[11]

$$X(t+h) = X(t) + a(X(t), t) \times h + \frac{1}{2}[\sigma(X(t+h), t) + \sigma(X(t), t)] \times \varepsilon(h)$$

Although smaller, the squared error would still be of order h and the scheme would require iterations since, here again, the unknown $X(t+h)$ appears on both sides of the equation.

13.2.4 The Doss or Nelson-and-Ramaswamy Transformation

In simulations of stochastic processes, all the troubles arise from changes of the value of the diffusion term within a time step. Any transformation that produces a constant diffusion is welcome. For instance, when simulating the Geometric Wiener process, one should simulate the logarithm of it.

---

11 See below, in section 13.5, the reason for that labeling.

A generalization of that idea is the following.[12] Suppose that the diffusion term of a one-dimensional process S is $\sigma(S)$. Suppose one introduces a change of variable: $X(S)$. By Itô's lemma, the diffusion of X will be: $\sigma(S)\partial X(S)/\partial S$. If we choose:

$$X(S) = \int^S \frac{du}{\sigma(u)}$$

X will have unit diffusion and will be easy to simulate. That is the Doss transformation.

As the reader can see, the scheme works only if $\sigma(S)$ does not vanish. And we are not aware of extensions to more than one dimension.

The scheme is useful in another context. A researcher is tempted to draw conclusions about the behavior of a process by looking at its drift. A plot of the drift of a process against its level is called a "phase diagram," as in Physics. The plot is meant to indicate what are the long-run properties of the process and whether it converges or not. When the diffusion of the process is not constant, a phase diagram can be extremely misleading, as the diffusion also influences the way in which the probability masses evolve over time. Here is a strong warning: if the reader wants to draw conclusions from a phase diagram, he must first apply the Doss transformation.[13]

13.2.5   The Use of "Variational Calculus" in Simulations

Suppose one wants to calculate the delta of an option in cases where no explicit formula exists. It is, of course, possible to calculate the value of the option by simulation for two values of the underlying price that are close to each other and then calculate the difference. But there is a way to obtain the δ directly by simulation. Consider an example in which the volatility is a function $\sigma(S, t)$ of the price of the underlying. The Black-Scholes PDE is:

$$\frac{\partial}{\partial S}C(S, t)r(t)S + \frac{1}{2}\frac{\partial^2}{\partial S^2}C(S, t)\sigma^2(S, t)S^2 + \frac{\partial}{\partial t}C(S, t) = r(t)C(S, t) \tag{13.13}$$

Differentiate both sides of this equation with respect to S and introduce the notation $\delta(S, t) \triangleq \frac{\partial}{\partial S}C(S, t)$:

$$\frac{1}{2}\frac{\partial^2}{\partial S^2}\delta(S, t)\sigma^2(S, t)S^2 + \frac{\partial}{\partial S}\delta(S, t)\left[r(t)S + \sigma^2(S, t)S + \frac{1}{2}\frac{\partial}{\partial S}\sigma^2(S, t)S^2\right]$$
$$+ \frac{\partial}{\partial t}\delta(S, t) = 0$$

This is a PDE that the function $\delta(S, t)$ must satisfy. It says that δ must be a (local) martingale under a probability measure under which the process for S has drift equal

---

12 See Doss (1977), Nelson and Ramaswamy (1990), and Detemple *et al.* (2006). Nelson and Ramaswamy (1990) used the idea in the context of a binomial tree rather than in the context of a simulation.

13 For a warning against that potential pitfall, see Dumas (1992).

to: $r(t)S + \sigma^2(S,t)S + \frac{1}{2}\frac{\partial}{\partial S}\sigma^2(S,t)S^2$. If it is martingale, δ at time t is equal to the expected value of δ at time T ($t < T$) under that measure. The value of δ at time T (the terminal condition) is evidently given by a step function (for a call): {0 if $S < \mathcal{K}$; 1 if $S > \mathcal{K}$}.

Therefore, one can get the value of δ by simulating the process S using the artificial drift and taking an average of the terminal values of the step function.

The simulation to obtain the value of the option and the value of its delta can be done jointly. Figure 13.1 is a sample output of a simulation with 5,000 runs for the plain Geometric Wiener process.

The mathematical elaboration of variational calculus is called the "Malliavin calculus." The corresponding simulation techniques have been enhanced in a number of ways.[14]

Detemple, Garcia, and Rindisbacher (2003) have shown how the Malliavin calculus coupled with simulations can serve to obtain investors' portfolio choices at the equilibrium of a financial market. To understand the link between the calculation of the δ of an option and the calculation of portfolio positions, observe that the δ is the number of units held of the underlying in the portfolio replicating the option (see chapter 6).

The reader may want to solve exercise 13.7.

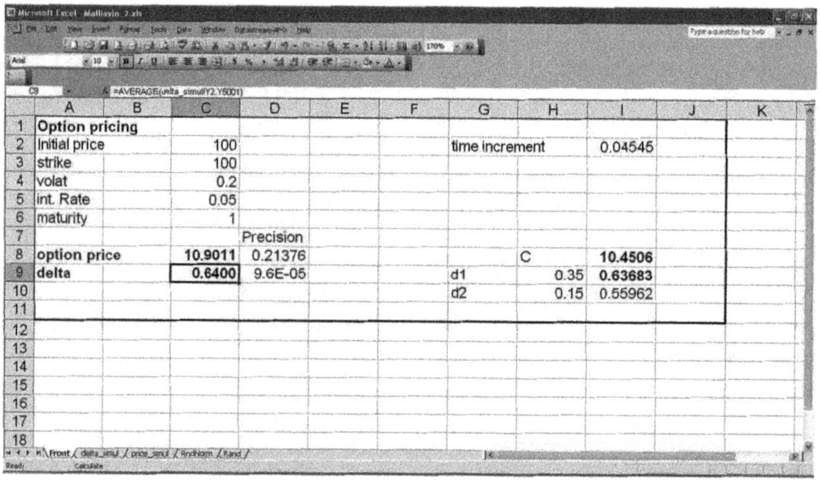

Figure 13.1
Simultaneous price and delta simulations: the option price in cell C8 and the delta in cell C9 obtained by simulation should be compared to the exact Black-Scholes price in cell I8 and the analytical delta (or $N(d_1)$) in cell I9.

---

14 Surveys of this matter are available: for example, Nualart (1995) and Montero and Kohatsu-Higa (2003). See also the detailed description of simulation applications of the Malliavin calculus in Fournié *et al.* (1999, 2001).

13.3   Analytical Methods

In some stylized financial models one sometimes encounters linear differential equations, that is, equations in which the unknown function appears linearly (for example, without squares or exponent of it). When these are linear ODEs and the coefficients are constant, there are well-known explicit solutions in the form of exponential functions. When the coefficients are linear, there are explicit solutions in the form of power functions. When the coefficients are affine functions, there are explicit solutions in the form of confluent hyper-geometric functions. The reader can find a gallery of solutions in the handbook by Abramowitz and Stigum (1964).

Most of the time, however, the differential equations in question are PDEs (such as the Black-Scholes PDE). And, more often yet, they are nonlinear PDEs. We cover below linear PDEs and a form of quadratic ODE known as a Riccati equation.

13.3.1   Solutions of *Linear* PDEs

For linear PDEs, we do not provide solution methods because many easily readable textbooks are available on that topic.[15] We only provide some classification so that the reader can find his/her way in the forest of equations. Linear second-order PDEs in two variables are equations of the general form:

$$A\frac{\partial^2 u}{\partial x^2}(x,y) + B\frac{\partial^2 u}{\partial x \partial y}(x,y) + C\frac{\partial^2 u}{\partial y^2}(x,y)$$

$$+D\frac{\partial u}{\partial x}(x,y) + E\frac{\partial u}{\partial y}(x,y) + Fu(x,y) = G$$

where u is the unknown function and the so-called "coefficients" A, B, C, D, E, F, and G are constants or given functions of x and y. When $G = 0$, the equation is said to be linear homogeneous. G is the inhomogeneous term of the equation.

There are three basic types of second-order linear PDEs:

1. Parabolic equations: $B^2 - 4AC = 0$. Heat-flow, diffusion, and Finance problems mostly lead to parabolic equations. For instance, in the Black-Scholes PDE (the variable y is t), $B^2 - 4AC = 0 - 4 \times \sigma^2 x^2 \times 0 = 0$. The second term of this calculation is equal to zero because the Black-Scholes equation is second order in x but first order only in t.

2. Hyperbolic equations: $B^2 - 4AC > 0$.

3. Elliptic equations: $B^2 - 4AC < 0$.

---

15 See, for example, Farlow (1993).

Equations of the last two types can be encountered in Finance when there are two state variables x and y other than time. Solution techniques differ across the three equation types. Boundary conditions also serve to classify problems:

1. Initial (or terminal) value and *initial-boundary value problems*, in which the boundary values are given along a straight line $x =$ constant or $y =$ constant in the (x, y) plane. This is called the Cauchy problem. The Black-Scholes European-option-valuation problem for a fixed maturity option is a Cauchy problem of a simple kind because the equation is first order in t.

2. *Two-point boundary value problem*, in which some boundary conditions are imposed along a fixed curve in the (x, y) plane. These problems can be further subclassified into the *Dirichlet problem*, in which the value of the unknown function is specified on the boundary, and the *Neumann problem* in which the derivatives of the unknown function are specified on the boundary.

3. Floating-boundary or free-boundary problem in which some boundary conditions is specified on some curve in the (x, y) plane but the location of the curve is unknown and must be derived from the boundary conditions and the PDE. The valuation of an American type option is a free-boundary problem. The boundary in question is the exercise boundary (see exercise 13.4 on the perpetual American put).

13.3.2   The Affine Framework and Solutions of Riccati Equations

Riccati equations are ODEs that involve the square of the unknown function. They are useful in a special but fairly flexible framework that is called the affine framework and which will be brought to bear in chapter 16 dealing with the term structure of interest rates.

Consider a set of n state variables Y driven by the diffusion process:

$$dY(t) = \mu_Y(Y(t), t)dt + \sigma_Y(Y(t), t)dw^*(t) \tag{13.14}$$

where w^* is a K-dimensional Wiener process under P^*; μ_Y and σ_Y take values respectively in $\mathbb{R}^n$ and in the space of the matrices $n \times K$. This process is named "affine" if the following holds:

Definition 13.2   *A multidimensional process Y is affine if and only if each element of the vector of its drift and of its variance-covariance matrix is affine in Y.*

That is, all coefficients in the associated PDE are affine.

Affine processes are convenient because their characteristic functions can be obtained in closed form via a Riccati equation.[16]

---

16 Here we consider only continuous-time affine processes but a similar mathematical framework can be developed in discrete time. See chapter 5 of Singleton (2006).

Definition 13.3 *A function $\varphi(x, t; \chi, u)$ is exponential affine in $x \in \mathbb{R}^n$ if it is in the form:*

$$\varphi(x, t; \chi, u) = e^{A(u-t)+B(u-t).x} \tag{13.15}$$

where $A(u - t)$ (a scalar function) and $B(u - t)$ (a vector function) are functions of time to future date (that is, time to a maturity date) only.

Theorem 13.1 *(Duffie, Pan, and Singleton (2000)) When technical conditions are satisfied (see Duffie, Filipovic, and Schachermayer (2003)), a process is affine if and only if its conditional characteristic function is exponential affine.*

Proof. To keep notation down, we sketch the proof for a one-dimensional process Y:

$$dY(t) = (a + b \times Y(t))dt + \sqrt{c + d \times Y(t)} \times dw^*(t) \tag{13.16}$$

For a given χ, the characteristic function of an affine process (13.16), seen as a function of x, being a conditional expected value satisfies the backward PDE:

$$0 = \frac{\partial \varphi}{\partial t} + \frac{\partial \varphi}{\partial x}(a + b \times x) + \frac{1}{2}\frac{\partial^2 \varphi}{\partial x^2}(c + d \times x) \tag{13.17}$$

subject to the boundary (that is, terminal) condition:

$$\varphi(x, u; \chi, u) \equiv e^{\chi x}$$

Substituting (13.15) as a trial solution:

$$0 = -\varphi(x)\big(A'(u - t) + B'(u - t) \times x\big)$$
$$+ \varphi(x)B(u - t)(a + b \times x) + \frac{1}{2}\varphi(x)B^2(u - t)(c + d \times x)$$

$$0 = -\big(A'(u - t) + B'(u - t) \times x\big) + B(u - t)(a + b \times x)$$
$$+ \frac{1}{2}B^2(u - t)(c + d \times x)$$

The PDE (13.17) can be satisfied for every value of x if and only if the functions A and B satisfy the following system of ODEs:

$$0 = -A'(u - t) + B(u - t)a + \frac{1}{2}B^2(u - t)c$$

$$0 = -B'(u - t) + B(u - t)b + \frac{1}{2}B^2(u - t)d \tag{13.18}$$

with boundary conditions:

$$A(0) = 0; \, B(0) = \chi$$

(because these will imply $e^{A(u-t)+B(u-t).x} = e^{\chi x}$ at $t = u$). The first equation is linear and poses no problem. *The second equation is a nonlinear ODE, of second degree, called a Riccati equation.*

A solution can be found by means of *Radon's lemma*.[17] Postulate a solution in the form:

$$B(u - t) \equiv \frac{f(u - t)}{g(u - t)}$$

and substitute into (13.18):

$$0 = -\left[\frac{f'(u - t)}{g(u - t)} - \frac{f(u - t)}{g^2(u - t)}g'(u - t)\right] + \frac{f(u - t)}{g(u - t)}b + \frac{1}{2}\left(\frac{f(u - t)}{g(u - t)}\right)^2 d$$

$$0 = -\left[f'(u - t) - f(u - t)\frac{g'(u - t)}{g(u - t)}\right] + f(u - t)b + \frac{1}{2}\frac{f^2(u - t)}{g(u - t)}d$$

A sufficient condition for this equation to be satisfied is that simultaneously:

$$0 = -f'(u - t) + f(u - t)b$$

$$0 = g'(u - t) + \frac{1}{2}f(u - t)d$$

which can easily be solved since this is a linear system of ODEs in the unknown functions $f(u - t)$ and $g(u - t)$. The boundary conditions are:

$$f(0) = \chi ; g(0) = 1$$

The reader will find a special case of the above problem in exercise 13.8.   □

13.4   Approximate Analytical Method: Perturbation Method

A perturbation method is a method to obtain an approximate solution to a system of equations or to a PDE.[18] It can be applied when an exact solution is known for a special combination of parameter values. Then the approximate solution is obtained in the form of a Taylor expansion taken with respect to the parameter values.[19] For the purpose of finding solutions to a system of equations, Taylor series may be very inconvenient as sometimes the exact equation has one solution and the approximate one has several (example: $e^x = b > 0$).[20]

---

17 For conditions under which an explicit solution is possible, see Grasselli and Tebaldi (2008). See Peng and Scaillet (2007), who make use of Radon's lemma and also provide a powerful generalization of the affine framework to an affine-quadratic one. An application of that extension to an equilibrium model was made in Dumas, Kurshev, and Uppal (2009).

18 There is no connection between "perturbation methods" of approximation, to be described now, and the "perturbation reasoning," which is a method of optimization expounded in Appendix B and used at several points in the book.

19 See Judd (1996).

20 Lagrange (1770) has proposed inverse series as a way to express the solution $w = g(z)$ of a system of equations $f(w) = z$. See: http://en.wikipedia.org/wiki/Lagrange_inversion_theorem. For an application to the derivation of complete-market sharing rules, see Bhamra and Uppal (2014).

Suppose the function giving the solution of an equilibrium or security-pricing problem is $f(x, \lambda_1)$ where x here is a state variable or underlying-security price and λ_1 is a set of fixed, real parameters. There are two conceivable series approaches. One can imagine an expansion of $f(x, \lambda_1)$ against x around some value a and calculate the unknown coefficients of the series that solve as closely as possible the equation system. These can be obtained sequentially: first the zeroth-order coefficient, then the first-order coefficient, and so on.

Or, one can imbed the problem into a sequence of problems seeking the function $f(x, \lambda)$ for $\lambda \in [\lambda_0, \lambda_1]$. One can then imagine an expansion of $f(x, \lambda)$ against λ around λ_0. Suppose that, for $\lambda = \lambda_0$, the function $f(x, \lambda_0) = g_0(x)$ and all its derivatives, $g_n(x)$, with respect to λ can be obtained exactly. The expansion can give an approximate solution function for $\lambda = \lambda_1$. The functions $g_n(x)$, $n = 0, \ldots$ are obtained by successively differentiating with respect to λ the system of equilibrium conditions (first-order conditions and market-clearing) and solving the resulting system for the functions g.

To compute the solution of an equilibrium problem, Judd and Guu (2001) have proposed an approach in which the parameter λ is the standard deviation σ of the shocks received exogenously by the economy. The expansion is around the value $\sigma = 0$, at which the system is deterministic. The expansion gives the stationary solution of the stochastic system if the deterministic system admits a deterministic steady state.[21]

In Finance, we are fortunate that logarithmic utility often yields an explicit solution. Kogan and Uppal (2001) have obtained approximate solutions of the portfolio-choice problem (and even of the financial-market equilibrium problem) for levels of risk aversion in a neighborhood of one. Consider the Merton portfolio choice problem with isoelastic utility and one risky security, and a single scalar Wiener process w, which is an example of the model in section 9.4

$$\max_{\{c(t)\}, \{\theta(t)\}} \mathbb{E}_0 \left\{ \psi \times \int_0^T e^{-\beta(s-t)} \frac{c(s)^\gamma - 1}{\gamma} ds + (1 - \psi) \times e^{-\beta(T-t)} \frac{W(T)^\gamma - 1}{\gamma} \right\}$$

subject to:

$$dW(t) = \{r(Y(t), t)W(t) + W(t)[\theta[\mu(Y(t), t) - r(Y(t), t)]]$$
$$- c(t)\} dt + W(t)\theta\sigma(Y(t), t)dw(t);$$
$$W(0) = e_0$$

since:

$$dS(t) = \mu(Y(t), t)dt + \sigma(Y(t), t) \times dw(t)$$
$$dY(t) = \mu_Y(Y(t), t)dt + \sigma_Y(Y(t), t) \times dw(t) \tag{13.19}$$

---

21 Dynare is an open-source software (http://www.dynare.org/download), which is callable from MatLab and automatically calculates a Taylor expansion of the equilibrium functions of an economic model.

The HJB equation is:

$$
0 = \max_{c,\theta}\left\{\psi \times e^{-\beta(s-t)}\frac{c(s)^\gamma - 1}{\gamma}\right.
$$

$$
+\frac{\partial J}{\partial W}(W,Y,t)\{r(Y,t)W + W[\mu(Y,t) - r(Y,t)]\theta - c\}
$$

$$
+\frac{\partial J}{\partial Y}(W,Y,t)\mu_Y\alpha(Y,t) + \frac{1}{2}\frac{\partial^2 J}{\partial W^2}(W,Y,t)W^2\theta\sigma(Y,t)\sigma(Y,t)^\mathsf{T}\theta
$$

$$
+\frac{1}{2}\frac{\partial^2 J}{\partial Y^2}(W,Y,t)\sigma_Y(Y,t)\sigma_Y(Y,t)^\mathsf{T}
$$

$$
\left.+\frac{\partial^2 J}{\partial W\partial Y}(W,Y,t)W\sigma_Y(Y,t)\sigma(Y,t)^\mathsf{T}\theta + \frac{\partial J}{\partial t}(W,Y,t)\right\} \tag{13.20}
$$

Given the homogeneity of the utility function, the solution to this equation subject to the terminal condition takes the following functional form:

$$
J(W,Y,t) = A(t)\frac{\left[e^{g(Y,t)}W\right]^\gamma - 1}{\gamma}
$$

$$
A(t) = \left(1 - \psi\frac{1+\beta}{\beta}\right)e^{-\beta(T-t)} + \frac{\psi}{\beta}
$$

from which consumption and portfolio rules could be calculated from the first-order conditions.

However, except in the case of log utility, the function $g(Y,t)$ cannot be computed in closed form. Kogan and Uppal look for $g(Y,t)$ as a power series in γ:

$$
g(Y,t) = g_0(Y,t) + \gamma g_1(Y,t) + O\left(\gamma^2\right)
$$

The function $g_0(Y,t)$ can be obtained from the value function of an investor with logarithmic utility:

$$
J(W,Y,t) = A(t)[\ln W + g_0(Y,t)]
$$

where:

$$
g_0(Y,t) = \psi\ln\psi\frac{1 - e^{-\rho(T-t)}}{\rho A(t)} - \psi \times \frac{1}{A(t)}\int_t^T e^{-\beta(s-t)}\ln(A(s))ds
$$

$$
+\frac{1}{A(t)}\mathbb{E}_t\int_t^T\left(A(t) - \frac{\psi}{\beta}\left(1 - e^{-\beta(s-t)}\right)\right)
$$

$$
\times\left(-\frac{1}{A(s)} + r(Y) + \frac{\varkappa^2(Y,t)}{2}\sigma(Y,t)\sigma(Y,t)^\mathsf{T}\right)ds
$$

and:

$$
\varkappa(Y,t) \triangleq \frac{\mu(Y,t) - r(Y,t)}{\sigma(Y,t)\sigma(Y,t)^\mathsf{T}}
$$

as can be verified by substituting the postulated value function, the optimal consumption, and portfolio policies of the log investor into the HJB equation (13.20) written for the log investor.

As mentioned above, differentiation of the equation system with respect to γ would produce a new system, which would be used to proceed to the next-order approximation and to the function $g_1(Y, t)$, and so on. The nth-order approximate consumption and portfolio choices of the non-log investor can be derived from the function $g_{n-1}(Y, t)$ only, while the function $g_n(Y, t)$ need not be known. Using the equations above, the reader can verify that fact for the zeroth order (see exercise 13.9).

13.5   Numerical Methods: Approximations of Continuous Systems

When no solution is available in the form of an explicit function, numerical methods are used. Because available computers are digital, these methods require either a system that is discrete in space and time to start with or one that is a discretized version of a continuous system. In Part I (chapters 2, 3, and 4), we have studied discrete systems. The canonical discrete systems are lattices such as the binomial tree (section 2.2.6) and the Markov chain.[22] Here we focus on discretized versions of continuous systems.

13.5.1   Lattice Approximations

We saw in section 2.2.6 that, as one subdivides time intervals forever, the first and second moments of constant-volatility and constant-drift binomial trees approach the first and second moments of a Brownian motion. In fact, Cox, Ross, and Rubinstein (1979) clearly intended their binomial construction to be used as an approximation of the underlying security's price behavior for the purpose of pricing derivatives, such as finite-maturity American options, that could not be priced with an explicit formula.[23]

A tree is analogous to an exhaustive simulation, so that some of the same principles of discrete time-step simulations that we saw in section 13.2 are also relevant in building them. All processes can be approximated by a tree of sufficient dimension. The difficulty arises from our desire to keep this tree from becoming excessively "bushy" because the computational burden would grow beyond the feasible. We want the tree to be recombining. When the tree is recombining the number of nodes grows in proportion to the number of time steps. When it is not, it grows exponentially.

Another requirement we place on approximation trees is that they do not jeopardize the notion of completeness versus incompleteness of a given market model. We know

---

22 For an application of lattice structures to equilibrium modeling, see Dumas and Lyasoff (2012).

23 They go as far as to show that not only the first and second moments of the approximate tree approach those of the continuous-time process but also the entire distribution approaches the continuous-time one.

that a continuous-time market model containing K Brownians requires $K + 1$ securities to be complete. The same must be true for the market model approximated by a tree. He (1990) "generalizes the Cox, Ross, and Rubinstein (1979) binomial option-pricing model, and establishes a convergence from discrete-time multivariate multinomial models to continuous-time multidimensional diffusion models for contingent claims prices. *The key to the approach is to approximate the K-dimensional diffusion price process by a sequence of K-variate, $(K + 1)$-nomial processes.*"[24] He shows that "contingent claims prices and dynamic replicating portfolio strategies derived from the discrete time models converge to their corresponding continuous-time limits." In his textbook, Ingersoll (1987, page 336) shows the way to approximate a two-dimensional Brownian. One might be tempted to approximate it with a quadrinomial tree, it being the product of two binomial trees. That would not be parsimonious and, above all, would violate our requirement. It should be approximated with a trinomial tree. Ingersoll shows how to write the five first and second moments of the trinomial trees and adjust the parameters of a trinomial tree (up and down movements and probabilities) so that first and second moments are equal to those of the two-dimensional Brownian we are approximating.

Please see exercise 13.10.

In fact, that principle reveals the reason for which continuous-time models tend to be easier to solve than discrete-time models with continuous state, or discrete states with an unrestricted number of possible values: continuous-time models implicitly assume a number of successor nodes (the "splitting index" of chapter 2) equal to the number of Brownians plus one, and no more.

That restriction simplifies the mathematics; it explains the mean-variance property, that is, the fact that only the first two moments of random variables play a role when we apply Itô's lemma. Continuous-time models that violated that assumption could be constructed but would be much more cumbersome.

It is harder to approximate mean-reverting processes, if we want the tree to remain recombining. Fitting the first moments and fitting the second moments together in that case becomes much more difficult. Tuckman (1995, page 238), in his textbook on fixed-income securities, provides an ingenious scheme to approximate a two-dimensional Ornstein-Uhlenbeck process with a recombining tree. Unfortunately, the scheme cannot be extended to more dimensions. Please see exercise 13.11.

As has been noted several times, under martingale pricing, prices of securities are expected values of future dividends and future prices. Expected values are, of course, integrals, which can be calculated numerically by so-called "quadrature" techniques. Tauchen

---

24 Our emphasis.

and Hussey (1991) have proposed a way to approximate the expected value of any stationary, discrete-time, continuous-state Markovian process by means of a Markov chain. The number of states in the Markov chain is a function of the desired approximation precision. Unfortunately, we are unaware of a way to apply their method to the approximation of a continous-time process.

13.5.2 Finite-Difference Approximations

In this approach, the unknown functions are approximated with a series of points along a mesh or a grid. To be specific, we consider the solution of a parabolic PDE such as:

$$\frac{\partial^2 u}{\partial x^2}(x,t) = \frac{\partial u}{\partial t}(x,t) \tag{13.21}$$

Letting h be the grid size in the x dimension and k be the grid size in the t dimension, the requisite derivatives can be approximated in the following possible ways:

- $\frac{\partial u}{\partial t}(x,t)$:

  - forward difference:
  $$\frac{\partial u}{\partial t}(x,t) \cong \frac{u(x,t+k) - u(x,t)}{k} \tag{13.22}$$

  - backward difference:
  $$\frac{\partial u}{\partial t}(x,t) \cong \frac{u(x,t) - u(x,t-k)}{k} \tag{13.23}$$

  - central difference:
  $$\frac{\partial u}{\partial t}(x,t) \cong \frac{u(x,t+k) - u(x,t-k)}{2k} \tag{13.24}$$

- $\frac{\partial^2 u}{\partial x^2}(x,t)$:

$$\frac{\partial^2 u}{\partial x^2}(x,t) \cong \frac{u(x+h,t) - 2u(x,t) + u(x-h,t)}{h^2} \tag{13.25}$$

13.5.2.1 Errors and convergence

Errors that arise from the numerical scheme are of three kinds:

1. Rounding errors: numbers have a finite number of decimals

2. Truncation errors: even if the approximating differences were applied to the exact solution of the PDE (13.21), they would induce a gap between the RHS and the LHS. That is the total truncation error. To calculate the order of magnitude of the truncation error, one would expand u in a Taylor series within the approximation equations (13.22 - 13.25) and obtain in this way the largest-order term of the difference between the RHS and the LHS. In an attempt to reduce the truncation error, quadratic approximations

involving three or more points could be used instead of (13.22 - 13.25) but then the numerical solution scheme becomes more painful.

3. Discretization error: the resulting difference between the true and the approximate solutions for u after the numerical scheme is completed.

A numerical scheme can have three desirable properties:

1. Convergence: when h and $k \to 0$, the approximate numerical solution approaches the true solution. The discretization error goes to zero.

2. Stability: the approximate numerical solution remains bounded at every step of the algorithm.

3. Consistency: when h and $k \to 0$, the truncation error goes to zero.

The following theorem relates these properties to each other:

Theorem 13.2 (Lax equivalence theorem) *Given a properly posed linear initial-value problem[25] and a linear finite difference approximation to it that satisfies the consistency requirement, stability is the necessary and sufficient condition for convergence.*

13.5.2.2   The explicit numerical scheme for solving PDE (13.21)

The so-called "explicit numerical scheme" uses the forward difference (13.22) for the derivative with respect to time:

$$\frac{u(x, t+k) - u(x, t)}{k} = \frac{u(x+h, t) - 2u(x, t) + u(x-h, t)}{h^2}$$

$$u(x, t+k) = u(x, t) + k\frac{u(x+h, t) - 2u(x, t) + u(x-h, t)}{h^2}$$

$$= \rho \times u(x+h, t) + (1 - 2\rho) \times u(x, t) + \rho \times u(x-h, t)$$

$$(13.26)$$

where $\rho = k/h^2$. In other words, the value of the function at each point x for the current stage $t + k$ is obtained "explicitly" from the values at three points $x - h$, x, $x + h$ of the previous stage t.

Two end points are "lost" at each stage. The scheme must be completed by artificial side conditions if the domain of integration is to remain constant from stage to stage.

The explicit scheme has the following property:

Theorem 13.3 *(Gerschgorin) The explicit scheme is stable if $\rho < 1/2$.*

---

25 A PDE is properly posed if: (i) the solution is unique when it exists, (ii) the solution depends continuously on the data of the initial condition, (iii) a solution always exists for initial data that is arbitrarily close to initial data for which no solution exists.

Proof. (Idea of proof) Interpret (13.26) as a linear operator A that one applies at each stage: $[u(x, t + k)] = A \times [u(x, t)]$ where:[26]

$$A \triangleq \begin{bmatrix} ? & ? & 0 & 0 & 0 & 0 & 0 \\ \rho & 1-2\rho & \rho & 0 & 0 & 0 & 0 \\ 0 & \rho & 1-2\rho & \rho & 0 & 0 & 0 \\ 0 & 0 & 0 & \rho & 1-2\rho & \rho & 0 & 0 \\ 0 & 0 & 0 & 0 & \rho & 1-2\rho & \rho & 0 \\ 0 & 0 & 0 & 0 & \rho & 1-2\rho & \rho \\ 0 & 0 & 0 & 0 & 0 & ? & ? \end{bmatrix}$$

That same operator will be applied to errors if any arise. The necessary condition for stability of a linear dynamic system is that the eigenvalues should all have absolute values smaller than one. Calculating the eigenvalues of the matrix, one gets the desired result. □

13.5.2.3 The implicit numerical scheme for solving PDE (13.21)

The so-called "implicit numerical scheme" uses the backward difference (13.23) for the derivative with respect to time:

$$\frac{u(x, t) - u(x, t - k)}{k} = \frac{u(x + h, t) - 2u(x, t) + u(x - h, t)}{h^2}$$

$$u(x, t) = u(x, t - k) + k \frac{u(x + h, t) - 2u(x, t) + u(x - h, t)}{h^2}$$

$$-u(x, t - k) = \rho \times u(x + h, t) + (-1 - 2\rho) \times u(x, t) + \rho \times u(x - h, t)$$

The value of the function at each point x for the current stage t can only be obtained if the values at the neighboring points $x - h$, x, $x + h$ of the *same stage* are determined simultaneously.[27] Hence, a system of simultaneous linear equations with as many unknowns as there are unknown points must be solved: $B \times [u(x, t)] = -[u(x, t - k)]$ where:

$$B \triangleq \begin{bmatrix} ? & ? & 0 & 0 & 0 & 0 & 0 \\ \rho & -1-2\rho & \rho & 0 & 0 & 0 & 0 \\ 0 & \rho & -1-2\rho & \rho & 0 & 0 & 0 \\ 0 & 0 & 0 & \rho & -1-2\rho & \rho & 0 & 0 \\ 0 & 0 & 0 & 0 & \rho & -1-2\rho & \rho & 0 \\ 0 & 0 & 0 & 0 & \rho & -1-2\rho & \rho \\ 0 & 0 & 0 & 0 & 0 & ? & ? \end{bmatrix}$$

---

26 The question marks "?" stand in for the side conditions that have to be specified.

27 Here again, two endpoints are "lost" at each stage. Side conditions must be appended. Without them, the scheme is not applicable.

The linear system can be solved by direct methods of elimination. That is easy because the system is tridiagonal and there exist simple, explicit formulas for the inverse of a tridiagonal matrix. Alternatively, the system can be solved by iterative methods, calculating the value at one point x at a time. Of these, the most convenient is the Gauss-Seidel method (which uses for the neighboring points indifferently the values of the current iteration, if they have already been calculated, and those of the previous iteration, if not).

The implicit scheme is unconditionally stable.

13.5.2.4   The Crank-Nicholson numerical scheme for solving PDE (13.21)

This scheme is based on an average (with weights equal to one-half) of the explicit and the implicit schemes. The new values at each stage are equally weighted averages of the explicit and the implicit values of the unknown function:

$$
\frac{u(x,t) - u(x, t-k)}{k} = \frac{1}{2} \frac{u(x+h,t) - 2u(x,t) + u(x-h,t)}{h^2}
$$
$$
+ \frac{1}{2} \frac{u(x+h, t-k) - 2u(x, t-k) + u(x-h, t-k)}{h^2}
$$

The motivation for this scheme is that both the explicit and the implicit schemes introduce a bias in the equation. The derivative with respect to x is calculated at time t in both cases but the approximating value for the time derivative, by the mean value theorem, correspond to some point in time somewhere in-between times t and $t - k$.

The Crank-Nicholson scheme is unconditionally stable.

13.6   Conclusion

After writing first-order conditions of optimality and market-clearing conditions, a researcher faces the problem of solving the system of equations that he or she faces. The choice then is either to artificially twist and modify the assumptions until one is able to obtain an explicit solution – at the cost perhaps of solving an economic problem quite different from the one that he had set out to solve – or to go ahead and solve numerically and analyze the numbers obtained. The more insightful route is up to the beholder. It is safe to say that a numerical solution is often better than the analytical solution to an artificial problem.

Exercises

13.1. Denote by $p(x; y, T - t)$ the probability density of a transition of the *time-homogeneous* Markovian process S from level x at time t to level y at time T; $T \geq t$, its drift being $r(S, t)$ and its diffusion $\sigma(S, t)$. Obtain the Fokker-Planck equation (13.4) from the Chapman-Kolmogorov equation (13.1) by integration by parts, making appropriate assumptions about the tail behavior of the probability distributions.

13.2. If the process with drift $r(S, t)S$ and diffusion $\sigma(S, t)S$ admits a long-run stationary density $\pi(y)$ (for example, when $r(y) = r$ and $\sigma(y) = \sigma$), the stationary density function can be obtained by solving the following Fokker-Planck equation:

$$-\frac{\partial}{\partial y}[r(y)y\pi(y)] + \frac{\partial^2}{\partial y^2}\left[\frac{1}{2}\sigma^2(y)y^2\pi(y)\right] = 0$$

subject to:

$$\pi(y) \geq 0; \int \pi(y)dy = 1$$

Please, find an explicit form for the solution of this equation.

13.3. Consider the Black-Scholes model with zero rate of interest and volatility $\sigma(S, t)$ function of the underlying price S. Denote by $C(x; y, T - t)$ the price of a European call option when the underlying process S is at x at date t, when the strike price is y and the maturity is at date T; $T \geq t$. This option price function can be viewed in two ways:

- Holding the terminal point (y, T) fixed, the option-price function $C(x; y, T - t)$ can be viewed as a function of x and t, which must satisfy the Black-Scholes PDE (6.13). This is the "backward approach."

- Holding the initial point (x, t) fixed, the same option-price function $C(x; y, T - t)$ can be viewed as a function of the strike y and T. This is the "forward approach."

Determine a partial differential equation (which we shall call the "forward equation") that must be satisfied by C as a function of y and T. This can be done by implementing the following steps:

- write down the Fokker-Planck equation (13.4), which is the forward equation for probability densities

- multiply all terms of that equation by the option payoff and integrate over the terminal stock price

- evaluate one of the terms by integration by parts

- interpret the resulting equation as an equation involving the derivatives of the option price with respect to strike and maturity.

13.4. Obtain an explicit valuation formula for an American-type put option that would have infinite maturity. [This exercise is a bit premature. In chapter 19, we study the boundary condition for the American put. Here, you should pick an arbitrary exercise point, get the value of the infinite-maturity put as a function of the exercise point, and then maximize the value of the put with respect to the choice of the exercise point.]

13.5. We are looking for the value of:

$$\phi(x) = \mathbb{E}\left[\int_t^\infty e^{-\rho(s-t)} f(X(s)) ds | X(t) = x\right]; \rho > 0; x > 0 \qquad (13.27)$$

where X follows a Geometric Brownian motion:

$$\frac{dX(t)}{X(t)} = \mu dt + \sigma dw(t)$$

The unknown ϕ satisfies the ODE:

$$f(x) - \rho\phi(x) + \frac{\partial\phi(x)}{\partial x}\mu x + \frac{1}{2}\frac{\partial^2\phi(x)}{\partial x^2}\sigma^2 x^2 = 0$$

Use the theory of ODEs to find an explicit solution $\phi(x)$ to that ODE that will, indeed, be equal to the starting expected value (13.27), in the form of the sum of two integrals.

Hint: in the special case in which $f(x) = x^\alpha$, you can verify that you have picked the right solution of the ODE by comparing it with the result of an explicit calculation of the expected value.

13.6. Write a small MatLab (or Mathematica) program to calculate the Gram-Charlier corrected price of a call option written on an underlying security that has volatility 0.15 per unit of time, skewness -1, kurtosis 4, and time to expiry 0.25 at a time when moneyness $((S - \mathcal{K})/\mathcal{K})$ is equal to -5%.

13.7. Reproduce figure 13.1 on an Excel spreadsheet or by any other means.

13.8. Consider a bivariate process $\{\delta, \widehat{f}^B\}$ driven by the following SDE system:

$$\frac{d\delta(t)}{\delta_t} = \widehat{f}^B(t)dt + \sigma_\delta dw_\delta^B(t)$$

$$d\widehat{f}^B(t) = -\zeta\left(\widehat{f}^B(t) - \overline{f}\right)dt + \frac{\gamma^B}{\sigma_\delta}dw_\delta^B(t) + \frac{\gamma^B}{\sigma_s}dw_s^B(t)$$

Calculate explicitly $\mathbb{E}_t^B[\delta^\alpha(u)]; u > t$. Note that this calculation can be used to obtain the characteristic function $\mathbb{E}_t^B[\delta^{i\chi}(u)]$ of the distribution of δ.

13.9. In section 13.4, we wrote, "The nth-order approximate consumption and portfolio choices of the non-log investor can be derived from the function $g_{n-1}(Y,t)$ only, while the function $g_n(Y,t)$ need not be known. Using the equations above, the reader can verify that fact for the zeroth order." Please, do so.

13.10. Construct a trinomial tree that will approximate a two-dimensional IID diffusion process with given, constant drifts, variances, and covariance.

13.11. Provide a scheme to approximate with a recombining tree a two-dimensional Ornstein-Uhlenbeck process.

13.12. Show that, when using the forward-difference approximation to solve

$$\frac{\partial^2 u}{\partial x^2}(x, t) = \frac{\partial u}{\partial t}(x, t)$$

the truncation error is of order k but of order h^2 (as defined in section 13.5).

14 Portfolio Choice and Equilibrium Restrictions in Incomplete Markets

This chapter addresses the investor optimization problem in incomplete markets, and some equilibrium restrictions that follow from its solution.[1] In complete markets, we studied the problem first in single-period economies, then in multiperiod ones, and finally in continuous time. We split its solution into several steps: first, thanks to state prices, we switched from a large number of one-period dynamic budget constraints to a single, lifetime constraint. Then we solved the global problem for consumption and reconstructed portfolios via a replication argument.

Can we perform these steps again in incomplete markets?[2] We know from chapter 2 that, in the one-period case already, uniqueness of state prices fails to hold. Here, we again start from the analysis of the single-period case, narrow down the search for possible state prices and ask whether we can still separate optimal consumption from portfolio allocation at the investor level. This provides us with the mathematical and economic insights for the continuous-time treatment that follows.

The chapter unfolds as follows. Section 14.1 goes back to single-period economies. It recalls the transformation of the primal problem into a dual, where there is a single, lifetime budget constraint. Section 14.2 sets up an incomplete, continuous-time market model; builds the dual, recovers state prices; comments on their "optimality"; and solves for consumption and portfolio choices. Section 14.3 briefly considers the case in which the investor can only choose a portfolio that satisfies some constraints concerning the positions that are taken.[3] Section 14.4 develops minimum-squared deviation hedging, an alternative approach to optimization in incomplete, continuous-time markets. Remark 14.3 discusses an example of incomplete market under a special CRRA utility, the log one.

---

1 Thanks to Astrid Schornick and Lucie Tepla for reading and commenting on this chapter.

2 We do not discuss the case of limited accessibility, often referred to as partial market segmentation in which some people have access to some securities. But the same method would apply to it.

3 As in Tepla (2000) and Schornick (2009).

14.1   Single-Period Analysis

By further developing the material of chapter 3, this section examines the optimality conditions of the original, or primal, problem. It emphasizes their relation with the *marketability* of a subspace of consumption bundles, and the characterization they provide of state prices. State prices are not unique, but must satisfy the "*kernel condition*," stating that the differences between acceptable state prices must stay in the kernel of the payoff matrix of tradable securities. This is another way of saying that state prices combine into quoted prices of marketed securities that are given. The section then transforms the optimization problem into its dual, which is subject to a lifetime constraint and from which portfolio choices have been eliminated. Once the dual problem is solved for consumption, portfolio choices are reconstructed. Unlike in the case of complete markets, however, there is no true separation of the calculation into two stages. Individual state prices and portfolio choices have to be determined jointly.

14.1.1   Model Setup

The set of available securities is defined as usual by the payoff matrix Σ, with time-0 securities prices $S = \{S_i, i = 1..N\}$ given. The market is incomplete, in that the payoff matrix is rectangular, of full row rank (that is, no redundant securities) but not of full column rank. Specifically, the rank of the payoff matrix is equal to the number N of traded securities with $N < K$. The crucial issue in assessing incompleteness is the inability of the rows of Σ to span the whole $\mathbb{R}^K$, that is, to make all states insurable or all affordable consumption bundles marketed.

   Each investor has access to all existing securities and chooses a portfolio $\Theta = \{\theta_i\}$ so as to maximize utility from consumption today and tomorrow, under the budget constraints for times 0 and 1. Recall the material of section 3.1.4, the definition of the "primal" problem of maximizing (3.15) subject to the $K + 1$ budget constraints (3.13) and (3.14), and the corresponding Lagrangean L (3.16). As we know, the optimization program entails finding a saddle point for the Lagrangean function:

$$\min_{\lambda_0, \{\phi(s)\}} \max_{c(0), \{c(s)\}, \{\theta_i\}} L \qquad (14.1)$$

Recall also the first-order conditions for this problem: (3.17), (3.18), (3.22), (3.13), and (3.14).

   In order to understand how different state prices can be combined into a common set of prices for traded securities, we need to answer some preliminary questions: given the multiplicity of state prices, can the problem (3.15) be reformulated in the Arrow-Debreu form, in which the investor directly chooses his state-dependent consumption while portfolio choices are eliminated? What do the resulting state prices look like?

14.1.2   The Dual Reformulation and State Prices

Recall now the material of section 3.1.6, where we defined the dual optimization problem (3.23), in which portfolio choices had disappeared and the constraints were one budget condition (3.24) and the pricing condition was (3.25).

The dual problem (3.23) is a "global" or lifetime reformulation, in that a single budget constraint (3.24) holds, relating, via state prices, today's consumption and endowment to tomorrow's analogous quantities. The optimization problem is reformulated to look like a consumption choice problem under complete markets, except that the prices of the state single-payment securities are not given; they must be endogenized by each investor by minimization. The "min" means that the state prices must be those least favorable to the investor, among all those that satisfy the kernel condition. Every investor interprets incompleteness as imposing on him *the minimal value of utility among the maximal ones.* State prices achieve the minimization, while consumption achieves maximization.[4]

***Remark* 14.1** *In section 4.3, we saw how to rewrite the pricing condition as a* kernel condition *(differences between state prices v must stay in the kernel of the matrix Σ) so that another way of writing the problem (3.23) is:*

$$\min_{v \in \ker \Sigma} \max_{c(0), \{c(s)\}} \sum_{s=1}^{K} \pi(s) u(c(0), c(s)) \tag{14.2}$$

$$subject\ to: c(0) + \sum_{s=1}^{K} (\kappa(s) + v(s))(c(s) - e(s)) = e(0) \tag{14.3}$$

where κ is defined by

$$\kappa = \Sigma^{\mathsf{T}} \left[\Sigma \Sigma^{\mathsf{T}} \right]^{-1} S \tag{14.4}$$

as suggested in chapter 2.

14.1.3   Consumption and Portfolios

Given the global, dual reformulation in (3.23), one can proceed to a solution, reconstructing the standard Lagrangean. We show now that the kernel condition acting as a constraint has the effect of forcing the consumption decisions of the investor to be marketable. The point is more subtle than in the complete-market case, where investors choose their consumption all facing the same state prices.

---

4 Intuitively, the minimization is done, on top of the maximization, with respect to consumption and portfolio choices, because one must satisfy the *most binding* set of constraints, among all those written with different sets of state prices.

Calling $\lambda_0\theta_i$ the Lagrange multiplier associated with the pricing or kernel condition, the Lagrange objective function associated with problem (3.23) is:

$$\min_{\lambda_0,\{\phi(s)\}} \max_{c(0),\{c(s)\},\{\theta_i\}} \sum_{s=1}^{K} \pi(s)u(c(0),c(s))$$

$$+\lambda_0\left[e(0) - c(0) - \sum_{s=1}^{K}\phi(s)(c(s) - e(s))\right] + \sum_{i=1}^{N}\lambda_0\theta_i\left[\sum_{s=1}^{K}\phi(s)q_i(s) - S_i\right]$$

The first-order condition with respect to consumption at time 0 gives, as usual

$$\sum_{s=1}^{K} \pi(s)\frac{\partial u}{\partial c(0)}(c(0),c(s)) = \lambda_0 \tag{14.5}$$

The first-order condition with respect to consumption in state s, $c(s)$, gives

$$\pi(s)\frac{\partial u}{\partial c(s)}(c(0),c(s)) - \lambda_0\phi(s) = 0$$

which would give us straight away consumption in the future, if consumption at time 0 and state prices were set. Consumption at time 0 is determined as usual with the help of the first-order condition with respect to the multiplier λ_0 of the lifetime budget constraint (3.24).

The two together produce

$$\phi(s) = \pi(s)\frac{\frac{\partial u}{\partial c(s)}(c(0),c(s))}{\sum_{s=1}^{K}\pi(s)\frac{\partial u}{\partial c(0)}(c(0),c(s))} \tag{14.6}$$

The state prices require more attention. The first-order conditions with respect to $\phi(s)$ is still $C - E = \Sigma^{\top}\Theta$, or

$$c(s) - e(s) = \sum_{i=1}^{N}\theta_i q_i(s) \tag{14.7}$$

which says that net trade in state s, $c(s) - e(s)$, must be obtained, by linear combination, in a portfolio of the payoffs of the N securities in that state. This means that the kernel condition serves to impose the *marketability condition* on consumption. Picking the least favorable state prices through the "min" of the Lagrangean is tantamount to forcing the investor's consumption program to be marketable. Such is the role of the kernel condition. In the absence of a marketability constraint, the investor would have achieved a more favorable consumption plan. The marketability constraint can only make him worse off. Hence, the "least favorable" part of the proposition.

The first-order conditions (14.7) form a system of K equations in N unknowns $\Theta = \{\theta_i\}$. The constraint on the choice of $\{\phi(s)\}$ is again (3.25) (or $\Sigma\nu = 0$, which is (4.18)), a system of N equations in K unknowns (Φ or $\nu = \Phi - \kappa$). If we put the two sets of conditions together we have a total of $N + K$ equations in $N + K$ unknowns, which are security holdings and state prices. We see that, in the incomplete-market case, we cannot truly eliminate portfolios from the calculation. They return through the back door as we must solve jointly for state prices and portfolios.

Furthermore, since (14.7) involves consumption, we must also consider (14.6), the conditions regarding future consumption, which form a system of K equations in K unknowns C as well as lifetime budget constraint (3.24), which is the first-order condition with respect to λ_0, and finally (14.5), the optimality condition for consumption at time 0. Overall, we have $N + 2K + 2$ equations in $N + 2K + 2$ unknowns.

As an example of the contemporaneous choice of state prices and consumption, consider the two-states, one-security case, in which

$$\Sigma = [q(1)\, q(2)]$$
$$S = S_1$$

and there is no endowment of goods after time 0.

Let κ be $\kappa = \Sigma^\mathsf{T}[\Sigma\Sigma^\mathsf{T}]^{-1} S$, or

$$\kappa^\mathsf{T} = \left[q^2(1) + q^2(2)\right]^{-1} \left[q(1)S_1 \; q(2)S_1\right]$$

κ is given, once the dividend matrix and the traded security prices are given. The kernel condition is

$$q(1)v(1) + q(2)v(2) = 0$$

which represents the appropriate specification of $\Sigma v = 0$; condition (14.7) gives:

$$c(s) = \theta q(s) \qquad s = 1,2 \tag{14.8}$$

The last three conditions form a system of three equations in the three unknowns $v(1), v(2), \theta$. We need to put them together with the choice of future consumption, as in (14.6), and the choice of $c(0)$ and λ_0, as in (3.24) and (14.5), for a total of seven equations in seven unknowns, in accordance with the general rule. In total, we have:

$$q(1)v(1) + q(2)v(2) = 0$$

$$c(s) = \theta q(s) \qquad\qquad s = 1,2,$$

$$v(s) = \pi(s)\frac{\frac{\partial u}{\partial c(s)}(c(0), c(s))}{\sum_{s=1}^{2} \pi(s)\frac{\partial u}{\partial c(0)}(c(0), c(s))} - \kappa(s)$$

$$\sum_{s=1}^{2} \pi(s)\frac{\partial u}{\partial c(0)}(c(0), c(s)) = \lambda_0$$

$$e(0) - c(0) = \sum_{s=1}^{2}(v(s) + \kappa(s))c(s)$$

which must be solved for $\theta, v(s), c(s), c(0), \lambda_0$, for given $\pi(s), \kappa(s), q(s), e(0)$.

14.2   The Dynamic Setting in Continuous Time

This section returns to continuous-time economies. It transforms the primal problem into its dual, which includes a lifetime constraint. Portfolio choices do not appear explicitly in the dual problem. The state prices, which are the multipliers of the lifetime constraint, are not unique. The dual problem is solved for consumption and state prices.

14.2.1   Model Setup

Our continuous-time setup is identical to the one in chapters 8 and 10, with the exception of dimensionality.[5] A riskless security and N risky securities are available:

$$B(t) = B(0)e^{\int_0^t r(s)ds} \tag{14.9}$$

$$S(t) + \int_0^t \iota(s)ds = S(0) + \int_0^t \mu(s)ds + \int_0^t \sigma(s)dw(s) \tag{14.10}$$

with $B(0) = 1$, $S(0) = S_0 \in \mathbb{R}^N$. The assumptions on the coefficients are chosen to guarantee existence (while not imposing Markovianity) of the integrals as discussed in chapter 7; $w(t)$ is a K-dimensional Wiener process. We now assume that $N < K$. The matrix σ has fewer rows than columns.[6]

Here is the *primal* problem:

$$\max_{\{c(t)\},\{\alpha(t),\Theta(t)\}} \mathbb{E}\left\{\int_0^T u(c(s),s)ds + \wp(W(T))\right\} \tag{14.11}$$

subject to:

$$\alpha(0)B(0) + \Theta(0)^\mathsf{T}S(0) \leq W_0 \tag{14.12}$$

$$\alpha(t)B(t) + \Theta(t)^\mathsf{T}S(t) + \int_0^t c(s)ds \leq$$

$$\alpha(0)B(0) + \Theta(0)^\mathsf{T}S(0)$$

$$+ \int_0^t \left[\alpha(s)B(s)r(s) + \Theta(s)^\mathsf{T}\mu(s)\right]ds + \int_0^t \Theta(s)^\mathsf{T}\sigma(s)dw(s); t \in (0,T) \tag{14.13}$$

$$W(T) \leq \alpha(T)B(T) + \Theta(T)^\mathsf{T}S(T) \tag{14.14}$$

---

5 Reminder: unless doing otherwise is necessary for comprehension, we simplify the notation for processes. All processes are stochastic but we suppress the reference to the state ω. Therefore, $X(t)$ actually means $X(\omega, t)$. In special cases, we also use the notation $f(t)$ to refer to a deterministic function of time. When this happens, we say so explicitly.

6 Notations remain what they were in chapter 8: numbers of units held in the riskless and risky securities are $\alpha(t)$ and $\Theta(t)$ respectively. And we keep the assumptions on the feasible consumption and final wealth, $\{c, W\}$. The assumptions of chapter 10 on the interim utility function, u, and the final one, $\wp$, are maintained. The individual dynamic program is, as usual, that of maximizing the utility of interim and final consumption by choosing appropriately a consumption path and an investment strategy in the riskless and risky securities. For simplicity, we assume that there are no endowments after time 0.

or, using Itô's lemma on (14.13) and the riskless and risky security Itô processes (14.9) and (14.10),

$$\int_0^t d\alpha(s) \times B(s) - \int_0^t \Theta(s)^{\mathsf{T}} \iota(s) ds$$

$$+ \int_0^t \left[d\Theta(s)^{\mathsf{T}} \mathcal{S}(s) + d\Theta(s)^{\mathsf{T}} d\mathcal{S}(s) \right] + \int_0^t c(s) ds \leq 0; \forall t \in [0, T]$$

which is nothing other than the continuous-time budget constraint (9.21) that we derived and used in chapter 9.

Using this formulation, we can write down the Lagrangean:

$$\max_{\{c(t)\}, \{\alpha(t), \Theta(t)\}} \min_{\{\lambda_0, \lambda(t)\}} \mathbb{E}_0 \left\{ \int_0^T u(c(s), s) ds + \wp(W(T)) \right\} \qquad (14.15)$$

$$+ \lambda_0 \times \left[W_0 - \left(\alpha(0) B(0) + \Theta(0)^{\mathsf{T}} \mathcal{S}(0) \right) \right]$$

$$+ \mathbb{E}_0 \left\{ - \int_0^T \lambda(t) \times \left[d\alpha(t) \times B(t) - \Theta(t)^{\mathsf{T}} \iota(t) dt + d\Theta(t)^{\mathsf{T}} \mathcal{S}(t) \right. \right.$$

$$\left. \left. + d\Theta(t)^{\mathsf{T}} d\mathcal{S}(t) + c(t) dt \right] + \lambda(T) \times \left[\alpha(T) B(T) + \Theta(T)^{\mathsf{T}} \mathcal{S}(T) - W(T) \right] \right\}$$

We now discuss the dual approach as a method to obtain the solution.

14.2.2 Dual

We are now ready to obtain the (quasi-)dual of the primal dynamic program.[7] That is done in the appendix to this chapter, where we show that the Lagrangean (14.15) is also the Lagrangean of the program:[8]

$$\max_{\{c(t)\}} \min_{\{\lambda_0, \lambda(t)\}} \mathbb{E}_0 \left\{ \int_0^T u(c(s), s) ds + \wp(W(T)) \right\} \qquad (14.16)$$

subject to:

$$\mathbb{E}_t[\lambda(T) \times B(T)] = \lambda(t) \times B(t); \forall t : 0 \leq t \leq T \qquad (14.17)$$

$$\mathbb{E}_t \left[\int_t^T \lambda(s) \times \iota(s) ds + \lambda(T) \times \mathcal{S}(T) \right] = \lambda(t) \times \mathcal{S}(t); \forall t : 0 \leq t \leq T \qquad (14.18)$$

and subject to a lifetime budget constraint:

$$\mathbb{E}_0 \left[\int_0^T \frac{\lambda(t)}{\lambda_0} \times c(t) dt + \frac{\lambda(T)}{\lambda_0} \times W(T) \right] = W_0 \qquad (14.19)$$

---

7 What we write here is not the full dual since we keep among the decision variables consumption, which is a primal variable. See also footnote 13 of chapter 3. Hence the reference to a (quasi) dual.

8 See He and Pearson (1991).

In the dual problem so written, we minimize, by a proper choice of the Lagrange multipliers $\{\lambda(t)\}$, the maximum expected utility from consumption and final wealth. Compared with utility maximization in complete markets, there is here an additional minimization.[9]

***Remark* 14.2**   *The investor cannot minimize directly with respect to λ since λ is a process that can be expected to contain the Brownians, over which he has no control. In section 14.2.3 below, we give the process λ the specific form:*

$$\lambda(t) \triangleq \lambda_0 \times \exp\left\{ -\int_0^t r(s)ds - \frac{1}{2}\int_0^t \|\kappa(s) + v(s)\|^2 ds \right.$$
$$\left. -\int_0^t [\kappa(s) + v(s)]^\mathsf{T} dw(s) \right\}$$

where r is given (if a riskless security is available for trade) and κ is also a given process, which we define as (14.20) below, so that v is truly the control variable over which the investor performs his minimization. Cuoco (1997) points out that the value of the optimal investment problem (14.16) subject to (14.17–14.9) does not define a convex function relative to v (because v appears as an exponent) so that minimization may not have a solution.

The constraints (14.17) and (14.18) to the problem say that security prices, once discounted using the Lagrange multipliers, are martingales.

14.2.3   Implied State Prices

The constraints (14.17) and (14.18) are the usual pricing or kernel equations of each security, which allow us to interpret the *multipliers as (being proportional to) stochastic discount factors*. Indeed, the values of the Lagrange multipliers that attain the minimum in the dual, admit a representation as an exponential martingale, can be transformed into stochastic discount factors and define a change of measure to a risk-neutral probability.

In order to show this, we proceed in a manner similar to the single-period case of section 14.1, by defining the generalized inverse of the diffusion matrix $\sigma : \sigma(t)^\mathsf{T}[\sigma(t)\sigma(t)^\mathsf{T}]^{-1}$. Construct from it a "market-price of risk" process κ in $\mathbb{R}^K$:[10]

$$\kappa(t) \triangleq \sigma(t)^\mathsf{T}\left[\sigma(t)\sigma(t)^\mathsf{T}\right]^{-1}[\mu(t) - r(t) \times \mathcal{S}(t)] \tag{14.20}$$

---

9 This is the main result of He and Pearson (1991). See also Karatzas, Lehoczky, and Shreve (1991), Shreve and Xu (1992).

10 This choice of κ is arbitrary. For purposes of obtaining individual choices, any κ that solves the equation:

$$\sigma(t)\kappa(t) = \mu(t) - r(t) \times S(t)$$

would have worked equally well. These κs differ from the one chosen in the text by a vector $\hat{v}$ which is in the kernel of σ. This is because the span of σ^T and the kernel of σ are two orthogonal subspaces. Any vector (and, at any fixed point in time, any process) can be projected onto these two subspaces to give two components, one in each space. The κ of the complete market would have been a nice choice but it is not acceptable as it is not generally in the span.

Note that κ is an adapted process, which, as in the single-period case, is in the span of the diffusion matrix σ^T of marketed claims, since: $\kappa(t) = \sigma(t)^\mathsf{T} x$ for this value of x:

$$x = \left[\sigma(t)\sigma(t)^\mathsf{T}\right]^{-1}[\mu(t) - r(t) \times \mathcal{S}(t)]$$

Also, denote as $v(t)$ any process that is in the kernel of $\sigma(t)$ at all times with probability one ($\sigma(t)v(t) = 0$). Consider the augmented set of market prices of risk $\kappa(t) + v(t)$, of which there is an infinite number. They all satisfy the equation:

$$\sigma(t)(\kappa(t) + v(t)) = [\mu(t) - r(t) \times \mathcal{S}(t)] \tag{14.21}$$

And consider their associated exponential martingales η:

$$\eta(t) \triangleq \exp\left\{-\frac{1}{2}\int_0^t \|\kappa(s) + v(s)\|^2 ds - \int_0^t [\kappa(s) + v(s)]^\mathsf{T} dw(s)\right\} \tag{14.22}$$

For the process η, Itô's lemma gives as usual

$$\frac{d\eta(t)}{\eta(t)} = -[\kappa(t) + v(t)]^\mathsf{T} dw(t) \tag{14.23}$$

and for η/B, it gives

$$d\left(\frac{\eta(t)}{B(t)}\right) = \frac{d\eta(t)}{B(t)} - \frac{\eta(t)}{B(t)^2}r(t)B(t)dt = -\frac{\eta(t)}{B(t)}r(t)dt - \eta(t)\frac{[\kappa(t) + v(t)]^\mathsf{T}}{B(t)}dw(t) \tag{14.24}$$

We show now that η/B is proportional to the Lagrange multiplier λ.

Proposition 14.1 *If we used for λ the process η/B, the constraints of the dual problem, (14.17) and (14.18), would be satisfied.*

Indeed, let $\lambda(t) = \lambda_0\eta(t)/B(t)$, $\lambda_0 \neq 0$. Once it is written in differential form, the first constraint (14.17) says that the expected change in the product of the multiplier and the riskless security's price is equal to zero:

$$\mathbb{E}_t d[\lambda(t) \times B(t)] = 0$$

while the second constraint (14.18) requires that, except for the drift created by dividends ι, the same holds for the N stock prices:

$$\mathbb{E}_t\{\lambda(t) \times \iota(t)dt + d[\lambda(t) \times \mathcal{S}(t)]\} = 0$$

Proof. To verify that the constraints are satisfied in differential form, let us compute the LHS of the first constraint. We have:

$$\mathbb{E}_t d[\lambda(t) \times B(t)] = \lambda(t) \times r(t) \times B(t)dt + \mathbb{E}_t[d\lambda(t) \times B(t)]$$

With $\lambda(t) = \lambda_0\eta(t)/B(t)$, the previous expression is equal to zero since its first part is

$$\lambda(t) \times r(t) \times B(t)dt = \lambda_0\eta(t)r(t)dt$$

and, based on (14.24), its second part is

$$\mathbb{E}_t\left[d\left(\frac{\eta(t)}{B(t)}\lambda_0\right) \times B(t)\right] = -\lambda_0\eta(t)r(t)dt$$

So, overall, the first constraint is satisfied when we use $\lambda_0 \eta(t)/B(t)$ as a Lagrange multiplier. This means that η/B is a stochastic discount factor for the riskless security. A process η with such properties is called a *minimax (local) martingale measure*.

Let us compute the LHS of the second constraint. We have:

$$\mathbb{E}_t[\lambda(t) \times \iota(t)dt] + \mathbb{E}_t d[\lambda(t) \times \mathcal{S}(t)] = \lambda(t) \times \iota(t)dt + \mathbb{E}_t d[\lambda(t) \times \mathcal{S}(t)]$$

$$= \lambda(t) \times \iota(t)dt + \mathbb{E}_t[d\lambda(t) \times \mathcal{S}(t) + \lambda(t) \times d\mathcal{S}(t) + d\lambda(t) \times d\mathcal{S}(t)]$$

This is equal to zero when $\lambda = \lambda_0 \eta/B$, since, dividing by λ_0, the differential in the expectation is

$$d\frac{\eta}{B}(t) \times \mathcal{S}(t) + \frac{\eta}{B}(t) \times d\mathcal{S}(t) + d\frac{\eta}{B}(t) \times d\mathcal{S}(t)$$

$$= \left(\frac{\eta}{B}(t)\mu(t) - \frac{\eta}{B}(t)\iota(t) \right) dt + \frac{\eta}{B}(t)\sigma(t)dw(t)$$

$$- \frac{\eta}{B}(t)\sigma(t)[\kappa(t) + v(t)]^\mathsf{T} dt$$

$$+ \mathcal{S}(t)\left(-\frac{\eta}{B}(t)r(t)dt - [\kappa(t) + v(t)]^\mathsf{T} dw(t) \right)$$

It follows that the expectation is

$$\left(\frac{\eta}{B}(t)\mu(t) - \frac{\eta}{B}(t)\iota(t) \right) dt - \frac{\eta}{B}(t)\sigma(t)[\kappa(t) + v(t)]^\mathsf{T} dt - \frac{\eta}{B}(t)r(t)\mathcal{S}(t)dt$$

and the LHS of the second constraint reduces to

$$\frac{\eta}{B}(t)\big\{ \mu(t)dt - \sigma(t)[\kappa(t) + v(t)]^\mathsf{T} - r(t)\mathcal{S}(t) \big\} dt$$

which is equal to zero by virtue of equality (14.21). This means that η/B is a stochastic discount factor for the risky securities as well. ☐

The reader can solve exercise 14.1 to show how this stochastic discount factor can be used to write the PDE for derivatives.

In conclusion, every η/B is proportional to a Lagrange multiplier and to a stochastic discount factor, and satisfies the constraints. For any $\lambda/\lambda_0 = \eta/B$, it is true that

$$\frac{d\lambda(t)}{\lambda(t)} = -r(t)dt - [\kappa(t) + v(t)]^\mathsf{T} dw(t) \tag{14.25}$$

As in complete markets, the drift of the stochastic-discount factor process is (the opposite of) the riskless rate. And the diffusion of the stochastic-discount factor process is (the opposite of) the market prices of risk, $\kappa(t) + v(t)$.

The stochastic-discount factor process that attains the minimum in the dual formulation is the one that induces each investor to not bear or hedge the risks that, because of market incompleteness, cannot be borne or hedged. It drives to zero the demand for non-marketed securities, exactly as it did in the corresponding discrete-time version (14.7). In a sense, market completeness obtains after the fact by setting equal to zero, via state prices, the demand and the supply of non-marketed securities. Restated yet another way, investors who face the marketability condition of incompleteness act as if they were fictitiously unconstrained and faced a modified price of risk.[11]

While the primal was subject to an infinity of budget constraints, thanks to state prices and to the kernel condition, the dual is subject to a single "global" constraint (14.19) for lifetime consumption. The constraint says, as in the complete-market case, that the expected value of lifetime consumption is equal to initial wealth, $W(0) = W_0$. In incomplete markets as well, we have been able to write the infinity of budget constraints as a single one, while portfolio holdings dropped out.

We have one possibility to rewrite the constraints for each η choice. Now use η as a change of measure to construct the risk-neutral probability P^*. Under (each) P^* the single budget constraint is written as:

$$\mathbb{E}_0^* \left[\int_0^T \frac{c(t)}{B(t)} dt + \frac{W(T)}{B(T)} \right] = W_0 \qquad (14.26)$$

The reader can verify this by solving exercise 14.2.

We still have to obtain ν, and consequently η. We do that in section 14.2.5 below.

14.2.4 Consumption

For each stochastic discount factor, first-order conditions for the consumption choice in program (14.16) are formally identical to what they were in the complete-market case:

$$\frac{\partial}{\partial c} u(c(t), t) = \lambda_0 \frac{\eta(t)}{B(t)} \quad (= \lambda(t)) \qquad (14.27)$$

$$\frac{\partial}{\partial W} \wp(W(T)) = \lambda_0 \frac{\eta(T)}{B(T)} \quad (= \lambda(T)) \qquad (14.28)$$

Call $\mathfrak{h}(\lambda(t), t)$ the solution of (14.27) and $\mathfrak{G}(\lambda(T))$ the solution of (14.28).

In the incomplete-market case, however, these solutions for optimal consumption enter the portfolio choice and are determined together with it, not separately from it, as we now show.

14.2.5 Portfolios

Since λ appears linearly in the Lagrangean (14.15), minimizing with respect to λ amounts to solving the constraints (14.17), (14.18), and (14.19). That will allow us to jointly obtain the stochastic discount factors – more specifically ν – and to retrieve optimal portfolio

---

11 The idea of "fictitious completion" comes from Karatzas *et al.* (1991).

holdings. We proceed as in the complete-market case. Assume that a vector of Markov state variables Y drives the securities prices dynamics:[12]

$$B(t) = B(0)e^{\int_0^t r(Y(s),s)ds}$$

$$S(t) + \int_0^t \iota(Y(s),s)ds = S(0) + \int_0^t \mu(Y(s),s)ds + \int_0^t \sigma(Y(s),s)dw(s)$$

$$Y(t) = Y(0) + \int_0^t \mu_Y(Y(s),s)ds + \int_0^t \sigma_Y(Y(s),s)dw(s)$$

Under this Markovian assumption, the Y state variables, together with state prices, are sufficient knowledge for probability assessments and investor decision making. Any other variable should be a function of them. In particular, we expect wealth at time t to be a function F of the time-t values of the $(\lambda(t), Y(t))$-state variables.

Since by assumption there are no endowments after time 0, wealth coincides with financial wealth. It is composed of a mixture of the short-term asset and stocks. As such, it is a traded asset. Consequently, the constraints (14.17) and (14.18) imply that wealth is at all times the present value of expected future consumption plus final wealth, for given state variables:

$$F(\lambda(t), Y(t), t) = \frac{B(t)}{\eta(t)}\mathbb{E}\left[\int_t^T \frac{c(s)\eta(s)}{B(s)}ds + \frac{W(T)\eta(T)}{B(T)}\bigg| \lambda(t), Y(t)\right] \qquad (14.29)$$

The expectation can equivalently be computed under a risk-neutral measure:

$$F(\lambda(t), Y(t), t) = B(t)\mathbb{E}^*\left[\int_t^T B(s)^{-1}\mathfrak{h}(\lambda(s),s)ds \right.$$

$$\left. + B(T)^{-1}\mathfrak{G}(\lambda(T))\bigg| \lambda(t), Y(t)\right] \qquad (14.30)$$

In chapter 8, we resorted at this point to the same proof by which we showed that the solution of the Black-Scholes PDE was given by the Feynman-Kac formula. Here too, by the same proof, equation (14.30) tells us that the function F must satisfy:

$$\mathcal{D}^*(F) + F_t = rF - \mathfrak{h} \qquad (14.31)$$

subject to the terminal condition at T:

$$F(\lambda, Y, T) = \mathfrak{G}(\lambda)$$

where $\mathcal{D}^*$ is the Dynkin under P^* and optimal consumption enters.

To write the Dynkin we use Girsanov theorem. As we know, the theorem says that

$$dw^* = (\kappa + \nu)dt + dw$$

---

12 We allow the vector $S(t)$ to be part of the vector $Y(t)$, in which case, of course, μ is part of μ_Y and σ is part of σ_Y.

is a Wiener process under the new probability measure. Under the probability P^*, we know from (10.17) in chapter 10 that the state variables satisfy the following SDEs:

$$Y(t) = Y(0) + \int_0^t [\mu_Y(Y(s), s) - \sigma_Y(Y(s), s)[\kappa(Y(s), s)$$

$$+ v(\lambda(s), Y(s), s)]] ds + \int_0^t \sigma_Y(Y(s), s) dw^*(s)$$

As a consequence, we have the generator:

$$\mathcal{D}^*(F) \triangleq \frac{1}{2} F_{\lambda\lambda} \lambda^2 (\kappa + v)^\mathsf{T} (\kappa + v) + \frac{1}{2} \text{trace}[F_{YY} \sigma_Y^\mathsf{T} \sigma_Y] \tag{14.32}$$

$$- F_{Y\lambda}^\mathsf{T} \sigma_Y (\kappa + v) \lambda + F_Y^\mathsf{T} [\mu_Y - \sigma_Y (\kappa + v)] - F_\lambda [\lambda r - \lambda (\kappa + v)^\mathsf{T} (\kappa + v)]$$

In the complete-market case, F was our tool to compute optimal portfolios. In that case we had a linear PDE for F. In the present case, the coefficients of the partial derivatives of the function F depend on v, which we have not solved for yet. It would be linear if the coefficients were constant. They are not, because v depends on the derivatives of F, as we show in a moment.

To obtain v, suppose that we have solved (14.31). How do we obtain portfolios after we have computed the function F? Itô's lemma provides the dynamics of F as:

$$F(\lambda(t), Y(t), t) - F(\lambda_0, Y(0), 0)$$

$$= \int_0^t \left[\mathcal{D}^*(F(\lambda(s), Y(s), s)) + F_t(\lambda(s), Y(s), s) \right] ds$$

$$+ \int_0^t \left\{ F_Y(\lambda(s), Y(s), s)^\mathsf{T} \sigma_Y(Y(s), s) \right.$$

$$\left. - F_\lambda(\lambda(s), Y(s), s) \lambda(s) [\kappa(Y(s), s) + v(\lambda(s), Y(s), s)]^\mathsf{T} \right\} dw^*(s)$$

Comparing with the budget constraint of the primal, the martingale representation theorem indicates that:

$$\Theta(t)^\mathsf{T} \sigma(Y(t), t) = F_Y(\lambda(t), Y(t), t)^\mathsf{T} \sigma_Y(Y(t), t)$$

$$- F_\lambda(\lambda(t), Y(t), t) \lambda(t) [\kappa(Y(t), t) + v(\lambda(t), Y(t), t)]^\mathsf{T} \tag{14.33}$$

or, dropping arguments:

$$\Theta(t)^\mathsf{T} \sigma(t) = F_Y(t)^\mathsf{T} \sigma_Y(t) - F_\lambda(t) \lambda(t) [\kappa(t) + v(t)]^\mathsf{T}$$

At each point in time t, this is a system of K equations in only N unknowns $\Theta(t)$. However, we can turn it into a system of $N + K$ equations in $N + K$ unknowns given that we also have the freedom to treat the elements of v as unknowns as soon as κ is fixed. Indeed, v has K elements and it must belong to the kernel of σ, or $\sigma v = 0$. This makes N equations. As a whole, we have $N + K$ equations and unknowns. As in the static case, state prices and portfolios must be solved for jointly.

Putting the two sets of equations together as follows:

$$\begin{bmatrix} \Theta^\mathsf{T} & \nu^\mathsf{T} \end{bmatrix} \begin{bmatrix} \sigma & 0_{N \times N} \\ F_\lambda \lambda I_K & \sigma^\mathsf{T} \end{bmatrix} = \begin{bmatrix} F_Y^\mathsf{T} \sigma_Y - F_\lambda \lambda \kappa^\mathsf{T} & 0_{1 \times N} \end{bmatrix}$$

and solving (assuming $F_\lambda \neq 0$ and recalling that κ is in the span of σ^T) we get:[13]

$$\nu(t)^\mathsf{T} = \frac{F_Y(t)^\mathsf{T} \sigma_Y(t) \left[I_K - \sigma(t)^\mathsf{T} \left(\sigma(t)\sigma(t)^\mathsf{T} \right)^{-1} \sigma(t) \right]}{F_\lambda(t)\lambda(t)} \tag{14.34}$$

as a solution for the K unknowns ν, as well as:

$$\Theta(t)^\mathsf{T} = \left\{ F_Y(t)^\mathsf{T} \sigma_Y(t) - F_\lambda(t)\lambda(t)\kappa(t)^\mathsf{T} \right\} \sigma(t)^\mathsf{T} \left[\sigma(t)\sigma(t)^\mathsf{T} \right]^{-1}$$

or:

$$\Theta(t) = -F_\lambda(t)\lambda(t) \left[\sigma(t)\sigma(t)^\mathsf{T} \right]^{-1} [\mu(t) - r(t) \times \mathcal{S}(t)]$$
$$+ \left[\sigma(t)\sigma(t)^\mathsf{T} \right]^{-1} \sigma(t)\sigma_Y(t)^\mathsf{T} F_Y(t)$$

as a solution for the remaining N unknowns Θ, and, of course:

$$\alpha(t)B(t) = F(\lambda(t), Y(t), t) - \Theta^\mathsf{T}(t)\mathcal{S}(t)$$

which gives us the optimal investment in the riskless security.

The expression (14.34) for ν depends on the function F causing the PDE (14.31) to be only *quasi-linear*. Its role, however, is similar to that of the linear PDE (10.19) in chapter 10. Substituting the expression for ν, which involves F_λ and F_Y, gives the complete PDE to be solved to obtain the function F. After simplifications, it is exactly identical to the PDE (9.34) that we obtained by applying the Cox-Huang transformation to the Bellman equation of Merton. While not linear, it is usually easier to attack numerically than the Bellman equation from dynamic programming (please solve exercise 14.3 on this issue; see also our discussion of numerical methods in chapter 13).

Remark 14.3 *In the special case in which the investor has logarithmic utility for interim consumption and for terminal wealth, F defined by (14.29) is only related to the variables*

---

13 Here are the details of the derivation. Equation (14.34) is obtained from (14.33) simply by postmultiplying by σ^T and using the fact that $\nu^\mathsf{T}\sigma^\mathsf{T} = 0$. Then, from (14.33):

$$\nu^\mathsf{T} = \frac{1}{F_\lambda \lambda} \left[F_Y^\mathsf{T} \sigma_Y - F_\lambda \lambda \kappa^\mathsf{T} \right] \times \left\{ I_K - \sigma^\mathsf{T} \left[\sigma\sigma^\mathsf{T} \right]^{-1} \sigma \right\}$$

Because of (14.20), κ^T is of the form $x^\mathsf{T}\sigma$ for some x:

$$\nu^\mathsf{T} = \frac{1}{F_\lambda \lambda} \left[F_Y^\mathsf{T} \sigma_Y - F_\lambda \lambda x^\mathsf{T}\sigma \right] \times \left\{ I_K - \sigma^\mathsf{T} \left[\sigma\sigma^\mathsf{T} \right]^{-1} \sigma \right\}$$

Multiplying through gives equation (14.34).

λ and t, and not to Y, because of (14.27) and (14.28). Hence, $F_Y = 0$ and $v = 0$ whether the market is complete or not.[14] This case is studied in exercise 14.4. The portfolio of that investor is

$$\Theta(t)^\mathsf{T} = -F_\lambda(t)\lambda(t)\big[\sigma(t)\sigma(t)^\mathsf{T}\big]^{-1}[\mu(t) - r(t) \times \mathcal{S}(t)]$$

and is called the "growth optimal" portfolio.

As in the discrete case, the solution for Θ sets to zero the demand for non-marketed securities, or makes the desired consumption path marketed, since it is obtained from the requirement that, via F, we span the same uncertainty as under the original variables.

At each point in time, wealth is invested either in the riskless security or in the risky ones. Hence the solution for α is simply the complement to total financial wealth.

14.3 Portfolio Constraints

Suppose we are given to solve the problem (14.11) subject to the constraints (14.12) and (14.13), in a complete market $N = K$ (as in chapter 10) – so that the matrix σ is square and invertible – but with additional inequality constraints of the type:

$$\Theta(t) \geq \underline{\Theta}(t)$$
$$\alpha(t) \geq \underline{\alpha}(t)$$

In other words, the investor faces lower bounds on the positions he can take. Then the Lagrangean instead of being (14.15) would have two more multiplier processes, here called $\varphi(t)$ and $\chi(t)$:

$$\max_{\{c(t)\},\{\alpha(t),\Theta(t)\}}\min_{\{\lambda(t),\varphi(t),\chi(t)\}} \mathbb{E}_0\left\{\int_0^T u(c(s),s)ds + \wp(W(T))\right\}$$
$$+\lambda_0 \times \big[W_0 - (\alpha(0)B(0) + \Theta(0)^\mathsf{T}\mathcal{S}(0))\big]$$
$$+\mathbb{E}_0\left\{-\int_0^T \lambda(t) \times \big[d\alpha(t) \times B(t) - \Theta(t)^\mathsf{T}\iota(t)dt + d\Theta(t)^\mathsf{T}\mathcal{S}(t)\right.$$
$$+d\Theta(t)^\mathsf{T}d\mathcal{S}(t) + c(t)dt\big] + \lambda(T) \times \big[\alpha(T)B(T) + \Theta(T)^\mathsf{T}\mathcal{S}(T) - W(T)\big]\Big\}$$
$$+\mathbb{E}_0\left[\int_0^T [\Theta(t) - \underline{\Theta}(t)]^\mathsf{T}\varphi(t)dt\right] + \mathbb{E}_0\left[\int_0^T [\alpha(t) - \underline{\alpha}(t)]\chi(t)dt\right]$$

and the (semi-)dual program would be:

$$\max_{\{c(t)\}}\min_{\{\lambda(t),\varphi(t),\chi(t)\}} \mathbb{E}_0\left\{\int_0^T u(c(t),t)dt + \wp(W(T))\right\}$$

---

14 Warning: the result does not extend to the case in which the log investor collects an endowment after time 0.

subject to:

$$\mathbb{E}_t\left[\int_t^T \chi(s)ds + \lambda(T) \times \mathcal{S}(T)\right] = \lambda(t) \times B(t); \forall t : 0 \le t \le T \qquad (14.35)$$

$$\mathbb{E}_t\left[\int_t^T \lambda(s) \times \iota(s)ds + \varphi(s)ds + \lambda(T) \times \mathcal{S}(T)\right] = \lambda(t) \times \mathcal{S}(t);$$

$$\forall t : 0 \le t \le T \qquad (14.36)$$

$$\varphi(t) \ge 0; \chi(t) \ge 0$$

and subject to a lifetime budget constraint:

$$\mathbb{E}_t\left[\int_0^T \lambda(s) \times c(s)ds + \lambda(T) \times W(T)\right] = \lambda_0 \times W(0)$$

One set of necessary conditions of optimality of both the primal and the dual are the complementary-slackness conditions

$$\left[\Theta(t) - \underline{\Theta}(t)\right]^\mathsf{T} \varphi(t) = 0; \left[\alpha(t) - \underline{\alpha}(t)\right] \chi(t) = 0 \qquad (14.37)$$

which say that the dual variables are different from zero if and only the primal constraints are binding. The dual program, therefore, is seen to be one in which, whenever the constraint $\Theta(t) \ge \underline{\Theta}(t)$ is binding, the dividends ι are artificially increased by the value of the dual variable φ/λ. The purpose is to encourage the investor to hold securities that they are required to hold. For a similar purpose, an artificial income χ/λ is added to the riskless asset whenever the constraint $\alpha(t) \ge \underline{\alpha}(t)$ is binding.

Define

$$\kappa(Y(t),t) \triangleq \sigma(Y(t),t)^{-1}\left[\mu(Y(t),t) + \frac{\varphi(t)}{\lambda(t)} - r(t) \times \mathcal{S}(t) - \frac{\chi(t)}{\lambda(t)}\frac{\mathcal{S}(t)}{B(t)}\right] \qquad (14.38)$$

and postulate that:

$$\lambda(t) \triangleq \exp\left\{\int_0^t\left[-\frac{\chi(s)}{B(s)} - \lambda(s)r(s) - \frac{1}{2}\|\kappa(s)\|^2\right]ds - \int_0^t [\kappa(s)]^\mathsf{T}dw(s)\right\}$$

We can verify that dual constraints (14.35) and (14.36) are then satisfied in their stochastic differential form (see exercise 14.5):

$$\chi(t)dt + \mathbb{E}_t d[\lambda(t) \times B(t)] = 0$$

$$\mathbb{E}_t\{\lambda(t) \times \iota(t)dt + \varphi(t)dt + d[\lambda(t) \times \mathcal{S}(t)]\} = 0$$

Wealth is again defined as (14.29) or (14.30) and the consumption choices are again given by (14.27) and (14.28). The portfolios are given by

$$\Theta(t)^\mathsf{T}\sigma(Y(t),t) = F_Y(\lambda(t),Y(t),t)^\mathsf{T}\sigma_Y(Y(t),t)$$

$$-F_\lambda(\lambda(t),Y(t),t)\lambda(t)\kappa(Y(t),t)^\mathsf{T}$$

or, κ being given by (14.38):

$$\Theta(t)^\mathsf{T} = F_Y(\lambda(t), Y(t), t)^\mathsf{T} \sigma_Y(Y(t), t) \sigma(Y(t), t)^{-1}$$
$$-F_\lambda(\lambda(t), Y(t), t)\lambda(t)\left[\mu(Y(t), t) + \frac{\varphi(t)}{\lambda(t)} - r(t) \times S(t)\right.$$
$$\left. -\frac{\chi(t)}{\lambda(t)}\frac{S(t)}{B(t)}\right]^\mathsf{T} \left(\sigma(Y(t), t)\sigma(t)^\mathsf{T}\right)^{-1} \qquad (14.39)$$

In conjunction with the complementary-slackness conditions (14.37), equations (14.39), and the residual equation $\alpha B + \Theta S = F$ make up a system of $2 \times (N + 1)$ equations in as many unknowns: $\Theta(t), \alpha(t), \varphi(t)$, and $\chi(t)$. That system, however, is nonlinear in the unknowns because the portfolios multiply the dual variables in (14.37).

The incomplete-market case of section 14.2 is a special case of the portfolio constraints considered here: in the incomplete-market case, we constrain some positions to be equal to zero. In the case of *equality* constraints, complementary slackness conditions are not needed, the system (14.39) becomes linear and can be solved straightforwardly as in the previous section.

14.4   The Minimum-Squared Deviation Approach

We return to an incomplete financial market. Instead of working out the solution of the utility-based global formulation, and in an attempt to pin down a unique state price process, the following idea can be pursued. State prices and equilibrium quantities in an incomplete market should be "close" to what they would be in a complete market. That is a correct statement in some economic sense of closeness (think of an Edgeworth box, as in chapter 4). One can think of implementing the idea by replacing the unspecified economic distance by the Euclidean norm (see Schweizer (1992)).

14.4.1   The One-Period Case

Let an investor have a target net payoff $C - E$ that he tries to attain by means of a portfolio Θ. In an incomplete market that is not always possible but he/she can come ε-close:

$$C - E = \Sigma^\mathsf{T}\Theta + \varepsilon$$

The Euclidean distance is:

$$\varepsilon^\mathsf{T}\varepsilon = \left(C - E - \Sigma^\mathsf{T}\Theta\right)^\mathsf{T}\left(C - E - \Sigma^\mathsf{T}\Theta\right)$$
$$= (C - E)^\mathsf{T}(C - E) + \Theta^\mathsf{T}\Sigma\Sigma^\mathsf{T}\Theta - 2(C - E)^\mathsf{T}\Sigma^\mathsf{T}\Theta$$

Minimize it:[15]

$$2\Sigma\Sigma^\mathsf{T}\Theta - 2\Sigma(C - E) = 0 \qquad (14.40)$$
$$\Theta = \left[\Sigma\Sigma^\mathsf{T}\right]^{-1}\Sigma(C - E) \qquad (14.41)$$

---

15 Equation (14.40) means $\Sigma\left\{\Sigma^\mathsf{T}\Theta - (C - E)\right\} = 0$ or $\Sigma\varepsilon = 0$.

For prices, we must have:

$$S = \Sigma \Phi$$

However, as we remarked in section 14.1, there are many possible solutions to this last system of equations, in more unknowns (K of them) than there are equations (N of them).

Which one of the solutions corresponds to investor portfolio behavior (14.41)? To answer this question, let us observe that $S^\mathsf{T} \Theta = \Phi^\mathsf{T}(C - E)$ must hold:

$$\underbrace{S^\mathsf{T}\left[\Sigma\Sigma^\mathsf{T}\right]^{-1}\Sigma(C - E)}_{\Theta} = \Phi^\mathsf{T}(C - E)$$

Also, since this must be true for any payoff $C - E$ that one might choose to replicate, evidently:

$$\Phi = \Sigma^\mathsf{T}\left[\Sigma\Sigma^\mathsf{T}\right]^{-1}S \qquad (14.42)$$

This choice of state prices corresponds to the choice $\nu = 0$ in the formulation (14.2, 14.3) in which κ has been set equal to the generalized-inverse solution.

14.4.2   Continuous Time: The "Minimal" Martingale Measure

We now develop a similar reasoning in continuous time. Given an incomplete market, we have seen that a whole family of pricing measures η can be entertained. The pricing measure that is being selected when implementing the minimum-squared deviation approach is the one for $\nu = 0$:

$$\eta_{\min}(t) = \exp\left\{-\int_0^t \kappa(s)^\mathsf{T}dw(s) - \frac{1}{2}\int_0^t \|\kappa(s)\|^2 ds\right\} \qquad (14.43)$$

where κ is defined as in (14.20) on the basis of the generalized inverse, which puts it in the span of σ^T.

This measure is called the *minimal martingale measure* because, of all the measures built on $\kappa + \nu$, it is the one that has the minimum norm:

$$0 = \arg\min_{\nu\in\ker(\sigma)} \|\kappa(s) + \nu(s)\|^2$$

Since investors tend to smooth their consumption, minimizing the variance of their marginal utility is certainly a good idea. But no more precise economic rationale for the above measure seems to be available.

An example can be built as follows. In order to extend the two-states, one-security case we built for discrete time, suppose that the price of a single security is driven by two independent Wiener processes in the following way:

$$dS(t) = \mu[S(t), w_1(t), t]dt$$
$$+\sigma_1[S(t), w_1(t), t]dw_1(t) + \sigma_2[S(t), w_1(t), t]dw_2(t)$$

Then, provided that both σ_1 and σ_2 are not zero with probability one at the same time, the generalized inverse solution is

$$\kappa = \begin{pmatrix} \frac{\sigma_1(t)}{\sigma_1^2(t)+\sigma_2^2(t)}[\mu(t) - r(t) \times S(t)] \\ \frac{\sigma_2(t)}{\sigma_1^2(t)+\sigma_2^2(t)}[\mu(t) - r(t) \times S(t)] \end{pmatrix}$$

Itô's lemma, applied to the exponential martingale $\eta_{\min}$, gives the following percentage change:

$$\frac{d\eta_{\min}}{\eta_{\min}} = -\frac{\sigma_1(t)dw_1(t) + \sigma_2(t)dw_2(t)}{\sigma_1^2(t) + \sigma_2^2(t)}[\mu(t) - r(t) \times S(t)]$$

Let the rate of interest be a given function $r = r(S, w_1, t)$. In this incomplete market, under the minimal pricing measure, any price process is a martingale, once multiplied by $\eta_{\min}$ and discounted. Its value $V(S, w_1, t)$ follows the PDE:

$$\frac{1}{dt}\frac{1}{\eta_{\min}}\mathbb{E}[d(\eta_{\min}V)] = V_S r(t)S(t) + \frac{1}{2}V_{SS}\left[\sigma_1^2(t) + \sigma_2^2(t)\right] + \frac{1}{2}V_{w_1w_1}$$

$$+V_{Sw_1}\sigma_1 - \frac{\mu(t) - r(t)S(t)}{\sqrt{\sigma_1^2(t) + \sigma_2^2(t)}}\frac{\sigma_1}{\sqrt{\sigma_1^2(t) + \sigma_2^2(t)}}V_{w_1} + V_t = r(t)V \qquad (14.44)$$

The drift μ of S does not cancel out of the PDE. It serves indirectly to price the risk w_1, via the correlation coefficient

$$\frac{\sigma_1}{\sqrt{\sigma_1^2(t) + \sigma_2^2(t)}}.$$

Under the minimal pricing measure, all risks are priced on the basis of the price of risk of the underlying security under consideration, to the tune of their correlation with it. By analogy with the model of Cox, Ingersoll, and Ross (chapter 11), it is as though the security-price risk stood for the risk of aggregate consumption.

In the next lines, we develop an interpretation of the PDE (14.44).

♠

The "self-financing-in-the-mean" argument:

By analogy with the complete-market case, one wonders whether equation (14.44) can be interpreted as a self-financing condition. Consider a portfolio with value $V(S, w_1, t)$ containing $\theta(S, w_1, t)$ shares of the underlying security and $\alpha(S, w_1, t)$ shares of the instantaneously riskless bank deposit:

$$V(S, w_1, t) = \theta(S, w_1, t)S + \alpha(S, w_1, t)B$$

The condition for it to be self-financing would be that the difference between the change in the replicating portfolio and the gains is null, namely $dV - dG = 0$, where $G = \theta S + \alpha B$:

$$\left[V_S\mu(t) + \frac{1}{2}V_{SS}\left[\sigma_1^2(t) + \sigma_2^2(t)\right] + \frac{1}{2}V_{w_1w_1} + V_{Sw_1}\sigma_1 + V_t\right]dt$$

$$+V_S[\sigma_1(t)dw_1(t) + \sigma_2(t)dw_2(t)] + V_{w_1}dw_1 \qquad (14.45)$$

$$-\theta(t)[\mu(t)dt + \sigma_1(t)dw_1(t) + \sigma_2(t)dw_2(t)] - r(t)[V - \theta(t)S]dt = 0$$

Obviously, this condition cannot be satisfied exactly, or with probability one. Interpret $dV - dG$ – which was equal to zero in complete markets but is no longer so – as a replication error. Suppose we pick θ to minimize the variance of the replication error:

$$\text{var}_t\{[V_S - \theta(t)] \times [\sigma_1(t)dw_1(t) + \sigma_2(t)dw_2(t)] + V_{w_1}dw_1\}$$
$$= [V_S - \theta(t)]^2\left[\sigma_1^2(t) + \sigma_2^2(t)\right] + V_{w_1}^2 + 2[V_S - \theta(t)]\sigma_1(t)V_{w_1}$$

Then:

$$-2[V_S - \theta(t)]\left[\sigma_1^2(t) + \sigma_2^2(t)\right] - 2\sigma_1(t)V_{w_1} = 0$$

$$\theta(t) = V_S + \frac{\sigma_1(t)}{\sigma_1^2(t) + \sigma_2^2(t)}V_{w_1}$$

This is the replication-error, variance-minimizing ratio. We can interpret it, as Basak and Chabakauri (2012) do in a similar setting, as a generalized Greek that comprises the standard Black-Scholes, complete-market term (V_S) plus a term $\sigma_1(t)V_{w_1}/\left(\sigma_1^2(t) + \sigma_2^2(t)\right)$ that accounts for market incompleteness.

Substituting back into (14.45), we get:

$$\left[V_S r(t)S + \frac{1}{2}V_{SS}\left[\sigma_1^2(t) + \sigma_2^2(t)\right] + \frac{1}{2}V_{w_1w_1} + V_{Sw_1}\sigma_1 + V_t\right]dt + V_{w_1}dw_1$$
$$- \left[\frac{\sigma_1(t)}{\sigma_1^2(t) + \sigma_2^2(t)}V_{w_1}\right][\mu(t)dt + \sigma_1(t)dw_1(t) + \sigma_2(t)dw_2(t)]$$
$$+ r(t)\left[\frac{\sigma_1(t)}{\sigma_1^2(t) + \sigma_2^2(t)}V_{w_1}\right]Sdt = r(t)Vdt$$

Taking the conditional expected value of the LHS, we obtain:

$$V_S r(t)S + \frac{1}{2}V_{SS}\left[\sigma_1^2(t) + \sigma_2^2(t)\right] + \frac{1}{2}V_{w_1w_1} + V_{Sw_1}\sigma_1 + V_t \qquad (14.46)$$
$$- \left[\frac{\sigma_1(t)}{\sigma_1^2(t) + \sigma_2^2(t)}V_{w_1}\right]\mu(t) + r(t)\left[\frac{\sigma_1(t)}{\sigma_1^2(t) + \sigma_2^2(t)}V_{w_1}\right]S = r(t)V$$

which is exactly (14.44).

The equation means that the replication policy that minimizes the variance of the replication error entails zero expected value of cash flows at each point in time.

14.5 Conclusion

Duality, an implication of the Lagrangean optimization technique, is a powerful tool in incomplete markets. It has allowed us to disentangle somewhat the problem of consumption choice from the problem of portfolio choice and to write a lifetime budget constraint, which is a very nice way to elucidate the decisions made by the investor. But, ultimately the problem of consumption and portfolio choice is more intricate in an incomplete market than it was in a complete market. In particular, it is not possible to obtain consumption choices without simultaneously solving for portfolio choices.

14.6   Appendix: Derivation of the Dual Problem 14.16

We start from the Lagrangean (14.15) and obtain first-order conditions for portfolio choice. In discrete time, it is easy to do that just by expanding terms: when we modify an exiting portfolio at time t, we can easily look up the effect this has in the time $t + 1$ budget constraint. In continuous time, the notation does not guide us as easily.

To keep track of the effect over time of a modification of a portfolio, we use an argument that involves a "perturbation" in the time path of the portfolio. The perturbation argument is familiar to applied mathematicians since the time of Euler and Lagrange and their variational calculus.

To perform the optimization of the portfolio $\max_{\{\alpha(t),\Theta(t)\}}$, consider a stochastic process $\eta(t)$:

$$\eta_{\tau_1,\tau_2}(t) \triangleq \begin{cases} 0, & t \leq \tau_1 \text{ and } t \geq \tau_2 \\ \text{arbitrary (but same class as } \alpha) \text{ on } \tau_1 < t < \tau_2 \end{cases}$$

where τ_1 and τ_2 are fixed points in time $0 < \tau_1 < \tau_2 < T$. Consider a perturbation of $\alpha(t)$ in the direction $\eta(t)$ and name $\Phi(\varepsilon)$ its effect on the Lagrangean (14.15):

$$\Phi(\varepsilon) \triangleq \lambda_0 \times \left[W_0 - \left(\alpha(0)B(0) + \Theta(0)^{\mathsf{T}} S(0) \right) \right]$$

$$- \int_0^T \mathbb{E}_0 \Big\{ \lambda(t) \times \big\{ \left[d\alpha(t) + \varepsilon \times d\eta_{\tau_1,\tau_2}(t) \right] \times B(t) - \Theta(t)^{\mathsf{T}} \iota(t)dt$$

$$+ d\Theta(t)^{\mathsf{T}} S(t) + d\Theta(t)^{\mathsf{T}} dS(t) \big\} \Big\}$$

$$+ \mathbb{E}_0 \Big\{ \lambda(T) \times \left[\alpha(T)B(T) + \Theta(T)^{\mathsf{T}} S(T) \right] \Big\}$$

Differentiate with respect to ε:

$$\Phi'(\varepsilon) = \mathbb{E}_0 \left[- \int_{\tau_1}^{\tau_2} \lambda(t) \times B(t) \times d\eta_{\tau_1,\tau_2}(t) \right]$$

To optimize α, we equate $\Phi'(\varepsilon)$ to zero, which implies:[16]

$$\mathbb{E}_0 \left[- \int_{\tau_1}^{\tau_2} \lambda(t) \times B(t) \times d\eta_{\tau_1,\tau_2}(t) \right] = 0 \tag{14.47}$$

The last equation must hold for any τ_1 and τ_2 and any process η. This implies that the product $\lambda \times B$ of the Lagrange multiplier and the riskless security's price is a martingale or that its prices, once discounted by the Lagrange multipliers, are martingales:

$$\mathbb{E}_{\tau_1}[\lambda(t) \times B(t)] = \lambda(\tau_1) \times B(\tau_1) \, ; \, \tau_1 < t < \tau_2 \tag{14.48}$$

---

16 Second order conditions are not examined.

Indeed, consider the operation of buying an arbitrary random but $\mathcal{F}(t_1)$-measurable amount ς_{t_1} of the bank account at date t_1 and reselling it at date t_2, where $\tau_1 < t_1 < t_2 < \tau_2$. That is a particular process η:

$$\eta_{\tau_1,\tau_2}(t) = \begin{cases} 0, & t \leq t_1 \text{ and } t \geq t_2 \\ \varsigma_{t_1} & \text{on } t_1 < t < t_2 \end{cases}$$

$$d\eta_{\tau_1,\tau_2}(t) = \begin{cases} \varsigma_{t_1} \text{ at } t = t_1 \\ -\varsigma_{t_1} \text{ at } t = t_2 \end{cases}$$

for which

$$\mathbb{E}_0\left[-\int_{\tau_1}^{\tau_2} \lambda(t) \times B(t) \times d\eta_{\tau_1,\tau_2}(t) \right]$$
$$= \mathbb{E}_0\left[-\varsigma_{t_1} \times (\lambda(t_1) \times B(t_1) - \lambda(t_2) \times B(t_2)) \right]$$
$$= \mathbb{E}_0\left[-\varsigma_{t_1} \times \left(\lambda(t_1) \times B(t_1) - \mathbb{E}_{t_1}\left[\lambda(t_2) \times B(t_2) \right] \right) \right]$$

Both $\lambda(t_1) \times B(t_1) - E_{t_1}\left[\lambda(t_2) \times B(t_2) \right]$ and ς_{t_1} are $\mathcal{F}(t_1)$-measurable random variables. The equation above says that these two random variables are orthogonal to each other. As ς_{t_1} is arbitrary, $\lambda(t_1) \times B(t_1) - E_{t_1}\left[\lambda(t_2) \times B(t_2) \right]$ is orthogonal to every $\mathcal{F}(t_1)$-measurable random variable. Condition (14.47) then implies:

$$\lambda(t_1) \times B(t_1) - \mathbb{E}_{t_1}\left[\lambda(t_2) \times B(t_2) \right] = 0$$

and, by continuity, (14.48) follows.[17] And (14.48) is nothing other than (14.17).

Consider now a perturbation of $\Theta(t)$ in the direction $\eta(t)$, where :

$$\eta_{\tau_1,\tau_2}(t) \triangleq \begin{cases} 0, t \leq \tau_1 \text{ and } t \geq \tau_2 \\ \text{arbitrary (but same class as } \Theta) \text{ on } \tau_1 < t < \tau_2 \end{cases}$$

and call $\Phi(\varepsilon)$ its effect on the Lagrangean:

$$\Phi(\varepsilon) \triangleq \lambda_0 \times \left[W_0 - \left(\alpha(0)B(0) + \Theta(0)^\mathsf{T} \mathcal{S}(0) \right) \right]$$

$$- \int_0^T \mathbb{E}_0 \left\{ \lambda(t) \times \left\{ d\alpha(t) \times B(t) - \left[\Theta(t) + \varepsilon \times \eta_{\tau_1,\tau_2}(t) \right]^\mathsf{T} \iota(t)dt \right. \right.$$

$$\left. + \left[d\Theta(t) + \varepsilon \times d\eta_{\tau_1,\tau_2}(t) \right]^\mathsf{T} \mathcal{S}(t) + d\Theta(t)^\mathsf{T} d\mathcal{S}(t) \right\} \right\}$$

$$+ \mathbb{E}_0 \left\{ \lambda(T) \times \left[\alpha(T)B(T) + \Theta(T)^\mathsf{T} \mathcal{S}(T) \right] \right\}$$

Differentiate with respect to ε:

$$\Phi'(\varepsilon) = \mathbb{E}_0 \left\{ -\int_{\tau_1}^{\tau_2} \lambda(t) \times \left\{ -\eta_{\tau_1,\tau_2}(t)^\mathsf{T} \iota(t)dt + d\eta_{\tau_1,\tau_2}(t)^\mathsf{T} [\mathcal{S}(t) + d\mathcal{S}(t)] \right\} \right\}$$

---

17 For help in the last part of the proof, we thank Tan Wang without implicating him.

To optimize Θ, equate $\Phi'(\varepsilon)$ to zero, which implies:

$$\mathbb{E}_0\left\{-\int_{\tau_1}^{\tau_2}\lambda(t)\times\left\{-\eta_{\tau_1,\tau_2}(t)^{\mathsf{T}}\iota(t)dt+d\eta_{\tau_1,\tau_2}(t)^{\mathsf{T}}[S(t)+dS(t)]\right\}\right\}=0$$

The last equation must hold for any τ_1 and τ_2 and any process η. This implies that the product $\lambda\times S$ of the Lagrange multiplier and risky security prices is a martingale, or that security prices, once discounted using the Lagrange multipliers, are martingales:

$$\mathbb{E}_{\tau_1}\left[\int_{\tau_1}^{t}\lambda(s)\times\iota(s)ds+\lambda(t)\times S(t)\right]=\lambda(\tau_1)\times S(\tau_1)\,;\,\tau_1<t<\tau_2 \qquad (14.49)$$

Indeed, consider the operation of buying an arbitrary random but $\mathcal{F}(t_1)$-measurable amount ς_{t_1} of any of the risky securities at date t_1 and reselling it at date t_2, where $\tau_1<t_1<t_2<\tau_2$. That is a particular process η:

$$\eta_{\tau_1,\tau_2}(t)=\begin{cases} 0, & t\leq t_1 \text{ and } t\geq t_2 \\ \varsigma_{t_1} & \text{on } t_1<t<t_2 \end{cases}$$

$$d\eta_{\tau_1,\tau_2}(t)=\begin{cases} \varsigma_{t_1} \text{ at } t=t_1 \\ -\varsigma_{t_1} \text{ at } t=t_2 \end{cases}$$

For this process η, we have:

$$\mathbb{E}_0\left\{\varsigma_{t_1}\times\left[\int_{t_1}^{t_2}\lambda(t)\times\iota(t)dt-\lambda(t_1)S(t_1)+\lambda(t_2)S(t_2)\right]\right\}=0$$

Hence, by a reasoning similar to the one pertaining to the riskless security:

$$\lambda(t_1)\times S(t_1)=\mathbb{E}_{t_1}\left[\int_{t_1}^{t_2}\lambda(t)\times\iota(t)dt+\lambda(t_2)\times S(t_2)\right]$$

and, by continuity, (14.49) follows. And (14.49) is nothing other than (14.18).

Since by assumption there are no endowments after time 0, wealth coincides with financial wealth. It is made of a mixture of the short-term assets and stocks. As such, it is a traded asset. Consequently, as we remark in the text, the constraints (14.17) and (14.18) imply that wealth is at all times the present value of expected future consumption plus final wealth. That fact follows from the constraints already in place and is in no sense an additional constraint, except for the purpose of meeting the time-0 initial conditions. At time 0, we need to write that the present value of expected future consumption plus final wealth is equal to the initial endowment (e_0 or W_0) given to the investor. That is accomplished by constraint (14.19) of the dual.

Exercises

14.1. Consider an option pricing problem with random interest rate. As in the standard Black-Scholes problem, the economy is endowed with two financial assets only: the option's underlying security and a bank deposit that pays an instantaneously riskless rate of interest. The variations of the underlying security's price and interest rate are governed by:

$$\frac{dS(t)}{S} = \mu dt + \sigma dw_1(t)$$

$$\frac{dr(t)}{r(t)} = \sigma_r dw_2(t)$$

μ, σ, and σ_r are constants. The correlation between w_1 and w_2 is arbitrary but constant. No bond exists that would have the same maturity date as the option. Write the PDE for the option value $V(S, r, t)$ under the minimax pricing measure.

14.2. Verify by applying Itô's lemma to $\eta W / B$ (where $W(t) = \alpha(t)B(t) + \Theta(t)^{\mathsf{T}} S(t)$) that the dynamic budget constraints

$$\alpha(t)B(t) + \Theta(t)^{\mathsf{T}} S(t) + \int_0^t c(s)ds =$$

$$\alpha(0)B(0) + \Theta(0)^{\mathsf{T}} S(0) + \int_0^t \left[\alpha(s)B(s)r(s) + \Theta(s)^{\mathsf{T}} \mu(s) \right] ds$$

$$+ \int_0^t \Theta(s)^{\mathsf{T}} \sigma(s)dw(s)$$

$$W(T) = \alpha(T)B(T) + \Theta(T)^{\mathsf{T}} S(T)$$

lead to the lifetime one:

$$B(0)\mathbb{E}\left[\int_0^T \frac{c(t)\eta(t)}{B(t)}dt + \frac{W(T)\eta(T)}{B(T)} \right] = \alpha(0)B(0) + \Theta(0)^{\mathsf{T}} S(0)$$

when:

$$\eta(t) = \exp\left[-\int_0^t [\kappa(S(s), s) + \nu(S(s), s)]^{\mathsf{T}} dw(s) \right.$$

$$\left. -\frac{1}{2} \int_0^t \|\kappa(S(s), s) + \nu(S(s), s)\| ds \right]$$

and w is a K-dimensional Wiener process, S and Θ are N-vectors with $N < K$, κ is defined as in (14.20) and $\nu \in \ker(\sigma)$, where σ is a $N \times K$ matrix.

14.3. Show that, substituting the expression for ν, which involves F_λ and F_Y, into the PDE (14.31), gives the complete PDE to be solved to obtain the function F in section 14.2.5. Demonstrate also that, after simplifications, it is exactly identical to the PDE (9.34) that we obtained by applying the Cox-Huang transformation to the HJB equation of Merton.

14.4. Show that remark 14.3 is true.

14.5. Verify that the dual constraints (14.35) and (14.36) of section 14.3 are satisfied in their stochastic differential form.

15 Incomplete-Market Equilibrium

As has been mentioned several times already, the data that can be collected from financial markets lead to a rejection of the classic complete-market equilibrium of chapter 12. Financial economists have been busy exploring generalizations of, or deviations from, the model that could explain the facts. The first priority is essentially to account for more volatility in the market and larger risk premia than the classic model can produce. The rest of this book is largely devoted to some of these avenues of exploration. In this chapter, we venture down one of these avenues: incomplete-market equilibria.

We discuss equilibria in which investors face unspanned or unhedgeable risks. In section 15.1, we summarize some key concepts that concern these equilibria in a static setting. In section 15.2, we explain a method to obtain dynamic-equilibrium solutions in continuous time. Then, in section 15.3 we ask whether incomplete markets can potentially explain observed risk premia. As an illustration, we discuss in section 15.4 a model of restricted participation, which serves to address the so-called *interest-rate and equity-premium puzzles*, described below. The same ideas and methods are applied to the benchmark example in section 15.5.1. When markets are incomplete, "bubbles" can develop. They are treated in section 15.5.

15.1 Various Concepts of Incomplete-Market Equilibrium, Existence, and Welfare Properties

15.1.1 One-Good, Static Setting

Corresponding to the two different optimization problems (3.15) and (3.23) of chapter 3 repeated in the previous chapter, one can define two types of competitive equilibrium.

The definition of the first type introduces a minor nuance relative to that of definition 4.1. The difference is that only time-0 markets – among them, of course, the financial market – are required to clear, so that we need not include direct future consumption choice (3.18) among the requirements of the definition:[1]

---

[1] We know, however, that, via the budget constraints, it will follow that time-1 markets also clear.

Definition 15.1 *A financial-market equilibrium is a vector of securities prices S, an allocation of consumption* $\{c^m(0)\}$, *a set of Lagrange multipliers* $\{\lambda_0^m\}$, *and a choice of portfolios* $\{\Theta^m\}$ *for the various investors, m = 1 ... M, for which each investor's first-order conditions (3.17, 3.20, 3.13, 3.14) are satisfied and the time-0 goods and financial markets clear:*

$$\sum_{m=1}^{M} \Theta^m = 0$$

$$\sum_{m=1}^{M} c^m(0) = \sum_{m=1}^{M} e^m(0)$$

The second type of equilibrium is similar to the Arrow-Debreu equilibrium (definition 4.2) with a crucial adaptation to incomplete markets:

Definition 15.2 *A no-arbitrage equilibrium[2] is a vector of securities prices S, an allocation of consumption* $\{c^m(0), c^m(s)\}$ *to the various investors, m = 1 ... M, a set of state prices* $\{\phi^m(s)\}$, *and a set of Lagrange multipliers* $\{\lambda_0^m\}$ *for which each investor's first-order conditions for min-max problem (3.23) are satisfied and goods-market clearing conditions (4.7) and (4.8) are satisfied:*

$$\sum_{m} c^m(0) = \sum_{m} e^m(0)$$

$$\sum_{m} c^m(s) = \sum_{m} e^m(s)$$

By contrast with definition 4.2, which was applicable to complete markets only, this new definition involves securities prices (coming from the kernel restriction (3.25) in (3.23)) and it involves different state prices $\{\phi^m(s)\}$ for different investors. Please, note also the difference between definitions 15.1 and 15.2: the first definition includes portfolios; the second definition refers to a direct choice of consumption (although portfolios will reappear in the course of the solution as Lagrange multipliers of the kernel restriction; see section 14.1.3).

Theorem 15.1 *In a one-good, static setting, every no-arbitrage equilibrium is a financial-market equilibrium and vice versa.*

One can show (see, for example, Magill and Quinzii (1996), page 86) that *a no-arbitrage equilibrium exists* provided each investor's endowment is positive at time 0 and in every state and that investors have strictly increasing and strictly quasi-concave utility functions.[3]

---

2 The term is loosely adapted from Magill and Quinzii (1996, page 84).

3 A function f is quasi-concave if $A = \{x \in R^n; f(x) \geq a\}$ is a convex set.

Therefore, a financial-market equilibrium also exists. For an in-depth treatment of this subject, the reader is referred to the textbook by Magill and Quinzii (1996)

As in the case of complete markets, unicity would require more stringent conditions. An elaborate mathematical theory (see Balasko (1988)) is used to count the number of equilibria.

15.1.2   Problems in More General Settings

In multigood or multiperiod settings, problems arise as soon as some of a complete set of Arrow-Debreu securities are missing at time 0, so that investors will have to make do with *spot trading in commodities (or securities)* taking place at future times. In the multi-period case, it is very important to observe *that each time period's payoffs on securities are endogenous as they include capital gains on them,* unless only one-period (or short-lived) securities, which by definition have a fixed next-period payoff, are available for trade.[4] When future spot trading is assumed, investors must form expectations about future spot prices. An appealing assumption is that they will anticipate the spot prices predicted by the model itself (Radner equilibrium). But at least two sets of difficulties arise.

15.1.2.1   Sunspots
One difficulty arises in the frequent cases in which the model admits several possible sets of spot prices, as when there exist several equilibria. In that case, investors have no way of knowing in advance which one of a finite number of sets of spot prices will actually prevail, since there exists no mechanism to coordinate their expectations.

A similar coordination problem can cause *new types of equilibria* to exist in which a dimension of uncertainty that does not exist objectively in the endowments, preferences, or technological opportunities of people, is nonetheless taken into account by investors in their portfolio decisions. The outcome depends on an "extrinsic" random variable, meaning a random influence that matters only because people expect it to matter to others and, therefore, to themselves. This can occur because, unlike in a complete market, no security exists with an equilibrium price that would indicate that this dimension of uncertainty receives or should receive a zero price. These are called "sunspot equilibria."[5]

15.1.2.2   Drop of rank
A second difficulty arises when securities payoffs are expressed in units of different goods and, in one candidate equilibrium, the random behavior of the future spot prices is so

---

4 Existence of the equilibrium extends to a multiperiod, one-good setting if there exist only short-lived securities.

5 See Cass and Shell (1982) and Cass (1992). Equilibria involving extrinsic uncertainty can arise for reasons other than market incompleteness, such as heterogeneous expectations. These are also called sunspot equilibria. For a survey see Shell (2008).

special as to cause some securities to become linearly dependent. As the rank of the matrix of payoffs is then reduced, portfolio choice becomes indeterminate.[6] But suppose, as is generally the case, that, in a new candidate equilibrium with a trimmed down number of securities, the future spot prices no longer cause the matrix of payoffs of the original securities to have a reduced rank. Then that candidate cannot be an equilibrium either. We must conclude that no equilibrium exists. This is the sense of the famous multi-good counter-example of Hart (1975).

The same drop-of-rank problem arises in the multiperiod case with long-lived securities.[7] But one can show then that equilibrium exists except at some points of the state space that are coincidental or "rare" (they form a subset of measure zero): these are the points where the drop of rank occurs. That form of existence is called "generic existence." See Duffie and Shafer (1985).[8]

15.1.3   Example: The Role of Idiosyncratic Risk

In an insightful article Mankiw (1986) provides a wonderful motivation for the study of incomplete-market equilibria. What follows is a series of quotes from the article. "There are two points of time in the model. At time zero, while the endowment of the consumption good is uncertain, portfolio choices are made. At time one, the endowment is realized and consumption takes place.

Per capita consumption in the economy takes on two values: a good value of μ, and a bad value of $(1 - \phi) \times \mu$, where $0 < \phi < 1$. Each state occurs with probability $1/2$."

"Suppose there are an infinite number of individuals that are identical *ex ante*. That is, as of time zero, the distribution of consumption is the same for all individuals. [Mankiw] assumes, however, that their consumption is not the same *ex post*. In particular, [he] assumes that, *in the bad state*, the shortfall in aggregate consumption, $\phi \times \mu$, is concentrated among a fraction ϱ of the population ($\phi < \varrho \le 1$)."[9] "The parameter ϱ measures the concentration of the aggregate shock. If $\varrho = 1$, then all individuals have the same consumption *ex post*. As ϱ approaches ϕ, the aggregate shock becomes more highly concentrated. At $\varrho = \phi$, the aggregate shock is fully concentrated on a few individuals whose consumption falls to zero."

---

6 Another way is to say that the agents' demand functions are discontinuous against the set of possible prices.

7 One way out of the problem is to prevent investors from taking unbounded positions, as they do in the neighborhood of the equilibrium in which the matrix drops rank. This was the assumption made by Radner. However, in cases in which positions are constrained by the bounds, the equilibrium depends on the artificially imposed bounds, an unreasonable economic model indeed!

8 As we saw in footnote 4 of chapter 12, when the market is complete, there is no such difficulty.

9 Emphasis added by us.

Remark **15.1** *Notice that it is in the bad aggregate state that the dispersion of consumption in the population is increased.*[10] *This is called* "Counter-cyclical Cross-sectional Variance" *(CCV).*

Mankiw considers a single security "that pays -1 in the bad state and pays $1 + \pi$ in the good state, where π is the premium. This security is equivalent to "a short position in an asset that pays off in both states (Treasury bills) together with a long position in an asset that pays off only in the good state (equity)."

"The stochastic environment facing any given individual is, therefore, as follows. With probability $1/2$, a good state occurs: his consumption is μ and the [security] pays $1 + \pi$. With probability $1/2$, a bad state occurs. In the bad state, the [security] pays -1; his consumption is μ with probability $1 - \varrho$ and is $(1 - \phi/\varrho) \times \mu$ with probability $\varrho \geq \phi$. [Mankiw] assumes there do not exist contingent-claims markets through which individuals can diversify away this latter risk."

This is the sense in which the market is incomplete. Mankiw's description of "consumptions" is really a description of endowments. *However, because of missing markets, in equilibrium, the consumptions just described cannot be altered by investors and remain equal to exogenous endowments. This is going to be a no-trade equilibrium.*

We assume independence between the occurrence of the bad state and the event for an individual of being affected by the shock. Hence the probability of, say, being in the bad state and not being affected by the shock is $(1 - \varrho)/2$. We call c_1 consumption in the good state at time 1, c_2 consumption in the bad state if the individual is not affected by the shock, c_3 consumption in the bad state if the individual is affected by the shock. We let θ be the investment in the security, ρ the rate of time preference. The objective function is:

$$\max_{\theta} \left\{ \rho \times \frac{1}{2} \left[u(c_1) + (1 - \varrho)u(c_2) + \varrho u(c_3) \right] \right\}$$

where:

$$c_1 = \mu + \theta \times (1 + \pi)$$
$$c_2 = \mu - \theta$$
$$c_3 = \left(1 - \frac{\phi}{\varrho} \right) \times \mu - \theta$$

Because of no trade, the first-order condition of portfolio choice must hold at $\theta = 0$, which means:

$$(1 + \pi)u'(\mu) - \left[(1 - \varrho)u'(\mu) + \varrho u' \left(\left(1 - \frac{\phi}{\varrho} \right) \times \mu \right) \right] = 0$$

---

10 For the empirical plausibility of this assumption, see Storesletten *et al.* (2004).

"The premium is, therefore,[11]

$$
\pi = \varrho \, \frac{u'\!\left(\left(1 - \frac{\phi}{\varrho}\right) \times \mu\right) - u'(\mu)}{u'(\mu)}
$$

The premium (π) in general depends not only on the size of the aggregate shock (μ, ϕ) but also on its distribution within the population (ϱ)."

Proposition 15.1 *(Mankiw (1986)) If the third derivative of the utility function is positive, then an increase in the concentration of the aggregate shock increases the premium: if* $u''' > 0$, *then:*

$$
\frac{\partial \pi}{\partial \varrho} < 0
$$

This is a manifestation of the familiar *"precautionary motive,"* which describes how much an investor's total saving is increased by an increase in non-traded (or "background") risk. In the Mankiw equilibrium, saving cannot be altered and the motive shows up as a modification of the premium.[12]

Mankiw also shows that, under the Inada assumption, as $\varrho \to \phi$, the premium becomes infinite. The equity premium can be made arbitrarily large by making the shock more and more concentrated.

The Mankiw setting is somewhat unusual: there is no consumption at time 0 and the menu of securities includes only one forward contract with zero cost at time 0. That could mean that the "premium" he defines is not akin to the real-world equity premium, which is the expected-return difference between equity and a riskless asset. For that reason, we examine in the appendix to this chapter other incomplete-market settings. In the setting labeled "New Version 1," we introduce consumption at time 0 and we let two securities be traded. One is riskless and the other pays in one state only. In "New Version 2" the second, the risky security pays off in both states. We reach similar conclusions as Mankiw did.

15.1.4 Incomplete Markets and Welfare: Equilibrium and Constrained Pareto Optimality in the Static Setting

Needless to say, in an incomplete market the allocation of consumption need not be Pareto optimal. Indeed, we know that marginal rates of substitution of different economic investors are not equated for each state of nature. However, there is a case in which it can be shown to be *constrained* Pareto optimal:

---

11 Since there is no trade, this is a virtual price premium (as in Lucas (1978)).

12 The same point is made in a multiperiod setting by Constantinides and Duffie (1996).

Theorem 15.2 *In a static, one-good economy, if the financial market is incomplete and a competitive equilibrium prevails, the allocation of consumption across individuals is* constrained *Pareto optimal. There exists a representative individual (or social planner) who can allocate consumption to individuals, taking into account constraints of aggregate resources and of marketability of consumption plans.*

Proof. Consider the following central-planner problem:

$$\max_{c^m(0),\{c^m(s)\}} \sum_m \frac{1}{\lambda^m} \sum_{s=1}^K \pi^m(s) u^m\left(c^m(0), c^m(s)\right); \lambda^m > 0$$

subject to:

$$c^m(s) - e^m(s) = \sum_i \theta_i^m q_{i,s} \text{ for some } \theta_i^m \qquad \text{(marketability constraint)}$$

$$\sum_m c^m(0) = \sum_m e^m(0); \qquad \sum_m \theta_i^m = 0 \qquad (15.1)$$

The Lagrangean is:

$$\max_{c^m(0),\{c^m(s)\},\{\theta_i^m\}} \sum_m \frac{1}{\lambda^m} \sum_s \pi^m(s) u^m\left(c^m(0), c^m(s)\right) \qquad (15.2)$$

$$+ \min_{\mu,\{\mu\phi^m(s)\},\{\mu S_i\}} \left\{ \mu \times \left[\sum_m e^m(0) - \sum_m c^m(0) \right] \right.$$

$$\left. + \sum_s \sum_m \mu \times \phi^m(s) \left[\sum_i \theta_i^m q_{i,s} - \left(c^m(s) - e^m(s)\right) \right] - \mu \times \left[\sum_i S_i \sum_m \theta_i^m \right] \right\}$$

where μ is the Lagrange multiplier for the time-0 resource constraint and $\mu \times \phi^m(s)$ denotes the Lagrange multiplier for the state-s marketability constraint of investor m, and $\mu \times S_i$ is the multiplier for the constraint $\sum_m \theta_i^m = 0$. The first-order conditions are:

$$\frac{1}{\lambda^m} \sum_s \pi^m(s) \frac{\partial u^m}{\partial c^m(0)}\left(c^m(0), c^m(s)\right) = \mu \qquad (15.3)$$

$$\frac{1}{\lambda^m} \pi^m(s) \frac{\partial u^m}{\partial c^m(s)}\left(c^m(0), c^m(s)\right) = \mu\phi^m(s)$$

$$\sum_m c^m(0) = \sum_m e^m(0);$$

$$\sum_i \theta_i^m q_{i,s} = c^m(s) - e^m(s)$$

$$\sum_s \phi^m(s) q_{i,s} = S_i \qquad (15.4)$$

$$\sum_m \theta_i^m = 0$$

We want to show that, with a proper set of the weights that define the central planner, a solution of the system of equations defining equilibrium is also a solution of the above system. *Choose the central-planner weights* $\{1/\lambda^m\}$ *to be the reciprocals of the Lagrange multipliers* $\{\lambda_0^m\}$ *of the equilibrium problem* ($\lambda^m = \lambda_0^m$), which satisfy the first-order conditions (3.13, 3.14, 3.17, and 3.18). Then comparing the two systems of equations, it is clear that they have a solution in common, with $\mu = 1$. $\square$

The existence of a representative individual in this restricted case implies that we can, as in the case of a complete market, obtain the equilibrium by a straight optimization of welfare, and then adjust the weights of the welfare functions to match the budget constraints of the equilibrium problem.

In more general settings, such as multigood or multiperiod economies, incomplete-market equilibria, when they exist, generally fail to be constrained Pareto optimal, as a counter-example in chapter 4 of Magill and Quinzii (1986, page 271) demonstrates. No representative individual built *with constant weights* exists.[13]

15.2   Obtaining Continuous-Time Incomplete-Market Equilibria

Assuming away the existence problems mentioned in the previous section, we can undertake to develop a method that will provide us with the dynamics of equilibrium quantities in an incomplete market. To do that, we can think of generalizing the method of Cox and Huang (1989) of chapter 12 to the case of an incomplete market. That task was undertaken by Cuoco and He (1994).[14] The method can be presented either as a direct calculation or as involving a representative investor (with stochastic weights).

15.2.1   Direct Calculation

The necessary ingredients, to which market clearing only needs to be added, have been developed in the previous chapter, section 14.2.2. There we showed the first-order conditions of the dual program (14.16) of each and every investor. First, there were the first-order

---

13 There are also consequences for production/physical investment decisions. Generally, in an incomplete market, even if a firm maximizes its market value some of its shareholders, because their marginal rates of substitutions differ, may find the resulting decisions not to their liking. A lack of unanimity of shareholders and a loss of theoretical support for value maximization follows. See Magill and Quinzii (1996), chapter 6.

14 In an exchange economy, investors cannot consume time after time unless they receive some dividends from equity securities in positive net supply or at least some of them receive endowments time after time. In the presence of interim endowments, the dual method expounded in the previous chapter runs into the mathematical difficulty pointed out in remark 14.2. Here we continue to assume that the only output is in the form of dividends ι. Otherwise total "output," that is, the total amount $\bar{c}$ available for consumption, would be total dividend *plus* total endowment.

conditions for consumption (14.27):[15]

$$u_c(c(t),t) = \lambda_0 \xi(t) \quad \left(\triangleq \lambda(t) \right) \tag{15.5}$$

solved as:

$$c(t) = \mathfrak{h}(\lambda(t),t) \tag{15.6}$$

***Remark* 15.2**   *Since* $\mathfrak{h}(u_c(c,t),t) \equiv c$ *for all values of* c, *the derivatives of* $\mathfrak{h}$ *(denoted* $\mathfrak{h}_\lambda$, *etc.) are related to the derivatives of* u_c *(which serve to define the risk aversion* $A(t) \triangleq -u_{cc}/u_c$ *and the prudence* $P(t) \triangleq -u_{ccc}/u_{cc}$ *of the investor):*

$$\mathfrak{h}_t \equiv -\mathfrak{h}_\lambda u_{ct}; \ \mathfrak{h}_\lambda \equiv \frac{1}{u_{cc}}; \ \mathfrak{h}_{\lambda\lambda} \equiv -\frac{u_{ccc}}{u_{cc}^3} \tag{15.7}$$

We make use of that interpretation in remark 15.3 below and in the example of section 15.4. See also chapter 18.

In equilibrium, the Lagrange multiplier (or dual or "co-state") variables λs are state variables that behave as in (14.25):

$$\frac{d\lambda(t)}{\lambda(t)} = -r(t)dt - [\kappa(t) + \nu(t)]^{\mathsf{T}} dw(t) \tag{15.8}$$

and that must be recognized as *endogenous* state variables because r, κ, and ν will be the results of the decisions made in equilibrium by investors, so that these, and not λ, are the real unknowns of the problem we are trying to solve.

In an incomplete market, the distribution of consumption – roughly corresponding to the distribution of wealth – is needed as a set of endogenous state variables for the reason that investors make windfall gains and losses that, in a complete market, would have been hedged away but here cannot be hedged for lack of the needed securities.[16] The windfall gains of some investors accompanied by the windfall losses of others shift the distribution of wealth in the population. These additional variables – as many as there are investors in the market (minus one) – constitute a gigantic burden on the computation of equilibrium. The one-to-one relation between an investor's λ process and his consumption implies that the current consumptions of all investors can be used as endogenous state variables instead of their dual variables or Lagrange multipliers.[17]

---

15 In this equilibrium analysis of an exchange economy, where there is no physical capital stock to be transferred from one generation to the next, we could assume no bequest motive and disregard first-order condition (14.28).

16 In a complete market, we saw in chapter 12 that the Negishi weights would be constants, not stochastic processes.

17 One can show easily that, putting aside the initial conditions, the entire system that we are about to solve is homogeneous of degree zero in the individual λs. As a result the distribution of consumption among investors or their consumption shares are the needed endogenous state variables. For an implementation of the idea of using consumptions as state variables, see Dumas and Lyasoff (2012). Consumptions are more convenient numerically speaking than the marginal utilities λ because – under the Inada assumption commonly made for reasons discussed previously – the latter become extremely large numbers as one approaches zero consumption. Chabakauri (2013) also uses consumption shares as state variables.

One way to write market clearing is to write the aggregate-resource restriction that says that the sum of individual consumption is equal to total dividend.[18] For that, we need to postulate the stochastic process for total dividend ($\sum_i \iota_i = \bar{c}$), in the following form:

$$\bar{c}(t) = \bar{c}(0) + \int_0^t \mu_{\bar{c}}(s)ds + \int_0^t \sigma_{\bar{c}}(s)dw(s) \tag{15.9}$$

Applying Itô's lemma to both sides of (15.6), we get:

$$dc(t) = \mathfrak{h}_t\left(\lambda(t),t\right)dt + \mathfrak{h}_\lambda\left(\lambda(t),t\right)d\lambda(t) + \frac{1}{2}\mathfrak{h}_{\lambda\lambda}\left(\lambda(t),t\right)(d\lambda(t))^2$$

$$= \mathfrak{h}_t dt + \mathfrak{h}_\lambda\left\{-r(t)dt - [\kappa(t)+v(t)]^\mathsf{T}dw(t)\right\}\lambda(t)$$

$$+\frac{1}{2}\mathfrak{h}_{\lambda\lambda}[\kappa(t)+v(t)]^\mathsf{T}[\kappa(t)+v(t)]\lambda^2(t)dt \tag{15.10}$$

If there are M investors indexed by $m = 1,\ldots,M$, we can sum equation (15.10) over all investors and use the market-clearing condition $\sum_{m=1}^M c^m = \bar{c}$ to write:

$$\mu_{\bar{c}}(t)dt + \sigma_{\bar{c}}(t)dw(t)$$

$$= \sum_{m=1}^M \mathfrak{h}_t^m\left(\lambda^m(t),t\right)dt + \sum_{m=1}^M \mathfrak{h}_\lambda^m\left(\lambda^m(t),t\right)\lambda^m(t)$$

$$\times\left\{-r(t)dt - [\kappa(t)+v^m(t)]^\mathsf{T}dw(t)\right\}$$

$$+\frac{1}{2}\sum_{m=1}^M \mathfrak{h}_{\lambda\lambda}^m\left(\lambda^m(t),t\right)(\lambda^m(t))^2\left[\kappa(t)+v^m(t)\right]^\mathsf{T}\left[\kappa(t)+v^m(t)\right]dt$$

We have assumed that, in this incomplete market, a riskless short-term security with a rate of interest r is actually available for trade. Hence the rate of interest r is the same for all investors. That is the reason for which we have placed no superscript m on r. Identifying terms:

$$\sigma_{\bar{c}}(t) = -\sum_{m=1}^M \mathfrak{h}_\lambda^m\left(\lambda^m(t),t\right)\lambda^m(t)\left[\kappa(t)+v^m(t)\right]^\mathsf{T} \tag{15.11}$$

$$\mu_{\bar{c}}(t) = \sum_{m=1}^M \mathfrak{h}_t^m\left(\lambda^m(t),t\right) - \sum_{m=1}^M \mathfrak{h}_\lambda^m\left(\lambda^m(t),t\right)\lambda^m(t)r(t) \tag{15.12}$$

$$+\frac{1}{2}\sum_{m=1}^M \mathfrak{h}_{\lambda\lambda}^m\left(\lambda^m(t),t\right)(\lambda^m(t))^2\left[\kappa(t)+v^m(t)\right]^\mathsf{T}\left[\kappa(t)+v^m(t)\right]$$

---

18 The other way is to write that the financial markets clear. By virtue of theorem 15.1 above, which can be extended to multiperiod settings, they are equivalent. But the unknowns κ (K in number) in the system below would need to be replaced by the unknowns μ (expected returns on risky securities, N in number).

These equations are linear algebraic in the unknowns $\kappa(t)$ and $r(t)$ and can be solved for them at every point in time. Please, observe that the solution for κ and r depends on the entire distribution of pairs $\{\lambda^m(t), \nu^m(t)\}_{m=1}^M$ in the population of investors.

Remark 15.3   *The solution can be interpreted by means of (15.5) and (15.7): The market-wide price of risk κ and the rate of interest r are given by:*

$$\kappa(t)^{\mathsf{T}} = \frac{\sigma_{\bar{c}}(t) - \sum_{m=1}^M \frac{1}{A^m(t)} \nu^m(t)^{\mathsf{T}}}{\sum_{m=1}^M \frac{1}{A^m(t)}} \tag{15.13}$$

$$r(t) = \frac{1}{\sum_{m=1}^M \frac{1}{A^m(t)}} \left[\mu_{\bar{c}}(t) - \sum_{m=1}^M \mathfrak{h}_t^m\left(\lambda^m(t), t\right) \right. \tag{15.14}$$

$$\left. -\frac{1}{2} \sum_{m=1}^M P^m(t) \left(\frac{1}{A^m(t)}\right)^2 \left[\kappa(t) + \nu^m(t)\right]^{\mathsf{T}} \left[\kappa(t) + \nu^m(t)\right] \right]$$

We must now solve for the unknowns ν^m. We saw in section 14.2.5 that individual investors' νs were given by (14.34):

$$\nu^m(t)^{\mathsf{T}} = \frac{F_Y^m(t)^{\mathsf{T}} \sigma_Y(t) \left[I_K - \sigma(t)^{\mathsf{T}}(\sigma(t)\sigma(t)^{\mathsf{T}})^{-1}\sigma(t)\right]}{F_\lambda^m(t)\lambda^m(t)} \tag{15.15}$$

which forces us to solve for the functions $\left\{ F^m\left(\{\lambda^m\}_{m=1}^M, Y, t\right)\right\}$ and for the securities' diffusion matrices σ, which can only be obtained from the price functions $\mathcal{S}\left(\{\lambda^m\}_{m=1}^M, Y, t\right)$ of risky securities. We saw that each investor's financial wealth function $F^m\left(\{\lambda^m\}_{m=1}^M, Y, t\right)$ satisfied the PDE (14.31):[19,20]

$$\mathcal{D}^*(F) + F_t = rF - \mathfrak{h} \tag{15.16}$$

subject to the terminal condition:

$$F = \mathfrak{G} \qquad \text{at } T$$

where the Dynkin $\mathcal{D}^*$ is defined as (14.32). Recall also that the decisions of all investors had to be such that the securities' price functions satisfied the first-order conditions of the primal portfolio choice, which were also the constraints (14.17) and (14.18)

---

19 The notation for the process Y is identical to what it was in previous chapters (equations (9.20, 10.17) and section 14.2.5).

20 In equilibrium, the functions $F^m\left(\{\lambda\}_{m=1}^M, Y, t\right)$ of all investors and the price functions $\mathcal{S}\left(\{\lambda\}_{m=1}^M, Y, t\right)$ are functions of the λs of all investors because κ and r are functions of all λs, which justifies our notation $\{\lambda\}_{m=1}^M$. For given κ and r, however, the implicit m superscript on $\mathcal{D}^*$ was suppressed because the calculation of $\mathcal{D}^*$ can be done by differentiating with respect to any investor's λ^m provided one also uses the corresponding individual ν^m diffusions. The kernel condition guarantees that, for traded assets, the result will be the same no matter which investor's point of view is adopted. An investor's financial wealth being a traded asset, the principle also applies to it.

of the dual program. These imply that the prices $S_i(\{\lambda\}, Y, t)$ solve the following linear PDEs:

$$\iota_i - r \times S_i + S_{i,t} + \mathcal{D}^*(S_i) = 0 \tag{15.17}$$

The backward-induction method thus works as follows:[21]

- start from the terminal date T and set:

$$F^m(\{\lambda^m\}, Y, T) = \mathfrak{G}^m(\lambda^m) \quad \forall \lambda^m, Y$$

for each investor and:

$$S(\{\lambda^m\}, Y, T) = 0 \quad \forall \{\lambda^m\}, Y$$

for each risky security. S is set equal to zero at the terminal date because S is the ex-dividend price of the stock. By convention we have set the value of the riskless bank account B at date 0 equal to 1. There is no definite value of B at date T. That does not prevent us from starting a backward-induction or recursive calculation because the process B does not appear in any of the equations.
There is no need to solve for anything at date T.

- assuming the problem has been solved at later dates, at date t we face an algebro-differential system, which must be discretized for numerical solution (see chapter 13). We have to solve for the $2 + M \times K$ unknowns $\{\kappa, r, \{v^m\}\}$ from (15.11, 15.12, and 15.15) and the $M + N$ unknowns $\{F^m(\{\lambda\}, Y, t)\}$ and $S(\{\lambda\}, Y, t)$ from the PDEs (15.16) and (15.17), after incorporating a substitution for the diffusion matrix σ:

$$\sigma(\{\lambda\}, Y, t) = \sum_{m=1}^{M} S_{\lambda^m}(\kappa + v^m)^\mathsf{T} + S_Y^\mathsf{T} \sigma_Y$$

The values of all the unknowns are obtained for every possible value of the state variables $(\{\lambda\}, Y)$, in a manner similar to dynamic programming except that we are now solving for the equilibrium of an entire population of investors.

- at date 0, perform the same calculation and then choose the initial values of the Lagrange multipliers $\{\lambda_0^m\}$ in such a way that $F^m(\{\lambda_0\}, Y(0), 0)$ matches the initial wealth endowment of each investor.

- once that is all done, economists can start from date 0 again and obtain multiple simulated paths of the economy moving forward, based on the functions obtained at each time step.

---

21 For the discrete-time analog of this procedure, which can be implemented on any lattice such as a tree or a Markov chain, see Dumas and Lyasoff (2012). As is true with any backward-induction or recursive procedure, it goes awry if the solution of each stage is not unique.

15.2.2 Representative Investor

Although an incomplete-market equilibrium is not constrained-Pareto optimal overall and we cannot define a representative individual or central planner with constant weights as we did in a complete market, it is at least "one-step ahead" constrained Pareto optimal, as can be inferred from theorem 15.2. Although that does not simplify the derivation of the equilibrium in any way, Cuoco and He (1994) introduce an elegant concept of representative agent with stochastic weights $1/\lambda(t)$. Define at each point in time a representative investor (a different one at different points in time), with utility or welfare function $\bar{u}$:

$$\bar{u}\left(\bar{c}, \left\{\lambda^m\right\}_{m=1}^{M}, t\right) \triangleq \max_{\{c^m\}} \sum_m \frac{1}{\lambda^m} u^m\left(c^m, t\right); \ \lambda^m > 0$$

subject to the ARC:

$$\sum_m c^m = \bar{c}$$

with first-order conditions:

$$\frac{1}{\lambda^m} u_c^m\left(c^m, t\right) = \mu$$

where μ is the Lagrange multiplier of the ARC.

But the weights have to be chosen in such a way that the individual consumptions can be financed by means of existing securities to allow the marketability or budget constraints to be satisfied at each point in time and every state of nature. Thus *the weights have to be stochastic* as did the λs of the direct calculation (see equation (15.8)). Indeed, one can easily verify that the equilibrium consumption allocation of the direct calculation could be viewed as the result of a central planning allocation in which each investor m would receive a weight:

$$\frac{1}{\lambda_0^m \exp\left[-\frac{1}{2}\int_0^t \|v^m(s)\|^2\, ds - \int_0^t v^m(s)^\mathsf{T}\, dw(s)\right]} \tag{15.18}$$

If the only purpose is to find the allocation of consumption, the central planner or representative investor is not terribly useful.

15.3 Revisiting the Breeden CAPM: The Effect of Incompleteness on Risk Premia in General Equilibrium

Among the equations of the previous section that are needed to get the position of the economy at every point in time, equation (15.17), which means $\mathbb{E}^*[dS] = (r \times S - \iota)dt$, has received a lot of attention in earlier chapters. Whenever utility is of the von Neumann-Morgenstern category and lifetime utility is time additive, it boils down to equation (11.6) of section 11.3, which is the CCAPM, written at the level of each individual investor.

Equation (15.17) involves the individual Lagrange multipliers λ and the market prices of risk $\kappa + \nu$ of individual investors, which are the diffusions of individual stochastic discount factors. One might expect that these market prices of risk could generate sizable risk premia. State prices are one-to-one related to individual consumptions, which are much more volatile than aggregate consumption. Individual households are exposed to idiosyncratic risks (unemployment, health hazards, life events, and so on), which are precisely those for which full hedging is not available in incomplete financial markets.

But, in section 11.3, we have also seen that the individual consumption-CAPM (11.6) can be aggregated into a CAPM (11.7) involving only aggregate consumption. So, for as long as utility is of the von Neumann-Morgenstern category and lifetime utility is time-additive and aggregate consumption, in continuous time, is a given continuous process built on Wiener processes, idiosyncratic risk borne by investors because of market incompleteness can only play a limited role in increasing the quantity of risk being priced.[22] The only way in which incompleteness can increase risk premia is by increasing the market price of risk, that is, by increasing the market's effective risk aversion.

As we shall see in chapter 21, however, lifetime utility can belong to a more general class and need not be time-additive. In that case, the consumption-CAPM will be invalid but the derivations of this section will remain valid and idiosyncratic risk will be able to have an effect on risk premia in continuous time. Furthermore, even when utility is time additive, it is possible for idiosyncratic risk to increase risk premia in a continuous-time model, provided the premia are measured over a finite period of time.[23]

It remains anyway that market incompleteness affects the rate of interest via the precautionary-saving motive.

15.4 Benchmark Example: Restricted Participation

The first example of incomplete-market equilibrium we study to point out the role and consequences of incompleteness, is the restricted or limited-participation equilibrium of Basak and Cuoco (1998).[24]

---

22 Cochrane (2005) makes the same remark. He draws a contrast between this conclusion and the discrete-time result of Constantinides and Duffie (1998) who show that the variance of idiosyncratic risk causes risk premia to be markedly affected under CCV.

23 See Christensen and Larsen (2014).

24 Dumas and Lyasoff (2012) generalize this example by means of a numerical method.

15.4.1   Endowment and Securities Markets

In the case of the incomplete-market equilibrium, all investors have access to a limited menu of securities and the menu is the same for all investors. The case of limited accessibility (sometimes called "partial segmentation") is more general. It would be one in which each investor is assigned a list of securities to which he/she has access.

But the situation considered by Basak and Cuoco is not quite as complex as that. There is only one Wiener process in the economy, one risky security, whose price is S, one instantaneously riskless security in zero net supply, whose value is B, and just two (or two categories of) finitely-lived investors. The economy is a pure-exchange one.

Agent a has access to both securities, whereas investor b has access to the riskless security only. Denote with $\alpha^m(t)$ the position of investor m ($m = a, b$) in the riskless asset, with $\theta^m(t)$ the position in the risky security. In order for the investors' strategies to be admissible, we also assume, when they receive no endowment stream of goods, that they maintain non-negative wealth at all times: $\alpha^m(t) + \theta^m(t)S(t) \geq 0$ for all t (alternatively, we could restrict portfolio strategies to $\mathcal{H}^2$.)

The restriction on participation in the risky-security market means that $\theta^a(t) = 1$ and $\theta^b(t) = 0$ for all t. The value of the risky-security position of investor a is the security price as well. No trading of it actually takes place at any time. Agents of category a are endowed with it and cannot trade it away. Agents of category a are the only ones receiving an income, which is exogenously given by equation (15.9). Obviously, this is also total consumption at each point in time. That income is in the form of a dividend paid on the entire stock market.

Agents of the two categories share the total zero net supply of the riskless security, which yields an endogenous rate of interest. At time 0 investors of category a are endowed with a short position $\alpha^a(0) = \beta < 0$ shares of the bank deposit (they are forced to be borrowers), while investors of category b are endowed with the long position $-\beta$. On average, category-a investors consume less than their endowment because they start out with a short position of the bond. This allows category-b investors to consume something out of category a's flow endowment.

Since the riskless security is tradable by all, the initial endowment of bank deposits serves to specify the initial distribution of financial wealth.[25]

The utility of both investors is separable in time and consumption, with the same time impatience ρ and infinite horizon. Both functions are isoelastic, defined over intermediate consumption, with investors of category b *having log utility and being, therefore, myopic*.

For purposes of calculating the equilibrium, we can also view this market as an incomplete market in which the only traded security is the instantaneously riskless one, the risky

---

[25] As Basak and Cuoco point out, the initial distribution of wealth, in their setup, also determines whether an equilibrium exists (β must be negative, but not so large that agents of category a could never repay their initial short position in the bond).

security being absent and the outside income received by category a being not a dividend but an endowment stream of goods.[26] That pins down the diffusion matrix of *traded* securities to the 1×1 matrix: $\sigma = 0$. The price and volatility of the risky security can be determined separately after calculating the equilibrium allocation.[27] Since κ should be in the span of $\sigma^{\top}$, it follows from $\sigma = 0$ that $\kappa = 0$ and that there is no kernel restriction on the choice of ν^a and ν^b.[28]

The equilibrium is defined as a quadruple of $(c^a(t), c^b(t), r(t), S(t))$.

15.4.2 Consumption Choices and State Prices

Each individual $m = a, b$ chooses consumption as in (15.6) above. Let λ_0^m be the Lagrange multiplier of his lifetime budget constraint. Consumption is not in closed form as long as state prices have not been made explicit. The state price of the logarithmic investor has been shown by He and Pearson to have $\nu^b = 0$ (see remark 14.3). Because $\kappa = 0$, this gives $\eta^b(t) = 1, \xi^b(t) = 1/B(t), \lambda^b(t) = \lambda_0^b/B(t)$.

In order to reconstruct the stochastic discount factor of category a, recall that, in equilibrium, the drift and diffusion of aggregate consumption must equal those of the exogenous endowment, which gave us equations (15.13) and (15.14).

In this special case, there is no need to solve a PDE. Equation (15.13) is all we need to obtain ν^a. Since $\kappa = \nu^b = 0$, it gives:

$$\nu^a(t) = A^a(c^a(t))\sigma_{\bar{c}}(t) \tag{15.19}$$

which says that the price of risk for investor a is directly proportional to the diffusion of the endowment $\bar{c}$ and to his risk aversion, at the optimal consumption plan.

Now that we have the stochastic discount factors (ξ^a, ξ^b), we can go back to consumption. If the initial Lagrange multipliers are given so that the process for (λ^a, λ^b) is known, equation (15.6) provides equilibrium consumption. That makes consumption of unrestricted investors covary with aggregate consumption, since ν^a does. Consumption of restricted investors, however, has zero conditional covariance with aggregate consumption (or the stock price):

$$c^b(t) = \mathfrak{h}^b\left(\lambda_0^b B^{-1}(t), t\right)$$

15.4.2.1 Riskless security

We now use the drift condition (15.12) on aggregate consumption to obtain the rate of interest. Substituting in it once more the fact that the diffusion of the stochastic discount

---

26 Here we ignore the warning of footnote 14 above.

27 However, see section 15.5 below.

28 Here the notation differs from that of Basak and Cuoco. They call κ the price of risk in the market for the risky security. Our analog is denoted ν^a. Indeed, the risky security is priced by agents of category a only. The riskless security price is the only one the two categories of agents have to agree on.

factor for the log investor is equal to zero, while c^b obeys the last expression above, we get the equilibrium interest rate, which, with the same rate of impatience ρ for both investors, becomes:

$$r = \rho + A(t)\left[\mu_{\bar{c}}(t) - \frac{1}{2}P^a(t)\sigma_{\bar{c}}^2(t)\right] \tag{15.20}$$

where the formula contains aggregate risk aversion $A(t)$, defined as the harmonic average of the investors' risk aversions:

$$A(t) \triangleq \frac{1}{-\sum_{m=a}^{b} \frac{u_c^m(c^m(t),t)}{u_{cc}^m(c^m(t),t)}}$$

and the prudence of unconstrained investors only:

$$P^a(t) \triangleq -\frac{u_{ccc}^a(c^a(t),t)}{u_{cc}^a(c^a(t),t)}$$

As usual, the interest rate differs from time impatience in proportion to aggregate risk aversion. The proportionality is dictated directly by the expected growth in aggregate consumption ($\mu_{\bar{c}}(t)$) and inversely by its variance ($\sigma_{\bar{c}}^2(t)$), filtered through the prudence of unrestricted investors. Since the consumption of investor a is locally risky, while consumption of investor b is riskless, the former investor is the one who exhibits precautionary saving. The difference between this interest rate and what would be the unrestricted-participation one, is that the former depends on prudence of the unrestricted investor, while the latter would have depended on the representative investor's prudence (see section 12.4).

The rate of interest is plotted in figure 15.1 as a function of the consumption level c^b of the restricted investor, which reflects the distribution of wealth. The figure is built for an unrestricted investor with risk aversion levels: $\gamma = -1, -3, -7, -10$. Output $\bar{c}(t)$ is normalized to 1. In all cases the rate is a decreasing function of the consumption level of restricted investors. The other parameters are $\mu_{\bar{c}}(t) = 1.83\%$, $\sigma_{\bar{c}}(t) = 3.57\%$, because these numbers match the aggregate data of Mehra and Prescott (1985) for the US economy, 1889-1978. Figure 15.1 displays also the rate level $r = 0.008$, as estimated by Mehra and Prescott. The rate produced by restricted participation crosses the horizontal line. This means that the corresponding economy is able to match empirical evidence, for some "wealth" distribution, for very reasonable levels of risk aversion. This means that even a simple incomplete-market model may solve the *interest-rate puzzle*.[29]

In figure 15.2 we report the drift for the optimal consumption of the unrestricted investor:

$$dc^a(t) = \left\{\frac{A(t)}{A^a(t)}\left[\mu_{\bar{c}}(t) - \frac{1}{2}P^a(t)\sigma_{\bar{c}}^2(t)\right] + \frac{1}{2}P^a(t)\sigma_{\bar{c}}^2(t)\right\}dt + \sigma_{\bar{c}}(t)dw(t) \tag{15.21}$$

---

29 The "solution" is short-lived, however, as the variable on the x axis – the consumption share – moves endogenously to the left, and quickly so. See section 15.5.1, especially figure 15.4.

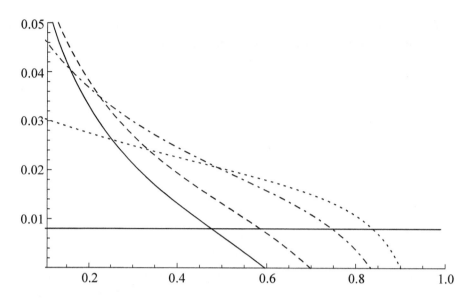

Figure 15.1

Interest rate r in the incomplete market of Basak and Cuoco as a function of the restricted investor's share of consumption $c^b/\bar{c}$ (on the x-axis), for different levels of risk aversion of the unrestricted investor ($\gamma = -1$ (solid curve), -3 (dashed line), -7 (dot-dashed), -10 (dotted)). The horizontal line is at the level 0.008, which is Mehra-Prescott's estimate of the real interest rate for the US economy, 1889-1978.

The consumption drift is increasing and convex in the share of the restricted investor; consequently it is decreasing and convex in the share of the unrestricted investor himself. The volatility is instead constant, and it simply matches the volatility of aggregate consumption.

15.4.2.2 Risky security

We know that the market price of risk is the return/volatility ratio (15.19) from the point of view of the unrestricted investor, who is the only participant in the risky-asset market. In the complete market, it would have been

$$A(c(t))\sigma_{\bar{c}}(t),$$

where A – the aggregate risk aversion – would have been the representative investor's risk aversion. If unrestricted investors are more risk-averse than restricted ones (as in Basak and Cuoco) – an unrealistic assumption – then the risk premium in the incomplete market is higher than the one in complete markets, everything else being equal.

For the isoelastic utility of the unrestricted investor the premium is

$$v^a(t) = \frac{1-\gamma}{c^a(t)}\sigma_{\bar{c}}(t) \tag{15.22}$$

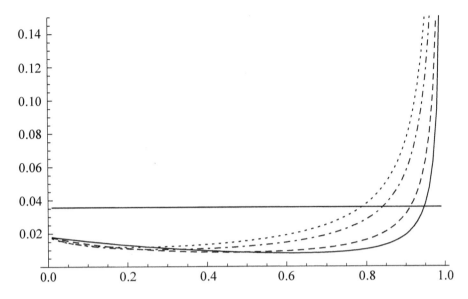

Figure 15.2
Consumption drift of the unrestricted investor (as in (15.21)) in the incomplete market of Basak and Cuoco as a function of the restricted investor's share of consumption $c^b/\bar{c}$ (on the horizontal axis), for different levels of risk aversion of the unrestricted investor ($\gamma = -1$ (solid curve), -3 (dashed line), -7 (dot-dashed), -10 (dotted)). The horizontal line is set at 0.0357, the historical US volatility.

The risk premium is increasing in the dividend volatility, decreasing in the unrestricted-investor's consumption c^a, and increasing in his relative risk-aversion coefficient, $1 - \gamma$. Following Basak and Cuoco, we plot in figure 15.3 the risk premium ν^a as a function of the consumption level of the restricted investor. ν^a matches the US risk premium, as measured by Mehra and Prescott, 0.37, for the reasonable levels of risk aversion assumed above and a dividend volatility equal to $\sigma_{\bar{c}}(t) = 3.57\%$, while we take $\rho = 0.001$. As a consequence, the incomplete-market model of Basak and Cuoco can solve also the *risk-premium puzzle*.[30]

Other potential solutions of the puzzle will be examined in later chapters. They involve other forms of incompleteness or frictions (see chapter 19), fluctuating beliefs (chapter 18) or non-separable expected-utility decision criteria (see, for instance, chapter 21 below).

---

30 However, see footnote 29. Here the consumption-CAPM based on *aggregate* consumption does not hold in the risky market because restricted investors have no access to it.

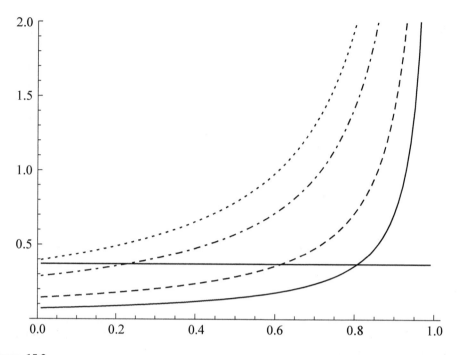

Figure 15.3

Risk premium per unit of volatility ν^a in the incomplete market of Basak and Cuoco as a function of the restricted investor's share of consumption $c^b/\bar{c}$ (on the horizontal axis), for different levels of risk aversion of the unrestricted investor ($\gamma = -1$ (solid curve), -3 (dashed line), -7 (dot-dashed), -10 (dotted)). The horizontal line is set at 0.37, which is Mehra-Prescott's estimate of the risk premium for the US economy, 1889-1978.

15.5   Bubbles in Equilibrium

In section 7.5, we saw that a security can have a bubble in the sense that there may exist "a (at least one) self-financing portfolio that not only has non-negative (pathwise) value but that costs less than the security and replicates its payoff." The replication cost can be referred to as the fundamental value of the security. And, to put oneself in an equilibrium context, we can think of the security in question as providing not a generic payoff, but a consumption stream. The bubble, which is, the difference between the market price and the fundamental value, could not exist in equilibrium in a complete market, even if investors were limited to portfolio strategies in $\mathcal{H}^2$ or, alternatively, had to maintain non-negative wealth. Hugonnier (2012) shows that it may exist in an incomplete market, where incompleteness arises from portfolio constraints for some investors, such as restricted participation. To illustrate that point, we first solve more explicitly a special case of the Basak-and-Cuoco equilibrium of section 15.4.

15.5.1 Benchmark Example (continued)

A simple subcase of the Basak and Cuoco model is the one in which *both* investors have logarithmic utility and are myopic.

We now revert to the original interpretation of this economy in which investors of category *a* are endowed with the risky security at time 0, so that they are entitled to receive the future dividends ι on it, but will not receive future endowments of goods. We also assume that the dividend follows a *Geometric* Brownian motion, the drift and the volatility of the dividend being now renamed $\mu_\iota \times \iota$ and $\sigma_\iota \times \iota$, respectively.

Despite the fact that their utility is log and the fact that they receive no endowment stream of goods, the market price of risk of category *a* investors is not equal to zero. Instead, it is still equal to the positive number (15.19) that we calculated previously, which can be viewed as the shadow cost of category *a* investors being forced in equilibrium to hold the risky asset. For the same reason, the constraint brings the rate of interest down. Hugonnier (2012) comments:

"...the limited participation always implies a higher market price of risk and a lower interest rate than in an unconstrained economy. To understand this feature, note that in the absence of portfolio constraints the investors do not trade in the riskless asset since they have homogeneous preferences. In the constrained economy, however, the second investor is forced to invest [...] his wealth in the riskless asset. The unconstrained investor must therefore be induced to become a net borrower in equilibrium and it follows that the rate of interest must decrease and the market price of risk must increase compared to an unconstrained economy."

We also take the opportunity of this special case to illustrate the representative-investor interpretation of section 15.2.2. With logarithmic utility, there exists an equilibrium where the weighting process $\hat{\lambda}(t)$ defining the representative individual is the ratio of the inverse Lagrange multipliers of the two investors:

$$\hat{\lambda}(t) = \frac{1/\lambda^b(t)}{1/\lambda^a(t)}$$

From (15.22) and (15.20) and given that:

$$e^{-\rho t} \frac{1}{c^m(t)} = \lambda_0^m \xi^m(t) \ \left(\triangleq \lambda^m(t) \right); m = a, b \tag{15.23}$$

it follows that:

$$\hat{\lambda}(t) = \frac{c^b(t)}{c^a(t)}$$

so that, given that $c^a(t) + c^b(t) = \iota(t)$:

$$\frac{c^a(t)}{\iota(t)} = \frac{1}{1 + \hat{\lambda}(t)}; \frac{c^b(t)}{\iota(t)} = \frac{\hat{\lambda}(t)}{1 + \hat{\lambda}(t)}$$

and following (15.22) and (15.20):

$$v^a(t) = \sigma_\iota \times \left(1 + \hat{\lambda}(t)\right) \tag{15.24}$$

$$r(t) = \rho + \mu_\iota - \left(1 + \hat{\lambda}(t)\right)\sigma_\iota^2 \tag{15.25}$$

Equation (15.24) further illustrates the impact of the market-participation restriction on the market price of risk of investor a.

Therefore, the stochastic discount factors can be written as:

$$\xi^a(t) = \exp\left[-\int_0^t r(s)ds - \sigma_\iota \times \int_0^t \left(1 + \hat{\lambda}(s)\right)dw(s)\right. \tag{15.26}$$
$$\left. - \frac{1}{2}\int_0^t \sigma_\iota^2 \times \left(1 + \hat{\lambda}(s)\right)^2 ds\right]$$

$$\xi^b(t) = \exp\left[-\int_0^t r(s)ds\right] \tag{15.27}$$

and the weight $\hat{\lambda}$ follows the SDE:

$$d\hat{\lambda}(t) = -\hat{\lambda}(t)\left(1 + \hat{\lambda}(t)\right)\sigma_\iota dw(t) \tag{15.28}$$

The relative weight $\hat{\lambda}$ plays a crucial role in this equilibrium as an endogenous state variable. While the Lipschitz condition is violated by SDE (15.28), Basak and Cuoco (1998; Lemma 1) show that its solution exists and is unique.

It is clearly a local martingale since its drift is zero. But it is not a true martingale (see chapter 7). Indeed, its conditional expectation is not $\hat{\lambda}(0)$. The expected value is found to be:[31]

$$\mathbb{E}\left[\hat{\lambda}(t) \mid \hat{\lambda}(0)\right] = \hat{\lambda}(0)\left[1 - \frac{1 + \hat{\lambda}(t)}{\hat{\lambda}(t)}H\left(t, \frac{\hat{\lambda}(t)}{1 + \hat{\lambda}(t)}; 1\right)\right]$$

where

$$H(t, s; x) \triangleq s^{\frac{1+x}{2}}N(d_+(t,s)) + s^{\frac{1-x}{2}}N(d_-(t,s))$$

$$d_+(t,s) \triangleq \frac{1}{\sigma_\iota\sqrt{t}}\log s + \frac{\sigma_\iota\sqrt{t}}{2}$$

$$d_-(t,s) \triangleq \frac{1}{\sigma_\iota\sqrt{t}}\log s - \frac{\sigma_\iota\sqrt{t}}{2}$$

and where N is the standard Gaussian distribution function. The behavior of $\hat{\lambda}$ is presented in figure 15.4. The expected consumption share is thus seen to move more swiftly in disfavor of the constrained investor than a true martingale would.

---

31 Like PDE (7.11), the PDE associated with the SDE (15.28) has several solutions. Direct probability calculation is used to determine which solution is the expected value. See Hugonnier (2012), lemma A.2.

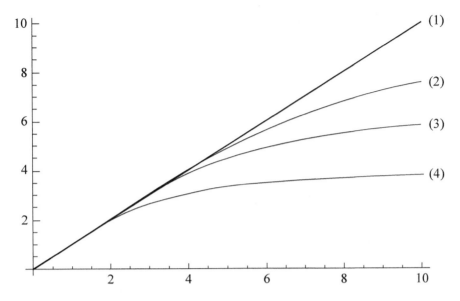

Figure 15.4

The expected value $\mathbb{E}\left[\hat{\lambda}(T) \mid \hat{\lambda}(0)\right]$ for $T = 5, 10$, and 25 (curves marked (2), (3), and (4) respectively). The initial value $\hat{\lambda}(0)$ is on the x-axis. The line marked (1) is shown for comparison. It is just the 45° line, which would give the conditional expected value if $\hat{\lambda}$ were a true martingale. The parameter value is: $\sigma_\iota = 3.57\%$.

We may evaluate each investor's wealth *using his own marginal utility* and applying it to his future consumption. Given the stochastic discount factors and the marginal utilities (15.23), the result is completely straightforward:[32]

$$W^m(t) = \mathbb{E}_t\left[\int_t^T \frac{\xi^m(s)}{\xi^m(t)} c^m(s)ds\right] \tag{15.29}$$

$$= c^m(t)\int_t^T e^{-\rho(s-t)}ds = \frac{1 - e^{\rho(T-t)}}{\rho}c^m(t)$$

Exercise 15.1 asks the reader to finish the characterization of the equilibrium, by studying the SDEs for the interest rate, risk premium, and consumption of the two investors, and the way it depends on the initial distribution of wealth. Exercise 15.2, instead, asks the reader to make a comparison with the corresponding complete-market equilibrium, and to determine in which equilibrium welfare is higher.

---

32 From the two wealths at time 0, and from the initial endowments, it follows that the process $\hat{\lambda}$ starts at:

$$\hat{\lambda}(0) = \frac{\beta}{-\beta + \frac{1-e^{\rho T}}{\rho}\iota(0)}$$

15.5.2 Bubble Interpretation

Since only category a investors participate in the stock market, the price of the stock should be obtained as:

$$F(t) = \mathbb{E}_t \left[\int_t^T \frac{\xi^a(s)}{\xi^a(t)} \iota(s)ds \right] \qquad (15.30)$$

which is the reflection of the first-order condition of portfolio choice of category a investors. Hugonnier (2012) says that that is also the cost in terms of time-t consumption units, at which each of the unrestricted investors of category a could replicate the future dividend stream ι.

Solving the PDE that says that

$$\mathbb{E}_t \left[d\big(\xi^a(t)F(t)\big) \right] + \xi^a(t)\iota(t)dt = 0$$

with terminal condition $F(t) = 0$, one would get:

$$F(t) = \frac{1 - e^{\rho(T-t)}}{\rho} \iota(t) \left(1 - \mathfrak{b}\left(t, \frac{\hat{\lambda}(t)}{1 + \hat{\lambda}(t)} \right) \right) \qquad (15.31)$$

where:

$$\mathfrak{b}(t,s) \triangleq \frac{1}{1 - e^{\rho(T-t)}} H(T-t), s; x_1) + e^{\rho(T-t)} H(T-t, s; 1)$$

$$x_1 = \sqrt{1 + 8 \frac{\rho}{\sigma_\iota^2}}$$

Aggregate wealth in this example economy is the sum of (15.29) over $m = a, b$:

$$S(t) = \frac{1 - e^{\rho(T-t)}}{\rho} \iota(t) \qquad (15.32)$$

There is no aggregate wealth in this economy other than the one created by the prospect of future dividends paid by the stock, which will be split into the consumption of a and of b. For that reason Basak and Cuoco (1998) and Hugonnier (2012) propose the value S in (15.32) as a candidate for the value of the stock market. Observe, however, the way it was computed; investors of category a, who will consume the stream $c^a(t)$, valued that consumption at the stochastic discount factor $\xi^a(t)$ and investors of category b, who will consume the stream $c^b(t)$, valued that consumption at their own stochastic discount factor $\xi^b(t)$. That is definitely the price at which each group values its own future consumption in the equilibrium, in which it is anticipated that there will be trades by which category b (the non-stockholders or rentiers) will gradually relinquish some of its initial endowment of the riskless security in order to consume out of the dividend to be paid to category a, who are the only investors holding the stock.

Now, it is true that $S > F$.[33] Hugonnier (2012) calls the difference between quantity (15.32) and quantity (15.30) a "bubble." The bubble arises from the valuation gap between the two groups of investors, a valuation gap that is not allowed directly to be closed by stock trading and can only be partially bridged by a flow of income.[34]

Is it conceivable that the value of the stock market be S instead of F and that a bubble exist? If it did, the positive valuation gap between $S(t)$ and $F(t)$ would offer an arbitrage opportunity to an investor of category a. At any time t, he could synthesize by a replication the future dividend stream for a total cost $F(t)$ and sell it short for the actual market price $S(t)$. He would invest the difference in the riskless asset. This would provide him with a gain at $T > t$ equal to $(S(t) - F(t)) \times \int_t^T \exp(r \times s)ds$, where the rate r is (15.25). Hugonnier points out that, were a small investor a to try to implement the arbitrage in question, he would run into negative financial wealth with positive probability (or violate the $\mathcal{H}^2$ requirement of continuous-time integrals).[35] Indeed, his wealth at $\tau > t$ would be equal to

$$F(\tau) - S(\tau) + (S(t) - F(t)) \times \int_t^\tau \exp(r \times s)ds$$

and would be negative for any dividend path which makes

$$S(\tau) > F(\tau) + (S(t) - F(t)) \times \int_t^\tau \exp(r \times s)ds$$

Since, for that reason, that apparent arbitrage opportunity cannot be exploited, the bubble can survive if it is there.[36]

The bubble that is allowed to exist on the stock is displayed in figure 15.5.

Remark 15.4   *The bubbles identified by Hugonnier are related to the ability of an investor in continuous time to trade an infinite number of times during a finite period of time, thus raising issues of integrability and local martingality. It should be clear from the above that the valuation gap that we have identified between S and F would be present as well in a discrete-time version of the economy. However, in a discrete-time economy of the type*

---

33 Mathematically, that fact coincides with the fact that the weight $\hat{\lambda}$ is not a true martingale but a local martingale. The weight process enters into the market price of risk (15.24) and, therefore, into the stochastic discount factor (15.26), which serves to calculate F.

34 In the case of two identical log investors considered here, the valuation quantity (15.32) is equal to what would be the price of the stock market in an unrestricted economy. But that is not generally true.

35 More basically, he could only trade with other investors of category a. If all of them tried to do that, they would find no one in equilibrium to trade with. Hugonnier removes that objection by allowing category b investors to trade a restricted amount of the stock. But equilibrium or counterparty considerations need not enter the reasoning of an arbitrageur, who considers himself small relative to the market. The price gap and the way to use market prices to pocket it is the only consideration.

36 Hugonnier and Prieto (2014) introduce a third class of agents called arbitrageurs, who have access to a credit facility. As they are allowed to go into more and more debt, they are more and more able to exploit the arbitrage opportunity. The size of the bubble is reduced accordingly.

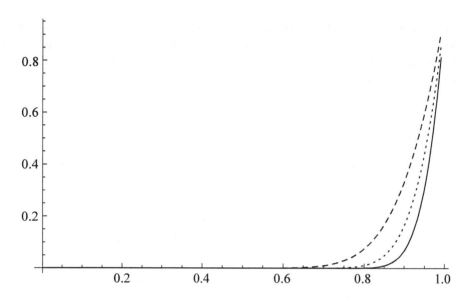

Figure 15.5
The relative bubble for the risky asset as a function of the initial value of the consumption share
$\hat{\lambda}(0)/\left(1+\hat{\lambda}(0)\right)$ of the restricted agents, for various values $T = 5, 10, 25$ (solid, small-dashed, and
dashed curves respectively) of the terminal date of the economy. The parameter value is $\sigma_\iota = 0.0357$.

*we studied in this book, where random variables have finite support, the bubble could and
would be arbitraged away so that the value of the stock market would be F unambiguously.*

15.6   Conclusion

We have summarized various properties of incomplete markets, explored a technique to
compute their equilibrium, which is analogous to the technique of chapter 12 applicable to
complete markets, and speculated on the ability of incomplete markets to generate larger
stock-return risk and risk premia, as compared to Breeden's consumption risk premium.
We have pointed out that the ability to trade in continuous time generates the possibility of
bubbles arising.

15.7   Appendix: Idiosyncratic Risk Revisited

New Version 1
Let us modify Mankiw's setting a bit and introduce time-0 consumption with unit endowment at
that time. And let there be two securities: a security that pays off in both states (Treasury bill) and
a security, with price p, that pays off some amount $2 + \pi$ in the good state only. The positions to be

taken in the two assets are denoted as usual with α and θ. We still assume independency between the occurrence of a specific state and belonging to a specific group of investors and we still call c_1 consumption in the good state at time 1, c_2 consumption in the bad state if the individual is not affected by the shock, and c_3 consumption in the bad state if the individual is affected by the shock. The objective function is now:

$$\max_{\alpha,\theta} \left\{ u(c_0) + \rho \times \frac{1}{2} \left[u(c_1) + (1-\varrho)u(c_2) + \varrho u(c_3) \right] \right\}$$

where:

$$c_0 = 1 - \alpha - p \times \theta$$
$$c_1 = \mu + \alpha \times (1+r) + \theta \times (2+\pi)$$
$$c_2 = \mu + \alpha \times (1+r)$$
$$c_3 = (1 - \frac{\phi}{\varrho}) \times \mu + \alpha \times (1+r)$$

The first-order conditions are:

$$-u'(c_0) + \rho \times \frac{1}{2} \left[u'(c_1) + (1-\varrho)u'(c_2) + \varrho u'(c_3) \right] \times (1+r) = 0$$

$$-u'(c_0) \times p + \rho \times \frac{1}{2} u'(c_1) \times (2+\pi) = 0$$

At equilibrium $\alpha = 0$ and $\theta = 0$, which gives the following prices for the two securities:

$$\frac{1}{1+r} = \rho \times \frac{1}{2} \frac{u'(\mu) + (1-\varrho)u'(\mu) + \varrho u'\left(\left(1 - \frac{\phi}{\varrho}\right) \times \mu \right)}{u'(1)}$$

$$p = \rho \times \frac{1}{2} \frac{u'(\mu) \times (2+\pi)}{u'(1)}$$

The gross expected rate of return on the risky asset is:

$$\frac{1}{2} \frac{(2+\pi)}{p}$$

and does not depend on ϱ. The gross risk premium is:[37]

$$\frac{1}{2} \frac{(2+\pi)}{p \times (1+r)} = \frac{1}{2} \frac{u'(\mu) + (1-\varrho)u'(\mu) + \varrho u'\left(\left(1 - \frac{\phi}{\varrho}\right) \times \mu \right)}{u'(\mu)}$$

Its derivative with respect to ϱ is:

$$\frac{1}{2} \frac{-u'(\mu) + u'\left(\left(1 - \frac{\phi}{\varrho}\right) \times \mu \right) + u''\left(\left(1 - \frac{\phi}{\varrho}\right) \times \mu \right) \frac{\phi}{\varrho} \times \mu}{u'(\mu)}$$

$$= \frac{1}{2} \frac{-\frac{u'(\mu) - u'\left(\left(1 - \frac{\phi}{\varrho}\right) \times \mu \right)}{\frac{\phi}{\varrho} \times \mu} + u''\left(\left(1 - \frac{\phi}{\varrho}\right) \times \mu \right)}{\frac{u'(\mu)}{\frac{\phi}{\varrho} \times \mu}}$$

---

37 We write the risk premium in ratio form but the conclusion would be identical if we had written it in the form of a difference.

If we take the limit of the ratio

$$\frac{u'(\mu) - u'\left((1 - \frac{\phi}{\varrho}) \times \mu\right)}{\frac{\phi}{\varrho} \times \mu}$$

when $\frac{\phi}{\varrho}$ tends to zero, we get $u''(\mu)$. If $u''' > 0$, the difference

$$-u''(\mu) + u''\left((1 - \frac{\phi}{\varrho}) \times \mu\right)$$

is negative, and the whole derivative is. This means that, as Mankiw predicted, an increase in the concentration of the aggregate shock increases the premium but, in the slightly modified setting, that is entirely due to its effect on the rate of interest.

New Version 2

Let us modify the setting again and let there be two securities: a security that pays off in both states (Treasury bill) and a security, with price p, that pays off the aggregate output in each state. The second security can then properly be regarded as equity in the usual sense. The objective function is:

$$\max_{\alpha, \theta} u(c_0) + \rho \times \frac{1}{2}\left[u(c_1) + (1 - \varrho)u(c_2) + \varrho u(c_3)\right]$$

subject to:

$$c_0 = 1 - \alpha - p \times \theta$$
$$c_1 = \mu + \alpha \times (1 + r) + \theta \times \mu$$
$$c_2 = \mu + \alpha \times (1 + r) + \theta \times (1 - \phi) \times \mu$$
$$c_3 = (1 - \frac{\phi}{\varrho}) \times \mu + \alpha \times (1 + r) + \theta \times (1 - \phi) \times \mu$$

The first-order conditions are:

$$-u'(c_0) + \rho \times \frac{1}{2}\left[u'(c_1) + (1 - \varrho)u'(c_2) + \varrho u'(c_3)\right] \times (1 + r) = 0$$

$$-u'(c_0) \times p + \rho \times \frac{1}{2}\left[u'(c_1) \times \mu + (1 - \varrho) u'(c_2) \times (1 - \phi) \times \mu \right.$$
$$\left. + \varrho u'(c_3) \times (1 - \phi) \times \mu\right] = 0$$

At equilibrium $\alpha = 0$ and $\theta = 0$, which gives the following prices for the two securities:

$$\frac{1}{1 + r} = \rho \times \frac{1}{2} \frac{u'(\mu) + (1 - \varrho)u'(\mu) + \varrho u'\left((1 - \frac{\phi}{\varrho}) \times \mu\right)}{u'(1)} \tag{15.33}$$

$$p = \rho \times \frac{1}{2} \frac{1}{u'(1)} \times \left[u'(\mu) \times \mu + (1 - \varrho)u'(\mu) \times (1 - \phi) \times \mu \right.$$

$$\left. + \varrho u'\left((1 - \frac{\phi}{\varrho}) \times \mu\right) \times (1 - \phi) \times \mu\right] \tag{15.34}$$

The derivatives of both prices are negative if $u''' > 0$:

$$\frac{\partial}{\partial \varrho}\left(\frac{1}{1+r}\right) = \rho \times \frac{1}{2}\frac{1}{u'(1)}$$

$$\times \left[-u'(\mu) + u'\left((1 - \frac{\phi}{\varrho}) \times \mu\right) + u''\left((1 - \frac{\phi}{\varrho}) \times \mu\right)\frac{\phi}{\varrho} \times \mu\right] < 0$$

$$\frac{\partial}{\partial \varrho}p = \rho \times \frac{1}{2}\frac{1}{u'(1)} \times \left[-u'(\mu) + u'\left((1 - \frac{\phi}{\varrho}) \times \mu\right)\right.$$

$$\left. +u''\left((1 - \frac{\phi}{\varrho}) \times \mu\right)\frac{\phi}{\varrho} \times \mu\right] \times (1 - \phi) \times \mu < 0$$

The gross expected rate of return is:

$$\frac{1}{2}\frac{\mu + (1 - \phi) \times \mu}{p}$$

which does depend on ϱ positively. The gross risk premium is:

$$\frac{1}{2}\frac{\mu + (1 - \phi) \times \mu}{p \times (1 + r)}$$

Its derivative with respect to ϱ is:

$$\frac{1}{2}\frac{\mu + (1 - \phi) \times \mu}{p} \times \left[\frac{\partial}{\partial \varrho}\left(\frac{1}{1+r}\right) - \frac{p'(\varrho)}{p \times (1 + r)}\right]$$

$$= \frac{1}{2}\frac{\mu + (1 - \phi) \times \mu}{p} \times \left[1 - \frac{(1 - \phi) \times \mu}{p \times (1 + r)}\right] \times \rho$$

$$\times \frac{1}{2}\frac{-u'(\mu) + u'\left((1 - \frac{\phi}{\varrho}) \times \mu\right) + u''\left((1 - \frac{\phi}{\varrho}) \times \mu\right)\frac{\phi}{\varrho} \times \mu}{u'(1)}$$

The term in brackets is positive, as one can show by substituting for $1 + r$ and p. In the last line we have the same expression that permitted us to sign the last derivative in "New Version 1," so that the last line is negative and the risk premium is a decreasing function of ϱ. As Mankiw predicted, an increase in the concentration of the aggregate shock increases the premium and, in this third setting, that is not entirely due to its effect on the rate of interest. The expected rate of return on equity and the rate of interest both increase in ϱ (drop in concentration), with the latter increasing less than the former. Their relative effects depend on the difference between the undiscounted price $p \times (1 + r)$ and the lower value $(1 - \phi) \times \mu$ of aggregate output. That depends on risk aversion.

15.8   Exercises

15.1. Write down the interest-rate level and the risk premium for the restricted-participation equilibrium of section 15.5.1. Write down also their SDEs, as well as the SDE for the consumption of the two investors, and determine whether and how the rates of growth or volatility of the previous three quantities are affected by the initial distribution of wealth.

15.2. Characterize the complete-market equilibrium that corresponds to the Basak-Cuoco economy with two logarithmic investors (hint: write down the representative

investor's problem and use the approach of chapter 10 to the solution of his optimization problem). In particular, write down the interest rate, the risk premium, the
optimal consumption of the two investors and compare it with the constrained-case
one of section 15.5.1. Use the results on consumption to determine whether welfare of either the first or the second investor decreases in the incomplete versus the
complete market.

16 Interest Rates and Bond Modeling

The only rate of interest we have considered so far has been the one for immediate maturity. The market for government and corporate bonds of all maturities is very large and so is the market for derivatives written on bonds and on rates of interest.

In this chapter, we undertake to perform for bonds the valuation of redundant derivative securities that was done for stocks in chapters 5 to 8. We face one big difficulty in this undertaking. Black and Scholes were able to specify the SDE for the price of a single stock without having to specify simultaneously the prices of all stocks. Stocks can be partially correlated with each other but, as long as they are perpetual securities, they can never reach zero volatility or perfect correlation with each other. Bonds are finite-maturity securities. As they approach maturity, their volatility must be brought down to zero. Furthermore, we cannot postulate arbitrarily the SDEs for two pure-discount bonds with maturity dates that are close to each other. If we did, we might open arbitrage opportunities. One way or the other, we must specify the behavior of all bonds together in an internally consistent fashion.[1]

In section 16.1 we introduce forward rates and yields to maturity. In section 16.2 we present some popular Markov models. We examine so-called affine models in section 16.3. Section 16.4 examines the implications of absence of arbitrage in an interest-rate model, when the latter is specified in the form of bond prices, forward rates, or the short rate. In section 16.4.4, we obtain the general conditions needed for interest-rate models to be

---

1 The first models to value interest rate sensitive options were based on models of the term structure of interest rates. This was a two-stage procedure. The first stage aimed to obtain a theoretical representation of the prices of bonds of various maturities on the basis of a one-factor or two-factor model. The second stage valued options on the term structure. See Brennan and Schwartz (1982).

The two-stage approach concerning bond options differed markedly from the approach of Black and Scholes concerning stock options. In the Black-Scholes stock option pricing theory, the behavior of the underlying asset price is postulated and the theory proceeds directly to value options on the basis of absence of arbitrage. This is a one-stage procedure.

The two-stage approach applied to bond options increased the chance of a poor fit of the theory with the data, because the errors of the first-stage model of the term structure had repercussions on the valuation of options. In other words, the first-stage bond prices did not generally fit exactly the actual term structure prevailing at the time the option was being valued while the second-stage valued the option on the basis of theoretical prices, as opposed to observed prices, of the underlying asset.

Markovian. Section 16.5 shows how to change the effective into the risk-neutral measure and vice versa. The next section provides an application. Section 16.7 investigates another change of measure, to the so-called forward measure, which is a matter of convenience as it avoids some difficulties one encounters when attempting to price some derivatives under the risk-neutral measure. Section 16.8 discusses interest rates in equilibrium; we use CIR's equilibrium as an example. In section 16.9 we provide an interpretation of the state variables that appear in Markovian or affine models.

16.1   Definitions: Short Rate, Yields, and Forward Rates

Let us consider a filtered probability space $(\Omega, \mathcal{F}, P, \mathbf{F})$ with the usual properties. Let the securities defined on it have generalized Black-Scholes prices and returns, and let consumption be the numeraire.[2] We want to make sure that these prices do not open arbitrage opportunities in the sense of definition 7.9 and that the conditions of theorem 8.2 and conjecture 8.1 hold, so that we may assume that a risk-neutral measure P^* exists. Before doing that, let us introduce the distinction between the short-term interest rate, which is a single number, the yields to maturity (one for each possible maturity or future point in time), and the instantaneous forward rates (one for each maturity).

By way of caveat, the reader is invited to answer the question in exercise 16.1.

Short rate
Up to now we have been working with a single instantaneously riskless security, a bank account. From now on, we call *"short rate"* the (instantaneously) *riskless rate r*, which is the return accruing on the usual bank account over the next instant and which varies stochastically over time. At time $t \geq 0$:[3]

$$dB(t) = r(t)B(t)dt$$

The bank account at $T > t$ has value

$$B(T) = \exp \int_0^T r(s)ds = B(t)\exp \int_t^T r(s)ds$$

This is the process that we have used to discount asset prices under the risk-neutral measure.

---

2 This means that interest rates are real, not nominal, and they are allowed to be negative. A negative interest rate is not an arbitrage opportunity.

3 Reminder: unless doing otherwise is necessary for comprehension, we simplify the notation for processes. All processes are stochastic but we suppress the reference to the state ω. Therefore, $X(t)$ actually means $X(\omega, t)$. In special cases, we also use the notation $f(t)$ to refer to a deterministic function of time. When this happens, we say so explicitly.

Bond prices

Let $\mathcal{P}(\omega, t, T)$, or $\mathcal{P}(t, T)$ for brevity, be the price at date t of a *zero-coupon bond* with unit face value or terminal value, maturing at date $T > t$. This bond pays one unit of account at maturity, $\mathcal{P}[T, T] = 1$. Under the no-arbitrage condition, the bond price, discounted at the riskless rate, like any other security price, is a martingale:

$$\mathcal{P}(t, T) = B(t)\mathbb{E}^*\left[\frac{1}{B(T)}\right] = \mathbb{E}^*\left[\exp\left(-\int_t^T r(u)du\right)\right] \tag{16.1}$$

where $\mathbb{E}^*$ is the expected value under the risk-neutral measure P^*, equivalent to P.[4]

Yields to maturity

The *yield-to-maturity* T, $R(t, T)$, is the internal rate of return of the zero-coupon bond $\mathcal{P}$, or the constant interest rate that can be earned by investing in the bond from time t to maturity. R makes the compound amount of $\mathcal{P}$ equal to one unit of account:

$$\mathcal{P}(t, T)\exp(R(t, T)(T - t)) = 1$$

It follows that R is defined as:

$$R(t, T) \triangleq -\frac{\ln \mathcal{P}(t, T)}{T - t} \tag{16.2}$$

The reader can now solve exercise 16.2.

Forward rates

Consider now two points in time in the future, T_1 and T_2, with $t \leq T_1 < T_2 \leq T$. The value at time t of the interest rate one can earn between those two dates using instruments available today, called the time-t *simple forward rate* for the period between T_1 and T_2, $f(t, T_1, T_2)$, is determined by a no-arbitrage reasoning, as follows. One has two possibilities to invest a unit of account from time 0 to time T_2: either directly, by means of a T_2-maturity bond, or by buying bonds with maturity T_1, and committing to invest at the forward rate f from T_1 to T_2. In the former case one buys $1/\mathcal{P}(t, T_2)$ bonds at time t. Each pays off one unit at maturity, so that the payoff at T_2 is also $1/\mathcal{P}(t, T_2)$. In the latter case one first buys $1/\mathcal{P}(t, T_1)$ zero-coupon bonds at time t, gets $1/\mathcal{P}(t, T_1)$ units of account at T_1, and reinvests those at the forward rate $f(t, T_1, T_2)$. At T_2, the payoff is:

$$\frac{1}{\mathcal{P}(t, T_1)}\exp(f(t, T_1, T_2)(T_2 - T_1))$$

To exclude arbitrage, the two amounts must be equal:

$$\frac{1}{\mathcal{P}(t, T_1)}\exp(f(t, T_1, T_2)(T_2 - T_1)) = \frac{1}{\mathcal{P}(t, T_2)}$$

It follows that the no-arbitrage value of the simple forward rate is

$$f(t, T_1, T_2) \triangleq \frac{\ln \mathcal{P}(t, T_1) - \ln \mathcal{P}(t, T_2)}{T_2 - T_1} \tag{16.3}$$

---

4 Here we take no stance on market completeness. Consequently, the change of measure might be unique or not.

By letting the reinvestment period go to zero, that is, $T_1 \to T_2 = T$, one gets the time-t value of the *instantaneous forward rate* for the date T, $f(t,T)$, as the negative of the log derivative of the zero-coupon bond price with respect to the maturity T:[5],[6]

$$f(t,T) \triangleq -\frac{\partial}{\partial T} \ln \mathcal{P}(t,T) \tag{16.4}$$

There is a relation between the yield and the forward rate for the same maturity. Using (16.2) we get:

$$f(t,T) = \frac{\partial[R(t,T)(T-t)]}{\partial T} = R(t,T) + \frac{\partial R(t,T)}{\partial T}(T-t)$$

which says that the forward rate and the yield over the same time span differ by a negative or positive amount, depending on the yield being decreasing or increasing as a function of the maturity date.

The short rate is included in the sequence of forward rates. Letting $T \to t$ in (16.4), we get the short rate:

$$\lim_{T \to t} f(t,T) = f(t,t) \equiv r(t) \tag{16.5}$$

Using the notions introduced so far, we can write down the bond price in three equivalent ways, using the sequence of forward rates quoted today, the yield to maturity, or the expected sequence of future short rates. An expectation is involved in the third expression only:

$$\mathcal{P}(t,T) = \exp\left(-\int_t^T f(t,u)du\right) \tag{16.6}$$

$$\mathcal{P}(t,T) = \exp(-(T-t)R(t,T)) \tag{16.7}$$

$$\mathcal{P}(t,T) = \mathbb{E}^*\left[\exp\left(-\int_t^T r(u)du\right)\right] \tag{16.8}$$

When, for a given initial date t, we consider either yields or forward rates as functions of their maturity date T, we name these the *term structure of interest rates (or of yields or of forwards)*. The term structure of interest rates can present different shapes, which are consistent with different economic theories of the reward required by market participants for lending in the bond market. Typically, the bond price is decreasing as a function of the maturity. We read from the last formulation above, (16.8), that when this is true the process for the short rate is expected to remain non-negative under the risk-neutral measure.

---

5 We assume here and below that the drift and volatilities, as well as the bond prices, are sufficiently smooth to allow differentiability with respect to maturity T at least up to the second order.

6 We ask forgiveness for using the same symbol f for the simple forward rate $f(t,T_1,T_2)$ and the instantaneous one, $f(t,T)$.

16.2   Examples of Markov Models

If we ever want to specify the coefficients for either the bond, the forward or the short process, we need a guideline to select interesting models that facilitate implementation, while maintaining tractability and giving a good empirical fit. In the models that follow, it is posited *ab initio* that the short rate follows a Markovian process. In section 16.4 below, we state the conditions under which that property is satisfied. We start in this section from a single Wiener process and a single-state variable model and work out in section 16.3 an extension to multi-Wiener (or multi-factor) models. In the current section, the single state variable is the short rate.

16.2.1   Vasicek

Vasicek (1977) posits an Ornstein-Uhlenbeck process for the short rate under the risk-neutral measure:

$$dr(t) = \varrho \times (\bar{r} - r(t))dt + \sigma_r dw^*(t); \ r_0 > 0 \text{ given} \tag{16.9}$$

where ϱ, $\bar{r}$, and σ_r are positive constants. The drift and variance are affine in the short rate. The main feature of the Vasicek process is its mean-reversion. The spot rate r rises in expected value whenever it is below the level $\bar{r}$, and decreases otherwise. The parameter ϱ represents the speed of reversion towards $\bar{r}$, which is usually interpreted as a long-run value of the rate (imposed, for instance, by a monetary authority), since we have:

$$r(t) = \bar{r} + e^{-\varrho t}(r_0 - \bar{r}) + \sigma_r \int_0^t e^{-\varrho(t-u)} dw^*(u)$$

and $\lim_{t \to \infty} \mathbb{E}^*[r(t)] = \bar{r}$. From the short rate we obtain the bond price, the yield and the forward rate, using the relations of section 16.1. This is done in small characters below. We also show that the long-run value of the yield, named R_∞, is

$$\bar{r} - \frac{1}{2}\frac{\sigma_r^2}{\varrho^2}$$

and that the forward rate has drift

$$\mu_f^*(t, T) = \frac{\sigma_r^2}{\varrho} e^{-\varrho(T-t)}(1 - e^{-\varrho(T-t)})$$

and volatility

$$\sigma_f(t, T) = e^{-\varrho(T-t)}\sigma_r$$

so that the diffusion of the bond price is

$$\sigma(t, T) = -\frac{1}{\varrho}\left(1 - e^{-\varrho(T-t)}\right)\sigma_r$$

The Vasicek model is a simple example of what we later call "affine" Gaussian models. It is so according to the definitions of section 13.3.2 and of example 7.1 because:

- the SDEs for the short rate has affine drift and variance terms (relative to the short rate);
- yields are affine in the short rate.

The transition densities for the Ornstein-Uhlenbeck short rate process are normally distributed; that is, the short rate is Gaussian.[7] The same happens for the forward rate. We provide later general conditions also for Gaussianity of affine models.

The reader can now solve exercises 16.3, 16.4, and 16.5.

———————————◆———————————

By applying the risk-neutral pricing formula (16.1), one can verify that the Vasicek bond price equals

$$\mathcal{P}(t,T) = \exp\left\{\frac{1}{\varrho}\left(1 - e^{-\varrho(T-t)}\right)(R_\infty - r) - (T-t)R_\infty - \frac{\sigma_r^2}{4\varrho^3}\left(1 - e^{-\varrho(T-t)}\right)^2\right\} \quad (16.10)$$

where:

$$R_\infty \triangleq \bar{r} - \frac{1}{2}\frac{\sigma_r^2}{\varrho^2}$$

Using the definition (16.2), it is immediate to prove from the bond price expression that the yield is affine in the short rate:

$$R(t,T) = R_\infty - \left\{\frac{1}{\varrho}\left(1 - e^{-\varrho(T-t)}\right)(R_\infty - r) - \frac{\sigma_r^2}{4\varrho^3}\left(1 - e^{-\varrho(T-t)}\right)^2\right\}\frac{1}{T-t} \quad (16.11)$$

Using the latter, one can verify that R_∞ is the level towards which yields converge when maturity goes to infinity:

$$\lim_{T\to\infty} R(t,T) = R_\infty$$

This long-run yield is below the long-run short-rate $\bar{r}$ and the spread between the two is increasing in the variance of the short-rate (σ_r) and decreasing in the speed of adjustment ϱ.

From the bond price expression it follows immediately that the log bond price is

$$\ln \mathcal{P}(t,T) = \frac{1}{\varrho}\left(1 - e^{-\varrho(T-t)}\right)(R_\infty - r) - (T-t)R_\infty - \frac{\sigma_r^2}{4\varrho^3}\left(1 - e^{-\varrho(T-t)}\right)^2$$

Taking its derivative with respect to T, according to definition (16.4), we get the forward rate:

$$f(t,T) = -e^{-\varrho(T-t)}(R_\infty - r) + R_\infty + \frac{1}{2}\frac{\sigma_r^2}{\varrho^2}\left(1 - e^{-\varrho(T-t)}\right)e^{-\varrho(T-t)} \quad (16.12)$$

———————————

7 Recall example 7.1. See also Arnold (1974).

Its dynamics are

$$df(t,T) = e^{-\varrho(T-t)}dr + e^{-\varrho(T-t)} \times \Bigg[-(R_\infty - r)\varrho$$

$$-\frac{1}{2}\frac{\sigma_r^2}{\varrho^2}e^{-\varrho(T-t)}\varrho + \frac{1}{2}\frac{\sigma_r^2}{\varrho^2}\Big(1 - e^{-\varrho(T-t)}\Big)\varrho \Bigg] dt$$

Substituting in the last expression the SDE for the short rate we get

$$df(t,T) = e^{-\varrho(T-t)}$$

$$\times \Bigg[\varrho(\bar{r} - r) - \varrho\Big(\bar{r} - r - \frac{1}{2}\frac{\sigma_r^2}{\varrho^2}\Big)$$

$$+ \frac{1}{2}\frac{\sigma_r^2}{\varrho^2}\Big(1 - 2e^{-\varrho(T-t)}\Big)\varrho \Bigg] dt + \sigma_r dw^*(t)$$

$$= \frac{\sigma_r^2}{\varrho}e^{-\varrho(T-t)}(1 - e^{-\varrho(T-t)})dt + e^{-\varrho(T-t)}\sigma_r dw^*(t)$$

We immediately observe that the drift of the forward rates is

$$\mu_f^*(t,T) = \frac{\sigma_r^2}{\varrho}e^{-\varrho(T-t)}(1 - e^{-\varrho(T-t)}) \tag{16.13}$$

while the instantaneous volatility is

$$\sigma_f(t,T) = e^{-\varrho(T-t)}\sigma_r \tag{16.14}$$

It will later be apparent (from (16.25)), that the latter volatility can be used to prove that the diffusion of the bond price is

$$\sigma(t,T) = -\frac{1}{\varrho}\Big(1 - e^{-\varrho(T-t)}\Big)\sigma_r \tag{16.15}$$

Let us focus now on the calibration of the model. For it to be consistent with a given initial term structure of forward rates, the RHS of (16.12) for $t = 0$ must coincide with it. The RHS is a function of the parameters $R_\infty, r_0, \sigma_r/\varrho$, or, equivalently, $\bar{r}, r_0, \sigma_r/\varrho$. Since these parameters are constant, the initial structure is an exponential function of T. Imagine that one wants to calibrate those parameters to a given, observed initial curve, or even to a finite number of its points. There is no guarantee that, taking a finite number of forward rates at time $0, f(0; T_i), i = 1, 2, ..M$, formula (16.12) can produce those rates for some values of the parameters $\bar{r}, r_0, \sigma_r/\varrho$ to be found.

16.2.2 Modified Vasicek Models

The Vasicek model is said to be extended or modified whenever the (risk-neutral) parameters of the short rate are time-varying:

$$dr(t) = (\chi(t) - \varrho(t)r(t))\,dt + \sigma_r(t)dw^*(t);$$

$$r_0 > 0 \text{ given}$$

where $\varrho(t)$, $\chi(t)$ and $\sigma_r(t)$ are positively-valued, *deterministic* functions of time.

The two versions of that model that are most well known are the so-called Ho and Lee (1986) and the Hull and White (1993a) models, which obtain when $\varrho(t) \equiv 0, \sigma_r \in \mathbb{R}$, and $\varrho, \sigma_r \in \mathbb{R}$, respectively. In the first case, there is zero mean reversion and the short rate volatility is constant. In the second, the rate reverts to a non-constant level, with a constant volatility; the adjustment speed is time independent.

The insertion of a time-varying parameter $\chi(t)$ provides more flexibility in fitting an initial term structure as compared to the Vasicek case. Keeping the instantaneous volatility of the short rate σ_r constant and the speed of adjustment ϱ either null or constant preserves the manageability of the Vasicek model. In particular, we show below that, in the Ho-and-Lee model, a shock ($dw^*(t)$) generates parallel shifts of the term structure, while in the Hull-and-White model it may generate a non-parallel shift, with an effect on the term structure that is larger for short than for long maturities, as empirically observed.

16.2.2.1 Ho and Lee
Let:

$$dr(t) = \chi(t)dt + \sigma_r dw^*(t)$$

One can show that the bond and forward volatilities are:

$$\sigma(t, T) = \lim_{\varrho \to 0} -\frac{1}{\varrho}\left(1 - e^{-\varrho(T-t)}\right)\sigma_r = (T - t)\sigma_r$$

$$\sigma_f(t, T) = \lim_{\varrho \to 0} e^{-\varrho(T-t)}\sigma_r = \sigma_r$$

So, zero-coupon bonds have a diffusion that is linear in maturity and linearly decreasing in the time-to-maturity $T - t$. Forward rates have a constant instantaneous diffusion. As a consequence, the drift of forward rates is

$$\mu_f^*(t, T) = \sigma(t, T)\frac{\partial}{\partial T}\sigma(t, T) = (T - t)\sigma_r^2$$

Overall, the dynamics of the forward rates is

$$df(t, T) = (T - t)\sigma_r^2 dt + \sigma_r dw^*(t)$$

Integrating, we get

$$f(t, T) = f(0, T) + \sigma_r w^*(t) + \sigma_r^2 t \times \left(T - \frac{t}{2}\right)$$

The last expression tells us that, for any $t > 0$, shocks to the term structure of forward rates (realizations of the Wiener process $w^*(t)$) produce a parallel shift of the term structure, since they enter the expression of the forward rate by means of a constant coefficient σ_r.

16.2.2.2 Hull and White

Let:

$$dr(t) = (\chi(t) - \varrho r(t))dt + \sigma_r dw^*(t)$$

The zero-coupon bond and the forward rate volatilities are as in the Vasicek case. As compared to the Ho-and-Lee model, the volatility of zero-coupon bonds does not decrease linearly as the final maturity approaches. It decreases exponentially. Also the volatility of forward rates is decreasing exponentially over maturities. The drift of the forward rates is exactly as in the Vasicek case. Overall, the dynamics of the forward rates are

$$df(t, T) = \frac{1}{\varrho}\left(1 - e^{-\varrho(T-t)}\right)e^{-\varrho(T-t)}\sigma_r^2 dt + e^{-\varrho(T-t)}\sigma_r dw^*(t)$$

Integrating with respect to t, we get

$$f(t, T) = f(0, T) + \sigma_r \int_0^t e^{-\varrho(T-s)}dw^*(s) - \frac{\sigma_r^2}{2\varrho^2}\left(1 - e^{-\varrho(T-t)}\right)^2$$

We see from this expression that, for any $t > 0$, shocks to the term structure of forward rates (realizations of the Wiener process $w^*(t)$) have a higher impact on short maturity forward rates and a smaller impact on long maturity ones. They enter with a negative exponential coefficient ($e^{-\varrho(T-s)}$), instead of a constant one. This is consistent with the fact that there is mean reversion in the Hull-and-White model, while there was no reversion in the Ho-and-Lee one.

The reader can now solve exercises 16.6, 16.7, and 16.8.

16.2.3 Cox, Ingersoll, and Ross

Cox, Ingersoll, and Ross (1985b) (CIR) posit a "square-root" process for the short rate under the risk-neutral measure:

$$dr(t) = \varrho(\bar{r} - r(t))dt + \psi \sqrt{r(t)}dw^*(t); \; r_0 > 0 \text{ given} \tag{16.16}$$

where ϱ, $\bar{r}$, and ψ are positive constants. The drift and variance are affine in r. There is still mean reversion, towards the level $\bar{r}$, with speed of adjustment ϱ. Both are constant. It is evident from the above process for the short rate that the CIR model satisfies also the two properties required in section 13.3.2 for a model to be affine.

Using (16.1), one can verify that the bond price is exponential in the short rate:

$$\mathcal{P}(t, T) = \bar{A}(t, T)e^{-D(t,T)r}$$

where

$$\bar{A}(t,T) \triangleq \left[\frac{2\gamma \exp\left[\frac{1}{2}(\varrho + \gamma)(T - t)\right]}{(\gamma + \varrho)\left(e^{\bar{r}(T-t)} - 1\right) + 2\bar{r}} \right]^{\frac{2\varrho\bar{r}}{\psi^2}}$$

$$D(t,T) \triangleq \frac{2\left(e^{\gamma(T-t)} - 1\right)}{(\gamma + \varrho)\left(e^{\gamma(T-t)} - 1\right) + 2\bar{r}}$$

$$\gamma \triangleq \left(\varrho^2 + 2\psi^2\right)^{1/2}$$

Using the relation between bond prices and yields (16.2), it can be verified that the yield is

$$R(t,T) = \frac{D(t,T)r - \ln \bar{A}(t,T)}{T - t}$$

and is again affine in the short rate.

If we take the log of price, then its derivative with respect to T, according to (16.4), gives the forward rate:

$$\ln \mathcal{P}(t,T) = -D(t,T)r + \ln \bar{A}(t,T)$$

$$f(t,T) = \frac{\partial}{\partial T}D(t,T)r - \frac{1}{\bar{A}(t,T)}\frac{\partial}{\partial T}\bar{A}(t,T) \tag{16.17}$$

The dynamics of the price and the forward rate, $d\mathcal{P}$ and df, can be used to show that

$$\sigma(t,T) = -D(t,T)\psi\sqrt{r} = -D(t,T)\sigma_r \tag{16.18}$$

$$\sigma_f(t,T) = \frac{\partial}{\partial T}D(t,T)\psi\sqrt{r} = \frac{\partial}{\partial T}D(t,T)\sigma_r \tag{16.19}$$

We can show that the drift of the forward rates under the risk-neutral measure is equal to those of the Vasicek as well as Hull-and-White model.

The reader can now solve exercises 16.9 and 16.10.

———————————♠———————————

Let us consider the fit to an initial term structure. For the CIR model to be consistent with a given initial term structure, it must be true that:

$$f(0;T) = \frac{\partial}{\partial T}D(0,T)r_0 - \frac{1}{\bar{A}(0,T)}\frac{\partial}{\partial T}\bar{A}(0,T)$$

where the RHS is a function of the parameters $\varrho, \bar{r}, \psi$. As in the Vasicek case, we are in a situation in which the choice of three parameters determines the fit to a given initial term structure. We cannot expect perfect fit.

16.3   Affine Models

The Vasicek and CIR examples belong to the class of *exponential-affine* (or simply *affine* for short) term-structure models, for which elegant solutions for bond prices and rates exist.

As in chapter 13, consider a set of n state variables Y driven by the diffusion process:

$$dY(t) = \mu_Y^*(Y(t), t)dt + \sigma_Y(Y(t), t)dw^*(t) \tag{16.20}$$

where w^* is a K-dimensional Wiener process under P^*, μ_Y^* and σ_Y take values respectively in $\mathbb{R}^n$, and in the space of the matrices $n \times K$. This process is called affine if μ_Y^*, $\sigma_Y(\sigma_Y)^\mathsf{T}$ are linear affine functions of Y. Recall that we saw in section 13.1.2 the definition of a characteristic function. And we saw in section 13.3.2 that a process is affine if and only if its conditional characteristic function is exponential affine (theorem 13.1).

We are now ready to apply the affine mathematical framework to the term structure. Consider an economy in which state variables Y follow an affine process (16.20) under the risk-neutral measure P^* (*assumption 1*) where, in addition, the riskless short rate at each point in time is affine in Y (*assumption 2*):

$$r(Y) = a_0 + a_1 Y \tag{16.21}$$

with a_0 a scalar and a_1 a vector.

Then the price at date t of a pure-discount bond maturing at subsequent date T is exponential affine, that is,

$$\mathcal{P}(t, T) = \mathbb{E}^*\left[e^{-\int_t^T r(Y(u))du}|Y(t) = y\right] = e^{A(T-t) + C(T-t)y}$$

where these $A(T - t)$ and $C(T - t)$ are integrals over time of the solution of the Riccati system (13.18) of section 13.3.2. The reason is that all the terms $\mathbb{E}^*\left[e^{-r(Y(u))}|Y(t) = y\right]$ are given values of the characteristic function calculated for different target dates u. The converse result holds too, thus:

Theorem 16.1 $\mathcal{P}$ *is exponential affine if and only if* μ_Y^*, $\sigma_Y(\sigma_Y)^\mathsf{T}$ *and r are affine in Y.*

Given the definition of the yield on a bond $R(t, T)$:

$$e^{R(t,T) \times (T-t)} = e^{A(T-t) + C(T-t)y}$$

in affine models (and in them only) it happens that:

$$R(t, T) = \frac{A(T - t)}{T - t} + \frac{C(T - t)}{T - t}y \tag{16.22}$$

meaning that the yield is affine in the state variables.[8] Equivalently, one can say that the sensitivities of the yield curve to the state variables are deterministic.

---

8 For the instantaneous yield, which is the rate of interest:

$$\lim_{T \to t} \frac{A(T - t)}{T - t} = a_0; \quad \lim_{T \to t} \frac{C(T - t)}{T - t} = a_1$$

Using the definitions above, one shows easily that also the forward rates are affine functions of the state variables. Hence the popular appeal of affine models.

One can distinguish two main classes of exponential affine models: the *Gaussian* and the *square-root* ones.

A model is *Gaussian* if the variance-covariance matrix of the state variables, $\sigma_Y \sigma_Y^\mathsf{T}$, is at most dependent on time, while it does not depend on the level of the state variables themselves. The most prominent example of Gaussian exponential affine processes is the Vasicek model; other examples of Gaussian models are those of Ho and Lee and Hull and White.

A model is a *square-root* model whenever the elements of the variance-covariance matrix of the state variables are affine in the state variables themselves, with constant coefficients and appropriate non-negativity constraints:

$$\left[\sigma_Y \sigma_Y^\mathsf{T}\right]_{ij} = \bar{\sigma}_{ij} + Y^\mathsf{T} \breve{\sigma}_{ij} \qquad\qquad i,j = 1,..,n$$

where $\bar{\sigma}_{ij} \in \mathbb{R}, \breve{\sigma}_{ij} \in \mathbb{R}^n$. The most prominent example of square-root process is the CIR one.

One might wonder whether an affine term structure model can arise in equilibrium and how the nature and number of state variables can be determined. The general equilibrium question is studied in section 16.8, using the specification of CIR, which produces the corresponding short rates. In order to give an answer to the second question, we need an interpretation of the state variables, which we also give below (section 16.9). Before covering these two issues, we study the change of measures in the interest-rate domain.

The reader can now solve exercise 16.11.

16.4   Various Ways of Specifying the Behavior of the Bond Market

In all the previous examples of this chapter, we have specified *ab initio* the behavior of the short rate. We observed how the term structures of bond prices or yields and forwards that followed from most of these specifications would not generally fit the empirical term structure of any initial time. Could we instead postulate joint processes for all the bond prices or all the forward rates? One cannot impose separate, arbitrary dynamics on the two sequences. The absence of arbitrage imposes non-trivial restrictions on the dynamics (drift and diffusion) of bonds and interest rates under the risk-neutral measure. This can be interpreted as *dynamic no-arbitrage*, since it affects the dynamics of rates as stochastic processes, instead of their level at a specific point in time. We first specify the implications for bond prices, as did El Karoui and Rochet (1989) and Hull and White (1993a). We then examine the implications for forward rates, as did Heath, Jarrow, and Morton (1992), and on the instantaneous short rate as in Hull and White (1990). The three implications (or restrictions) are equivalent, initial conditions apart.

16.4.1 Specifying the Behavior of Bond Prices

When developing the theory of Black and Scholes, we started with the behavior of only one stock price under the risk-neutral measure. Now, we must specify the initial conditions and the behavior over time of the entire structure of bond prices $\mathcal{P}(t, T)$ for different T. When doing that, we need to impose some restrictions on the assumed future behavior of bond prices, to make sure that arbitrage possibilities are ruled out.

Let us specify directly the behavior of prices under some risk-neutral probability measure. Under P^*, we know that the drift of the prices of all bonds is r, since they are traded securities. Their diffusions, however, remain to be chosen. At time $t > 0$, for all $T > t \in \mathbb{R}_{++}$, we can write:

$$\frac{d\mathcal{P}(t, T)}{\mathcal{P}(t, T)} = r(t)dt + \sigma(t, T)dw^*(t) \tag{16.23}$$

$$\mathcal{P}(0, T) \text{ given}$$

where $w^*(t)$ is a K-dimensional Wiener process under the risk-neutral measure.

The formulation (16.23) seems incomplete without some knowledge of the behavior of the instantaneous short rate $r(t)$ over time. Even if we specify $r(t)$, the diffusion remains to be specified under the restriction that $\sigma(T, T) = 0$, which must hold since the terminal price of a bond is certain: $\mathcal{P}(t, T) = 1$. Despite the assumed existence of the P^* measure and the fact that all bonds return the same r, we cannot guarantee absence of arbitrage, since we have a possible conflict between terminal conditions, $\mathcal{P}(T, T) = 1$, and the initial conditions $\mathcal{P}(0, T)$ provided by the time-0 observed term structure of all bond prices. We are not sure that every diffusion σ is consistent with the fact that, with $\mathcal{P}(0, T)$ and $\mathcal{P}(t, T)$ being given, the relation (16.23) holds. We show in section 16.4.3 that the behavior of r cannot be arbitrary between time t and time T if we give ourselves the term structure at time t for all maturity dates till T.

To clarify that point, it is useful to draw the implications of (16.23) for forward rates and the spot rate.

16.4.2 Specifying the Behavior of Forward Rates

To make sure that the boundary condition $\sigma(T, T) = 0$ is satisfied with probability 1, the most readily available assumption would seem to be to assume that the derivative $\partial\sigma(t, s)/\partial s$ is finite, which, by integration over s from t to T, would place the required restriction on the function $\sigma(t, T)$. That integral would automatically satisfy the boundary condition. From there comes the idea of specifying the behavior of forward rates, which must be related to the behavior of bond prices.

From equation (16.23), we derive the behavior of forward rates over time, and show that the existence of a common drift for all bonds under the risk-neutral measure, namely, in the absence of arbitrage opportunities, implies a restriction relating the drift of forward rates to their diffusion, as well as a relation between the SDE coefficients of bonds and those of forward rates.[9]

The forward rate implied in the time-t term structure, for the future period $[T_1, T_2]$ is given by (16.3). Applying Itô's lemma to the logarithm of bond prices in (16.3), using (16.23) and observing that, under the risk-neutral measure, all bonds have the same drift, we get the following SDE for (discrete) forward rates, under the risk-neutral measure:

$$df(t, T_1, T_2) = \frac{\sigma(t, T_2)\sigma(t, T_2)^\mathsf{T} - \sigma(t, T_1)\sigma(t, T_1)^\mathsf{T}}{2(T_2 - T_1)} dt$$
$$+ \frac{\sigma(t, T_1) - \sigma(t, T_2)}{T_2 - T_1} dw^*(t)$$

The process for the instantaneous forward rate is obtained by taking the limit of the above expression as $T_2 \to T_1 = T$:[10]

$$df(t, T) = \sigma(t, T)\left(\frac{\partial}{\partial T}\sigma(t, T)\right)^\mathsf{T} dt - \frac{\partial}{\partial T}\sigma(t, T) dw^*(t) \qquad (16.24)$$

Denote as $\sigma_f(t, T)$ the volatilities of forward rates. From the last equation:

$$\sigma_f(t, T) \triangleq -\frac{\partial}{\partial T}\sigma(t, T) \qquad (16.25)$$

This proves that:

Proposition 16.1 *Under the risk-neutral measure, the diffusion of the forward rate is equal to the negative of the derivative with respect to maturity date of the volatility of the bond price. Equivalently, the volatility of the bond is the negative integral of the volatility of the forwards:*

$$\sigma(t, T) = -\int_t^T \sigma_f(t, s) ds \qquad (16.26)$$

Using that fact, the SDE for forward rates is:

$$df(t, T) = \mu_f^*(t, T) dt + \sigma_f(t, T) dw^*(t) \qquad (16.27)$$

where, according to (16.24):

$$\mu_f^*(t, T) = \left[\int_t^T \sigma_f(t, s) ds\right] \times \left(\sigma_f(t, T)\right)^\mathsf{T} \qquad (16.28)$$

This proves that

Proposition 16.2 Forward-rate drift restriction *(Heath, Jarrow, and Morton (1992), or HJM) The drift of forward rates under a risk-neutral measure is equal to their diffusion times the integral of their diffusions over all maturities.*

---

9 Equivalently, we could have derived from (16.23) an expression for yields to maturities of the various bonds. See exercise 16.2.

10 T is a fixed date in this equation.

According to (16.25), the drift and diffusion terms of the stochastic process for forward rates, under a risk-neutral probability, depend only on the volatilities of the rates of return on bonds. They do not depend on the prices of bonds nor on the riskless interest rate, except perhaps indirectly by means of their impact on the volatility of bond returns. Once the volatilities of bond returns are specified for all maturities, the process for forward rates under the risk-neutral measure follows uniquely. This restriction tells us that modeling the process for forward rates, as was done by HJM, is equivalent to modeling the process for bond prices. Indeed, as can be seen in (16.23), the latter dynamics involve r as a drift and $\sigma(t, T)$ as a diffusion, where $\sigma(t, T)$ is related to the drift and diffusion of forward rates by (16.25).

It is easy to shift from one formulation (giving the volatility of the forward rate and using (16.28) for its drift) to the other (giving the short interest rate and the volatility of bonds as in (16.23)). The choice of formulation is a matter of convenience. In fact both formulations are useful. On the one hand, the process for the bond price provides information about the drift: the drift is r and that implies a drift restriction on forward rates. The diffusion of the forward rate process, on the other hand, can be specified freely and it implies the diffusion of the bond prices, which could not have been specified freely to start with because of the terminal restriction $\sigma(T, T) = 0$.

We conclude that

Remark 16.1 *The most convenient way to specify the behavior of bond prices under a risk-neutral measure is to write:*

$$\frac{d\mathcal{P}(t, T)}{\mathcal{P}(t, T)} = r(t)dt - \left[\int_t^T \sigma_f(t, s)ds\right] dw^*(t) \qquad (16.29)$$

where $\sigma_f(t, s)$, viewed as a process over time t, can be specified freely (in $\mathcal{H}^2$).

The reader can verify that all the models of section 16.2 satisfy the HJM restrictions, as they must. An exercise on the forward rate restriction is given as exercise 16.12.

16.4.3 Specifying the Behavior of the Short Rate

The remaining point to be clarified is the relation between bonds and forward rates on the one hand, and short rates on the other, imagining that the entire term structure at some starting date t is given. We know from (16.5) that the instantaneous short interest rate is one of the instantaneous forward rates, $r(t) = f(t, T)$. Let us use this fact to give an integral expression for the short rate at time t and to write down its dynamics. By definition

$$f(t, t) = f(0, t) + \int_0^t df(s, t)$$

Substituting *df* from equation (16.24) above, we obtain the following expression for the short rate:

$$r(t) = f(0,t) + \int_0^t \sigma(s,t)\left(\frac{\partial}{\partial T}\sigma(s,t)\right)^\mathsf{T} ds - \int_0^t \frac{\partial}{\partial T}\sigma(s,t)dw^*(s) \tag{16.30}$$

The SDE for the short rate—imagining a single Wiener for simplicity—can then be obtained by stochastic differentiation:

$$dr(t) = \frac{\partial}{\partial T}f(0,t)dt \tag{16.31}$$

$$+ \left\{\int_0^t\left[\sigma(s,t)\frac{\partial^2}{\partial T^2}\sigma(s,t) + \left(\frac{\partial}{\partial T}\sigma(s,t)\right)^2\right]ds\right\}dt$$

$$+\sigma(t,t)\frac{\partial}{\partial T}\sigma(t,t)dt$$

$$-\frac{\partial}{\partial T}\sigma(t,t)dw^*(t) - \left\{\int_0^t\frac{\partial^2}{\partial T^2}\sigma(s,t)dw^*(s)\right\}dt$$

If we make use of the requirement that, at maturity, the volatility of the return on a bond is zero, $\sigma(t,t) \equiv 0$, the last expression simplifies to:[11]

$$dr(t) = \left\{\frac{\partial}{\partial T}f(0,t)+\right.$$

$$\int_0^t\left[\sigma(s,t)\frac{\partial^2}{\partial T^2}\sigma(s,t)ds + \left(\frac{\partial}{\partial T}\sigma(s,t)\right)^2ds - \frac{\partial^2}{\partial T^2}\sigma(s,t)dw^*(s)\right]\left.\right\}dt$$

$$-\frac{\partial}{\partial T}\sigma(t,t)dw^*(t) \tag{16.32}$$

which tells us that specifying the *whole dynamics* of the short rates – or the LHS for all *t* – is equivalent to specifying the drifts and diffusions of bond prices for all *t* and, by the HJM conditions, the drift and diffusion of forward rates, which make up the RHS of this equation.

Not only do the HJM no-arbitrage restrictions provide a telling expression (16.30) for the short rates, they also dictate the evolution of the short rate of interest from time *t* onwards based on the current forward rates, $f(0,t)$, and on the current and past bond volatilities $\sigma(s,t)$, $s \in [0,t]$, their derivatives and the *past* trajectory of the Wiener process $w^*(t)$, which are on the RHS of (16.32).

---

11 The stochastic differential equation (16.32) is not a special case of the equation (16.24) for forward rates, even though $r(t)$ is a special forward rate: $r(t) = f(t,t)$. Equation (16.24) was written for a fixed maturity date T, whereas $dr(t) = df(t,t)$; that is, the increment (16.32) in the instantaneous short rate is calculated with a "sliding" or "rolling" immediate maturity date t.

16.4.4   Condition for the Short Rate to Be Markovian

Equation (16.32) shows that, in general, short rates are not Markovian. The short rate may be non-Markovian even when the formulation for forward rates (16.24) is chosen to be Markovian. Two is the minimum number of state variables required to capture the path dependency. From there, it is not hard to pin down the conditions under which a short rate that satisfies the HJM properties (and, as a consequence, the forward rates and bond prices which correspond to it) is Markovian.

We develop the theory for the single-Wiener process case, even though a similar proof can be provided for the case of K Wiener processes.[12] The volatility of the forward rate is the short-rate volatility, when $T \to t$. We denote it accordingly as $\sigma_f(t, T) = \sigma_r(t)$.

Proposition 16.3 *(Ritchken and Sanakarasubramaniam (1995)) A necessary and sufficient condition for HJM-short rates at time t to be determined by a two-state-variable Markov process is that the volatility of forward rates admit the representation*

$$\sigma_f(t, T) = \sigma_r(t) \exp\left(-\int_t^T k(u)du\right)$$

where $k(u)$ is a scalar, deterministic function of time. The two state *variables are the short rate itself and the integrated forward-rate variance, defined as*

$$\phi(t) \triangleq \int_0^t \left[\sigma_f(x, t)\right]^2 dx$$

The proof is in the appendix of this chapter.

The consequences on bond prices are as follows. Under the assumption of the theorem, the volatility of bond prices is

$$\sigma(t, T) = -\sigma_r(t) \int_t^T \exp\left(-\int_t^x k(u)du\right)dx \tag{16.33}$$

or

$$\sigma(t, T) = -\sigma_r(t) \int_t^T k(t, x)dx$$

where we took the liberty of using the notation:

$$k(t, x) \triangleq \exp\left(-\int_t^x k(u)du\right)$$

which is a deterministic function of time. It follows that forward rates from any point in time t to any maturity T can be written in terms of their initial values (at time 0) and the

---

12 The discrete-time representation of Markovian processes can be accomplished by means of a "recombining" binomial tree. This is a big advantage for the numerical calculation of the prices of options. The Markovian character is necessary for the tree to be recombining.

same two state-variables above, or, equivalently, in terms of the difference between the short rate and its "best forecast" at time $0, f(0,t)$:

$$I(t) \triangleq r(t) - f(0,t)$$

and the integrated variance:

$$f(t,T) = f(0,T) + k(t,T)I(t) - k(t,T)\left[\int_t^T k(t,u)du\right]\phi(t) \tag{16.34}$$

Bond prices at $t > 0$ can also be written in terms of their initial values (at time 0) and the same pair of state variables:

$$\mathcal{P}(t,T) = \frac{\mathcal{P}(0,T)}{\mathcal{P}(0,t)} \exp\left[X(t,T)I(t) - \frac{1}{2}X^2(t,T)\phi(t)\right] \tag{16.35}$$

where:

$$X(t,T) \triangleq -\frac{\sigma(t,T)}{\sigma_f(t,T)} = \int_t^T k(t,x)dx$$

The state variables are common to all bonds, independently of their maturity T.

When does the two-state variable model become a one-variable model? Since a deterministic short rate is not interesting in the current context, we consider the case in which the other factor, the integrated variance, is deterministic. That is so if the volatility of the short rate is constant and non-zero at all times, $\sigma_r(t) = \sigma_r \neq 0$, but the volatility of the forward rate is a deterministic function of time, of the type

$$\sigma_f(t,T) = \sigma_r e^{-\varrho(T-t)} \tag{16.36}$$

for $\varrho \in \mathbb{R}$. In this case the function $\phi(t)$ is deterministic, and no variance risk is present. The reader can verify that all the models of section 16.2 are indeed one-factor Markovian.

Expression (16.35) lends itself nicely to considerations on bond hedging, which we write in small characters below.

———————————◆———————————

To hedge the bond values against unexpected changes in the state variables, expand the bond value (16.35) as follows

$$\Delta\mathcal{P}(t,T) = \frac{\partial\mathcal{P}}{\partial t}\Delta t + \frac{\partial\mathcal{P}}{\partial I}\Delta I + \frac{1}{2}\frac{\partial^2\mathcal{P}}{\partial I^2}(\Delta I)^2 + \frac{\partial\mathcal{P}}{\partial\phi}\Delta\phi$$

$$+ \frac{1}{2}\frac{\partial^2\mathcal{P}}{\partial\phi^2}(\Delta\phi)^2 + \frac{\partial^2\mathcal{P}}{\partial I\partial\phi}\Delta I\Delta\phi\ldots$$

and, using expression (16.35), observe that the derivatives of the price with respect to the factors can be written in closed form

$$\frac{\partial\mathcal{P}}{\partial I} = X(t,T)\mathcal{P}(t,T) \geq 0; \quad \frac{\partial^2\mathcal{P}}{\partial I^2} = X^2(t,T)\mathcal{P}(t,T) \geq 0$$

$$\frac{\partial\mathcal{P}}{\partial\phi} = -\frac{1}{2}X^2(t,T)P(t,T) \leq 0; \quad \frac{\partial^2\mathcal{P}}{\partial\phi^2} = \frac{1}{4}X^4(t,T)P(t,T) \geq 0$$

$$\frac{\partial^2\mathcal{P}}{\partial\phi\partial I} = -\frac{1}{2}X^3(t,T)P(t,T) \leq 0$$

In contrast to the Black-Scholes model and the hedging of derivatives on stocks, the presence of two risk factors prevents us from hedging bonds using the first and the second pure derivatives, which correspond to the delta and gamma in the Black-Scholes model. We also need the second cross-derivative, $\partial^2 \mathcal{P}/\partial\phi\partial I$, even if we want to hedge up to first-order changes in the short rate and the forward variance, unless the two are uncorrelated.

16.5   Effective versus Risk-Neutral Measures

The short rate in the short-term-based models, as well as the forward rate in the HJM approach, were written down directly under the risk-neutral measure P^*.

But, in most applications, one parametrizes the short, forward, and bond price processes using observed time series of bond prices. For that reason, one needs to know the manner in which one passes from the risk-neutral measure to the effective one, P, and *vice versa*. Observed prices are evidently expectations under a risk-neutral measure. How can we reconstruct the effective measure? Conversely, if one starts from time series of rate observations in the past, and knows how to get a martingale pricing measure from the effective one, he can parametrize the drifts and diffusions under P and then switch to P^* for derivative pricing. How does one do this? By Girsanov's theorem, the key variable is the market price of risk.

Suppose we know that the term structure is driven by a Wiener process of dimension K. And suppose that we observe the short rate $r(t)$ and (under the effective measure) the following process for K "reference" bonds:

$$\frac{d\mathcal{P}(t, T_i)}{\mathcal{P}(t, T_i)} = \mu(t, T_i)dt + \sigma(t, T_i)dw(t)$$
$$i = 1, \dots, K$$

where the diffusion matrices of the K bonds are consistent with each other in the sense that there exists a common process $\sigma_f(t, T)$ for all T such that:[13]

$$\sigma(t, T_i) = -\int_t^{T_i} \sigma_f(t, s)ds \quad \forall i = 1, \dots, K$$

Then we can define the market price of risk vector:

$$\kappa(t) \triangleq \sigma_K(t)^{-1}[\mu_K(t) - r(t)\mathbf{1}_K]$$

where $\sigma_K(t) \triangleq \{\sigma(t, T_i)\}_{i=1}^K$ and $\mu_K(t) \triangleq \{\mu(t, T_i)\}_{i=1}^K$. From this κ we can define an exponential martingale η that will serve as a change of measure and that will allow us to price all bonds other than the K reference bonds as well as any derivative written on any bonds. Equivalently, we can define a Wiener process under the risk-neutral measure:

$$dw^*(t) = dw(t) + \kappa(t)dt$$

---

13 Although it is required to exist, we need not observe it, the prices of K bonds only being observable.

Remark 16.2 *The market price of risk vector applies to all bonds. The resulting term structure of yields or forwards may very well be upward or downward sloping. The slope of the term structure is not an indication of a segmentation or even of a clientele effect applying to bond prices. It certainly does not mean that the price of risk is different for different maturities. To wit, the yield curve (16.11) in the Vasicek model is not flat even though the prices of all bonds are calculated under the same pricing measure.*

Remark 16.3 *Given the existence of more than K bonds of many different maturities, the bond market may appear to be complete if the SDE for bond returns contains K independent Brownians w. Then, as we just showed, we can obtain the corresponding Brownians w^* under the risk-neutral measure and price a derivative written on bonds as an expected value of its payoff. However, to actually compute that expected value, we need to know the entire system of SDEs driving bond returns, that is, we need to know also the process of the diffusion matrix $\sigma(t, T)$ of the bond returns. Suppose that that matrix is driven by a separate or a larger set of Brownians. For those, we do not necessarily know the corresponding risk-neutral Brownians, unless additional securities are available that can tell us their market price of risk. That issue is referred to as "unspanned stochastic volatility." Stochastic volatility will be covered in chapter 15 in the context of the stock market. In the context of the bond market, the issue is studied empirically in great detail in several papers by Collin-Dufresne and co-authors (2002, 2005, 2009).*

Instead of observing bond prices, we could observe over time the short rate and the process for *all* (not just K) forward rates:

$$df(t, T) = \mu_f(t, T)dt + \sigma_f(t, T)dw(t); \qquad \forall\, T \tag{16.37}$$

We can reconstruct the drifts of bonds as follows:[14]

$$\mu(t, T) = r(t) - \int_t^T \mu_f(t, s)ds + \int_t^T \mu_f^*(t, s)ds; \quad \forall\, T \tag{16.38}$$

That equation is true because the definition (16.4) of forward rates implies:

$$\mu_f(t, T) = -\frac{\partial}{\partial T}\mu(t, T) + \mu_f^*(t, T); \quad \forall\, T$$

$\mu_f^*(t, T)$ being the risk-neutral forward-rate drift (16.28). Integrating over T and recalling that for a bond of immediate maturity $\mu(t, t) = r(t)$, we get (16.38). Extracting $\mu_K(t) = \{\mu(t, T_i)\}_{i=1}^K$, we can construct κ.

The procedure based on observing forwards is less parsimonious than the one based on prices because we need to observe them all even though they are related to each other.

---

14 We need to observe the process for all (not just K) forward rates because we take its integral over maturities.

Indeed, the drifts $\mu_f(t, T)$ of all the forward rates in (16.37) cannot be arbitrary or independent of each other since they are all based on K of them:

$$df(t, T) = \left\{ \mu_f^*(t, T) \right.$$
$$+ \sigma_f(t, T)\sigma_K(t)^{-1} \left[\mu_K(t) - r(t)\mathbf{1}_K \right] \Big\} dt$$
$$+ \sigma_f(t, T)dw(t); \qquad \forall\, T$$

That means that there exists a restriction.

Proposition 16.4 *Drifts of forwards under the effective measure are restricted as follows:*

$$\mu_f(t, T) = \left[\int_t^T \sigma_f(t, s)ds \right] \times (\sigma_f(t, T))^\mathsf{T}$$
$$+ \sigma_f(t, T)\sigma_K(t)^{-1} \left[\mu_K(t) - r(t)\mathbf{1}_K \right]; \qquad \forall\, T$$

if and only if there are no arbitrage opportunities.

Finally, we could have observed over time the diffusion vectors of all forward rates and the process for the short rate and again obtained the change of measure. That third procedure is cumbersome unless the short rate is Markovian. Please see the Markovian case in Veronesi (2010), page 631.

We conclude this section by pointing out that the logic of the Heath-Jarrow-Morton framework assigns a comparatively minor role to the drift restriction (16.28). The central role is instead played by the specification of the *diffusion* of the forwards, which allows one to write the prices of all bonds in the form (16.29).

16.6   Application: Pricing of Redundant Assets

Knowing κ and the risk-neutral probability from the observation of the short rate and the process of K reference bonds, one may evaluate any interest-sensitive security, simply by calculating a conditional expected value. For instance, the behavior of all bonds follows from that of the K reference bonds. The SDE on any bond under the effective measure, and thereby their empirical expected rate of return, would be given by:

$$\frac{d\mathcal{P}(t, T)}{\mathcal{P}(t, T)} = \left\{ r(t) + \sigma(t, T)\sigma_K(t)^{-1} \left[\mu_K(t) - r(t)\mathbf{1}_K \right] \right\} dt$$
$$+ \sigma(t, T)dw(t); \qquad \forall\, T$$

provided that:

$$\sigma(t, T) = - \int_t^T \sigma_f(t, s)ds \quad \forall\, T$$

for a process $\sigma_f(t, T)$ that coincides at the points $\{T_i\}_{i=1}^K$ with the one that was common to all the K reference bonds.

Derivatives can also be priced. For instance, under the assumption that the volatility of pure discount bond returns depends only on time t and maturity date T of the bond in an exponential fashion (*deterministic volatility structure of bond prices*), Hull and White (1993b) show that the price of an option written on a pure discount bond paying 1 unit of consumption at T, with an exercise price equal to K and a maturity date denoted $T_O < T$ is equal to:

$$C(P(t,T), P(t,T_O), t; T_O, T, \mathcal{K}) = P(t,T) \times N(h + \sigma_P)$$
$$-\mathcal{K} \times P(t,T_O) \times N(h)$$

where:

$$h = \frac{1}{\sigma_P} \ln \left[\frac{P(t,T)}{\mathcal{K} \times P(t,T_O)} \right] - \frac{\sigma_P}{2}$$
$$\sigma_P^2 = \int_t^{T_O} [\sigma(s,t) - \sigma(s,T_O)]^2 \, ds$$

Other formulas have been obtained under the assumption that the volatility of forward rates depends only on time, t, and maturity date, T.[15] And Black, Derman, and Toy (1990) constructed a binomial tree, in the vein of Cox, Ross, and Rubinstein (section 2.2.6), to price bond options.

———————————◆———————————

Some interest-rate derivatives, such as Forward-Rate Agreements (FRA) and swaps, can be easily priced under the risk-neutral measure. For others, such as caps, it is advisable to switch to another measure, called the forward measure. We explain why.

In a FRA, one party commits to pay a fixed rate in exchange for a floating, short rate, such as the LIBOR (London Interbank Offered Rate). Denote as $L(s, s + \Delta s)$ the variable interest rate, with F the fixed rate. The payment is done at a future point in time $s + \Delta s$, over a fixed notional N, and with reference to a pre-specified period of time Δs (a quarter, a semester or so). The long part pays $F \times \Delta s \times N$ and receives $L(s, s + \Delta s) \times \Delta s \times N$:

$$[L(s, s + \Delta s) - F] \times \Delta s \times N$$

Using the fact that discrete compounding holds for $L(s, s + \Delta s)$, that is, that the corresponding compound factor $\mathcal{P}^{-1}$ is

$$1 + L(s, s + \Delta s) \times \Delta s = \mathcal{P}(s, s + \Delta s)^{-1} \tag{16.39}$$

and making the standard no-arbitrage assumption, which requires discounted payoffs to be martingales under the risk-neutral measure, one can easily show that the value FRA$(0, s, s + \Delta s)$ at time $s > 0$ of the FRA is the difference between two positions in zero-coupon bonds, a long position in N bonds with maturity s, a short position in $N \times (1 - F \times \Delta s)$ bonds with maturity $s + \Delta s$:

$$\text{FRA}(0, s, s + \Delta s) = N \times [\mathcal{P}(0, s) - (1 - F \times \Delta s)\mathcal{P}(0, s + \Delta s)]$$

———————————————————————

15 El Karoui and Rochet (1989) price options on coupon-paying bonds.

A swap is a sequence of FRA, and can be priced as such. So, interest-rate swaps can be priced in closed form using the risk-neutral measure.

For most interest-rate derivatives, however, both a future rate (a short rate, according to the definition of the previous sections, or its discrete-time counterpart, such as the LIBOR) and the bank-account value appear in the risk-neutral expectation, which then becomes the expectation of correlated quantities. Consider for instance a so-called "caplet," that is, a derivative that has the payoff of a FRA if positive, a null payoff otherwise, or, in other words, an option on the LIBOR with strike F. Its payoff is

$$\max[L(s, s + \Delta s) - F, 0] \times \Delta s \times N$$

and its no-arbitrage value, using conditional expectations, is

$$\Delta s \times N \times \mathbb{E}^* \left[\frac{\max[L(s, s + \Delta s) - F, 0]}{B(s + \Delta s)} \right]$$

$$\Delta s \times N \times \mathbb{E}^* \left[\mathcal{P}(s, s + \Delta s) \frac{\max[L(s, s + \Delta s) - F, 0]}{B(s)} \right] \tag{16.40}$$

Using (16.39) again, we can write it as

$$\Delta s \times N \times \mathbb{E}^* \left[\frac{1}{B(s)} \max \left[\frac{1}{\Delta s} (1 - \mathcal{P}(s, s + \Delta s)) - F\mathcal{P}(s, s + \Delta s), 0 \right] \right]$$

$$= N \times \mathbb{E}^* \left[\frac{1}{B(s)} \max[1 - (1 + F\Delta s)\mathcal{P}(s, s + \Delta s), 0] \right]$$

$$= N(1 + F\Delta s) \times \mathbb{E}^* \left[\frac{1}{B(s)} \max \left[(1 + F\Delta s)^{-1} - \mathcal{P}(s, s + \Delta s), 0 \right] \right] \tag{16.41}$$

This shows that the price of a caplet is a multiple of the price of a put with strike $(1 + F\Delta s)^{-1}$, written on a zero-coupon bond with maturity $s + \Delta s$. The put expires at s. The exponential involves both the bank account and the bond value, which are not independent: this is why computing the cap value this way is cumbersome. If we price a caplet then we can price any call or put option on zero-coupon bonds too.

16.7   A Convenient Change of Numeraire

As we saw repeatedly, under no arbitrage, the price of any attainable claim X – including any asset price – normalized by the bank account B is a martingale:

$$\frac{X(t)}{B(t)} = \mathbb{E}^* \left[\frac{X(T)}{B(T)} \,\Big|\, \mathcal{F}_t \right] \tag{16.42}$$

Up to this point we always used the bank account for discounting. It would be helpful, however, to switch to a measure, whose expectation we denote as $\mathbb{E}^T$, under which the bank account factors out of the expectation, so that we would be left with the problem of computing: $\mathbb{E}^T[X(T) \mid \mathcal{F}_t]$.[16]

16.7.1   Change of Discounting Asset as a Change of Measure

Such a reformulation is actually possible if we recall that the same martingale principle applies if we normalize the price of the attainable claim by any traded non-dividend paying claim with price $S_0 > 0$. X/S_0 is then a martingale under some measure. The martingale measure is different for different normalizing asset prices S_0. We must, therefore, be more precise and restate the same result by specifying that the measure is P^{S_0}, because it is specific to reference asset price S_0. Correspondingly, let us call $\mathbb{E}^{S_0}$ the expectation under P^{S_0}. The pricing formula is:

$$\frac{X(t)}{S_0(t)} = \mathbb{E}^{S_0}\left[\frac{X(T)}{S_0(T)} \,\bigg|\, \mathcal{F}_t\right] \tag{16.43}$$

We still denote as $\mathbb{E}^*$ the expectation when the bank account is used as a discount factor. As a subcase of the previous formula we can write that, if S_0 is a traded asset, S_0/B is itself a martingale under P^*:

$$\frac{S_0(t)}{B(t)} = \mathbb{E}^*\left[\frac{S_0(T)}{B(T)} \,\bigg|\, \mathcal{F}_t\right]$$

We must specify the Radon-Nikodym derivative that permits to shift from $\mathbb{E}^*$ to $\mathbb{E}^{S_0}$. We show now that, for any positive process, we can find a Radon-Nikodym derivative such that X discounted using S_0 is a martingale, as indicated by (16.43). Notice that the risk-neutral expectation of $X(T)/S_0(T)$, by proposition 8.1, is related to its expectation under P^{S_0} by

$$\mathbb{E}^*\left[\frac{dP^{S_0}}{dP^*}\frac{X(T)}{S_0(T)} \,\bigg|\, \mathcal{F}_t\right] = \mathbb{E}^{S_0}\left[\frac{X(T)}{S_0(T)} \,\bigg|\, \mathcal{F}_t\right] \times \mathbb{E}^*\left[\frac{dP^{S_0}}{dP^*} \,\bigg|\, \mathcal{F}_t\right] \tag{16.44}$$

If we take as Radon-Nikodym derivative

$$\frac{dP^{S_0}}{dP^*} = \frac{S_0(T)}{S_0(0)B(T)} \tag{16.45}$$

then the expectations under the risk-neutral measure in (16.44) become:

$$\mathbb{E}^*\left[\frac{dP^{S_0}}{dP^*}\frac{X(T)}{S_0(T)} \,\bigg|\, \mathcal{F}_t\right] = \mathbb{E}^*\left[\frac{S_0(T)}{S_0(0)B(T)}\frac{X(T)}{S_0(T)} \,\bigg|\, \mathcal{F}_t\right]$$

$$= \mathbb{E}^*\left[\frac{X(T)}{S_0(0)B(T)} \,\bigg|\, \mathcal{F}_t\right] = \frac{X(t)}{S_0(0)B(t)}$$

---

16 For instance, the price of a caplet (16.41) could be rewritten so that we would be left with the problem of computing:

$$\mathbb{E}^T\left[\max\left[(1 + F\Delta s)^{-1} - \mathcal{P}(s, s + \Delta s), 0\right]\right]$$

In this case indeed we could use any assumption on the distribution of bond prices (lognormal, for instance) and get closed-form, or easy-to-handle, analytical forms.

$$\mathbb{E}^*\left[\frac{dP^{S_0}}{dP^*}\,\Big|\,\mathcal{F}_t\right] = \mathbb{E}^*\left[\frac{S_0(T)}{S_0(0)B(T)}\,\Big|\,\mathcal{F}_t\right] = \frac{S_0(t)}{S_0(0)B(t)}$$

Substituting in (16.44) we finally have:

$$\frac{X(t)}{S_0(t)} = \mathbb{E}^{S_0}\left[\frac{X(T)}{S_0(T)}\,\Big|\,\mathcal{F}_t\right]$$

which shows that, indeed, X/S_0 is a martingale under the new measure, provided the change of measure is (16.45).

16.7.2 Using Bond Prices for Discounting: The Forward Measure

It is often advisable to use, as a discounting asset, the zero-coupon bond price $\mathcal{P}$ for a specific maturity T instead of the bank account. Denote as P^T the corresponding probability measure. According to (16.45), the Radon-Nikodym derivative for the bond maturing at T, $\mathcal{P}(t,T)$, is

$$\frac{dP^T}{dP^*} = \frac{\mathcal{P}(T,T)}{\mathcal{P}(0,T)B(T)} = \frac{1}{\mathcal{P}(0,T)B(T)} \tag{16.46}$$

and

$$\mathbb{E}^*\left[\frac{dP^T}{dP^*}\,\Big|\,\mathcal{F}_t\right] = \frac{1}{B(t)}\frac{1}{\mathcal{P}(0,t)}$$

Any asset, discounted using that bond, has the martingale property, and:

$$\frac{X(t)}{\mathcal{P}(t,T)} = \mathbb{E}^T\left[\frac{X(T)}{\mathcal{P}(T,T)}\,\Big|\,\mathcal{F}_t\right] = \frac{\mathcal{P}(0,T)B(t)}{\mathcal{P}(t,T)}\mathbb{E}^*\left[\frac{1}{B(T)}\frac{X(T)}{\mathcal{P}(0,T)}\,\Big|\,\mathcal{F}_t\right]$$

$$= \frac{B(t)}{\mathcal{P}(t,T)}\mathbb{E}^*\left[\frac{X(T)}{B(T)}\,\Big|\,\mathcal{F}_t\right] \tag{16.47}$$

The quantity on the LHS is the forward price of X, while the RHS is its expectation under the forward measure. So, under the measure in which discounting is done using the bond value, forward prices are martingales. That is why this measure is called the *forward measure* (see Geman *et al.* (1995), Jarrow (1996)).

We saw in section 16.1, equations (16.6) to (16.8), above that the sequence of forward rates over maturities is related under the risk-neutral measure to the sequence of spot rates over the future. We show now that

Proposition 16.5 *Under the forward measure, each forward rate is equal to the expected value of a future short rate:*

$$f(t,T) = \mathbb{E}^T[r(T)\mid \mathcal{F}_t]$$

To prove the proposition, observe that, from (16.47):

$$\mathbb{E}^{T}[r(T) \mid \mathcal{F}_t] = \frac{B(t)}{\mathcal{P}(t,T)} \mathbb{E}^{*}\left[r(T) \frac{1}{B(T)} \,\middle|\, \mathcal{F}_t \right]$$

$$= \frac{1}{\mathcal{P}(t,T)} \mathbb{E}^{*}\left[r(T) \exp\left(-\int_t^T r(t)dt \right) \,\middle|\, \mathcal{F}_t \right]$$

$$= -\frac{1}{\mathcal{P}(t,T)} \frac{\partial \mathcal{P}(t,T)}{\partial T} = f(t,T)$$

♠

As could be anticipated, the measure is very helpful in pricing derivatives on bonds, including caplets, since it permits to factor the bank account out of the expectation. Consider the case of the caplet (16.41), where we need to evaluate an option on the **LIBOR** with strike F. In the previous section, we transformed the risk-neutral expectation of its payoff, once discounted, into (16.40). Putting aside the terms $\Delta s \times N$, we need to evaluate

$$\mathbb{E}^{*}\left[\frac{\mathcal{P}(s,s+\Delta s)}{B(s)} \max[L(s,s+\Delta s) - F, 0] \right] \tag{16.48}$$

According to (16.46), modified to take into consideration that the forward measure now needed is for $T = s + \Delta s$ for any asset with maturity s the expectation of the payoff under the risk-neutral measure, discounted at the riskless rate, can be written as

$$\mathbb{E}^{*}\left[\frac{X(s)}{B(s)} \right] = \mathbb{E}^{s+\Delta s}\left[\frac{dP^{*}}{dP^{s+\Delta s}} \frac{X(s)}{B(s)} \right] = \mathbb{E}^{s+\Delta s}\left[\mathcal{P}(0,s)B(s) \frac{X(s)}{B(s)} \right]$$

$$= \mathcal{P}(0,s+\Delta s)\mathbb{E}^{s+\Delta s}\left[\frac{X(s)}{\mathcal{P}(s,s+\Delta s)} \right]$$

Therefore, we can evaluate (16.48) as

$$\mathcal{P}(0,s+\Delta s)\mathbb{E}^{T}\left[\frac{\mathcal{P}(s,s+\Delta s)\max[L(s,s+\Delta s) - F, 0]}{\mathcal{P}(s,s+\Delta s)} \right]$$

$$= \mathcal{P}(0,s)\mathbb{E}^{T}[\max[L(s,s+\Delta s) - F, 0]] \tag{16.49}$$

Even though the term into square brackets has a non-linear dependence on the **LIBOR** rate from s to $s + \Delta s$, the expectation can be computed quite easily as soon as a specific assumption on the distribution of the rate $L(s, s + \Delta s)$ is introduced. A standard example is the Black formula for pricing caplets, which assumes that such rates are Geometric Brownian motions. Proposition 16.5 holds also for **LIBOR** rates, and states that the time-0 forward rate for the period $(s, s + \Delta s), f(0, s, s + \Delta s)$, is equal to the forward expectation of the corresponding **LIBOR** rate, namely

$$f(0,s,s+\Delta s) = \mathbb{E}^{T}[L(s,s+\Delta s)]$$

If we apply this property to the denominator of (16.49), we get

$$\mathcal{P}(0,s+\Delta s)\mathbb{E}^{T}[\max(L(s,s+\Delta s) - F, 0)]$$

Assuming lognormal **LIBOR** rates with instantaneous volatility σ and reintroducing the terms N and Δs, the cap value at 0 is

$$\mathcal{P}(0,+\Delta s) \times N \times \Delta s(f(0,s,s+\Delta s)N(d_1) - FN(d_2))$$

where

$$d_1 = \frac{\ln(f/F) + \left(\frac{\sigma^2}{2}\right)s}{\sigma\sqrt{s}}$$

$$d_2 = d_1 - \sigma\sqrt{s}$$

and N is the distribution function of the standard Gaussian. As explained in small characters in the previous section, once caps and caplets are priced, options on bonds can also be priced.

16.8 General Equilibrium Considerations

Cox, Ingersoll, and Ross (1985b) show that their affine interest-rate specification is consistent with the general equilibrium of a particular economy. The point of departure is their own general-equilibrium model, which we studied in section 11.4. Consider the special case of the model of that section in which the utility of the representative investor is logarithmic (section 11.5), there exists only one production facility and the rates of transmission of the drift and diffusion of Y to the capital stock are h and ε, with $h > \varepsilon^2$:

$$\mu_Q(Y,t) = h \times Y$$
$$\sigma_Q(Y,t) = \varepsilon\sqrt{Y} \qquad (16.50)$$

The exogenous state variable Y is assumed to follow a square-root process as in SDE:[17]

$$dY(t) = (b - \varrho Y(t))dt + k\sqrt{Y(t)}dw(t)$$
$$Y_0 = y \in \mathbb{R}^+, t > 0$$

where b, ϱ and k are strictly positive scalars with $2b > k^2$, and where w is a one-dimensional Wiener process.[18] In the notation of section 11.4:

$$\mu_Y(Y,t) = b - \varrho Y$$
$$\sigma_Y(Y,t) = k\sqrt{Y}$$

Applying the result (11.23):

$$r(t) = (h - \varepsilon^2)Y(t) \qquad (16.51)$$

The short rate is then affine in Y, as desired.[19] For any t, applying Itô's lemma to (16.51), the process for r under P is:

$$dr(t) = \left[\left(h - \varepsilon^2\right)b - \varrho r(t)\right]dt + \sqrt{h - \varepsilon^2}k\sqrt{r(t)}dw(t) \qquad (16.52)$$

---

[17] The fact that, in this model, variance is linear in Y, would allow one to interpret the stochastic process for Y as the stochastic process for volatility. This is the interpretation that was given to it by Heston (1993) and that is adopted in chapter 17.

[18] The inequality restriction guarantees non-negativity at all times.

[19] The conditional distribution of Y is a non-central chi square, so that the distribution of the instantaneous rate is chi square also.

where

$$\sqrt{h - \varepsilon^2}\sqrt{r(t)} = \left(h - \varepsilon^2\right)\sqrt{Y(t)}$$

The percent diffusion of aggregate wealth being equal to $\varepsilon\sqrt{Y}$ (see equation (16.50), and the marginal utility of wealth being the reciprocal of wealth in the log case, the percent diffusion of the stochastic discount factor is equal to $-\varepsilon\sqrt{Y}$. Hence the price of risk $\kappa(t)$ is equal to $\varepsilon\sqrt{Y(t)}$. The change of Brownian to effect the change of measure is then

$$dw^*(t) = dw(t) + \varepsilon\sqrt{Y(t)}dt$$

Substituting into (16.52), the process for the rate of interest under P^* is:

$$dr(t) = \left[\left(h - \varepsilon^2\right)b - \varrho r(t)\right]dt$$
$$+\sqrt{h - \varepsilon^2}k\sqrt{r(t)}\left[dw^*(t) - \varepsilon\sqrt{\frac{r(t)}{h - \varepsilon^2}}dt\right]$$
$$= \left[\left(h - \varepsilon^2\right)b - (\varrho + k\varepsilon)r(t)\right]dt + \sqrt{h - \varepsilon^2}k\sqrt{r(t)}dw^*(t)$$

which justifies the form of the instantaneous rate presented in section 16.2.3 above, namely (16.16). For that, one just has to redefine the parameters as follows:

$$\varrho \triangleq (\varrho + k\varepsilon); \; \bar{r} \triangleq b\frac{h - \varepsilon^2}{\varrho}; \; \psi \triangleq \sqrt{h - \varepsilon^2}k$$

The form (16.16) is thus consistent with a log-investor equilibrium, in which there exists a unique square-root state variable and the price of risk is proportional to its square root.

We claimed in section 16.4.4 that the CIR model is a two-factor Markov model. This is true because it satisfies the necessary and sufficient condition in proposition 16.3 for being a Markov process, but not the sufficient condition (16.36) for being a one-factor process. Indeed, since the deterministic function D in section 16.2.3 depends only on the difference between T and t, we can write the forward volatility

$$\sigma_f = \frac{\partial}{\partial T}D(t, T)\sigma_r$$

as

$$\sigma_f = \exp(\varrho(T - t))\sigma_r$$

by choosing $\varrho = (\partial \ln D(t, T)/\partial T)/(T - t)$. This shows that the process of r is Markovian. However, since the short rate volatility $\sigma_r = \psi\sqrt{r}$ is not constant, the model is two-factor Markovian, with the factors being the short rate and the forward cumulated variance.

16.9 Interpretation of Factors

A huge body of literature uses statistical tools, mainly *principal-component* analysis, to identify three main factors that drive the dynamics of forward, bond, and short curves. Even over quite a long time series, the first three factors are usually able to explain more than

90% of the variances of interest rates of different maturities. Unfortunately, these factors, given the type of analysis they emerge from, do not have a unique economic interpretation. They are identified empirically as driving the level, the slope, and the curvature of the term structure. Although quite popular, they are not easy to reconcile with an equilibrium view. We refer the interested reader to the work of Litterman and Scheinkman (1991) for an account of their interpretation.

Cochrane and Piazzesi (2005) identify a single factor as a linear combination of forward rates, and find that it explains long-maturity (from two- to five-year) bond holding returns in excess of the short (one-year) rate. The factor they identify then is a robust one: in a no-arbitrage model like the ones we have been describing in this chapter, it can be used as a state variable for different maturities. Their factor is unrelated to the three standard, "statistically" identified factors, namely the level, slope, and curvature.[20]

A more recent approach consists in identifying state variables by economic reasoning, using macroeconomic variables to give an economic interpretation of the factors. Some contributions in this field are Ang and Piazzesi (2003), Ang et al. (2004), and Piazzesi (2005). Ang and Piazzesi (2003), as well as Ang et al. (2004), consider as observable factors inflation and the level of real GDP. Their measures are constructed from a number of standard macro-indicators. The authors study the way their dynamics affect those of the rates. They show that GDP shocks change the level of intermediate-maturity rates and the curvature of the term structure (the third factor in the purely statistical approach). Inflation has an impact on the level of the entire term structure (the first factor). Piazzesi (2005) uses the target rate of the Federal Reserve and assumes that the instantaneous short rate deviates only temporarily from it. The hypothesis that the Fed rate is the state variable cannot be rejected by Piazzesi. The decisions of the Fed on its rate change the slope of the term structure (the second factor in the statistical approach).

This seems to be a promising research area, not only because it helps unify, under a common economic interpretation, different models and approaches in interest-rate studies, but also because of its potential spillover into the domain of equity.

16.10   Conclusion

The chapter has been largely methodological in nature. It has been a challenge simultaneously to specify the dynamics of prices of many securities. The challenge arose from two sources. First, bonds have a maturity. Their returns cannot be IID. We had to let their volatility reach zero as the bond approached its maturity date. Second, if K Wiener processes are the sources of risk in the bond market, $K + 1$ bonds suffice to make the market

---

20 The same factor is able to predict also stock returns somewhat. In this sense, it could be also applied as a factor in the analysis we conducted from chapter 9 onwards.

complete. All other bonds are redundant. Their dynamics are tied to the dynamics of the first $K + 1$ we specify.

Both difficulties were solved by specifying jointly the behavior of bond prices and the behavior of forward interest rates implied by the term structure of bond prices. We found that we could specify freely the diffusion of forward rates and that the volatilities of bond returns followed from it. The specification of the drift of forward rates was constrained by the Heath-Jarrow-Morton drift restriction. Under the risk-neutral measure, we have enough information on drifts on the bond-return side: the expected returns of all bonds must be equal to the riskless short rate.

In the next chapter, the same challenge will arise but in more dimensions.

16.11   Appendix: Proof of Proposition 16.3

In order to prove the proposition, it is sufficient to exploit the formal resemblance between the expression (16.30) for the short rate — which will become a state variable — and the RHS of its stochastic differential, (16.32). Write the former and the latter in terms of the forward-rate volatility:

$$r(t) = f(0,t) - \int_0^t \sigma(s,t)\sigma_f(s,t)ds + \int_0^t \sigma_f(s,t)dw^*(s) \tag{16.53}$$

$$dr(t) = \left\{ \frac{\partial}{\partial t}f(0,t) + \int_0^t \sigma_f(s,t)^2 ds \right. \tag{16.54}$$
$$\left. + \int_0^t \left[-\sigma(s,t)\frac{\partial}{\partial t}\sigma_f(s,t)ds + \frac{\partial}{\partial t}\sigma_f(s,t)dw^*(s) \right] \right\} dt$$
$$+ \sigma_f(t,T)dw^*(t)$$

and identify a class of volatility functions by the following restriction:

$$\frac{\partial}{\partial t}\sigma_f(s,t) = -k(t)\sigma_f(s,t) \tag{16.55}$$

which holds for any t, including T, and means that

$$\frac{\partial}{\partial t}\ln\sigma_f(t,T) = -k(T)$$

or, equivalently:

$$\sigma_f(t,T) = \sigma_f(t,T)\exp\left(-\int_t^T k(s)ds \right) \tag{16.56}$$

In (16.54) the following quantity shows up:

$$\int_0^t \left[-\sigma(s,t)\frac{\partial}{\partial t}\sigma_f(s,t)ds + \frac{\partial}{\partial t}\sigma_f(s,t)dw^*(s) \right]$$

Using first (16.55) then (16.53), it becomes

$$-k(t)\int_0^t \left[-\sigma(s,t)\sigma_f(s,t)ds + \int_0^t \sigma_f(s,t)dw^*(s) \right] = -k(t)\left[r(t) - f(0,t) \right]$$

Plugging this into (16.54), we get the short-rate differential as a function of the two state variables $r(t)$ and $\phi(t)$:

$$dr(t) = \left\{ \frac{\partial}{\partial t} f(0,t) + k(t)\big[f(0,t) - r(t)\big] + \phi(t) \right\} dt + \sigma_f(t,T)dw^*(t)$$

as desired. $\square$

Exercises

16.1. Consider a given stochastic process for bond prices (called the Brownian bridge) under P^*:

$$dP(t,T) = \varrho \frac{1 - P(t,T)}{T - t} dt + \sigma(t,T)dw^*(t), \quad T \in \mathbb{R}_{++}$$

There exists besides a riskless money market account with a rate of interest r. Can we construct a risk-neutral measure?

16.2. Define the bond price as in the text:

$$\frac{dP(t,T)}{P(t,T)} = r(t)dt + \sigma(t,T)dw^*(t), \quad T \in \mathbb{R}_{++}$$

$$P(0,T) \text{ given}$$

where w^* is a K-dimensional Brownian. Remark that $\sigma(T,T) = 0$, since the terminal price of a bond is certain: $P(T,T) = 1$. Derive an expression for the dynamics of the yields to maturities

$$R(t,T) \triangleq -\frac{\ln P(t,T)}{T - t}$$

of the various bonds.

16.3. Prove that the price of a bond in Vasicek's model is equal to:

$$P(t,T) = \exp\left(\frac{1}{\varrho}\left(1 - e^{-\varrho(T-t)}\right)(R_\infty - r) - (T-t)R_\infty \right.$$

$$\left. -\frac{(\sigma_r)^2}{4\varrho^3}\left(1 - e^{-\varrho(T-t)}\right)^2 \right)$$

where: $R_\infty \triangleq \bar{r} - \frac{1}{2}\frac{(\sigma_r)^2}{\varrho^2}$. (Hint: use the fact that

$$P(t,T) = \mathbb{E}^*[e^{-\int_t^T r(s)ds}]$$

and the expression for $r(t)$).

16.4. By substituting the forward rate and the bond volatility consistent with

$$f(0;T) = -e^{-\varrho T}(R_\infty - r_0) + R_\infty + \frac{1}{2}\frac{(\sigma_r)^2}{\varrho^2}\left(1 - e^{-\varrho T}\right)e^{-\varrho T}$$

and

$$\sigma(t,T) = -\frac{1}{\varrho}\left(1 - e^{-\varrho(T-t)}\right)\sigma_r$$

into (16.32) provide the verification of the fact that the bond price proved in the previous exercise and the short-rate dynamics

$$dr(t) = \varrho\left(\bar{r} - r(t)\right)dt + \sigma_r dw^*(t); \quad r_0 > 0 \text{ given}$$

are compatible with each other.

16.5. Consider a one-state variable economy in the manner of Vasicek, but assuming a process with a constant drift for the short rate of interest under $P^* : dr = \mu dt + \sigma dw^*$. (This process was actually considered by Merton). Obtain the time-t price of a zero-coupon bond with maturity T. Show that the price of a bond so computed has at least one unacceptable property.

16.6. Consider a European call option on a zero-coupon bond with maturity T, priced $P(t,T)$ at time t. The option has maturity $T_O \leq T$ and strike $\mathcal{K}$. Assume that the volatility of the pure discount bond returns depends only on time, t, and maturity date, T, of the bond. Demonstrate that the price of the call is

$$C(P(t,T), P(t,T_O), t; T_O, T, \mathcal{K}) = P(t,T) \times N(h + \sigma_P)$$
$$-\mathcal{K} \times P(t,T_O) \times N(h)$$

where:

$$h = \frac{1}{\sigma_P}\ln\left[\frac{P(t,T)}{\mathcal{K} \times P(t,T_O)}\right] - \frac{\sigma_P}{2}$$
$$\sigma_P^2 = \int_t^{T_O}[\sigma(s,t) - \sigma(s,T_O)]^2\,ds$$

Find the specification of the call price for the Ho-and-Lee and Hull-and-White models. (Hint: show the general HJM solution, then for Ho and Lee and for Hull and White just substitute their specification of $\sigma(t,T)$, that is, $(T-t)\sigma_r$ and $-\left(1 - e^{-\varrho(T-t)}\right)\sigma_r/\varrho$ respectively).

16.7. Consider both the Ho-and-Lee and the Hull-and-White models. Find the bond price expressions, using the risk-neutral pricing formula

$$\mathcal{P}(t,T) = \mathbb{E}^*\left[\exp\left(-\int_t^T r(u)du\right)\right]$$

Show, using the definition

$$f(t,T) \triangleq -\frac{\partial}{\partial T}\ln\mathcal{P}(t,T)$$

that the instantaneous forward rate is as in the text:

$$f(t,T) = f(0,T) + \sigma_r w^*(t) + (\sigma_r)^2\left(Tt - \frac{t^2}{2}\right)$$

for Ho and Lee,

$$f(t,T) = f(0,T) + \sigma_r \int_0^t e^{-\varrho(T-s)} dw^*(s) - \frac{(\sigma_r)^2}{2\varrho^2}\left(1 - e^{-\varrho(T-t)}\right)^2$$

for Hull and White.

16.8. Prove that in the Hull-and-White case – and, as a subcase, in Ho and Lee – the HJM restrictions permit to write the price of a zero-coupon as:

$$\mathcal{P}(t,T) = \frac{\mathcal{P}(0,T)}{\mathcal{P}(0,t)} \exp[-B(t,T)I(t) - a(t,T)]$$

where:

$$I(t) \triangleq r(t) - f(0,t)$$

$$B(t,T) \triangleq \left\{1 - \exp\left[-\varrho(T-t)\right]\right\}\frac{1}{\varrho}$$

$$a(t,T) \triangleq \frac{(\sigma_r)^2}{4\varrho} B^2(t,T)\left[1 - \exp(-2\varrho t)\right]$$

16.9. Verify that, in CIR's model, the price of a bond is equal to:

$$\mathcal{P}(t,T) = \bar{A}(t,T) e^{-D(t,T)r}$$

where

$$\bar{A}(t,T) \triangleq \left[\frac{2\gamma \exp\left[\frac{1}{2}(\varrho + \gamma)(T-t)\right]}{(\gamma + \varrho)\left(e^{\bar{r}(T-t)} - 1\right) + 2\bar{r}}\right]^{\frac{2\varrho\bar{r}}{\psi^2}}$$

$$D(t,T) \triangleq \frac{2\left(e^{\gamma(T-t)} - 1\right)}{(\gamma + \varrho)\left(e^{\gamma(T-t)} - 1\right) + 2\bar{r}}$$

$$\gamma \triangleq \left(\varrho^2 + 2\psi^2\right)^{1/2}$$

(Hint: use the fact that

$$\mathcal{P}(t,T) = \mathbb{E}^*\left[\exp\left(-\int_t^T r(u)du\right)\right]$$

and the expression for $r(t)$).

16.10. Verify that, in CIR's model, the forward rate is

$$f(t,T) = \frac{\partial}{\partial T}D(t,T)r - \frac{1}{A(t,T)}\frac{\partial}{\partial T}A(t,T)$$

and that its volatility is

$$\sigma_f(t,T) = \frac{\partial}{\partial T}D(t,T)\sigma_r\sqrt{r}$$

(Hint: use the definition

$$f(t, T) \triangleq -\frac{\partial}{\partial T} \ln \mathcal{P}(t, T)$$

and the expression for $\mathcal{P}(t, T)$ for the first part, Itô's lemma for the second).

16.11. Consider an economy in which the short rate r is driven by the following process involving two state variables, the short rate itself and its drift:

$$dr(t) = \varrho_1 [\mu(t) - r(t)] \, dt + \sigma_1 dw_1(t); \; \varrho_1 > 0$$
$$d\mu(t) = \varrho_2 [\theta - \mu(t)] \, dt + \sigma_2 dw_2(t); \; \varrho_2 > 0$$

where the two Wiener processes w_1 and w_2 are correlated, with a constant correlation equal to ρ. It is assumed that the market prices, κ_1 and κ_2, for the two dimensions of risk are constant. This means that:

$$dr(t) = \varrho_1 [\mu(t) - r(t) - \kappa_1 \sigma_1] \, dt + \sigma_1 dw_1^*(t)$$
$$d\mu(t) = \varrho_2 [\theta - \mu(t) - \kappa_2 \sigma_2] \, dt + \sigma_2 dw_2^*(t)$$

where w_1^* and w_2^* are Wiener processes under the risk-neutral measure. This model is sometimes called the "double-decay" or "Gaussian central tendency" model.

a. Indicate whether this model belongs to the class of exponential-affine (sometimes simply called "affine") models of the term structure.

b. Write down the partial differential equation that must be satisfied, under that model, by the price of a bond of fixed maturity date, as a function of the two state variables.

c. Based on similar problems you have encountered in this book, postulate a functional form for the bond price function and solve the partial differential equation.

d. Deduce the form of the function giving the value of a forward rate as a function of the two state variables.

16.12. Consider a one-dimensional diffusion process $m(t)$. Suppose that the forward interest rate $f(t, T)$ satisfies the stochastic differential equation:

$$df(t, T) = \left[-K_m \left(2C_1 + m(t) \right) e^{-2K_m(T-t)} + \frac{1}{K_m} e^{-K_m(T-t)} \gamma^2(t) \right] dt$$
$$+ e^{-K_m(T-t)} \gamma(t) dw^*(t)$$

where K_m and C_1 are constants, w^* is a Wiener process under the risk-neutral measure, and $\gamma(t)$ is a one-dimensional diffusion process to be specified. Verify that there exists a specification of $\gamma(t)$ such that the HJM drift restriction is satisfied.

17 Stochastic Volatility

In the strict-sense Black-Scholes model, which we used as a benchmark example above, the volatility of a single stock as well as the instantaneous variance-covariance matrix of the marketed assets were constant over time. That was a convenient simplification. Unfortunately, it does not agree with many empirical phenomena. The main motivation for expanding the benchmark complete-market model to include non-constant volatility is, therefore, empirical. We briefly summarize it below, in the form of the "smile" and the "leverage" effects (section 17.1.1).

The extended models can be separated into two main classes: models that preserve market completeness (section 17.1.2) and models that do not (section 17.2), as they include the additional dimension of risk called "stochastic volatility." Stochastic volatility is the archetypical example of an incomplete-market situation. The relation between these two approaches is studied in section 17.7. We then study so-called forward-volatility models (section 17.3), together with the modern no-arbitrage, Heath-Jarrow-Morton-like, restrictions for volatility.[1] The next section, 17.4, is devoted to the VIX index. Last, we ask under what circumstances stochastic volatility arises in general equilibrium (section 17.5). Parallel to the continuous-time literature on stochastic volatility, a discrete-time literature has grown, resulting in the renowned ARCH and GARCH models. We map out the correspondence between the two approaches in the appendix to this chapter.

17.1 Motivation

17.1.1 Empirics

The prices of options written on the same underlying asset contain information about the volatility of the underlying. Let $\sigma_I(\mathcal{K}; T)$ be the volatility number that is implicit in the option price observed at date 0 for a given maturity T and strike $\mathcal{K}$. Imagining that volatility

---

1 These will be similar to restriction (16.26) on the volatility of bond prices.

is constant, the Black-Scholes formula applies and σ_I is the solution to the following equation

$$C_0(\mathcal{K}; T) = S_0 N(d_1(\sigma_I)) - \mathcal{K} \exp(-rT) N(d_2(\sigma_I))$$

where C_0 is the observed call price at time 0 for the strike $\mathcal{K}$, $d_1(\sigma)$ and $d_2(\sigma)$ are as defined in chapter 6 and the parameter σ in them is set to the unknown σ_I (similar equations for puts exist). σ_I is the only unknown, all the other parameters of the Black-Scholes price being observed directly. The solution is the volatility σ_I implicit in C_0. Because the Black-Scholes pricing function is continuous, monotonic, and bounded for any value of the underlying, the solution exists, is unique, and is increasing in C_0.

By varying the strike, we obtain a whole *implied volatility function* $\sigma_I(\mathcal{K}; T)$. As a matter of fact, the implied volatility is a one-to-one function of observed prices. Traders often use it to quote options, instead of prices of options themselves. We can extend the exercise to different maturities, keeping the underlying the same. By so doing, we obtain a family of functions $\sigma_I(\mathcal{K}; T)$ for different maturities T or a whole *implied volatility surface* $\sigma_I(\mathcal{K}, T)$. If the assumptions of the strict-sense Black-Scholes formula were correct, the function would be constant.

The standard empirical phenomenon that questions the validity of the strict-sense Black-Scholes model as a description of the actual dynamics of asset prices is the so-called option "smile." Far from being constant, empirical observations for a given maturity exhibit higher implicit volatility for far in-the-money and far-out-of-the-money options, smaller volatility for close-to-the-money options. Implicit volatility as a function of moneyness is therefore U-shaped, like a smile (often a smirk, in fact). The phenomenon is persistent across maturities. Figure 17.1 presents the example of options on the S&P500, showing a smirk for every maturity of the options.

A somewhat related phenomenon is the so-called "leverage effect," which consists in a negative correlation between market returns and changes in volatility. Empirically, volatility is usually high while market prices are low or volatility is low when the market is high, as figure 17.2 shows. One intuitive explanation for that phenomenon is the following. When equity prices rise, firms' leverage, everything else being equal, drops; their stocks become less risky; and the volatility of equity returns is lower. In empirical tests the numbers do not match this leverage explanation, but the label "leverage effect" serves to describe the negative correlation between volatility and stock-price level. For the time being, let us just observe that we need to consider alternatives to the strict-sense Black-Scholes model.

How can we capture these related phenomena in a model for the underlying that would be richer than the strict Black-Scholes? In principle, we could construct a structural model for volatility. In order to do this, we should have good theoretical foundations for the way in which conditional volatility (along with the volume of trade) evolves over time in a financial market. This obviously depends on the way information arrives and on what type

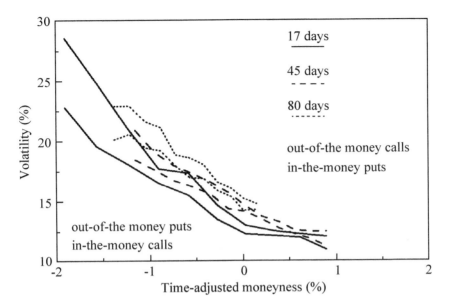

Figure 17.1

Volatility smiles on the S&P over different expiry dates. Black-Scholes implied volatilities on April 1, 1992. Implied volatilities are computed from the S&P500 index call option prices for the April, May, and June 1992 option expirations (with time to maturity T equal to 17, 45, and 80 days respectively). The lower line of each pair is based on the option's bid price, and the upper line is based on the ask. Moneyness, instead of being defined as $K/S - 1$, as with options for the same maturity and without dividends, is adjusted for maturity as follows: $(K/(S - pvD) - 1)/\sqrt{T}$, where pvD is the present value of dividends. Source: Dumas *et al.* (1998).

of information arrives, public *versus* private. Roughly speaking, "purely public" information arriving repeatedly generates unconditional volatility but no trading volume.[2,3] "Purely private" information generates volume but no change in price.

In practice, the approach that has been followed is that of producing reduced-form models, which do not model information processing explicitly, but postulate a dynamics for volatility. We can try to do that while preserving market completeness or build a more flexible model, where market completeness is abandoned.

---

2 However, Green (2004) shows empirically that belief dispersion increases following the release of public information. That observation supports models of Difference of Opinion, such as the one of section 18.4.

3 If more information arrives into a market and gets incorporated into prices, the conditional volatility is reduced when the information arrives (uncertainty is reduced at that point since consumers learn). But, as this happens day in and day out, there is more movement in price: unconditional volatility increase.

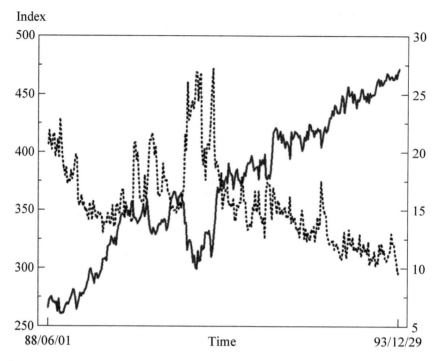

Figure 17.2

S&P 500 index level and Black-Scholes implied volatility and S&P500 index each Wednesday during the period June 1988 through December 1993. On the horizontal axis moneyness adjusted for the time horizon is shown. Source: Dumas *et al.* (1998).

17.1.2   Time-Varying Volatility with Market Completeness

The most straightforward way to extend the strict Black-Scholes model and its constant volatility is to make volatility either a deterministic function of time, or a non-deterministic one that would be driven by the same Wiener processes that appear in the asset price processes. For the sake of simplicity, we explain the point with a single (risky) asset, single-Wiener space and its generated filtration.

- Assume that the asset price includes a Deterministic Volatility Function (DVF):

$$\frac{dS(t)}{S(t)} = \mu(t)dt + \sigma(S,t)dw(t)$$

where $\sigma(S,t)$ is a deterministic function of time t and the asset price S at the most, capturing the leverage effect. The volatility at any future point in time is uniquely determined by calendar time and the value attained at that point by the underlying. This formulation allows for variation over time, but keeps the market complete. It suffices to postulate a function $\sigma(S, t)$ with some parameters to be determined; to solve the Black-Scholes PDE for the corresponding option price and fit it to the volatility smile. This time the fit serves to determine the parameters of the volatility function, not the implied volatility as a number. A well-known example is the so-called Constant-Elasticity of Variance (CEV) model, already seen in section 7.5 in which the volatility is proportional to S^{α} with $\alpha < 1$. Since the market is complete and technical conditions are satisfied, the pricing measure is unique and replication along the lines of chapter 6 is still possible. While straightforward, the DVF specifications, including the CEV, have unfortunately done a poor job in capturing the behavior of volatility. For instance, Dumas *et al.* (1998), using weekly S&P data over the period June 1988 to December 1993, show that the empirical performance of any deterministic-volatility model is poor. The calibrated parameters are very unstable. Parameters estimated from one cross section of option prices observed on one day and fitting the smile that day, regularly become invalid just one week later. In addition to its lack of robustness, hedging performance of DVF models is poor. Quite paradoxically, the strict Black-Scholes model performs better in-sample, and its hedge ratios are more effective than the DVF ones.

- The DVF specification has been generalized by Hobson and Rogers (1998). Define the log excess-return index on discounted asset prices $P(t)$, $Z(t) = \ln\left(P(t)e^{-rt}\right)$. Introduce the so-called "offset function of order m," $S^{(m)}(t)$, which "sums" the difference between the current return and previous returns $(Z(t-u), u \le t)$, raised to the power m, and gives exponentially decreasing importance to returns far in the past (by multiplying them with $e^{-\lambda u}$):

$$S^{(m)}(t) = \int_0^\infty \lambda e^{-\lambda u}(Z(t) - Z(t-u))^m du$$

Then use these as arguments of the volatility functions:

$$\sigma\left(t, Z(t), S^{(1)}(t), \ldots S^{(n)}(t)\right)$$

The volatility of the log-prices $Z(t)$ depends on the offsets of the log-price from its exponentially weighted moving averages. In this way, the model allows volatility to depend not just on the level of the stock price, but also on stock *price changes* and their powers, appropriately weighted. For instance, using only the offset function of order one, one has:

$$dZ(t) = dS^{(1)}(t) + \lambda S^{(1)}(t)dt$$

The advantage of this model is that it captures past price changes while preserving a complete-market and allowing an easy derivation of the PDE for option prices. The empirical investigations of this model are not many: however, they show a clear superiority of the model with respect to the Heston model (section 17.2.2), at least as far as options written on the S&P are concerned. See Platania and Rogers (2005).

- Another way of modeling time-varying volatility without abandoning the safe harbor of complete-market models is to assume that the same Wiener process drives the underlying and the volatility level, as in the following equations:

$$\frac{dS}{S} = \mu(t)dt + \sigma(S, Y, t)dw(t) \tag{17.1}$$

$$dY = \mu_Y(t)dt + \sigma_Y(S, Y, t)dw(t) \tag{17.2}$$

where w is a one-dimensional Wiener process and Y is a (latent) state variable that, together with the underlying asset price, drives the function σ. The other functions have the usual properties that guarantee existence of a solution for the system (17.1, 17.2). Volatility is perfectly correlated with the price (negatively or positively, according to the sign of the parameters and functions), so as to be able to accommodate both the smile and leverage effects. With this approach, the market is still complete. The possible empirical failures in capturing the relevant phenomena are not known, since, to our knowledge, this avenue has not been explored empirically. However, the model is a special case of models presented below, which are tested.

17.2 Examples of Markov Models with Stochastic Volatility

Much attention has been devoted to extensions of the previous approaches that are known as "stochastic volatility models." In these models, volatility, or the latent variable behind it named Y, entails the introduction of a second Wiener process:

$$\frac{dS}{S} = \mu(t)dt + \sigma(S, Y, t)dw(t)$$

$$dY = \mu_Y(t)dt + \sigma_Y(S, Y, t)dw(t)$$

where w is now a *two-dimensional* Wiener process. These models are flexible and can capture any source of randomness in the volatility that is not caused by movements in the underlying. But they make the market incomplete, and this opens valuation problems. There arise difficulties in capturing the "market price of volatility risk." The latter difficulty will be apparent when we examine some renowned models of stochastic volatility, namely the Hull-and-White and the Heston models. The closed or semi-closed formulas they provide allow calibration. Even then calibration is not trivial.

17.2.1 Hull and White

This section briefly summarizes the Hull-and-White (1987) model and the way we can calibrate it, using options data. We start by supposing that, *under the risk-neutral probability*, the joint stochastic process for a stock price and its volatility is

$$\frac{dS(t)}{S(t)} = rdt + \sigma(t)dw_1^*(t)$$

$$V(t) = \sigma^2(t)$$

$$dV(t) = \mu_Y(\sigma(t), t)dt + \sigma_Y(\sigma(t), t)dw_2^*(t) \qquad (17.3)$$

where w_1^* and w_2^* are two *independent* scalar Wiener processes under P^*. In addition, σ is a stochastic process evidently adapted with respect to the filtration generated by (w_1^*, w_2^*) and r is a constant. Observe that the variance process V evolves on its own, independently of w_1^* or S.

Applying Itô's lemma over the interval $[0, T]$, we get

$$\ln S(T) - \ln S(0) = \int_0^T \left[r - \frac{1}{2}\sigma^2(t)\right]dt + \int_0^T \sigma(t)dw_1^*(t) \qquad (17.4)$$

To calibrate the model, we first price options. To do that, we try to establish a connection with Black and Scholes. Let T be the life of a derivative. Introduce a quantity that is usually labeled "realized variance of $\ln S(T)$," that is, the true realization of the variance of log returns over an interval $[0, T]$, equal to: $\int_0^T \sigma^2(t)dt$. Define its average $\overline{V}$ as

$$\overline{V} = \frac{1}{T}\int_0^T \sigma^2(t)dt$$

Suppose for a second that we give ourselves $\overline{V}$ in (17.4)

$$\ln S(T) - \ln S(0) = [r - \frac{1}{2}\overline{V}]T + \int_0^T \sigma(t)dw_1^*(t)$$

Since σ is adapted and evolves independently of w_1^*, or S for that matter, $\int_0^T \sigma(t)dw_1^*(t)$, for a given volatility path, or conditionally on $\overline{V}$, is a weighted sum of normal increments $dw_1^*(t)$ where the weights are unrelated to the increments. For that reason, conditional on $\overline{V}$, log returns on the underlying are normally distributed (with zero expected value and a variance equal to $\overline{V} \times T$). Hence the price of a call option can be written as the expectation conditioned down of a risk-neutral process

$$C(x, y) = \int_0^\infty \mathbb{E}^*\left\{[S(T) - \mathcal{K}]^+ \mid \overline{V}, S(0) = x\right\} \times h\left(\overline{V} \mid V(0) = y\right) d\overline{V}$$

where h is the density of $\overline{V}$. Given the normality of $\ln(S(T)|\overline{V})$, we also have an explicit formula for $\mathbb{E}\{[S(T) - \mathcal{K}]^+ \mid \overline{V}, x\}$. It is just the Black-Scholes formula with volatility $\overline{V}$.

♠

Our solution for the Hull-White option is not complete until we obtain the density of the realized volatility $h(\overline{V}|\ V(0) = y)$. In their article, Hull and White provide expressions for all the moments of that density when $\mu = 0$.

Still, the model is not completely specified, neither under the risk-neutral nor under the effective measure, unless we calibrate the parameters $\sigma_Y(\sigma, t)$ and $\mu_Y(\sigma, t)$, which drive the volatility process under the risk-neutral measure, and unless we provide an estimate of the volatility-risk premium. This is usually done by minimizing the so-called pricing error, that is, the distance between theoretical and actual prices. Distance can be measured by taking the mean square error of the pricing errors, their mean absolute value, or other measures. Given that the Hull-White model, because of the density h, does not provide fully closed-form formulas, computing the pricing error is computationally demanding. The volatility risk premium is even more challenging to obtain. Using for instance Cox, Ingersoll, and Ross, we know that the drift adjustment ought to depend on the marginal utility function and its covariance with volatility in the following way:

$$-\begin{bmatrix} -\frac{\partial^2 J}{\partial W^2} & -\frac{\partial^2 J}{\partial W \partial V} \\ \frac{\partial J}{\partial W} & \frac{\partial J}{\partial W} \end{bmatrix} \begin{bmatrix} \mathrm{cov}[W, V] \\ \mathrm{var}[V] \end{bmatrix} = \frac{1}{\frac{\partial J}{\partial W}} \mathrm{cov}\left[\frac{\partial J}{\partial W}, V\right] = \frac{1}{\frac{\partial u}{\partial c}} \mathrm{cov}\left[\frac{\partial u}{\partial c}, V\right]$$

If we want to utilize the Hull-and-White model as is, and switch from the risk-neutral to the effective measure without changing the calibrated drift, we need to assume that this covariance is zero or, in other words, that volatility risk is not priced. This is the main restriction of the model: there is volatility "risk," in the sense that volatility is stochastic, with an additional Wiener process entering the picture, but any estimation of the parameters of the model valid under both measures requires that investors give the new source of risk a price of zero.

17.2.2   Heston

The Heston (1993) model is another specification of stochastic volatility, which reflects mean reversion in volatility, is able to reproduce the leverage effect and permits calibration. Again, we introduce the model, specify its calibration possibilities, and conjecture the form of volatility risk premia.

Under a risk-neutral measure P^*, as above, let the stock and variance processes be:[4]

$$\frac{dS(t)}{S(t)} = rdt + \sqrt{V(t)}dw_1^*(t)$$

$$dV(t) = \{\varrho \times [\theta - V(t)] - kV(t)\}\,dt + k\sqrt{V(t)}dw_2^*(t) \tag{17.5}$$

where r is a constant rate of interest, k is a constant "skewness" coefficient, and the two scalar Wiener processes *are correlated* with correlation denoted $\breve{\rho}$. The leverage effect would be incorporated by means of a negative correlation. The reason for which the parameter k represents skewness is that when the volatility is high, the effect that a large negative

---

4 In the notation of section 16.8, $\varepsilon = 1$.

value of the shock dw_2^* produces on the volatility is high as well, while it cannot be high when volatility is low. So, it tends to make volatility movements asymmetric.

The *very special* case of this model in which the correlation of the Wiener processes is equal to one is consistent with a version of the special Cox-Ingersoll-and-Ross general-equilibrium economic model that we presented in chapter 11. In that model, the premium on the risk of exogenous state variables (Y but, in the present case, V) was:[5]

$$\frac{1}{\frac{\partial J}{\partial W}}\mathrm{cov}\left[\frac{\partial J}{\partial W}, V\right]$$

In the notation of section 16.8, with a log-utility specification, we found a market price of risk equal to $\kappa = \sqrt{V}$ so the value for the risk premium is: $-\sqrt{V} \times k\sqrt{V} = -kV$, as supposed in SDE (17.5). So, Heston's model, unlike the Hull-and-White model, does allow non-zero risk pricing relative to the marginal utility of wealth. At the same time, it has the clear term of mean reversion that we already found in the CIR interest-rate case.

But there is a cost: option pricing is more involved than in the Hull-White case, since the transition densities of the process S are not known. Because their characteristic functions can be obtained, the option price can be calculated by a Fourier inversion, as follows. Recall from chapter 13 that the characteristic function of the distribution of the logarithm of $S(T)$ is defined as:

$$f(x, y, t; \phi, T) \triangleq \mathbb{E}^*\left[(S(T))^{i\phi} \mid S(t) = x, V(t) = y\right] \tag{17.6}$$

where i is the imaginary number and $\phi \in \mathbb{R}$. Note that the expected value is taken over the terminal stock price $S(T)$, under the risk-neutral joint probability of the underlying and its variance, started at x and y at time t.

As we did in chapter 13, we can write the PDE for the characteristic function:

$$rx\frac{\partial f}{\partial x}(x, y, t; \phi, T) + \frac{1}{2}yx^2\frac{\partial^2 f}{\partial x^2}(x, y, t; \phi, T) \tag{17.7}$$

$$+\left[\varrho(\theta - y) - ky\right]\frac{\partial f}{\partial y}(x, y, t; \phi, T) + \frac{1}{2}k^2y\frac{\partial^2 f}{\partial y^2}(x, y, t; \phi, T)$$

$$+\frac{\partial^2 f}{\partial x \partial y}k\breve{\rho}yx + \frac{\partial f}{\partial t}(x, y, t; \phi, T) = 0$$

with the obvious boundary condition:

$$f(x, y, T; \phi, T) = x^{i\phi} \tag{17.8}$$

---

5 See remark 11.1.

One can guess a solution of the form:

$$f(x, y, t, \phi, T) = x^{i\phi} e^{C(T-t)+D(T-t)y} \tag{17.9}$$

for which the boundary condition is $C(0) = 0$, $D(0) = 0$. Let us verify that the guessed solution works. Substituting (17.9) into (17.7) gives:

$$ri\phi - \frac{1}{2}y\left(\phi^2 + i\phi\right) + \left[\varrho(\theta - y) - ky\right]D + \frac{1}{2}k^2yD^2 + i\phi Dk\breve{p}y + \left[\frac{\partial C}{\partial t} + \frac{\partial D}{\partial t}y\right] = 0$$

If we collect the terms in y and distinguish them from the terms that do not depend on y, we get:

$$\begin{cases} ri\phi + \varrho\theta D + \frac{\partial C}{\partial t}(T - t) = 0 \\ -\frac{1}{2}\left(\phi^2 + i\phi\right) - (\varrho + k)D + \frac{1}{2}k^2D^2 + i\phi Dk\breve{p} + \frac{\partial D}{\partial t}(T - t) = 0 \end{cases} \tag{17.10}$$

These are two ODEs, for the functions C and D respectively, the first being linear, the second Riccati, which can be solved analytically.

The cumulative transition probability P^* (cumulative probability function of $S(T)$ from $\mathcal{K}$ to ∞) is then obtained by a kind of Fourier inversion, as was indicated in chapter 13:

$$P^*(x, y, t; \mathcal{K}, T) = \frac{1}{2} + \frac{1}{\pi} \int_0^\infty \text{Re}\left[\frac{\mathcal{K}^{-i\phi} f(x, y, t, \phi, T)}{i\phi}\right] d\phi \tag{17.11}$$

From this cumulative transition probability, the option price is easily obtained, since the option payoff depends on the underlying and the price is an expectation over the cumulative probability function of the underlying.

The reader can solve exercise 17.1.

By fitting as closely as possible the theoretical option prices to the observed ones, calibration of the model parameters, including the risk premium, can be obtained. This is the implied risk premium, corresponding to the specific risk-neutral measure dictated by market prices. Usually, the implied parameters are obtained from option quotes on a specific day (a single cross section of option prices). As a consequence, implied parameters tend to be somewhat unstable.

To sum up, stochastic volatility models present a number of complexities. First, they generate an incomplete market, with an infinity of possible risk premia, so that some arbitrary assumption must be made regarding the market price of volatility risk. Second, the analysis in Dumas et al. (1998) pointed to the difficulty of eliciting a model for volatility, a quantity that is not directly observable. The difficulty was present in the case of DVF. It is even more present when volatility is assumed to follow a separate stochastic process. One is caught in a perilous loop: in order to figure out the right option pricing model, one must know how volatility behaves, and one is able to elicit volatility out of option prices only when one has calibrated the right volatility process.

The problem will be addressed by the more recent local-volatility, arbitrage-free formulations, which we develop in section 17.3 below. Another, more pragmatic possibility is available in discrete time in the form of purely stastistical models such as "GARCH" models,[6] which make it possible to circumvent the calibration difficulties at least. Above all, one has to understand which modeling restrictions, if any, are needed in order to reap these calibration advantages. The workings of GARCH models and their relation with continuous-time models are covered in the appendix to this chapter.

17.3   Stochastic Volatility and Forward Variance

In the spirit of Black and Scholes (extended to a large number of securities by Heath *et al.* (1992), as in the previous chapter), one can try to return to complete markets by assuming we know that the entire system of prices of options written on the *same underlying security* is driven by a K-dimensional Wiener process, so that we can utilize their initial values as an indication of their future behavior.

Denote by $C(t, \mathcal{K}, T)$ the prices at date t of a *European* call option with strike $\mathcal{K}$ and maturity date T on the same underlying security.[7] As a function of strike and maturity date, these option prices form a *surface*. The underlying security is a particular element of that large vector or surface; its price is $S(t) \equiv C(t, 0, T)$, which does not depend on T. Let us specify directly the behavior of prices under some risk-neutral probability measure P^*. Under P^*, we know that the drift of the prices of all traded securities is the rate of interest r. The diffusion matrix of the options remains to be chosen. In the previous chapter, we dealt with stochastic interest rates. In this chapter we aim to deal with stochastic volatility. To simplify, let us assume that the rate of interest is constant and normalize that constant to be equal to 0. At time t, for all $\mathcal{K}, T > t$, we can write:[8]

$$\frac{dC(t, \mathcal{K}, T)}{C(t, \mathcal{K}, T)} = \sigma_C(t, \mathcal{K}, T) dw^*(t) \qquad (17.12)$$

$$C(0, \mathcal{K}, T) \text{ given}$$

$$C(t, \mathcal{K}, t) = [S(t) - \mathcal{K}]^+ \qquad (17.13)$$

and, in particular, for $\mathcal{K} = 0$:

$$\frac{dS(t)}{S(t)} = \sigma_S(t) dw^*(t) \qquad (17.14)$$

$$S(0) \text{ given}$$

---

6 "GARCH" stands for Generalized Autoregressive Conditional Heteroskedasticity.

7 No similar theory exists for American-type options.

8 As we have often done, $\sigma_C(t, X, T)$ stands for $\sigma_C(\omega, t, X, T)$.

where, $w^*(t)$ is a K-dimensional Wiener process under the risk-neutral measure and $\sigma_C(t, \mathcal{K}, T)$ contains K columns. These being prices of options written on the same underlying, they are restricted to satisfy some joint terminal and initial conditions and we need to impose some restrictions on $\sigma_C(t, \mathcal{K}, T)$. Otherwise, arbitrage opportunities would develop.

17.3.1 Static Arbitrage Restrictions

A number of static arbitrage restrictions were spelled out by Merton (1973). For instance, an option cannot be worth more than its underlying security. They all derive from the payoff conditions (17.13). It follows from them that:

- $[S(t) - \mathcal{K}]^+ \leq C(t, \mathcal{K}, T) \leq S(t)$
- $C(t, \mathcal{K}, T)$ is increasing in T, non-increasing and convex in $\mathcal{K}$
- $\lim_{\mathcal{K} \to \infty} C(t, \mathcal{K}, T) = 0$
- $\lim_{\mathcal{K} \to 0} C(t, \mathcal{K}, T) = S(t)$

Obviously, if we choose $\sigma_C(t, \mathcal{K}, T)$ in (17.12) arbitrarily, at some point one of these barriers or conditions will be breached. We need a way to specify the diffusion of C in such a way that that does not happen. This is analogous to, in the previous chapter, forcing the volatility of a bond price to approach zero as time approaches the maturity date. There, we achieved that goal by expressing the volatility of a bond return as (the opposite of) an integral of the volatility of forward rates. Here, we similarly define forward variance.

17.3.2 Definition of Forward Variance

Given an option price function or surface $C(t, \mathcal{K}, T)$ at a given point in time t for $\mathcal{K}, T > t$, keeping the underlying price S of time t as a parameter, we define:[9]

Definition 17.1 *Forward variance*

$$v(t, \mathcal{K}, T) \triangleq \frac{2 \frac{\partial}{\partial T} C(t, \mathcal{K}, T)}{\mathcal{K}^2 \frac{\partial^2}{\partial \mathcal{K}^2} C(t, \mathcal{K}, T)} \tag{17.15}$$

If the static arbitrage conditions are satisfied,

$$v(t, \mathcal{K}, T) > 0 \text{ for } T \geq t, \mathcal{K} \geq 0 \tag{17.16}$$

---

9 Evidently, since in practice options are traded only for a finite number of maturities and strikes, in any specific practical circumstance, the surface available is one for a discrete grid only. Interpolation methods can be used to fill in the gaps.

In the reverse, if we give ourselves a forward-variance surface $v(t, \mathcal{K}, T)$, we can introduce at time t the procedure of solving the PDE:

$$\frac{1}{2}v(t, \mathcal{K}, T)\mathcal{K}^2\frac{\partial^2}{\partial \mathcal{K}^2}C(t, \mathcal{K}, T) = \frac{\partial}{\partial T}C(t, \mathcal{K}, T) \tag{17.17}$$

for the unknown $C(t, \mathcal{K}, T)$ over $\mathcal{K} \in R_+$ and $T: t \le T \le \infty$ with *initial* condition (17.13). The solution is a function $C(t, \mathcal{K}, T)$ of $\mathcal{K}$ and T. Equation (17.17) is called the "forward equation" of Dupire (1994).[10] Let us give a name to that mapping:[11]

Dupire: $v(t, \mathcal{K}, T) \rightarrow C(t, \mathcal{K}, T)$ for fixed t

The procedure is analogous to the recovery of bond prices from forward rates by the integral (16.6). It is less straightforward than an integral but it is equally well defined, as there is a unique solution to that Cauchy problem (under some technical conditions that are similar to the Lipschitz and growth conditions).

We can also define the diffusion of forward variance from the diffusion of option prices and vice versa. Applying Itô's lemma to the definition (17.15), the diffusion of v is:

$$\sigma_v(t, \mathcal{K}, T) = 2\frac{\frac{\partial}{\partial T}\sigma_C(t, \mathcal{K}, T)}{\mathcal{K}^2\frac{\partial^2}{\partial \mathcal{K}^2}C(t, \mathcal{K}, T)} - 2\frac{\frac{\partial}{\partial T}C(t, \mathcal{K}, T)}{\mathcal{K}^2\left(\frac{\partial^2}{\partial \mathcal{K}^2}C(t, \mathcal{K}, T)\right)^2}\frac{\partial^2}{\partial \mathcal{K}^2}\sigma_C(t, \mathcal{K}, T)$$

In the reverse, suppose that we give ourselves the function $v(t, \mathcal{K}, T)$ and the diffusion $\sigma_v(t, \mathcal{K}, T)$ of v, can we get the diffusion of the options $\sigma_C(t, \mathcal{K}, T)$? Notice that, given the function $v(t, \mathcal{K}, T)$, the Dupire mapping is well defined and can be performed *at every fixed point in time* t independently of the behavior of v over time. For that reason, we can apply Itô's lemma to the terms of equation (17.17) to get:

$$\frac{1}{2}\sigma_v(t, \mathcal{K}, T)\mathcal{K}^2\frac{\partial^2}{\partial \mathcal{K}^2}C(t, \mathcal{K}, T) + \frac{1}{2}v(t, \mathcal{K}, T)\mathcal{K}^2\frac{\partial^2}{\partial \mathcal{K}^2}\sigma_C(t, \mathcal{K}, T)$$

$$= \frac{\partial}{\partial T}\sigma_C(t, \mathcal{K}, T) \tag{17.18}$$

For fixed t, the function $\sigma_v(t, \mathcal{K}, T)$ being given and the function $C(t, \mathcal{K}, T)$ being obtainable from the Dupire mapping, we can solve that PDE for the function $\sigma_C(t, \mathcal{K}, T)$ over $\mathcal{K} \in R^+$ and $T: t \le T \le \infty$ with *initial* condition

$$\sigma_C(t, \mathcal{K}, t) = \begin{cases} 0 & \text{if } \mathcal{K} > S \\ \sigma_S(t) & \text{otherwise} \end{cases}$$

---

10 See also Derman and Kani (1994, 1997). The forward PDE for European options is analogous to the Fokker-Planck equation (13.4) for transition probabilities, while the Black-Scholes PDE is a backward equation analogous to the Chapman-Kolmogorov equation (13.1). See exercises 13.1 and 13.3 of chapter 13.

11 The mapping is not defined for $X = 0$. It needs to be extended by taking the limit $X \rightarrow 0$.

Let us give a name to that mapping:

$$\text{DDupire: } \sigma_v(t, \mathcal{K}, T) \to \sigma_C(t, \mathcal{K}, T) \text{ for fixed } t$$

Proposition 17.1   *The function $\sigma_C(t, \mathcal{K}, T)$ so defined satisfies the static arbitrage restrictions automatically.*

17.3.3   Interpretation of Forward Variance

The forward variance has a very telling interpretation, which justifies its name:

Theorem 17.1   *The forward variance is equal to the expected value at time t under the risk-neutral measure of the variance of the underlying at time T conditional on the underlying price being equal to $\mathcal{K}$ at that time:*

$$v(t, \mathcal{K}, T) = \mathbb{E}_t^* \left[\sigma_S^2(T) \mid S(T) = \mathcal{K} \right] \tag{17.19}$$

Proof. We give the proof only for the case in which the underlying price $S(t)$ and its scalar volatility $\sigma_S(t)$ follow a joint Markov process with transition density $p^*(S(t), \sigma_S(t); S(T), \sigma_S(T), T - t)$ from time t to time T under the risk-neutral measure.[12] Within the confines of this proof, let the drift of volatility σ_S be μ_S, its volatility be γ, and its correlation with the process of S be ρ. The rate of interest is equal to zero. The price of the option is:

$$C(S, \sigma_S, \mathcal{K}, T - t) = \int_{\mathcal{K}}^{\infty} \int_0^{\infty} p^*(S, \sigma_S; x, y, T - t)\,(x - \mathcal{K})\,dx\,dy \tag{17.20}$$

It is obvious that one can generalize to stochastic volatility the Breeden-Litzenberger equation of section 6.6. Indeed, taking a second derivative of both sides of (17.20) gives:

$$\frac{\partial^2}{\partial \mathcal{K}^2} C(S, \sigma_S, \mathcal{K}, T - t) = \int_0^{\infty} p^*(S, \sigma_S; \mathcal{K}, y, T - t)\,dy$$

which is the risk-neutral probability density that $\mathcal{K} \leq S(T) < \mathcal{K} + d\mathcal{K}$. Similarly:

$$\frac{\partial}{\partial T} C(S, \sigma_S, \mathcal{K}, T - t) = \int_{\mathcal{K}}^{\infty} \int_0^{\infty} \frac{\partial}{\partial T} p^*(S, \sigma_S; x, y, T - t)\,(x - \mathcal{K})\,dx\,dy$$

---

12 This heuristic proof was given in an unpublished note by Dumas (1995) and is a generalization of the appendix in Derman and Kani (1994). See also Carr and Madan (1998) and Britten-Jones and Neuberger (2000). A general and rigorous proof is to be found in Carmona and Nadtochiy (2009).

Now, multiply by $x - \mathcal{K}$ both sides of the Fokker-Planck equation (13.4) extended to two dimensions and integrate with respect to x and y:

$$-\int_0^\infty \int_{\mathcal{K}}^\infty \frac{\partial}{\partial y} \left[\mu_S \times p^*(S, \sigma_S; x, y, T - t) \right] (x - \mathcal{K}) dx dy$$

$$+\int_0^\infty \int_{\mathcal{K}}^\infty \frac{\partial^2}{\partial x^2} \left[\frac{1}{2} y^2 x^2 p^*(S, \sigma_S; x, y, T - t) \right] (x - \mathcal{K}) dx dy$$

$$+\int_0^\infty \int_{\mathcal{K}}^\infty \frac{\partial^2}{\partial y^2} \left[\frac{1}{2} \gamma^2 p^*(S, \sigma_S; x, y, T - t) \right] (x - \mathcal{K}) dx dy$$

$$+\int_0^\infty \int_{\mathcal{K}}^\infty \frac{\partial^2}{\partial x \partial y} \left[\rho x y \gamma p^*(S, \sigma_S; x, y, T - t) \right] (x - \mathcal{K}) dx dy$$

$$= \int_0^\infty \int_{\mathcal{K}}^\infty \frac{\partial}{\partial T} p^*(S, \sigma_S; x, y, T - t) (x - \mathcal{K}) dx dy$$

Integrating by parts and/or integrating depending on the terms, and assuming that the transition density function p^* has the property that $p^* = 0$ and $\partial p^* / \partial y = 0$ at $y = 0$ and $y = \infty$, the first, third, and fourth terms vanish and we are left with:

$$\int_0^\infty \frac{1}{2} y^2 \mathcal{K}^2 p^*(S, \sigma_S; \mathcal{K}, y, T - t) \, dy = \int_0^\infty \int_{\mathcal{K}}^\infty \frac{\partial}{\partial T} p^*(S, \sigma_S; x, y, T - t) (x - \mathcal{K}) \, dx dy$$

But the left-hand side is

$$\frac{1}{2} \mathcal{K}^2 \mathbb{E}_t^* \left[\sigma^2(T) \mid S(T) = \mathcal{K} \right] \times \frac{\partial^2}{\partial \mathcal{K}^2} C(S, \sigma_S, \mathcal{K}, T - t)$$

and the right-hand side is $\partial C / \partial T$ so that, comparing with definition (17.15), we can identify the conditional expected value with the forward variance $v(t, \mathcal{K}, T)$. $\square$

Since forward variances are expectations of the future variance of the underlying, somewhat like forward interest rates are expectations of future instantaneous rates, they are named *forward* variances. In a manner analogous to forward interest rates, they give back the spot variance $\sigma_S^2(t)$ when $\mathcal{K} \to 0$.

Notice that the forward variance is not the implied variance. To put it simply, while the implied variance is model-dependent (it derives from Black-Scholes), the forward variance is "model free," as is the result of Breeden and Litzenberger. The theoretical construction we develop in the next section assumes that call prices for all strikes and maturities are quoted and observed. This makes the market *de facto* complete, and makes the measure P^* that is implicit in market prices, the unique equivalent measure of the market.

17.3.4 Summary of the Option Valuation Procedure

Suppose we know that the option price surface is driven by a Wiener process of dimension K. And suppose that we observe under the effective measure the following process for K "reference" options all written on the same underlying security:

$$\frac{dC(t, \mathcal{K}_i, T_i)}{C(t, \mathcal{K}_i, T_i)} = \mu_C(t, \mathcal{K}_i, T_i)\, dt + \sigma_C(t, \mathcal{K}_i, T_i)\, dw(t)$$

$$i = 1, \ldots, K$$

where the diffusion matrices of the K options are consistent with each other in the sense that

$$\sigma_v(t, \mathcal{K}, T) \quad \overset{\text{DDupire}}{\longrightarrow} \quad \sigma_C(t, \mathcal{K}_i, T_i) \quad \text{for fixed } t \quad \forall i = 1, \ldots, K$$

for some common process $\sigma_v(t, \mathcal{K}, T)$.

Then we can define the market-price of risk vector (still assuming a zero rate of interest):

$$\kappa(t) \triangleq \sigma_K(t)^{-1} \mu_K(t)$$

where $\sigma_K(t) \triangleq \{\sigma_C(t, \mathcal{K}_i, T_i)\}_{i=1}^{K}$ and $\mu_K(t) \triangleq \{\mu_C(t, \mathcal{K}_i, T_i)\}_{i=1}^{K}$. Then from this κ we can define an exponential martingale η that will serve as a change of measure and that will allow us to price all options other than the K reference options as well as any derivative written on the same underlying. Equivalently, we can define a process that is a Wiener process under the risk-neutral measure:

$$dw^*(t) = dw(t) + \kappa(t)dt$$

Knowing κ, η, and the risk-neutral probability from the observation of the process of K reference options, one may evaluate any derivative written on the same underlying security, including exotic options, simply by calculating a conditional expected value. For instance, the behavior of all options, beyond the K reference ones, follows. The SDE on any option under the effective measure, and thereby their empirical expected rate of return, would be given by:

$$\frac{dC(t, \mathcal{K}, T)}{C(t, \mathcal{K}, T)} = \sigma_C(t, \mathcal{K}, T)\sigma_K(t)^{-1}\mu_K(t)dt + \sigma_C(t, \mathcal{K}, T)dw(t); \quad \forall T$$

provided that:

$$\sigma_v(t, \mathcal{K}, T) \quad \overset{\text{DDupire}}{\longrightarrow} \quad \sigma_C(t, \mathcal{K}, T) \quad \forall \mathcal{K}, T$$

for a process $\sigma_v(t, \mathcal{K}, T)$ that coincides at the points $\{\mathcal{K}_i, T_i\}_{i=1}^{K}$ with the one that was common to all the K reference options.

17.4 VIX

Using the conditional expectation of theorem 17.1, one can obtain from current option prices an estimate of the market's *unconditional*, risk-neutral expectation of the future variance. One only has to condition down by multiplying the expression (17.15) by the conditional probability $\frac{\partial^2 C}{\partial \mathcal{K}^2}$ and integrating over $\mathcal{K}$:

$$\mathbb{E}_t^*\left[\sigma_S^2(T)\right] = 2\int_0^\infty \frac{1}{\mathcal{K}^2}\frac{\partial}{\partial T}C(t,\mathcal{K},T)\,d\mathcal{K}$$

Finally, suppose one wanted to obtain an average of this expected value over a future period of time $[t_1, t_2]$ $(t < t_1 < t_2)$:

$$\int_{t_1}^{t_2}\mathbb{E}_t^*\left[\sigma_S^2(u)\right]du = 2\int_0^\infty \frac{1}{\mathcal{K}^2}[C(t,\mathcal{K},t_2) - C(t,\mathcal{K},t_1)]\,d\mathcal{K} \tag{17.21}$$

This says that the market price of a contract on future variance of the underlying can be obtained directly by integrating over their strike prices a continuum of differences between option prices of *identical strikes and different maturity dates*. This is the "price of a variance swap" as defined in Carr and Madan (1998) and Britten-Jones and Neuberger (2000).

The Chicago Board Options Exchange (CBOE) publishes daily an index called "the VIX," which has been much in the news during the 2008 crisis and in more recent years. Since 2003, it is calculated according to formula (17.21).[13] The description is available at: http://www.cboe.com/micro/vix/vixwhite.pdf.

Comparing the price of a variance swap to the actual realized variance (and making a correction for the covariance between realized variance and consumption growth (or market return as a proxy)), one can then determine empirically whether volatility risk is priced in the market (over and beyond their consumption-risk content). In their paper suggestively entitled "The Price of a Smile," Buraschi and Jackwerth (2001) took up that task, based on data on stock-market index options. They use the Generalized Method of Moments (GMM) to test that the two are equal. Overwhelmingly, they reject the null hypothesis of zero price. Options on the index are not redundant assets: they allow one to take bets on volatility.[14]

Observing that the smile is usually much less pronounced on individual securities than on the index, Driessen, Maenhout, and Vilkov (2009) decomposed the variance of the index

---

13 It used to be calculated from the Black-Scholes formula as a mix of option prices, where the weight of each option depended on the volume traded. Under the new definition, VIX contracts could be exactly replicated if a continuum of options were available.

14 Stochastic variance can receive a price in the financial market (over and above consumption risk) only if the utility of the representative investor (imagining there exists one) is not a time-additive von Neumann-Morgenstern utility. Volatility is a "delayed risk"; a change in volatility will only have an effect on the process after the immediate period of investment. See chapter 21.

into the average variance of the components and the pairwise covariances. Since the variance of the components receives a small price, they reasoned that the price of index variance risk was mostly the price of fluctuations in the correlation between the assets that make up the index. They derived a risk-neutral valuation of correlation risk and tested whether correlation risk was priced. They found that it was.

The reader can solve exercise 17.2.

17.5   Stochastic Volatility in Equilibrium

As usual, we conclude our review of stochastic volatility by mentioning how it would appear in a competitive equilibrium.

While some of the previous models have addressed mainly the smile effect under the risk-neutral measure, an equilibrium model should be able to capture the leverage effect, that is, the fact that higher returns under the effective measure are usually accompanied by higher volatility. As mentioned already, the effect is connected to leverage because of the "naive" explanation for it. With a higher return, equity prices rise and firms, everything else equal, are less levered so that their stocks become less risky and the volatility of stock prices is lower. However, empirical tests are hardly consistent with the naive leverage explanation.

Since we observe negative correlation, but cannot ascertain causality, the effect could also go the other way: it could be the case that an anticipated increase in volatility commands a higher return, which, everything else equal, can take place only if prices fall in the short run (the so-called "volatility-feedback" effect). Whatever the direction of causality is, the equilibrium models described so far are too simple to capture stochastic volatility and the market incompleteness that it may entail.

We saw in section 17.2.2 that the *very special* case of the Heston model, when the correlation between the two Wiener processes is set equal to 1, is consistent with a version of the special Cox-Ingersoll-Ross general-equilibrium economic model that we presented in chapter 11. So, Heston's model does allow non-zero risk pricing *relative to the marginal utility of wealth*. However, it would be possible to incorporate the leverage effect only by setting the correlation to a negative number.

Models capable of assigning a non-zero price to stochastic utility, relative to the marginal utility of consumption, generally use recursive or Epstein-Zin preferences instead of time-additive utility. Equilibrium models of stochastic volatility can, therefore, be addressed in the setting of chapter 21.

17.6   Conclusion

Lacking a rendition of the way information arrives to financial markets, it is impossible at this point to construct a structural model of volatility behavior. Information could be arriving smoothly and continuously or in big chunks at isolated times, with very different behavior for resulting volatility. Like the previous chapter, this chapter has been mostly methodological as we had to capture the simultaneous behavior of several securities, such as several derivatives written on the same stock. In the previous chapter, we found that we could specify freely the volatilities of forward interest rates. In this chapter, we introduced the concept of forward volatility – very much related to modern VIX – and found that we could specify freely the volatility of forward volatility.

Once equipped with this device, it became possible, for instance, to price exotic options written on a stock based on the specified behavior of some reference plain-vanilla options written on the same stock.

17.7   Appendix: GARCH

A Generalized Autoregressive Conditional Heteroskedasticity process of order p and q, briefly a GARCH(p, q) model, is a discrete-time joint stochastic process for a variable $\ln S(t)$ and its variance $h(t)$ described, under the historical (not the risk-neutral) measure, by

$$\ln S(t) = \ln S(t - \Delta) + r\Delta - \frac{1}{2}h(t) + \varepsilon\sqrt{h(t)} + \sqrt{h(t)}z(t) \tag{17.22}$$

$$h(t) = \varpi + \sum_{i=1}^{p}\beta_i h(t - i\Delta) + \sum_{i=1}^{q}\alpha_i h(t - i\Delta)z^2(t - i\Delta)$$

where r is the continuously compounded interest rate for the time interval Δ, $z(t)$ is a standard normal disturbance, $h(t)$ is the conditional variance of the log return between $t - \Delta$ and t, and is known from the information set at time $t - \Delta$. The conditional variance $h(t)$ appears in the first equation as a return premium for which the risk premium per units of risk is assumed constant. Indeed, the equation says that, conditional on a given variance h, known at the beginning of the period, gross log returns are normally distributed, with expectation $\exp(r\Delta + \varepsilon\sqrt{h(t)})$. In this sense, the parameter κ is the additional expected return per unit of risk. The second equation describes the level of the conditional variance at time t as the sum of a constant ϖ, a weighted average of past conditional variances $h(t - i\Delta)$, up to p periods before, and a weighted average of past, squared price innovations, $h(t - i\Delta)z^2(t - i\Delta)$, up to the order q. The obvious restrictions on the parameters are $p \geq 0, q \geq 0, \alpha_i \geq 0, \beta_i \geq 0$. For stationarity, the weights have to sum up to less than one:

$$\sum_{i=1}^{p}\beta_i + \sum_{i=1}^{q}\alpha_i < 1$$

The GARCH model captures both stochastic correlation and, most advantageously, the correlation between volatility and underlying prices. As stated, it is not two–factor Markovian: current volatility and the current asset price are not sufficient statistics for representing current information. The knowledge of $z^2(t - i\Delta), i = 1, .., q$, is also needed. This model, originally introduced by Bollerslev (1986), has been extended in various ways and has proven to be very successful in capturing heteroskedasticity in financial data. Since it is cast in discrete time, and it proved to be effective in fitting time-series data, it has been used extensively in empirical work. It is quite easily amenable to parameter estimation: almost any econometric software contains functions for estimating the parameters of most GARCH specifications. The parameters governing the volatility can be obtained from a time series of returns. As we will see, the option pricing that is consistent with it provides option prices as a function of the current underlying price, as the Black-Scholes formula does, and the past history of those prices. As a consequence, a GARCH model, if it also permits closed-form option pricing, allows us to parametrize the volatility process by exploiting both option prices and a whole time series of asset price observations, instead of using only the current implied volatility, or a cross section of option prices at one point in time. In this way, the parameter estimates obtained from it are more stable and statistically reliable than are estimates of the stochastic volatility models described so far.

In order to illustrate the practical and theoretical properties of the GARCH model for stochastic volatility, we first describe how, and under which restrictions, it can be used for option pricing, so as to fully exploit the robustness just described. Subsequently, we provide conditions under which a discrete-time GARCH model admits a continuous-time counterpart.

17.7.1 Parameter Specification and Estimate

Not all GARCH models admit closed-form option price solutions. A remarkable case is the following quasi-GARCH process, slightly different from the previous one, for which Heston and Nandi (2000) provide explicit option valuation:

$$\ln S(t) = \ln S(t - \Delta) + r\Delta - \frac{1}{2}h(t) + \varepsilon h(t) + \sqrt{h(t)}z(t) \tag{17.23}$$

$$h(t) = \varpi + \sum_{i=1}^{p} \beta_i h(t - i\Delta) + \sum_{i=1}^{q} \alpha_i \left[z(t - i\Delta) - \gamma_i \sqrt{h(t - i\Delta)} \right]^2$$

As compared to the more general formulation above, this specification makes current conditional variance depend on past conditional variances, but not on squared past price innovations. The tilt is in the last term, which is altered from $z^2(t - i\Delta)\sqrt{h(t - i\Delta)}$ to $z(t - i\Delta) - \gamma_i\sqrt{h(t - i\Delta)}$. Instead of a central one, innovations have a non-central chi-square distribution, whose non-centrality depends on the parameter γ_i. In spite of this technicality, the model maintains most of the traditional GARCH properties, including stationarity and correlation between the underlying price and variance. In the simplest, but most commonly used case, $p = q = 1$, correlation is negative and depends both on the weight of past "innovations" in the conditional variance and on the parameter that determines non-centrality:

$$\text{cov}_{t-\Delta}[h(t + \Delta), \ln S(t)] = -2\alpha_1\gamma_1 h(t)$$

Since γ_1 controls such covariance, it is responsible for capturing the leverage effect that we described at the beginning of this chapter.

Derivative valuation is provided under the assumption that, over an interval of time of length Δ, the one-period-ahead variance does not change from the statistical to the risk-neutral measure. This "local risk-neutrality" assumption, which is tenable under various utility and return/volatility distributions, makes it possible to price an option by the usual martingale device, that is, as the risk-neutral expectation of its final payoff, discounted. So, to introduce pricing, Heston and Nandi first switch to a pricing measure P^*:

$$\ln S(t) = \ln S(t - \Delta) + r\Delta - \frac{1}{2}h(t) + \sqrt{h(t)}z^*(t) \tag{17.24}$$

$$h(t) = \varpi + \sum_{i=1}^{p} \beta_i h(t - i\Delta) + \sum_{i=1}^{q} \alpha_i \left[z^*(t - i\Delta) - \gamma_i \sqrt{h(t - i\Delta)} \right]^2$$

$$+\alpha_1 \left[z^*(t - \Delta) - \left(\gamma_1 + \varepsilon + \frac{1}{2} \right) \sqrt{h(t - \Delta)} \right]^2$$

The effect on the asset process of switching to the risk-neutral measure is almost standard:

$$z^*(t) = \left(\varepsilon + \frac{1}{2} \right) \sqrt{h(t)} + z(t)$$

while it is novel in the variance case, where, for the last innovation ($i = 1$), past volatilities (and non-centrality) are increased by a multiple of the risk premium ε. Heston and Nandi proceed to show that, under the assumption that a Black-Scholes-type pricing formula (with normal innovations) can be used, which in turn requires a reasoning of the "local risk-neutrality" type, such a formula can be written explicitly in terms of the characteristic functions of the transition densities corresponding to (17.24). These characteristic functions are somewhat similar to those found by Heston:

$$f(x, t, \phi, T) = x^{i\phi} \exp \left[A(t, i\phi, T) + \sum_{i=1}^{p} B_i(t, i\phi, T)h(t + 2\Delta - i\Delta) \right. \tag{17.25}$$

$$\left. + \sum_{i=1}^{q} C_i(t, i\phi, T) \left[z^*(t + \Delta - i\Delta) - (\gamma_i + \varepsilon) \sqrt{h(t + \Delta - i\Delta)} \right]^2 \right]$$

where A, B_1, C_1 are functions of time obtainable from ordinary first-difference equations and where B_i, C_i for $i > 1$ are calculated recursively. Transition densities can be obtained by inversion but, above all, calibration of the model is possible and quite robust. Indeed, time series data can be used to provide the parameters of the volatility process, preferably using Maximum Likelihood Estimation. These estimates can be used in connection with panel data of option prices (a time series of cross section option prices across strikes and maturities) or cross sections of them, so as to capture the "forward looking" informational content of option prices. Heston and Nandi show that the out-of-sample fit of their model on S&P index data is not only better than the fit of the Black-Scholes model, but also of a version of the latter model "enriched" to give to it more flexibility. The intuition for the superior ability of their GARCH model to fit observed data is that the model itself incorporates the leverage effect, or a negative correlation between volatility and asset returns.

17.7.2   GARCH versus Continuous-Time Stochastic Volatility

It is possible to reconcile the GARCH model studied so far with the continuous-time models presented in the previous sections. This section shows that one of the GARCH specification, the Heston and Nandi one, includes the Heston model as a continuous-limit specification.[15] In order to specify

---

15 On this topic, see Nelson (1990).

this continuous-time counterpart, we consider only a subcase of the Heston and Nandi model, which is a GARCH process of order 1.

Consider, indeed, the Heston and Nandi formulation (17.23) in the special case $p = 0$, $q = 1$. Let $\Delta \to 0$ in a way that we are going to specify. First, define the variance per unit of time: $V(t) = h(t)/\Delta$. The equation for h in (17.23) becomes

$$V(t + \Delta) = \frac{\varpi}{\Delta} + \frac{\alpha_1}{\Delta}\left[z(t) - \gamma_1\sqrt{\Delta}\sqrt{V(t)}\right]^2$$

Now, let us specify the behavior of each parameter as $\Delta \to 0$. Let both α and ϖ be quadratic in time, and let γ_1 be hyperbolic:

$$\alpha_1(\Delta) = \frac{1}{4}k^2\Delta^2$$

$$\varpi(\Delta) = \left(\varrho\theta - \frac{1}{4}k^2\right)\Delta^2$$

$$\gamma_1(\Delta) = \frac{2}{k\Delta} - \frac{\varrho}{k}$$

Then, the process approaches in probability distribution the following continuous-time process:

$$dV(t) = \varrho[\theta - V(t)]dt - k\sqrt{V(t)}dw(t) \tag{17.26}$$

which the reader can recognize as the Heston model, while at the same time, the process for the asset price becomes

$$d\ln S(t) = \left[r + \left(\varepsilon - \frac{1}{2}\right)V(t)\right]dt + \sqrt{V(t)}dw(t)$$

Note that the same Wiener process drives the spot asset price and the variance. Hence, in this special case, the two risks – price risk and volatility risk – are perfectly correlated. Since only one Wiener process is involved, it would have been possible to derive the option pricing formula in the Heston model as a special case of (17.25) and vice versa. The continuous-time limit, therefore, shows that we can justify (17.25) even without resorting to the local-risk-neutrality assumption, which the reader can deem quite artificial.

To demonstrate the asserted convergence, observe that from the expression of $\alpha_1(\Delta), \varpi(\Delta)$ and $\gamma_1(\Delta)$ it follows that

$$V(t + \Delta) = \left(\varrho\theta - \frac{1}{4}k^2\right)\Delta + \frac{1}{4}k^2\Delta\left[z(t) - \left(\frac{2}{k\Delta} - \frac{\varrho}{k}\right)\sqrt{\Delta}\sqrt{V(t)}\right]^2$$

$$= \left(\varrho\theta - \frac{1}{4}k^2\right)\Delta + \frac{1}{4}k^2\Delta\left[z^2(t) - 2z(t)\left(\frac{2}{k\Delta} - \frac{\varrho}{k}\right)\sqrt{\Delta}\sqrt{V(t)}\right]$$

$$\quad + \frac{1}{4}k^2\Delta\left[\frac{2}{k\Delta} - \frac{\varrho}{k}\right]^2 \Delta V(t)$$

$$= \left(\varrho\theta - \frac{1}{4}k^2\right)\Delta + \frac{1}{4}k^2\Delta\left[z^2(t) - 2z(t)\left(\frac{2}{k\Delta} - \frac{\varrho}{k}\right)\sqrt{\Delta}\sqrt{V(t)}\right]$$

$$\quad + \left[1 - \Delta\varrho + \frac{1}{4}\Delta^2\varrho^2\right]V(t) \tag{17.27}$$

$$\frac{V(t+\Delta)-V(t)}{\Delta}=\left(\varrho\theta-\frac{1}{4}k^2\right) \qquad (17.28)$$

$$+\frac{1}{4}k^2\left[z^2(t)-2z(t)\left(\frac{2}{k\Delta}-\frac{\varrho}{k}\right)\sqrt{\Delta}\sigma(t)\right]$$

$$+\left(-\varrho+\frac{1}{4}\Delta\varrho^2\right)V(t)$$

From (17.28):

$$\frac{1}{\Delta}\mathbb{E}_t[V(t+\Delta)-V(t)] \to \varrho[\theta-V(t)]$$

From (17.27):

$$V(t+\Delta)-V(t)-\mathbb{E}_t[V(t+\Delta)-V(t)] \to -k\sqrt{V(t)}\sqrt{\Delta}z(t)$$

(17.26) follows.

Exercises

17.1. This exercise contains a numerical illustration of the Heston model:

a. Solve explicitly the system of ODEs (17.10). The functions C and D thus obtained provide you with the characteristic function (17.9).

b. Using that explicit solution, write a code to calculate numerically the cumulative distribution (17.11). Of course, the numerical integration cannot be done to infinity. You can set a high upper bound and check the sensitivity of the solution.

c. How would you proceed to use the cumulative distribution to obtain the price of an option under stochastic volatility?

17.2. (from a discussion with Pascal Maenhout)
Consider a pure-exchange economy with two risky "trees." The dividend attached to risky tree i ($i=1,2$) over a small period of time dt is equal to $\delta_i(t)dt$. The sum of the two dividends $\delta_1(t)+\delta_2(t)$ is the total flow of physical resources available for consumption in the economy over the time interval t to $t+dt$. The stochastic differential equations governing processes δ_i are as follows:

$$\frac{d\delta_1(t)}{\delta_1(t)}=f_1(t)dt+\frac{\sigma_1}{\sqrt{1+(\rho(t))^2}}\times(dw_1(t)+\rho(t)dw_2(t))$$

$$\frac{d\delta_2(t)}{\delta_2(t)}=f_2(t)dt+\frac{\sigma_2}{\sqrt{1+(\rho(t))^2}}\times(\rho(t)dw_1(t)+dw_2(t))$$

$$d\rho(t)=f_3(t)dt+(s_1dw_1(t)+s_2dw_2(t)+s_3dw_3(t))$$

where w_1, w_2, and w_3 are independent Wiener processes and σ_1, σ_2, s_1, s_2, and s_3 are constants. $\rho(t)$ is evidently interpretable as the correlation between the two rates of growth of the two trees. The correlation is risky since it follows a stochastic process of its own.

a. Assume that there exists a representative investor and assume at first that he has a time-additive von-Neumann-Morgenstern utility function. Indicate whether correlation risk is priced in this economy. Recall that the risk of a risky variable x is said to be priced if a financial security whose rate of return in the financial market correlates with x receives, for that reason, a different expected return from an asset that would have zero correlation with x.

b. Can you imagine a utility function of known type for the representative investor that would cause correlation risk to be priced? If not, read chapter 21 or go to exercise 21.4 of chapter 21.

18 Heterogeneous Expectations

In this chapter,[1] we focus on the way publicly available information is processed by market participants and we study the properties of a market where information processing makes investors heterogeneous in their probability beliefs. The arrival of information moves securities prices and is, therefore, a source of risk. We ask in which way this risk is priced. We do not consider the case in which some investors receive information that others do not receive, which is the case of private (sometimes called "asymmetric") information.[2]

In section 18.1, we construct a scenario in which some variable of the economy is not observable by investors. They harbor beliefs about the unobservable variable, which they adjust as public information arrives.

Then, we ask how investors may have developed these heterogeneous beliefs. They do so by some learning process. In section 18.2, we discuss an example in which they learn by means of Bayes' formula. They start from different priors, which are the only source of heterogeneity in their beliefs. They disagree because of that and they know it. We go on to show the impact of their Bayesian learning on their portfolio choice and ask whether diversifying a portfolio and buying information are complements or substitutes.

In section 18.3, we go back to the situation of section 18.1 in which beliefs are taken as given and develop an equilibrium in which the market is complete but investors harbor heterogeneous and fluctuating probability beliefs. These cause the market to be *more volatile*, so that prices of securities can deviate from the "fundamental" value that they would have under full information. We refer to these stochastic deviations as "difference-of-opinion" risk, also called "valuation" or "sentiment" risk. It is the risk that is created for one investor by the fickleness of other investors (and, as a matter of fact, also his own). The behavior

---

1 Professor Astrid Schornick of INSEAD is a co-author of this chapter. For sections 18.1.1, 18.1.2, 18.1.3, 18.2.1, and 18.3.1, the exposition owes a lot to Basak (2000, 2005), except for one methodological deviation noted below in remark 18.2.

2 Models in which agents receive *different information (private signals)*, belong to the vast "Noisy-Rational Expectations" literature originating from the work of Grossman and Stiglitz (1980), Hellwig (1980), and Wang (1993), in which agents learn also from price, a channel that we do not consider here.

of others is a source of risk on a par with the risk of the economy. We show how that risk is priced. We ask in particular (in section 18.3.2), whether the difference of opinion across investors tends to increase or decrease securities' prices.

When they receive the same public information time after time, Bayesian learners, unless they have infinite trust in their separate priors, tend to converge to common probability beliefs. The heterogeneity of beliefs between agents needs to be regenerated; otherwise Bayes' law causes it to die out. In section 18.4, we discuss the equilibrium that prevails when different investors process public information differently.

One can distinguish three stages in the development of the literature on incomplete information and learning. In the first stage, papers such as Detemple (1986), Dothan and Feldman (1986), and Gennotte (1986) developed the theory of portfolio choice for a single, imperfectly informed investor facing a given price process, thus extending to learning the theory covered in chapters 9 and 10. Brennan (1998) made an important contribution to this literature by showing that an investor's own future learning is a source of risk that he or she will want to hedge, as a form of intertemporal hedging. Further work was done by Xia (2001). This stage of the literature is the foundation for section 18.2. In a second stage, researchers developed models of equilibrium with imperfect information and with a single representative agent.[3] Papers that have done so include Timmerman (1993, 1996); Detemple and Murthy (1994), who study a production economy, using logarithmic utility; David (1997); Brennan and Xia (1998); Veronesi (1999, 2000); and Collin-Dufresne, Johannes and Lochstoer (2016). The third stage of development has consisted in developing models of equilibrium with two groups of investors as in Zapatero (1998), who studies a pure-exchange economy with logarithmic utility; Basak (2000) who maintains the exchange economy but extends the model to general utility functions. In this book, we skip the second stage. Sections 18.1, 18.3, and 18.4 of this chapter directly consider two groups of investors.[4]

18.1 Difference of Opinion

As noted, all aspects of investor heterogeneity covered in this chapter are set in the context of incomplete-information models, not asymmetric-information models (in which investors receive private information). This means that all investors knowingly differ in their views. Rightly or wrongly, each investor does not consider the other investors as having information that he does not possess and, therefore, makes no effort to learn from others' behavior, that is, from their investment activities or from the resulting market price. They

3 Lintner (1969) first developed the CAPM with heterogeneous beliefs.
4 An excellent survey is available in Ziegler (2003).

"agree to disagree."[5] That means we adopt an approach called the "difference-of-opinion" approach.[6]

18.1.1   Endowment and Securities Markets

To fix ideas, imagine that the economy is populated by two, or two groups of, competitive investors, $m = a, b$, who receive in the aggregate an exogenous endowment process $\bar{c}$:

$$d\bar{c}(t) = \mu_{\bar{c}}(t)\bar{c}(t)dt + \sigma_{\bar{c}}(t)\bar{c}(t)dw(t) \tag{18.1}$$

where w is a one-dimensional Wiener process under the effective measure, and the drift $\mu_{\bar{c}}$ is itself a stochastic process. Both processes $\mu_{\bar{c}}$ and $\bar{c}$ are defined on the probability space $(\Omega, \mathcal{F}, P)$.

We consider a situation in which investors do not observe the shocks w. Their filtration is coarser than the filtration $\mathcal{F}^w$ generated by the process w. For example, assume that, at any time $t > 0$, investors observe the increments $d\bar{c}(t)$ in the endowment, so that their common filtration is the filtration $\mathcal{F}^{\bar{c}}$ generated by the process $\bar{c}$ – or a finer one, if they receive additional information that we do not discuss at this point. But they do not observe the split of $d\bar{c}$ into a drift component $\mu_{\bar{c}}(t)\bar{c}(t)dt$ and a diffusion component $\sigma_{\bar{c}}(t)\bar{c}(t)dw(t)$.

Still, the volatility is known to both investors since they are assumed to infer it from the quadratic variation of the endowment, $(d\bar{c})^2$, which makes it observable since $(d\bar{c})^2 = \bar{c}^2\sigma_{\bar{c}}^2 dt$. But, because of limited observability, each investor m may infer the drift $\mu_{\bar{c}}$ differently and develop his own subjective estimate $\hat{\mu}_{\bar{c}}^m$ of it, so that he harbors his own beliefs about the endowment process:

$$d\bar{c}(t) = \hat{\mu}_{\bar{c}}^m(t)\bar{c}(t)dt + \sigma_{\bar{c}}(t)\bar{c}(t)dw^m(t) \tag{18.2}$$

where w^m is a *one-dimensional* Wiener process under the subjective probability measure P^m of investor m (see below) and $\hat{\mu}_{\bar{c}}^m$ is itself a stochastic process.

We elaborate further on that example in sections 18.2.1 and 18.4. Suffice it to say for now that each investor m works in the probability space $(\Omega, \mathcal{F}^{\bar{c}}, P^m)$, not in the original space $(\Omega, \mathcal{F}, P)$. His probability measure P^m may be different from that of the other investors. We assume that the measures P^m are equivalent: investors agree on which events have zero probability of occurring. We are now contemplating three probability measures: (i) the effective measure P (with endowment drift $\mu_{\bar{c}}$), (ii, iii) the subjective or "perceived" measures P^a and P^b of the two investors (with endowment drifts $\hat{\mu}_{\bar{c}}^a$, $\hat{\mu}_{\bar{c}}^b$ respectively). There exists a change of probability measure $\varkappa$, which is a strictly positive martingale

---

5 Aumann (1976) shows that "if two people have the same priors, and their posteriors for an event A are common knowledge, then these posteriors are equal." The example considered below involves different priors.

6 See Harris and Raviv (1993), Kandel and Pearson (1995), and Cecchetti, Lam, and Mark (2000). See Morris (1995) for a discussion of this approach.

process, that translates the probabilities of events as seen by investor b into the probabilities of the same event as seen by investor a:[7]

$$\mathbb{E}^a\left[\mathbf{1}_{E_u}|\mathcal{F}_t^{\bar{c}}\right] = \mathbb{E}^b\left[\frac{\varkappa_u}{\varkappa_t}\mathbf{1}_{E_u}|\mathcal{F}_t^{\bar{c}}\right] \tag{18.3}$$

where $\mathbf{1}_{E_u}$ is the indicator function for an event E_u occurring at date u and belonging to the σ-algebra $\mathcal{F}_u^{\bar{c}}$. *Let us call $\varkappa$ the "difference of opinion" because it is the ratio of the probability beliefs of investor a over those of investor b.*

Substituting (18.2) into (18.1), the relation between investor m's Wiener process and the effective Wiener process is found:

$$dw^m(t) = \frac{1}{\sigma_{\bar{c}}(t)}\left[\mu_{\bar{c}}(t)dt + \sigma_{\bar{c}}(t)dw(t) - \hat{\mu}_{\bar{c}}^m(t)dt\right]$$

$$dw(t) = \frac{\hat{\mu}_{\bar{c}}^m(t) - \mu_{\bar{c}}(t)}{\sigma_{\bar{c}}(t)}dt + dw^m(t) \tag{18.4}$$

Let us denote as $\hat{g}(t)$ the difference between the investors' estimates of growth rates, *normalized by the endowment standard deviation* and call it a "disagreement process:"

$$\hat{g}(t) \triangleq \frac{\hat{\mu}_{\bar{c}}^a(t) - \hat{\mu}_{\bar{c}}^b(t)}{\sigma_{\bar{c}}(t)}$$

Equation (18.4) gives

$$dw^b(t) = dw^a(t) + \hat{g}(t)dt \tag{18.5}$$

A value $\hat{g}(t) > 0$ implies that investor a is more "optimistic," that is, he expects a higher growth rate of the endowment over the next time interval dt than investor b does.

The difference of opinion process $\varkappa$ and the disagreement process $\hat{g}$ are different but there is a relation between them. Equation (18.3) implies, by Girsanov's theorem:[8]

Proposition 18.1 *The disagreement process is the diffusion term in the difference of opinion:*

$$\frac{d\varkappa(t)}{\varkappa(t)} = \hat{g}(t)dw^b(t) \tag{18.6}$$

***Remark* 18.1** *Not only is the difference of opinion $\varkappa(t)$ stochastic, its volatility $\hat{g}(t)$ may also be stochastic (see sections 18.2.1 and 18.4). If so, the disagreement creates heteroskedasticity or stochastic volatility (in the sense of chapter 17).*

Agents are allowed to trade two assets: a bond and a stock, both in zero-net supply, with the usual notations.[9] The stock depends on the same Wiener process as the endowment

---

7 The process $\varkappa$ is a strictly positive martingale under the measure of b. The process $1/\varkappa$, which would effect the reverse change of measure, is a strictly positive martingale under the measure of a.

8 This is one more illustration of Girsanov's theorem: the difference between the two agents' subjective probability measures translates into a change of drift.

9 Endowments are the only physical resources of the economy.

but, because of (18.4), its dynamics is also written in terms of the Wiener process of each investor, with the following notation:

$$\frac{dS(t)}{S(t)} = \mu(t)dt + \sigma(t)dw(t)$$

$$= \mu(t)dt + \sigma(t)dw^m(t) - \frac{\sigma(t)}{\sigma_{\bar{c}}(t)}\left[\mu_{\bar{c}}(t) - \hat{\mu}_{\bar{c}}^m(t)\right]dt$$

$$= \mu^m(t)dt + \sigma(t)dw^m(t) \tag{18.7}$$

where we define $\mu^m(t)$ as:

$$\mu^m(t) \triangleq \mu(t) - \frac{\sigma(t)}{\sigma_{\bar{c}}(t)}\left[\mu_{\bar{c}}(t) - \hat{\mu}_{\bar{c}}^m(t)\right]$$

This last formulation (18.7) of the price process is the operational one since *the truth is not available to investors and, therefore, cannot be reflected in securities prices.*

The previous construction warrants three comments. First, investors, being in the situation of not knowing the true value of the drift, replace the endowment process (18.1), the drift of which is unknown, with a process (18.2), the drift of which is their own and the Wiener process, w^m of which is a Wiener under their own probability measure. With the multiple specifications of beliefs, it is still possible to compute portfolio optimization and equilibrium with the tools introduced in the previous chapters.

Second, when investors cannot observe some variables, they may not be able to estimate some components of the entire Wiener process system, including those driving $\mu_{\bar{c}}(t)$. Then, we must adjust the definition of a complete market. A market is complete when the number of securities is equal to one plus the number of Wiener processes that can be estimated by both investors. An example of that distinction is provided in section 18.4. In this chapter, we make the assumption of completeness.

Third, both investors, of course, must agree on prices S: all of them will trade at these prices and obviously a buyer and a seller must agree on the price they transact at. Since their filtrations all coincide, there exist prices of securities that are adapted to the common filtration.

Therefore, investors agree on the same complete market, and there is scope for building an equilibrium for it.

18.1.2   The Several Risk Premia

Since the source of uncertainty driving the output process is the same as the one driving the returns on risky investment, the heterogeneity of beliefs about the endowment affects securities' demand and carries over into the financial markets although, at a minimum, investors must agree on observed asset prices, so that (18.7) holds for both investors $m = a, b$. Simplifying we get:

$$\mu^a(t)dt + \sigma(t)dw^a(t) = \mu^b(t)dt + \sigma(t)dw^b(t)$$

This reveals the way the two investors' perceptions of *securities'* growth rates or conditionally expected returns – as distinct from the endowment growth rates – must be related:

$$\mu^a(t) - \mu^b(t) = \sigma(t)\hat{g}(t) \tag{18.8}$$

This relation feeds directly into the differences across investors' "perceived market prices of risk." Recall the standard definition of $\kappa(t)$, the market price of risk in this economy with a single Brownian motion that would prevail in the absence of belief heterogeneity (section 8.2, equation 8.11). Since both investors $m = a, b$ are able to observe the instantaneous risk-free interest rate as well as diffusion parameters of any stochastic process, differences in perceived market prices of risk follow directly:

$$\kappa^a(t) - \kappa^b(t) = \frac{\mu^a(t) - \mu^b(t)}{\sigma(t)} = \hat{g}(t) \tag{18.9}$$

We can consider now that each investor m faces his own stochastic discount factor $\xi^m(t)$ for $m = a, b$. The two investor-specific stochastic-discount factor processes $(\xi^m(t) = \eta^m(t)/B(t))$ are:

$$\xi^m(t) = \exp\left\{ -\int_0^t r(s)ds - \int_0^t \kappa^m(s)dw^m(s) - \frac{1}{2}\int_0^t \left(\kappa^m(s)\right)^2 \times ds \right\} \frac{1}{B(t)} \tag{18.10}$$

However, the market being complete, it would perhaps be more natural to consider that they all face the same stochastic discount factor but compute their expected values with different probability measures. For instance, because of the mapping (18.3), the lifetime budget constraint of investor a can equally well be written as:

$$\mathbb{E}^a\left[\int_0^T \xi^a(t)\left(c^a(t) - e^a(t)\right)dt \right] \leq W_0^a$$

or as:

$$\mathbb{E}^b\left[\int_0^T \xi^b(t)\left(c^a(t) - e^a(t)\right)dt \right] \leq W_0^a$$

In effect, we are now working with four probability measures: in addition to the three probability measures mentioned earlier (with endowment drifts $\mu_{\bar{c}}$, $\hat{\mu}_{\bar{c}}^a$, and $\hat{\mu}_{\bar{c}}^b$ respectively), there is the pricing measure under which all discounted prices are martingales. Obviously, the change of measure η^a going from investor a's measure to his pricing measure differs from the change of measure η^b going from investor b's measure to his pricing measure by exactly the difference of opinion:

$$\varkappa \times \eta^a = \eta^b$$

and, if short-term bonds are traded, similarly:

$$\varkappa \times \xi^a = \xi^b$$

The stochastic discount factors ξ^a and ξ^b "of investors a and b" *should not be viewed as different stochastic discount factors*. Instead, they are the same, in two guises, translated one from the other, to jibe with different probability beliefs and expected-value operators.

18.1.3 Investor Optimization

We proceed now with a direct application of the technique learned in chapters 10 and 12. Each investor m is endowed with a fraction of the aggregate output stream $\bar{c}(t)$ so that $e^a(t) + e^b(t) = \bar{c}(t)$. The resulting dynamic budget constraint follows the notation given in previous chapters, $W^m(t)$ indicates investor m's wealth at time t, $c^m(t)$ his consumption, and $\theta^m(t)$ the number of units he holds of the risky asset with price $S(t)$.

Investors maximize their expected utility from consumption over the finite-horizon economy; their respective utility functions $u^m(c^m)$ satisfy all standard conditions. To ease notations, we assume an absence of time preference; utility depends on consumption only, not time. Rewriting the dynamic budget constraint in its lifetime form (as in (10.10)) using investor b's stochastic discount factor density gives the following formulation:

- for investor b:

$$\max_{c^b} \mathbb{E}^b \left[\int_0^T u^b(c^b(t))dt \right] \tag{18.11}$$

subject to:

$$\mathbb{E}^b \left[\int_0^T \xi^b \left(c^b(t) - e^b(t) \right) dt \right] \leq W_0^b$$

with first-order condition for consumption:

$$u_c^b(c^b(t)) = \lambda_0^b \xi^b(t)$$

- for investor a:

$$\max_{c^a} \mathbb{E}^b \left[\int_0^T \varkappa(t) u^a(c^a(t))dt \right] \tag{18.12}$$

subject to:

$$\mathbb{E}^b \left[\int_0^T \xi^b(t) \left(c^a(t) - e^a(t) \right) dt \right] \leq W_0^a$$

with first-order condition for consumption:

$$\varkappa(t) u_c^a(c^a(t)) = \lambda_0^a \xi^b(t)$$

In this way, we use in this calculation only one pair of pricing and probability measures: that of investor b.

Lagrange multipliers λ_0^m ensure that the lifetime budget constraints hold (are actually binding) at the optimum. Inverting the investors' first-order conditions gives the optimal consumption policies:

$$c^b(t) = \mathfrak{h}^b \left(\lambda_0^b \xi^b(t) \right) \tag{18.13}$$

$$c^a(t) = \mathfrak{h}^a \left(\lambda_0^a \xi^a(t) \right) = \mathfrak{h}^a \left(\lambda_0^a \frac{\xi^b(t)}{\varkappa(t)} \right) \tag{18.14}$$

18.1.4 Comparative Analysis of a Change in Disagreement

We now discuss briefly the change in an investor's growth rate of consumption that will result from an increase in the disagreement, which, as we have seen (equation (18.6)), is an increase in the risk of the difference of opinion. We adopt the one-period, discrete-time comparative-statics methods of Gollier and Kimball (1996), Gollier (2001), Gollier and Eeckhoudt (2002), and especially Gollier (2008). Unlike them, we focus on the substitution effect and neglect the wealth effect, which would be reflected in the Lagrange multipliers.

Applying Itô's lemma to the demand function (18.13) of investor b, for fixed λ_0^b, and using (15.7), we get the increase of his consumption from time t to time $t + dt$ under his own measure for a given value of his own version ξ^b of the stochastic discount factor:

$$dc^b(t) = \mathfrak{h}^{b\prime}\left(\lambda_0^b\xi^b(t)\right)\lambda_0^b d\xi^b(t) + \frac{1}{2}\mathfrak{h}^{b\prime\prime}\left(\lambda_0^b\xi^b(t)\right)\left(\lambda_0^b d\xi^b(t)\right)^2$$

$$= \frac{1}{A^b(t)}\left\{\left[r(t) + \frac{1}{2}\frac{P^b(t)}{A^b(t)}\left(\kappa^b(t)\right)^2\right]\times dt + \kappa^b(t)dw^b(t)\right\}$$

where A^b and P^b are the absolute risk aversion and prudence of the investor. In this expression, the disagreement $\hat{g}$ does not appear because investor b lives in his own world.

We need to consider two amendments to this expression. First, the increase of consumption could be computed under the measure of investor a:

$$dc^b(t) = \frac{1}{A^b(t)}\left\{\left[r(t) + \frac{1}{2}\frac{P^b(t)}{A^b(t)}\left(\kappa^b(t)\right)^2 + \kappa^b(t)\hat{g}(t)\right]\times dt + \kappa^b(t)dw^a(t)\right\}$$

which, in case $\kappa^b > 0$, says that investor a expects investor b to consume more at time $t + dt$ (or less at time t) if $\hat{g} > 0$, that is, if investor b is comparatively pessimistic, than he would otherwise. Being pessimistic, he restricts his current relative to his future consumption.

Second, in performing the comparison between two levels of disagreement, the assumption of price taking under perfect competition must be clarified. It is clear that the investor should take as given the rate of interest r since a riskless asset is assumed to be traded but, in view of equation (18.9), investor b could hardly take his own price of risk κ^b as given when the disagreement $\hat{g}$ is changed. He needs someone to trade with. Suppose, for instance, that he takes as given the market price of risk κ^a of the other investor. Then the change of consumption over time must be written:

$$dc^b(t) = \frac{1}{A^b(t)}\left\{\left[r(t) + \frac{1}{2}\frac{P^b(t)}{A^b(t)}\left(\kappa^a(t) - \hat{g}(t)\right)^2\right.\right.$$

$$\left.\left. + \left(\kappa^a(t) - \hat{g}(t)\right)\hat{g}(t)\right]\times dt + \left(\kappa^a(t) - \hat{g}(t)\right)dw^a(t)\right\}$$

or expanding:

$$dc^b(t) = \frac{1}{A^b(t)}\left\{\left[r(t) + \frac{1}{2}\frac{P^b(t)}{A^b(t)}\kappa^a(t)^2 + \left(-1 + \frac{1}{2}\frac{P^b(t)}{A^b(t)}\right)\hat{g}(t)^2\right.\right.$$
$$\left.\left. + \left(1 - \frac{P^b(t)}{A^b(t)}\right)\kappa^a(t)\hat{g}(t)\right] \times dt + \left(\kappa^a(t) - \hat{g}(t)\right)dw^a(t)\right\}$$

which, in case $\kappa^a > 0$, says that investor a expects investor b to consume more at time $t + dt$ (or less at time t) if $\hat{g} > 0$ and $P^b/A^b < 1$. As for the difference-of-opinion risk created by the disagreement, which appears as $\hat{g}^2$, its effect is to increase consumption at $t + dt$ (or reduce it at t) if $P^b > 2A^b$. This effect arises from a double reaction of the investor. First, the disagreement causes his own beliefs to become more volatile relative to that of the other investor (hence -1). Second, it also causes his own state price to become more volatile (hence $(1/2) \times P^b/A^b$). The two reactions work in opposite directions.

18.2 The Value of Information

So far, we have taken as given the heterogeneous probability beliefs of investors. We have only postulated a disagreement $\hat{g}$ (and a consequent difference of opinion $\varkappa$) between investors without specifying more precisely where they come from and how they behave over time. It was possible to do that because investors' learning and investors' decisions are separable. In this section, we examine one way in which investors might derive their probability beliefs and in which they might make portfolio decisions on that basis.

18.2.1 Bayesian Updating and Disagreement between Investors

Assume that investors start with prior probabilities but receive no further information than the realized values of the endowment. They form expectations about endowment growth on that basis. The investors' information filtration is now the product of $\mathcal{F}^{\bar{c}}$, the filtration generated by $\bar{c}$, and $\mathcal{H}$, a σ-field on which the priors of the investors are defined. But they differ in their beliefs because they start from heterogeneous priors so that estimates $\hat{\mu}_{\bar{c}}^a$ and $\hat{\mu}_{\bar{c}}^b$ about the endowment drift are different at any point in time. That means each investor m works in his probability space $(\Omega, \mathcal{H} \times \mathcal{F}^{\bar{c}}, P^m)$ but not in the original space $(\Omega, \mathcal{H} \times \mathcal{F}^{\bar{c}}, P)$. The probability measures of the two investors differ from each other, because the priors do and their resulting estimated drift do.

The disagreement process $\hat{g}(t)$ is determined, by the investors' initial priors and, as they learn over time, the process by which they update their estimates. The estimates are formed by taking the expectation of the process $\mu_{\bar{c}}$ under the investor-specific probability measure:

$$\hat{\mu}_{\bar{c}}^m(t) = \mathbb{E}^m\left[\mu_{\bar{c}}(t)|\mathcal{H} \times \mathcal{F}_t^{\bar{c}}\right]$$

For a given current value of the endowment $\bar{c}(t)$, observation of its change $d\bar{c}(t)$, variance $\sigma_{\bar{c}}^2$, and estimated drift $\hat{\mu}_{\bar{c}}^m(t)$, each investor interprets the change $d\bar{c}(t)$ as a *surprise about the drift*. The surprise or shock $dw^m(t)$ is given by

$$dw^m(t) = \frac{1}{\sigma_{\bar{c}}(t)} \left[\frac{d\bar{c}(t)}{\bar{c}(t)} - \hat{\mu}_{\bar{c}}^m(t)dt \right] \tag{18.15}$$

This is the process that enters expression (18.2) above. Equation (18.15) embodies the basic principle of Kalman *filtering*, which is just another formulation of Bayes' formula.[10]

The lines below take up the case of a Geometric Brownian motion with constant coefficients for the endowment. They illustrate the general principle stated in the introduction saying that, when they receive the same public information time after time, Bayesian learners, unless they place infinite trust in their priors, tend to converge to common probability beliefs and the disagreement process is pulled towards zero. Convergence may be deterministic or stochastic (the disagreement becomes a process that mean reverts to zero). In both cases, heterogeneity of beliefs "vanishes" over time.

———————————— ♠ ————————————

To understand better the evolution of the disagreement, let us take as an example the case in which the endowment (here the signal) $\bar{c}(t)$ follows a Geometric Brownian motion, with parameters $\mu_{\bar{c}}$ and $\sigma_{\bar{c}}$ constant:

$$d\bar{c}(t) = \mu_{\bar{c}}\bar{c}(t)dt + \sigma_{\bar{c}}\bar{c}(t)dw(t)$$

Instead of the drift being a process, we just consider a constant relative drift that investors do not observe. Assume that investor m's initial prior on $\mu_{\bar{c}}$ is normally distributed around the mean $\mu_{\bar{c},0}^m$, with variance V_0^m:

$$\mu_{\bar{c},0} \sim \mathcal{N}\left(\mu_{\bar{c},0}^m, V_0^m \right)$$

Obviously, the more uncertain an investor is regarding the true (unknown) value of $\mu_{\bar{c}}$, the higher is the prior variance V_0^m. Applying Kalman filtering, it can be shown that updated beliefs $\hat{\mu}_{\bar{c}}^m(t)$ are also normally distributed at all times t, and the posterior on $\mu_{\bar{c}}$ follows the process

$$d\hat{\mu}_{\bar{c}}^m(t) = \frac{V^m(t)}{\sigma_{\bar{c}}^2} \left[\frac{d\bar{c}(t)}{\bar{c}(t)} - \hat{\mu}_{\bar{c}}^m(t)dt \right] \tag{18.16}$$

which says that investor m updates his estimate of the drift $\hat{\mu}_{\bar{c}}^m(t)$ based on the way the realization $d\bar{c}(t)/\bar{c}(t)$ differs from his prior estimate. The posterior variance is computed as

$$V^m(t) = \mathbb{E}_t^m \left[\left(\hat{\mu}_{\bar{c}}^m(t) - \mu_{\bar{c}}(t) \right)^2 \right] = \frac{V_0^m \sigma_{\bar{c}}^2}{V_0^m t + \sigma_{\bar{c}}^2} \tag{18.17}$$

The change in $\hat{\mu}_{\bar{c}}^m(t)$ is inversely proportional to the volatility of the endowment. A high level of $\sigma_{\bar{c}}$ indicates that the endowment process is noisy, and thus will be weighted less by investor m in

————————————————————————

10 See theorem 12.7, page 36 of Liptser and Shiryaev (2001).

his updated expected growth rate. From the posterior variance expression (18.17), one can see that $V^m(t)$ is increasing in V_0^m: the higher the investor's prior variance V_0^m is, the more the new time-t signal of observing output will contribute to his new, updated belief $\hat{\mu}_{\bar{c}}^m(t)$. As more information is accumulated, (18.17) says that the posterior variance $V^m(t)$ shrinks deterministically over time.

While both investors a and b use the same signal to update their prior, they may be subject to varying degrees of uncertainty about their respective prior: $V_0^a \neq V_0^b$. Equation (18.16) can also be written as

$$d\hat{\mu}_{\bar{c}}^m(t) = \frac{V^m(t)}{\sigma_{\bar{c}}} dw^m(t) \tag{18.18}$$

From (18.18) it follows directly that

Proposition 18.2 $\hat{g}(t)$ *follows the mean-reverting dynamics*

$$d\hat{g}(t) = -\frac{V_0^b}{\sigma_{\bar{c}}^2}\hat{g}(t)dt + \frac{V_0^a - V_0^b}{\sigma_{\bar{c}}^2}dw^a(t)$$

$$= -\frac{V_0^a}{\sigma_{\bar{c}}^2}\hat{g}(t)dt + \frac{V_0^a - V_0^b}{\sigma_{\bar{c}}^2}dw^b(t)$$

We have here an example of an elementary situation in which, following remark 18.1, the process of $\hat{g}$ is stochastic. This is true if prior variances V_0^a and V_0^b are different. In the special case in which both investors have the same prior variance, beliefs will converge deterministically over time, and time-t beliefs are a deterministic function of prior mean, prior variance, and the variance of the endowment process. But even when they do not, the mean reversion $-V_0^a/\sigma_{\bar{c}}^2$ in $\hat{g}$ will pull the disagreement towards zero, stochastically so.

For a second example, one can examine the case of a mean-reverting drift. See Scheinkman and Xiong (2003) and Dumas, Kurshev, and Uppal (2009), also discussed in section 18.4 below. The reader is invited to solve exercise 18.1.

18.2.2   Information and Portfolio Choice

Information received and processed, possibly in the Bayesian way, is used, of course, for decision making – in our case, for portfolio choice. Models of incomplete information can be used to ask whether information is a complement or substitute of portfolio diversification.[11],[12] Consider an investor who can invest in a riskless asset and participate either in a market in which a risky asset subject to one risk source is traded or in a market where an asset subject to two risk sources is traded.

---

11 The following example builds on an application in Luciano and Tolomeo (2016a).

12 Here is a statement by a smart MBA student, who was taking the asset-management class at INSEAD: "Diversification is an excuse for lack of analysis."

In market #1, a riskless asset, with zero rate of return, and risky security #1, with price $S_1(t)$ at time t, are traded. In market #2, a riskless asset, with zero rate of return, and risky security #2, with price $S_2(t)$ at time t, are traded.

The dynamics of the risky asset S_1, on $(\Omega, \mathcal{F}, P, \mathcal{F})$, where $\mathcal{F}$ is the filtration generated by the Brownian motion w_1, is

$$\frac{dS_1(t)}{S_1(t)} = \mu dt + \sigma d\Im_1(t); S_1(0) > 0 \qquad (18.19)$$

and the state variable $\Im_1$ is specified as an Ornstein-Uhlenbeck process:

$$d\Im_1(t) = -\vartheta_1 \Im_1(t)dt + dw_1(t); \Im_1(0) = 0 \qquad (18.20)$$

with $\vartheta_1 > 0$. Notice that the conditionally expected rate of return of the security is time varying and equal to: $\mu - \sigma\vartheta_1\Im_1(t)$. And $\Im_1$ (and S_1) are fully observed.

Assume that the utility function of the investor is logarithmic so that he maximizes the long-run rate of growth of his wealth. This means that his objective function is:[13]

$$\max_x \left(\lim_{T \to \infty} \frac{1}{T} \ln(W) \right)$$

where x is the share of wealth W invested in the risky asset. If the investor participates in market #1 and buys security #1, the maximization problem is solved under the constraint

$$\frac{dW(t)}{W(t)} = x(t)\frac{dS_1(t)}{S_1(t)}$$

with dS_1/S_1 given by (18.19, 18.20). In market #1, the optimal strategy x^* and value function J computed at time 0 are

$$x^*(t) = \frac{\mu - \sigma\vartheta_1\Im_1(t)}{\sigma^2}$$

$$J(x) = \frac{\mu}{2\sigma^2} + \frac{\vartheta_1}{4}. \qquad (18.21)$$

The dynamics of security #2 of market #2 incorporate one additional source of risk:

$$\frac{dS_2(t)}{S_2(t)} = \mu dt + \sigma dY(t); S_2(0) > 0 \qquad (18.22)$$

$$Y(t) = p_1\Im_1(t) + p_2\Im_2(t)$$

$$d\Im_2(t) = -\vartheta_2\Im_2(t)dt + dw_2(t); \Im_2(0) = 0$$

---

13 This form of objective function simplifies the derivations because the HJB equation for it is linear. In chapter 19, we encounter again this kind of objective function.

The weights p_j of the state variables $\Im_j$ in the "pooled signal" Y are positive $p_1, p_2 > 0$, and their square sum up to 1: $\sum_{j=1}^{2} p_j^2 = 1$.[14] The Brownian motions w_1, w_2 are independent, $\vartheta_1, \vartheta_2 > 0$ and $\vartheta_1 \neq \vartheta_2$. The parameters ϑ_j are positive to guarantee mean reversion. Mean reversion is different across processes of the $\Im$ type to distinguish between signals with different persistence, or that "fade out" at different speeds. Notice that the conditionally expected rate of return of the security is time varying and equal to: $\mu - p_1\sigma\vartheta_1\Im_1(t) - p_2\sigma\vartheta_2\Im_2(t)$.

If the investor invests in market #2, his portfolio is more diversified than it is when he invests in market #1. But he has incomplete information because, while he knows μ and σ and the weights p_j, he does not observe separately the realizations of the processes $\Im_j$. He observes only Y, which provides incomplete information, since the conditional correlation between Y and $\Im_1$ is equal to $p_1 < 1$ and the conditional correlation between Y and $\Im_2$ is equal to $p_2 < 1$. His filtration, called $\mathcal{F}^U$, is the filtration generated by Y. Here and below, the superscript U stands for "uninformed." He develops *estimates* $\hat{\Im}_1(t)$, $\hat{\Im}_2(t)$ of the current values of $\Im_1(t)$ and $\Im_2(t)$. Under his own filtration and probability measure, the risky asset follows the SDE:

$$\frac{dS_2(t)}{S_2(t)} = \left[\mu - p_1\sigma\vartheta_1\hat{\Im}_1(t) - p_2\sigma\vartheta_2\hat{\Im}_2(t)\right]dt + \sigma\,dw^U(t)$$

where $\hat{\Im}_1$, $\hat{\Im}_2$ are obtained from filtering, as was done above in (18.15) and (18.16) above:[15]

$$d\hat{\Im}_1(t) = -\vartheta_1\hat{J}_1(t)dt + \hat{j}_1 dw^U(t)$$
$$d\hat{\Im}_2(t) = -\vartheta_2\hat{J}_2(t)dt + \hat{j}_2 dw^U(t)$$

and where:

$$\hat{j}_1 = \frac{\vartheta_1 - \sqrt{p_1^2\vartheta_2^2 + p_2^2\vartheta_1^2}}{p_1(\vartheta_1 - \vartheta_2)}; \qquad \hat{j}_2 = \frac{-\vartheta_2 + \sqrt{p_1^2\vartheta_2^2 + p_2^2\vartheta_1^2}}{p_2(\vartheta_1 - \vartheta_2)}$$

In market #2, the optimal strategy x^{*U} of the uninformed investor and his value function J^U computed at time 0 are

$$x^{*U}(t) = \frac{\mu + \sigma\left(\hat{\Im}_1(t) + \hat{\Im}_2(t)\right)}{\sigma^2}$$

$$J^U(x) = \frac{\mu^2}{2\sigma^2} + \frac{\vartheta_1(1+p_2^2) + \vartheta_2(1+p_1^2) - 2\sqrt{\vartheta_2^2 p_1^2 + \vartheta_1^2 p_2^2}}{4} \tag{18.23}$$

By paying an information fee of ϕ utility units per unit of time, however, the investor can gain access to full information about the separate state variables $\Im_1$ and $\Im_2$ so that

---

14 The restriction on the sum of the squared weights p_j just serves the purpose of making the instantaneous variance of Y equal to one.

15 Again, see theorem 12.7, page 36 of Liptser and Shiryaev (2001).

the process for S_2 under his filtration is as in equation (18.22). In market #2, the optimal strategy x^I of the informed investor and his value function J^I are

$$x^{*I}(t) = \frac{\mu - \vartheta_1 \sigma p_1 \Im_1(t) - \vartheta_2 \sigma p_2 \Im_2(t)}{\sigma^2}$$

$$J^I(x, \phi) = \frac{\mu^2}{2\sigma^2} + \frac{(1 - p_1^2)\vartheta_2 + p_1^2 \vartheta_1}{4} - \phi \qquad (18.24)$$

There exists a level of information fee ϕ^* above which the indirect utility of the investor if uninformed becomes greater than the one if informed, so that staying uninformed is preferable:

$$\phi^* = \frac{1}{2}\left(\sqrt{\vartheta_2^2 p_1^2 + \vartheta_1^2 p_2^2} - \vartheta_2 p_1^2 - \vartheta_1 p_2^2 \right)$$

To decide at time 0 which market to enter and, if one enters market #2, whether to pay the information fee, we compare the three indirect utilities J, J^U, and J^I. For that, one must make assumptions on the weights of the risk factors in Y, as well as on their mean reversion, that is, on the parameters $\{p_j\}$ and $\{\vartheta_j\}$.

Luciano and Tolomeo (2016a) study first the case in which the first signal mean reverts more slowly than the second, meaning that it is more persistent. They take the case in which the mean reversion parameters are increasing in arithmetic sequence: $\vartheta_1 < \vartheta_2, \vartheta_1 = \vartheta_2/2$. By comparing the derived utility functions J, J^U, and J^I, they show that the optimal policy of the investor is:

- to diversify (that is, enter market #2) and buy information, as long as $\phi < \phi^*$ ($J < J^U < J^I$),

- to stay uninformed but still diversify when $\phi > \phi^*$ ($J < J^I < J^U$).

Diversification and information are complements as long as $\phi < \phi^*$, that is, when information is not very costly. They are not when $\phi > \phi^*$.

Consider now the case in which the mean reversion parameters are decreasing in arithmetic sequence, from the first to the second factor, so that the first factor is less persistent than the second. The optimal choice of the investor is to stay undiversified in market #1, independently of the cost of information. Buying information on an asset which diversifies but is more noisy than the less diversified asset is of no value ($J > J^I > J^U$).

The model permits to study also under-diversification, that always occurs, in similar models, specifically van Nieuwerburgh and Veldkamp (2010), if the utility function is myopic (or CRRA) and returns are Gaussian. In van Nieuwerburgh and Veldkamp (2010) the phenomenon of under-diversification is studied in a static setting: information is released once; portfolio selection occurs once. Luciano and Tolomeo (2016a) show that, with risk factors – that can also be interpreted as "signals" – with different persistence, under-diversification does not always occur: it does only if the costs of acquiring information are high and the signal has low persistence. So, in comparison with the existing, static literature, a dynamic model of contemporaneous choice of information and diversification permits to explore much better the links between the importance of the signals over time and the cost of information.

18.3   Equilibrium

In this section, we revert to the situation of section 18.1 and take as given the heterogeneous probability beliefs of investors. We draw implications for equilibrium that hold irrespective of the way investors derived their expectations.

In an economy with heterogeneous investors, the equilibrium to be determined is a set of *price process parameters* $(\mu^m(t), r(t), \sigma(t))$ as well as investors' consumption and trading strategies $(c^m(t), \theta^m(t))$. Investor m's consumption strategy $c^m(t)$ is optimal given m's perception about the processes $d\bar{c}(t)$, $dS(t)$, and $dB(t)$, and the chosen trading strategy $\theta^m(t)$ finances this consumption policy. We can either calculate an equilibrium using market clearing or maximize an aggregate welfare function built from both investors' objective functions (18.11, 18.12) weighted by *fixed weights* $1/\lambda_0^b$ and $1/\lambda_0^a$ as follows:[16]

$$\bar{u}^b(\bar{c}, \varkappa) \triangleq \max_{\{c^a, c^b\}} \frac{1}{\lambda_0^a} \varkappa \times u^a(c^a) + \frac{1}{\lambda_0^b} u^b(c^b) \tag{18.25}$$

subject to:

$$c^a + c^b \leq \bar{c}$$

***Remark* 18.2**   *Basak (2000, 2005) introduces fluctuating weights to construct a representative agent. In a complete market, Negishi weights are constant. Negishi weights* multiplied by probability beliefs *such as $\varkappa(t)/\lambda_0^a$ fluctuate. And they do so exogenously following, for instance, the Bayesian rules outlined in section 18.2.1 above. The situation here is very different from the case of incomplete markets. There – although that was not very useful (see section 15.2) – we did construct a representative agent, as Cuoco and He (1994) had done. But the weights fluctuated stochastically and* endogenously.

If we choose the direct calculation based on market clearing, we write:

$$c^a(t) + c^b(t) = \bar{c}(t)$$
$$\theta^a(t) + \theta^b(t) = 0$$
$$W^a(t) + W^b(t) = 0$$

Aggregate output must be consumed in its entirety, and both assets are in zero net supply, so that aggregate financial wealth must also be zero. Writing the first equation more explicitly,

---

16 We write $\bar{u}^b$ to keep track of the fact that, with this definition, the expected value of that utility function is to be taken under the probability measure of investor b. $\bar{u}^a$ would be equal to $\bar{u}^b/\varkappa$.

as in (18.14) and (18.13), to take account of first-order conditions:

$$\mathfrak{h}^a\left(\lambda_0^a\frac{\xi^b(t)}{\varkappa(t)}\right) + \mathfrak{h}^b\left(\lambda_0^b\xi^b(t)\right) = \bar{c}(t) \tag{18.26}$$

That is a nonlinear algebraic equation where the unknown is the stochastic discount factor $\xi^b(t)$. Given the assumptions, the solution exists but it can be obtained explicitly only under restrictive assumptions. It has the following property:

Proposition 18.3 *The stochastic discount factor depends on the two exogenous processes $\bar{c}$, aggregate output, and $\varkappa$, the difference of opinion.*

These two are, in this special case, perfectly conditionally correlated with each other with a sign of the correlation that depends on disagreement $\hat{g}$ (see (18.6)). Here the shock w serves both as a physical shock and as an information shock. But, in general, $\bar{c}$ and $\varkappa$ would not be perfectly correlated. As we show below, the difference of opinion $\varkappa$ is *an additional risk factor*, which can increase the size of risk premia and make them more erratic (and harder to measure over time).[17]

18.3.1 Equilibrium Consumption and Price Parameters

Applying Itô's lemma to both sides of (18.26) and *identifying diffusion terms*, by a calculation analogous to the one that led to (15.13), we get that:

$$\kappa^b(t) = \bar{A}(t)\left[\sigma_{\bar{c}}(t)\bar{c}(t) - \frac{\hat{g}(t)}{A^a(t)}\right] \tag{18.27}$$

$$\kappa^a(t) = \bar{A}(t)\left[\sigma_{\bar{c}}(t)\bar{c}(t) + \frac{\hat{g}(t)}{A^b(t)}\right]$$

where:

$$\bar{A}(t) \triangleq \frac{1}{\frac{1}{A^a(c^a(t))} + \frac{1}{A^b(c^b(t))}}$$

is the "aggregate risk aversion," which is equal to the risk aversion of the representative agent defined in (18.25). Equation (18.27) can also be obtained from (minus) the diffusion of the marginal utility of the representative agent (18.25).

This formula shows that disagreement adds a layer of time-varying market price of risk and may perhaps be used to explain the *excess volatility puzzle*. By excess volatility puzzle we mean the assertion, on which there is no general consensus, that the volatility of

---

17 But it is not, in the special case under study, a risk factor or a dimension of risk that can be viewed as separate since it is correlated with $\bar{c}$. In the example of section 18.4 below, we present a specification in which $\hat{g}$ is actually a risk factor, which, however, receives a zero price because of the time-additivity of the utility function. With more general lifetime utility functions than the time-additive one, such as those to be seen in chapter 21, $\hat{g}$ would be a third risk factor, which would be priced over and above the risk of output e and the risk of the difference of opinion $\varkappa$.

the stock market is excessive with respect to what it "should" be. In this model the market prices of risk κ^a and κ^b differ from, and their volatility is excessive relative to what they would be in the absence of disagreement, when formula (18.27) reduces to the first component. It is in this sense that here we can state that there is excess volatility.

The reader can now solve exercises 18.2 and 18.3.

Next, identifying drift terms, following a calculation analogous to the one that led to (15.14), we obtain equilibrium interest rates in the economy:

$$
\begin{aligned}
r(t) = {}& \bar{A}(t)\left(\frac{\bar{A}(t)}{A^a(t)}\hat{\mu}_{\bar{c}}^a(t) + \frac{\bar{A}(t)}{A^b(t)}\hat{\mu}_{\bar{c}}^b(t)\right)\bar{c}(t) - \frac{1}{2}\bar{A}(t)\bar{P}(t)\bar{c}(t)^2\sigma_{\bar{c}}(t)^2 \\
& -\frac{1}{2}\frac{\bar{A}(t)}{A^a(t)+A^b(t)}\left[-2 + \frac{P^b(t)+P^a(t)}{A^a(t)+A^b(t)}\right]\hat{g}(t)^2 \\
& -\frac{\bar{A}(t)^2}{A^a(t)+A^b(t)}\left(\frac{P^a(t)}{A^a(t)} - \frac{P^b(t)}{A^b(t)}\right)\bar{c}(t)\sigma_{\bar{c}}(t)\hat{g}(t)
\end{aligned}
\tag{18.28}
$$

where:

$$
\bar{P}(t) \triangleq \left(\frac{\bar{A}(t)}{A^a(t)}\right)^2 P^a(t) + \left(\frac{\bar{A}(t)}{A^b(t)}\right)^2 P^b(t)
$$

is "aggregate prudence." Equation (18.28) can also be obtained as (minus) the drift of the marginal utility of the representative agent (18.25).

Expression (18.28) may be compared to the analogous expression (12.17) obtained in the chapter on complete-market equilibrium with homogeneous expectations.[18] As can be expected intuitively, the degree of disagreement matters in the aggregate (second line of the expression), but also in the way the disagreement process covaries with the fundamental risk (third line). We might expect that the higher the risk created by the difference-of-opinion process is (that is, the higher $\hat{g}(t)^2$), the lower interest rates have to be as investors will have a desire to save more, thus lowering interest rates. We examine this matter in more detail in the next section.

———————————◆———————————

Recall that $\hat{g}(t) > 0$ implies that investor a is the more optimistic of the two investors. Hence (18.27) shows that market prices of risk, which will be reflected in investors' portfolios, will accordingly transfer risk across investors – towards the investor that is more willing to bear risk, or rather, more optimistic about the return he will receive for bearing this risk. Before determining in detail the equilibrium risk-free rate, we can obtain from (18.27) a version of the CCAPM that accommodates

---

18 Recall that in that case the interest rate is fully determined by the representative agent's preference parameters (risk aversion $\bar{A}(t)$ and prudence $\bar{P}(t)$), the anticipated expected growth rate of output, and aggregate consumption risk. The higher expected growth rate of output is, the higher the interest rate must be to prevent excess aggregate demand for borrowing in order to invest into the risky asset. Conversely, the more risky the output process is (higher $\sigma_e(t)$), the lower interest rates have to be as investors will have a desire to save more, thus lowering interest rates.

heterogeneity in beliefs across investors using the definition of $\kappa^m(t) = \sigma^{-1}(t)(\mu^m(t) - r(t))$:

$$\mu^b(t) - r(t) = \bar{A}(t)\sigma_{\bar{c}}(t)\sigma(t)\bar{c}(t) - \frac{\bar{A}(t)}{A^a(t)}\hat{g}(t)\sigma(t)$$

$$\mu(t) - r(t) = \frac{\sigma(t)}{\sigma_{\bar{c}}(t)}\left[\mu_{\bar{c}}(t) - \hat{\mu}_{\bar{c}}^b(t)\right] + \bar{A}(t)\frac{\mathrm{cov}(S(t), \bar{c}(t))}{S(t)}$$

$$- \frac{\bar{A}(t)}{A^b(t)}\frac{\mathrm{cov}(S(t), \varkappa(t))}{S(t)\varkappa(t)}$$

where, based on our definition of (conditional, instantaneous) variance and covariance of continuous processes in chapter 5, the first covariance is between the percentage returns on S and the ones in the endowment, while the second is between the former and the percentage changes in $\varkappa(t)$. For any given risk aversion, the difference of opinions introduces additional terms in the CAPM. Furthermore, we have seen that $\bar{c}$ and κ are perfectly, sometimes positively, sometimes negatively correlated. Empirically speaking, it is not straightforward to measure $\hat{\mu}_{\bar{c}}^b$ and $\varkappa$. Survey data of analysts' forecasts of earnings would help. Agent b's perception on equilibrium compensation for carrying risk – as well as the observed compensation $\mu(t) - r(t)$ – are determined by systematic risks, that is, by the way the stock covaries with aggregate consumption risk and with the difference of opinion, captured by $\varkappa(t)$.

18.3.2   Consensus Beliefs

Recall that we have been working with four probability measures: (i) the effective measure (with endowment drift $\mu_{\bar{c}}$), which is of no use to investors because they do not know the truth, (ii, iii) the subjective or "perceived" measures P^a and P^b of the two investors and (iv) the pricing measure (in various forms). We introduce now a fifth probability measure, called the "consensus probability measure" $\bar{P}$ that would aggregate the beliefs P^a and P^b of both investors.

Following Jouini and Napp (2007), we define a pseudo-representative investor with fixed weights $1/\lambda_0^m$. Let his utility function $\bar{u}$ be defined state by state exactly as in (12.11). This pseudo-representative investor is fictional as it would be the right representative investor for the case in which investors had identical beliefs. It is not the same as the proper representative investor that was defined in (18.25) above and that was capable of replicating the competitive-market equilibrium under the investors' subjective beliefs.[19]

---

19 If beliefs had been identical, the consumptions of the two investors and their Lagrange multipliers would have been different from what they are in this economy. But we imagine artificially that the Lagrange multipliers remain the same as they were in the heterogeneous-expectations economy. For that to be true, we adjust the individual endowments, keeping the aggregate endowment the same.

We now choose the consensus measure. Consider a process $\varkappa$ such that the problem:

$$\max_c \mathbb{E}^b \left[\int_0^T \varkappa(t) \bar{u}(c(t)) dt \right]$$

$$\text{subject to } \mathbb{E}^b \left[\int_0^T \xi^b(t) \left(c(t) - \bar{c}(t) \right) dt \right] \leq W_0^a + W_0^b$$

admits a solution $c(t) = \bar{c}(t)$ with the same prices of risk ξ^b as in the equilibrium with heterogeneous beliefs. We interpret $\varkappa$ below. We write the first-order condition (with a Lagrange multiplier equal to 1 because of the definition of $\bar{u}$):

$$\varkappa(t) \bar{u}_{\bar{c}}(\bar{c}(t)) = \xi^b(t)$$

This last equation entirely defines $\varkappa$:[20]

$$\varkappa(t) \triangleq \frac{\xi^b(t)}{\bar{u}_{\bar{c}}(\bar{c}(t))}$$

We show now that:

Proposition 18.4 $\varkappa$ *so defined is not a martingale under* P^b.

Proof. The drift under P^b is:

$$\frac{-r(t)\xi^b(t)}{\bar{u}_{\bar{c}}(\bar{c}(t))} - \frac{\xi^b(t)}{\bar{u}_{\bar{c}}(\bar{c}(t))^2} \bar{u}_{\bar{c}\bar{c}}(\bar{c}(t)) \hat{\mu}_{\bar{c}}^b(t) \bar{c}(t)$$

$$+ \frac{1}{2} \xi^b(t) \left[-\frac{\bar{u}_{\bar{c}\bar{c}\bar{c}}(\bar{c}(t))}{\bar{u}_{\bar{c}}^2(\bar{c}(t))} + 2\frac{\bar{u}_{\bar{c}\bar{c}}^2(\bar{c}(t))}{\bar{u}_{\bar{c}}^3(\bar{c}(t))} \right] (\sigma_{\bar{c}}(t) \bar{c}(t))^2$$

$$+ \kappa^b(t) \xi^b(t) \frac{\bar{u}_{\bar{c}\bar{c}}(\bar{c}(t))}{\bar{u}_{\bar{c}}^2(\bar{c}(t))} \sigma_{\bar{c}}(t) \bar{c}(t)$$

which is not equal to zero because

$$r(t) \neq \bar{A}(t) \hat{\mu}_{\bar{c}}^b(t) \bar{c}(t) + \frac{1}{2} \left[-\bar{P} \times \bar{A} + 2\bar{A}^2 \right] (\sigma_{\bar{c}}(t) \bar{c}(t))^2$$

$$- \bar{A}(t)^2 \left[\sigma_{\bar{c}}(t) \bar{c}(t) - \frac{\hat{g}(t)}{A^a(t)} \right] \sigma_{\bar{c}}(t) \bar{c}(t)$$

$$= \bar{A}(t) \hat{\mu}_{\bar{c}}^b(t) \bar{c}(t) + \frac{1}{2} [-\bar{P} \times \bar{A}] (\sigma_{\bar{c}}(t) \bar{c}(t))^2 + \bar{A}(t)^2 \frac{\hat{g}(t)}{A^a(t)} \sigma_{\bar{c}}(t) \bar{c}(t)$$

$$r(t) \neq \bar{A}(t) \left(\frac{\bar{A}(t)}{A^a(t)} \hat{\mu}_{\bar{c}}^a(t) + \frac{\bar{A}(t)}{A^b(t)} \hat{\mu}_{\bar{c}}^b(t) \right) \bar{c}(t) - \frac{1}{2} \bar{P}(t) \bar{A}(t) (\sigma_{\bar{c}}(t) \bar{c}(t))^2 \qquad (18.29)$$

as can be seen by comparing (18.29) to (18.28). $\qquad \square$

---

20 Warning: $\bar{u}_{\bar{c}}(\bar{c}(t)) \neq \bar{u}_{\bar{c}}^b(\bar{c}(t))$. Again these are the two utility functions of two different representative investors.

Because it deviates from martingality, $\varkappa$ is not a change of measure from P^b to any measure. Removing the drift (or "default of martingality") from $\varkappa$ leaves a proper change of measure, which we call $\bar{\varkappa}$.[21] Our definition of the consensus probability measure is $\bar{P} \triangleq \bar{\varkappa} \times P^b$.

Consider any security paying a dividend process ι. Its price is:

$$S(t) = \mathbb{E}^b \int_t^\infty \frac{\xi^b(s)}{\xi^b(t)} \iota(s) ds = \mathbb{E}^b \int_t^\infty \frac{\varkappa(s)}{\varkappa(t)} \frac{\bar{u}_c(\bar{c}(s))}{\bar{u}_c(\bar{c}(t))} \iota(s) ds$$

$$\neq \mathbb{E}^b \int_t^\infty \frac{\bar{\varkappa}(s)}{\bar{\varkappa}(t)} \frac{\bar{u}_c(\bar{c}(s))}{\bar{u}_c(\bar{c}(t))} \iota(s) ds = \overline{\mathbb{E}} \int_t^\infty \frac{\bar{u}_c(\bar{c}(s))}{\bar{u}_c(\bar{c}(t))} \iota(s) ds$$

We would like to know how the price $S(t)$ that actually prevails compares with the price shown in the second line just above, which would prevail in the modified economy where both investors held probability beliefs $\bar{P}$. For that we need to know the sign of the terms by which the rate of interest in the heterogeneous-expectations economy differs from the value given by the RHS of (18.29). These are:

$$-\frac{1}{2} \frac{\bar{A}(t)}{A^a(t) + A^b(t)} \left[-2 + \frac{P^b(t) + P^a(t)}{A^a(t) + A^b(t)} \right] \hat{g}(t)^2 \qquad (18.30)$$

$$-\frac{\bar{A}(t)^2}{A^a(t) + A^b(t)} \left(\frac{P^a(t)}{A^a(t)} - \frac{P^b(t)}{A^b(t)} \right) \bar{c}(t) \sigma_{\bar{c}}(t) \hat{g}(t)$$

The concept of consensus beliefs so defined allows us to derive the following theorems:

Theorem 18.1   *For $A^a = A^b$, the rate of interest under heterogeneous beliefs is higher than under the corresponding consensus beliefs if $2A^a > P^b > P^a$ and $\hat{g} > 0$.*

For the same risk aversion, rates under heterogeneous beliefs are higher if the more prudent agent is also the more pessimistic agent. General intuition would suggest that more pessimistic investors push interest rates down. Likewise, more prudent investors (higher P) push interest rates down. But this theorem says that in a heterogeneous-expectations environment, if the pessimist is also the more prudent, interest rates are higher.

Theorem 18.2   *For $P^a/A^a = P^b/A^b$, the rate of interest under heterogeneous beliefs is higher than under the corresponding consensus beliefs if $2A^a > P^a$.*

For identical ratios P^m/A^m, rates under heterogeneous beliefs are higher if the common value of the ratios is less than 2.

---

21 Needless to say, the diffusion of $\bar{\varkappa}$ is equal to the diffusion of $\varkappa$.

The results on the rate of interest extend to some degree to short-term securities. But even if $P^m(t) < 2A^m(t)$ at all times with probability 1, we cannot extend the theorem to long-term securities because future interest rates might covary with future cash flows, thus providing an effect that could offset the effect on the level of the rate of interest. In figure 18.1 below, we illustrate in a specific setting the impact of heterogeneous beliefs on the prices of long-term securities. It goes in the direction we indicated just now.

Example 18.1   If the utility functions of both investors are quadratic (possibly with unequal risk aversions), prudence is equal to zero for both of them and expression (18.30) is unambiguously positive. Heterogeneity of beliefs reduces short-term securities prices relative to the consensus beliefs defined above.

Example 18.2   If the utility functions of both investors are negative exponentials, risk aversion is constant and prudence is equal to risk aversion. The last term of expression (18.30) is equal to zero. The first term is positive. Heterogeneity of beliefs reduces short-term securities prices relative to the consensus beliefs.

The reader can now solve exercise 18.4.

18.4   Sentiment Risk

We have seen in section 18.2.1 that, when they receive the same public information time after time, Bayesian learners tend to converge to common probability beliefs. To be sustained over long horizons, the heterogeneity of beliefs between investors needs to be regenerated. In this section, we assume that *different investors process differently the public information they receive.*[22] Agents disagree steadfastly about the basic model they believe in, or about some model parameter. Under this approach, agents are viewed as being non-Bayesian, in which case the model belongs in the category of *behavioral asset pricing models* (as do Barberis *et al.* (1998), Daniel, Hirshleifer, and Subrahmanyam (1998), and Hong and Stein (1999)).[23]

Dumas, Kurshev, and Uppal (2009) flesh out this aspect and provide a complete equilibrium theory. They assume that the endowment of the economy behaves as in (18.1) above

---

[22] The alternative is to let investors receive different, private information. See footnote 2. The approach adopted here is more easily tractable while capturing some of the same phenomena as the first one. It is also adopted in the related work of David (2008).

[23] Perhaps one can say equally well, as do Biais and Bossaerts (1998), that agents remain Bayesian and place infinite trust on some aspect of their prior.

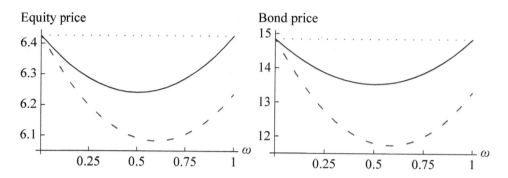

Figure 18.1

The prices of equity and bonds are plotted against ω the relative consumption weight of the sentiment-prone group in the population, for $\varphi = 0$ (higher dotted line) as well as $\varphi = 0.95$ (lower dashed curve and intermediate solid curve). The intermediate, solid curve represents the pure effect of sentiment fluctuations on price. The difference between the solid and the dashed lines is the effect of the covariation between the fundamental and sentiment. The plots are drawn for the case of zero disagreement, $\hat{g} = 0$ (as defined in section 18.1.1). Utility is isoelastic with a risk aversion equal to 3 (see exercise 18.4).

and that the conditionally expected rate of growth is itself a random process, specifically an Ornstein-Uhlenbeck process:

$$d\mu_{\bar{c}}(t) = \varrho \times \left(\bar{\mu}_{\bar{c}} - \mu_{\bar{c}}(t)\right)dt + \sigma_\mu dw_\mu(t)$$

They assume that $\mu_{\bar{c}}$ is not observable by market participants who must all infer the current value of $\mu_{\bar{c}}$ by observing not only the realization of the endowment but also a *public signal s* with stochastic differential equation:

$$ds(t) = \sigma_s dw_s(t)$$

The signal is truly noise in the sense that it has zero correlation ($dw_\mu(t)dw_s(t) = 0$) with the unobserved variable $\mu_{\bar{c}}$ and provides, therefore, no information about it.

However, Dumas *et al.* (2009) let the market participants fall into two categories. Some are "rational" and have figured out by Bayesian methods that the correlation is zero. Others are "sentiment prone" or overconfident about the signal and believe steadfastly that the correlation is a number φ greater than zero.[24]

Because of that, the sentiment-prone investors take the signal seriously and react to it. That is, by construction, an overreaction. They adjust their estimate $\hat{\mu}_{\bar{c}}$ of the conditionally

---

24 Before Dumas *et al.* (2009), Scheinkman and Xiong (2003) had considered two categories of agents, both of which were overconfident but in opposite ways. The more recent literature includes an international version of the sentiment-risk model in Dumas, Lewis and Osambela (2017) and a model by Andrei and Hasler (2015) in which the correlation φ fluctuates to reflect the time-varying attention to news paid by stock market investors.

expected rate of growth of the endowment according to whether the signal indicates positive or negative growth, whereas the rational, Bayesian agents do not. That is the mechanism by which heterogeneity of beliefs is regenerated and a motive for trading (or "speculating") is created.

Depending on the signal, the sentiment-prone investors buy or sell the risky security, in this way creating excess volatility in the returns. Given their probability beliefs, both categories of investors optimize their respective decisions, thinking that the other category is wrong: they "agree to disagree" but take into account the vagaries of the others and the risk or "noise" they create in the market place.

Assuming isoelastic utility with equal risk aversions for both categories of investors, Dumas *et al.* are able to solve explicitly for the equilibrium using the exponential affine-quadratic class of functions, which the reader encountered already in chapters 13 and 16, and compute the optimal reaction of the rational investors.

Figure 18.1 – somewhat in the spirit of theorem 18.2 – illustrates that, in this specific setup the prices of long-term securities are lower when expectations are heterogeneous. Figure 18.2 illustrates that this heterogeneous-investor model just described produces "excess" volatility in comparison with the corresponding homogeneous-market model. The figure is drawn for a zero current value of the disagreement $\hat{g}$ but reflects the fact that investors will disagree in the future. Unfortunately, the same effect also produces excess volatility in the bond market, over and above what the data would indicate, and excess correlation between the two markets.

The risk created by the vagaries of others, which is internal to the financial market and is added to the pure economic risk of output, is called "*sentiment risk.*" It is the risk that a security will be valued in the future at a price different from the rational-expectations price. Others have called it "valuation risk" or "trading risk."[25] The presence of sentiment-prone investors not only provides a separate risk factor, which distorts the stock and bond markets, but also scares away rational, risk-averse investors. In the words of De Long *et al.* (1990), "noise traders create their own space."

Dumas *et al.* also show that, for this reason, the sentiment-prone investors lose money only very slowly.[26] Their consumption share remains close to its initial level for hundreds of years. Because they are not eliminated quickly by a process akin to a Darwinian one and, therefore, survive for a long time, the hypothetical presence of such investors should be taken into account by economists. Heterogeneity of beliefs is a legitimate way to model heterogeneity of agents even in the fairly long run.

---

25 See Albuquerque *et al.* (2016).

26 Kogan *et al.* (2006) and Yan (2008) had done the same before, with non-time-varying expectations.

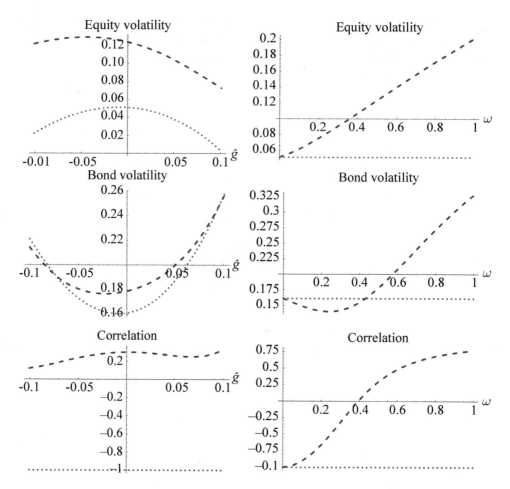

Figure 18.2

Conditional volatilities of equity and bond returns and their conditional correlation. The first column of this figure plots against disagreement, $\hat{g}$ as defined in section 18.1.1 (except that, here, $\hat{g}$ is not normalized by $\sigma_{\tilde{c}}$), the volatilities of equity and bond returns and their correlation, assuming that the two groups of investors have equal weight. In the second column of this figure, the same quantities are plotted but now against the relative consumption weight of the sentiment-prone group in the population, assuming that $\hat{g} = 0.03$. There are two curves in each plot: the dotted curve is for the case of proper beliefs ($\varphi = 0$) and the dashed curve is for sentiment-prone beliefs ($\varphi = 0.95$). Source: Figure 2 in Dumas *et al.* (2009).

18.5   Conclusion

We have developed a complete-market equilibrium in which investors' expectations are heterogeneous and fluctuate over time. The risk created by changes in the beliefs of others is priced, over and beyond the consumption risk premium. We refer to that risk as "sentiment risk" or "valuation risk." We showed that differences of opinions and disagreement create excess volatility.

Exercises

18.1. Assume that the endowment of the economy behaves as in equation (18.1) and that the conditionally expected rate of growth is itself a random process, specifically an Ornstein-Uhlenbeck process:

$$d\mu_{\bar{c}}(t) = -\varrho \times \left(\mu_{\bar{c}}(t) - \bar{\mu}_{\bar{c}}\right)dt + \sigma_\mu dw_\mu(t)$$

Assume that $\mu_{\bar{c}}$ is not observable by any investor m so that he infers the current value of $\mu_{\bar{c}}$ by observing only the realization of the endowment. Assume that investor m's initial prior on $\mu_{\bar{c}}$ is normally distributed around some mean $\mu_{\bar{c},0}^m$, with variance V_0^m but that the process has been running for a long period of time and has reached a steady state so that the role of these initial prior values has vanished. Calculate the process $\left\{\hat{\mu}_{\bar{c}}^m(t)\right\}$ and the process for the disagreement between any two investors $\{a,b\}$.

18.2. Specify the equilibrium of section 18.3.1 for the case in which investors are CRRA, and for the case in which they are logarithmic. In particular, obtain the risk premium and the CCAPM.

18.3. Consider the equilibrium of section 18.3.1. There the only resources of the economy were the endowments received by investors. It was assumed that the market was complete and that any security available was in zero net supply. Otherwise, the exact menu of available securities was not specified. How would you modify the equations describing this equilibrium to include additional resources in the form of dividends or coupons received from firms the liabilities of which are in positive supply?

18.4. Suppose that the utility functions of two investors are of the power type with equal exponent, that is, equal relative risk aversion, show that heterogeneity of beliefs reduces short-term securities prices relative to the consensus beliefs if and only if relative risk aversion is greater than one.

19 Stopping, Regulation, Portfolio Selection, and Pricing under Trading Costs

The financial sector of the economy issues and trades securities. But, more importantly, it provides a *service* to clients, such as the service of accessing the financial market and trading. This service is provided at a cost. Understanding this cost and its effect on financial-market equilibrium is as important to the financial industry as is the cost of producing chickpeas to the chickpea industry.

In this chapter, we do not provide microfoundations for the cost of Finance. We take the cost function as given but we choose the functional form in such a way that it reflects one special and important feature of the cost of financial services. The distinguishing feature is this. Producers of chickpeas only produce chickpeas and consumers only buy chickpeas. Producers collect a revenue and the consumers pay it. Philippon (2015) writes the user cost of Finance as the sum of the rate of return to a saver plus the unit cost of financial intermediation. The cost of financial intermediation is then the spread between the borrowing and the lending rates. That formulation presupposes that a saver is always a saver and a borrower always a borrower. The question of choosing between being a saver or a borrower is not on the table.

But financial-market investors sometimes buy and at some other times sell the very same security. In both cases they pay a unit cost to the institution that organizes the market. The cost of trading is always positive irrespective of the direction of the trade. The absence of frictions, which was assumed in the first part of the book, implied, among other things, the optimality of continual interventions on the portfolio mix, which may not be realistic. The cost of trading creates a friction in the trading activity and induces investors not to trade when they otherwise would have. In the real world, investors buy financial securities and for a while do no re-trade them, a behavior consistent with trading costs.

We want to draw the consequences for investment decisions. In the presence of trading costs, be they fixed with respect to the amount of the transaction or proportional to it, realistic, non-continual rebalancing policies can be explained in a utility-based, perfectly rational model of portfolio selection. When costs are fixed, policies involving adjustment at all times would evidently be a suicide. When costs are variable, these policies, together with the infinite-variation nature of Wiener processes, would produce infinite costs over any finite period of time. Still a suicide.

While we do not investigate the origin of the cost of Finance, we must show that its size is not negligible. For that, we need to be aware of what it includes. Trading costs have to be interpreted not only as bid-ask spreads or brokerage fees, but also as the opportunity cost of time devoted to portfolio selection and, above all, to information acquisition. When these activities are delegated to an intermediary, the opportunity cost becomes an effective, pecuniary one for the investor. Three recent papers throw a lot of light on this issue.

French (2008) shows that the magnitude of spreads, fees, and other trading costs, in spite of increasing competition and technological advances, is not negligible. At the same time, it is not very large. He provides an estimate of the difference between these costs and the costs one would pay simply holding the market portfolio. This estimate, which he names "the cost of active investing," can be interpreted as a lower bound of the actual costs for spreads and fees. His estimate, averaged over the period 1980-2006, is 0.67% of the aggregate market value of financial securities, per year. That means that, relative to the inventory to be adjusted (as opposed to the size of the trade), trading costs represent on average at least 0.67% of it. Going into some more detail, in French's estimates, spreads are not differentiated across investors: they are measured by the revenues of brokerage firms and dealers. They amount to 146 basis point in 1980, down to 11 basis points in 2006. As concerns information-gathering costs, the cost of time devoted to portfolio selection and, above all, to information acquisition, is quite difficult to estimate. It can be proxied by the fees paid in order to get the service offered by a third party. French calls this the "cost of price discovery." Fees are differentiated for different categories of investors. US mutual funds (including Exchange Traded Funds, closed and open-end funds), for instance, used to spend more than 2% in 1980, which went down to less than 1% in 2006. Institutional investors spent 34 basis points in 1980, 23 in 2006. On average, funds of hedge funds required a fee of more than 6.5% of managed assets, over the period 1996 to 2007.

The second paper we mention is by Philippon (2015). It provides the most comprehensive account to date of the cost of Finance. He writes: "We can think of the finance industry as providing three types of services: (i) liquidity (means of payments, cash management); (ii) transfer of funds (pooling funds from savers, screening, and monitoring borrowers); (iii) information (price signals, advising on mergers and acquisitions). Financial firms typically produce a bundle of such services. For instance, risk management uses all three types of activities. Services of type (i) and (ii) typically involve the creation of various financial assets and liabilities." With this definition, he shows that the total value added of the financial industry is remarkably proportional to the total amount "intermediated," where the latter is defined as a mix of stocks of debt and equity outstanding, and flows occurring in the financial industry. The coefficient of proportionality is remarkably constant at 2% throughout the twentieth century.[1]

The third paper is by Novy-Marx and Velikov (2015). We are all aware of the enormous amount of research work that went into the empirical analysis of "pricing anomalies," revealed by investment strategies the average return of which cannot be explained by some kind of CAPM. Pricing anomalies discovered by academics and eagerly sought by professional investors number in the hundred. Novy-Marx and Velikov carefully estimate the cost of implementing each of twenty-three strategies. The costs they find range from 0.03%/month for the "Gross Profitability" strategy to 1.78%/month for the "Industry Relative Reversals" strategy. They conclude that most known asset pricing anomalies do not remain profitable after accounting for transaction costs. In particular, only two of the strategies that have more than 50% one-sided monthly turnover remain profitable. However, if the trading time is chosen so that transaction costs are minimized, most of the latter strategies remain profitable. And the most effective minimization technique is of the type we will describe in sections 19.3 and 19.4 below, the theoretically rational one. The message of Novy-Marx and Velikov then is that transaction costs do matter and must be taken into account when testing the validity of a CAPM.

In this chapter, we examine optimal portfolio and trading decisions that are either irreversible or reversible at a cost. Section 19.1 links the costs to different mathematical formulations. Whatever be the size of the costs involved, the decision rules to be considered and the resulting behavior of investors are different in nature from the classical controls adopted so far in the book. These decisions are either of the *optimal stopping* type, if they consist in stopping a stochastic process, or of the *singular or impulse control* type, if they consist in intervening on the process and then letting it go on further. In section 19.2 we describe an irreversible decision and summarize the mathematical tools needed to solve for it. In section 19.2.1 we provide an example, namely the American-option exercise, and comment on its solution for finite and infinite horizon. In section 19.3 we present a reversible decision and the mathematical tools needed for its solution under an infinite-horizon hypothesis. In sections 19.4 and 19.5 we study, as its main application, the portfolio selection with trading costs. The two sections are devoted to variable and fixed adjustment costs, respectively. In section 19.6 we examine option pricing with trading cost. Section 19.7 is devoted to equilibrium, the ensuing section concludes.

The mathematics that back this chapter are different from that used in the rest of the book. They are in fact quite recent and still under development. We put the emphasis on

---

1 The total amount intermediated is a composite of the level and flow series is created by averaging the two, where flows are scaled by a factor of 8.48 to make the two series comparable. Hence the cost is much more than 2% of the value of trades.

interpretation rather than on the mathematical development *per se*.[2] The basic mathematical tools are relegated to Appendix B of the book.

19.1 Cost Functions and Mathematical Tools

We consider three kinds of cost functions. In all three kinds a kink is present and the cost function is convex. The cost function of the first kind is proportional. The cost of buying securities is proportional to the value of the securities purchased. And the cost of selling is proportional to the absolute value of the value of the securities sold. The second kind is a fixed cost; that is, as soon as even a small amount of securities is traded a finite cost is incurred. The third kind is a limiting case. The cost of trading in one direction is proportional or even zero while the cost of trading in the opposite direction is infinite. In the third case, one talks of an irreversible decision, while in the case of cost functions of the first two kinds decisions should be seen as reversible at a cost. Irreversibility and costly reversibility produce *hysteresis*; if an investor receives two successive shocks in opposite directions, he will not upon the second shock reverse the decision he made upon the first shock.

Irreversibility is present, for instance, when an option, which can be exercised before maturity, that is, an *American option*, is actually exercised, or when a physical investment decision (a "real option"), which can be postponed, is actually taken by a firm. In both cases, the dice are cast; one cannot change his mind later. Reversibility at a cost can prevail in the physical investment case, as a realistic alternative to total irreversibility. It is also the right way to look at portfolio selection with trading cost: one cannot change the security mix for free but one can change it in all directions. It is also the right way to tackle derivative pricing with trading costs: one cannot replicate the option perfectly at each point in time, given that replication is costly.

In the category of irreversible decisions, we concentrate on the American option problem and, in the category of reversible decisions, on the portfolio selection and derivative pricing problems. We refer the interested reader to the article by Pindyck (1988) for real-options decisions. Often the difference between irreversible and reversible decisions is that, in the first case, one has to decide only *when* to act while, in the second one, has to decide *when and how* (or by which amount), since he can still postpone further action to a later date. The first decisions are taken *once and for all*, the second ones are *repeated*. From the modeling point of view, the difference is that the former problems are optimal-stopping ones while the latter are either singular stochastic control or impulse control ones.

Optimal stopping: when the decision consists in intervention on a process, so as to stop it from further wanderings, we are in the classical optimal-stopping framework. The most well-known financial problem involving optimal stopping pertains to the American option.

---

2 See Kabanov and Safarian (2009).

For American options what is relevant is the decision (that is, when to exercise) and the "value" produced by the decision criterion (that is, the ensuing option price). We argue that the intervention or exercise criterion consists in fixing a threshold, above which one does not intervene, but below which exercise is optimal. There is a no-intervention or no-trade region, and an intervention region. Since the time at which the threshold will be reached is stochastic (a "stopping time"; see definition 5.2), the no-arbitrage price of the option is the expectation of the discounted payoff, under the risk-neutral distribution, inclusive of the distribution of that stopping time. When the underlying is Markov, one way to pose the problem of optimal exercise consists in transforming it into a *free-boundary* problem. This permits us to relate the optimal stopping problem to the ones (singular and impulse control) that follow, and to understand the nature of the *boundary conditions* that characterize the free boundary.[3]

Singular or instantaneous stochastic control applies when, unlike in classical control, some of the controls of the problem cannot be described by absolutely continuous functions.[4] It can be proven that, in the presence of costs of interventions that vary non-smoothly with the size of the transaction, optimal portfolio policies are non-classical, that is, not absolutely continuous. Suppose, for illustration, that there exist only a riskless and a risky security with IID returns, that utility is isoelastic, and that trading costs are proportional (non-smooth at zero). Then, optimal policies can be loosely described as follows. Do not intervene as long as the ratio of the risky to riskless security value is within a no-intervention or no-trade interval. Intervene at the maximum admissible rate, as soon as the boundaries of the no-trade region are reached.[5] Do this so as to kick the ratio back just inside the boundaries. Overall, regulate the ratio so that it does not leave the no-trade region or its boundaries.

For singular stochastic control the dynamic-programming approach and its verification theorem hold, as we explain in section B.4 of book Appendix B. It can be shown that a solution exists for specific problems and that the optimal value function is C^2 in the region of no intervention. The HJB equation then applies, and a verification theorem analogous to the one we developed in Appendix B and used in chapter 9 can be developed. We will devote our attention to the *boundary conditions* of the HJB equation, since these make the difference, both from a methodological and an interpretative point of view.[6]

---

3 A comprehensive reference for optimal stopping as applied to Finance is the book by Peskir and Shyriaev (2006), which treats also the non-Markovian case.

4 An absolutely continuous function can be represented as the integral of a *bounded* function of time, using the standard (Riemann or Lebesgue) definition of an integral.

5 For example, if the horizon of the optimization problem is infinite, if the risky asset follows a Geometric Brownian motion and the utility function has CRRA, these boundaries are straight lines in the plane of values of riskless and risky holdings, as in figure 19.2 below.

6 Well-known references for singular control are chapter 8 in Fleming and Soner (1993) and the book by Harrison (1985).

Impulse control applies in the presence of trading costs of a size that is fixed with respect to the transaction, or include a fixed component. In a nutshell, fixed adjustment costs still entail a no-trade interval and a prompt, infinite-rate intervention at its boundaries. However, while in the variable cost case the optimal policy consists in transacting so as to stay just inside the boundaries; in the pure fixed-cost case, as one can easily imagine, the optimal policy consists in reestablishing the portfolio mix that would be optimal in the absence of costs. That mix is positioned inside the no-trade interval. When there are variable costs, in addition to fixed ones, the optimal policy is characterized by two additional ratios, which are on both sides of the optimal frictionless mix, and to which the mix must be returned when the upper and lower frontiers of the no-trade region are reached. While for singular stochastic control we justify in Appendix B the use of a verification approach, for impulse control we omit a similar justification. We refer the reader to Bensoussan and Lions (1982).

19.2 An Irreversible Decision: To Exercise or Not to Exercise

Irreversible decisions of the type "exercise an American option" are important, for at least three reasons:

1. they entail intervention, or *optimal stopping*, when the state variables are in a closed set (the exercise region) or reach its boundary;

2. they permit the introduction in the simplest setting of the *value-matching* or *continuous-fit* and of the *smooth-pasting* or *smooth-fit boundary conditions*, which must be imposed on both singular and impulse controls;

3. they can be attacked, in the finite-horizon case, via a number of equivalent techniques, which will be applicable also to singular control.

We address points 1 and 2 in general terms in this section, while we emphasize the specific case of finite horizon when discussing the American option example, in the next section.

The classical problem of optimal stopping for Markovian processes in continuous time can be formalized as

$$\max_{0 \leq \tau \leq T} \mathbb{E}\big[g[X(\tau)]\big] \tag{19.1}$$

where g is measurable and the process X is Markov, takes values in $\mathbb{R}^N$, and is continuous. We consider the natural filtration of X, which is continuous from the right.[7] This guarantees that the first time at which X enters into a closed set is a stopping time, a property that we use in the sequel. We consider only finite stopping times, even when $T = \infty$.

---

7 See section 2.2.1.

With the Markovian assumption, the problem can be turned into the solution of a *free-boundary problem*. A free-boundary problem is formulated as a PDE together with some boundary conditions. The points at which these conditions apply are not prespecified, but must be found when solving the problem itself.[8]

The Markov setup is special in that, by observing the current state of the system, and without looking at its past behavior, one should be able to decide whether to stop the process or to optimally continue. The space in which X takes values is naturally partitioned into a continuation or no-trade (*NT*) region, and a stopping region, R, whose closedness properties depend on the continuity of the value function of the problem

$$J(x) \triangleq \max_{0 \leq \tau \leq T} \mathbb{E}g[X(\tau)] \tag{19.2}$$

where $X(0) = x \in \mathbb{R}^N$.

If the horizon is infinite, it can be demonstrated that the value function J is the smallest function F that is at once

- greater than or equal to g, for all x:

$$F(x) \geq g(x) \tag{19.3}$$

- superharmonic, that is, such that:

$$\mathbb{E}[F(X(\tau))] \leq F(x) \tag{19.4}$$

over all stopping times τ and starting values x of X.

If the horizon is finite, an extended version of the previous results applies, in which the value function depends on state variables and time.

In order to find J and R we need a technique. The one we analyze here is the transformation into a *free-boundary* problem.

When the horizon is infinite and the process X is a time-homogeneous diffusion:

$$dX = \mu(x)dt + \sigma(x)dw$$

the value function must satisfy the infinitesimal version of the inequality (19.4)

$$0 \geq \mathcal{D}(J) \tag{19.5}$$

where $\mathcal{D}(J)$ is the Dynkin (or differential operator) of J, that is,

$$0 \geq \frac{\partial}{\partial x}J(x)\mu(x) + \frac{1}{2}\sigma^{\mathsf{T}}(x)\frac{\partial^2}{\partial x^2}J(x)\sigma(x)$$

According to (19.3), J should be greater than g on the continuation region *NT* and equal to it on the stopping one, R:

$$J \geq g \tag{19.6}$$

---

8 If, for instance, one sets a single boundary condition for a PDE at some fixed point, the problem is not a free-boundary problem. When one is asked to find a function which solves the PDE *and* also the point at which the boundary condition is true, the problem is a free-boundary one.

Suppose that the boundary of the continuation region, ∂NT, is "smooth." The conditions on J and R, (19.5) and (19.6), are satisfied as equalities but at different points:

$$\begin{cases} 0 = \frac{\partial}{\partial x}J(x)\mu(x) + \frac{1}{2}\sigma^{\mathsf{T}}(x)\frac{\partial^2}{\partial x^2}J(x)\sigma(x) & x \in NT \\ J(x) = g(x) & x \in \partial NT \\ \frac{\partial}{\partial x}J(x) = \frac{\partial}{\partial x}g(x) & x \in \partial NT \end{cases} \tag{19.7}$$

The first is a linear, second-order ODE in J. The value-matching condition, $J = g$, holds on the boundary ∂NT, and it holds independently of the location of the boundary. The third, which requires equality of the derivatives of J and g, is the so-called *smooth-pasting* condition, first introduced in Mikhalevish (1956, 1958), which is a first-order necessary condition of optimality.

Overall, the ODE and its boundary condition give a set of sufficient conditions that give the value function and the transaction and the no-transaction regions. If a function $J(x,t)$ and a number $x^*(t)$ that solve the ODE and its boundary conditions exist, then they are the value function and the boundary location of the no-transaction region (see Van Moerbeke (1974)).

When the problem of finding J and R has to be solved under a finite horizon, the value function cannot be time-independent, $J = J(x,t)$. Then a PDE analogous to the ODE for the infinite horizon case holds, with the boundary conditions appropriately modified.

We illustrate the two cases via the American-option optimal exercise and pricing.

19.2.1   The American Put

Let a security price S follow the Markovian process:

$$\frac{dS(t)}{S(t)} = \mu\,(S,t)\,dt + \sigma\,(S,t)\,dw(t)$$

and let the instantaneous rate of interest be denoted by $r > 0$.

We are interested in pricing an American put option on S.[9] Let its price be some function $P(S,t)$. Because of the no-arbitrage condition, this price is the discounted expectation of the put payoff, when optimal exercise occurs. The exercise value of the put is $[\mathcal{K} - S]^+$.

We are going to verify that, consistently with the previous section, the optimal control policy is of the type: "do not exercise as long as S is above a threshold; exercise when it is at or below it." The optimal exercise boundary is denoted $\widehat{S}(t)$. The problem is to figure out $\widehat{S}(t)$ and the value of the put $P(S,t)$.[10]

As long as the put is alive (that is, not exercised), a replication reasoning analogous to the one in chapter 6 permits us to state that, if P is C^2, it must satisfy the (generalized)

---

9 The call option case is not studied since rational investors never exercise before maturity an American call written on an underlying that pays no dividend.

10 The heuristic argument we present was offered, for the case in which the underlying is Geometric Brownian motion, by Merton (1973b), following Samuelson (1965) and McKean (1965).

Black-Scholes PDE:

$$\mathcal{D}^*(P) + \frac{\partial P}{\partial t} = rP \tag{19.8}$$

Before the exercise time τ_R, the option is worth at least as much alive (P) as dead $([\mathcal{K} - S]^+)$. The option is exercised, that is, we are at τ_R, as soon as it becomes worth the same alive or dead: $P = [\mathcal{K} - S]^+$. This reasoning provides us with two boundary conditions:

$$\text{at } t < \tau_R: \qquad P \geq [\mathcal{K} - S]^+$$
$$\text{at } t = \tau_R: \qquad P = [\mathcal{K} - S]^+$$

We now transform the boundary conditions so that they are formulated in terms of the exercise threshold $\widehat{S}(t)$ instead of the exit time τ_R. Because the put payoff is decreasing in the underlying price, exercise will occur when the latter is *low* enough, or the first time $S(t)$ enters the right-closed set $R = (-\infty, \widehat{S}(t)]$. The above conditions can be written as

$$P(S, t; \widehat{S}) \geq \mathcal{K} - S \text{ for all } S \leq \widehat{S} \tag{19.9}$$

$$P(S, t; \widehat{S}) = \mathcal{K} - S \text{ for } S = \widehat{S} \tag{19.10}$$

Condition (19.10) is the value-matching condition.

Let us add a basic condition applicable to all puts, that follows from their definition:

$$\lim_{S \to +\infty} P = 0 \tag{19.11}$$

This condition reinforces the decreasing property against the underlying price by guaranteeing that the price tends towards zero when the underlying tends to infinity.

We now use the boundary condition to optimally choose $\widehat{S}$. Among all the solutions of the PDE (19.8), satisfying (19.10) and (19.11), we look for the ones that maximize the value of the put by a choice of $\widehat{S}(t)$. The necessary condition is that the first derivative of P be null:

$$\left. \frac{\partial}{\partial \widehat{S}} P(S, t; \widehat{S}) \right|_{S = \widehat{S}} = 0 \tag{19.12}$$

Since equation (19.10) is true for all $S = \widehat{S}$, we can differentiate it with respect to S and $\widehat{S}$ kept equal to each other:

$$\left. \frac{\partial}{\partial S} P(S, t; \widehat{S}) \right|_{S = \widehat{S}} + \left. \frac{\partial}{\partial \widehat{S}} P(\widehat{S}, t; \widehat{S}) \right|_{S = \widehat{S}} = -1$$

and substitute for (19.12). Hence:

$$\left. \frac{\partial}{\partial S} P(S, t; \widehat{S}) \right|_{S = \widehat{S}} = -1 \tag{19.13}$$

This is the smooth-pasting condition of optimality that we had already mentioned in the general optimal stopping setup, (19.7).

Dixit (1993, page 36) explains this condition in the following terms (notation altered by us): "We can get a better intuition for smooth pasting by using the discrete approximation to Brownian motion. At the supposed optimum $\widehat{S}$ [...] the slopes of $P(S, t)$ and $\mathcal{K} - S$ are equal [...]. Suppose the contrary, and show that a suitably constructed alternative policy can do better. The slopes could have been unequal in either of two ways. First we could have $\partial P(S,t)/\partial S|_{S=\widehat{S}} < -1$. That would give $P < \mathcal{K} - S$ to the right of $\widehat{S}$, making immediate termination optimal there, contradicting the supposed optimality of $\widehat{S}$. Or we could have $\partial P(S,t)/\partial S|_{S=\widehat{S}} > -1$. We show that this implies a clear preference for inaction at $S = \widehat{S}$.

Starting at $\widehat{S}$, immediate stopping yields the terminal payoff $\mathcal{K} - S$. Instead, consider the following policy, defined using the discrete approximation. Do not stop the process right away; wait for the next small finite time step Δt, and then reassess the situation. If the next increment is [negative], stop, and if it is [positive], continue. Under our assumption $\partial P(S,t)/\partial S|_{S=\widehat{S}} > -1$, this alternative policy offers a positive net gain over the supposedly optimal policy of stopping at $\widehat{S}$, because we get an average of a move to the [left] up a steeper curve and a move to the [right] along a flatter curve."

Now consider the infinitely-lived put. When the perpetual American option is written on a Geometric Brownian motion underlying and the riskless rate is constant, the partial derivative with respect to time drops out of the equation (19.8), which becomes a second-order ODE. Its coefficients are constant. Also the optimal boundary simplifies: according to the previous section, it is a constant, $\widehat{S}(t) = \widehat{S} \in \mathbb{R}$. As a result of this simplification, the American option pricing admits an explicit solution (see exercise 19.1).

With a finite horizon, existence, and optimality of a control policy of the type "exercise when the underlying goes under a (deterministically time-varying) threshold" can still be guaranteed, according to the optimal stopping results with a finite horizon in Van Moerbeke (1974). However, the PDE (19.8) cannot be turned into an ODE. To the best of our knowledge, no one has provided an analytical, closed-form solution to the corresponding Geometric Brownian motion, free-boundary problem. What we know is that the optimal boundary is unique and satisfies a nonlinear Volterra integral equation of the second kind. Comforted by existence and uniqueness of the boundary, and, as a consequence, of the price, one can then proceed to approximate them via a number of techniques.[11]

One approach works on "variational inequalities" of the type (19.5). The pioneering paper in the field is due to Brennan and Schwartz (1977). It can be backed by the optimal stopping approach of Bensoussan and Lions (1982), as in Jaillet, Lamberton, and Lapeyre (1990). Another approximation approach, which is quite intuitive and simple, consists in randomizing the maturity of the option. For the American case, this approach has been suggested by Carr (1998). See also Peskir and Shyriayev (2006).

---

11 We do not survey here, beyond a reference to chapter 13, the American-option pricing literature which uses numerical techniques. Among these, the most popular one uses a binomial process as an approximation of the Geometric Brownian motion.

To sum up, in the American-option problem restricted to diffusion processes, according to the general theory of optimal stopping, there are two distinct boundary conditions, value-matching and smooth-pasting. What the option example permitted us to understand is the intuition for the two conditions:

- Value matching holds *for any arbitrary choice of the exercise boundary*. It arises only from the fact that the filtration is generated by a continuous process w. The filtration being continuous, there can be no surprise in the value function when reaching the set R. The value function, the price in the option case, must assume the same value it would have in the no-transaction region.

- Smooth-pasting instead is an *optimality condition*, imposed only when the positioning of the boundary is optimized. Indeed, we have obtained it as a necessary condition of optimality.

19.3   Reversible Decisions: How to Regulate

The optimization of reversible decisions is an issue that arises, for instance, in portfolio-choice problems. One is allowed to transact any quantity today, and transacting today does not preclude transacting tomorrow. Portfolio rebalancing differs from option exercise because it is a decision that is reversible at a cost, not a discrete, irreversible decision.

We consider an enlarged class of controls, whose cumulative interventions, which increase and decrease the state of the system, regulate it between an upper and a lower barrier. Two example situations are examined: a basic situation in which a profit function is maximized and a portfolio-choice situation.

In the basic situation, the state variable is controlled at a cost, infinitesimal or not, at an upper barrier and at zero cost at a lower barrier. Between the two barriers, the state variable moves randomly and a flow payoff is produced as a function of the value of the state variable. Overall, the purpose of controlling it is to maximize the present value of such a payoff, net of the costs of control. The upper barrier is chosen optimally. The second is not; it is normalized to zero. This will allow us to discuss:

- the differences between regulating the process at a fixed versus an optimally chosen barrier;
- the effect of different cost structures (variable versus fixed).

In the presence of variable costs only, the adjustment is infinitesimal. In the presence of fixed costs, the control jumps to a lower barrier, $v < u$.

In the portfolio situation, both intervention barriers are chosen optimally. They are denoted l and u. With our specifications, l and u are two constants, not two functions of time. When costs are variable, regulation makes the state variable a diffusion reflected between the barriers l and u. When costs have a fixed component, the optimal policy still entails interventions at some l and u, but the regulated variable is transported to additional barriers located between u and l: $l' > l$ applicable if the process hits l, $u' < u$ applicable if the process hits u.

In sections 19.3.1, 19.3.2, 19.3.3, and 19.3.4, we obtain the controls for the basic situation by means of a heuristic that is motivated by the sufficient conditions of Harrison and Taylor (1978), Harrison and Taksar (1983). In section 19.3.5, we compare them to traditional interventions, and show why the "regulator" class – as opposed to the classical class of intervention at all times – is appropriate.

The portfolio problem is studied in section 19.4.

19.3.1   Base Case: Calculating the Value Function

As in the American option case, we show that, if the control policy is of the regulation type, then the value function satisfies the differential equation and boundary conditions of Harrison and Taylor (1978).[12]

The underlying process
Consider a state variable X that follows an Itô diffusive process regulated between two barriers at 0 and u. Let the coefficients be time-independent. Let L represent cumulative contributions to X, U cumulative withdrawals. The processes L and U are adapted, non-decreasing, with $L(0) = U(0) = 0$. At $X = l = 0$, a costless and rewardless infinitesimal regulator is applied to bring X back just above 0. At $X = u$ another regulator is applied that instantaneously takes X below u, to a level $v < u$. The regulators are positive and negative contributions, dL and dU respectively.[13] In addition, we specify that U increases (by an amount $u - v$ denoted dU) only when $x = u$ while L is continuous, and increases, by an amount $dL > 0$, only when $x = 0$. The regulated process $X + L - U$ behaves as a diffusion that is *reflected* to stay between 0 and u. Overall, the SDE for X is:

$$dX(t) = \mu(X(t))dt + \sigma(X(t))dw(t) + dL(t) - dU(t) \qquad (19.14)$$

Regulation costs
Let the upper regulator dU be operated at a cost dC. Similarly to U, C is a non-negative, non-decreasing process; C increases only when U does, that is, when $X = u$. When it does,

---

12 The problem has been studied, for the case of constant coefficients and linear flow payoff, in Harrison and Taylor (1978) and extended to convex payoffs in Harrison and Taksar (1983). Their achievements are collected in Harrison (1985). Both Harrison and Taylor (1978) and Harrison and Taksar (1983) provide a differential equation and some boundary conditions (value-matching and smooth-pasting) that are sufficient to characterize the value function of the problem.

13 Please notice that here d is not a differential in the sense of ordinary calculus.

the increase is given by a linear cost function $c(dU)$:

$$dC = c(dU) = c_0 + \rho dU$$

where c_0 is a fixed cost component and ρ is a coefficient for the proportional cost component.

ODE for the value function

Let $\phi(x)$ be a strictly concave, increasing, bounded flow-payoff function, and let $\delta > 0$ be the discount rate. Define the value function $e^{-\delta t}F$, which is the discounted value of the payoff stream, or the performance of the (u, v) policy over an infinite horizon:[14]

$$e^{-\delta t}F(x; u, v) = \mathbb{E}\left[\int_t^\infty e^{-\delta s}[\phi(X(s))ds - dC(s)] \,|\, X(t) = x\right]$$

where X follows the SDE (19.14).

In the zone of no regulation $(0 < X(t) < u)$, the process X moves of its own accord. It follows (19.14) with $dL = dU = 0$. The expected change in F is brought about by the flow payoff $\phi(x)$ and the effect of discounting:

$$0 = \phi(x) - \delta F(x) + \frac{\partial}{\partial x}F(x)\mu(x) + \frac{1}{2}\frac{\partial^2}{\partial x^2}F(x)\sigma^2(x) \tag{19.15}$$

This is a second-order, linear, inhomogeneous ODE in F. As we know, its general solution is made of the sum of a particular solution of the corresponding homogeneous equation and a particular solution of the inhomogeneous one. Call $V(x)$ a particular solution of the linear ODE, $F_1(x)$ and $F_2(x)$ two solutions of the associated homogenous equation. Then the general solution is:

$$F(x; A_1, A_2) = V(x) + A_1 F_1(x) + A_2 F_2(x) \tag{19.16}$$

where A_1 and A_2 are two integration constants.

We need a method for calculating $F(x; u, v)$ and, when u and v are choice variables, a method for optimizing them. That will provide us with boundary conditions for the above ODE.

19.3.2 Boundary Conditions: Value Matching

Let us consider the upper barrier first. As long as $dC = 0$, $F(x)$ is defined as the expected value of an integral whose kernel is a bounded flow. The expected value is taken with respect to a continuous filtration. The trajectory of the associated process F, therefore, cannot be discontinuous. Only when a cost dC is paid can a discontinuity exist. When $x = u$, the behavior of F depends on the cost being paid. Let us distinguish the case of finite and infinitely small costs.

---

14 Under an infinite horizon, the control barriers are usually independent of time. At least, they are such when X is an arithmetic Brownian motion. Examples in which the horizon is infinite but the control policies are not independent of time are provided by Guo and Tomecek (2009).

If the cost dC is finite, a jump dF occurs, with $dF = dC$. We write the discontinuity of the value function that occurs because of costs, as follows:

$$F(u; u, v) = F(u - dU; u, v) - c(dU) \equiv F(v; u, v) - c(u - v) \qquad (19.17)$$

This is the value-matching condition again. It simply says that the value function after the adjustment (at v) differs from the pre-adjustment one (at u) because of the costs just incurred c.

If the cost dC is infinitely small when the regulator $dU = u - v$ is of a small magnitude, or v is close to u, equation (19.17) can be expanded into differential terms:[15]

$$F(u) = F(u) - F'(u)dU - c'(0)dU$$

which yields:

$$F'(u; u, u) = -c'(0) \qquad (19.18)$$

In the case of infinitesimal moves and rewards, the value-matching condition, which usually involves the function F itself as in (19.17), takes the form of a condition involving the first derivative F'.

Let us consider the lower barrier. At $X = 0$, the infinitesimal regulator dL applies, the value-matching condition is trivially satisfied. As for smooth pasting, one must have, by symmetry with (19.18):

$$F'(0; u, v) = 0 \qquad (19.19)$$

Applying (19.17) or (19.18), as the case may be, and (19.19), for given u and v, we can find $A_1(u, v)$ and $A_2(u, v)$ from (19.16). Hence, we now have the full value function:

$$F(x; u, v) = V(x) + A_1(u, v)F_1(x) + A_2(u, v)F_2(x)$$

Since the levels u and v are choice variables, it remains to choose them. We study the optimization problem for fixed costs first, for purely variable ones second.

19.3.3 Optimizing the Regulator via Smooth-Pasting Boundary Conditions: The Case of Impulse Control

In this section we seek to optimize the choice of u and v when there are fixed costs; that is, $c(0) > 0$.

It could be shown easily, as Dixit (1989, 1991) did in the special case of Arithmetic Brownian motion, that the derivative of $F(x; u, v)$ with respect to u or v has the same sign

---

15 Here we use the shortcut F' for derivatives of functions of a real variable:

$$F'(x; y, z) \triangleq \frac{\partial}{\partial x} F(x; y, z)$$

for all values of x. Hence, maximizing the performance $F(x; u, v)$ with respect to u and v is equivalent to maximizing $A_1(u, v)$ or $A_2(u, v)$ with respect to u and v. Improving boundary behavior increases the value of the performance index everywhere. A change in u or v either shifts the whole function $F(x)$ up or shifts the whole of it down.

Using the fact that the partials of A_1 and A_2 must be zero for the optimum to obtain, we differentiate (19.17) with respect to u and v. We keep A_1 and A_2 fixed, which are being maximized, because of the envelope theorem. The resulting conditions are:

$$V'(u) + A_1 F_1'(u) + A_2 F_2'(u) = -c'(u - v) \tag{19.20}$$

$$0 = V'(v) + A_1 F_1'(v) + A_2 F_2'(v) + c'(u - v)$$

Write them as:

$$F'(u) = -c'(u - v) \tag{19.21}$$

$$0 = F'(v) + c'(u - v) \tag{19.22}$$

Conditions (19.21) and (19.22) serve to determine the two unknowns u and v. They are the smooth-pasting conditions and indicate that, for optimality, the *time-path* of F' is continuous:

$$F'(u) = F'(v)$$

The marginal value function takes the same value at the point one jumps from and at the point one jumps to. Since we also have the continuity condition (19.17), the solutions for u and v are, in general, not equal to each other, despite the equality in the values of the derivatives.

19.3.4 Optimizing the Regulator via Smooth-Pasting Boundary Conditions: The Case of Instantaneous Control

We now consider the case in which $c(0) = 0$ and the cost is strictly proportional to the distance $u - v$. The cost per unit distance is a constant ρ. There is no fixed component in the cost or reward of regulation. Equations (19.17), (19.21), and (19.22) above, which are still valid, say that the optimal values of u and v become equal to each other. Due to the unbounded variation of X, the process U, which is designed to prevent X from escaping above $u = v$, executes infinite small jumps. In mathematical terms, the optimal process U is continuous with probability one, without being absolutely continuous.[16] This is called a *singular control* process. Consistently with the need to keep a process of unbounded variation at or below a fixed barrier, intervention occurs at the "highest possible speed."

The finding makes economic sense: under purely proportional cost to regulation, there is no sense in taking discrete actions. If one did, one would only increase the probability of having to reverse the move in the future. Infinitesimal moves are optimal. But they must be

---

16 See footnote 4.

done at infinite speed as otherwise the Brownian, which is quick and nimble, would escape from the *NT* region.

Now, if $u = v$, not only do conditions (19.21) and (19.22) merge into one condition, but we have also seen, under equation (19.18) above, that this same condition holds identically for any choice of the trigger point u. We seem to be left without any condition for the optimal choice of u!

Fortunately, we can regenerate an optimality condition. Consider the value-matching condition (19.18) which, under the current solution for F, is

$$V'(u) + A_1 F_1'(u) + A_2 F'(u) = 0$$

Noting again that optimizing F is equivalent to finding stationary values for A_1 and A_2, the last equation can be differentiated with respect to u, keeping A_1 and A_2 constant, to yield:

$$V''(u) + A_1 F_1''(u) + A_2 F_2''(u) = 0 \tag{19.23}$$

We recognize the LHS of this equation as $F''(u)$. Hence, we have as an optimality condition:

$$F''(u) = 0 \tag{19.24}$$

Dumas (1991) called this condition a *super-contact condition*: it is a smooth-pasting condition that now involves the second derivative of the unknown function F. Requirement (19.24) is a natural extension of the smooth-pasting conditions (19.21) and (19.22) to the limiting case of the infinitesimal regulator. Indeed, write and expand (19.21) and (19.22) as follows:

$$F'(u) = -\rho$$

$$0 = \rho + F'(u - dU)$$

or, after further expansion:

$$0 = \rho + F'(u) - F''(u)dU$$

which together yield: $0 = F''(u)$ as in (19.24).

To sum up, when the upper boundary u, and the adjustment level v, are optimized, while the lower boundary is normalized to zero with infinitesimal adjustment, the ODE has to be solved under the value-matching and smooth-pasting conditions, as follows.

If upper adjustment costs have a fixed component, the value-matching and smooth-pasting conditions at the upper barrier u are

$$F(u) = F(v) - c(u - v)$$

$$F'(u) = F'(v) = -c'(u - v)$$

These two equations need to be solved for u and v.

If adjustment costs do not have a fixed component, the value-matching and smooth-pasting conditions at u are

$$F'(u) = -c'(0)$$

$$F''(u) = 0$$

The second implies the first, and has to be solved with respect to u.

At the lower, costless barrier the value-matching condition is

$$F'(0) = 0$$

There is no smooth-pasting condition, since no optimization of the barrier is involved.

The reader can now address exercise 19.2.

19.3.5 Why Not Classical Control?

We can ask ourselves whether the class of classical interventions were not sufficient in order to regulate X. Consider the variable-cost case:

$$dC = \begin{cases} \rho dU \text{ when } dL = 0 \\ \xi dL \text{ when } dU = 0 \end{cases}$$

Imagine that the controls were classical, that is, with bounded derivative against time, which means that we could write them as

$$L(t) = \int_0^t \bar{l}(s)ds \qquad\qquad 0 \le \bar{l}(s) \le \Gamma$$

$$U(t) = \int_0^t \bar{u}(s)ds \qquad\qquad 0 \le \bar{u}(s) \le \Gamma$$

with $\Gamma < \infty$. We show that, if the value function is concave,

- they must be applied at the maximum rate
- they entail intervention at a fixed level of the state variable.

Substituting into the SDE for the state variable X we get:

$$dX(t) = \left[\mu(X(t)) + \bar{l}(t) - \bar{u}(t)\right]dt + \sigma(X(t))dw(t)$$

Apply the tools of classical dynamic programming to this SDE. According to Appendix B, we can then define the value function of the problem, $F(x)$, and write for it at each point in time t the ODE:

$$\max_{\{\bar{l}(t), \bar{u}(t)\}} \left\{ \phi(x) - \rho\bar{l}(t) - \xi\bar{u}(t) - \delta F(x) \right.$$

$$\left. + \frac{\partial}{\partial x}F(x)\left[\mu(x) + \bar{l}(t) - \bar{u}(t)\right] + \frac{1}{2}\frac{\partial^2}{\partial x^2}F(x)\sigma^2(x) \right\} = 0$$

The first-order conditions for $\bar{l}$ and $\bar{u}$ become:

$$\bar{l}(t) = \begin{cases} \Gamma & \text{if } \frac{\partial F}{\partial x} \geq \rho \\ 0 & \text{otherwise} \end{cases}$$

$$\bar{u}(t) = \begin{cases} \Gamma & \text{if } \frac{\partial F}{\partial x} \leq -\xi \\ 0 & \text{otherwise} \end{cases}$$

These conditions tell us that the control is "bang-bang": either one intervenes on X (increasing or decreasing it) at the maximum rate, or one should not intervene. Suppose that the value function is concave. This is true in most applications, including the previous one.[17] Then the first derivative of F, $\partial F/\partial x$ is decreasing. As figure 19.1 shows, it is greater than ρ under a given threshold, call it l, and smaller than $-\xi$ above u.

The previous conditions become:

$$\bar{l}(t) = \begin{cases} \Gamma & \text{if } x(t) \leq l \\ 0 & \text{otherwise} \end{cases}$$

$$\bar{u}(t) = \begin{cases} \Gamma & \text{if } x(t) \geq u \\ 0 & \text{otherwise} \end{cases}$$

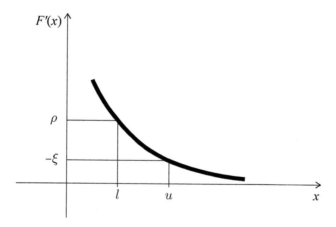

Figure 19.1
The function $\partial F/\partial x$ being decreasing, it is greater than ρ under a given threshold, call it l, and smaller than $-\xi$ above u.

---

17 Sufficient conditions for concavity are given by Harrison and Taksar (1983). It can be considered a consequence of the link between regulation and optimal stopping – which is studied, for instance, by Karatzas and Shreve (1986) – since a smooth function is superharmonic if and only if it is concave.

That is why one should sell and buy at the maximum admissible rate below l and above u, respectively.

This reasoning shows heuristically that a singular control was, indeed, necessary, and that absolutely continuous controls were not appropriate. An analogous reasoning applies to the fixed-costs and impulse-control cases.

19.4   The Portfolio Problem under Proportional Trading Costs

Consider an investor who is facing two securities: a risky security with diffusive price S, of which he currently holds a Euro amount Y, and a riskless security with price B, of which he currently holds a Euro amount X. Let the two state variables: X and Y describe his current securities *inventory*. Note that, under trading costs, wealth, defined perhaps as the sum $X + Y$, is no longer a sufficient state variable. Each position in the inventory is now a state variable.

When no transactions take place, X and Y evolve as prices do, except for the fact that the investor dips into the riskless-security balance (let us call it "cash") to consume:

$$dY(t) = \mu Y(t)dt + \sigma Y(t)dw(t)$$
$$dX(t) = (rX(t) - c(t))dt$$

where c is the consumption rate, $Y(0) > 0, X(0) > 0$.

Every time the investor undertakes a transaction to exchange one security for the other, he/she pays, out of cash, a trading cost equal to $1 - s$ times the value of the transaction, with $0 < s < 1$. Let cumulative values of transactions be denoted by U and L, where U are sales of the risky security and L are sales of the riskless security. Overall, the system of SDEs becomes:

$$dY(t) = \mu Y(t)dt + \sigma Y(t)dw(t) + sdL(t) - dU(t)$$
$$dX(t) = (rX(t) - c(t))dt + sdU(t) - dL(t)$$

Let the objective function of the investor be:

$$\max_{\{c,L,U\}} \mathbb{E}\left[\int_0^T u(c,t)\, dt + \wp(X(T), Y(T)) \,\Big|\, X(0) = x, Y(0) = y \right]$$

where u is the utility of interim consumption, while $\wp$ is the bequest function. The formal and rigorous mathematical treatment of existence of a solution is usually restricted to the case of Geometric Brownian motion with power utility, which we consider in section 19.4.1 below. The intuition we provided above, however, opens the way to the following extension to general cases.

Define the value function

$$J(X,Y,t) \triangleq \max_{\{c,L,U\}} \mathbb{E}_t \left[\int_t^T u(c,z)dz + \wp(X(T),Y(T)) \right]$$

(19.25)

Within the inaction region, the following PDE applies:

$$\max_{\{c\}} \left[u(c,t) + \mathcal{D}^c(J) + \frac{\partial J}{\partial t} \right] = 0$$

(19.26)

where

$$\mathcal{D}^c(J) = \frac{1}{2} \frac{\partial^2}{\partial Y^2} J(X,Y,t)\sigma^2 y^2 + \frac{\partial}{\partial Y} J(X,Y,t)\mu y + \frac{\partial}{\partial X} J(X,Y,t)(rx - c)$$

When a transaction takes place at some stopping time τ_u or τ_l, value-matching must hold:[18]

$$J(x_u + sdU, y_u - dU, \tau_u) = J(x_u, y_u, \tau_u)$$

$$J(x_l - dL, y_l + sdL, \tau_l) = J(x_l, y_l, \tau_l)$$

Expanding:

$$\frac{\partial}{\partial X} J(x_u, y_u, \tau_u)sdU - \frac{\partial}{\partial Y} J(x_u, y_u, \tau_u)dU = 0$$

$$-\frac{\partial}{\partial X} J(x_l, y_l, \tau_l)dL + \frac{\partial}{\partial Y} J(x_l, y_l, \tau_l)sdL = 0$$

we get the value-matching conditions:

$$\frac{\partial}{\partial X} J(x_u, y_u, \tau_u)s - \frac{\partial}{\partial Y} J(x_u, y_u, \tau_u) = 0$$

(19.27)

$$\frac{\partial}{\partial X} J(x_l, y_l, \tau_l) - \frac{\partial}{\partial Y} J(x_l, y_l, \tau_l)s = 0$$

(19.28)

For optimality, smooth-pasting with respect to the stochastic variable Y must hold at the upper action point:

$$\frac{\partial}{\partial Y} J(x_u + sdU, y_u - dU, \tau_u) - \frac{\partial}{\partial Y} J(x_u, y_u, \tau_u) = 0$$

Expanding:

$$\frac{\partial^2}{\partial X \partial Y} J(x_u, y_u, \tau_u)s - \frac{\partial^2}{\partial Y^2} J(x_u, y_u, \tau_u) = 0$$

(19.29)

And similarly at the lower action point:

$$\frac{\partial^2}{\partial X \partial Y} J(x_l, y_l, \tau_l) - \frac{\partial^2}{\partial Y^2} J(x_l, y_l, \tau_l)s = 0$$

(19.30)

---

18 Notation: at time τ_u, $Y(\tau_u) = y_u$; $X(\tau_u) = x_u$; at time τ_l, $Y(\tau_l) = y_l$; $X(\tau_l) = x_l$.

It can be shown, at least under regularity assumptions and specific utility choices, that a solution of the portfolio optimization program will be a solution of the PDE (19.26) subject to the boundary conditions (19.27-19.28; 19.29-19.30) and to the terminal condition

$$J(X, Y, T) = \wp(X, Y)$$

The unknowns are the function J and the position of the trigger points: (x_u, y_u) and (x_l, y_l).

19.4.1   A Semi-explicit Policy Case: Power Utility

The infinite-horizon portfolio problem with trading costs, with a Geometric Brownian motion risky security and isoelastic utility function, has been addressed by Magill and Constantinides (1976) and Constantinides (1986). In order to produce an explicit solution, they assumed a specific, suboptimal consumption policy. Consumption was supposed to be a constant fraction of the riskless security position.

This simplifying assumption was removed in the later literature. Davis and Norman (1990) studied the full problem under constraints on the security parameters that make Merton's optimal portfolio stay between the intervention barriers with trading cost. Their optimal policy keeps the investor "solvent," in the sense that wealth does not become negative. Shreve and Soner (1994) extended the results to parameter combinations that do not make the Merton's portfolio stay between the barriers and do not keep the investor solvent automatically. Both of them provide the appropriate PDE and boundary conditions for the value function, and prove that there is a solution to the corresponding free-boundary problem and that its regulation policy is optimal. The control policy makes the ratio of the risky to riskless security a regulated process. The mathematical background to build upon is given by the existence and regularity of a value function, discussed in the last section of our book's Appendix B. From the computational point of view, they succeed in transforming the free-boundary problem into a system of two nonlinear ODEs with four boundary conditions.

Dumas and Luciano (1991) studied the corresponding problem when the investor aims at maximizing the utility of final wealth, with no consumption on the way and an infinite horizon. The resulting ODE is linear. They provided a semi-explicit solution for the portfolio problem, in the sense that both the value function and the control barriers are determined up to a unique constant, which has to be determined numerically as the solution of an *algebraic* equation. One can also study the problem of maximizing the long-run growth rate of wealth, which is the log-utility special case.

Here we follow the approach in Dumas and Luciano, which proceeds by verification: the candidate optimal policy and value function, determined using the separability and homogeneity properties embedded in the power utility, are shown to satisfy the appropriate free-boundary problem. The boundary conditions include optimality of the intervention region. As a consequence, the control policy is optimal. The only requirement is that the value function be C^2. That will turn out to be true when smooth-pasting is imposed.

It is convenient to assume that the utility function u is isoelastic, since it is then reasonable to postulate that $J(X, Y, t)$ is a homogeneous function in X and Y and that the decision to undertake a transaction is a function of the portfolio composition $\theta = Y/X$ only, with no consideration given to the portfolio size. Then, the region of no transactions in the space (X, Y) is a cone with edges: $\theta = u$ and $\theta = l < u$. The former triggers an increase in U, the latter an increase in L. The no-transaction region is exemplified in the graph of figure 19.2. The amounts invested form a pair: the amount in the riskless asset is on the x-axis while the amount invested in the risky asset is on the y-axis. These two amounts fluctuate randomly as risky-security returns come in and as the riskless interest rate gradually increases the amount invested in the riskless security. The upper straight line is the boundary that, when reached, causes the investor to sell the risky security and buy the riskless one, thereby "kicking in" the pair just below the boundary in the direction set by the proportional cost of trading. The lower straight line is the boundary at which he does the opposite. The middle straight line is the portfolio mix that would be chosen in the absence of trading costs.

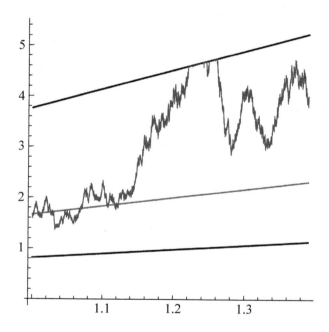

Figure 19.2
The no-transaction region for the problem of portfolio choice with proportional transactions costs. The amounts invested form a pair: the amount in the riskless asset is on the x-axis while the amount invested in the risky asset is on the y-axis. The upper straight line is the boundary that, when reached, causes the investor to sell the risky security and buy the riskless one. The lower straight line is the boundary at which he does the opposite. The middle straight line is the portfolio mix that would be chosen in the absence of trading costs.

The dynamics of the portfolio components without trade are:

$$dY(t) = \mu Y(t)dt + \sigma Y(t)dw(t) \tag{19.31}$$

$$dX(t) = rX(t)dt \tag{19.32}$$

with μ and σ constant, $Y(0) > 0, X(0) > 0$.

The investor problem to be solved is

$$\max_{\{L,U\}} \lim_{T \to \infty} \mathbb{E}\left[\frac{(X(T) + sY(T))^\gamma}{\gamma}\right]$$

In the final-consumption case, any time-discounting factor such as $\exp(-\rho T)$ would be superfluous. Instead, what is essential is to find a factor that keeps the value function bounded when the horizon tends to infinity.

Achieving boundedness in the absence of trading costs

Consider first the same problem without trading costs:

$$\max_{\{Y,X\}} \lim_{T \to \infty} \mathbb{E}\left[\frac{(X(T) + Y(T))^\gamma}{\gamma} \,\middle|\, X(0) = x, Y(0) = y\right] \tag{19.33}$$

subject to (19.31), (19.32). But start from its finite-horizon version:

$$\max_{\{Y,X\}} \mathbb{E}\left[\frac{(X(T) + Y(T))^\gamma}{\gamma} \,\middle|\, X(0) = x, Y(0) = y\right] \tag{19.34}$$

We studied a closely related problem in section 9.2.2. As in chapter 9, there exists a value function for problem (19.34), namely the finite-horizon, no trading costs case. It is the one that solves the corresponding HJB equation:

$$\max\left(rXJ_X + \mu YJ_Y + \frac{1}{2}J_{YY}\sigma^2 Y^2 + J_t\right) = 0$$

with terminal condition $J(X, Y, T) = (X + Y)^\gamma / \gamma$. The solution is

$$\exp\left[-a(1 - \gamma)(T - t)\right]\frac{(X + Y)^\gamma}{\gamma}$$

Here a is given by equation (9.15) in chapter 9, with ρ set at 0 and

$$X + Y = X \times \left(1 + \frac{\mu - r}{(1 - \gamma)\sigma^2 - \mu + r}\right)$$

Now, take the horizon date to infinity as in (19.33), while attempting to keep this value function finite (that is, neither going to 0 nor to ∞). To do this, we have to introduce discounting at the rate $-a(1 - \gamma)$ so that the discounted value function is

$$\exp\left[a(1 - \gamma)(T - t)\right]\exp\left[-a(1 - \gamma)(T - t)\right]\frac{(X + Y)}{\gamma} = \frac{(X + Y)^\gamma}{\gamma} \tag{19.35}$$

which solves the modified HJB equation:

$$\max(\mathcal{D}(J) + a(1 - \gamma)J) = 0$$

where

$$\mathcal{D}(J) = rXJ_X + \mu YJ_Y + \frac{1}{2}J_{YY}\sigma^2 Y^2$$

Stationarity having been achieved, we have set $J_t = 0$.

Achieving boundedness in the presence of trading costs

Analogously, in the infinite horizon case with trading costs, we define the value function $J = J(X, Y, t)$ as

$$J(X, Y, t) \triangleq \max_{\{L,U\}} \lim_{T \to \infty} \mathbb{E}_t\left[\exp(a'(T - t))\frac{(X(T) + sY(T))^\gamma}{\gamma}\right]$$

for some rate a' to be determined, that will keep J bounded. When boundedness is achieved so is stationarity, so that it is clear that $J(X, Y, t)$, in fact, does not depend on time. The PDE becomes

$$\mathcal{D}(J) + a'J = 0$$

while the boundary conditions are

$$J_X(X, lX) = sJ_Y(X, lX)$$
$$sJ_X(X, uX) = J_Y(X, uX)$$
$$J_{XY}(X, uX)s - J_{YY}(X, uX) = 0$$
$$-J_{XY}(X, lX) + J_{YY}(X, lX)s = 0$$

where the boundaries u and l are constant, under the presumption of homogeneity.

Using homogeneity

A homogeneous value function will satisfy both the PDE and the terminal condition. Hence we can write that $J(x, y) = x^\gamma I(\theta)/\gamma$, where $\theta = y/x$. Then the PDE becomes a *linear ODE*

$$\frac{1}{2}I_{\theta\theta}\theta^2\sigma^2 + (\mu - r)\theta I_\theta + \underbrace{(a' + r\gamma)}_{\triangleq \delta}I = 0 \tag{19.36}$$

The boundary conditions become

$$I'(l) = \frac{\gamma}{s+l}I(l) \tag{19.37}$$

$$I'(u) = \frac{\gamma s}{1+us}I(u) \tag{19.38}$$

$$I''(l) = \frac{(\gamma - 1)I'(l)}{1 + \dfrac{l}{s}}\frac{1}{s}$$

$$I''(u)\frac{(\gamma - 1)I'(u)}{1 + us}s \tag{19.39}$$

Overall, the problem consists in finding a' and in solving the ODE (19.36) and its associated boundary conditions (19.37) to (19.39).

Reduction to an algebraic problem

The ODE can be further simplified, and become a constant-coefficient one, by a change of variable, from θ to $z = \ln\theta$. Let $I(\theta) \equiv \bar{I}(z)$; the ODE becomes

$$\frac{1}{2}\bar{I}_{zz}\sigma^2 + \left(\mu - r - \frac{1}{2}\sigma^2\right)\bar{I}_z + \delta\bar{I} = 0$$

In this form, it admits a solution of the type

$$I(\theta) = A_1(l, u)\theta^{k_1} + A_2(l, u)\theta^{k_2} \tag{19.40}$$

where

- the constants k_1, k_2 solve the characteristic equation :

$$\frac{1}{2}k^2\sigma^2 + \left(\mu - r - \frac{1}{2}\sigma^2\right)k + \delta = 0$$

- the integration constants $A_1(l, u), A_2(l, u)$, together with l and u, satisfy the four algebraic equations obtained from the boundary conditions in which we substitute (19.40);

- the constant a' is chosen in such a way that these boundary conditions, which are linear in $A_1(l, u), A_2(l, u)$, admit a non-trivial (non-null) solution. This is achieved by equating the determinant of the corresponding matrix of coefficients to zero. In this way one gets the algebraic equation for a'.

As a whole, the problem is then 100% algebraic, and explicit up to the constant a'. Dumas and Luciano (1991) show that, if the Merton's line is inside the no-trade region, and for reasonable values of the other parameters, one can calculate the constant a'. The resulting policy is simple and the expected time between transactions can be quite large.

The reader can extend this case by solving exercise 19.3.

19.4.2   Comment on Quadratic Costs

One may wonder how restrictive the choice of proportional trading costs is. Variable trading costs could be concave or convex. Proportionality led to simple policies. Would such policies be inappropriate in the presence of other cost components? Suppose that costs are quadratic. Are optimal policies still simple or are they of a different nature?

The result we justify now is that a kink in the (convex) trading-cost function at zero is the crucial feature in determining the nature of the policies. Due to the properties of the Brownian motion, higher-order (such as quadratic) components affect total costs but do not affect optimal policies materially. When considering variable costs, omitting these components has no major consequences on portfolio allocation. This makes the results of the previous section more relevant than they might at first seem.

Suppose that trading costs were proportional to the square of the value of the transaction, with coefficient of proportionality κ. Denote the corresponding transaction $d\Delta$. The dynamics of X and Y would be:[19]

$$dY(t) = \mu Y(t)dt + \sigma Y(t)dw(t) + d\Delta$$
$$dX(t) = rX(t)dt - d\Delta - \kappa(d\Delta)^2$$

Suppose we addressed the portfolio problem in the standard way, as in Merton, with intervention at each point in time. At time t, the investor holds an inventory of securities (x, y). He/she would move to a new portfolio

$$x' = x - d\Delta - \kappa(d\Delta)^2; \, y' = y + d\Delta$$

and pay the corresponding cost. The cumulative trading cost over the life of the investor would be

$$\kappa \int_0^T (d\Delta)^2$$

Because Wiener processes have finite quadratic variation, these costs, even if wasteful (that is, suboptimal), would remain finite, no matter how often one transacted, over a finite horizon.

Compare now with proportional trading costs. A similar policy, of transacting at all times in response to Wiener shocks, would have produced costs equal to

$$\int_0^T |d\Delta|$$

That would have been suicidal, since $\int_0^T |d\Delta| = \infty$.

The contrast illustrates that, with quadratic costs,[20] the Merton approach, of action at all times, is still valid. That is why, if one wants to study the effects of trading costs, he can safely neglect variable, second-order components. However, he cannot disregard variable and first-order, or linear, components, as well as fixed components.

19.5   The Portfolio Problem under Fixed or Quasi-fixed Trading Costs

The study of optimal portfolio policies in the presence of purely fixed costs was initiated by Morton and Pliska (1995), who assumed Geometric Brownian motion risky securities and an infinite horizon. They aim to maximize the rate of growth of consumption, which is a problem similar to Dumas and Luciano (1991) but with $\gamma = 0$. Morton and Pliska wrote a system of six algebraic equations, to be solved numerically, which characterize the value function and optimal policy.

---

19 The equation below assumes that transactions costs are paid out of the cash account. That is not essential for the argument.

20 In a quadratic trading cost function, there is no kink at zero.

Korn (1998) attacked the problem both with fixed and variable trading cost, as well as intermediate consumption. He was able to provide sufficient conditions for the solution of quasi-variational inequalities to represent the value function of the optimality problem and for the corresponding impulse policy to be optimal. He provided the risk neutral and CRRA utility functions as examples, but could not achieve existence of a solution in all cases (power utility and Geometric Brownian motion, for instance).

With fixed costs, all in all, portfolio policies and value function characterizations are less flexible and explicit than in the proportional cost case.

As in the variable case, instead of providing a detailed account of existence and uniqueness of the optimal policy or value function, we give here a heuristic treatment of the problem, which can be used to verify the existence and features of an impulse-control policy. Consider purely fixed costs.

If a transaction involves a fixed-cost c_0, it will typically not be optimal to perform a small transaction. Let us assume that the fixed cost always comes out of the cash account. At the trigger point x_u, X will move from x_u to $x_u + dU$, where dU is now a finite value.

When a transaction takes place at some stopping time τ_u or τ_l, value matching must hold:

$$J(x_u + dU - c_0, y_u - dU, \tau_u) = J(x_u, y_u, \tau_u) \qquad (19.41)$$

$$J(x_l - dL - c_0, y_l + dL, \tau_l) = J(x_l, y_l, \tau_l)$$

For optimality, smooth-pasting must hold at the upper action points:

$$\frac{\partial}{\partial Y} J(x_u + dU - c_0, y_u - dU, \tau_u) = \frac{\partial}{\partial Y} J(x_u, y_u, \tau_u) \qquad (19.42)$$

and also, similarly, at the lower action points. A solution of the portfolio-optimization program will be a solution of the PDE (19.26), namely

$$\max_{\{c\}} \left[u(c, t) + \mathcal{D}(J) + \frac{\partial J}{\partial t} \right] = 0$$

where

$$\mathcal{D}^c(J) = \frac{1}{2} \frac{\partial^2}{\partial Y^2} J(X, Y, t) \sigma^2 Y^2 + \frac{\partial}{\partial Y} J(X, Y, t) \mu Y + \frac{\partial}{\partial X} J(X, Y, t)(rX - c)$$

subject to the boundary conditions (19.41-19.42). The unknowns are the function J and the location of the trigger points: (x_u, y_u) and (x_l, y_l). Typically, action will be triggered when the triplet (X, Y, t) reaches some outer boundary of the state-variables $\times$ time space. It consists in jumping to an inner set of the space strictly inside the outer boundary.

With purely fixed costs, the inner set equates the set that would be optimal in the absence of costs. With fixed and proportional costs, as we mentioned above, the inner set brackets it.

Consider now the case of isoelastic utility, infinite horizon, a Geometric Brownian motion risky security, proportional plus fixed costs. There could be two cones in the (x, y) plane. One is the outer cone: action is triggered when the ratio θ reaches its boundary. The other is an inner cone. One would jump to its edges.

19.6   Option Pricing under Trading Costs

19.6.1   The Inadequacy of the Replication and Super-Replication Approaches

As we argued in section 19.1 and as one can understand from sections 19.4 and 19.5, a policy of portfolio rebalancing at fixed points in time (Leland (1985)) is not optimal. The same is true when a derivative security is included in the portfolio. In the context of a discrete-time binomial representation of the stochastic process for the risky security price, it is possible to construct portfolio strategies that will replicate an option payoff exactly *and* will be self-financing at every node of the tree *inclusive of trading costs* (see Boyle and Vorst (1992)). However, the scheme collapses when one attempts to take the tree to its continuous-time limit, because replication inclusive of trading costs eats away the return from the underlying security. Exact replication is infinitely wasteful for the same reason for which continual portfolio rebalancing was: the (absolute) variation of a Wiener process is infinite.

One way to go is to admit non-exact hedging or replication, with trades occurring only from time to time. That is the approach taken in the article of Leland (1985), later commented upon by Kabanov and Safarian (1997). Leland, however, assumed the timing of trades to be fixed, which, as we shall see, is inconsistent with optimal portfolio policies under trading costs and can become very costly.

To remove the inconsistencies of committing to trades at fixed points in time, a number of authors, including Bensaid, Lesne, Pagès, and Scheinkman (1992), proposed super-replication instead of replication. But Soner, Shreve, and Cvitanic (1995) showed that the super-replicating strategy for a call option consists in buying and holding the underlying security until the maturity date of the option. Hence, the only bound on the price of a call option that the approach provides is the price of the underlying itself. That is not very interesting.

A policy of approximate replication minimizing the expected value of the squared deviations between the derivative and its replacing portfolio values (see for example, Lamberton, Pham, and Schweizer (1998)) would deliver a non-trivial result. It illustrates the idea that it will be necessary to allow deviations above *and* below the target payoff profile. Deviations of one type will have to be weighted against deviations of the other type. Risk cannot be eliminated completely, since perfect replication is infinitely costly and super-replication allows a wide gap at maturity between the derivative and the underlying. From the point of view of Economics, what is required is a utility approach.[21]

---

21 Minimization of squared deviations is a form of utility. It is hard to accept it as a paradigm from the standpoint of Economics. See also section 14.4.

The idea of building option pricing on utility is due to Hodges and Neuberger (1989) and was further developed in Davis, Panas, and Zariphopoulou (1993), Clewlow and Hodges (1997), Constantinides and Zariphopoulou (1999), and Constantinides and Perrakis (2002). The driving idea, which we will formalize below, is as follows. The bid and ask prices of an option are respectively the amount of cash one is willing to give away, or to receive, in order to be *indifferent* between having and not having one unit of option. Indifference is judged, as it should, via a utility function. As above, we give a heuristic treatment of the problem, the proof of existence of the bid and ask prices, of existence and smoothness of the value function, and of optimality of the portfolio policy being available in the literature mentioned above.

19.6.2   Option Pricing within a Portfolio Context

Let an investor buy and hold a call option for one share of stock. That investor also manages a portfolio containing the underlying security and the riskless security. The option will mature and deliver its payoff at some future date T.

The indirect utility of consumption of the portfolio problem, when the option is not included in the portfolio, is a function $V(x, y)$ (named $J(X, Y, t)$ in (19.25), but now stationary). Let the value function for a portfolio that includes the option be:[22]

$$J(X, Y, S, t) \triangleq \max_{\{L, U\}} \mathbb{E}_t \left[V \left(X(T) + [S(T) - \mathcal{K}]^+, Y(T) \right) \right]$$

and, of course:

$$J(X, Y, S, T) = V \left(X + [S - \mathcal{K}]^+, Y \right) \tag{19.43}$$

For the sake of simplicity, we assume proportional trading cost only and a Geometric Brownian motion risky security. The security dynamics are

$$\frac{dS}{S} = \mu dt + \sigma dw$$
$$dY = \mu Y dt + \sigma Y dw + s dL - dU$$
$$dX = rX dt + s dU - dL$$

Since costs are proportional, we can assume that a no-trade region exists and impose value-matching and smooth-pasting conditions.

Within the inaction region and for $t \leq T$, the following PDE applies:

$$\mathcal{D}(J) + \frac{\partial J}{\partial t} = 0$$

---

22 S and Y require separate notations because, as in section 19.4, Y is the total value of risky assets held, that is, the price S times the number of units of stock in the portfolio, while S is needed as the value of the option's underlying.

where

$$\mathcal{D}(J) = \frac{\partial}{\partial Y}J(X,Y,S,t)\mu Y + \frac{1}{2}\frac{\partial^2}{\partial Y^2}J(X,Y,S,t)\sigma^2 Y^2 + \frac{\partial}{\partial X}J(X,Y,t)rX$$
$$+\frac{1}{2}\frac{\partial^2}{\partial S^2}J(X,Y,S,t)\sigma^2 S^2 + \frac{\partial}{\partial S}J(X,Y,S,t)\mu S + \frac{\partial^2}{\partial S \partial Y}J\sigma^2 SY$$

with terminal condition (19.43). When a transaction takes place at some stopping time τ_u or τ_l, value matching must hold:

$$J(x_u + sdU, y_u - dU, S_u, \tau_u) = J(x_u, y_u, S_u, \tau_u)$$
$$J(x_l - dL, y_l + sdL, S_l, \tau_l) = J(x_l, y_l, S_l, \tau_l)$$

Expanding:

$$\frac{\partial}{\partial X}J(x_u, y_u, S_u, \tau_u)\,s = \frac{\partial}{\partial Y}J(x_u, y_u, S_u, \tau_u)$$
$$\frac{\partial}{\partial X}J(x_l, y_l, S_l, \tau_l) = \frac{\partial}{\partial Y}J(x_l, y_l, S_l, \tau_l)\,s$$

For optimality, smooth-pasting must hold at the upper action point:

$$\frac{\partial}{\partial Y}J(x_u + sdU, y_u - dU, S_u, \tau_u) = \frac{\partial}{\partial Y}J(x_u, y_u, S_u, \tau_u)$$

Expanding:

$$\frac{\partial^2}{\partial X \partial Y}J(x_u, y_u, S_u, \tau_u)\,s = \frac{\partial^2}{\partial Y^2}J(x_u, y_u, S_u, \tau_u)$$

And similarly at the lower action point:

$$\frac{\partial^2}{\partial X \partial Y}J(x_l, y_l, S_l, \tau_l) = \frac{\partial^2}{\partial Y^2}J(x_l, y_l, S_l, \tau_l)\,s$$

Then, one can define the buy price as the value C_b that makes the investor indifferent between buying *one* call and pay C_b out of cash or staying out of the option market. The buy price solves:

$$J(X - C_b, Y, S, t) = V(X, Y, t)$$

Analogously, one can define the ask or sell price as the one that makes the investor indifferent between keeping *one* option in the portfolio or selling it and cashing C_a. The sell price is the value C_a that solves:

$$J(X, Y, S, t) = V(X + C, Y, t)$$

Typically the former will be below the Black-Scholes price and the latter above (they differ from each other only because the option is assumed to be of finite size).

It is almost impossible to get analytical results because the inaction region corresponding to V and J is hard to characterize. See Davis, Panas, and Zariphopoulou (1993). The boundary of the inaction region is a function of time as one approaches the maturity of the option. Hodges and Neuberger (1989), Davis, Panas, and Zariphopoulou (1993), and Clewlow and Hodges (1997) work out the case of negative exponential utility and solve it numerically, under different approximations (binomial model for the Brownian motion, for instance).

The reader can now solve exercise 19.4.

19.7 Equilibria and Other Open Problems

The difficulties encountered in optimizing portfolios under trading costs are magnified when it comes to equilibrium. Equilibrium in the presence of frictions is important in terms both of *prices and of quantities*. When purchasing a security an investor needs not only have in mind the cash flows that the security will pay into the indefinite future, he/she must also anticipate his/her desire and ability to resell the security in the marketplace at a later point in time. The endogenous stochastic process of the liquidity of securities is as important to investment and valuation as is the exogenous stochastic process of their future cash flows.

Getting equilibrium prices would resolve the obvious internal inconsistency of the developments above. In a market with trading costs, there is no reason to believe that security prices could legitimately be modeled by an Itô diffusive process. Equilibrium prices would come in the form of a process for bid and ask prices, and the bid-ask spread. And the prices at which transactions actually occur would not be in the form of a continuous process but a "dotted" process. Last but not least, equilibrium could provide an explanation for the so-called *liquidity premium*, that is, the difference in the equilibrium prices at which a security would trade in markets without and with trading costs. It is intuitive that inaction, or trading in strategies of the "buy and hold-for-a-while" type, should produce a liquidity premium for securities depending on their level of trading costs. Liquidity risk is not fully captured by existing optimizing models.

Getting equilibrium quantities or trade is equally important: an economy in which investors adopt buy and hold-for-a-while strategies could solve some of the continuous-time puzzles of trade. Indeed, a frictionless model gives either no trade – for instance, with homogenous traders – or infinite trade resulting from the infinite variation of Brownian motion. Neither zero nor infinite trade is a convincing description of the world. Buy-and-hold strategies with trade of each investor in bunches or infinitesimal trade with investors' heterogeneity is expected to explain trade much better. The study of trade is in its infancy.

Vayanos (1998), Vayanos and Vila (1999), and Lo, Mamaysky, and Wang (2004) set up general equilibrium models in which the level of transaction costs is exogenous. Those costs are "physical" costs, such as information or taxes, and do not include bid-ask spreads and commissions paid to dealers, brokers, or to a specialist. If the costs have to be interpreted as bid-ask spreads, indeed, the equilibria are partial equilibria, since intermediaries who receive those costs are not modeled. The papers provide general-equilibrium trade but not equilibrium bid-ask spreads. Trade is not continuous in time, and buy-and-hold strategies occur in equilibrium. In Vayanos (1998) and Vayanos and Vila (1999), an investor's

only motive to trade is the fact that he has a finite lifetime. Transactions costs induce him
to trade twice in his life: when young, he buys some securities that he can resell in order to
be able to live during his old age. In the paper of Lo, Mamaysky, and Wang (2004), costs
of trading are fixed costs; all traders have the same negative exponential utility function;
individual investors' endowments provide the motive to trade but aggregate endowment is
not stochastic. Their model produces a reduction in investors' demand, with consequent
illiquidity premium, but above all a realistic, numerically calibrated, trading frequency.

Luciano and Tolomeo (2016b) endogenize both the bid-ask spread and trade. In order to
do so, they model also a (representative) intermediary, namely a specialist, and let investors
get immediate execution through the specialist or trade in a competitive market, where fees
are not paid. The switch to a competitive market occurs randomly, and serves as a proxy
for competition among intermediaries. Trade is infrequent, with a realistic frequency. The
competitive case also provides realistic bid-ask spreads and, interestingly, generates higher
fees for smaller investors. The model shows that partial equilibrium studies in the vein
of Constantinides (1986) overestimated the impact of bid-ask spreads on trade frequency.
It also shows that, in equilibrium, policy interventions in favour of disintermediation and
deterring speculation on the part of market makers, in the spirit of the Volcker rule, have a
positive effect on liquidity and reduce equilibrium spreads.

Recently Buss and Dumas (2017) have invoked trading fees to explain the empirical puzzle of slow-moving capital. In his address as president of the American Finance Associa-
tion, Darrell Duffie (2010) gives numerous examples – with supporting empirical evidence
– of situations in which investment capital does not adjust immediately and seems to move
slowly towards profitable trades. When a shock occurs, the price of a security reacts first,
before the quantities adjust. When they do, the price movement is reversed. Duffie's examples are: additions and deletions from the S&P 500 index, arrival of a new order in the
book, natural disasters impacting insurance markets, defaults affecting credit-default-swap
spreads, and issuance of U.S. Treasury securities affecting yields. Many other authors cited
by Duffie show evidence of "price-pressure" situations. Buss and Dumas (2017) show that
the *hysteresis* or path-dependence effect of trading frictions can explain slow price reversal.
When an impulse or shock (such as an endowment shock) hits, all investors adjust immediately, less so than they would in the absence of fees. However, on an equilibrium path with
ongoing shocks, the investors will also react later on. Indeed, the impulse has moved the
cost-paying investors closer to a trade boundary. When new shocks arrive, these investors
will act, more so than they would have acted in the absence of the prior impulse.

19.8   Conclusion

Trading is costly. There is friction in the financial market. When trading costs are proportional or contain a proportional component, this generates a kink at zero trade. The
investor's portfolio choice decision is crucially different from what it is without costs.

There is a region of the state space in which the investor chooses to do nothing. Two types of boundary conditions play a crucial role in determining the boundary of that "no-trade" area. The value-matching condition is a condition reflecting the continuous arrival of information; the value function of a decision maker cannot undergo a jump over time. It holds even if the no-trade region is set suboptimally. The smooth-pasting condition is the condition of optimality.

Effort is under way to draw the consequences of financial-market frictions. One of them is slow-moving capital. But there are also pricing implications, which may help to solve some of the empirical puzzles of asset pricing.

Exercises

19.1. In exercise 13.4 of chapter 13, the reader was asked to compute the perpetual American put option price when the underlying follows a Geometric Brownian motion and the riskless rate is constant. The reader was asked to impose the value-matching condition. Verify that the solution found there satisfies also the smooth-pasting condition.

19.2. Consider the base-case regulation of section 19.3. Assume that the flow payoff function and the cost functions are:

$$\phi(X) = e^{-\gamma X}$$

$$C(dU) = a + b dU$$

$$C(dL) = a' + b' dL,$$

that X follows a Brownian motion:

$$dX = \mu dt + \sigma dw$$

Assume also that, when it reaches the upper and lower barriers u and l, X reverts respectively to u' and l'. Find the corresponding particular solution of the ODE for the value function, $V(x)$, as well as the two solutions of the homogeneous equation, $F_1(x), F_2(x)$. Show by verification that the function

$$F(x) = V(x) + A_1 F_1(x) + A_2 F_2(x)$$

which solves the ODE is the value function. Write down the value-matching and smooth-pasting boundary conditions.

19.3. An investor with isoelastic utility, having access to a riskless deposit with constant interest rate r and to a risky equity share with IID rates of return seeks an investment policy under transactions costs that maximizes $\mathbb{E}[u(x(\tau) + sy(\tau))]$ where τ is exponentially distributed with parameter λ; that is, $P(\tau \in dt) = \lambda e^{-\lambda t} dt$, where $x(t)$ is the cash amount of riskless deposit held and $y(t)$ is the cash amount of equity held at any time t. The investor can trade out of the riskless deposit and into the equity share at no cost, but trading out of the equity share and into the riskless deposit has a cost equal to a fraction $1 - s$ of the cash amount of the equity sold.

a. Show that the maximization problem of the investor is equivalently written as:

$$\max \lambda \mathbb{E} \left[\int_0^\infty e^{-\lambda t} \frac{[x(t) + sy(t)]^\gamma}{\gamma} dt \right]; \gamma < 1, \gamma \neq 0$$

subject to a number of constraints that you will write.

b. Write the HJB PDE applicable in the no-trade zone as well as the boundary conditions that must be satisfied on the boundary of the no-trade zone.

c. Show that one candidate solution for the value function is homogeneous of degree one. Draw the implication of that fact for the shape of the no-trade region and rewrite the PDE and the boundary conditions in terms of an unknown function of one variable only.

d. As the resulting ODE is linear inhomogeneous, propose an explicit form for the general solution to the equation. Write the equations to be satisfied by all unknowns of the problem.

e. By elimination of all other variables, write down in full detail a system of two equations where the two unknowns are the slopes of the edges of the no-trade region. Is there a solution to that system?

19.4. Refer to the article Grenadier (2002). Derive step-by-step the result of example 5 on page 716 of the article. (The reader may look up the properties of the confluent hypergeometric function in a handbook of mathematical functions such as Abramovitz and Stigum (1964)).

20 Portfolio Selection and Equilibrium with Habit Formation

Our decision-theoretic setup, based on expected utility, is very convenient and axiomatically well-grounded. It seems now time to see whether a theory "close" to the one developed so far can be generated under a slightly more general decision-theory framework. We would like this more general framework to cope with the most remarkable mismatches between empirical regularities and financial theory. Let us focus on one major problem. The expected-utility, time-additive model that we have adopted so far, together with market completeness, does a poor job when faced with the *equity-premium puzzle*. We already encountered the puzzle in chapter 14, where we discussed the ability of market incompleteness to explain the puzzle. Another possibility to explain this and related puzzles consists in introducing assumptions not on the availability of trade and securities, but on the willingness to trade, as determined by utility. The literature has done this in two ways. One way consists in considering that "consumption," which is the argument of the utility function, is not the same as the consumption expense appearing in the budget constraint. The two processes can be transformations of each other.[1] That is the case of the economic model of *habit-formation*, which we study in this chapter. We first extend the expected-utility argument, from consumption to consumption in excess of habit. Habit formation can be the result of internal adaptation or external influences (the "Keeping up with the Joneses" effect). In the next chapter we cover the other way, namely *recursive preferences*, which are preferences covering current and future consumption. Both approaches in some ways violate the axioms of expected-utility, in a sense to be specified below. We show that they both act on the *relative preference* for today's versus tomorrow's consumption.

The plan of the chapter is as follows. We start by explaining in more depth the equity-premium puzzle and the interest rate puzzle and the way they are related to each other (section 20.1). Then we ask ourselves whether habit formation is able to solve the puzzles (section 20.2).

For the sake of tractability, most of the results are derived for our benchmark example of isoelastic utility function.

---

1 As an example, see equation (20.3) below.

20.1   Motivation: The Equity-Premium and Other Puzzles

We already encountered the equity-premium puzzle in chapter 14. We pointed out the extremely high level of relative risk aversion needed in a frictionless, complete market to explain the observed ratio of excess returns of the market over its volatility. Here we give a more comprehensive description of this and related puzzles. Our hope in doing that is to discover a hint of one possible solution.

The equity premium
Suppose that aggregate consumption follows an Itô process:

$$\frac{dc}{c} = \mu_c dt + \sigma_c dw$$

and let the utility of some representative investor be isoelastic, so that:

$$\frac{\partial u}{\partial c}(c) = c^{\gamma - 1}$$

By Itô's lemma, the percentage change in his marginal utility

$$\frac{d\frac{\partial u}{\partial c}(c)}{\frac{\partial u}{\partial c}(c)}$$

admits a diffusion coefficient, which is proportional to consumption volatility:

$$\frac{1}{\frac{\partial u}{\partial c}(c)} \sigma\left(\frac{\partial u}{\partial c}(c)\right) = (\gamma - 1) \times \sigma_c \tag{20.1}$$

where $(1 - \gamma)$, as we know, is the Arrow-Pratt relative risk-aversion parameter A_r. We also know, from the consumption CAPM, that the risk premium on the stock market should be equal to:[2]

$$-\frac{1}{\frac{\partial u}{\partial c}(c)} \text{cov}\left(R_M, \frac{\partial u}{\partial c}(c)\right) = (1 - \gamma) \times \frac{1}{c} \text{cov}(R_M, c)$$

and, since correlation is at most equal to 1, should be bounded above by

$$(1 - \gamma) \times \sigma(R_M) \times \sigma_c \tag{20.2}$$

Set the two volatilities that appear in the last expression to their average historical value over the period 1889–1978 in the US. The volatility of consumption has been $\sigma_c = 3.57\%$ per year and the volatility of the stock market has been $\sigma(R_M) = 16.67\%$ per year. Then *the risk premium on equity* should be at the most:

$$(1 - \gamma) \times 3.57\% \times 16.67\% = (1 - \gamma) \times 0.595\%$$

Historically, the risk premium in the United States has been equal to 6.18% per year. An excessively large risk aversion, as large as 10.38, would be necessary to rationalize the

---

2 Recall from section 5.4 that the symbols var() and cov() in continuous time denote variances and covariances of instantaneous *increases* of processes, with the exception of processes that are rates of return on securities.

observed risk premium, since

$$6.18\% = (1 - \gamma) \times 0.595\%$$

gives $1 - \gamma = 10.38$. This number is high as compared to behavioral experiments.

In short, consumption volatility being what it is, there is an excessive risk premium *for given stock market volatility*.

Stock market volatility

There is the added question of the *excessive volatility of the stock market*. It is a challenge to imagine a general-equilibrium model in which consumption volatility is of the order of magnitude of 3.57% per year while the volatility of financial wealth is 16.67%, since financial wealth is but the present value of future consumption in excess of endowments (or output, in a production economy). State prices have to be very, very volatile. This is the excess volatility puzzle of Shiller (1981). If the volatility of the stock market were about equal to, or less than, the volatility of consumption, then the premium on equity in (20.2) should be at most:

$$(1 - \gamma) \times 3.57\% \times 3.57\% = (1 - \gamma) \times 0.13\%$$

This would necessitate a risk aversion equal to 48.5 if one wanted to rationalize the equity premium, since

$$6.18\% = (1 - \gamma) \times 0.13\%$$

gives $\gamma = 48.5$.

The combined problems of excessive risk premium for given stock-market volatility and excessive stock-market volatility make up the *equity premium puzzle* of Mehra and Prescott (1985).

Closely related to the excess volatility puzzle is the *predictability puzzle*. According to the financial theory we have expounded, future risk-adjusted excess returns of securities should not be predictable from current information (under the effective measure) since their conditional expected value should be equal to zero, irrespective, therefore, of current information. There is evidence that they are predictable to a small but significant extent, which is an anomaly. Excess volatility will manifest itself in the form of predictability since it means that, when prices are low, they are "too low" and, when they are high, they are "too high" relative to the risk-pricing model.

Interest-rate puzzle

The equity-premium problem is coupled with a *rate-of-interest puzzle* (Weil (1989)). Since the rate of interest is equal to minus the drift of marginal utility,

$$r = -\mathbb{E}\left[\frac{d\xi}{\xi}\right]$$

the above assumptions give:

$$r = -(\gamma - 1)\mathbb{E}\left[\frac{dc}{c}\right] - \frac{1}{2}(\gamma - 1)(\gamma - 2)\left(\frac{dc}{c}\right)^2$$
$$\approx -(\gamma - 1) \times 1.83\% - 0.5 \times (\gamma - 1)(\gamma - 2)(3.57\%)^2$$

where the mean growth rate of consumption has been set at its historical average of 1.83% per year. In order to rationalize the observed real rate of interest, which historically has been about 0.8%, one would need a risk aversion $1 - \gamma$ equal approximately to 27.26. This is the *rate-of-interest* or *risk-free rate puzzle*.

An intuitive grasp of the puzzles

How can we cope with the previous puzzles? It appears from them that investors, if their behavior is described by the standard expected-utility model, give too much importance to consumption volatility; that is, unless we impose an unrealistically high risk aversion, the corresponding risk premium turns out to be too low to be consistent with reality. So, if we want to eliminate or reduce the puzzles, we could perhaps modify the argument of the investor utility function, making, for instance, our investor appreciate only consumption above a floor level.

Suppose, for instance, that utility is defined only over the consumption that exceeds a *subsistence* level X:

$$u(c) = \frac{1}{\gamma}(c - X)^\gamma; \gamma < 1$$

where X is a constant, which stands for the minimum living standard of the investor.[3]

With this new form of expected utility, the absolute and relative Arrow-Pratt risk-aversion coefficients are effectively

$$A(c) = \frac{1 - \gamma}{c - X}$$
$$A_r(c) = c\frac{1 - \gamma}{c - X}$$

They are greater than the corresponding coefficients without subsistence consumption. The volatility of marginal utility is given by:

$$\frac{d(c - X)^{\gamma - 1}}{(c - X)^{\gamma - 1}} = (\gamma - 1)\frac{dc}{c - X} = (\gamma - 1)\frac{dc}{c}\frac{c}{c - X}$$

It is now equal to the level that produced the puzzle, as in (20.1), times $c/(c - X)$, which can be a large enough number if c is not too far above X. The factor $c/(c - X)$ acts like a leverage effect. A more volatile marginal utility could rationalize at once a higher risk premium for a given level of stock market volatility and a higher stock market volatility.

---

3 We thank Philippe Weil for an enlightening discussion on this point.

Indeed, the marginal utility provides the discount factors that map future consumption into current wealth. If the discount factors are volatile, current wealth can be made volatile too.

Suppose for instance that[4]

$$\frac{c}{c - X} = \frac{16.67}{3.57} = 4.67$$

The previous form of utility, for a risk aversion $1 - \gamma$ equal to 2.22391, gives an equity premium equal to:

$$(1 - \gamma) \times 3.57\% \times 4.67 \times 16.67\%$$
$$= 2.22391 \times 3.57\% \times 4.67 \times 16.67\%$$
$$= 6.18\%$$

which is then consistent with the observed equity premium. This means that the simple insertion of a minimum consumption level provides some rationale for the main puzzle. Unfortunately, it is unable to solve the interest-rate puzzle. Indeed, it gives a rate of interest equal to:

$$2.22391 \times 1.83\% \times 4.67 - 0.5 \times 2.22391 \times 3.22391 \times (4.67 \times 3.57\%)^2 = 9\%$$

which is evidently too high to be reasonable. Still that is a line of thought to be pursued.[5] We do so now.

20.2   Habit Formation

If X is a constant and $\mu_c > 0$, c will grow to be much larger than X. What is needed is a utility model in which X grows gradually as consumption standards grow, preserving the increase in risk aversion achieved above. This gives rise to the idea of *habit formation*:

- Habit formation is expected to smooth the consumption path and to reduce its volatility relative to the volatility of wealth.

- State prices should nevertheless become more volatile. In particular, one should obtain a pro-cyclical effective risk aversion (higher in bad states, lower in good ones), which should add to the previous picture the ability to explain cyclicality of the risk premium. This is important, since, on top of the puzzles mentioned so far, empirical data imply counter-cyclicality of the risk premium, that is, high (low) risk premia when dividends and consumption are low (high). If effective risk aversion is cyclical, a risk premium

---

4 If so, c would be probably unreasonably close to x: $(c - X)/X \simeq 27\%$. The choice will be discussed more thoroughly in the next section.

5 We may, however, be fooling ourselves: effective risk aversion is now not $1 - \gamma$ but $(1 - \gamma)c/(c - X)$, which is just as high as it had to be under the model without subsistence level. Why focus on the number $1 - \gamma$ and claim victory when one has managed to keep it reasonably low?

higher than usual is needed in bad states of the world, to convince investors to hold risk assets. The opposite would follow for good states.

Let us see whether all these goals are indeed reachable.

The idea can be implemented in two ways. Habit formation may be due to *internal habits*, that is, one's own habits acquired over time. Or it may be due to so-called *external habits*, that is, the desire to consume at least as much as one's own "peers," the proverbial Joneses.

20.2.1 Internal Habit

The idea of *internal* habit formation has been developed by Ryder and Heal (1973), Sundaresan (1989), and Constantinides (1990). Constantinides chooses power utility with the following coding of the habit derived from past consumption:

$$X(t) = e^{-at}X_0 + b \int_0^t e^{a(s-t)}c(s)ds \qquad (20.3)$$

or:

$$dX(t) = [bc(t) - aX(t)]dt$$

Notice that, when substituting Constantinides' level X into the argument of the utility function, expected utility is no longer time-additive. Equation (20.3) introduces a transformation of the process of consumption of the kind we were referring to in the introduction.

Suppose that there exists one risky and one riskless security. The intertemporal maximization problem becomes

$$V(W(0), X(0)) = \max_{\{c(t), \theta(t)\}} \mathbb{E} \int_0^{+\infty} \exp(-\rho s)\frac{1}{\gamma}(c(s) - X(s))^\gamma ds$$

subject to: $c(t) \geq X(t)$ and a traditional budget constraint, a problem in which there are two state variables: W and X. Constantinides assumes that the risky security follows a Geometric Brownian motion with expected rate of return μ and volatility σ, and the rate of interest on the riskless security is fixed at r. He then restricts the parameters' range to ensure existence and uniqueness of a solution to the portfolio choice problem.

He calculates the value function of that problem as

$$V(W(t), X(t)) = \frac{(r+a-b)h^{\gamma-1}}{(r+a)\gamma}\left(W(t) - \frac{X(t)}{r+a-b}\right)^\gamma$$

where h is a positive constant related to $(r, a, b, \mu, \sigma, \gamma)$. More importantly, he obtains the stationary probability distributions of

$$y(t) = \frac{X(t)}{c(t) - X(t)}$$

and

$$z(t) = \frac{X(t)}{c(t)}$$

which represent respectively the optimal habit-over-non-habit level of consumption and the optimal habit-over-total consumption. The optimal consumption policy is

$$c(t) = X(t) + h \times \left(W(t) - \frac{X(t)}{r + a - b} \right)$$

The consumption level is higher than the level of habit and increases in the spread between the current level of wealth and the "adjusted" or capitalized habit $X/(r + a - b) > 0$.

Constantinides sets $\gamma = -1.2$, $\mu - r = 6\%$ and $\sigma = 16.5\%$, the last two as per US experience. He then calibrates the parameters a and b so that the mean growth rate of consumption is equal to 1.8% and the standard deviation of the growth rate of consumption is 3.6% as in the data. For these values of a and b, he finds a most likely value of $z(t)$ approximately equal to 0.8, which means that the ratio of current to excess consumption is

$$\frac{c}{c - X} = \frac{1}{1 - 0.8} = 5$$

which rationalizes the choice of the number 4.67 that we made above and which, so far, was not justified by optimal behavior. With these parameter values, he is then able to rationalize empirical evidence on the equity premium with a very reasonable risk-aversion parameter.

He then discusses the reasons that have allowed him to solve the puzzle. Risk aversion is defined not on the basis of the utility for consumption $u(c)$ but on the basis of the indirect utility function $V(W, X)$, since this is the notion of risk aversion that is relevant for security pricing.[6] The reason for which there is a difference between the two in the case of internal habit is that the first-order condition with respect to consumption is

$$(c - X)^{\gamma - 1} - \frac{\partial V}{\partial W} + b \frac{\partial V}{\partial X} = 0$$

The last, additional term appears because current consumption shifts habit, which is internal, and, therefore, future consumption. Hence, the marginal utility of consumption in his case is not equal to the marginal utility of wealth, which provides the stochastic discount factor.[7] This gap allows the marginal utility of consumption to be less volatile than the stochastic discount factor and rationalizes the large state-price volatility mentioned above. More important, however, is the fact that there is a gap between the volatility of the marginal utility of consumption $(c - X)^{\gamma - 1}$ and the volatility of consumption itself, over and beyond the factor $\gamma - 1$. That gap is created, as we saw, by the presence of the state variable X in the argument of consumption, with the attendant leverage effect. These are the advantages of Constantinides' approach.

But difficulties arise if one tries to model interest rates. Constantinides assumes that the rate of interest is fixed. At the optimum he describes, his investor is a net lender (the share

---

6 He also calculates from $u(c)$ the elasticity of intertemporal substitution (see section 20.3 below) and observes that its dissociated from risk aversion (whereas, with time-additive utility, they would be systematically related).

7 The consumption CAPM no longer holds: a additional, wealth-related term appears in the stochastic discount factor. That would a be two-factor CAPM, consumption and wealth being the two factors.

of wealth devoted to risky capital is smaller than one). That is because she wants to hold capital that will deliver the future habit level of consumption for sure. But, in reality, no such riskless production possibility exists in the real world. We want aggregate borrowing to be equal to zero. There are two ways in which one could think of closing that hole:

- One could impose that the representative investor be neither a borrower nor a lender and calculate the riskless rate that would achieve that result. One would find a rate of interest, if any, that is unsuitable. The Constantinides' model cannot be an equilibrium model, if one applies it in this way.

- One could argue that, although there exists no riskless technology in the real world, there does exist a menu of technologies of varying degrees of risk. They impose a physical trade-off between risk and return. But then, the standard deviation of equity return should be viewed as the standard deviation of the technological mix. If the standard deviation of the high risk technology is 16.5%, the standard deviation of the mix is much below 16.5%. But it is not clear how close to zero it can be.

The reader can now solve exercises 20.1 and 20.2.

20.2.2   External Habit

To model *external* habit, consider an exogenous random variable $X(t)$ reflecting the external level of consumption. For instance, X can be the aggregate consumption level with some lag.

Abel (1990) incorporates habits in an equilibrium model by letting the utility of a representative investor be a function of one's own consumption in the future, $c(t + s), s > 0$, relative to a (geometric) mix of both individual and aggregate consumptions in the past, namely $c^D(t - 1)X^{1-D}(t - 1)$. He introduces a utility function *in ratio form*:

$$u(c(t + s); c(t - 1), X(t - 1)) = \frac{1}{\gamma}\left(\frac{c(t + s)}{c^D(t - 1)X^{1-D}(t - 1)}\right)^{\gamma} \qquad s = 1, 2, \ldots$$

By changing the level of D between 0 and 1, he is able to model the case of external habits ($D = 0$), as well as pure internal habit formation ($D = 1$). He assumes a given external rate of growth for investor and aggregate consumption. With $D = 0$ he gets closer, but cannot fully capture the equity-premium puzzle.

Chan and Kogan (2002) take the work of Abel to continuous time and extend it to a population of investors with diverse values of the curvature parameter γ. The purpose of their work is to generate in the equity market a Sharpe ratio that is time varying, which it could not be, when utility is in the ratio form, if the curvature parameter of all investors were the same. Let aggregate endowment e in their pure-exchange economy follow a Geometric Brownian motion:

$$de(t) = \mu e(t) + \sigma e(t)dw(t)$$

Consider a continuum of investors, each of whom consumes c, has impatience parameter ρ, and curvature parameter $\gamma < 0$:

$$u(c(t), X(t); \gamma) = \frac{1}{\gamma} \left(\frac{c(t)}{X(t)} \right)^{\gamma}$$

where the external standard of living $X(t)$ is defined as a weighted geometric average of past realizations of the aggregate endowment process as in

$$\ln(X(t)) = \ln(X_0) \times \exp(-\lambda t) + \lambda \int_0^t \exp(-\lambda \times (t - s)) \ln(e_s) \, ds \qquad (20.4)$$

Defining the surplus $\chi(t) \triangleq \ln(e(t)) - \ln(X(t))$ to be log-aggregate consumption relative to the external standard of living, an application of Itô's lemma shows that, as $t \to \infty$, the behavior of χ approaches:

$$d\chi(t) = -\lambda \times (\chi(t) - \bar{\chi}) dt + \sigma \, dw(t)$$

where:

$$\bar{\chi} = \lim_{t \to +\infty} \mathbb{E}[\chi(t)|\chi_0] = \frac{\mu - \sigma^2/2}{\lambda}$$

The probability distribution of χ is stationary with

$$\lim_{t \to +\infty} \text{var}[\chi(t)|\chi_0] = \frac{\sigma^2}{2\lambda}$$

Calling $\phi(\gamma)$ the distribution density of curvature parameters in the population, Chan and Kogan show that the consumption-sharing rule at a Pareto optimum with equal weight on each investor has the following property:

$$\frac{c(\chi(t); \gamma)}{e(t)} = \phi(\gamma)^{\frac{1}{1-\gamma}} \exp\left[-\frac{z(\chi(t))}{1 - \gamma} - \chi(t) \right] \qquad (20.5)$$

where $z(\chi(t))$, the logarithm of the shadow price of the ARC, is such that ARC holds:

$$\int_{-\infty}^0 c(\chi(t); \gamma) d\gamma = e(t) \qquad (20.6)$$

It is a decreasing function of χ because the marginal utility of consumption of the average investor is a decreasing function of relative consumption.

The probability distribution of χ being stationary, equation (20.5) shows that the distribution of consumption in the population is not degenerate. That is in contrast to the result that would have held in the absence of habit formation. Indeed, with a population of time-additive CRRA investors, the consumption share of the least risk-averse investor would approach 100% as time goes by, the reason being that that investor holds more of the risky securities than anyone else and thus earns a higher return.

In this economy, because of habit formation, stochastic discount factors $\xi(t)$ are not equal to the (discounted) shadow price of the resource constraint $\exp[z(t)]$. Because of the ratio form of the utility functions, they are equal to

$$\xi(t) = \frac{\frac{\exp[-\rho t + z(t)]}{X(t)}}{\frac{\exp[z_0]}{X_0}}$$

where $X(t)$ is conditionally non-stochastic (see equation (20.4)). As usual, the Sharpe ratio (or risk premium κ on the aggregate risky asset per unit of risk) is equal to the negative of the percentage diffusion of $\xi(t)$, which is shown to be:

$$\kappa(t) = -\sigma z'(\chi(t))$$

Differentiating the aggregate resource constraint or ARC (20.6) then proves that κ is high when χ is low (a recession or trough), as in the data.

Campbell and Cochrane (1999) have also produced an equilibrium model of external habits, in a different form. They assume the existence of a representative investor, which basically requires a complete financial market, and use for it a power utility function where habit appears *in an additive or difference form*:

$$u(c(t), X(t)) = \frac{1}{\gamma}(c(t) - X(t))^\gamma; \gamma < 1$$

which produces the "leveraged" risk aversion:

$$A_r = \frac{(1 - \gamma)c(t)}{c(t) - X(t)}$$

Thanks to the utility hypothesis, risk aversion is high when consumption is low and increases steeply when consumption falls towards the habit level $X(t)$. Their choice was coupled with a lognormal assumption for the surplus consumption ratio $(c(t) - X(t))/c(t)$. The reliance on external habits allows for an easy equilibrium solution even if the population is heterogeneous in wealth.[8] The lognormal hypothesis makes the model calibration possible. Campbell and Cochrane obtain a better fit of the riskless rate in equilibrium, as compared to the no-habit model. Their interest rate is, indeed, equal to 0.94%.

Menzly *et al.* (2004) take up in continuous time the same task as Campbell and Cochrane and extend it to several risky assets. The paper is a contribution to the literature on the predictability of stock returns based on dividend yields (current dividend divided by current stock price). As discussed above, predictability and excess volatility are related to each other. Stock prices being equal to the present discounted values of future cash flows to shareholders, the dividend yield on an investor asset must forecast future cash flows, future stock returns, or both.[9] If one attempts to separate the two components by means of bivariate linear regressions of investor stocks' returns and cash flows on past dividend yields and past returns and cash flows, the results are empirically very weak. The reason may be that these relations are nonlinear and risk premia are time varying. We must

---

8 Under internal habit, there would be as many state variables in the economy as there are individuals.
9 See Cochrane (2001), pages 389 and following.

exploit asset-pricing theory to specify these relations. In Menzly *et al.*, the time-varying nature of risk premia is introduced by means of habit formation. Let $C(t)$ be an exogenous, aggregate consumption or output flow at time t assumed to follow a Geometric Brownian motion and let $c(t) = \ln C(t)$. Lifetime utility of a representative investor is assumed to be:

$$\mathbb{E}\left[\int_0^\infty e^{-\rho t} \ln[C(t) - X(t)] \, dt\right]$$

where $X(t)$ is an external habit level, the behavior of which is not specified as such. Instead, the *inverse* surplus ratio $Y(t) \triangleq C(t)/(C(t) - X(t))$ is set as a mean-reverting process, perfectly negatively correlated with innovations in consumption growth:

$$dY(t) = k \times \left(\bar{Y} - Y(t)\right) dt - \alpha \times (Y(t) - \lambda) \times (dc(t) - \mathbb{E}_t dc(t)); \quad \alpha > 0; \lambda > 0$$

The parameter α captures the impact of unexpected consumption growth on the inverse surplus ratio. Notice that the adjustment of habit is contemporaneous to the shock in consumption. However, in the applications the parameter is set much above one (precisely at 79.39) so that habit X, while literally containing, like consumption, a Brownian component, adopts a comparatively smooth behavior.

The cash flows attached to individual stock i ($i = 1, \ldots, n$) are specified not individually but as shares $s^i(t)$ of the aggregate flow $C(t)$ that follow mean-reverting processes:[10]

$$ds^i(t) = \phi^i \times \left(\bar{s}^i - s^i(t)\right) dt + s^i(t) \times \sigma^i(s(t)) \cdot dw(t) \qquad (20.7)$$

where $s(t) \triangleq \left\{s^i(t)\right\}_{i=0}^n$ and w is a K-dimensional Brownian motion. The diffusions $\sigma^i(s(t))$ are chosen in such a way that all the variances and covariances between cash flows and with aggregate consumption are affine with respect to $s(t)$. The share processes being mean reverting, no individual stock will eventually dominate the economy. It follows that cash-flow shares anticipate growth; when the cash-flow share of a stock is currently low, its expected growth rate must be high.

Menzly *et al.* derive the prices of stocks. The price-dividend ratio is found to be a linear function of the surplus ratio, of the stock's cash-flow share and of their product. They also derive explicitly the conditionally expected stock return on each individual stock. They develop a calibration and empirically match the model to the values of 20 industry portfolios. They summarize their contribution to the issue of predictability in the following terms:[11]

---

10 The inequality $\sum_{i=1}^n s_t^i < 1$ is enforced. A residual cash flow exists in the economy, representing non-shareholder income, such as labor income.

11 The next four paragraphs are a single, direct quote from their paper. The words within square brackets are, however, added by us.

"First, while changes in risk preferences [created by habit formation] generate the traditional negative relation between price/dividend ratios and expected returns, the variation in expected dividend growth generates a positive one. Intuitively, a higher expected dividend growth implies both a higher price/dividend ratio and a riskier asset since its cash flows are expected farther in the future. The asset's duration is longer, and thus the expected return is higher.

Second, these offsetting effects weaken the ability of the dividend yield to forecast returns and essentially eliminate its ability to predict future dividend growth.

Third, predictive regressions for returns should include both the dividend yield and the consumption/price ratio to disentangle the effect that changes in risk preferences and expected dividend growth have on prices and returns.

Fourth, there is a direct link between the predictability of future cash flows – by the share of dividends over consumption in our model – and the ability of the dividend yield to predict future returns."

Santos and Veronesi (2010) exploit some of the modeling devices in the Menzly *et al.* paper and enrich them to show that habit persistence can explain not just the general level but also one aspect of the cross section of stock returns. One more asset-pricing puzzle, which we have not so far mentioned, is the *value-premium puzzle*. The standard CAPM and CCAPM are unable to incorporate one more asset-pricing premium, commanded by *value stocks*. Value stocks are commonly defined as those the book/market ratio of which is high (see Fama and French (1993)). Empirically, they usually receive a return premium compared to the so-called growth stocks, for which the book/market ratio is low.

In the Santos and Veronesi paper, the definition of value and growth stocks is based not on book/market but on dividend/price. They show that either a value or a growth premium may emerge, depending on parameter values. Their model also solves the equity premium puzzle, and is able to fit the conditional CAPM and to replicate the effect of a high versus low book/market ratio as well.

In order to produce that variety of effects, Santos and Veronesi introduce heterogeneity in the firms' cash-flow risk, measured by the cash-flows' covariance with consumption, in the following way. First, they recall that one cannot posit inconsistent assumptions on dividends and consumption, since the former sum up to the latter, period by period. In their notation, where $C(t)$ is consumption at time t and $D^i(t)$ is the dividend of firm i, $C(t) = \sum_{i=1}^{n} D^i(t)$. The shares $s(t)$ are mean-reverting, as in (20.7), so that no firm takes over the economy in the long run, but w is n-dimensional and the restriction $\sum_i s^i(t) = 1$ is imposed by restricting the diffusions $\sigma^i(s(t))$ in the following way:

$$\sigma^i(s(t)) = \upsilon_i - \sum_{j=1}^{n} s^j(t)\upsilon_j$$

where the vectors υ_i are constants. Second, they assume that the diffusion vector σ_c of consumption growth is constant. Third and most importantly, consumption drift is the sum of a constant and a time-varying component that is stochastic and captures "long-run risk."[12] The predictable component is affine in the the stock shares $s(t)$:

$$\mu_C(t) = \bar{\mu}_C + s^{\mathsf{T}}(t)\theta_{CF}$$

The vector of coefficients is set as $\theta_{CF}^i = v_i^{\mathsf{T}}\sigma_c$ so that $\mu_C(t)$ is proportional to the covariance of the stock shares with consumption growth itself. The distribution of shares, as well as their relative behavior with respect to total consumption, are the engines of the long-run risk in this setting.

As a consequence of the previous assumptions, the covariance of the rate of growth of single dividends with the one of overall consumption at time t is

$$\sigma_{CF}^i(t) \triangleq \frac{1}{D^i(t)}\frac{1}{C(t)}\mathrm{cov}\big(D^i(t), C(t)\big) = \sigma_c^{\mathsf{T}}\sigma_c + \theta_{CF}^i - s^{\mathsf{T}}(t)\theta_{CF}$$

This covariance, which has constant expectation $(\sigma_c^{\mathsf{T}}\sigma_c + \theta_{CF}^i)$ is named *cash-flow risk* and it plays an important role in all the derivations. Its expressions shows that θ_{CF}^i determines the cash-flow risk of stock i with respect to the total.

As for the representative investor's choices, the assumption is as in Campbell and Cochrane (1999), that is, power utility defined on the excess of consumption over habits, $1 - \gamma$ being risk aversion. As in the previous models, the authors also introduce an assumption on the dynamics of excess consumption, as a ratio of total consumption, but they impose it on its power

$$G(t) \triangleq \left(\frac{C(t) - X(t)}{C(t)}\right)^{-\gamma}$$

At the cost of not specifying exactly the habit variable $X(t)$, they assume that the instantaneous diffusion of G depends on its difference with respect to a long-run value λ. That is, the diffusion of G is:

$$\sigma_G(t) \triangleq K \times (G(t) - \lambda) \times \sigma_c$$

with K and λ being positive constants. And they assume that G is mean-reverting to a constant value $\bar{G}$ with drift:

$$k \times (\bar{G} - G(t)) - \sigma_G(t)s^{\mathsf{T}}(t)\theta_{CF}$$

with k being a positive constant.

Starting from the stochastic discount factor

$$\exp(-\rho t)(C(t))^{-\gamma}G(t)$$

where ρ is the usual rate of intertemporal preferences, Santos and Veronesi derive the price/consumption ratio, the expected return on total wealth, its diffusion, the price/dividend ratio of single stocks, and the expected return on single stocks, in equilibrium.

---

12 This assumption, proposed by Bansal and Yaron (2004), will be encountered again in chapter 21 below.

In particular, they show that the latter is the sum of two components, $\mu_i^{disc}(t)$ and $\mu_i^{CF}(t)$. $\mu_i^{disc}(t)$, as its symbol says, is driven by the aggregate discount, proxied by $G(t)$, while $\mu_i^{CF}(t)$ is related to the cash-flow risk of asset i, $\sigma_{CF}^i(t)$, as well as to the cash-flow risk on the other assets. And they show that securities with a higher expected growth, as measured by the relative share $\bar{s}^i/s^i(t)$, which are also those with high price/dividend ratio, display stronger discount effects.[13]

When cash-flow risk does not exist, that is, $\sigma_{CF}^i(t) = 0$ for all stocks, as well as when its cross-sectional differences are small – the second component vanishes, and growth stocks, the price/dividend ratio of which is high, command a higher return than value stocks, the ratio of which is low. So, in the absence or cash-flow risk heterogeneity across stocks, a counterfactual growth premium arises.

However, when cash-flow risk dominates, the opposite effect holds true, and value stocks command a premium, as in the empirical findings. This is a result of value stocks having both high risk and low expected dividend growth.

All in all, their model is able to connect the value premium with cash-flow risk heterogeneity. However, in order to obtain the latter, cash-flow risk must be quantitatively too high in comparison to any reasonable calibrated value. So, the value-premium puzzle is solved, but a cash-flow risk puzzle arises, and even their model leaves further space for improvements in empirical asset pricing explanations.

As concerns the other empirical regularities, their model solves the equity-premium puzzle, as the previous habit-formation models did. Once empirically calibrated, the model explains that the conditional CAPM does better than its unconditional counterpart in explaining returns. It does so because value stocks become riskier, and deserve a bigger premium, in bad states of the world. Thanks to the last phenomenon and to the added level of heterogeneity in firms' returns, the model is also able to empirically reproduce a phenomenon first detected by Fama and French (1993), that is, the existence of a negative correlation between market returns and the returns on the HML factor. The latter indeed accounts for the spread in returns between value and growth stocks.[14]

20.3   Risk Aversion versus Elasticity of Intertemporal Substitution (EIS)

In this section, we point out that the curvature of the utility function of expected-utility models plays a double role. We know from Appendix A that it stands for risk aversion and determines the demand for risky assets or the preference for consumption across states,

---

13 Note that, in this model, the classification of securities as being value or growth stocks fluctuates endogenously depending on cash-flow shares.

14 Recall from chapter 12 that Fama and French (1993) obtain explanatory power with a factor model in which the factors are the spread between returns for firms with an high-market-to-book ratio and firms with a low ratio (the HML factor) and the spread between returns of small versus big firms (the SMB factor).

intratemporally. We show now that it also commands the elasticity of *intertemporal* substitutions (EIS) in comparative static analysis of the demand for consumption at different points in time. Then we ask whether habit formation may sort out this double role, which should be psychologically separate. We show that, unfortunately, habit formation does not disentangle them. In chapter 21, we propose recursive utility as a formulation that draws a better distinction between risk aversion and EIS.

The notion of EIS is well defined only under certainty. We perform the calculation in that setting.[15] Let us consider the comparative statics of *riskless choices over time*. For that, let us place ourselves in context of the Fisher economy of section 3.1.1.

Definition 20.1 *The EIS ε is the percentage change in the growth rate of consumption between two successive points in time, optimally chosen by an investor per unit of a percentage change in the rate of interest.*

At the optimum one over one plus the rate of interest is equated to the marginal rate of substitution u_2/u_1. Hence the definition means:

$$\varepsilon \triangleq -\frac{d\ln(\frac{c(2)}{c(1)})}{d\ln\left(\frac{u_2(c(1),c(2))}{u_1(c(1),c(2))}\right)}$$

Assume that the utility in each period is of the power type, so that the total utility over two periods, as evaluated at time 1, is:[16]

$$u(c(1),c(2)) = (c(1))^\rho + \beta(c(2))^\rho; \rho < 1$$

Since

$$\frac{u_2(c(1),c(2))}{u_1(c(1),c(2))} = \beta\left(\frac{c(2)}{c(1)}\right)^{\rho-1}$$

and

$$\ln\frac{u_2(c(1),c(2))}{u_1(c(1),c(2))} = \ln\beta - (1-\rho)\ln\left(\frac{c(2)}{c(1)}\right)$$

or

$$-\ln\left(\frac{c(2)}{c(1)}\right) = \frac{1}{1-\rho}\left(\ln\frac{u_2(c(1),c(2))}{u_1(c(1),c(2))} - \ln\beta\right)$$

the elasticity is

$$\varepsilon = \frac{d\frac{1}{\rho}\left(\ln\frac{u_2(c(1),c(2))}{u_1(c(1),c(2))} - \ln\beta\right)}{d\ln\left(\frac{u_2(c(1),c(2))}{u_1(c(1),c(2))}\right)} = \frac{1}{1-\rho}$$

---

15 Unfortunately, to our knowledge, the elasticity notion in the case of risky prospects does not exist, since there would be one elasticity for each future state of nature.

16 The derivation follows Lengwiler (2004).

The EIS is equal to one over what would be the relative risk aversion in a stochastic setting. It coincides with relative risk tolerance.

Let us examine whether the same is true with habit formation. First, under certainty, consider the following example. Let the reference habit level (*external* habit) be set equal to the initial consumption $c(1)$, that is,

$$u(c(1), c(2)) = (c(1))^\rho + \beta(z(c(1), c(2)))^\rho; \rho < 1$$

and let:

$$z(c(1), c(2)) \triangleq c(2)(c(1))^{-h}, \qquad\qquad 0 \le h \le 1$$

By performing the same steps as above, it is easy to see that we still have coincidence between EIS and relative risk tolerance:

$$\varepsilon = \frac{1}{1 - \rho}$$

Now, with the same example, reintroduce uncertainty, in the sense that the consumption stream is $(c(1), c(2))$, but $c(2)$ can - say - take the values $c_{2,s}, s = 1, ..K$. Habit formation – with time-1 consumption determining the habit level – gives

$$u(c(1), c(2)) = y(c(1)) + \beta \mathbb{E} y(z(c(1), c(2)))$$

which becomes

$$u(c(1), c(2)) = (c(1))^\rho + \beta(c(1))^{-h \times \rho} \mathbb{E}(c(2))^\rho$$

The way in which consumption at time 2 enters overall utility still depends on the same parameter ρ that determines the appreciation of utility at time 1 without habit formation. It is consumption at time 1 that determines the threshold for habit formation, but "distorted" since it enters into total utility as $(c(1))^\rho \left(1 + \beta(c(1))^{-h} \mathbb{E}(c(2))^\rho\right)$. We cannot compute the EIS since, strictly speaking, the EIS is not defined under uncertainty. However, it is clear intuitively that the exponent ρ should not serve to determine both intratemporal preferences and intertemporal substitution.

20.4   Conclusion

In this chapter, we have reviewed one category of the attempts made during the last decade to explain the asset pricing puzzles. It is the category based on the hypothesis of habit formation, while assuming a complete financial market. The formulation introduces a leverage effect in marginal utility, thus creating larger risk premia for a given risk.

Exercises

20.1. In the context of the "habit-formation" model of Constantinides (1990), attempt to endogenize the rate of interest. The equilibrium condition to be satisfied is that the representative investor should neither be a borrower nor a lender. As a first step, check whether the household is a net lender or a net borrower at the optimum calculated by Constantinides. (Hint: introduce a numerical calibration and check conditions about the optimal allocation policy).

20.2. If it is not possible for the household to be a net borrower at the optimum, explain what economic feature of the Constantinides model is responsible for that impossibility and discuss how serious a limitation this represents for the realism and applicability of the Constantinides solution of the equity-premium puzzle. If, however, that is possible, discuss the value of the rate of interest so obtained (for instance, the value in the calibration proposed by Constantinides) in relation to the rate-of-interest puzzle of Weil (1989).

21 Portfolio Selection and Equilibrium with Recursive Utility

So far, we have only considered utility specifications in which lifetime utility is defined as the sum (or integral) of the utilities of consumption of the successive points in time, possibly with the extension, seen in the previous chapter, in which "consumption" is in fact consumption compared to habit. In this chapter, we explore ways in which we can further generalize lifetime utility, by preserving time consistency, a feature underlying expected utility that we explain below, while trying to disentangle the roles of risk aversion, which concerns choices across states of nature, and of elasticity of behavior across time. As we saw, that disentangling is not accomplished by habit formation. For the purpose, we turn to recursive preferences. We first introduce the concept in discrete then in continuous time (sections 21.2, 21.4). We study the corresponding individual optimization problem in complete markets (section 21.5) and we address the equilibrium problem with heterogeneous investors (section 21.6). Last, we give examples of the way recursive preferences are able to tackle the asset-pricing puzzles, and discuss the limits of the recursive approach to puzzles (section 21.7). For the sake of tractability, most of the results are derived for our benchmark example of isoelastic utility function. Two appendices complete the chapter.

21.1 Modeling Strategy

As we embark on the recursive generalization of expected utility, we have to introduce some discipline by setting limits for the exercise and by clarifying the goal of our undertaking.

21.1.1 The Restriction: Time Consistency

Consider – in discrete time, to fix ideas – a stochastic process $\{c(t)\}_{t=0}^{T}$ of consumption, representing a lifetime consumption stream. In a head-on search for generality, one might want to postulate a utility ordering $u\left(\{c(t)\}_{t=0}^{T}\right)$ over the entire stream. Such a general form would require that one carry forward through the entire lifetime the consumption sequence that has been realized over the past. As one does that, inconsistencies would appear over time as the investor would prefer to deviate *ex post* from the preferences he had expressed and the decisions he had made *ex ante*.

A sequence of decisions determining the consumption stream over time is said to be *dynamically consistent* with respect to the maximization of an objective function if, when calculating the current control, the investor's strategy or control of a later point in time coincides with the control that solves the same problem at the later point in time, state by state. In other words, we can predict that the investor will implement what he was planning to do and not renege on it.

The objective functions we have considered so far did not raise any issue of dynamic inconsistency because they were additive over time and across states of nature, by virtue of the von Neumann-Morgenstern axioms imposed on time-state gambles. But utility of the more general type $u\big(\{c(t)\}_{t=0}^{T}\big)$ does not necessarily lead to consistent strategies. If we search for a consumption path able to maximize overall utility without requiring consistency, in most cases we end up with a non-consistent path, as the early work of Dreze and Modigliani (1972) and the work of Johnsen and Donaldson (1985) show.[1]

For that reason, we restrict our generalization to a class called *recursive preferences.* By its very definition, to be stated below, recursive utility is separable over time. Under certainty, that restriction is sufficient for dynamic consistency.[2] Under uncertainty, it is not quite enough because some dynamic inconsistency can also arise when the preference ordering depends on consumption in states other than the ones that are realized, an example of which is regret. We assume that problem away by maintaining the axioms von Neumann Morgenstern *for a given point in time* across the states that can prevail at the next point in time (called the successor states in earlier chapters).

Recursive utility is often called a "non-expected utility" preference ordering. Indeed, the utility of a consumption path $\{c(t)\}_{t=0}^{T}$, considered as a whole, does not statisfy the axioms of von Neumann and Morgenstern. Recursive utility is not of the von Neumann Morgenstern type for gambles over time and states.

21.1.2   The Motivation

Recursive utility is sometimes viewed as an attempt to disentangle the roles of risk aversion, which concerns choices across states of nature, and elasticity of behavior across time.

---

1 A paramount example of time-inconsistency is the dynamic mean-variance portfolio problem in which the objective function is to maximize a function of the expected value and the variance of terminal wealth. Dynamic inconsistency arises unless the investor behaves myopically or can precommit. Basak and Chabakauri (2010) derive the time-consistent solution in an incomplete market using dynamic programming.

2 The restriction would not be sufficient if, instead of adhering to a predetermined programming clock, the investor were to "reset" his time to time 0 every time he entered a new period, as is done in Strotz (1955) and Laibson (1997). That form of behavior is motivated by the quest for "immediate satisfaction" as when the utility of the first period under optimization differs from later utility. It does lead to time inconsistency. We do not introduce time reset in this entire book.

We have seen in the previous chapter that habit-based utility functions do not permit that differentiation.

Imagine that the utility functional over two points in time is the sum of two utilities: that of today's consumption and that of the certainty equivalent of tomorrow's consumption, where the certainty equivalent – which reflects risk aversion or intratemporal preferences – is computed using a function different from the one that governs intertemporal preferences. If the former is denoted with υ and the latter with y, the certainty equivalent is

$$\zeta \triangleq \upsilon^{-1}(\mathbb{E}(\upsilon(c(2))))$$

while the utility of the two-points in time consumption stream is

$$u(c(1), c(2)) = y(c(1)) + \beta y(\zeta)$$

The total utility of an investor is the sum of current utility plus the utility of the certainty equivalent of future consumption.

Let the utility of consumption be a power function with power ρ, while the certainty of tomorrow's consumption uses a power γ:

$$y(c) = (c)^\rho$$
$$\upsilon(c) = (c)^\gamma$$

The certainty equivalent is

$$(\mathbb{E}\left[(c(2))^\gamma\right])^{\frac{1}{\gamma}}$$

while total utility is

$$u(c(1), c(2)) = (c(1))^\rho + \beta \left(\mathbb{E}\left[(c(2))^\gamma\right]\right)^{\frac{\rho}{\gamma}} \tag{21.1}$$

It is clear that γ affects the way in which changes in consumption tomorrow are appreciated, because it affects the calculation of the certainty equivalent, for any given intertemporal discount β and for any given level of intertemporal substitutability ρ.

With recursive utility it is consumption tomorrow that is appreciated differently from the way it is under time-additive expected utility. So, in the power case, we see that recursive preferences and habit formation, though in different ways, change the *relative* preference of consumption at different points in time. While recursive utility, by definition, acts on the appreciation of future consumption, habit formation, in the current specification, acts on the appreciation of past consumption.

The general separation idea is to first take into account the random aspect of tomorrow's consumption by means of a certainty equivalent. That certainty equivalent takes care of the risk-aversion aspect of preferences. Second, the certainty equivalent of tomorrow's consumption is then weighed against today's consumption, thus reflecting the preference for consumption today versus tomorrow. In the next section, we extend the same idea to more than two points in time.[3]

21.2   Recursive Utility: Definition in Discrete-Time

Recursive utility can be defined axiomatically, exactly as expected utility; see, for instance, Skiadas (1998).[4] Here we present a functional construction. We first provide an intuitive extension of the two-points in time construction above. Then we improve on it by giving a proper definition.

Consider an economy with dates $t = 0, 1, ..T \leq \infty$ and a consumption stream $\{c(t)\}_{t=0}^{T}$ (generally a stochastic process) that starts at date 0 and call $u(\{c(t)\}_{t=0}^{T})$ the level of the preference index of that consumption stream. The consumption stream $\{c(t)\}_{t=0}^{T}$ can be split at time t into two substreams:

$$\{c(t)\}_{t=0}^{T} = \left\{ \{c(s)\}_{s=0}^{t}, \{c(s)\}_{s=t+1}^{T} \right\}$$

so that the preference index becomes $u\left(\left\{ \{c(s)\}_{s=0}^{t}, \{c(s)\}_{s=t+1}^{T} \right\}\right)$.

We first give the definition of a recursive preference index or ordering, then show how to construct such an index recursively using the notion of an aggregator.[5]

Definition 21.1   *An intertemporal preference ordering u is called "recursive" if, for all t and all processes $\{c(t)\}_{t=0}^{T}$ and $\{c'(s)\}_{t=0}^{T}$ such that:*

$$u\left(\left\{ \{c(s)\}_{s=0}^{t}, \{c(s)\}_{s=t+1}^{T} \right\}\right) \geq u\left(\left\{ \{c(s)\}_{s=0}^{t}, \{c'(s)\}_{s=t+1}^{T} \right\}\right)$$

it is also true that $\forall \left\{ c_t'' \right\}_{t=0}^{T}$:

$$u\left(\left\{ \{c''(s)\}_{s=0}^{t}, \{c(s)\}_{s=t+1}^{T} \right\}\right) \geq u\left(\left\{ \{c''(s)\}_{s=0}^{t}, \{c'(s)\}_{s=t+1}^{T} \right\}\right)$$

That is, the preference over consumption paths that start from t is independent of consumption prior to t. Hence, when the ordering is recursive, there is a meaning to the utility of a consumption path that starts at t. With an abuse of notation we use the same symbol u for that ordering, which is understood as follows:

$$u\left(\{c(s)\}_{s=t+1}^{T}\right) \geq u\left(\{c'(s)\}_{s=t+1}^{T}\right)$$

---

3 Schroder and Skiadas (2002) show that any utility model, including habit formation, can be written as a model without habit formation, by changing appropriately the Arrow-Debreu prices. Hence, one can construct a utility function that incorporates both the features of habit formation and those of recursive utility.

4 The axioms in Skiadas (1998) are enlarged so as to incorporate habit formation into recursions.

5 See Epstein (1987), assumption 4.

if and only if $\forall \{c(s)\}_{s=0}^{t}$,

$$u\left(\{\{c(s)\}_{s=0}^{t}, \{c(s)\}_{s=t+1}^{T}\}\right) \geq u\left(\left\{\{c(s)\}_{s=0}^{t}, \{c'(s)\}_{s=t+1}^{T}\right\}\right)$$

Under certainty, the above definition is sufficient.

Under uncertainty, we append to our definition of a recursive ordering *the requirement of independence from unrealized alternatives of the same point in time.*[6] Let $V(t) = u\left(\{c(s)\}_{s=t}^{T}\right)$ be the value of the intertemporal utility beginning at t, and let

$$\zeta_t = \zeta(V(t+1)|\mathcal{F}(t))$$

be the value of a certainty equivalent applied to the probability distribution of future utility $V(t+1)$ conditional upon time t information. Note that $V(t)$ is adapted to the time-t filtration. We construct the certainty equivalent from the von Neumann-Morgenstern axioms of choice under conditions of risk imposed separately at each point in time.

21.3 Recursive Utility in Discrete Time: Two Representations

21.3.1 Aggregator Representation

Following Koopmans (1960), Kreps and Porteus (1978), Epstein and Zin (1989) and others, who have generalized Koopmans' work to uncertainty, the value V of a recursive utility functional can be constructed recursively as follows:

Definition 21.2 *Intertemporal utility $V(t)$ is given by the recursion:*

$$V(t) = \mathcal{W}(c(t), \zeta_t), \; t \geq 0 \tag{21.2}$$

where $\mathcal{W}$ is a function increasing strictly in both arguments.

$\mathcal{W}$ is called an *aggregator function*, because it puts together time-t consumption $c(t)$ with an "index of subsequent consumption" to arrive at the current value of utility. Thanks to monotonicity, the index of subsequent consumption gives a functional form to a preference ordering that is recursive according to definition 21.1.

There exists an infinity of $(\mathcal{W}, \zeta)$ pairs that represent the same intertemporal preference ordering. The proof is given in small characters at the end of this section. It can be demonstrated that among the infinity of pairs equivalent to $(\mathcal{W}, \zeta)$, there exists one for which the certainty equivalence operator ζ is simply the expected-value operator $\mathbb{E}_t[V(t+1)]$. The corresponding aggregator is called the *normalized aggregator*. When the aggregator is normalized, we have

$$V(t) = \mathcal{W}(c(t), \mathbb{E}_t[V(t+1)]) \tag{21.3}$$

---

6 See Johnsen and Donaldson (1985).

In this form, it is obvious that time-additive expected utility is a special case:

$$V(t) = u(c(t)) + \mathbb{E}_t [V(t+1)]$$

When it has been normalized to the form (21.3), the aggregator alone captures the two psychologically separate aspects of intertemporal behavior and behavior towards risk. It will, of course, carry enough parameters to allow one to set the two behaviorally distinct traits. In other words, the aggregator $\mathcal{W}(c, u)$ (which will become $\mathfrak{f}(c, u)$ in continuous-time) captures both EIS (loosely defined) and intratemporal risk aversion.

Epstein and Zin (1989) have shown that the first-order condition (Euler equation) for portfolio choice, for each asset i, is:

$$\mathcal{W}_1(t) = \mathcal{W}_2(t) \times \mathbb{E}_t [\mathcal{W}_1(t+1) \times R_i(t+1)]$$

where $R_i(t+1)$ is the gross rate of return between times t and $t+1$ on security i and $\mathcal{W}_j(t)$ denotes the derivative of the aggregator function with respect to its jth argument, evaluated at $(c(t), \mathbb{E}_t[V(t+1)])$. Giovannini and Weil (1989) provided the intuition for this result:

Giving up one unit of consumption today costs $\mathcal{W}_1(t)$ time-t utils. An additional unit of consumption tomorrow provides $\mathcal{W}_1(t+1)$ time-$(t+1)$ utils, which are worth $\mathcal{W}_2(t)\mathcal{W}_1(t+1)$ time-t utils. In an optimum, investing one unit of consumption given at time t in any asset i, and eating the proceeds at $t+1$ should not, on average, increase utility.

This means that generally the personal stochastic discount factor of the investor at time $t+1$ relative to time t is given by:

$$\mathcal{W}_2(t)\frac{\mathcal{W}_1(t+1)}{\mathcal{W}_1(t)}$$

Consider the following example.

Example 21.1 The CES normalized aggregator, otherwise called the "isoelastic," or "Kreps-Porteus" aggregator is:

$$\mathcal{W}(c, u) = \left[c^\rho + \beta (\gamma u)^{\frac{\rho}{\gamma}} \right]^{\frac{\gamma}{\rho}} \frac{1}{\gamma} \tag{21.4}$$

$$\gamma < 1; \gamma \neq 0; \rho < 1; \rho \neq 0; \beta < 1$$

It implies the recursion:

$$V(t) = \left[(c(t))^\rho + \beta (\gamma \mathbb{E}_t[V(t+1)])^{\frac{\rho}{\gamma}} \right]^{\frac{\gamma}{\rho}} \frac{1}{\gamma}, \, t \geq 0$$

and it assigns to the pair $(1/(1-\rho), 1-\gamma)$ the roles of EIS (loosely defined) and intratemporal relative risk aversion, respectively.

The classic, time-additive expected-utility special case of that class is obtained with $\gamma = \rho$.

In the isoelastic case, Giovannini and Weil (1989) have shown that the investor's stochastic discount factor boils down to:

$$\beta^{\frac{\gamma}{\rho}} \left(\frac{c(t+1)}{c(t)} \right)^{(\rho-1)\frac{\gamma}{\rho}} (R(t+1))^{\frac{\gamma}{\rho}-1} \tag{21.5}$$

where $R(t+1)$ is the rate of return on *total* wealth, where total wealth is defined as usual as the present value of future consumption, calculated with the same stochastic discount factor. The proof is in the first appendix to this chapter.

There is one more feature that recursive preferences, unlike time-additive von Neumann-Morgenstern utility, may be able to capture. It is preference for the time at which uncertainty about a given gamble is resolved. The second appendix to this chapter shows that recursive utility introduces a preference for early versus late resolution. Unfortunately, it does not allow one separately to specify risk aversion and that other aspect of preferences.[7]

To demonstrate the multiplicity of equivalent $(\mathcal{W}, \zeta)$ pairs, let g be a strictly monotonically increasing, continuous function. Then $g(V(t))$ can be used instead of $V(t)$, to rank consumption bundles. Let $\left(\widehat{\mathcal{W}}, \hat{\zeta} \right)$ be defined by

$$\widehat{\mathcal{W}}(c,z) \triangleq g\left[\mathcal{W} \left(c, g^{-1}(z) \right) \right]$$

and

$$\hat{\zeta}(x) \triangleq g\left[\zeta \left(g^{-1}(x) \right) \right]$$

Then the pair $\left(\widehat{\mathcal{W}}, \hat{\zeta} \right)$ is equivalent to $(\mathcal{W}, \zeta)$. Indeed, consider the recursion:

$$V(t) = \mathcal{W}(c(t), \zeta_t(V(t+1))), \ t \geq 0$$

If we transform both the LHS and the RHS using g, and use the fact that $g^{-1} \circ g$ is the identity, we get

$$g(V(t)) = g\left[\mathcal{W} \left(c(t), g^{-1} \circ \ g \circ \zeta_t \left(g^{-1} \circ \ gV(t+1) \right) \right) \right]$$
$$\left[\hat{V}(t) \right] = [\qquad \widehat{\mathcal{W}} \qquad] \ [\quad \hat{\zeta}_t \quad] \ [\ \hat{V}(t+1) \ ]$$

It is easy to recognize a new, equivalent recursion: $\hat{V}(t) \triangleq g(V(t)) = \widehat{\mathcal{W}}(c(t), \hat{\zeta})$, as claimed.

21.3.2 Discount-Factor Representation

Consider the recursive-utility aggregator $\mathcal{W}(c, \zeta)$. If ζ is viewed as the derived utility from future consumptions, $\mathcal{W}(c, \zeta)$ may be interpreted as the "present utility value" of the utility flow from current and future consumptions. The present utility value may be decomposed

---

7 Technically speaking, the preference for early versus late resolution of the uncertainty of a given gamble is not a preference over random variables but a preference over filtrations.

into a component which represents the present value of next period's utility, and a component (denoted F) which represents the remainder (this period's utility plus any interaction between c and ζ). One way to write such a decomposition is:

$$\mathcal{W}(c, \zeta) = \mathfrak{F} + \mathcal{W}_\zeta(c, \zeta)\zeta$$

in which case $\mathcal{W}_\zeta(c, \zeta)\zeta$ may be interpreted as the present value of next period's utility and $\mathcal{W}_\zeta$ may be viewed as a "discount factor." In order to emphasize this role of $\mathcal{W}_\zeta$, define the "discount rate" ν as:

$$\mathcal{W}_\zeta = 1 - \nu$$

Assuming that $\mathcal{W}$ is concave in ζ, we may summarize the two equations above in the form of the following equivalent decompositions:[8]

$$\mathfrak{F}(c, \nu) = \max_{\zeta \in R} \{\mathcal{W}(c, \zeta) - (1 - \nu)\zeta\} \Leftrightarrow \mathcal{W}(c, \zeta) = \min_{\nu \in R} \{\mathfrak{F}(c, \nu) + (1 - \nu)\zeta\}$$

where $\mathfrak{F}(c, \nu)$, called the "felicity function," is the analog under recursive utility of the utility of one period's consumption under time-additive utility. Note that the discount rate ν is not given but is instead determined by a minimization.

Lifetime utility may then be written in a pseudo-additive variational utility form:

$$V(t) = \min_{\nu \in \Pi} \mathbb{E}_t \left\{ \sum_{s=t}^{T} \left[\prod_{\tau=t}^{s} (1 - \nu(\tau)) \right] \mathfrak{F}(c(s), \nu(s)) ds \right\} \tag{21.6}$$

where Π is an appropriate class of processes. We extend that same idea to continuous time under the name "variational utility" in section 21.4.2 below.

The central feature of this new formulation is that recursive utility is now written in a quasi time-additive form, but one in which the individual's discount factors $\left[\prod_{\tau=t}^{s} (1 - \nu(\tau)) \right]$ vary over time and are chosen endogenously.

21.4   Recursive Utility: Continuous Time

21.4.1   Stochastic Differential Utility

Under certainty, but in continuous time, Epstein (1987) shows, under the assumption of recursivity and other technical conditions, that there exists a "generating function" $\mathfrak{f}$, which we shall still call an aggregator function, such that utility changes over time depend on the

---

8 For example, if the aggregator function $\mathcal{W}(c, \zeta)$ is of the CES type (21.4), then the corresponding felicity function, $\mathfrak{F}(c, \nu) \equiv \max_\zeta [\mathcal{W}(c, \zeta) - (1 - \nu)\zeta]$, is:

$$\mathfrak{F}(c, \nu) = \frac{c^\gamma}{\gamma} \left\{ \left[1 + \beta \left[\left(\frac{1 - \nu}{\beta} \right)^{\frac{\gamma}{\gamma - \rho}} - \beta \right]^{-1} \right]^{\frac{\gamma}{\rho}} - (1 - \nu) \left[\left(\frac{1 - \nu}{\beta} \right)^{\frac{\rho}{\gamma - \rho}} - \beta \right]^{-\frac{\gamma}{\rho}} \right\}$$

current level of consumption and utility of consumption in the future through $\mathfrak{f}$:

$$\frac{du(\{c(s)\}_{s=t}^T)}{dt} = -\mathfrak{f}\left(c(t), u(\{c(s)\}_{s=t}^T)\right)$$

or

$$u(\{c(s)\}_{s=t}^T) = \int_t^T \mathfrak{f}\left(c(s), u\left(\{c(\tau)\}_{\tau=s}^T\right)\right) ds$$

In the case of uncertainty, Duffie and Epstein (1992) write recursive utility $V\left(\{c(s)\}_{s=t}^T\right)$ recursively, in the following form:[9]

$$V(t) = \mathbb{E}_t\left(\int_t^T \mathfrak{f}(c(s), V(s))ds\right) \tag{21.7}$$

$$V(T) = 0$$

They name it *stochastic differential utility*. Its formulation involves a certainty equivalent that is simply the expected-value operator. Hence, $\mathfrak{f}$ in the above must be regarded as the normalized aggregator. Writing (21.7) in differential form, we get:

$$\mathbb{E}_t[dV(t)] = -\mathfrak{f}(c(t), V(t))dt$$

Remark 21.1 *V is an "undiscounted" derived lifetime utility, in the sense that it is not discounted back to time 0. It is discounted back to the current time t only. Discounted lifetime utility is defined further below.*

Example 21.2 The continuous-time CES isoelastic aggregator in normalized form is:

$$\mathfrak{f}(c, u) \triangleq \frac{\beta}{\rho} \frac{c^\rho - (\gamma u)^{\frac{\rho}{\gamma}}}{(\gamma u)^{\frac{\rho}{\gamma}-1}} \tag{21.8}$$

$$\gamma < 1; \gamma \neq 0; \rho < 1; \rho \neq 0; \beta > 0$$

The classic, time-additive special case of that class is obtained with $\gamma = \rho$.

21.4.2 Variational Utility

The reformulation of the investor's optimization problem in terms of "variational utility" is based on Geoffard's characterization of recursive utility (Geoffard (1996)), which he developed in a deterministic continuous-time setting. It involves the Legendre (or convex-duality) transform of the aggregator of the recursive utility, in a manner similar to the transformation of the primal problem into a dual problem, as seen in section 14.2.2. In a continuous-time stochastic setting, the idea is briefly as follows.

---

9 The function $\mathfrak{f}$ must at least satisfy the Lipschitz and growth conditions of theorem 7.1.

Consider recursive utility (21.7). When the aggregator $\mathfrak{f}$ is concave in its second argument, define the Legendre transform:[10]

$$\mathfrak{F}(c, v) = \max_{u} \{\mathfrak{f}(c, u) + v \times u\}$$

which we call the "felicity function" associated with $\mathfrak{f}$ and which implies in the reverse:

$$\mathfrak{f}(c, u) = \min_{v} \{\mathfrak{F}(c, v) - u \times v\} \tag{21.9}$$

Remark 21.2

$$\mathfrak{f}_1(c, u) \equiv \mathfrak{F}_1(c, v)$$

Example 21.3   The continuous-time CES isoelastic felicity function associated with (21.8) is:

$$\mathfrak{F}(c, v) = \beta \frac{c^{\gamma}}{\gamma} \left[-\frac{\rho - \gamma}{\gamma - \rho \frac{v}{\beta}} \right]^{\frac{\gamma}{\rho} - 1}$$

with the same restrictions on parameter values.

Inserting equation (21.9) in the basic recursion (21.7) above, and using integration by parts, one obtains another characterization of $V\left(\{c(s)\}_{s=t}^{T}\right)$, known as

Definition 21.3   *Stochastic variational utility (SVU):*

$$V(t) = \min_{v} \mathbb{E}_t \left(\int_{t}^{T} e^{-\int_{t}^{s} v(\tau)d\tau} \mathfrak{F}(c(s), v(s))ds \right) \tag{21.10}$$

We can interpret the vs as time-varying utility-discount rates or "psychological discount rates" for future consumption. But these are endogenous discount rates chosen by the investor based on his felicity function. The choice of discount rate in this approach is just one more decision to be made by the investor, besides his choice of consumption.

Defining

$$\varkappa(t) \triangleq \exp\left[-\int_{0}^{t} v(\tau)d\tau \right] \tag{21.11}$$

an alternative way of writing the same as equation (21.10) is:

$$\varkappa(t)V(t) = \min_{v} \mathbb{E}_t \left\{ \int_{t}^{T} \varkappa(s)\mathfrak{F}(c(s), v(s))ds \right\} \tag{21.12}$$

subject to:

$$d\varkappa(t) = -v(t)\varkappa(t)dt \tag{21.13}$$

$$\varkappa(0) = 1$$

---

10 When $\mathfrak{f}$ is convex, define $\mathfrak{F}$ as:

$$\mathfrak{F}(c, v) = \min_{u} \{\mathfrak{f}(c, u) - vu\}$$

where $\varkappa$ is a psychological discount-factor process. Thus $\varkappa(t)V(t)$ is the derived lifetime utility discounted back to time 0. Notice that the SDE (21.13) for the factor process $\varkappa$ contains *no Brownian term*.

Consider a felicity function $\mathfrak{F}$; let $\mathfrak{F}$ be increasing in its first argument (consumption), strictly convex in its second argument (the adapted process that represents its discount rate) and continuously differentiable. Equation (21.10) tells us how the discount rates-processes $v(t)$ are obtained: in contrast to the time-additive expected utility, the discount rate here may depend on the consumption process for which the utility is being evaluated.[11] Equation (21.10) says that the stochastic variational utility of the consumption process c is *quasi time additive*, in the sense that it can be written as the discounted sum of values of the felicity function $\mathfrak{F}$. The discount rate, however, is endogenous and is obtained from a minimization.

The following theorem exploits the correspondence between aggregators and felicity functions to establish the equivalence between recursive utility and stochastic variational utility.

Theorem 21.1 *Let $\mathfrak{f}$ be an aggregator and $\mathfrak{F}$ be its associated felicity function. Suppose that the stochastic differential utility and the stochastic variational utility of c both exist. Then V is the stochastic differential utility with aggregator $\mathfrak{f}$ if and only if V is the stochastic variational utility with felicity function $\mathfrak{F}$.*

The full proof can be obtained by assembling El Karoui, Peng, and Quenez (1997) and Dumas, Uppal, and Wang (2000). We have just seen that one can go from stochastic differential utility to stochastic variational utility by simple substitution. We now give a one-line proof for the reverse implication. Start with the variational form (21.12), apply the Bellman principle and perform the minimization:[12]

$$0 = \min_v [\mathfrak{F}(c(t), v(t)) - v(t)V(t)] \, dt + \mathbb{E}_t[dV(t)]$$

but, by virtue of (21.9), this is:[13]

$$0 = \mathfrak{f}(c(t), V(t)) \, dt + \mathbb{E}_t[dV(t)]$$

---

11 Already Uzawa (1968) considered discount rates that were functions of the level of consumption.

12 Our application of the Bellman principle is only based on the additivity of the form (21.12). It does not require a Markovian assumption, which, in an implementation of dynamic programming, would be needed only to make $\mathbb{E}_t[dV(t)]$ explicit.

13 The first-order condition is obviously:

$$\mathfrak{F}_2(c(t), v(t)) = V(t) \tag{21.14}$$

and the solution is:

$$v(t) = -\mathfrak{f}_2(c(t), V(t)) \tag{21.15}$$

which is the definition of recursive utility. The value $V(t)$ of the minimum in (21.12) is identical to the recursive objective function (21.7).

21.5 Individual Investor Optimality

In complete markets, it is possible to transform the intertemporal optimization problems with recursive preferences into a global one, in the manner of Cox and Huang. As we saw in chapter 10, this approach brings two benefits: separability of portfolio selection from consumption decisions and construction of the optimal portfolio as a replication strategy. One way to do that has been proposed by Schroder and Skiadas (1999). A simplifying reformulation is based on variational utility. The latter opens the possibility of constructing a representative investor, a question we examine in section 21.6 below.

The first-order conditions of optimality for an investor who maximizes his stochastic differential utility (21.7) are shown to be fairly complex, in that they involve so-called forward-backward SDEs. These are SDEs for which some of the associated boundary conditions are initial conditions and others are terminal conditions.

21.5.1 Choice of the Consumption Path in Complete Markets

Consider the optimality problem of an investor who maximizes (21.10) or (21.7), receives no endowments on the way, starts from initial (financial and total) wealth W_0, and has access to exacly the same set of securities that we considered in chapter 10. As we saw there, it can be shown that, under technical conditions, the investor's problem can be written using a single, lifetime constraint, which says that, with the exogenous process $\{\xi(s)\}$, wealth is the present value of future consumption, just as under expected utility:

$$W_0 = \mathbb{E}_0\left[\int_0^T \xi(s)c(s)ds\right] \tag{21.16}$$

We can build, as usual, a Lagrangean, defined on the consumption process, the utility process, and a single Lagrangean multiplier λ_0:

$$\min_{\nu} \mathbb{E}_0\left[\int_0^T \varkappa(t)\mathfrak{F}(c(t), \nu(t))dt\right] + \lambda_0 \times \left(W_0 - \mathbb{E}_0\left[\int_0^T \xi(s)c(s)ds\right]\right)$$

The first-order conditions for its maximization with respect to the consumption stream can be obtained:

$$\varkappa(t)\mathfrak{F}_1(c(t), \nu(t)) = \lambda_0\xi(t)$$

which, given remark 21.2, is equivalent to:

$$\varkappa(t)\mathfrak{f}_1(c(t), V(t)) = \lambda_0\xi(t) \tag{21.17}$$

while (21.7) must hold along the way.

Remark 21.3   *The marginal utility of consumption in the form $\mathfrak{f}_1$ is a function not only of current c but also of the level of utility V, which is a stochastic variable. Similarly, the marginal utility in the form $\mathfrak{F}_1$ is a function of both c and the discount rate v, which is also a stochastic variable. These additional stochastic variables entering the pricing kernel open the possibility of generating risk premia larger than they are under time-additivity. See proposition 21.2 below. In discrete time, as we saw above, that observation was made in various forms by Epstein (1988), Epstein and Zin (1989), and Giovannini and Weil (1989).*

Under usual conditions including Inada conditions, these equations have a unique solution for c as a function of[14]

$$\lambda(t) \triangleq \lambda_0 \frac{\xi(t)}{\varkappa(t)}$$

Let us call $\mathfrak{h}$ the function giving the demand for consumption:

$$c(t) = \mathfrak{h}(V(t), \lambda(t)) \tag{21.19}$$

that is, the function inverse of (21.17).

Because the market is complete, the process ξ is given to us but the process $1/\varkappa$, with percentage drift v still needs to be calculated. Or, if we make use of the first-order condition (21.14), the process V needs to be calculated.

The situation we face is analogous to the one we encountered in chapter 14 on incomplete markets, with two crucial differences.

- There the unknown v was the *diffusion* of the investor-specific pricing process ξ while here the unknown v is the *drift* of the proces $\varkappa^{-1}$, which multiplies the universal pricing process, which is given.

- There the unknown diffusion could only be obtained jointly with the portfolios whereas here it is possible to solve for the unknown drift in a first Cox-Huang stage and then to solve for portfolios in a second-stage replication that is completely identical to the one in chapter 10.

Schroder and Skiadas (1999) view the system made of (21.17), (21.7), (21.11), and (21.15), to be solved for the processes c, v, λ, and V, as a backward-forward system of SDEs: forward SDE (21.18) for λ, with *initial* condition $\lambda(0) = \lambda_0$ and "backward" SDEs for V, with *terminal* condition $V(T) = 0$.[15] With a Markovian assumption, the system can also be solved by means of a backward PDE for the unknown function G: $V(t) = G(\lambda(t), Y(t), t)$, where $Y(t)$ is a vector of state variables capturing non IID aspects,

---

14 From (8.16) and (21.13), the SDE for λ is:

$$d\lambda(t) = -\lambda(t) \times (r - v(t)) \, dt - \lambda(t) \kappa(t)^{\mathsf{T}} \, dw(t) \tag{21.18}$$

15 The constant $\lambda_0 > 0$ then solves (21.16).

as in section 9.4.[16] The backward PDE for the function $G(\lambda, Y, t)$ is:

$$\mathfrak{f}(\mathfrak{h}(G, \lambda), G) - (r + \mathfrak{f}_2(\mathfrak{h}(G, \lambda), G))\frac{\partial G}{\partial \lambda}\lambda + \frac{1}{2}\|\kappa\|^2\frac{\partial^2 G}{\partial \lambda^2}\lambda^2 \qquad (21.20)$$

$$+ \frac{\partial G}{\partial Y}\mu_Y(Y, t) + \frac{1}{2}\text{trace}\left[\sigma_Y^{\mathsf{T}}\frac{\partial^2 G}{\partial Y^2}\sigma_Y\right] + \frac{\partial^2 G}{\partial Y \partial \lambda}\sigma_Y \kappa^{\mathsf{T}}\lambda + \frac{\partial G}{\partial t} = 0$$

with terminal condition:[17]

$$G(\lambda, Y, T) = 0$$

Once the function G is obtained, the rest of the first-stage solution follows:

$$\begin{cases} c(t) = \mathfrak{h}\left(G(t, \lambda(t), Y(t)), \lambda(t)\right) \\ v(t) = -\mathfrak{f}_2\left[c(t), G(t, \lambda(t), Y(t))\right] \end{cases}$$

which completely determines the joint process $\{c(t), \lambda(t)\}$. In the second stage, portfolios are obtained by replication of the c process.

In the example that follows, we illustrate the workings of the Cox-Huang first stage. However, since, in practice, it will be unavoidable in this case, when optimizing consumption, to make a Markovian assumption and to solve a PDE, one must recognize that the elegant Cox-Huang two-stage procedure loses some of its appeal as compared to dynamic programming, which solves for consumption and portfolio choice together as was done in chapter 9.

By solving exercise 21.3, the reader can verify that both approaches are equivalent.

21.5.2   Benchmark Example

We consider the same available securities as in section 9.2, with IID returns on one risky security and one riskless security with a constant rate of interest but utility is now stochastic differential utility.

In the case of the continuous-time CES isoelastic aggregator (21.8),

$$\mathfrak{f}_1(c, u) = \beta\frac{c^{\rho-1}}{(\gamma u)^{\frac{\rho}{\gamma}-1}}$$

so that the function $\mathfrak{h}(V, \lambda)$ giving the consumption choice is

$$c = \left[\lambda\frac{1}{\beta}(\gamma G)^{\frac{\rho}{\gamma}-1}\right]^{\frac{1}{\rho-1}}$$

and

$$\mathfrak{f}_2(c, u) = \frac{\beta}{\rho}\left[(\gamma - \rho)\frac{c^{\rho}}{(\gamma u)^{\frac{\rho}{\gamma}}} - \gamma\right]$$

---

16 Please, refer to the notation of that section for the process Y.

17 The lifetime utility function (21.7) ignores the bequest motive $\wp\,(W)$. Otherwise, we would write $G(\lambda, Y, T) = \wp\,(\mathfrak{G}\,(\lambda))$ where $\mathfrak{G}$ is the function inverse of $\partial\wp/\partial W$.

so that the PDE (21.20) for the function $G(\lambda, t)$ is

$$\frac{\beta}{\rho}\left[\left(\lambda\frac{1}{\beta}\right)^{\frac{\rho}{\rho-1}}(\gamma G)^{\left(\frac{\rho}{\gamma}-1\right)\frac{1}{\rho-1}} - \gamma G\right]$$

$$-\left(r + \frac{\beta}{\rho}\left[(\gamma - \rho)\left(\lambda\frac{1}{\beta}\right)^{\frac{\rho}{\rho-1}}(\gamma G)^{\left(\frac{\rho}{\gamma}-1\right)\frac{1}{\rho-1}-1} - \gamma\right]\right)\frac{\partial G}{\partial \lambda}\lambda$$

$$+\frac{1}{2}\kappa^2\frac{\partial^2 G}{\partial \lambda^2}\lambda^2 + \frac{\partial G}{\partial t} = 0$$

The solution is

$$G(\lambda, t) = \frac{1}{\gamma}A(t)^{\frac{1}{1-\gamma}}\lambda^{\frac{\gamma}{\gamma-1}}$$

with a function $A(t)$ that solves the following ODE:

$$\gamma\left(\frac{1}{\rho} - 1\right)\left(\frac{1}{\beta}\right)^{1/(\rho-1)}A(t)^{\left(\rho+\frac{\rho}{\gamma}-1\right)\frac{1}{\rho-1}} - A(t)\varrho + A'(t) = 0$$

$$\varrho = \frac{\gamma\beta}{\rho} - \gamma\left(r - \frac{1}{2}\frac{1}{(\gamma-1)}\left(\frac{\mu-r}{\sigma}\right)^2\right)$$

under boundary condition $A(T) = 0$.[18]
  Hence

$$c = \left[\frac{1}{\beta}\right]^{\frac{1}{\rho-1}}\lambda^{\frac{1}{\gamma-1}}A(t)^{\frac{1}{1-\gamma}\left(\frac{\rho}{\gamma}-1\right)\frac{1}{\rho-1}}$$

and

$$\nu = \frac{\gamma\beta}{\rho} + \left(1 - \frac{\gamma}{\rho}\right)\left[\frac{1}{\beta}A(t)^{\frac{\rho}{\gamma}}\right]^{\frac{1}{\rho-1}}$$

which is a deterministic function in this example. The behavior of ν entirely determines the behavior of λ except for the initial condition $\lambda(0) = \lambda_0$ where λ_0 should be chosen to match the lifetime budget constraint.

  We proceed to the second stage and calculate portfolios. For that, we write the PDE for wealth $W(\lambda, \xi, t)$, as in (10.19). It would generally be a degenerate PDE because ξ and λ are perfectly correlated. But, in this example, because the processes ν and, therefore $\varkappa$, are deterministic, ξ and λ are actually functions of each other and time. Hence, we can write a

---

18 The solution is:

$$A(t) = d\left(\frac{1 - e^{-a(T-t)}}{a}\right)^b; \quad d = \beta^{\gamma/\rho}; a = \varrho/b; b = \gamma\left(\frac{1}{\rho} - 1\right)$$

PDE (analogous to (10.19)) for a function $W(\lambda, t)$ of one of the two arguments ξ and λ:

$$\left(\frac{1}{\beta}\right)^{\frac{1}{\rho-1}} \lambda^{\frac{1}{\gamma-1}} A(t)^{\frac{1}{1-\gamma}\left(\frac{\rho}{\gamma}-1\right)\frac{1}{\rho-1}} - \frac{\partial W}{\partial \lambda} \times \left(r - \frac{\gamma\beta}{\rho} - \left(1 - \frac{\gamma}{\rho}\right)\left[\frac{1}{\beta}A(t)^{\frac{\rho}{\gamma}}\right]^{\frac{1}{\rho-1}}\right)\lambda$$

$$+\frac{1}{2}\frac{\partial^2 W}{\partial\lambda^2}\kappa^2\lambda^2 + \frac{\partial W}{\partial t} - r \times W + \frac{\partial W}{\partial\lambda}\kappa^2\lambda = 0$$

with a terminal condition $W(\lambda, T) = 0$. The solution is:

$$W = \lambda^{\frac{1}{\gamma-1}} A(t)^{\frac{1}{1-\gamma}}$$

from which it follows by Itô's lemma that the relative diffusion of wealth is $-\kappa/(\gamma-1)$. The budget equation in SDE form says that that same relative diffusion is given by $x_1\sigma$, if we call x_1 the fraction of wealth invested in the risky asset. Hence:

$$x_1(t) = \frac{1}{1-\gamma}\frac{\kappa}{\sigma}$$

which is a constant portfolio composition, identical to the composition under time-additive utility, as was pointed out some time ago by Svensson (1989).

21.6 Equilibrium with Recursive Utility in Complete Markets

We saw above that the formulation of recursive utility as (21.2) in discrete time, or (21.7) in continuous time, permits the solution of investor intertemporal optimization problems. In the Markovian case, thanks to the recursive property of the utility of a consumption stream, dynamic programming can be used, just as it was with time additivity because it is a technique that exploits recursivity. Problems of equilibrium and Pareto optimality, however, become difficult even in the complete-market case because of the functional difficulty in combining investor utility of that type into an overall welfare function. Let us consider such equilibrium issues.

21.6.1 Direct Calculation of Equilibrium

As was done in previous chapters, it is quite possible to calculate an equilibrium directly by putting together all the first-order conditions of each and every investor as well as the market-clearing condition, which, in a complete market, are equivalent to the ARC at each point in time and in each and every state:

$$\begin{cases} \sum_{m=1}^{M} c^m(t) = \sum_{m=1}^{M} \mathfrak{h}^m\left(V^m(t), \lambda_0^m \frac{\xi(t)}{\varkappa^m(t)}\right) \\ v^m(t) = -\mathfrak{f}_2\left(c^m(t), V^m(t), Y(t)\right) \end{cases}$$

where each $\varkappa^m(t)$ evolves as in (21.13) so that here $\varkappa^m(0) = 1$, and $V^m(t)$ is given by $G^m(\lambda(t), Y(t), t)$ where the function G^m is the solution of the PDE (21.20).

So, the calculation would proceed as follows:[19]

- start from the terminal date T and set:

$$G^m(\lambda, Y, T) = 0$$

for each investor m. There is no need to solve for anything at date T.

- assuming the problem has been solved at later dates, at date t use the solution $G^m(\lambda, Y, t)$ of the PDE (21.20) for each investor to write:

$$\sum_{m=1}^{M} c^m(t) = \sum_{m=1}^{M} \mathfrak{h}^m\left(G^m\left(\lambda_0^m \frac{\xi(t)}{\varkappa^m(t)}, Y, t\right), \lambda_0^m \frac{\xi(t)}{\varkappa^m(t)}\right)$$

and solve this equation for stochastic discount factors ξ, thus getting a function

$$\xi\left(\sum_{m=1}^{M} c^m, \left\{\frac{\lambda_0^m}{\varkappa^m}\right\}_{m=1}^{M}, Y, t\right) \tag{21.21}$$

- at date 0, perform the same calculation and use the process $\xi(t)$ obtained along the way to price the consumption stream of each investor as an expected value

$$\mathbb{E}_0\left[\int_0^T \xi\left(\left\{\frac{\lambda_0^m}{\varkappa^m(t)}\right\}_{m=1}^{M}, Y, t\right) \mathfrak{h}^m\left(G^m\left(\lambda_0^m \frac{\xi(t)}{\varkappa^m(t)}, Y, t\right),\right.\right.$$
$$\left.\left. \frac{\lambda_0^m}{\varkappa^m(t)} \xi\left(\sum_{m=1}^{M} c^m(t), \left\{\frac{\lambda_0^m}{\varkappa^m(t)}\right\}_{m=1}^{M}, Y\right)\right) dt\right]$$

(solving for the purpose a linear PDE derived from the Feynman-Kac formula, where the unknown is the function $W^m\left(\{\lambda_0^m\}_{m=1}^{M}, Y, 0\right)$). Then choose the initial values of the Lagrange multipliers $\{\lambda_0^m\}$ in such a way that $W^m(\{\lambda_0\}, Y(0), 0)$ matches the initial wealth endowment W_0^m of each investor.

- once that is all done, the economists can start from date 0 again and obtain multiple simulated paths of the economy moving forward, based on the functions obtained at each time step.

Because the direct calculation, in this case, is cumbersome, it is probably more efficient to calculate the equilibrium as a Pareto optimum.

---

19 Duffie, Geoffard, and Skiadas (1994) actually present this procedure as a way to calculate a Pareto optimal allocation.

21.6.2 Calculating a Pareto Optimum Conveniently

In an economy populated by M investors, Epstein (1987) defines efficient allocations as those that solve a problem of the type:

$$\max_{\{c^m(t)\}_{t=0}^T\}_{m=1}^M} \sum_{m=1}^M \alpha^m u^m \left(\{c^m(t)\}_{t=0}^T\right) \tag{21.22}$$

where $\{\alpha^m\}_{m=1}^M$ are non-negative numbers and where $\left\{\{c^m(t)\}_{t=0}^T\right\}_{m=1}^M$ must belong to an appropriately defined feasible set, such as the one defined by the ARC. The difficulty is that one cannot interchange the aggregation over time – which is nonlinear within each u^m – with the weighted average operator that serves to construct social welfare. Hence, it becomes difficult to solve the welfare problem sequentially. To solve this difficulty, Dumas, Uppal, and Wang (2000) exploit the quasi time additivity of the variational-utility formulation.

We formulate the α-efficient allocation problem (21.22) as an optimization problem with stochastic variational utility.

Using (21.12), the central planner's dynamic problem leading to a Pareto efficient allocation can be written as:

$$\max_{\{c^m\}_{m=1}^M} \min_{\{v^m\}_{m=1}^M} \sum_{m=1}^M \mathbb{E}_0 \left(\int_0^T \varkappa^m(s) \mathfrak{F}^m(c^m(s), v^m(s)) ds \right) \tag{21.23}$$

subject to the ARC and, for $m = 1, \ldots, M$:

$$d\varkappa^m(s) = -v^m(s)\varkappa^m(s)ds; \qquad \varkappa^m(0) = \alpha^m \tag{21.24}$$

where the α^ms are (scalar) investor's weights and the superscript m indicates the variable associated with investor m. In the Markovian case, this problem can be tackled using the standard dynamic programming approach.

It is best conceptually *not* to think of the time-varying $\varkappa^m$s as welfare weights (of Negishi). Instead, the constant α^ms are the welfare weights, which are appropriate to mimic equilibrium in a complete market. The time-varying weights $\varkappa^m$s are equal to the welfare weights times *each investor's* psychological discount factor.

***Remark* 21.4** *Under time-additive utility, the weights $\varkappa^m$s would be constant but, with recursive utility they evolve according to the SDE (21.24). That SDE contains no Brownian term. That is in sharp contrast with the evolution of the implied weights in an incomplete market with time-additive utility. See section 15.5.1. There the weights contain a Brownian term reflecting the unhedgeability of some risks. Of course, in an incomplete market with recursive utility, the two types of weights would multiply each other.*

When it is written in the form (21.23), it is immediately apparent why the welfare optimum, in an economy in which each investor's utility function is recursive, is an intricate problem:

Proposition 21.1 *The welfare function (21.23) is not a recursive utility function.*

Indeed, although the Negishi weights α^m are fixed numbers, as is always the case in a complete market, at time later than time 0, the felicity function at time t is weighted by time-varying factors $\varkappa^m(t)$, which reflect past decisions – including past consumption decisions. When solving the welfare problem (21.23) by dynamic programming, it is necessary to keep track of the $\varkappa^m$s, which are inherited from the past, thereby violating the condition of independence from past behavior stated in the definition 21.1 of recursive preferences. These time varying factors must be regarded as endogenous state variables of the welfare-maximization problem.

In other words, the aggregation of several investors each of whose utility belongs to the class of recursive utility functions does not produce a utility function belonging to that class. The class is not stable under aggregation. The proposition underscores one grievous fact. When an economic modeler postulates the existence of a "representative" investor with recursive utility, *he is in effect assuming that the utility functions of all investors are identical.*

21.6.3 The Markovian Case

Let $Y(t)$ be a (vector) state process such that

$$dY(t) = \mu_Y(Y(t), \vartheta(t), t)\, dt + \sigma_Y(Y(t), \vartheta(t), t) \times dw(t) \tag{21.25}$$

where μ_Y is an adapted process, w is a K-dimensional standard Wiener process, which generates the filtration, the matrix-valued process σ_Y is of dimension $H \times K$, and $\vartheta(t)$ is a k-dimensional control variable that may have $\{c^m\}_{m=1}^M$ as one of its components and portfolio choice as other components. We assume that the diffusion and drift coefficients, σ_Y and μ_Y, satisfy the usual uniform (for given ϑ) Lipschitz and linear growth conditions in $Y(t)$ so that the SDE in (21.25) has a unique solution. For any fixed ϑ and for any function g that is twice continuously differentiable in y and continuously differentiable in (y, t), call $\mathcal{D}^\vartheta g$ the differential operator associated with the state process $Y(t)$.

In view of the reformulation in the previous section, writing $\varkappa$ for $\{\varkappa^m\}_{m=1}^M$, the optimization problem we consider is

$$J(\{\varkappa\}, Y, t) \triangleq \max_{\{c, \vartheta\}} \min_{\{v\}} \mathbb{E}_t \left\{ \int_t^T \sum_{m=1}^M \varkappa^m(s) \mathfrak{F}^m(c^m(s), v^m(s))\, ds \right\} \tag{21.26}$$

with constraints, determined also by the endowments e. The constraints, written for $s \geq t$, are

$$\sum_{m=1}^{M} c^m(s) \leq e(Y(s)) \tag{21.27}$$

$$d\varkappa^m(s) = -\nu^m(s)\varkappa^m(s)ds; \; \varkappa^m(0) = \alpha^m \quad m = 1, \ldots, M \tag{21.28}$$

$$J(\varkappa, Y, T) = 0 \quad \forall \varkappa, Y \tag{21.29}$$

Now, we proceed to the characterization of these allocations using the above optimization problem. The Bellman equation of the problem in (21.26-21.29) is:

$$0 = \max_{\{c,\vartheta\}} \left\{ \min_{\{v\}} \left[\sum_{m=1}^{M} \varkappa^m \left[\mathfrak{F}^m(c^m, \nu^m) - J_{\varkappa^m}(\{\varkappa\}, Y, t)\nu^m \right] \right] + \mathcal{D}^\vartheta J(\varkappa, Y, t) \right\} \tag{21.30}$$

Remark 21.5 *It is clear by inspection that this Bellman equation admits a solution that is homogeneous of degree 1 in $\{\varkappa_m\}_{m=1}^{M}$. Hence, by Euler's theorem: $J(\{\varkappa\}, Y, t) = \sum_{m=1}^{M} \varkappa^m J_{\varkappa^m}(\varkappa, Y, t)$.*

Remark 21.6 *In equation (21.30), the* min *operator, by virtue of Legendre duality (21.9), is easily taken care of. Equation (21.30) can be rewritten:*

$$0 = \max_{\{c,\vartheta\}} \left\{ \sum_{m=1}^{M} \varkappa^m \mathfrak{f}^m(c^m, J_{\varkappa^m}(\{\varkappa\}, Y, t)) + \mathcal{D}^\vartheta J(\{\varkappa\}, Y, t) \right\} \tag{21.31}$$

The advantage of this characterization of α-efficient allocations based on variational utility (as compared to, say, Duffie *et al.* (1994) and to the direct calculation of equilibrium done above) is that it allows us to solve for the allocation using the familiar technique of dynamic programming *using only one PDE and one value function J*, namely the aggregate derived-social welfare function.[20]

The investors' utility levels remain implicit, being encapsulated inside the welfare function; at no point in the course of our method do we need to determine them explicitly. The relation between the aggregate welfare process and the investors' utility processes is: $V^m = J_{\varkappa^m}$. The investor utility levels are the gradients of the welfare level taken with respect to the weights.

21.6.4   The Market Prices of Risk

Once the function $J(\{\varkappa\}, Y, t)$ is obtained for a given set of Pareto weights $\{\alpha^m\}_{m=1}^{M}$, we can get securities' prices in a decentralized version of the same economy. First, as we just mentioned, the derivative with respect to $\varkappa^m$ is the utility V^m of investor m derived from

---

20 A superb application of this technique is made in Borovicka (2015) and in Osambela *et al.* (2016).

the continuation of the Pareto optimal program. Second, to obtain the state prices we sum the inverted first-order conditions for consumption of all investors:

$$\sum_{m=1}^{M} c^m = \sum_{m=1}^{M} \mathfrak{h}^m \left(J_{\varkappa^m}(\{\varkappa\}, Y, t), \frac{\xi}{\varkappa^m} \right) \tag{21.32}$$

That equation, in which aggregate consumption $\sum_{m=1}^{M} c^m$ is a given, is to be solved for ξ at each point in time and for all values of Y and $\{\varkappa^m\}_{m=1}^{M}$, thus getting a stochastic discount factor equal to:

$$\xi \left(\sum_{m=1}^{M} c^m, Y, \{\varkappa^m\}_{m=1}^{M}, t \right) \tag{21.33}$$

Third, at date 0, use the process $\xi(t)$ to price the consumption stream of each investor as an expected value

$$\mathbb{E}_0 \left[\int_0^T \xi \left(\sum_{m=1}^{M} c^m(t), Y(t), \{\varkappa^m(t)\}_{m=1}^{M}, t \right) \right.$$

$$\left. \times \mathfrak{h}^m \left(J_{\varkappa^m}(\{\varkappa(t)\}, Y(t), t), \frac{1}{\varkappa^m(t)} \xi \left(\sum_{m=1}^{M} c^m(t), Y(t), \{\varkappa^m(t)\}_{m=1}^{M}, t \right) \right) dt \right]$$

(solving for the purpose a linear PDE where, recalling that $\varkappa^m(0) = \alpha^m$, the unknown is the function $W^m(\{\alpha^m\}_{m=1}^{M}, Y, 0)$). Then, choose the Pareto weights $\{\alpha^m\}$ in such a way that $W^m(\{\alpha^m\}_{m=1}^{M}, Y(0), 0)$ matches the initial wealth endowment W_0^m of each investor.

The results (21.21) and (21.33) establish an important proposition about pricing:

Proposition 21.2   *Under recursive, non-additive utility, the risk of the evolution of the exogenous state variables Y is priced over and beyond the risk of aggregate consumption.*

The way we obtained the stochastic-discount factor function (21.33) makes clear the difference between time-additive and non-time-additive (but still recursive) utility functions. As we saw in previous chapters, had the utility functions been time-additive, the marginal utility of consumption would only have been a function of consumption and time and not a function of derived utility V. Then equation (21.32) would just have been:

$$\sum_{m=1}^{M} c^m = \sum_{m=1}^{M} \mathfrak{h}^m \left(\frac{\xi}{\alpha^m}, t \right)$$

so that the solution for the stochastic discount factor ξ would have been a function of aggregate consumption and time at the most. That was the message of the Breeden CAPM. Immediate aggregate consumption was the only form of risk that was priced.

When utility is not time-additive, *delayed risks*, captured by the derived utility V of subsequent consumption, are also priced.

The reader can solve exercise 21.4.

21.7   Back to the Puzzles: Pricing under Recursive Utility

Delayed risks – in the sense of risks that do not affect the immediate investment period – open one more avenue towards the solution of the asset pricing puzzles. Consider, for instance, an economic equilibrium in which consumption not only is stochastic but its volatility is also stochastic (being driven by some exogenous or endogenous state variable Y of the type considered in (21.25); see chapter 17). With time-additive utility, the risk of volatility receives a zero price over and beyond the price already charged for its covariance with immediate-period consumption risk. But, with recursive utility, the volatility of consumption can be, or can be driven by, a state variable Y of which we have seen in proposition 21.2 that it can be priced over and beyond consumption risk, thus contributing an additional risk premium.

In the model of Bansal and Yaron (2004), which is a single-investor (or rather homogeneous-investor) model, cast in discrete time, the volatility and the expected value of aggregate consumption follow an autoregressive process of order one. Their model seems to solve both the equity premium and the interest-rate puzzle.[21] Similar to Bansal and Yaron, other single-investor problems with recursive utility that appeared in the literature have done quite a good job in solving the empirical puzzles. They go under the label of "long-run risk models," because recursive utility is not used in isolation, but together with a state variable which contains a long-lasting or slow-moving component, to produce a sizable risk premium that can explain the puzzles. Here are several interpretations that have been made of the mysterious slow-moving state variable. In Kaltenbrunner and Lochstoer (2010), the variable is interpreted as the capital stock. In Kung and Schmid (2015) it is the level of technological knowledge. In Maurer (2014) and Favero, Gozlukla, and Tamoni (2011), it is demographics. In Bansal, Kiku, and Ochoa (2015), it is climate change. In Kung (2015) and in Gavazzoni (2012), it is inflation. And in Favilukis and Lin (2016) and in Kuehn, Petrosky-Nadeau, and Zhang (2013), it is sticky wages.

However, a caveat may be in order. It is quite common in the recursive-utility literature to build on the solution for optimal consumption under time-additive utility, or on solutions to similar problems, in which the EIS is equal to one, by using a linearization of the

---

21 The value of the EIS parameter assumed by Bansal and Yaron, above 1, is controversial. Indeed, the EIS is usually estimated by regressing consumption growth on securities's returns or the rate of interest, or vice versa. There is a lot of econometric debate on that matter. It was traditionally thought that the EIS had to be quite a bit smaller than 1 (in Hall (1978)'s historic article the number found was 0.3). But recent evidence that tracks the behavior of separate categories of households has produced numbers above 1 (see Attanasio and Weber (1989)). Bansal and Yaron add that, when volatility is stochastic, estimated values of the EIS are biased downward. So, they can be estimated to be lower than one when they are in fact greater.

Campbell and Shiller (1988) type. The linearization permits to solve the problem when the EIS is not one. This is the approach taken for instance in Bansal and Yaron (2004) and most of this literature. However, the approximation introduced by the Campbell and Shiller linearization is not negligible. This is proved in Kraft, Seifred, and Steffensen (2011) for the case in which the volatility is stochastic (of the Heston type).

In addition, those models exploit the properties of recursive utility but do not consider heterogeneous investors in a true equilibrium model of the manner of section 21.6.2. There is a lot of potential for future work in this subarea of asset pricing.

21.8   Conclusion

In this chapter, following chapter 20, we have reviewed the second attempt made during the last decade to explain asset pricing puzzles. It is based on recursive, but not time-additive, utility, which prices risks other than consumption risks, such as the risk of future long-run consumption. It also has the potential to create larger risk premia than the classic consumption model does.

21.9   Appendix 1: Proof of the Giovannini-Weil Stochastic Discount Factor, Equation (21.5)

With the CES aggregator,

$$
\mathcal{W}_1(t) = \frac{1}{\gamma} \frac{\gamma}{\rho} \left\{ (c(t))^\rho + \beta \times (\mathbb{E}_t [V(t+1)])^{\frac{\rho}{\gamma}} \right\}^{\frac{\gamma}{\rho}-1} \rho \, (c(t))^{\rho-1}
$$

$$
= \frac{1}{\gamma} \frac{\gamma}{\rho} \left\{ [\gamma \mathcal{W}]^{\frac{\rho}{\gamma}} \right\}^{\frac{\gamma}{\rho}-1} \rho \, (c(t))^{\rho-1}
$$

$$
= \gamma^{-\frac{\rho}{\gamma}} \frac{\gamma}{\rho} \mathcal{W}^{\frac{\frac{\gamma}{\rho}-1}{\frac{\gamma}{\rho}}} \rho \, (c(t))^{\rho-1}
$$

$$
\mathcal{W}_2(t) = \gamma^{1-\frac{\rho}{\gamma}} \frac{\gamma}{\rho} \mathcal{W}^{\frac{\frac{\gamma}{\rho}-1}{\frac{\gamma}{\rho}}} \beta \frac{\rho}{\gamma} (\gamma \mathbb{E}_t [V(t+1)])^{\frac{\rho}{\gamma}-1}
$$

$$
\mathcal{W}_2(t) \frac{\mathcal{W}_1(t+1)}{\mathcal{W}_1(t)} = \gamma^{1-\frac{\rho}{\gamma}} \frac{\gamma}{\rho} (V(t))^{\frac{\frac{\gamma}{\rho}-1}{\frac{\gamma}{\rho}}} \beta \frac{\rho}{\gamma} (\gamma \mathbb{E}_t [V(t+1)])^{\frac{\rho}{\gamma}-1}
$$

$$
\times \frac{\gamma^{-\frac{\rho}{\gamma}} \frac{\gamma}{\rho} (V(t))^{\frac{\frac{\gamma}{\rho}-1}{\frac{\gamma}{\rho}}} \rho \, (c(t))^{\rho-1}}{\gamma^{-\frac{\rho}{\gamma}} \frac{\gamma}{\rho} (V(t))^{\frac{\frac{\gamma}{\rho}-1}{\frac{\gamma}{\rho}}} \rho \, (c(t))^{\rho-1}}
$$

Notice that the CES aggregator is special in that $V(t)$ cancels from the stochastic discount factor:

$$\mathcal{W}_2(t)\frac{\mathcal{W}_1(t+1)}{\mathcal{W}_1(t)} = \beta \left(\mathbb{E}_t\left[V\left(t+1\right)\right]\right)^{\frac{\rho}{\gamma}-1}\frac{(V(t))^{\frac{\frac{\gamma}{\rho}-1}{}}\,(c(t))^{\rho-1}}{(c(t))^{\rho-1}}$$

$$= \beta \left(\frac{c(t+1)}{c(t)}\right)^{\rho-1}\left(\frac{V(t+1)}{\mathbb{E}_t\left[V\left(t+1\right)\right]}\right)^{1-\frac{\rho}{\gamma}}$$

Define $\upsilon(t)$:[22]

$$V(t) \triangleq \frac{1}{\gamma}\,(c(t))^{\gamma}\,(\upsilon\,(t))^{\frac{\gamma}{\rho}}$$

Then the stochastic discount factor is

$$\beta\frac{\left(\frac{c(t+1)}{c(t)}\right)^{\gamma-1}(\upsilon(t+1))^{\frac{\gamma}{\rho}-1}}{\left(\mathbb{E}_t\left[\left(\frac{c(t+1)}{c(t)}\right)^{\gamma}(\upsilon\,(t+1))^{\frac{\gamma}{\rho}}\right]\right)^{1-\frac{\rho}{\gamma}}}$$

and the recursion (21.3) implies

$$\upsilon(t) = 1 + \beta \left(\mathbb{E}_t\left[\left(\frac{c(t+1)}{c(t)}\right)^{\gamma}(\upsilon\,(t+1))^{\frac{\gamma}{\rho}}\right]\right)^{\frac{\rho}{\gamma}}$$

or:

$$\upsilon\,(t) - 1 = \beta\frac{\mathbb{E}_t\left[\left(\frac{c(t+1)}{c(t)}\right)^{\gamma}(\upsilon\,(t+1))^{\frac{\gamma}{\rho}-1}\,(1+\upsilon(t+1)-1)\right]}{\left(\mathbb{E}_t\left[\left(\frac{c(t+1)}{c(t)}\right)^{\gamma}(\upsilon\,(t+1))^{\frac{\gamma}{\rho}}\right]\right)^{1-\frac{\rho}{\gamma}}}$$

Meanwhile, consider an asset paying a stream $c(t)$. Its price at time t (not including time-t consumption), $\mathfrak{W}(t)$, satisfies:

$$\frac{\mathfrak{W}(t)}{c(t)} = \beta\frac{\mathbb{E}_t\left[\left(\frac{c(t+1)}{c(t)}\right)^{\gamma}(\upsilon(t+1))^{\frac{\gamma}{\rho}-1}\left(1+\frac{\mathfrak{W}(t+1)}{c(t+1)}\right)\right]}{\left(\mathbb{E}_t\left[\left(\frac{c(t+1)}{c(t)}\right)^{\gamma}(\upsilon(t+1))^{\frac{\gamma}{\rho}}\right]\right)^{1-\frac{\rho}{\gamma}}}$$

Comparing the last two equations shows that:[23]

$$\upsilon(t) - 1 \equiv \frac{\mathfrak{W}(t)}{c(t)}$$

and the gross return $R(t)$ on the consumption asset is:

$$R(t+1) \triangleq \frac{c(t+1)+\mathfrak{W}(t+1)}{\mathfrak{W}(t)} = \frac{c(t+1)}{c(t)}\frac{1+\frac{\mathfrak{W}(t+1)}{c(t+1)}}{\frac{\mathfrak{W}(t)}{c(t)}} = \frac{c(t+1)}{c(t)}\frac{\upsilon(t+1)}{\upsilon(t)-1}$$

---

22 This proof is adapted from a proof of Semyon Malamud (EPFL).

23 The terminal conditions are: $\mathfrak{W}(T) = 0$ and $\upsilon(T) = 1$.

and satisfies

$$
1 = \beta \frac{\mathbb{E}_t\left[\left(\frac{c(t+1)}{c(t)}\right)^{\gamma-1} (v(t+1))^{\frac{\gamma}{\rho}-1} R(t+1)\right]}{\left(\mathbb{E}_t\left[\left(\frac{c(t+1)}{c(t)}\right)^{\gamma} (v(t+1))^{\frac{\gamma}{\rho}}\right]\right)^{1-\frac{\rho}{\gamma}}}
$$

Therefore the stochastic discount factor becomes:

$$
\beta \frac{\left(\frac{c(t+1)}{c(t)}\right)^{\gamma-1}\left(R(t+1)\frac{\frac{v(t)-1}{c(t+1)}}{\frac{c(t+1)}{c(t)}}\right)^{\frac{\gamma}{\rho}-1}}{\left(\mathbb{E}_t\left[\left(\frac{c(t+1)}{c(t)}\right)^{\gamma}(v(t+1))^{\frac{\gamma}{\rho}}\right]\right)^{1-\frac{\rho}{\gamma}}}
$$

$$
= \beta \frac{\left(\frac{c(t+1)}{c(t)}\right)^{\gamma-1}\left(\frac{\frac{v(t)-1}{c(t+1)}}{\frac{c(t+1)}{c(t)}}\right)^{\frac{\gamma}{\rho}-1}(R(t+1))^{\frac{\gamma}{\rho}-1}}{\left(\mathbb{E}_t\left[\left(\frac{c(t+1)}{c(t)}\right)^{\gamma}(v(t+1))^{\frac{\gamma}{\rho}}\right]\right)^{1-\frac{\rho}{\gamma}}}
$$

$$
= \beta \frac{\left(\frac{c(t+1)}{c(t)}\right)^{\gamma-1}\left(\frac{\beta\left(\mathbb{E}_t\left[\left(\frac{c(t+1)}{c(t)}\right)^{\gamma}(v(t+1))^{\frac{\gamma}{\rho}}\right]\right)^{\frac{\rho}{\gamma}}}{\frac{c(t+1)}{c(t)}}\right)^{\frac{\rho}{\gamma}\cdot\frac{\gamma}{\rho}-1}(R(t+1))^{\frac{\gamma}{\rho}-1}}{\left(\mathbb{E}_t\left[\left(\frac{c(t+1)}{c(t)}\right)^{\gamma}(v(t+1))^{\frac{\gamma}{\rho}}\right]\right)^{1-\frac{\rho}{\gamma}}}
$$

$$
= \beta^{\frac{\gamma}{\rho}}\left(\frac{c(t+1)}{c(t)}\right)^{\gamma-1}\left(\frac{1}{\frac{c(t+1)}{c(t)}}\right)^{\frac{\gamma}{\rho}-1}(R(t+1))^{\frac{\gamma}{\rho}-1}
$$

which is equivalent to (21.5). $\qquad\square$

21.10 Appendix 2: Preference for the Timing of Uncertainty Resolution

When consumption is evaluated through expected utility, the investor is by construction indifferent to the time at which uncertainty is resolved over the life cycle, or over a specific consumption stream. Provided future consumption is random when the evaluation is done, the exact date at which this uncertainty will be unveiled is irrelevant. Expected utility ignores preference for early resolution of uncertainty—intuitively, knowing soon which values consumption in the future will take—versus late resolution of uncertainty. As a consequence, this trait of investors' preferences is seldom mentioned when the attention is restricted to expected utility. To be specific, suppose we are at time 1, consumption c_1 is given and equal to 5, while consumption c_2 at time 2 takes the values 0.1 and 10 with probability $1/2$, as the result of flipping a fair coin. Let us consider the following two prospects: $(c_1, c_2) = (5, 0.1)$ or $(5, 10)$ and note that consumption is not a choice variable. Its stream is exogenous, and greater or smaller information cannot be exploited to maximize utility.

We are just evaluating an exogenous consumption pattern. In a standard expected-utility framework, at time 1, the consumption stream is worth

$$u(c_1, \tilde{c}_2) = y(c_1) + \beta \mathbb{E} y(\tilde{c}_2)$$

$$= y(5) + \beta \times \left[\frac{1}{2} y(0.1) + \frac{1}{2} y(10) \right]$$

independently of whether the coin is tossed (or the state of nature in the future becomes known) just an instant after 1 or at time 2. We would like to know whether recursive preferences are able to embed preference for early or late revelation of information, namely whether, under recursive preferences, getting to know whether consumption at time 2 will be equal to 0.1 or 10 makes a difference. It is only the time at which the state of nature becomes known that changes.

It is easy to show that recursive preferences are indeed able to model early versus late preference and that – in the intuitive formulation of recursive preferences of section 21.1.2 – this depends on the relative concavity of u (the utility of current consumption) and v (the utility that serves to calculate the certainty equivalent of future consumption). When uncertainty is resolved at time 2, the overall utility is

$$u(c_1, \tilde{c}_2) = y(c_1) + \beta \times y(v^{-1}(\mathbb{E}(v(\tilde{c}_2)))) \tag{21.34}$$

$$= y(5) + \beta \times y \left[v^{-1} \left(\frac{1}{2} v(0.1) + \frac{1}{2} v(10) \right) \right]$$

When uncertainty is resolved just an instant after 1, overall time-1 utility conditional on knowing the realization of consumption at time 2 does not require the use of a certainty equivalent:

$$u(c_1, c_2) = y(c_1) + \beta y(c_2)$$

so that its unconditional value at 1 is

$$u(c_1, c_2) = y(c_1) + \beta \mathbb{E} y(\tilde{c}_2) \tag{21.35}$$

$$= y(5) + \beta \times \left[\frac{1}{2} y(0.1) + \frac{1}{2} y(10) \right]$$

as in the standard expected-utility framework. The investor is indifferent to the resolution time if (21.34) and (21.35) are the same. This happens if and only if

$$y \left[v^{-1} \left(\frac{1}{2} v(0.1) + \frac{1}{2} v(10) \right) \right]$$

$$= \frac{1}{2} y(0.1) + \frac{1}{2} y(10)$$

which means that the certainty equivalent under the y and v functions are equal:

$$v^{-1} \left(\frac{1}{2} v(0.1) + \frac{1}{2} v(10) \right)$$

$$= y^{-1} \left(\frac{1}{2} y(0.1) + \frac{1}{2} y(10) \right)$$

In the example early resolution will be preferred if and only if (21.35) is greater than (21.34), and, in general, if

$$\mathbb{E}y(\tilde{c}_2) > y(\upsilon^{-1}(\mathbb{E}(\upsilon(\tilde{c}_2))))$$

or

$$y^{-1}(\mathbb{E}y(\tilde{c}_2)) > \upsilon^{-1}(\mathbb{E}(\upsilon(\tilde{c}_2)))$$

That holds only when risk aversion as embedded by y – and measured by its Arrow-Pratt coefficient – is smaller than risk aversion as embedded in υ. These apply to different cases of information revelation. Investors who are less risk averse according to the function that determines their intratemporal choices are also the ones who prefer early information revelation.

Taking the more rigorous approach to recursive preferences of section 21.2, it can be shown (see Kreps and Porteus (1978)) that

Proposition 21.3 *Concavity (convexity) of $\mathcal{W}(c,u)$ with respect to u implies preference for earlier (later) resolution of uncertainty.*

Let us provide an example.

Example 21.4 Suppose that, faced with the consumption stream described above, the investor has as a "Kreps-Porteus" aggregator with $\beta = 0.99$, $\gamma = -1$ and $\rho = -2$:

$$\mathcal{W}(c,u) = -\left[c^{-2} + 0.99\,(-u)^2\right]^{1/2}$$

When the coin is flipped at time $t = 2$, his overall utility level is:

$$\mathcal{W}(c,u) = -\left[5^{-2} + 0.99 \times \left(\left(0.5 \times 10^{-1} + 0.5 \times 0.1^{-1}\right)\right)^2\right]^{\frac{1}{2}} = -5.0286$$

When the coin is flipped soon after time $t = 1$, his utility level is:

$$\mathcal{W}(c,u) = -0.5 \times \left[5^{-2} + 0.99 \times \left((10)^{-1}\right)^2\right]^{\frac{1}{2}}$$

$$-0.5 \times \left[5^{-2} + 0.99 \times \left((0.1)^{-1}\right)^2\right]^{\frac{1}{2}} = -5.0876$$

From the fact that the result in the first case is greater, we conclude that this investor prefers late resolution of uncertainty. The reason is that the aggregator is convex. Indeed, the first derivative of $\mathcal{W}$ is:

$$\frac{\partial}{\partial u}\left[c^\rho + \beta\,(\gamma u)^{\frac{\rho}{\gamma}}\right]^{\frac{\gamma}{\rho}} \frac{1}{\gamma} = \left[c^\rho + \beta\,(\gamma u)^{\frac{\rho}{\gamma}}\right]^{\frac{\gamma}{\rho}-1} \beta\,(\gamma u)^{\frac{\rho}{\gamma}-1}$$

Differentiate it once more:

$$\frac{\partial}{\partial u}\left\{\left[c^{\rho}+\beta\left(\gamma u\right)^{\frac{\rho}{\gamma}}\right]^{\frac{\gamma}{\rho}-1}\beta\left(\gamma u\right)^{\frac{\rho}{\gamma}-1}\right\}=\left(\frac{\gamma}{\rho}-1\right)\left[c^{\rho}+\beta\left(\gamma u\right)^{\frac{\rho}{\gamma}}\right]^{\frac{\gamma}{\rho}-2}\beta^2\rho\left(\gamma u\right)^{2\left(\frac{\rho}{\gamma}-1\right)}$$

$$+\left[c^{\rho}+\beta\left(\gamma u\right)^{\frac{\rho}{\gamma}}\right]^{\frac{\gamma}{\rho}-1}\beta\left(\frac{\rho}{\gamma}-1\right)\left(\gamma u\right)^{\frac{\rho}{\gamma}-2}\gamma$$

For negative values of both γ and ρ, this last expression has sign opposite to $\gamma/\rho-1$. In the numerical example $\gamma/\rho-1=-1/2<0$. So the second derivative is positive, and $\mathcal{W}$ is convex. That explains that the investor prefers late resolution.

If instead we assume that $\rho=-1/2$, the utility when the coin is flipped at $t=2$ is:

$$-\left[5^{-\frac{1}{2}}+0.99\times\left(\left(0.5\times10^{-1}+0.5\times0.1^{-1}\right)\right)^{\frac{1}{2}}\right]^2=-7.1396$$

and when the coin is flipped at $t=1$:

$$-0.5\times\left[5^{-\frac{1}{2}}+0.99\times\left(\left(10\right)^{-1}\right)^{\frac{1}{2}}\right]^2$$

$$-0.5\times\left[5^{\frac{1}{2}}+0.99\times\left(\left(0.1\right)^{-1}\right)^{\frac{1}{2}}\right]^2=-6.6897$$

So, the investor prefers earlier resolution of uncertainty. When $\rho=-1/2$, $\mathcal{W}$ is concave, since $\gamma/\rho-1=2-1=1>0$.

Exercises

21.1. Show that for the discrete-time utility 21.4 in the absence of uncertainty, the elasticity of intertemporal substitution equals $1/(1-\rho)$. Discuss a possible extension to the case of uncertainty. (Hint: see section 20.3).

21.2. Consider an economy with a representative investor characterized by the discrete-time recursive utility as in Epstein and Zin (1989), but with the added feature of an external habit process which proportionally affects per-period consumption. This means that the consumption index is given by $\hat{c}_{(t)}=c_{(t)}X_{(t)}$. Show that up to a constant the equilibrium stochastic discount factor is a geometric average of the growth rates for consumption and external habit and the market return. Discuss its properties.

21.3. Solve the benchmark-example problem of section 21.5.2 by means of dynamic programming as in chapter 9 and verify that the solution is identical to the one obtained in the section.

21.4. (This exercise is derived from Chacko and Viceira (2005)). We assume that wealth consists of only tradeable securities. Moreover, to keep the analysis simple, we assume that there are only two tradeable securities. One of them is riskless, with instantaneous return r, where r is a constant. The second security is risky, with instantaneous total return dynamics given by

$$\frac{dS(t)}{S(t)} = \mu dt + \sqrt{v(t)} dw_S(t)$$

where $v(t)$ is the time-varying instantaneous variance of the return on the risky security, w_S is a Wiener process, and $S(t)$ is the value of a fund that is fully invested in the security and that reinvests all dividends. μ is a constant.

The conditional variance of the risky security return varies stochastically over time, and this induces time variation in investment opportunities.

We assume the following dynamics for the inverse of this variance:

$$dy(t) = \varrho(\bar{y} - y(t)) dt + \sigma \sqrt{y(t)} dw_y(t)$$

where $y = 1/v$ is the precision of the risky security return process and w_y is a Wiener process. Precision follows a mean-reverting process with long-term mean equal to $\bar{y}$ and reversion parameter $\varrho > 0$. This process implies that volatility is mean-reverting and that proportional changes in volatility are more pronounced in times of high volatility than in times of low volatility.

We also assume that unexpected returns on the security are instantaneously correlated with innovations in precision: $\text{corr}_t(y, S)/(yS) = \rho$; $\text{corr}_t(v, S)/(vS) = -\rho$. Investors' preferences are described by a recursive but non-time-additive utility function, with unit elasticity of intertemporal substitution

$$V(t) = \mathbb{E}_t \left(\int_t^\infty \mathfrak{f}(c(s), V(s)) ds \right) \tag{21.36}$$

where:

$$\mathfrak{f}(c, V) = \beta (1 - \gamma) V \left[\ln(c) - \frac{1}{1 - \gamma} \ln((1 - \gamma) V) \right]$$

$$\beta, \gamma > 0$$

The investor maximizes (21.36) subject to the intertemporal budget constraint:

$$dW(t) = \{[\theta(t)(\mu - r) + r] W(t) - c(t)\} dt + \theta(t) W(t) \sqrt{v(t)} dw_S(t)$$

where W represents the investor's wealth, θ is the fraction of wealth invested in the risky security, and c represents the investor's instantaneous consumption.

a. Write the HJB equation corresponding to the above problem and show that one solution of that equation is:

$$V(W, y) = \exp[Ay + B] \frac{W^{1-\gamma}}{1 - \gamma}$$

where A and B are two constants to be determined.

b. Show that the optimal decisions corresponding to the above value function are:

$$c = \beta W$$

$$\theta = \frac{\mu - r}{\gamma v} + \frac{\rho \sigma}{\gamma} A \frac{1}{v}$$

c. Show this last result again by martingale methods.

d. Verify that the above utility function exhibits unit elasticity of intertemporal substitution and a risk aversion equal to γ.

An Afterword

Hirshleifer (1986) wrote: "Economic theory is and will remain an unfinished story. Starting with a basic structure of concepts and relations, it will always be possible to specialize the analysis in the interests of simplicity and concreteness, and to generalize it in the interest of wider applicability; to make new distinctions, and then to reunify ideas on a higher level; and to modify one principle or assumption after another, as called for in the effort to improve the prediction and exploration of behavior." This book has been inspired by Hirshleifer's words.

We moved from "a basic structure of concepts and relations," such as expected utility and the Fisher economic problem, in the absence of market frictions. We conducted a "specialized analysis" in discrete-time, finite-uncertainty models; we "generalized" it to continuous-time, infinite-uncertainty. We "distinguished" homogeneous from heterogeneous-agents' markets and provided the "re-unifying" concept of representative investor. We grounded it by studying equilibrium in depth. We "distinguished" redundant and non-redundant securities, and found for all of them the "re-unifying" fundamental security pricing rule. We "modified" our assumption of no frictions and expected utility to "improve the prediction," namely to face some empirical puzzles. We modified it also in order to "explore" different behavioral patterns, such as habit formation.

We revisited some basic financial theory, as well as more recent research. Not only have we left unmentioned some alternative extensions, such as the strategic use of information, but also valuable, recent contributions.

In spite of these limitations, we hope to have attained a compromise between careful mathematical modeling, the economic message that such modeling was meant to convey, and the possibility of implementing it.

In doing so, and in sharing Hirshleifer's view, we hope to have provided young scholars with a synthesis and interpretation of well-grounded, sound research, able to crystalize and distill empirical regularities and basic market mechanisms. Finance, after all, is still in its infancy, and fully deserves their *beautiful minds* and their strenuous efforts in this direction.

Basic Notation

Abbreviations

- "MRS" stands for "marginal rate of substitution"
- "RHS, LHS" stand for "right-hand side, left-hand side"
- "IID" stands for "identically, independently distributed"
- "ODE" stands for "ordinary differential equation"
- "SDE" stands for "stochastic differential equation"
- "PDE" stands for "partial differential equation"
- "EMM" stands for "equivalent martingale measure"
- "HARA" stands for "hyperbolic absolute risk aversion"
- "CRRA" stands for "constant relative risk aversion"
- "ARC" stands for "aggregate resource condition"
- "HJB" stands for "Hamilton-Jacobi-Bellman"

Equalities

- $=$ stands for "are two equal elements," as, for instance, in an equation to be solved
- $\equiv$ stands for an identity between a right-hand side and a left-hand side that are both variable
- $\triangleq$ stands for a particular form of identity that is a definition

Sets

- $\mathbb{N} = \{1, 2, .., N, ...\}$
- $\mathbb{R} = (-\infty, +\infty)$
- $\mathbb{R}^n$ is the space of n-dimensional real vectors
- $\mathbb{R}_+ = [0, +\infty)$
- $\mathbb{R}_{++} = (0, +\infty)$
- $\mathcal{B}$ is a Borel set. Borel sets are those obtained by union and intersection of intervals of $\mathbb{R}$.
- $\mathfrak{M}$ the set of consumption and portfolio and terminal wealth processes that are admissible in the sense of definition 7.7.

Vectors and matrices

- If x is a vector of $\mathbb{R}^N$, whose elements are x_i, we denote it indifferently as $x, \{x_i, i = 1, 2, ...N\}$ or $\{x_i\}_{i=1}^N$ or simply $\{x_i\}$.
- $\mathbf{1}$ is a vector of ones; $\mathbf{0}$ is a vector of zeros.
- $\mathrm{diag}(x)$ is a zero (square) matrix, whose main diagonal has been replaced by the vector x.

- $\underbrace{A}_{M \times N}$ says that the matrix A has M rows and N columns as does $A_{M \times N}$; sometimes we write dimensions as $A \in \mathbb{R}^{M \times N}$.
- $[A]_{ij}$ or a_{ij} is the element in row i, column j of the matrix A.
- trace $(A) = \sum_{i=1}^{n} a_{ii}$ is the trace of A.
- The transpose of a matrix or vector A is denoted A^{T}.
- $\|A\|$ is the Euclidean norm of the vector or matrix A: $\|A\|^2 = \mathrm{trace}(AA^{\mathsf{T}})$.
- rank(A) is the rank of matrix A.

Functions

- The function $f(x)$ is said to be increasing (decreasing) if it is increasing (decreasing) in a weak sense.
- The function $f(x)$ is said to be convex (concave) if it is convex (concave) in a weak sense. It is said to be strictly convex (concave) if it is convex (concave) in a strict sense.
- $\partial f(x,y)/\partial x$ is the partial derivative of $f(x,y) \colon \mathbb{R}^2 \to \mathbb{R}$. Also denoted f_x or f_1.
- We denote the derivative of $f(x) \colon \mathbb{R} \to \mathbb{R}$ with $f'(x)$ as well as with $\partial f(x)/\partial x$.
- $f \in C^n$ if it admits derivatives up to the order n, continuous
- $O(dx)$ is an infinitesimal of the same order as dx, $o(dx)$ is an infinitesimal of order higher than dx.

Random variables and processes

- $\mathcal{N}(0,1)$ is a standard Gaussian random variable. $N(x)$ is its distribution computed at the point $x \in \mathbb{R}$, $n(x)$ is its density at the same point.
- $\mathbb{E}[X]$ is the expected value of the random variable X, var(X) its variance, cov(X,Y) its covariance with random variable Y. If X and Y are processes, var(X) and cov(X,Y) are the instantaneous variances and covariances. cov(X,Y) is the covariance between changes over time of X and Y, except when the processes are themselves increases (such as rates of return on securities): cov(X,Y) = $dXdY/dt$.
- $\mathbb{E}_t(X) \triangleq \mathbb{E}[X|\mathcal{F}(t)]$ is the expected value conditional on the information available at time t. All variances and covariances are conditional ones but we omit the subscript t.
- $\mathbf{1}_{\{A\}}$ is the random variable "indicator of event A," which is worth 1 if A is true, 0 otherwise.
- "corr" is the correlation of two random variables.
- L^p is the space of random variables that admit moments up to p, $0 < p < \infty$. The norm is

$$\|X\| = \left(\int |x|^p \, dF(x) \right)^{1/p}$$

where F is the distribution function of X. A similar definition applies to random vectors.
- Positivity of random vectors (and variables) in L^p is defined as follows: if C is the set of all the random vectors $X \colon \Omega \to \mathbb{R}^n$ with the L^p norm, $0 < p < \infty$, then $X \in C_+$ if and only if $\Pr(X \geq 0) = 1$.
- L^∞ is the space of bounded measurable random variables.
- $X^+ = \max[X, 0]$.
- $X^- = -\min[X, 0]$.

Simplified notation

Unless doing otherwise is necessary for comprehension, we simplify the notation for processes. All processes are stochastic but we suppress the reference to the state ω. Therefore, $X(t)$ actually means $X(\omega, t)$. In special cases, we also use the notation $f(t)$ to refer to a deterministic function of time. When that is the case, we say so explicitly.

Appendix A
A Review of Utility Theory and Mean-Variance Theory

This appendix reviews the notions of

- expected utility,
- additivity over time and time impatience,
- risk aversion,
- prudence,
- and one-period mean-variance theory.

It introduces the relation between the one-period mean-variance predictions on expected returns and the non-mean-variance results we get in the setting of chapter 2, as well as in later chapters of the book. It makes no pretence of being exhaustive or rigorous from the point of view of decision theory. It just serves the purpose of recalling terminology and fixing notation.

A.1 Expected Utility

Assume that there exists one investor and one consumption good, which is the numeraire or the unit of account. There are only two points in time, 0 and 1.

- at time 0, the investor receives a non-random endowment $e(0) \in \mathbb{R}_+$, consumes an amount $c(0) \in \mathbb{R}_+$ of the good, and invests the difference between the two;
- at time 1, he receives a new, non-negative endowment and consumes it, together with accumulated savings. Both the time-1 endowment and accumulated savings have a value that is state-contingent or state-dependent. As seen from time 0, they are random variables. If randomness is represented by $s = 1, ..., K$ states of nature, these random variables can take K different values (they are discrete). We denote as $\pi(s)$ the probability that the investor assigns to state s occurring. All the states have positive probability.[1] The investor consumes $c(s) \in \mathbb{R}_+$ in state s. Consumption is generally random, since it is equal to the time-1 endowment $e(s) \in \mathbb{R}_{++}$ plus cumulated savings.

In this framework we fix the notion of expected utility, which we also will use, without further specification, in the case of more than two points in time and in the case of an infinity, both discrete and continuous, of states. In most of the book we assume that investors satisfy the axioms of von Neumann and Morgenstern (1944), in the Savage (1954) version. Under these axioms, the choices of each investor are represented by a (real-valued) utility function, the so-called von Neumann-Morgenstern utility, which is defined on consumption at time 0 and

---

1 Here – as in the text – we consider indistinguishable those random variables which differ only on zero-probability states. Accordingly, zero-probability states are ignored. We assume $\pi(s) > 0, s = 1, .., K$.

time 1:
$$u(c(0), c(s)): \mathbb{R}_+ \times \mathbb{R}_+ \to \mathbb{R}$$
Using von Neumann-Morgenstern utility, and computing its expected value, or expected utility
$$\sum_{s=1}^{K} \pi(s) u(c(0), c(s))$$
one obtains for the investor a complete, non-satiating, continuous and transitive ordering of consumption bundles $\{c(0), c(s); s = 1, ..., K\}$. The ranking is complete in that every bundle can be ordered with respect to all others. It is non-satiating because u is increasing in each of its arguments. It is continuous because u is taken to be a continuous function. It is transitive in that it satisfies the transitivity property. The expected utility is state independent, additively separable across states, and linear in the probabilities.[2]

We assume that the function u is twice differentiable with continuous derivatives (C^2). Because of non-satiation, the first derivatives, which represent marginal utility, are taken to be positive:
$$\frac{\partial u}{\partial c(i)}(c(0), c(s)) > 0 \qquad\qquad i = 0, s; \qquad 0 < c(i) < \infty$$
and strictly decreasing, which means that the utility function is strictly concave, when we consider consumption at time 0 and in the future:
$$\frac{\partial^2 u}{\partial c^2(i)}(c(0), c(s)) < 0 \qquad\qquad i = 0, s$$
and across states in the future. Positive marginal utility formalizes the idea that investors prefer higher consumption to smaller consumption. Decreasing marginal utility formalizes decreasing satisfaction from further consumption. As a consequence, curves of indifference between time-0 consumption and state-s consumption, whose equation are
$$\frac{\partial u}{\partial c(0)} dc(0) + \frac{\partial u}{\partial c(s)} dc(s) = 0$$
are strictly convex and represent a higher utility level as one moves to the northeast.

Last, we assume that marginal utility goes to infinity as soon as consumption becomes negligible:
$$\lim_{c(i) \to 0+} \frac{\partial u}{\partial c(i)}(c(0), c(s)) = +\infty \qquad\qquad i = 0, s$$

This condition, which is known as the first Inada condition, prevents zero or negative consumption from being optimal.

One recognizes a second Inada condition, which states that marginal utility vanishes when consumption tends to infinity:
$$\lim_{c(i) \to +\infty} \frac{\partial u}{\partial c(i)}(c(0), c(s)) = 0+ \qquad\qquad i = 0, s$$

Proposition A.1 *The two Inada conditions together guarantee that first-order conditions for consumption $c(i), i = 0, s$, such as:*
$$\frac{\partial u}{\partial c(i)}(c(0), c(s)) = \lambda(i) > 0$$
have a non-negative solution.

The inverse function (a consumption-demand function) is denoted $\mathfrak{h}(\{\lambda(i)\}, i)$. The inverse exists and is strictly decreasing in its first argument because of the strict concavity of u. The function $\mathfrak{h}$ plays a major role in our

---

2 State independence means that there is no preference for states of nature, in contrast to the case in which the utility function is state-dependent, and expected utility becomes: $\sum_s \pi(s) u(c(0), c(s), s)$.

developments: it maps the positive semi-axis onto itself, and has limits consistent with the Inada conditions, namely:

$$\lim_{\lambda(i) \to 0+} \mathfrak{h}(\{\lambda(i)\}, i) = +\infty$$

$$\lim_{\lambda(i) \to +\infty} \mathfrak{h}(\{\lambda(i)\}, i) = 0+$$

If $u \in C^2$, then $\mathfrak{h} \in C^1$.

A.1.1   Additivity and Time Impatience

Lifetime utility $u(c(0), c(s))$, over two points in time, may or may not be *additive over time*. When it is additive, the level of consumption experienced at time 0 does not affect the perception of goods consumed at time 1. Overall utility is the sum of the "satisfaction" from consumption at the two points in time. Additivity is violated when, say, habits formed at time 0 affect preferences over consumption at time 1, a case that we examine in chapter 20 of the book, or when the aggregation of utility over time is not done by means of the addition, as in chapter 21. Prior to these chapters, we assume utility to be additive over time.

Additive utility depends on time and on consumption of each specific point in time, which we write, with an abuse of notation, as

$$\sum_{s=1}^{K} \pi(s) u(c(0), c(s)) = u(0, c(0)) + \sum_{s=1}^{K} \pi(s) u(1, c(s))$$

The function u of each point in time has the properties listed in the previous section with respect to consumption. Its dependence on time must formalize the idea that it is better to consume a given amount of good at time 0 than at time 1, a phenomenon known as *time-impatience*:

$$u(0, c) > u(1, c).$$

In order to distinguish the impact of the level of consumption from its timing, in most of the book we sometimes further assume that in the utility function $u(t, c_t)$ *time factors out*, or is multiplicatively separable as in

$$u(t, c_t) = \beta^t \times v(c_t), \qquad\qquad 0 < \beta < 1$$

The time-discount factor β is smaller than one, in order to reflect time impatience: $u(0, c) = u(c) > u(1, c) = \beta \times v(c)$. Time impatience is the higher the smaller the coefficient β is. When time factors out, the expected utility index simplifies considerably:

$$\sum_{s=1}^{K} \pi(s) u(c(0), c(s)) = v(c(0)) + \beta \sum_{s=1}^{K} \pi(s) v(c(s))$$

That is the index we will use most of the time.

A.1.2   Risk Aversion and Prudence

When a utility function is additive and time factors out, we can easily elicit risk attitude, that is, the perception of the risk in realizations of consumption at one point of time. Three attitudes towards risk are possible: aversion for risk, love for risk, and risk neutrality.

Risk aversion is the reluctance to take bets or gambles, or to exchange a sure amount of consumption for a bet that brings state-dependent consumption, with equal expected value. A risk-averse investor derives from the bet a level of expected utility that is smaller than the utility of its expectation:

$$\sum_{s=1}^{K} \pi(s) u(c(s)) < u\left(\sum_{s=1}^{K} \pi(s) c(s)\right)$$

The opposite attitude, the desire to take bets, or love of risk, would be represented by the opposite inequality:

$$\sum_{s=1}^{K} \pi(s) u(c(s)) > u\left(\sum_{s=1}^{K} \pi(s) c(s)\right)$$

Risk neutrality, which is indifference between a bet and the amount of its expectation received for sure, would mean:

$$\sum_{s=1}^{K} \pi(s)u(c(s)) = u\left(\sum_{s=1}^{K} \pi(s)c(s)\right)$$

and would imply that the function u is affine. These three attitudes are modeled respectively using utility functions $u(c)$ strictly concave, strictly convex, and affine in consumption.

To understand why, consider u strictly concave. For illustration, consider the case in which there exist two states of the world. Since $\pi(2) = 1 - \pi(1)$, expected utility becomes

$$\pi(1)u(c(1)) + (1 - \pi(1))u(c(2)),$$

while the utility of the expectation is

$$u\left(\pi(1)c(1) + (1 - \pi(1))c(2)\right)$$

The former is strictly smaller than the latter, and expected utility is smaller than the utility of the expected value, for any positive probability $\pi(1)$, since the chord lies below the graph of a concave function (see figure A.1). An equivalent way to state the same idea is the following: the certainty equivalent of a bet is smaller than its expected value. The certainty equivalent CE is the sure amount that investors are willing to exchange for the bet between $c(1)$ and $c(2)$ and that gives the same utility as the bet:

$$u(CE) = \pi(1)u(c(1)) + (1 - \pi(1))u(c(2))$$

Indeed, in figure A.1 CE stays on the left of the expectation of the bet, $\bar{c} = \pi(1)c(1) + (1 - \pi(1))c(2)$.

With K states, the certainty equivalent remains smaller that the expected value of consumption

$$CE < \sum_{s=1}^{K} \pi(s)c(s)$$

for a strictly concave utility, or a risk-averse investor. The opposite inequality holds for risk-loving investors, while risk-neutral investors are the only ones for whom certainty equivalent and expectation are equal. When they

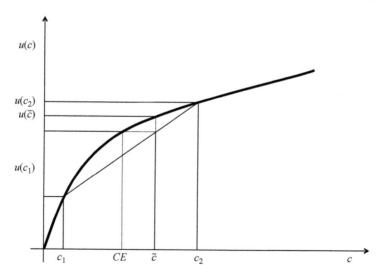

Figure A.1
Relative position of the certainty equivalent and the expected value when the utility function is concave.

evaluate random payoffs in the future, risk-neutral investors disregard dispersion and look only at the expected value.

The level of risk aversion, or risk preference, is loosely measured by the difference between the left- and the right-hand side of the previous inequalities. To quantify it, Arrow (1965) and Pratt (1964) resorted to the derivatives of the function u. Since the left-hand side and right-hand side are further apart as the concavity (convexity) of u is more pronounced, risk aversion is measured by the second-order derivative, normalized using the first-order one. The so-called Arrow-Pratt coefficient of absolute risk aversion is

$$A(c) \triangleq -\frac{u''(c)}{u'(c)}$$

for any $c \in \mathbb{R}_+$, while its relative counterpart is

$$A_r(c) \triangleq -c\frac{u''(c)}{u'(c)}$$

These measures are positive when $u'' < 0$, that is, when the decision maker is risk-averse. They are negative only if he is risk-loving, and equal to zero for every consumption level if he is risk-neutral.[3]

A third aspect of the investor's attitudes towards risk is the so-called (absolute) prudence. The definition and characterization of the prudence coefficient can be found in Kimball (1990). Prudence is defined only when $u''(c) \neq 0$ and is the ratio of the third to second derivative of u

$$P(c) \triangleq -\frac{u'''(c)}{u''(c)}$$

An investor is prudent if and only if this coefficient is positive. For risk-averse investors, this means that marginal utility is convex. Leland (1968) and Kimball demonstrate that the savings of a prudent investor increase with the level of risk of his future wealth. Faced with the latter, he accumulates "precautionary savings." An investor who is not prudent, while still being risk-averse, does not do so.

A.1.3   The HARA Class

The HARA (hyperbolic-absolute risk aversion) class of one-period utilities is defined as follows:

$$u(c) = \frac{1-\gamma}{\gamma} \left(\frac{\delta c}{1-\gamma} + \eta \right)^{\gamma}$$

Some restrictions have to be imposed on the parameters, to make sure that the function is well defined and to incorporate positive risk aversion. They are:

$$\gamma \neq 1$$
$$\delta > 0$$
$$\frac{\delta c}{1-\gamma} + \eta > 0$$
$$\eta = 1 \text{ if } \gamma \to -\infty$$

The corresponding aversion is hyperbolic in consumption, which justifies the name:

$$A(c) = \frac{1}{\frac{\delta c}{1-\gamma} + \eta}$$

This risk aversion can be either increasing, decreasing, or constant.

The hyperbolic class includes the exponential and quadratic utility function (see below). The so-called isoelastic case obtains for $\delta = 1, \eta = 0, \gamma < 1$, so that

$$u(c) = \frac{1-\gamma}{\gamma} \left(\frac{c}{1-\gamma} \right)^{\gamma}$$

---

3 Risk aversion coefficients can be equal to zero at single points also for risk-averse and risk-prone investors. Strictly concave or convex functions can exhibit null second derivatives at specific points, which form at most a countable set over the real line. In the text, the requirement on the sign of the risk-aversion coefficient disregards single points or countable sets. The coefficient is said to be positive for risk-averse individuals and negative for risk-loving ones.

which is usually simplified to

$$u(c) = \frac{c^{\gamma}}{\gamma}$$

The isoelastic utility is increasing, concave, and satisfies the Inada conditions. Its coefficients of risk aversion are easily found and reported in chapter 2, where we use this utility – our benchmark example – for the first time.

A.2 Mean-Variance Utility Theory

Under some conditions, the expected utility of consumption may be expressed as an increasing function of the expected value and a decreasing function of the variance of consumption, without any other moment of the probability distribution coming into the picture. These conditions may have to do with:

- the utility function u;
- the probability distribution of consumption at time 1.

Mean-variance analysis, which is ubiquitous in Finance, is then a special case of the expected-utility, two-dates specification in which either one of the following obtains:

- $u(c)$ is quadratic, $u(c) = -ac^2 + c$, with $a \in \mathbb{R}_{++}$ or
- u is simply increasing and concave, but the random variable c is a Gaussian or a monotonic transform of a Gaussian random variable; that is, it belongs to the family of "elliptical distributions" or
- risks are "small." Consumption at time 1 is basically a constant, with a random variable added which has a very small expected value μ but also a small variance σ^2, by which is meant that μ/σ^2 remains finite, as μ, σ^2 are driven to zero. Samuelson (1970) referred to these as "compact distributions."

Mean-variance analysis started with Markowitz (1952, 1959) and is pervasive in one-period Finance (see chapter 2). It is important also in order to interpret results in dynamic Finance, because the stochastic features of Brownian motion give a prominent role to expected value and variance even in complicated dynamic settings. At several places in the book we draw the comparison with one-period, mean-variance results.

Mean-variance analysis starts from a simple question. Assume no endowments, and assume that consumption is financed only by the returns from the portfolio of financial assets. Is it possible, for investors who satisfy the axioms of von Neumann and Morgenstern, to recast their objective utility function in a mathematically convenient form, involving two arguments only: expected portfolio return and variance of portfolio return?

Since the expected value of a square is equal to the square of the expected value plus the variance, one way in which this can be done is by assuming that investors have quadratic utility. This has two drawbacks: quadratic utility exhibits a satiation point (where the first derivative is zero) and increasing absolute risk aversion.

A better way of achieving the same goal is to assume that rates of return are normally distributed. Let future wealth $W = \overline{W} + \sigma\varepsilon$, where $\overline{W}$ is a constant and ε is a standard normal variate. An investor's expected utility is equal to:

$$V\left(\overline{W}, \sigma^2\right) = \int_{-\infty}^{+\infty} u\left(\overline{W} + \sigma\varepsilon\right) n(\varepsilon)d\varepsilon$$

where n is the normal density. Take the derivatives of the objective function:

$$\frac{\partial}{\partial \overline{W}} V\left(\overline{W}, \sigma^2\right) = \int_{-\infty}^{+\infty} u'\left(\overline{W} + \sigma\varepsilon\right) n(\varepsilon)d\varepsilon > 0$$

$$\frac{\partial}{\partial \sigma^2} V\left(\overline{W}, \sigma^2\right) = \frac{1}{2\sigma} \frac{\partial V}{\partial \sigma} = \frac{1}{2\sigma} \int_{-\infty}^{+\infty} u'\left(\overline{W} + \sigma\varepsilon\right) \varepsilon n(\varepsilon)d\varepsilon$$

$$= \frac{1}{2\sigma} \int_{0}^{+\infty} \left[u'\left(\overline{W} + \sigma\varepsilon\right) - u'\left(\overline{W} - \sigma\varepsilon\right)\right] \varepsilon n(\varepsilon)d\varepsilon < 0$$

where the latter formula obtains by symmetry of n and the negativity results from the concavity of of u. Hence, an investor "likes" expected returns and "dislikes" variance.

The same property holds not just for the normal distribution but for members of the family of so-called "elliptical distributions," which share the property that isoprobability contours are ellipses. They are defined by their multivariate density for the random vector R:

$$f(R) = |\Omega|^{-\frac{1}{2}} g\left[(R - \mu)^{\mathsf{T}} \Omega^{-1} (R - \mu)\right]$$

where g is any non-negative function properly normalized, Ω and μ are a matrix and a vector of parameters. Each member of this class indexed by the function g is stable under addition, even though the class taken as a whole is not stable. Stability under addition is important so that portfolio returns, which are averages of investor security returns, will have the mean-variance property.

A.2.1   The Mean-Variance Frontier

Given a multivariate distribution of securities' returns, the frontier describes the highest achievable expected portfolio return that can be achieved for a given variance of portfolio return. The calculation of the frontier in the case in which there exists a riskless asset is a degenerate case of the calculation in the absence of a riskless asset. The portfolios of the frontier are called "mean-variance efficient." We consider two cases.

Absence of a riskless asset

Endowed with either a quadratic objective function or an elliptical distribution for returns, one can recast the optimization problem of an investor in a one-period framework as that of maximizing returns from the portfolio, keeping its variance fixed. At first, we take all assets to have non-zero variance. Let the target level of variance be σ^2:[4]

$$\max_x x^{\mathsf{T}} \mathbb{E}[R] \tag{A.1}$$

$$\text{subject to} : x^{\mathsf{T}} \Omega x = \sigma^2$$

$$x^{\mathsf{T}} \mathbf{1} = 1$$

where x is the portfolio fractional composition ($x_i < 0$ is interpreted as a short sale),[5] $x^{\mathsf{T}} \mathbb{E}[R]$ is the expected value of the portfolio rate of return, Ω is the variance-covariance matrix of rates of return ($\Omega_{i,j} = \text{cov}[R_i, R_j]$), $x^{\mathsf{T}} \Omega x$ is the variance of the portfolio rate of return.

We can form a Lagrangean as follows:

$$L(x, \theta, \lambda) = x^{\mathsf{T}} \mathbb{E}[R] + \frac{1}{2}\theta \times \left(\sigma^2 - x^{\mathsf{T}} \Omega x\right) + \lambda \times \left(1 - x^{\mathsf{T}} \mathbf{1}\right)$$

The first Lagrange multiplier, $\theta/2$, is the shadow price of one unit of additional risk (variance), while the second, λ, is interpretable as the shadow interest rate on one unit of additional investible wealth.

The first-order conditions are:[6]

$$\mathbb{E}[R] - \theta \times \Omega x - \lambda \times \mathbf{1} = 0 \tag{A.2}$$

$$x^{\mathsf{T}} \Omega x = \sigma^2$$

$$x^{\mathsf{T}} \mathbf{1} = 1 \tag{A.3}$$

Solving the first-order conditions (A.2):

$$x = \frac{1}{\theta} \Omega^{-1} (\mathbb{E}[R] - \lambda \mathbf{1})$$

---

4 $x^{\mathsf{T}} \Omega x = \sum_i \sum_j x_i \times x_j \times \text{cov}[R_i, R_j]$.

5 x_i is the fraction of a person's wealth invested in security i. It is not the number of units of a security held (which, in other parts of the book, we call θ), though there is an obvious relationship between the two formulations: $x_i = \theta_i \times S_i/W$, where S_i is the price of security i.

6 These are necessary and sufficient because the variance-covariance matrix Ω is positive definite by construction. $\Omega x = \text{cov}[R, x^{\mathsf{T}} R]$.

Premultiplying by $\mathbf{1}^{\mathsf{T}}$ and recalling that the portfolio weights must sum up to one, $x^{\mathsf{T}}\mathbf{1} = 1$:

$$1 = \frac{1}{\theta}\mathbf{1}^{\mathsf{T}}\Omega^{-1}(\mathbb{E}(R) - \lambda\mathbf{1})$$

Therefore, the shadow interest rate is:

$$\lambda = \frac{\frac{1}{\theta}\mathbf{1}^{\mathsf{T}}\Omega^{-1}\mathbb{E}[R] - 1}{\frac{1}{\theta}\mathbf{1}^{\mathsf{T}}\Omega^{-1}\mathbf{1}} \tag{A.4}$$

Substituting into the first FOC we get the portfolio weights:

$$x = \frac{1}{\theta}\Omega^{-1}\left\{\mathbb{E}[R] - \frac{\frac{1}{\theta}\mathbf{1}^{\mathsf{T}}\Omega^{-1}\mathbb{E}[R] - 1}{\frac{1}{\theta}\mathbf{1}^{\mathsf{T}}\Omega^{-1}\mathbf{1}}\mathbf{1}\right\}$$

$$= \frac{1}{\theta}\Omega^{-1}\mathbb{E}[R] - \frac{\frac{1}{\theta}\mathbf{1}^{\mathsf{T}}\Omega^{-1}\mathbb{E}[R] - 1}{\mathbf{1}^{\mathsf{T}}\Omega^{-1}\mathbf{1}}\Omega^{-1}\mathbf{1} \tag{A.5}$$

The mean-variance frontier, which links the portfolio mean $x^{\mathsf{T}}\mathbb{E}[R]$ to its variance $x^{\mathsf{T}}\Omega x$, is given parametrically by varying the shadow price $1/\theta$. Since x is affine in $1/\theta$, the expected return on the portfolio is also affine in $1/\theta$ and the portfolio variance is quadratic in $1/\theta$, while the standard deviation is also affine. Hence, the frontier is a branch of a parabola in mean-variance space and the *mean-standard deviation frontier* is a branch of a hyperbola in mean×standard-deviation space. This would not generally be true if positions x in the portfolio were constrained to be within a set (for example, non-negative, as when no short selling is allowed).

Presence of a riskless asset

Now, suppose that there exists a riskless asset with a rate of return r. The riskless asset must be treated separately; Ω now designates the variance-covariance matrix of risky assets only and the vector x now designates, out of the unit stock of investible wealth, the amounts invested in the risky assets only.

The solution for the portfolio composition is even more straightforward than in the previous situation. The first-order condition of the type (A.2) corresponding to the riskless asset is simply:

$$r - \lambda = 0$$

so that the given riskless return pins down λ.

Then, restricting Ω and R to the risky securities:

$$x = \frac{1}{\theta}\Omega^{-1}\left[\mathbb{E}[R] - r\mathbf{1}\right] \tag{A.6}$$

while the fraction of wealth invested in the riskless security is equal to:

$$1 - x^{\mathsf{T}}\mathbf{1} = 1 - \frac{1}{\theta}\mathbf{1}^{\mathsf{T}}\Omega^{-1}\left[\mathbb{E}[R] - r\mathbf{1}\right]$$

Portfolio expected return and portfolio standard deviation are:

$$\mathbb{E}[R]^{\mathsf{T}}x = \frac{1}{\theta}\mathbb{E}[R]^{\mathsf{T}}\Omega^{-1}\left[\mathbb{E}[R] - r\mathbf{1}\right]$$

$$\sigma = \sqrt{x^{\mathsf{T}}\Omega x} = \frac{1}{\theta}\sqrt{\left[\mathbb{E}[R] - r\mathbf{1}\right]^{\mathsf{T}}\Omega^{-1}\left[\mathbb{E}[R] - r\mathbf{1}\right]}$$

The *mean-standard deviation frontier* is now a straight line tangent to the frontier of risky assets. The tangent portfolio composition is given by:

$$x_T = \frac{\Omega^{-1}\left[\mathbb{E}[R] - r\mathbf{1}\right]}{\mathbf{1}^{\mathsf{T}}\Omega^{-1}\left[\mathbb{E}[R] - r\mathbf{1}\right]} \tag{A.7}$$

Fund separation

Under the above hypotheses, portfolio allocation can be done indifferently either with the original risky assets (and the riskless one, if it exists) or with two funds. The result holds also in the dynamic context of chapters 9 and 11.

The set of mean-variance efficient portfolios (A.5) or (A.6), parametrized by $1/\theta$, satisfies a remarkable property. As we remarked above, their composition is affine in $1/\theta$. It is well known that any linear combination of two points of a straight line is also on the line and, conversely, that a straight line is entirely defined by two of its points. The theorem follows from the these simple observations:

Theorem A.1   *Black (1972)*

- *The linear combination of two mean-variance efficient portfolios gives a third mean-variance efficient portfolio, provided the new portfolio expected return is not smaller than that of the minimum-variance portfolio. (This is true in particular for convex combinations.)*

- *All mean-variance efficient portfolios can be described as linear combination of two mean-variance efficient portfolios chosen arbitrarily.*

This is a *two-fund separation theorem.* Two funds are all that is needed to represent completely the set of efficient portfolios. If there exists a riskless asset, it is natural to use it as one of the "funds" and use as the other fund the tangent portfolio, that is, the portfolio that belongs to both the mean-standard deviation efficient frontier without and with the riskless asset.

A.2.2   The Mean-Variance CAPM

We assume now that all investors in the financial marketplace differ by the value of $1/\theta$ and their wealth but each one of them chooses to hold a mean-variance efficient portfolio. Does that impose a restriction on the cross section of expected returns of different assets when demand equals supply, that is, all assets are held? One can use an algebraic or an intuitive derivation. Here we use the latter.[7] Since, by virtue of Black's theorem, any convex combination of efficient portfolios is an efficient portfolio and, when all securities are held (that is, demand equals supply), the market portfolio, which reflects the supply of all assets, is a convex combination of investors' portfolio demands, each of which is efficient. It follows that *the market portfolio is efficient.* It lies on the efficient frontier.

If the market portfolio, whose composition is denoted x_M, lies on the efficient frontier, there must exist a value θ_M of θ and a value λ_M of λ for which x_M satisfies (A.2):

$$\mathbb{E}[R] = \lambda_M \mathbf{1} + \theta_M \times \Omega x_M \tag{A.8}$$

Call R_M the return on the market portfolio, $R_M = x_M^\mathsf{T} R$. We have:

$$\mathbb{E}[R] = \lambda_M \mathbf{1} + \theta_M \times \mathrm{cov}\,[R, R_M] \tag{A.9}$$

This is the CAPM (Capital Asset Pricing Model) relation of Sharpe (1964) and Lintner (1965). Under (A.9), the expected rate of return of *each security* is affine in the security's covariance with the market portfolio. This is a result that we get in the one-period, non-mean-variance setting of chapter 2, and that we find again in the book, in discrete as well as continuous, non-mean-variance dynamic settings (see chapters 9 and 11).

The CAPM can be rewritten in its alternative, popular "β-version." The CAPM relation (A.9) holds for each security. It holds in particular for the market portfolio return itself:

$$\mathbb{E}[R_M] = \lambda_M + \theta_M \times \mathrm{var}\,[R_M]$$

Substituting, one can obviously write the CAPM relation as:

$$\mathbb{E}[R_i] = \lambda_M + (\mathbb{E}[R_M] - \lambda_M) \times \beta_{i|M}$$

---

7 The reader will find an algebraic derivation in the appendix to chapter 11.

where $\beta_{i|M}$ is the ratio of the covariance between a single asset return and the market portfolio return to the variance of the latter:

$$\beta_{i|M} \triangleq \frac{\text{cov}[R_i, R_M]}{\text{var}[R_M]}$$

This is the "β-version", similar to the result we obtain in chapter 2, outside the mean variance case, using marginal rates of substitution.

In fact, the CAPM (A.9) contains implied marginal rates of substitution in the sense of chapter 2. Compare it with one of the pricing relations in chapter 2, namely

$$\mathbb{E}[R_i] = \frac{1}{\mathbb{E}[\xi]} - 1 - \frac{1}{\mathbb{E}[\xi]} \text{cov}[R_i, \xi]$$

We find that, under the CAPM theory:

$$\frac{1}{\mathbb{E}[\xi]} - 1 = \lambda_M$$

$$(\mathbb{E}[R_M] - \lambda_M) \frac{\text{cov}[R_i, R_M]}{\text{var}[R_M]} = -\frac{1}{\mathbb{E}[\xi]} \text{cov}[R_i, \xi]$$

Looking at this equality as an equation in the unknown ξ, the general solution is:[8]

$$\xi = \frac{1 - \theta_M \times (R_M - \mathbb{E}[R_M]) + \varepsilon}{1 + \lambda_M}$$

where ε is *any* random variable with zero expected value and zero covariance with all the traded securities. This describes the set of marginal rates of substitution that are implicit in the mean-variance CAPM.

---

8 Check:

$$\mathbb{E}[R_i] = \lambda - (1 + \lambda) \frac{\theta}{1 + \lambda} \text{cov}[R_i, R_M]$$

Appendix B
Global and Recursive Optimization

This appendix recapitulates some basic notions concerning global optimization (called "static" optimization by some authors), which is used in chapters 3 and 10 and in the corresponding equilibrium of chapter 12. It then reviews recursive optimization, in the form of dynamic programming, which is used in chapters 3, 9, and 11 in its simplest form, then in the chapter on transaction costs (chapter 19), in a more sophisticated version.

Basic notions of static optimization are covered in section B.1. For a rigorous approach we suggest Mangasarian (1969) and Luenberger (1969). See also Boyd and Vandenberghe (2004).

Dynamic, recursive optimization is studied first in markets without frictions, both in discrete and continuous time (sections B.2 and B.3), then in markets with frictions, which are treated, as in the text, only in continuous time (section B.4). In all cases, we first provide a statement of Bellman's principle of dynamic programming. The principle states a necessary condition of optimality. We then provide a verification theorem, which verifies whether the necessary conditions of optimality are also sufficient. For a treatment more rigorous than the one we make available, we refer the interested reader to Bertsekas and Shreve (1978) in relation to section B.2, to Fleming-Rishel (1975) for section B.3, to Fleming and Soner (1993) as well as Shreve and Soner (1994) for section B.4. In particular, we limit our attention to finite-horizon and infinite-horizon but time-homogeneous problems, without discussing the delicate issue of the transversality conditions that must be imposed when the horizon becomes infinite. For a discussion of transversality conditions, we again refer the interested reader to the above references.

B.1 Global Optimization

Let us consider the following problem:

$$\max f(x, y)$$

subject to:

$$g(x, y) = b$$

where both f and g are real-valued and C^1 functions, x and y are real variables, and $b \in \mathbb{R}$. In stating the problem in this way, we are already assuming that the optimum exists (otherwise we should search for the sup, which is also a proper max whenever it is reached). Suppose that we want to distinguish local and global optima.[1] The first important result about this problem says that, if the gradient of g, noted ∇g, is different from zero at the (local) optimum (x_0, y_0), then there exists a scalar λ_0 such that

$$\nabla f(x_0, y_0) = \lambda_0 \nabla g(x_0, y_0)$$

---

1 Here we should warn the reader against a potential confusion in our vocabulary. We use the word "global" in two meanings. It can mean the opposite of "local," as is the case right now. Or it can mean the opposite of "recursive," as in most of the text. The term "global" has been adopted in the text to refer to the optimization of total, or lifetime, or global utility, in one fell swoop.

In that case, the constant λ_0 is called the Lagrange multiplier and the result can be restated by defining the Lagrangean function

$$L(x, y, \lambda) \triangleq f(x, y) + \lambda \times (b - g(x, y))$$

and by saying:

Theorem B.1   *If the gradient of g, ∇g, is different from zero at the (local) optimum (x_0, y_0), then there exists a scalar λ_0 such that (x_0, y_0, λ_0) is a stationary point of the Lagrangean.*

The theorem transforms a constrained problem for f into an unconstrained one for L. Usually, (x_0, y_0, λ_0) is not a maximum for L, but *a saddle point* for it (a maximum with respect x and y, a minimum with respect to λ):

$$L(x, y, \lambda_0) \leq L(x_0, y_0, \lambda_0) \leq L(x_0, y_0, \lambda)$$

The multiplier is unique. By defining the extended Lagrangean

$$L(x, y, \zeta, \lambda) \triangleq \zeta f(x, y) + \lambda(b - g(x, y))$$

the theorem can be extended to the case when the gradient of the constraint happens to be zero. Using the extended Lagrangean allows to relax the assumption made on the gradient of g. It applies as well to functions f and g of more than two variables, say n variables, collected in the vector x, and to more than one constraint, $b \in \mathbb{R}^m$. Suppose that there exist m constraints and that $m \leq n$. In this case we have one multiplier for each constraint. If the Jacobian matrix of the constraints $g(x): \mathbb{R}^n \to \mathbb{R}^m$ has maximum rank at the optimum x_0, that is, the latter point is regular, then there exist m multipliers, collected in the vector λ, such that

$$L(x, \lambda) \triangleq f(x) + \lambda \cdot (b - g(x))$$

is stationary at (x_0, λ_0).

Lagrange multipliers have an appealing economic interpretation. If you think of b as a parameter, and $L(x, \lambda)$ has a regular optimum at (x_0, λ_0), or, more precisely, $(x_0(b_0), \lambda_0(b_0))$, then the Lagrange multipliers represent the derivatives of the optimized value of f with respect to the components of b around b_0:

$$\frac{\partial f(x(b))}{\partial b_i} = \lambda_i(b)$$

$$i = 1, ..m$$

That is true under mild differentiability conditions (f and g of class C^2).

Second-order conditions are easy to state. At a maximum x_0, the quadratic form $h \cdot \nabla^2 L(x_0) \cdot h$ is negative semi-definite when $\nabla g_i(x_0) h = 0$. If the quadratic form is negative definite when $\nabla g_i(x_0) h = 0$, then x_0 is a maximum.

The Lagrangean technique is valid also for more general problems, in which *inequality constraints* are present, and the choice variables x must belong to a given set X, say, $x \geq 0$:

$$\max_x f(x) \qquad (B.1)$$

subject to:

$$g(x) \leq b, \quad x \in X$$

with $x \in \mathbb{R}^n, b \in \mathbb{R}^m$.

The first important observation about these problems is that, if one of the components of the vector b is perturbed by $\varepsilon > 0$, then the value of the function f in the new problem cannot be smaller than the one in the non-perturbed problem. It follows that, in contrast to the case of equality constraints, multipliers cannot be negative: $\lambda_i \geq 0, i = 1, ..., m$. Here, the following sufficient conditions hold:

Theorem B.2   *If the Lagrangean $X \times \mathbb{R}^m_+ \to \mathbb{R}$:*

$$L(x, \lambda) \triangleq f(x) + \lambda \cdot (b - g(x))$$

has a saddle point at (x_0, λ_0)

$$L(x, \lambda_0) \leq L(x_0, \lambda_0) \leq L(x_0, \lambda)$$

then x_0 solves (B.1) and the complementary-slackness conditions

$$\lambda_i \times (b_i - g_i(x_0)) = 0$$

hold.

That theorem is the foundation of the theory of *duality*. Before exploring it, let us make one observation. Let the real-values function L be defined over a space $X \times \Lambda$. Whether or not the maxima exist, the inequalities

$$\max_{x \in X} \underbrace{\min_{\lambda \in \Lambda} L(x, \lambda)}_{P(x)} \leq \min_{\lambda \in \Lambda} \underbrace{\max_{x \in X} L(x, \lambda)}_{D(\lambda)}$$

are true, since $P(x) \leq L(x, \lambda) \leq D(\lambda)$. Equality holds in the case of a saddle point:

$$\max_{x \in X} P(x) = L(x, \lambda) = \min_{\lambda \in \Lambda} D(\lambda) \tag{B.2}$$

Starting from (B.2), let us attach to the *primal problem* (B.1) the so-called *dual problem*

$$\min_{\lambda} L(x, \lambda)$$

$$\text{subject to}: \ \nabla_x L(x, \lambda) = 0, \lambda \geq 0, x \in X$$

One can give conditions under which a solution to the primal provides a solution to the dual and, more importantly, (weaker) conditions under which a solution to the dual provides a solution to the primal, namely

Theorem B.3 *If $f(x)$ is concave[2] and the g_i functions are quasi-convex,[3] a solution (x_0, λ_0) to the dual such that x_0 in the interior of X, $L(x, \lambda_0)$ is C^2 in a neighborhood of x_0 and the Hessian of L with respect to x is non-null at x_0, then x_0 solves the primal.*

B.2   Discrete-Time Recursive Optimality

B.2.1   Statement of the Optimization Problem

Consider the following finite-horizon problem:

$$\max_{\{v(s,t)\}} \left\{ u(e(0), v(0), 0) + \sum_{t=1}^{T-1} \sum_{s=1}^{K_t} \pi(s, t) u(e(s, t), v(s, t), t) + \sum_{s=1}^{K_T} \pi(s, T) \wp(e(s, T), T) \right\}$$

in which the max can be reached by choice of the variables $\{v(s, t), t = 0, 1, ..T - 1\}$, to be specified better below, and the objective function is additively separable over time. At each point in time $t < T$, the objective function depends on time, on the state of the system, as described by the (vector of) so-called *state variables* $e(s, t)$, and on the (vector of) so-called *control variables* $v(s, t)$. Let these vectors belong to $\mathbb{R}^N$. At time 0 in particular there is a single state, so that $e(s, 0) = e(0), v(s, 0) = v(0)$. For $0 < t < T$, both the state and control variables realizations may differ across states. They are (vector-valued) random variables, measurable at t:

$$e(t) \triangleq \{e(s, t), s = 1, ..K_t\}$$
$$v(t) \triangleq \{v(s, t), s = 1, ..K_t\} \tag{B.3}$$

Their joint probability distribution, as evaluated at time 0, is described by the probabilities $\pi(s, t)$. These form a vector of dimension $K_t < \infty$: the number of states of the world for each date is assumed to be finite. The expectation of the function $u(e(s, t), v(s, t), t)$ enters the objective function. We interpret u as the utility function of an investor at time t. The objective function at time T depends only on the controls and is formalized through a bequest function $\wp$.[4]

---

2 Pseudoconcavity would be a sufficient assumption. The nuance between concavity and pseudoconcavity is beyond the scope of this book.

3 For the definition, see footnote 3 of chapter 15.

4 See chapter 9.

We assume that the problem is Markovian, in the following sense. The probability distribution of the successors s' (at $t+1$) of state s (at time t) depends on the state and controls of time t only, $e(s,t), v(s,t), t$:

$$\pi\left(s', t+1\right) = f(e(s,t), v(s,t), t)$$

instead of depending on their values at all times before and up to t. State variables are controlled Markov processes. We assume that it is possible to link controls and state variables by an *evolution equation*, which says that the values the state variables will take at time $t+1$ depend on their value at t, on the corresponding controls, on time and on a vector of disturbances $\Upsilon(s, t+1)$ that are IID variables. The number of disturbances is unessential. We can state this condition state by state, as

$$e_{s', t+1} = g(e(s,t), v(s,t), t, \Upsilon(s, t+1))$$

or, taking all states together, as $e(t+1) = g(e(t), v(t), t, \Upsilon(t+1))$. Overall, the problem is $\mathcal{P}_0$:

$$\max_{v(t)} \left\{ u(e(0), v(0), 0) + \sum_{t=1}^{T-1} \mathbb{E}_0 u(e(t), v(t), t) + \mathbb{E}_0 \wp(e(T), T) \right\}$$

subject to:

$$e(t+1) = g(e(t), v(t), t, \Upsilon(t+1))$$

where the choice of the controls is meant to be made state-by-state, because of (B.3). The controls can be subject to constraints.

B.2.2   Bellman's Principle in Discrete Time

Let us define the *value function*, or indirect-utility or derived-utility function, of the problem $\mathcal{P}_0$ as the maximized value of the utility the investor can get over his whole lifetime:

$$J(e(0), 0) \triangleq \max_{\{v(t)\}} \left\{ u(e(0), v(0), 0) + \sum_{t=1}^{T-1} \mathbb{E}_0 u(e(t), v(t), t) + \mathbb{E}_0 \wp(e(T), T) \right\}$$

The problem to be solved can be embedded in a family of problems $\mathcal{P}_t$, each of which starts at time t, when the state of the system is represented by $e(t)$:

$$\max_{\{v(j)\}} \left\{ \sum_{j=t}^{T-1} \mathbb{E}_t u(e(j), v(j), j) + \mathbb{E}_t \wp(e(T), T) \right\}$$

subject to:

$$e(j+1) = g(e(j), v(j), j, \Upsilon(j+1))$$

Their value function $J(e(t), t)$ is defined in a way analogous to $J(e(0), 0)$:[5]

$$J(e(t), t) \triangleq \max_{\{v(j)\}} \left\{ \sum_{j=t}^{T-1} \mathbb{E}_t u(e(j), v(j), j) + \mathbb{E}_t \wp(e(T), T) \right\} \tag{B.4}$$

The value function at t is the maximized value of the utility that we can get from t onwards. The value function at the last date, T, is set as:

$$J(e(T), T) \equiv \wp(e(T), T) \tag{B.5}$$

---

5 For as long as the horizon is finite, both in discrete and in continuous time, one can define the value function as the maximized utility evaluated either at time 0, or as evaluated at time t. Here we leave unspecified the dependence of u on time.

We proceed backwards. At time $T - 1$, we have:

$$J(e(T - 1), T - 1) \triangleq \max_{v(T-1)} \left\{ u(e(T - 1), v(T - 1), T - 1) + \mathbb{E}_{T-1} \wp(e(T), T) \right\}$$

which, because of (B.5) and Markovianity, is *equivalent* to

$$J(e(T - 1), T - 1) = \max_{v(T-1)} \{ u(e(T - 1), v(T - 1), T - 1)$$
$$+ \mathbb{E}_{T-1} J(g(e(T - 1), v(T - 1), T - 1, \Upsilon(T)), T) \}$$

This means that the controls at $T - 1$ are chosen so as to maximize the current utility and the expectation of the future, *derived* utility. At time $T - 2$, we can hope to transform problem $\mathcal{P}_{T-2}$, which, due to (B.4), involves the choice of all future controls

$$J(e(T - 2), T - 2) = \max_{v(T-2), v(T-1)} \{ u(e(T - 2), v(T - 2), T - 2)$$
$$+ \mathbb{E}_{T-2} u(e(T - 1), v(T - 1), T - 1) + \mathbb{E}_{T-2} \wp(e(T), T) \}$$

into a problem that entails choosing only the current controls, namely:

$$J(e(T - 2), T - 2) = \max_{v(T-2)} \{ u(e(T - 2), v(T - 2), T - 2)$$
$$+ \mathbb{E}_{T-2} \left[\max_{v(T-1)} \left\{ u(e(T - 1), v(T - 1), T - 1) + \mathbb{E}_{T-2} \wp(e(T), T) \right\} \right] \}$$
$$= \max_{v(T-2)} \left\{ u(e(T - 2), v(T - 2), T - 2) + \mathbb{E}_{T-2} J(e(T - 1), T - 1) \right\}$$
$$= \max_{v(T-2)} \{ u(e(T - 2), v(T - 2), T - 2)$$
$$+ \mathbb{E}_{T-2} J(g(e(T - 2), v(T - 2), T - 2, \Upsilon(T - 1)), T - 1) \}$$

In the former formulation, we have to choose the controls for dates $T - 2$ and $T - 1$, while in the latter we have to choose the control for the current period, $T - 2$, only. Utility at $T - 2$ depends on those controls and not on the ones at $T - 1$. As for utility at $T - 1$ and after, the idea is that, no matter how (with which control values) the investor enters into one state at time $T - 1$, he will proceed optimally from that point onwards, by choosing the controls that optimize his future utility (at $T - 1$ and T). Since the latter controls bring him to $J(e(T - 1), T - 1)$ at $T - 1$, the best thing to do at $T - 2$, consistently with maximizing expected utility, is to maximize the expectation of $J(e(T - 1), T - 1)$. This is achieved by making the best for the time being, that is, choosing $v(T - 2)$ only.

Analogously, we can hope to transform any t-problem $\mathcal{P}_t$ into $\mathcal{P}'_t$:

$$J(e(t), t) = \max_{v(t)} \{ u(e(t), v(t), t) + \mathbb{E}_t J(g(e(t), v(t), t, \Upsilon(t + 1)), t + 1) \}$$

We restrict the attention, when selecting the controls from time t onward, to the ones that guarantee optimality at t. Conditional on these, we pursue optimality from $t + 1$ onwards. It means that, no matter what is the state realization at $t + 1$, from that point onward we act according to $J(e(t + 1), t + 1)$. As a consequence, as in $T - 2$, we have just one thing to do: act optimally from t to $t + 1$, via $v(t)$.

This reformulation is, indeed, possible, as intuition suggests, because of the separation of the objective function over time. It is made simpler to implement by the assumption of Markovianity. It is the so-called *dynamic programming* or *Bellman's principle of optimality*, which is stated as a necessary optimality condition. If the solution to each and every problem starting at t, $J(e(t), t)$, exists, then it solves the recurrence equation written above (see Bellman (1957)):

Theorem B.4 *(Bellman's principle of optimality)* *The value function satisfies the recurrence equation*

$$J(e(t), t) = \max_{v(s,t)} \{ u(e(s, t), v(s, t), t) + \mathbb{E}_t J(g(e(t), v(t), t, \Upsilon(t + 1)), t + 1) \} \tag{B.6}$$
$$t = 0, 1, \ldots T - 1$$

with terminal condition (B.5).

In practical applications of the theory, a verification theorem is needed. Embed the problem starting in state $e(0)$ at time 0 into the family of problems starting in state $e(t)$ at time t. Start from the last date, where (B.5) gives the value function, and proceed backward, *deciding at each point in time t only the immediate controls instead of deciding the whole stream of them, from t to T*. At each point in time t, substitute the optimal controls into the recurrence equations (B.6) and solve for $J(e(t), t)$. $J(e(0), 0)$ encapsulates the optimal solution for the original problem. The difference between the value-function form of the maximization problem, $\mathcal{P}'_t$, and the original one, $\mathcal{P}_t$, is the following, as given by Bellman's principle. In the original, global formulation we have to solve for all controls at once, namely

$$K_0 + K_1 + .. + K_{T-1} = 1 + K_1 + .. + K_{T-1}$$

control values. In the value-function formulation we have to solve for K_t controls at each point in time.

The problem becomes *time-homogeneous* when

- the horizon is infinite,
- the utility function is separable in time and the other variables: with abuse of notation, $u(e(s, t), v(s, t), t) = \beta^t u(e(s, t), v(s, t)), 0 < \beta < 1$,
- the transition probability of the Markov state process is time-homogeneous, $g(e(t), v(t), t, \Upsilon(t + 1)) = g(e(t), v(t), \Upsilon(t + 1))$,
- and the admissible set of controls, if these are constrained, is time independent.

B.3   Continuous-Time Recursive Optimality: Classical Control

B.3.1   Statement of the Optimization Problem

Let us assume, as usual, a filtered probability space $(\Omega, \mathcal{F}, P)$. Let the space and the filtration $\mathbf{F} = \{\mathcal{F}_t\}$ have the usual properties, namely completeness of the space and augmented filtration. The dynamics of the $\mathbb{R}^N$-valued *state variables* is assumed to be of the following type:

$$de(t) = a(e, v, t)dt + b(e, v, t)dw(t) \tag{B.7}$$

with a an $\mathbb{R}^N$-valued coefficient, b a matrix of coefficients of dimension $N \times K$, w a K-dimensional Wiener process, $e(0) = e_0 \in \mathbb{R}^N$.[6] We assume that, for any control path, the coefficients a and b guarantee not only that a solution to (B.7) exists and is unique, but also that it is a Markov diffusion process (see chapter 7). State variables are adapted.

With a notation and terminology similar to the one we adopted for discrete time, let the problem to be solved be $\mathcal{P}_0$:

$$\max_{\{v(t)\}} \mathbb{E}_0 \left\{ \int_0^T u(e(t), v(t), t)dt + \wp(e(T), T) \right\}$$

subject to:

$$de(t) = a(e, v, t)dt + b(e, v, t)dw(t)$$

where $\{v(t)\} = \{v(t), t \in [0, T]\}$. The *controls* are assumed to follow an *absolutely continuous*, adapted process. In addition, we restrict the attention to a class of controls that are called *feedback controls*. Their value at time t is a (measurable) function of the value of the state variable at time t and time t itself:[7]

$$v(t) = v(e(t), t)$$

The exact definition is embedded in theorem B.6 below. Roughly speaking, the past does not matter for controls. Only the current state of the system does. Without loss of generality, we can think of the controls as being $\mathbb{R}^N$-valued too.

The utility and bequest functions satisfy the regularity conditions assumed throughout the book. They are bounded, twice differentiable, and strictly concave. This is a *classical control problem*.

---

6 The filtration can be the one generated by the Brownian motion.

7 But, even if a larger class of controls were admitted, the optimal controls would always be feedback ones.

B.3.2   Bellman's Principle and Its Verification Theorem

As in the discrete-time case, we embed the original problem, $\mathcal{P}_0$, into a family of problems $\mathcal{P}_t$:

$$\max_{\{v(s)\}} \mathbb{E}_t \left\{ \int_t^T u(e(s), v(s), s)ds + \wp(e(T), T) \right\}$$

subject to:

$$de(s) = a(e, v, s)ds + b(e, v, s)dw(s)$$

We define the function J, called the *value function* of the program:

$$J(e(t), t) \triangleq \max_{\{v(s)\}} \mathbb{E}_t \left\{ \int_t^T u(e(s), v(s), s)ds + \wp(e(T), T) \right\}$$

$$t < T$$

$$J(e, T) \equiv \wp(e, T) \tag{B.8}$$

As in the discrete-time case, it can be shown, under technical conditions, that the *Bellman's principle of optimality* holds (as a statement of a necessary condition). If the solution to each and every problem starting at t, $J(e_t, t)$ exists, then it solves the following:

Theorem B.5   (Bellman's principle of optimality)   *The value function satisfies the HJB equation:*

$$\max_{\{v(t)\}} \left\{ u(e, v, t) + \frac{\partial J(e, t)}{\partial e} a(e, v, t) \right. \tag{B.9}$$

$$\left. + \frac{1}{2} trace \left[b(e, v, t)^{\mathsf{T}} \frac{\partial^2 J(e, t)}{\partial e^2} b(e, v, t) \right] \right\} + \frac{\partial J(e, t)}{\partial t} = 0$$

with terminal condition (B.8).

We do not give a proof, which requires some technicalities but follows from the same intuition as in the discrete-time case. Indeed, the HJB equation can be obtained, under appropriate boundedness and measurability, as a limit of the discrete-time recursions.

It can also be shown that a verification theorem holds. The verification approach provides a sufficient condition, under appropriate hypotheses.[8] We omit some technical details but sketch its proof, since the theorem is used very often in the textbook:

Theorem B.6   *Suppose that $J \in C^{2,1}\left(\mathbb{R}^N \times \mathbb{R}\right)$ satisfies the HJB equation (B.9) with boundary condition $J(e, T) \equiv \wp(e, T)$. Suppose, moreover, there exist admissible, measurable functions $v^*(e, t)$ that satisfy the first-order conditions of optimality for the continuous-time problem $\mathcal{P}_t$. Finally, suppose that e^* is the unique square-integrable process solving the SDEs (B.7) with $v = v^*(e, t)$. Let $\left(\bar{v}^*\right)$ be the corresponding feedback control, that is, the process defined by: $\bar{v}^*(t) = v^*(e^*(t), t)$.*
If $\left(\bar{v}^*\right) \in \mathcal{L}^2$, then J is the value function of the control problem and $\left(\bar{v}^*\right)$ is an optimal control.

Proof.   (Sketch) Let v be any control $\in \mathcal{L}^2$ and let V^v be the utility process corresponding to v:

$$V^v(t) \triangleq \mathbb{E}_t \left\{ \int_t^T u(e(s), v(s), s)ds + \wp(e(T), T) \right\}$$

Let $\left(e^v(t); t \geq 0\right)$ denote the solution of the state process equations (B.7), initialized at $e(0)$ at time 0, when the value of the controls is v.

---

8 Necessity is studied in Fleming and Rishel (1975).

By Itô's lemma, since $J(e(T),T) \equiv \wp(e,T)$,

$$
J(e(t),t) = \mathbb{E}_t \left\{ \int_t^T - \left\{ \frac{\partial J(e^v(s),s)}{\partial e} a + \frac{1}{2} \text{trace}\left(b^\mathsf{T} \frac{\partial^2 J(e^v(s),s)}{\partial e^2} b \right) \right. \right.
$$
$$
\left. \left. + \frac{\partial J(e^v(s),s)}{\partial t} \right\} ds + \wp\left(e^v(T),T\right) \right\}
$$

(B.10)

Hence

$$
J(e(t),t) - V^v(t) = \mathbb{E}_t \left\{ \int_t^T - \left\{ \frac{\partial J(e^v(s),s)}{\partial e} a + \frac{1}{2} \text{trace}\left(b^\mathsf{T} \frac{\partial^2 J(e^v(s),s)}{\partial e^2} b \right) \right. \right.
$$
$$
\left. \left. + \frac{\partial J(e^v(s),s)}{\partial t} + u(c,v,s) \right\} ds \right\}
$$

The Bellman equation (B.9) implies that

$$
- \left\{ u(c,v,s) + \frac{\partial J(e^v(s),s)}{\partial e} a + \frac{1}{2} \text{trace}\left(b^\mathsf{T} \frac{\partial^2 J(e^v(s),s)}{\partial e^2} b \right) + \frac{\partial J(e^v(s),s)}{\partial t} \right\} \geq 0
$$

Hence: $V^v(0) \leq J(e(0),0)$. In the special case in which $v = v^*$, the inequality is an equality. Since v in the above inequality is arbitrary, v^* is optimal. In particular this is true for feedback controls.   □

Also, in the continuous-time case, controls can be subject to constraints. The problem becomes *time-homogeneous* when

- the utility function is separable in time and the other variables: with abuse of notation, $u(e,v,t) = \exp(-\rho t) u(e,v), \rho > 0$;
- the transition probability of the Markov state process is time-homogeneous, in that its coefficients are independent of time;
- the horizon is infinite;
- and the admissible set of controls, if the latter are constrained, is time independent.

In this case the feedback controls are a function of the state only and, with a single state variable, the HJB equation can turn into an ODE. This will be the case for the example to follow.

Remark B.1 *Sometimes we do not wish to control the system over $[0,T]$, but over the time span $(0,\tau)$, where τ is the exit time of the Markov diffusion state process from a given, open set. Let A be its frontier (or a part of it). We are interested in the state process stopped at τ. The HJB equation is unaffected. For $e \in A$ the terminal condition becomes $J(e,\tau) \equiv \wp(e,\tau)$.*

B.3.3   Perturbation Reasoning or Variational Calculus

We saw above, when considering the static problem (B.1), that relaxing an inequality constraint by $\varepsilon > 0$, that is, perturbing it by ε, led to a higher value of the objective function. This intuitive idea, of getting hints by perturbing the controls or the constraints, works in greater generality and provides a straightforward way to solve a static maximization problem. As we know, in an unconstrained problem, or in a constrained one, provided the constraint remains satisfied, perturbation leads to the first-order condition for optimality. Imagine perturbing the control by ε; compute the derivative of the objective function with respect to the perturbation, and set it equal to zero when $\varepsilon = 0$. If you are at a maximum, the derivative must be zero. Otherwise said, the derivative equated to zero is a necessary (but not sufficient) condition for optimality.

One would like to have available a corresponding method also for dynamic problems. The idea is the following. Imagine perturbing the optimal control path by a function of time, in such a way that constraints are still satisfied. Equate to zero the derivative of the objective function with respect to the size of the perturbation. By so doing, you get a difference equation (in discrete time) or a differential equation (in continuous time) that is an intertemporal first-order condition for a dynamic choice problem. It is known as the *Euler equation*. It describes the evolution of the problem variables along an optimal path.

To present an example, let us consider a simplified version of the problem $\mathcal{P}_0$ above, where the controls are the state variables themselves, $e(t)$, the objective function depends on them and their rates of change of $e'(t)$, the function $\wp$ is identically zero and there is no uncertainty:

$$\sup_{\{e(t)\}} \int_0^T u\big(e(t), e'(t), t\big)\, dt$$

subject to

$$de(t) = a(e, t)dt$$

To fix ideas, let the initial and final value of the state variables be given:

$$e(0) = e_0$$
$$e(T) = e_T$$

Under mild regularity and differentiability properties, the following procedure can be adopted to obtain the Euler equation.[9] Suppose that $e^*(t)$ provides a maximum for $\mathcal{P}_0$ and consider a perturbation to such a path equal to $h(t)$, such that the perturbed path still satisfies the initial and terminal conditions:

$$h(0) = h(T) = 0$$

Call $e(t)$ the perturbed path and assume it is admissible, in the sense that it preserves regularity

$$e(t) = e^*(t) + h(t)$$

Then also

$$e^*(t) + \varepsilon \times h(t)$$

with ε a positive constant, is admissible. Compute the value of the objective function of the problem $\mathcal{P}_0$ for the perturbed trajectory and consider it as a function $f(\varepsilon)$ of ε

$$f(\varepsilon) = \int_0^T u\big(e^*(t) + \varepsilon h(t), e^{*\prime}(t) + \varepsilon h'(t), t\big)$$

As a function of a real variable, we require that the first-order derivative of f be equal to zero at $\varepsilon = 0$. This simply follows from the fact that $e^*(t)$ provides a maximum for $\mathcal{P}_0$. Observe that the derivative of the integrand is

$$u'(\varepsilon) = \frac{du(e^*(t) + \varepsilon h(t), e^{*\prime}(t) + \varepsilon h'(t), t)}{de} h(t) + \frac{du(e^*(t) + \varepsilon h(t), e^{*\prime}(t) + \varepsilon h'(t), t)}{de'} h'(t)$$

The derivative of f is simply the integral of $u'(\varepsilon)$:

$$f'(\varepsilon) = \int_0^T \left[\frac{du}{de} h(t) + \frac{du}{de'} h'(t) \right] dt$$

where u is still computed at $\big(e^*(t) + \varepsilon h(t), e^{*\prime}(t) + \varepsilon h'(t), t\big)$. Compute this derivative when $\varepsilon = 0$ and set it to zero:

$$f'(\varepsilon)\,|_{\varepsilon=0} = \int_0^T \left[\frac{du(e^*(t), e^{*\prime}(t), t)}{de} h(t) + \frac{du(e^*(t), e^{*\prime}(t), t)}{de'} h'(t) \right] dt = 0$$

Compute by parts the second integral, namely

$$\int_0^T \frac{du}{de'} h'(t) dt = \frac{du(e^*(T), e^{*\prime}(T), T)}{de'} h(T) - \frac{du(e^*(0), e^{*\prime}(0), 0)}{de'} h(0) - \int_0^T \frac{d}{dt}\left(\frac{du}{de'} \right) h(t) dt$$

---

9 See Kamien and Schwartz (1981).

which simplifies to

$$-\int_0^T \frac{d}{dt}\left(\frac{du}{de'}\right)h(t)dt$$

because $h(0) = h(T) = 0$. Substituting in $f'(\varepsilon)\,|_{\varepsilon=0} = 0$ we get

$$f'(\varepsilon)\,|_{\varepsilon=0} = \int_0^T \left[\frac{du(e^*(t), e^{*\prime}(t), t)}{de} - \frac{d}{dt}\left(\frac{du(e^*(t), e^{*\prime}(t), t)}{de'}\right)\right]h(t)dt = 0$$

which, as we said, must hold for any $h(t)$ with the features listed above. It does if and only if

$$\frac{du(e^*(t), e^{*\prime}(t), t)}{de} = \frac{d}{dt}\left(\frac{du(e^*(t), e^{*\prime}(t), t)}{de'}\right)$$

which is a differential equation in e called the Euler equation.

B.4   Continuous-Time Optimality under Frictions: Singular Control

The presentation of this topic is restricted to the case in which

- the utility function depends on consumption only, is multiplicatively separable in time and consumption and is of the power type:

$$u(e, v, t) = u(v, t) = u(c, t) = \exp(-\rho t)\frac{c^\gamma}{\gamma},$$

- the horizon is infinite
- there is a single, Geometric-Brownian motion, risky security, held in the portfolio in an amount denoted y at market price
- the riskless security – with market value in the portfolio denoted x – has a constant rate of return r
- frictions are represented by transactions costs, proportional to the amount of the transaction. In percentage terms, transactions costs are $1 - s$ times the value of the risky security sold or bought, $0 < s < 1$.[10] The trades between the two securities constitute the other control variables.

In this case, consumption remains an absolutely continuous control. But assets sales and purchases become *singular stochastic controls*. The process of these controls is only "singularly" continuous and not absolutely continuous. That is, it cannot be represented as the integral of a bounded function of time using the standard (Riemann or Lebesgue) definition of an integral. Intuitively, controls can be applied *at a rate that is not finite*. The *state variable process* is bivariate:

$$e = \begin{bmatrix} x \\ y \end{bmatrix}$$

In the region of the state space with no trades, the state variables have the following, constant-coefficient dynamics:

$$dx = (rx - c)dt$$
$$dy = \mu y dt + \sigma y dw(t)$$

The *control process* is bivariate as well:

$$v = \begin{bmatrix} L \\ U \end{bmatrix}$$

---

10 Costs are symmetric for sales and purchases: the extension to asymmetric costs is straightforward.

L represents cumulative reductions of the state variable y, U cumulative increases. They are sales and purchases of the risky security, respectively. The processes L and U are right-continuous with left limits, adapted, non-decreasing, with $L(0) = U(0) = 0$. The cum-trade equations for the state variables are:

$$\begin{cases} dx = (rx - c)dt - dL + sdU \\ dy = \mu ydt + \sigma ydw(t) + sdL - dU \end{cases} \tag{B.11}$$

Since these controlled processes are not continuous, we denote with τ the first time they hit the boundaries of the region in which they are continuous. In the applications of interest in the book, the region is a cone in the plane (x, y), which includes the origin. The boundaries of the cone are the lines $y = l \times x$ and $y = u \times x$.

B.4.1 Bellman's Principle

In a manner analogous to what we did in discrete and continous time, in the absence of frictions, we consider the family of problems $\mathcal{P}_t$:

$$\max_{\{v(s), L(s), U(s)\}} \mathbb{E}_t \left\{ \int_t^{+\infty} \exp(-\rho s) \frac{c(s)^\gamma}{\gamma} ds \right\}$$

subject to (B.11).

We define the function J, called the *value function* of the program:

$$J(x, y) \triangleq \max_{\{c(s), L(s), U(s)\}} \mathbb{E}_t \left\{ \int_t^{+\infty} \exp(-\rho s) \frac{c(s)^\gamma}{\gamma} ds \right\}$$

Now, instead of assuming that J is C^2, as we did in the corresponding problem without frictions, we simply assume that it is finite. In the case in which the controls are constrained by a "solvency requirement" of the type

$$\left\{ (x, y) : x + \frac{y}{s} \geq 0, x + sy \geq 0 \right\}$$

that property is enough to show that J solves the *dynamic programming principle* in a non-infinitesimal version in which the controls would be adjusted by finite moves.

In order to show that, for the problem at hand, it solves also the version with infinitesimal moves, namely

$$\min_{\{c(s), L, U\}} \left\{ \delta J - rx \frac{\partial J(x, y)}{\partial x} - \mu y \frac{\partial J(x, y)}{\partial y} - \frac{1}{2} \sigma^2 y^2 \frac{\partial^2 J(x, y)}{\partial y^2} - c^*, \right. \tag{B.12}$$
$$\left. -s \frac{\partial J(x, y)}{\partial x} + \frac{\partial J(x, y)}{\partial y}, \frac{\partial J(x, y)}{\partial x} - s \frac{\partial J(x, y)}{\partial y} \right\} = 0$$

– where c^* satisfies the first-order condition for consumption – we need sufficient smoothness on J. The way to go is the following. First, it can be shown that the HJB equation has a solution J in the so-called "viscosity sense." This means that there are simultaneously a so-called "viscosity supersolution" and a "subsolution." The supersolution is a continuous function, which is the upper bound of all the C^2 functions that make the LHS of (B.12) non-negative. The subsolution is a continuous function, which is the lower bound of all the the C^2 functions that make the LHS of (B.12) non-positive. A function that acts both as a supersolution and subsolution is a viscosity solution. For the problem at hand, the viscosity solution is smooth enough; J is C^2 (see Fleming and Soner (1993) or Shreve and Soner (1994)).

As in classical cases, if a solution exists, the corresponding policy is optimal among the singular ones. This means that a verification theorem holds, if J is C^2.

That is why in the text, restricting our attention to C^2 solutions, we proceed by verification also in the singular control case.

References

Abel, A., 1990, Asset Prices under Habit Formation and Catching Up with the Joneses, *The American Economic Review,* 80, 38–42.

Abramovitz, M. and I. A. Stigum, 1964, *Handbook of Mathematical Formulas*, National Bureau of Standards: NY.

Aït-Sahalia, Y. and J. Yu, 2006, Saddlepoint Approximations for Continuous-Time Markov Processes, *Journal of Econometrics*, 134, 507–551.

Albuquerque, R., M. Eichenbaum, V. Luo, and S. Rebelo, 2016, Valuation Risk and Asset Pricing, *The Journal of Finance,* 71, 2861–2903.

Anderson, R. and R. Raimondo, 2008, Equilibrium in Continuous-Time Financial Markets: Endogenously Dynamically Complete Markets, *Econometrica,* 76, 841–907.

Andrei, D. and M. Hasler, 2015, Investor Attention and Stock Market Volatility, *Review of Financial Studies*, 28: 33–72.

Ang, A. and M. Piazzesi, 2003, A No-Arbitrage Vector Autoregression of Term Structure Dynamics with Macroeconomic and Latent Variables, *Journal of Monetary Economics* 50, 745–787.

Ang, A., S. Dong, and M. Piazzesi, 2004, No Arbitrage Taylor's Rules, NBER Working Paper 13448, Chicago University.

Arnold, L.,1974, *Stochastic Differential Equations: Theory and Applications*, Wiley-Interscience: New York, NY.

Arrow, K. J., 1951, An Extension of the Basic Theorems of Classical Welfare Economics, in J. Neyman (Ed.) *Proceedings of the Second Berkeley Symposium on Mathematical Statistics,* University of California Press: Berkeley, CA.

Arrow, K. J., 1953, Le rôle des valeurs boursières pour la répartition la meilleure des risques, *Économétrie, Colloques Internationaux du Centre National de la Recherche Scientifique* 40, 41–47; English version: 1963, The Role of Securities in the Optimal Allocation of Risk Bearing, *Review of Economic Studies* 31, 91–96.

Arrow, K. J., 1965, *The Theory of Risk Aversion, in Aspects of the Theory of Risk Bearing*, Yrjo Foundation: Helsinki.

Arrow, K. J., 1970, *Essays in the Theory of Risk-Bearing,* Markham: Chicago, IL.

Arrow, K. J. and G. Debreu, 1954, Existence of an Equilibrium for a Competitive Economy, *Econometrica,* 22, 265–292.

Attanasio, P. O. and G. Weber, 1989, Intertemporal Substitution, Risk Aversion, and the Euler Equation for Consumption, *Economic Journal*, 99, 59–73.

Aumann, R. J., 1976, Agreeing to Disagree, *The Annals of Statistics*, 4, 1236–1239.

Back, K., 1992, Insider Trading in Continuous Time, *Review of Financial Studies*, 5, 387–409.

Back, K., 2010, *Asset Pricing and Portfolio Choice Theory*, Oxford University Press: New York, NY.

Back, K. and D. Paulsen, 2009, Open-loop Equilibria and Perfect Competition in Option Exercise Games, *Review of Financial Studies*, 22, 4531–4552.

Backus, D., S. Foresi, and L. Wu, 1997, Accounting for Biases in Black-Scholes, CRIF Working Paper series http://fordham.bepress.com/crif_working_papers/30

Balasko, Y., 1988, *Foundations of the Theory of General Equilibrium*, Academic Press: Orlando, FL.

Bansal, R. and A. Yaron, 2004, Risks for the Long Run: A Potential Resolution of Asset Pricing Puzzles, *The Journal of Finance*, 59, 1481–1509.

Bansal, R., D. Kiku, and M. Ochoa, 2015, Climate Change and Growth Risks, Working Paper, Fuqua School of Business, Duke University.

Barberis, N., A. Shleifer, and R. Vishny, 1998, A Model of Investor Sentiment, *Journal of Financial Economics*, 49, 307–343.

Basak, S. 2000, A Model of Dynamic Equilibrium Asset Pricing with Heterogeneous Beliefs and Extraneous Risk, *Journal of Economic Dynamics and Control*, 24, 63–95.

Basak, S. 2005, Asset Pricing with Heterogeneous Beliefs, 2005, *Journal of Banking and Finance*, 29, 2849–2881.

Basak, S. and G. Chabakauri, 2010, Dynamic Mean-Variance Asset Allocation, *Review of Financial Studies*, 23, 2970–3016.

Basak, S. and G. Chabakauri, 2012, Dynamic Hedging in Incomplete Markets: A Simple Solution, *Review of Financial Studies*, 25, 1845–1896.

Basak, S. and D. Cuoco, 1998, An Equilibrium Model with Restricted Market Participation, *Review of Financial Studies* 11, 309–341.

Bellman, R., 1957, *Dynamic Programming,* Princeton University Press: Princeton, NJ.

Bensaïd, B., J. Lesne, H. Pagès, and J. A. Scheinkman, 1992, Derivative Asset Pricing with Transactions Costs, *Mathematical Finance*, 2, 63–86.

Bensoussan, A. and J.-L. Lions, 1982, *Applications of Variational Inequalities in Stochastic Control*, North Holland: Amsterdam.

Berk, J., R. Green, and V. Naik 1999, Optimal Investment, Growth Options, and Security Returns, *The Journal of Finance*, 54, 1153–1607.

Bertsekas, D. and S. E. Shreve, 1978, *Stochastic Optimal Control: The Discrete Time Case*, Academic Press: New York, NY.

Bhamra, H. S. and R. Uppal, 2014, Asset Prices with Heterogeneity in Preferences and Beliefs, *Review of Financial Studies*, 27, 519–580.

Biais, B. and P. Bossaerts, 1998, Asset Prices and Trading Volume in a Beauty Contest, *Review of Economic Studies*, 65, 307–340.

Black, F., 1972, Capital-Market Equilibrium with Restricted Borrowing, *Journal of Business*, 45, 444–455.

Black, F., E. Derman, and W. Toy, 1990, A One-Factor Model of Interest Rates and Its Application to Treasury Bond Options, *Financial Analysts Journal*, 46, 33–39.

Black, F. and M. Scholes, 1973, The Pricing of Options and Corporate Liabilities, *Journal of Political Economy* 81, 637–654.

Blume, M. E., and I. Friend, 1975, The Demand for Risky Assets, *American Economic Review* 65, 900–922.

Borovicka, J., 2015, Survival and Long-Run Dynamics with Heterogeneous Beliefs under Recursive Preferences, Working Paper, New York University.

Boyd, S. and L. Vandenberghe, 2004, *Convex Optimization*, Cambridge University Press: New York, NY.

Boyle, P. and T. Vorst, 1992, Option Replication in Discrete Time with Transactions Costs, *The Journal of Finance* 47, 271.

Breeden, D. T., 1979, An Intertemporal Asset Pricing Model with Stochastic Consumption and Investment Opportunities, *Journal of Financial Economics*, 7, 265–296.

Breeden, D. T. and R. Litzenberger, 1978, Prices of State-Contingent Claims Implicit in Option Prices, *Journal of Business*, 51, 4, 621–651.

Brennan, M. J., 1998, The Role of Learning in Dynamic Portfolio Decisions, *European Finance Review*, 1, 295–306.

Brennan, M. J. and E. Schwartz, 1976, The Valuation of American Put Options, *Journal of Finance* 32, 449–462.

Brennan, M. J. and E. Schwartz, 1982, An Equilibrium Model of Bond Pricing and a Test of Market Efficiency, *Journal of Financial and Quantitative Analysis*, 17, 301–329.

Brennan, M. J., A. W. Wang, and Y. Xia, 2004, Estimation and Test of a Simple Model of Intertemporal Capital Asset Pricing, *The Journal of Finance,* 59, 1743–1775.

Brennan, M. J. and Y. Xia, 1998, Stock Price Volatility and Equity Premium, *Journal of Monetary Economics*, 47, 249–283.

Britten-Jones, M. and A. Neuberger, 2000, Option Prices, Implied Price Processes, and Stochastic Volatility, *The Journal of Finance*, 55, 839–866.

Bru, B. and M. Yor, 2002, Comments on the Life and Mathematical Legacy of Wolfgang Doeblin, *Finance and Stochastics*, 6, 3–47.

Buraschi, A. and J. Jackwerth, 2001, The Price of a Smile: Hedging and Spanning in Option Markets, *Review of Financial Studies*, 14, 495–527.

Buss, A. and B. Dumas, 2017, The Dynamic Properties of Financial-Market Equilibrium with Trading Fees, INSEAD working paper.

Campbell, J., 1993, Intertemporal Asset Pricing without Consumption Data, *American Economic Review* 83, 487–512.

Campbell, J. and J. Cochrane, 1999, By Force of Habit: A Consumption-Based Explanation of Aggregate Stock Market Behavior, *Journal of Political Economy,* 107, 205–251.

Campbell, J. Y. and R. J. Shiller, 1988, Stock Prices, Earnings and Expected Dividends, *Journal of Finance,* 43, 661–676.

Carmona, R. and S. Nadtochiy, 2009, Local Volatility Dynamic Models, *Finance and Stochastics*, 13, 1–48.

Carr, P., 1998, Randomization and the American Put, *Review of Financial Studies*, 11, 597–626.

Carr, P. and D. Madan, 1998, Towards a Theory of Volatility Trading, in R. Jarrow (Ed.), *Volatility: New Estimation Techniques for Pricing Derivatives*, London: Risk Books, 417–427.

Casassus, J., P. Collin-Dufresne, and R. S. Goldstein, 2005, Unspanned Stochastic Volatility and Fixed-income Derivative Pricing, *The Journal of Banking and Finance*, 2005, 29, 2723–2749.

Cass, D., 1992, Sunspots and Incomplete Markets: The General Case, *Economic Theory*, 2, 341–358.

Cass, D. and K. Shell, 1983, Do Sunspots Matter? *Journal of Political Economy*, 91, 193–227.

Cecchetti, S. G., P.-S. Lam, and N. C. Mark, 2000, Asset Pricing with Distorted Beliefs: Are Equity Returns Too Good to Be True?, *American Economic Review*, 90, 787–805.

Chabakauri, G., 2013, Dynamic Equilibrium with Two Stocks, Heterogeneous Investors, and Portfolio Constraints, *Review of Financial Studies*, 26, 3104–3141.

Chacko, G. and L. Viceira, 2005, Dynamic Consumption and Portfolio Choice with Stochastic Volatility in Incomplete Markets, *Review of Financial Studies*, 18, 1369–1402.

Chan, Y. L. and L. Kogan, 2002, Catching Up with the Joneses: Heterogeneous Preferences and the Dynamics of Asset Prices, *Journal of Political Economy*, 110, 1255–1285.

Cheng, S. T., 1991, On the Feasibility of Arbitrage-based Option Pricing When Stochastic Bond Price Processes Are Involved, *Journal of Economic Theory*, 53, 185-198.

Chiarella, C., A. Kucera and A. Ziogas, 2004, A Survey of the Integral Representation of American Option Prices, University of Technology, Sydney, QFRC Paper #118.

Christensen, P. O. and K. Larsen, 2014, Incomplete Continuous-Time Securities Markets with Stochastic Income Volatility, *Review of Asset Pricing Studies*, 4, 247–285.

Clewlow, L. and S. Hodges, 1997, Optimal Delta-Hedging under Transactions Costs, *Journal of Economic Dynamics and Control* 21, 1353–1376.

Cochrane, J. H., 1991, Production-based Asset Pricing and the Link between Stock Returns and Economic Fluctuations, *The Journal of Finance*, 46, 209–237.

Cochrane, J. H., 2001, *Asset Pricing*, Princeton University Press: Princeton, NJ.

Cochrane, J. H., 2005, Financial Markets and the Real Economy, chapter in Rajnish Mehra, (Eds.), *Handbook of the Equity Risk Premium,* Elsevier: Boston, MA, 2011.

Cochrane J. H. and M. Piazzesi, 2005, Bond Risk Premia, *American Economic Review*, 95, 138–160.

Collard, F., 2001, Stochastic Simulations with DYNARE, A Practical Guide, GREMAQ, University of Toulouse.

Collin-Dufresne, P. and R.S. Goldstein, 2002, Do Bonds Span the Fixed-income Markets? Theory and Evidence for Unspanned Stochastic Volatility, *The Journal of Finance*, 57, 1685–1730.

Collin-Dufresne, P., R.S. Goldstein, and C. Jones, 2009, Can Interest-rate Volatility be Extracted from the Cross Section of Bond Yields?, *The Journal of Financial Economics*, 94, October 2009, 47–66.

Collin-Dufresne, P., M. Johannes, and L. Lochstoer, 2016, Parameter Learning in General Equilibrium: Asset Pricing Implications, *American Economic Review*, 106, 664–98.

Constantinides, G. M. 1986, Capital Market Equilibrium with Transaction Costs, *Journal of Political Economy* 94, 842–862.

Constantinides, G. M., 1990, Habit Formation: A Resolution of the Equity Premium Puzzle, *Journal of Political Economy* 98, 519–543.

Constantinides, G. M. and D. Duffie, 1996, Asset Pricing with Heterogenous Consumers, *Journal of Political Economy,* 104, 219–240.

Constantinides, G. M. and S. Perrakis, 2002, Stochastic Dominance Bounds on Derivative Prices in a Multiperiod Economy with Proportional Transaction Costs, *Journal of Economic Dynamics and Control*, 26, 1323–1352.

Constantinides, G. M. and T. Zariphopoulou, Bounds on Prices of Contingent Claims in an Intertemporal Economy with Proportional Transaction Costs and General Preferences, *Finance and Stochastics* 3, 345–369.

Cox, J. C. and C.-F. Huang, 1989, Optimum Consumption and Portfolio Policies When Asset Prices Follow a Diffusion Process, *Journal of Economic Theory* 49, 33–83.

Cox, J. C., J. Ingersoll, and S. Ross, 1985a, An Intertemporal General Equilibrium Model of Asset Prices, *Econometrica,* 53, 363–384.

Cox, J. C. J. Ingersoll, and S. Ross, 1985b, A Theory of the Term Structure of Interest Rates, *Econometrica* 55, 385–407.

Cox, J. C. and H. Leland, 2000, On Dynamic Investment Strategies, *Journal of Economic Dynamics and Control* 24, 1859–1880.

Cox, J. C. and S. Ross, 1976, The Valuation of Options for Alternative Stochastic Processes, *Journal of Financial Economics* 3, 145–166.

Cox, J. C., S. Ross, and M. Rubinstein, 1979, Option Pricing: A Simplified Approach, *Journal of Financial Economics* 7, 229–263.

Cuoco, D., 1997, Optimal Consumption and Portfolio Constraints and Stochastic Income, *Journal of Economic Theory* 72, 33–73.

Daniel, K., D. Hirshleifer, and A. Subrahmanyam, 1998, Investor Psychology and Security Market Under- and Over-reactions, *The Journal of Finance*, 53, 1839–1885.

David, A., 1997, Fluctuating Confidence in Stock Markets: Implications for Returns and Volatility, *Journal of Financial and Quantitative Analysis*, 32, 427–462.

David, A., 2008, Heterogenous Beliefs, Speculation, and the Equity Premium, *The Journal of Finance*, 63, 41–83.

Davis, M. and R. Norman, 1990, Portfolio Selection with Transactions Costs, *Mathematics of Operations Research* 15, 676–713.

Davis, M., V. Panas, and T. Zariphopoulou, 1993, European Option Pricing with Transactions Costs, *SIAM Journal of Control and Optimization* 31, 470–549.

Debreu, G., 1959, *Theory of Value*, John Wiley: New York, NY.

Delbaen, F. and W. Schachermayer, 1994, A General Version of the Fundamental Theorem of Asset Pricing, *Mathematische Annalen* 300, 463–520.

De Long, J. B., A. Shleifer, L. H. Summers, and R. J. Waldmann, 1990, Noise Trader Risk in Financial Markets, *Journal of Political Economy*, 98, 703–738.

Derman, E. and I. Kani, 1994, Riding on a Smile, *Risk*, 7, 32–39.

Derman, E. and I. Kani, 1997, Stochastic Implied Trees: Arbitrage Pricing With Stochastic Term and Strike Structure of Volatility, Goldman Sachs Quantitative Strategies Research Notes.

Detemple, J., R. Garcia, and M. Rindisbacher, 2003, A Monte Carlo Method for Optimal Portfolios, *The Journal of Finance*, 58, 401–446.

Detemple, J., R. Garcia, and M. Rindisbacher, 2006, Asymptotic Properties of Monte Carlo Estimators of Diffusion Processes, *Journal of Econometrics*, 134, 1–68.

Detemple, J. and S. Murthy, 1994, Intertemporal Asset Pricing with Heterogeneous Beliefs, *Journal of Economic Theory*, 62, 294–320.

Dixit, A., 1989, Entry and Exit Decisions under Uncertainty, *Journal of Political Economy* 97, 205–228.

Dixit, A., 1991, A Simplified Treatment of Some Results Concerning Regulated Brownian Motion, *Journal of Economic Dynamics and Control* 15, 657–674.

Dixit, A., 1993, *The Art of Smooth-Pasting*, Harwood Academic Publishers: Chur, Switzerland.

Doss, H., 1977, Liens entre équations différentielles stochastiques et ordinaires, *Annales de l'Institut H. Poincaré* 13, 99–125.

Dothan, M. U. and D Feldman, 1986, Equilibrium Interest Rates and Multiperiod Bonds in a Partially Observable Economy, *The Journal of Finance*, 41, 369–382

Drèze, J. and F. Modigliani, 1972, Consumption Decisions under Uncertainty, *Journal of Economic Theory*, 5, 308–335.

Driessen, J., P. J. Maenhout, and G. Vilkov, 2009, The Price of Correlation Risk: Evidence from Equity Options, *The Journal of Finance*, 64, 1377–1406.

Dudley, R. M., 1977, Wiener Functionals as Itô Integrals, *The Annals of Probability*, 5, 140–141.

Duffie, D., 1986, Stochastic Equilibria: Existence, Spanning Number, and the "No Expected Financial Gain from Trade" Hypothesis, *Econometrica* 54, 1161–1184.

Duffie, D., 2010, Presidential Address: Asset Price Dynamics with Slow-Moving Capital, *The Journal of Finance*, 55, 1237–1267.

Duffie, D. and L. Epstein, 1992, Stochastic Differential Utility, *Econometrica* 60, 353–394.

Duffie, D., D. Filipović, and W. Schachermayer 2003, Affine Processes and Applications in Finance, *Annals of Applied Probability*, 13, 984–1053.

Duffie, D., P.-Y. Geoffard, and C. Skiadas, 1994, Efficient and Equilibrium Allocations with Stochastic Differential Utility, *Journal of Mathematical Economists*, 23, 133–146.

Duffie, D., J. Pan, and K. Singleton, 2000, Transform Analysis and Asset Pricing for Affine Jump-diffusions, *Econometrica*, 68, 1343–1376.

Duffie, D. and W. Shafer, 1985, Equilibrium in Incomplete Markets I: A Basic Model of Generic Existence, *Journal of Mathematical Economics*, 14, 285–300.

Duffie, D. and W. Zame, 1989, The Consumption-Based Capital Asset Pricing Model, *Econometrica* 57, 1279–1297.

Dumas, B., 1989, Two-Person Dynamic Equilibrium in the Capital Market, *Review of Financial Studies* 2, 157–188.

Dumas, B., 1991, Super Contact and Related Optimality Conditions, *Journal of Economic Dynamics and Control* 15, 675–685.

Dumas, B., 1992, Capital Market Equilibrium and the Real Exchange Rate in a Spatially Separated World, *Review of Financial Studies*, 5, 153–180.

Dumas, B., 1995, The Meaning of the Implicit Volatility Function in Case of Stochastic Volatility, unpublished note (meant to be an appendix to Dumas *et al.* (1998)) available at: http://faculty.insead.edu/bernard-dumas/research

Dumas, B., J. Fleming, and R. E. Whaley, 1998, Implied Volatility Functions: Empirical Tests, *Journal of Finance*, 53, 2059–2106.

Dumas, B., A. Kurshev, and R. Uppal, 2009, Equilibrium Portfolio Strategies in the Presence of Sentiment Risk and Excess Volatility, *The Journal of Finance*, 64, 581–632.

Dumas, B., K. Lewis, and E. Osambela, 2017, Differences of Opinion and International Equity Markets, *Review of Financial Studies*, 30, 750–800.

Dumas, B. and E. Luciano, 1991, An Exact Solution to a Portfolio Choice Problem under Transactions Costs, *The Journal of Finance*, 46, 577–595.

Dumas, B. and A. Lyasoff, 2012, Incomplete-Market Equilibria Solved Recursively on an Event Tree, *The Journal of Finance*, 67, 1887–1931.

Dumas, B., R. Uppal, and T. Wang, 2000, Efficient Inter-temporal Allocations with Recursive Utility, *Journal of Economic Theory* 93, 240–259.

Dupire, B., 1994, Pricing with a Smile, *Risk*, 7, 32–39.

Dybvig, P. and C. Huang, 1987, Non-negative Wealth, Absence of Arbitrage and Feasible Consumption Plans, *Review of Financial Studies* 1, 377–401.

El Karoui, N., S. Peng and M.-C. Quenez, Backward Stochastic Differential Equations in Finance, *Mathematical Finance*, 7, 1–71.

El Karoui, N. and J.-C. Rochet, 1989, A Pricing Formula for Options on Coupon Bonds, Working Paper, Université Paris VI.

Emmanuel, D. and J. D. MacBeth, 1982, Further Results on the Constant Elasticity of Variance Call Option Pricing Model, *Journal of Financial and Quantitative Analysis* 17, 533–554.

Epstein, L. G., 1987, The Global Stability of Efficient Intertemporal Allocation, *Econometrica* 55, 329–355.

Epstein, L. G., 1988, Risk Aversion and Asset Prices, *Journal of Monetary Economics*, 22, 179–192.

Epstein, L. G. and S. E. Zin, 1989, Substitution, Risk Aversion and the Temporal Behavior of Consumption and Asset Returns: A Theoretical Framework, *Econometrica*, 57, 937–969.

Fama, E. and K. French, 1993, Common Risk Factors in the Returns on Stock and Bonds, *Journal of Financial Economics* 33, 1, 3–56.

Farlow, S. J., 1993, *Partial Differential Equations for Scientists and Engineers*, Dover Books on Mathematics: New York, NY.

Favero, C. A., A. E. Gozluklu, and A. Tamoni, 2011, Demographic Trends, the Dividend-Price Ratio and the Predictability of Long-Run Stock Market Returns, *Journal of Financial and Quantitative Analysis*, 46, 1493–1520.

Favilukis, J. and X. Lin, 2016, Wage Rigidity: A Quantitative Solution to Several Asset Pricing Puzzles, *Review of Financial Studies*, 29, 148–192.

Fisher, I., 1930, *The Theory of Interest, as Determined by Impatience to Spend Income and Opportunity to Invest It*, The Macmillan Co: New York, NY.

Fleming, W. and R. Rishel, 1975, *Deterministic and Stochastic Optimal Control*, Springer-Verlag: Berlin-New York, NY.

Fleming, W. and H. Soner, 1993, *Controlled Markov Processes and Viscosity Solutions*, Springer-Verlag: New York, NY.

Fournié, E., J.-M. Lasry, J. Lebuchoux, P.-L. Lions, and N. Touzi, 1999, Applications of Malliavin Calculus to Monte-Carlo Methods in Finance, *Finance and Stochastics*, 3, 391–412.

Fournié, E., J.-M. Lasry, J. Lebuchoux, and P.-L. Lions, 2001, Applications of Malliavin Calculus to Monte-Carlo Methods in Finance II, *Finance and Stochastics* 5, 201–236.

French, K., 2008, The Cost of Active Investing, *The Journal of Finance*, 63, 1537–1573.

Friend, I. and E. Blume, 1975, The Demand for Risky Assets, *American Economic Review*, 65, 900–922.

Fusai, G. and A. Roncoroni, 2008, *Implementing Models in Quantitative Finance: Methods and Cases*, Springer Verlag, Heidelberg.

Gavazzoni, F., 2012, Nominal Frictions, Monetary Policy, and Long-Run Risk, Working Paper, INSEAD.

Gennotte, G., 1986, Optimal Portfolio Choice Under Incomplete Information, *The Journal of Finance*, 41, 733–746.

Geoffard, P.-Y., 1996, Discounting and Optimizing: Capital Accumulation as a Variational Min-max Problem, *Journal of Economic Theory*, 69, 53 70.

Giovannini, A., and P. Weil, 1989, Risk Aversion and Intertemporal Substitution in the Capital Asset Pricing Model, NBER, Working Paper 2824.

Gollier, C., 2008, Understanding Saving and Portfolio Choices with Predictable Changes in Asset Returns, *Journal of Mathematical Economics*, 44, 445–458.

Gollier, C., 2001, *The Economics of Risk and Time*, MIT Press: Cambridge, MA.

Gollier, C. and L. Eeckhoudt, 2001, Are Independent Optimal Risks Substitutes? Working Paper, University of Toulouse.

Gollier, C. and M. S. Kimball, 1994, New Methods in the Classical Economics of Uncertainty: Characterizing Utility Functions, Working Paper, University of Toulouse.

Gomes, J., L. Kogan and L. Zhang, 2003, Equilibrium Cross-Section of Returns, *Journal of Political Economy*, 111, 693–732.

Grasselli, M. and C. Tebaldi, 2008, Solvable Affine Term Structure Models, *Mathematical Finance*, 18, 135–153.

Green, T. C., 2004, Economic News and the Impact of Trading on Bond Prices, *The Journal of Finance*, 59, 1201–1234.

Grenadier, S. R., 2002, Option Exercise Games: An Application to the Equilibrium Investment Strategies of Firms, *Review of Financial Studies*, 15, 691–722.

Grossman, S. J. and J. E. Stiglitz, 1980, On the Impossibility of Informationally Efficient Markets, *American Economic Review*, 70, 393–408.

Guo, X. and P. Tomecek, 2009, A Class of Singular Control Problems and the Smooth-Fit Principle, *Siam Journal on Control and Optimization*, 47, 3076–99.

Harris, M. and A. Raviv, 1993, Differences of Opinion Make a Horse Race, *Review of Financial Studies*, 6, 473–506.

Harrison, J. M. and D. M. Kreps, 1979, Martingales and Arbitrage in Multiperiod Securities Markets, *Journal of Economic Theory* 20, 381–408.

Harrison, J. M. and S. R. Pliska, 1981, Martingales and Stochastic Integrals in the Theory of Continuous Trading, *Stochastic Processes and Their Applications*, 11, 215–260.

Harrison, J. M. and M. Taksar, 1983, Instantaneous Control of Brownian Motion, *Mathematics of Operations Research* 8, 439–453.

Harrison, J. M. and A. Taylor, 1978, Optimal Control of a Brownian Storage System, *Stochastic Processes and Their Applications*, 6, 179–194.

Hart, O., 1975, On the Optimality of Equilibrium when the Market Structure is Incomplete, *Journal of Economic Theory*, 11, 418–443.

He, H., 1990, Convergence from Discrete- to Continuous-Time Contingent Claims Prices, *Review of Financial Studies*, 3, 523–546.

He, H., and H. Leland, 1993, On Equilibrium Asset Price Processes, *Review of Financial Studies* 6, 593–617.

He, H., and N. D. Pearson, 1991, Consumption and Portfolio Policies with Incomplete Markets and Short-Sale Constraints: the Infinite Dimensional Case, *Journal of Economic Theory* 54, 259–304.

Heath, D., R. Jarrow, and A. Morton, 1992, Bond Pricing and the Term Structure of Interest Rates: a New Methodology for Contingent Claims Valuation, *Econometrica* 60, 77–105.

Hellwig, M. F., 1980, On the Aggregation of Information in Complete Markets, *Journal of Economic Theory*, 26, 279–312.

Heston, S. L., 1993, A Closed-Form Solution for Options with Stochastic Volatility with Applications to Bond and Currency Options, *Review of Financial Studies* 6, 327–343.

Heston, S. L., M. Loewenstein, and G. A. Willard, 2007, Options and Bubbles, *Review of Financial Studies* 20, 359–390.

Heston, S. L., and S. Nandi, 2000, A Closed-Form GARCH Option Valuation Model, *Review of Financial Studies*, 13, 585–625.

Higham, D. J., 2001, An Algorithmic Introduction to Numerical Simulation of Stochastic Differential Equations, *SIAM Review* 43, 525–546.

Hirshleifer, J., 1970, *Investment, Interest, and Capital*, Prentice-Hall: Englewood Cliffs, NJ.

Hirshleifer, J., 1989, *Time, Uncertainty, and Information*, Blackwell: Willstone, VT.

Ho, T. S. Y. and S.-B. Lee, 1986, Term Structure Movements and Pricing Interest Rate Contingent Claims, *The Journal of Finance* 41, 1011–1029.

Hobson, D. G., and L. C. G. Rogers, 1998, Complete Models with Stochastic Volatility, *Mathematical Finance*, 8, 27–48.

Hodges, S. D. and A. Neuberger, 1989, Optimal Replication of Contingent Claims Under Transactions Costs, *The Review of Futures Markets*, 8, 222–239.

Hong, H. and J. C. Stein, 1999, A Unified Theory of Underreaction, Momentum Trading, and Overreaction in Asset Markets, *The Journal of Finance*, 54, 2143–2184.

Huang, C., 1987, An Intertemporal General Equilibrium Asset Pricing Model: The Case of Diffusion Information, *Econometrica* 55, 117–142.

Hugonnier, J., 2012, Rational Asset Pricing Bubbles and Portfolio Constraints, *Journal of Economic Theory*, 147, 2260–2302.

Hugonnier, J., S. Malamud, and E. Trubowitz, 2012, Endogenous Completeness of Diffusion Driven Equilibrium Markets, *Econometrica*, 80, 1249–1270.

Hugonnier, J. and R. Prieto, 2014, Asset Pricing with Arbitrage Activity, *Journal of Financial Economics*, forthcoming.

Hull, J. and A. White, 1987, The Pricing of Options on Assets with Stochastic Volatilities, *The Journal of Finance* 42, 281–300.

Hull, J. and A. White, 1990, Pricing Interest Rate Derivative Securities, *Review of Financial Studies* 3, 573–592.

Hull, J. and A. White, 1993a, Bond Option Pricing Based on a Model for the Evolution of Bond Prices, *Advances in Futures and Options Research* 6, 1–13.

Hull, J. and A. White, 1993b, One-Factor Interest Rate Models and the Valuation of Interest Rate Derivative Securities, *Journal of Financial and Quantitative Analysis* 28, 235–254.

Ingersoll, J., 1987, *Theory of Financial Decision Making*, Rowman and Littlefield Publishers: Totowa, NJ.

Itô, K., 1942, On stochastic processes (I) (Infinitely divisible laws of probability), *Japanese Journal of Mathematics*, 18, 261–301.

Itô, K., 1944, Stochastic Integral, *Proceedings of the Imperial Academy Tokyo* 20, 519–524.

Itô, K., 1951, On a Formula Concerning Stochastic Differentials, *Nagoya Mathematical Journal* 3, 55–65.

Jaillet, P., D. Lamberton, and B. Lapeyre, 1990, Variational Inequalities and the Pricing of American Options, *Acta Applicandae Mathematicae 21*, 263–289.

Jarrow, R. and A. Rudd, 1982, Approximate Option Valuation for Arbitrary Stochastic Processes, *Journal of Financial Economics,* 10, 347–369.

Jeanblanc, M., M. Yor, and M. Chesney, 2009, *Mathematical Methods for Financial Markets*, Springer: Heidelberg, Germany.

Jermann, U., 1998, Asset Pricing in Production Economies, *Journal of Monetary Economics*, 41, 257–275.

Johnsen, T. H. and J. B. Donaldson, 1985, The Structure of Intertemporal Preferences under Uncertainty and Time Consistent Plans, *Econometrica*, 53, 1451–1458.

Johnson, N. L. and S. Kotz, 1970, *Distributions in Statistics, Continuous Univariate Distributions - 2*, John Wiley and Sons: New York, NY.

Jondeau, E. and M. Rockinger, 2001, Gram-Charlier Densities, *Journal of Economic Dynamics and Control*, 25, 1457–1483.

Jouini, E. and C. Napp, 2007, Consensus Consumer and Intertemporal Asset Pricing with Heterogeneous Beliefs, *Review of Economic Studies*, 74, 1149–1174.

Judd, K. L., 1996, Approximation, Perturbation, and Projection Methods in Economics, in H. Amman, D. Kendrick, and J. Rust, (Eds.), *Handbook of Computational Economics*, North Holland: Amsterdam, The Netherlands.

Judd, K. L. and S. M. Guu, 2001, Asymptotic Methods for Asset Market Equilibrium Analysis, *Economic Theory*, Springer, 18, 1, 127–157.

Kabanov, Y. and M. Safarian, 1997, On Leland's Strategy of Option Pricing with Transaction Costs, *Finance and Stochastics 1*, 239–250.

Kabanov, Y. and M. Safrian, 2009, *Markets with Transactions Costs*, Springer: Heidelberg, Germany.

Kaltenbrunner, G. and L. A. Lochstoer, 2010, Long-run Risk through Consumption Smoothing, *Review of Financial Studies*, 23, 3190–3224.

Kamien, M. I. and N. L. Schwartz, 1991, *Dynamic Optimization. The Calculus of Variations and Optimal Control in Economics and Management*, North Holland, Amsterdam, The Netherlands.

Kandel, E. and N. D. Pearson, 1995, Differential Interpretation of Public Signals and Trade in Speculative Markets, *Journal of Political Economy*, 103, 831–872.

Karatzas, I., J. Lehoczky, and S. E. Shreve, 1987, Optimal Portfolio and Consumption Decisions for a Small Investor on a Finite Horizon, *SIAM Journal of Control and Optimization*, 25, 1157–1186.

Karatzas, I., J. P. Lehoczky, S. E. Shreve, and G. L. Xu, 1991, Martingale and Duality Methods for Utility Maximization in an Incomplete Market, *SIAM Journal of Control and Optimization*, 29, 702–730.

Karatzas, I. and S. E. Shreve, 1986, Equivalent Models for Finite Fuel Stochastic Control, *Stochastics*, 18, 245–276.

Karatzas, I. and S. E. Shreve, 1991, *Brownian Motion and Stochastic Calculus*, Springer-Verlag: New York, NY.

Karatzas, I. and S. E. Shreve, 1998, *Methods of Mathematical Finance*, Springer-Verlag: New York, NY.

Kimball, M. S., 1990, Precautionary Saving in the Small and in the Large, *Econometrica* 58, 53–73.

Klebaner, F., 2005, *Introduction to Stochastic Calculus with Applications*, 2nd edition, Imperial College Press, London.

Kloeden, P. E. and E. Platen, 1999, *Numerical Solution of Stochastic Differential Equations*, Springer-Verlag: Berlin, Germany.

Kogan, L., 2001, An Equilibrium Model of Irreversible Investment, *Journal of Financial Economics*, 62, 201–245.

Kogan, L., 2004, Asset Prices and Real Investment, *Journal of Financial Economics*, 73, 411–432.

Kogan, L., S. Ross, and M. Westerfield, 2006, The Price Impact and Survival of Irrational Traders, *The Journal of Finance*, 61, 195–220.

Kogan, L. and R. Uppal, 2000 and 2001, Risk Aversion and Optimal Portfolio Policies in Partial and General Equilibrium Economics, Working Paper, MIT and London Business School.

Koopmans, T. C., 1960, Stationary Ordinal Utility and Impatience, *Econometrica*, 28, 287–309.

Korn, R., 1997, *Optimal Portfolios: Stochastic Models for Optimal Investment and Risk Management in Continuous Time*, World Scientific: Singapore.

Kraft, H., F. T. Seifried, and M. Steffensen, 2013, Consumption-Portfolio Optimization with Recursive Utility in Incomplete Markets, *Finance and Stochastics*, 17, 161–196.

Kreps D. M., 1981, Arbitrage and Equilibrium in Economies with Infinitely Many Commodities, *Journal of Mathematical Economics* 8, 15–35.

Kreps, D. M. and E. L. Porteus, 1978, Temporal Resolution of Uncertainty and Dynamic Choice Theory, *Econometrica* 46, 185–200.

Krylov, N., 1980, *Controlled Diffusion Processes*, Springer-Verlag: Berlin.

Kuehn, L. A., N. Petrosky-Nadeau, and L. Zhang, 2013, An Equilibrium Asset Pricing Model with Labor Market Search, Working Paper, Tepper School of Business, Carnegie-Mellon University.

Kung, H., 2015, Macroeconomic Linkages Between Monetary Policy and the Term Structure of Interest Rates, *Journal of Financial Economics*, 115, 42–57.

Kung, H. and L. Schmid, 2015, Innovation, Growth, and Asset Prices, *The Journal of Finance*, 70, 1001–1037.

Kyle, A. S., 1985, Continuous Auctions and Insider Trading, *Econometrica*, 53, 1315–1336.

Lagrange, J.-L., 1770, Nouvelle méthode pour résoudre les équations littérales par le moyen des séries, *Mémoires de l'Académie Royale des Sciences et Belles-Lettres de Berlin*, 24, 251–326.

Laibson, D., 1997, Golden Eggs and Hyperbolic Discounting, *Quarterly Journal of Economics*, 62, 443–478.

Lamberton, D., H. Pham, and M. Schweizer, 1998, Local Risk-Minimization Under Transaction Costs, *Mathematics of Operations, Research*, 23, 585–612.

Leland, H. E., 1968, Saving and Uncertainty: The Precautionary Demand for Saving, *The Quarterly Journal of Economics*, 82, 465–473.

Leland, H., 1985, Option Pricing and Replication with Transaction Costs, *Journal of Finance* 40, 1283–1301.

Lengwiler, Y., 2004, *Microfoundations of Financial Economics: An Introduction to General Equilibrium Asset Pricing*, Princeton University Press: Princeton, NJ.

Lintner, J., 1965, The Valuation of Risk Assets and the Selection of Risky Investments in Stock Portfolios and Capital Budgets, *Review of Economics and Statistics* 47, 768–783.

Liptser, R. S. and A. N. Shiryaev, 2001, *Statistics of Random Processes II, Applications*, 2nd edition, Springer Verlag: New York, NY.

Litterman, R., and J. A. Scheinkman, 1991, Common Factors Affecting Bonds Returns, *Journal of Fixed Income*, 1, 54–61.

Lo, A., H. Mamaysky, and J. Wang, 2004, Asset Pricing and Trading Volume under Fixed Transaction Costs, *Journal of Political Economy*, 112, 1054–1090.

Lo, A. W. and J. Wang, 2000, Trading Volume: Definitions, Data Analysis, and Implications of Portfolio Theory, *Review of Financial Studies* 13, 257–300.

Lucas, R., 1978, Asset Prices in an Exchange Economy, *Econometrica* 46, 1429–1445.

Luciano, E., 2008, Spark Spread Options when Commodity Prices Are Represented as Time-Changed Processes, in Geman, H., (Ed.), *Financial Risk Management in Commodity Markets: From Shipping to Agriculturals and Energy*, J. Wiley Financial Series: New York, NY.

Luciano, E., M. Marena, and P. Semeraro, 2015, Dependence Calibration and Portfolio Fit with Factor-based Time Changes, *Quantitative Finance*, forthcoming, DOI:10.1080/14697688.2015.1114661.

Luciano, E. and W. Schoutens, 2006, A Multivariate Jump-Driven Financial Asset Model, *Quantitative Finance*, 6, 385–402.

Luciano, E. and P. Semeraro, 2010a, A Generalized Normal Mean Variance Mixture for Return Processes in Finance, *International Journal of Theoretical and Applied Finance*, 13, 415–440.

Luciano, E. and P. Semeraro, 2010b, Multivariate Time Changes for Lévy Asset Models: Characterization and Calibration, *Journal of Computational and Applied Mathematics,* 233, 1937–1953.

Luciano, E. and A. Tolomeo, 2016a, Information Effects in Longevity-Linked versus Purely Financial Portfolios, Cerp-Collegio Carlo Alberto, Working Paper.

Luciano, E. and A. Tolomeo, 2016b, Equilibrium bid-ask spreads and the effect of competitive trading delays, Collegio Carlo Alberto Notebook 467/2016.

Luenberger, D. G., 1969, *Optimization by Vector Space Methods*, John Wiley and Sons, Inc: New York, NY.

Magill, M., and M. Quinzii, 1996, *Theory of Incomplete Markets*, Vol. 1, MIT Press: Cambridge, MA.

Mangasarian, O., 1969, *Nonlinear Programming*, McGraw-Hill: New York, NY.

Mankiw, G. N., 1986, The Equity Premium and the Concentration of Aggregate Shocks, *Journal of Financial Economics,* 17, 211–219.

Markowitz, H. M., 1952, Portfolio Selection, *Journal of Finance* 1, 77–91.

Markowitz, H. M., 1959, *Portfolio Selection*, Yale University Press: New Haven, CT.

Martin, I, 2013, The Lucas Orchard, *Econometrica*, 81, 55–111.

Mas-Colell, A., M. D. Whinston, and J. R. Green, *Microeconomic Theory*, Oxford University Press, 1995.

Maurer, T. A., 2014, Asset Pricing Implications of Demographic Change, Working Paper, Olin School of Business, Washington University of Saint-Louis.

McKean, H., 1965, Appendix: A Free Boundary Problem for the Heat Equation Arising from a Problem in Mathematical Economics, *Industrial Management Review* 6, 32–39.

Mehra, R. and E. Prescott, 1985, The Equity Premium: A Puzzle, *Journal of Monetary Economics* 15, 145–161.

Menzly, L., T. Santos, and P. Veronesi, 2004, Understanding Predictability, *Journal of Political Economy*, 112, 1–47.

Merton, R. C., 1969, Lifetime Portfolio Selection under Uncertainty: The Continuous-time Case, *Review of Economics and Statistics* 51, 247–257.

Merton, R. C., 1971, Optimum Consumption and Portfolio Rules in a Continuous-time Model, *Journal of Economic Theory* 3, 373–413.

Merton, R. C., 1973a, An Intertemporal Asset Pricing Model, *Econometrica* 41, 867–888.

Merton, R. C., 1973b, Theory of Rational Option Pricing, *Bell Journal of Economics and Management Science* 4, 141–183.

Merton, R. C., 1977, On the Pricing of Contingent Claims and the Modigliani-Miller Theorem, *Journal of Financial Economics* 5, 241–250.

Merton, R. C., 1982, On the Mathematics and Economic Assumptions of Continuous-time Models, in W. F. Sharpe, (Ed.,) *Financial Economics: Essays in Honor of Paul Cootner*, Prentice-Hall: Englewood Cliffs, NJ.

Merton, R. C., 1990, *Continuous-time Finance*, Basil Blackwell: Gateshead.

Mikhalevish, V. S., 1956, Sequential Bayes Solutions to Optimal Methods of Statistical Acceptance Control, *Theory of Probability and its Applications* 1, 395–421.

Mikhalevish, V. S., 1958, A Bayes Test of Two Hypotheses Concerning the Mean of a Normal Process, (in Ukrainian) *Visnik Kiiv Univ.* 1, 101–104.

Montero, M. and A. Kohatsu-Higa, 2003, Malliavin Calculus Applied to Finance, *Physica A*, 320, 548–570.

Morris, S., 1995, The Common Prior Assumption in Economic Theory, *Economics and Philosophy*, 11, 227–253.

Morton, A. J. and S. R. Pliska, S. R., 1995, Optimal Portfolio Management with Fixed Transactions Costs, *Mathematical Finance*, 5, 337–356.

Negishi, T., 1960, Welfare Economics and the Existence of an Equilibrium for a Competitive Economy, *Metroeconomica* 12, 92–97.

Nelson, D., 1990, ARCH Models as Diffusion Approximations, *Journal of Econometrics* 45, 7–38.

Nelson, D. and K. Ramaswamy, 1990, Simple Binomial Processes as Diffusion Approximations in Financial Models, *Review of Financial Studies*, 3, 393–430.

Nielsen, L. T., 1999, *Pricing and Hedging of Derivative Securities*, Oxford University Press: Oxford.

Nielsen, L. T. and M. Vassalou, 2006, The Instantaneous Capital Market Line, *Economic Theory*, 28, 651–664.

Novy-Marx, R. and M. Velikov, 2015, A Taxonomy of Anomalies and Their Trading Costs, *Review of Financial Studies*, forthcoming.

Nualart, D., 1995, *Malliavin Calculus and Related Topics*, Springer Verlag: Berlin.

Osambela, E., B. Hollifield, and S. Baker, 2016, Disagreement, Speculation, and Aggregate Investment, *Journal of Financial Economics*, 119, 210–225.

Peng, C. and O. Scaillet, 2007, Linear-Quadratic Jump-Diffusion Modeling, *Mathematical Finance*, 17, 575–598.

Peskir, G. and A. Shyriaev, 2006, *Optimal Stopping and Free-Boundary Problems,* Springer Verlag: Berlin.

Philippon, T., 2015, Has the US Finance Industry Become Less Efficient? On the Theory and Measurement of Financial Intermediation, *American Economic Review*, 105, 1408–1438.

Piazzesi, M., 2005, Bond Yields and the Federal Reserve, *Journal of Political Economy* 113, 311–344.

Pindyck, R., 1988, Irreversible Investment, Capacity Choice, and the Value of the Firm, *American Economic Review* 78, 969–985.

Platania, A. and L. C. G. Rogers, 2005, Putting the Hobson-Rogers Model to the Test, Working Paper, University of Padova.

Pliska, S. R., 1986, A Stochastic Calculus Model of Continuous Trading: Optimal Portfolios, *Mathematical Operations Research*, 11, 371–382.

Pratt, J., 1964, Risk Aversion in the Small and the Large, *Econometrica* 32, 122–136.

Quarteroni, A., R. Sacco, and F. Saleri, 2000, *Numerical Mathematics*, Springer-Verlag: New York, NY.

Radner, R., 1972, Existence of Equilibrium of Plans, Prices, and Price Expectations in a Sequence of Markets, *Econometrica* 40, 289–303.

Ritschken, P. and L. Sanakarasubramanian, 1995, Volatility Structures of Forward Rates and the Dynamics of the Term Structure, *Mathematical Finance* 5, 55–72.

Rogers, L. C. G. and O. Zane, 1999, Saddle-Point Approximations to Option Prices, *Annals of Applied Probability,* 9, 493–503.

Ross, S., 1973, Return, Risk and Arbitrage, published in I. Friend and J. Bicksler, (Eds.), *Risk and Return in Finance*, Ballinger: Cambridge, 1976, 189–217.

Ross, S., 1976, Options and Efficiency, *Quarterly Journal of Economics* 90, 75–98.

Ross, S., 1978, A Simpler Approach to the Valuation of Risky Streams, *Journal of Business,* 51, 453–475.

Ryder, H. E., Jr. and G. M. Heal, 1973, Optimum Growth with Intertemporally Dependent Preferences, *Review of Economic Studies*, 40, 1–33.

Samuelson, P. A., 1965, Rational Theory of Warrant Pricing, *Industrial Management Review,* 6, 13.

Samuelson, P. A., 1969, Lifetime Portfolio Selection by Dynamic Stochastic Programming, *Review of Economics and Statistics,* 60, 239–246.

Samuelson, P. A., 1970, The Fundamental Approximation Theorem of Portfolio Analysis in Terms of Means, Variances, and Higher Moments, *Review of Economic Studies*, 37, 4, 537–542.

Santos, T. and P. Veronesi, 2010, Habit Formation, the Cross Section of Stock Returns and the Cash Flow Risk Puzzle, *Journal of Financial Economics*, 98, 385–413.

Savage, L. J., 1954, *The Foundations of Statistics*, J. Wiley and Sons: New York.

Scheinkman, J. A. and W. Xiong, 2003, Overconfidence and Speculative Bubbles, *Journal of Political Economy*, 111, 1183–1219.

Schornick, A. V., 2009, International Capital Constraints and Stock Market Dynamics, Working Paper, INSEAD.

Schroder, M. and C. Skiadas, 1999, Optimal Consumption and Portfolio Selection with Stochastic Differential Utility, *Journal of Economic Theory*, 89, 68–126.

Schroder, M. and C. Skiadas, 2002, An Isomorphism between Asset Pricing Models with and without Linear Habit Formation, *The Review of Financial Studies* 15, 1189–1222.

Schweizer, M., 1992, Mean-variance Hedging for General Claims, *Annals of Applied Probabilities* 2, 171–179.

Sharpe, W. F., 1964, Capital Asset Prices: A Theory of Market Equilibrium under Conditions of Risk, *Journal of Finance* 19, 425–442.

Sharpe, W. F., 1966, Mutual Fund Performance, *Journal of Business,* 39, 119–138.

Sharpe, W. F., 1994, The Sharpe Ratio, *The Journal of Portfolio Management,* 21, 49–58.

Shaw, W. T., 1998, *Modeling Financial Derivatives with Mathematica*, Cambridge University Press: Cambridge, MA.

Shell, K., 2008, Sunspot Equilibrium, *The New Palgrave: A Dictionary of Economics*, 2nd Edition, L. Blume and S. Durlauf, (Eds.), Palgrave Macmillan: New York, NY.

Shiller, R. J., 1981, Do Stock Prices Move Too Much to Be Justified by Subsequent Changes in Dividends?, *American Economic Review* 71, 421–436.

Shreve, S. E. and H. M. Soner, 1994, Optimal Investment and Consumption with Transaction Costs, *Annals of Applied Probability* 4, 609–692.

Shreve, S. E. and G. L. Xu, 1992a, A Duality Method for Optimal Consumption and Under Short Selling Prohibition: I, General Market Coefficients, *Annals of Applied Probability* 2, 87–112.

Shreve, S. E. and G. L. Xu, 1992b, A Duality Method for Optimal Consumption and Under Short Selling Prohibition: II. Constant Market Coefficients, *Annals of Applied Probability* 2, 314–328.

Singleton, K., 2006, *Empirical Dynamic Asset Pricing*, Princeton University Press: Princeton, NJ.

Skiadas, C., 1998, Recursive Utility and Preferences for Information, *Economic Theory*, 12, 293–312.

Solnik, B., 1974, An Equilibrium Model of the International Capital Market, *Journal of Economic Theory*, 8, 500–524.

Soner, H. M., S. E. Shreve, and J. Cvitanic, 1995, There Is No Nontrivial Hedging Portfolio for Option Pricing with Transactions Costs, *Annals of Applied Probability* 5, 327–355.

Steffensen, M., 2011, On the Theory of Continuous-Time Recursive Utility, SSRN:http://ssrn.com/abstract=1954655

Storesletten, K., C. Telmer, and A. Yaron, 2004, Cyclical Dynamics in Idiosyncratic Labor Market Risk, *Journal of Political Economy*, 112, 695–716.

Strotz, R. H., 1955, Myopia and Inconsistency in Dynamic Utility Maximization, *The Review of Economic Studies*, 23, 165–180.

Sundaresan, S. M., 1989, Intertemporally Dependent Preferences and the Volatility of Consumption and Wealth, *Review of Financial Studies*, 2, 73–89.

Svensson, L. E. O., 1989, Portfolio Choice with Non-expected Utility in Continuous Time, *Economic Letters*, 30, 313–317.

Talay, D., Simulation of Stochastic Differential Systems, in *Probabilistic Methods in Applied Physics*, P. Kree and W. Wedig (Eds.), Lecture Notes in Physics, Springer-Verlag: Berlin.

Tauchen, G. and R. Hussey, 1991, Quadrature-based Methods for Obtaining Approximate Solutions to Nonlinear Asset Pricing Models, *Econometrica*, 59, 371–396.

Tepla, L., 2000, Optimal Portfolio Policies with Borrowing and Short Sale Constraints, *Journal of Economic Dynamics and Control*, 24, 1623–1639.

Timmerman, A. G., 1993, How Learning in Financial Markets Generates Excess Volatility and Predictability in Stock Prices, *Quarterly Journal of Economics*, 108, 1135–1145.

Timmerman, A. G., 1996, Excess Volatility and Predictability of Stock Prices in Autoregressive Dividend Models with Learning, *Review of Economic Studies*, 63, 523–557.

Tuckman, B., 1995, *Fixed Income Securities: Tools for Today's Markets*, John Wiley: New York, NY.

Uzawa, H., 1968, Time Preference, the Consumption Function, and Optimum Asset Holdings, in J. N. Wolfe, (Ed.), *Value, Capital and Growth: Papers in Honour of Sir John Hicks*, Chicago: Aldine.

Van Moerbeke, P. L., 1974, An Optimal Stopping Problem with Linear Reward, *Acta Mathematica* 132, 111–154.

Van Nieuwerburgh and L. Veldkamp, 2010, Information Acquisition and Under-Diversification, *The Review of Economic Studies*, 77, 779–805.

Vasicek, O., 1977, An Equilibrium Characterization of the Term Structure, *Journal of Financial Economics* 5, 177–188.

Vassalou, M., 2003, News Related to Future GDP Growth as a Risk Factor in Equity Returns, *Journal of Financial Economics* 68, 47–73.

Vayanos, D., 1998, Transaction Costs and Asset Prices: A Dynamic Equilibrium Model, *Review of Financial Studies*, 11, 1–58.

Vayanos, D. and J.-L. Vila, 1999, Equilibrium Interest Rate and Liquidity Premium with Transaction Costs, *Economic Theory*, 13, 509–539.

Veronesi, P., 1999, Stock Market Overreaction to Bad News in Good Times: A Rational Expectations Equilibrium Model, *Review of Financial Studies*, 1999, 12, 975–1007.

Veronesi, P., 2000, How Does Information Quality Affect Stock Returns? *The Journal of Finance*, 55, 807–837.

Veronesi, P., 2010, *Fixed Income Securities: Valuation, Risk, and Risk Management*, John Wiley: New York, NY.

Von Neumann J. and O. Morgenstern, 1944, *Theory of Games and Economic Behavior*, Princeton University Press: Princeton, NJ.

Walras, L., 1874/1877, *Elements d'économie politique pure*, 4th edition, (L. Corbaz: Lausanne), English translation in *Elements of Pure Economics*, W. Jeffé (Ed.), Allen and Unwin: London.

Wang, J., 1993, A Model of Intertemporal Asset Prices under Asymmetric Information, *Review of Economic Studies*, 60, 249–282.

Weil, P., 1989, The Equity Premium Puzzle and the Risk-Free Rate Puzzle, *Journal of Monetary Economics* 24, 401–421.

Yan, H., 2008, Natural Selection in Financial Markets: Does It Work? *Management Science*, 2008, 54, 1935–1950.

Zapatero, F., 1998, Effects of Financial Innovations on Market Volatility When Beliefs are Heterogeneous, *Journal of Economic Dynamics and Control,* 22, 597–626.

Zhang, L., 2005, The Value Premium, *The Journal of Finance*, 60, 67–103.

Ziegler, A. C., 2003, *Incomplete Information and Heterogeneous Beliefs in Continuous-Time Finance*, Springer Verlag: Berlin.

Author Index

Index